THE GERMAN IDEOLOGY

including
Theses on Feuerbach
and
Introduction to the Critique
of Political Economy

THE GERMAN IDEOLOGY

including
Theses on Feuerbach
and
Introduction to the Critique
of Political Economy

Karl Marx
(With Friedrich Engels)

GREAT BOOKS IN PHILOSOPHY

Prometheus Books
59 John Glenn Drive
Amherst, New York 14228-2119

Published 1998 by Prometheus Books

Inquiries should be addressed to
Prometheus Books
59 John Glenn Drive
Amherst, New York 14228–2119
VOICE: 716–691–0133, ext. 210
FAX: 716–691–0137
WWW.PROMETHEUSBOOKS.COM

21 20 19 18 17   16 15 14 13 12

Library of Congress Cataloging-in-Publication Data

Marx, Karl, 1818–1883.
[Deutsche Ideologie. English]
The German ideology : including Theses on Feuerbach and introduction to The critique of political economy / Karl Marx, with
Friedrich Engels.
p.   cm. — (Great books in philosophy)
Includes bibliographical references.
ISBN 1–57392–258–7 (alk. paper)
1. Feuerbach, Ludwig, 1804–1872. 2. Dialectical materialism.
3. Socialism. I. Engels, Friedrich, 1820–1895. II. Marx, Karl,
1818–1883. Thesen über Feuerbach. English. III. Title. IV. Series.
HX273.M23713   1998
335.4′11—dc21   98–31715
                                                              CIP

Printed in the United States of America on acid-free paper

Additional Titles on Social and Political Philosophy in Prometheus's Great Books in Philosophy Series

Aristotle
The Politics

Francis Bacon
Essays

Mikhail Bakunin
The Basic Bakunin:
Writings, 1869–1871

Edmund Burke
Reflections on the Revolution
in France

John Dewey
Freedom and Culture

G. W. F. Hegel
The Philosophy of History

G. W. F. Hegel
Philosophy of Right

Thomas Hobbes
The Leviathan

Sidney Hook
Paradoxes of Freedom

Sidney Hook
Reason, Social Myths, and
Democracy

John Locke
Second Treatise on Civil Government

Niccolo Machiavelli
The Prince

Karl Marx
The Poverty of Philosophy

Karl Marx and Friedrich Engels
The Economic and Philosophical
Manuscripts of 1844 and
The Communist Manifesto

John Stuart Mill
Considerations on
Representative Government

John Stuart Mill
On Liberty

John Stuart Mill
On Socialism

John Stuart Mill
The Subjection of Women

Friedrich Nietzsche
Thus Spake Zarathustra

Thomas Paine
Common Sense

Thomas Paine
Rights of Man

Plato
Lysis, Phaedrus, and *Symposium*

Plato
The Republic

Jean-Jacques Rousseau
The Social Contract

Mary Wollstonecraft
A Vindication of the Rights of Men

Mary Wollstonecraft
A Vindication of the Rights of Women

See the back of this volume for a complete list of titles in Prometheus's Great Books in Philosophy and Great Minds series.

KARL MARX was born in Trier, Prussia, on May 5, 1818, to an intellectual Jewish family. At seventeen he enrolled at the University of Bonn and a year later transferred to the University of Berlin, where he became interested in the philosophy of G. W. F. Hegel. In 1841, Marx obtained his doctorate in philosophy, having presented a thesis on post-Aristotelian Greek philosophy.

As a young graduate deeply involved with the radical Hegelian movement, Marx found it difficult to secure a teaching post in the autocratic environment of Prussian society. In 1842 he became editor of the Cologne newspaper *Rheinische Zeitung*, but his probing economic critiques prompted the government to close the publication, whereupon Marx left for France.

While in Paris, Marx quickly became involved with émigré German workers and French socialists, and soon he was persuaded to the communist point of view. His first expression of these views occurred in the *Economic and Philosophic Manuscripts of 1844,* which remained unpublished until 1930. It was during this brief initial stay in France that Marx became associated with Friedrich Engels.

For his radical political activities, Marx was expelled from Paris toward the end of 1844. He moved, with Engels, to Brussels, where he was to remain for the next three years, except for occasional short trips to England. Here Marx wrote the manuscript for *The German Ideology* (1845, co-authored by Friedrich Engels) and the polemic *The Poverty of Philosophy* (1847) against idealistic socialism. Marx later joined the Communist League, a German workers group, for which he and Engels were to become the primary spokespersons. In 1847 Marx and Engels were asked to write a manifesto for the league conference in London. This resulted in the creation of the *Communist Manifesto,* one of the most influential popular political documents ever written. Its publication coincided with a wave of revolutions in Europe in 1848.

Marx returned to Paris in 1848 but soon after left for Germany, where in Cologne he founded the *Neue Rheinische Zeitung,* a radical newspaper that attacked Prussian rule. As revolutionary fervor waned, the government suppressed his paper and Marx fled to England in 1849. For the next thirty-four years Marx remained in England absorbed in his work.

During this period Marx wrote voluminously, although many of his works were published only after his death: *The Class Struggles in France* (1848); *The Eighteenth Brumaire of Louis Bonaparte*

(1848); *Grundrisse,* or *Outlines* (1857–58; published in Moscow in 1941 and in the West in the 1950s); *Theories of Surplus Value* (1860); *Capital* (vol. 1, 1867; vols. 2 and 3 in 1885 and 1894); and *The Civil War in France* (1871). Karl Marx died in London on March 13, 1883.

CONTENTS

Karl Marx

INTRODUCTION TO THE CRITIQUE OF POLITICAL ECONOMY

1. PRODUCTION IN GENERAL

The subject of our discussion is first of all *material* production by individuals as determined by society, naturally constitutes the starting point. The individual and isolated hunter or fisher who forms the starting point with Smith and Ricardo, belongs to the insipid illusions of the eighteenth century. They are Robinsonades which do not by any means represent, as students of the history of civilization imagine, a reaction against over-refinement and a return to a misunderstood natural life. They are no more based on such a naturalism than is Rosseau's "contrat social," which makes naturally independent individuals come in contact and have mutual intercourse by contract. They are the fiction and only the aesthetic fiction of the small and great Robinsonades. They are, moreover, the anticipation of "bourgeois society," which had been in course of development since the sixteenth century and made gigantic strides towards maturity in the eighteenth. In this society of free competition the individual appears free from the bonds of nature, etc., which in former epochs of history made him a part of a definite, limited human conglomeration. To the prophets of the eighteenth century, on whose shoulders Smith and Ricardo are still standing, this eighteenth-century individual, constituting the joint product of the dissolution of the feudal form of society and of the new forces of production which had developed since the sixteenth century, appears as an ideal whose existence belongs to the past; not as a result of history, but as its starting point.

1

Since that individual appeared to be in conformity with nature and [corresponded] to their conception of human nature, [he was regarded] not as a product of history, but of nature. This illusion has been characteristic of every new epoch in the past. Steuart, who, as an aristocrat, stood more firmly on historical ground, contrary to the spirit of the eighteenth century, escaped this simplicity of view. The further back we go into history, the more the individual and, therefore, the producing individual seems to depend on and constitute a part of a larger whole: at first it is, quite naturally, the family and the clan, which is but an enlarged family; later on, it is the community growing up in its different forms out of the clash and the amalgamation of clans. It is but in the eighteenth century, in "bourgeois society," that the different forms of social union confront the individual as a mere means to his private ends, as an outward necessity. But the period in which this view of the isolated individual becomes prevalent, is the very one in which the interrelations of society (general from this point of view) have reached the highest state of development. Man is in the most literal sense of the word a *zoon politikon,* not only a social animal, but an animal which can develop into an individual only in society. Production by isolated individuals outside of society—something which might happen as an exception to a civilized man who by accident got into the wilderness and already dynamically possessed within himself the forces of society— is as great an absurdity as the idea of the development of language without individuals living together and talking to one another. We need not dwell on this any longer. It would not be necessary to touch upon this point at all, were not the vagary which had its justification and sense with the people of the eighteenth century transplanted In all earnest into the field of political economy by Bastiat, Carey, Proudhon and others. Proudhon and others naturally find it very pleasant, when they do not know the historical origin of a certain economic phenomenon, to give it a quasi historico-philosophical explanation by going into mythology. Adam or Prometheus bit upon the scheme cut and dried, whereupon it was adopted, etc. Nothing is more tediously dry than the dreaming *locus communis.*

Whenever we speak, therefore, of production, we always have in mind production at a certain stage of social development, or production by social individuals. Hence, it might seem that in order to speak of production at all, we must either trace the historical process of development through its Various phases, or declare at the outset that we are dealing with a certain historical period, as, e.g., with modern capitalistic production which, as a matter of fact, constitutes the subject proper of this work. But all stages of production have certain landmarks in common, common purposes. *Production in general* is an abstraction, but it is a rational abstraction, in so far as it singles out and fixes the common features, thereby saving us repetition. Yet these general or common features discovered by comparison constitute something very complex, whose constituent elements have different destinations. Some of these elements belong to all epochs, others are common to a few. Some of them are common to the most modern as well as to the most ancient epochs. No production is conceivable without them; but while even the most completely developed languages have laws and conditions in common with the least developed ones, what is characteristic of their development are the points of departure from the general and common. The conditions which generally govern production must be differentiated in order that the essential points of difference be not lost sight of in view of the general uniformity which is due to the fact that the subject, mankind, and the object, nature, remain the same. The failure to remember this one fact is the source of all the wisdom of modern economists who are trying to prove the eternal nature and harmony of existing social conditions. Thus they say, e.g., that no production is possible without some instrument of production, let that instrument be only the hand; that none is possible without past accumulated labor, even if that labor consist of mere skill which has been accumulated and concentrated in the hand of the savage by repeated exercise. Capital is, among other things, also an instrument of production, also past impersonal labor. Hence capital is a universal, eternal natural phenomenon; which is true if we disregard the specific properties which turn an "instrument of production" and "stored-up labor" into capital. The entire history of production appears to a man like Carey, e.g., as a malicious perversion on the part of governments.

If there is no production in general, there is also no general production. Production is always some special branch of production or an aggregate, as, e.g., agriculture, stock raising, manufactures, etc. But political economy is not technology. The connection between the general destinations of production at a given stage of social development and the particular forms of production, is to be developed elsewhere (later on).

Finally, production is not only of a special kind. It is always a certain body politic, a social personality that is engaged on a larger or smaller aggregate of branches of production. The connection between the real process and its scientific presentation also falls outside of the scope of this treatise. [We must thus distinguish between] production in general, special branches of production and production as a whole.

It is the fashion with economists to open their works with a general introduction, which is entitled "production" (see, e.g., John Stuart Mill) and deals with the general "requisites of production."

This general introductory part treats or is supposed to treat:

1. Of the conditions without which production is impossible, i.e., of the most essential conditions of production. As a matter of fact, however, it dwindles down, as we shall see, to a few very simple definitions, which flatten out into shallow tautologies;

2. Of conditions which further production more or less, as, e.g., Adam Smith's [discussion of] a progressive and stagnant state of society.

In order to give scientific value to what serves with him as a mere summary, it would be necessary to study the *degree of productivity* by periods in the development of individual nations; such a study falls outside of the scope of the present subject, and in so far as it does belong here is to be brought out in connection with the discussion of competition, accumulation, etc. The commonly accepted view of the matter gives a general answer to the effect that an industrial nation is at the height of its production at the moment when it reaches its historical climax in all respects. Or, that certain races, climates, natural conditions, such as distance from the sea, fertility of the soil, etc., are more favorable to production than others. That again comes down to the tautology that the facility of creating wealth depends on the extent to which its elements are present both subjectively and objectively. As a matter of fact a nation is at its industrial height so long as its main object is not gain, but the process of gaining. In that respect the Yankees stand above the English.

But all that is not what the economists are really after in the general introductory part. Their object is rather to represent production in contradistinction to distribution—see Mill, e.g.—as subject to eternal laws independent of history, and then to substitute bourgeois relations, in an underhand way, as immutable natural laws of society *in abstracto.* This is the more or less conscious aim of the entire proceeding. On the contrary, when it comes to distribution, mankind is supposed to have indulged in all sorts of arbitrary action. Quite apart from the fact that they violently break the ties which bind production and distribution together, so much must be clear from the outset: that, no matter bow greatly the systems of distribution may vary at different stages of society, it should be possible here, as in the case of production, to discover the common features and to confound and eliminate all historical differences in formulating *general human* laws. E.g., the slave, the serf, the wage-worker—all receive a quantity of food, which enables them to exist as slave, serf, and wage-worker. The conqueror, the official, the landlord, the monk, or the levite, who respectively live on tribute, taxes, rent, alms, and the tithe,—all receive [a part] of the social product which is determined by laws different from those which determine the part received by the slave, etc. The two main points which all economists place under this head, are: first, property; second, the protection of the latter by the administration of justice, police, etc. The objections to these two points can be stated very briefly.

1. All production is appropriation of nature by the individual within and through a definite form of society. In that sense it is a tautology to say that property (appropriation) is a condition of production. But it becomes ridiculous, when from that one jumps at once to a definite form of property, e.g., private property (which implies, besides, as a prerequisite the existence of an opposite form, viz. absence of property). History points rather to common property (e.g., among the Hindoos, Slavs, ancient Celts, etc.) as the primitive form, which still plays an important part at a much later period as communal property. The question as to whether wealth grows more rapidly under this or that form of property, is not even raised here as yet. But that there can be no such a thing as production, nor, consequently, society, where property does not exist in any form, is a tautology. Appropriation which does not appropriate is a *contradictio in subjecto*.

2. Protection of property, etc. Reduced to their real meaning, these commonplaces express more than what their preachers know, namely, that every form of production creates its own legal relations, forms of government, etc. The crudity and the shortcomings of the conception lie in the tendency to see but an accidental reflective connection in what constitutes an organic union. The bourgeois economists have a vague notion that it is better to carry on production under the modern police, than it was, e.g., under club-law. They forget that club law is also law, and that the right of the stronger continues to exist in other forms even under their "government of law."

When the social conditions corresponding to a certain stage of production are in a state of formation or disappearance, disturbances of production naturally arise, although differing in extent and effect.

To sum up: all the stages of production have certain destinations in common, which we generalize in thought; but the so-called general conditions of all production are nothing but abstract conceptions which do not go to make up any real stage in the history of production.

2. THE GENERAL RELATION OF PRODUCTION TO DISTRIBUTION, EXCHANGE, AND CONSUMPTION

Before going into a further analysis of production, it is necessary to look at the various divisions which economists put side by side with it. The most shallow conception is as follows: By production, the members of society appropriate (produce and shape) the products of nature to human wants; distribution determines the proportion in which the individual participates in this production; exchange brings him the particular products into which he wishes to turn the quantity secured by him through distribution; finally, through consumption the products become objects of use and enjoyment, of individual appropriation. Production yields goods adopted to our needs; distribution distributes them according to social laws; exchange distributes further what has already been distributed, according to individual wants; finally, in consumption the product drops out of the social movement, becoming the direct object of the individual want which it serves and satisfies in use. Production thus appears as the starting point; consumption as the final end; and distribution and exchange as the middle; the latter has a double aspect, distribution being defined as a process carried on by society, while exchange, as one proceeding from the individual. In production the person is embodied in things, in [consumption] things are embodied in persons; in distribution, society assumes the part of go-between of production and consumption in the form of generally prevailing rules; in exchange this is accomplished by the accidental make-up of the individual.

Distribution determines what proportion (quantity) of the products the individual is to receive; exchange determines the products in which the individual desires to receive his share allotted to him by distribution.

Production, distribution, exchange, and consumption thus form a perfect connection, production standing for the general, distribution and exchange for the special, and consumption for the individual, in which all are joined together. To be sure this is a connection, but it does not go very deep. Production is determined [according to the economists] by universal natural laws, while distribution depends on social chance: distribution can, therefore, have a more or less stimulating effect on production: exchange lies between the two as a formal (?) social movement, and the final act of consumption which is considered not only as a final purpose, but also as a final aim, falls, properly, outside of the scope of economics, except in so far as it reacts on the starting point and causes the entire process to begin all over again.

The opponents of the economists—whether economists themselves or not—who reproach them with tearing apart, like barbarians, what is an organic whole, either stand on common ground with them or are *below* them. Nothing is more common than the charge that the economists have been considering production as an end in itself, too much to the exclusion of everything else. The same has been said with regard to distribution. This accusation is itself based on the economic conception that distribution exists side by side with production as a self-contained, independent sphere. Or [they are accused] that the various factors are not treated by them in their connection as a whole. As though it were the text books that impress this separation upon life and not life upon the text books; and the subject at issue were a dialectic balancing of conceptions and not an analysis of real conditions.

a. *Production is at the same time also consumption.* Twofold consumption, subjective and objective. The individual who develops his faculties in production, is also expending them, consuming them in the act of production, just as procreation is in its way a consumption of vital powers. In the second place, production is consumption of means of production which are used and used up and partly (as e.g., in burning) reduced to their natural elements. The same is true of the consumption of raw materials which do not remain in their natural form and state, being greatly absorbed in the process. The act of production is, therefore, in all its aspects an act of consumption as well. But this is admitted by economists. Production as directly identical with consumption, consumption as directly coincident with production, they call productive consumption. This identity of production and consumption finds its expression in Spinoza's proposition, *Determinatio est negatio.* But this definition of productive consumption is resorted to just for the purpose of distinguishing between consumption as identical with production and consumption proper, which is defined as its destructive counterpart. Let us then consider consumption proper.

Consumption is directly also production, just as in nature the consumption of the elements and of chemical matter constitutes production of plants. It is clear, that in nutrition, e.g., which is but one form of consumption, man produces his own body; but it is equally true of every kind of consumption, which goes to produce the human being in one way or another. [It is] consumptive production. But, say the economists, this production which is identical with consumption, is a second production resulting from the destruction of the product of the first. In the first, the producer transforms himself into things; in the second, things are transformed into human beings. Consequently, this consumptive production—although constituting a direct unity of production and consumption—differs essentially from production proper. The direct unity in which production coincides with consumption and consumption with production, does not interfere with their direct duality.

Production is thus at the same time consumption, and consump-

tion is at the same time production. Each is directly its own counterpart. But at the same time an intermediary movement goes on
between the two. Production furthers consumption by creating material for the latter which otherwise would lack its object. But consumption in its turn furthers production, by providing for the products the individual for whom they are products. The product receives
its last finishing touches in consumption. A railroad on which no one
rides, which is, consequently not used up, not consumed, is but a
potential railroad, and not a real one. Without production, no consumption; but, on the other hand, without consumption, no production; since production would then be without a purpose. Consumption produces production in two ways.

In the first place, in that the product first becomes a real product
in consumption; e.g., a garment becomes a real garment only
through the act of being worn; a dwelling which is not inhabited, is
really no dwelling; consequently, a product as distinguished from a
mere natural object, proves to be such, first *becomes* a product in
consumption. Consumption gives the product the finishing touch by
annihilating it, since a product is the [result] of production not only
as the material embodiment of activity, but also as a mere object for
the active subject.

In the second place, consumption produces production by creating the necessity for new production, i.e., by providing the ideal,
inward, impelling cause which constitutes the prerequisite of production. Consumption furnishes the impulse for production as well
as its object, which plays in production the part of its guiding aim. It
is clear that while production furnishes the material object of consumption, consumption provides the ideal object of production, as
its image, its want, its impulse and its purpose. It furnishes the object
of production in its subjective form. No wants, no production. But
consumption reproduces the want.

In its turn, production

First, furnishes consumption with its material, its object. Consumption without an object is no consumption, hence production
works in this direction by producing consumption.

Second. But it is not only the object that production provides for
consumption. It gives consumption its definite outline, its character,
its finish. Just as consumption gives the product its finishing touch
as a product, production puts the finishing touch on consumption.
For the object is not simply an object in general, but a definite
object, which is consumed in a certain definite manner prescribed in
its turn by production. Hunger is hunger; but the hunger that is satisfied with cooked meat eaten with fork and knife is a different kind
of hunger from the one that devours raw meat with the aid of hands,

nails, and teeth. Not only the object of consumption, but also the manner of consumption is produced by production; that is to say, consumption is created by production not only objectively, but also subjectively. Production thus creates the consumers.

Third. Production not only supplies the want with material, but supplies the material with a want. When consumption emerges from its first stage of natural crudeness and directness—and its continuation in that state would in itself be the result of a production still remaining in a state of natural crudeness—it is itself furthered by its object as a moving spring. The want of it which consumption experiences is created by its appreciation of the product. The object of art, as well as any other product, creates an artistic and beauty-enjoying public. Production thus produces not only an object for the individual, but also an individual for the object.

Production thus produces consumption: first, by furnishing the latter with material; second, by determining the manner of consumption; third, by creating in consumers a want for its products as objects of consumption. It thus produces the object, the manner, and the moving spring of consumption. In the same manner, consumption [creates] the *disposition* of the producer by setting (?) him up as an aim and by stimulating wants. The identity of consumption and production thus appears to be a threefold one.

First, direct identity: production is consumption; consumption is production. Consumptive production. Productive consumption. Economists call both productive consumption, but make one distinction by calling the former reproduction, and the latter productive consumption. All inquiries into the former deal with productive and unproductive labor; those into the latter treat of productive and unproductive consumption.

Second. Each appears as the means of the other and as being brought about by the other, which is expressed as their mutual interdependence; a relation, by virtue of which they appear as mutually connected and indispensable, yet remaining outside of each other.

Production creates the material as the outward object of consumption; consumption creates the want as the inward object, the purpose of production. Without production, no consumption; without consumption, no production; this maxim figures (?) in political economy in many forms.

Third. Production is not only directly consumption and consumption directly production; nor is production merely a means of consumption and consumption the purpose of production. In other words, not only does each furnish the other with its object; production, the material object of consumption; consumption, the ideal object of production. On the contrary, either one is not only directly the other, not (?) only a means of furthering the other, but while it is taking place, creates the other as such for itself (?). Consumption completes the act of production by giving the finishing touch to the product as such, by destroying the latter, by breaking up its independent material form; by bringing to a state of readiness, through the necessity of repetition, the disposition to produce developed in the first act of production; that is to say, it is not only the concluding act through which the product becomes a product, but also [the one] through which the producer becomes a producer. On the other hand, production produces consumption, by determining the manner of consumption, and further, by creating the incentive for consumption, the very ability to consume, in the form of want. This latter identity mentioned under point 3, is much discussed in political economy in connection with the treatment of the relations of demand and supply, of objects and wants, of natural wants and those created by society.

Hence, it is the simplest matter with a Hegelian to treat production and consumption as identical. And this has been done not only by socialist writers of fiction but even by economists, e.g., Say; the latter maintained that if we consider a nation as a whole, or mankind *in abstracto*—her production is at the same time her consumption. Storch pointed out Say's error by calling attention to the fact that a nation does not entirely consume her product, but also creates means of production, fixed capital, etc. To consider society as a single individual is moreover a false mode of speculative reasoning. With an individual, production and consumption appear as different aspects of one act. The important point to be emphasized here is that if production and consumption be considered as activities of one individual or of separate individuals, they appear at any rate as aspects of one process in which production forms the actual starting point and is, therefore, the predominating factor. Consumption, as a natural necessity, as a want, constitutes an internal factor of productive activity, but the latter is the starting point of realization and, therefore, its predominating factor, the act into which the entire process resolves itself in the end. The individual produces a certain article and turns again into himself by consuming it; but he returns as a productive and a self-reproducing, individual. Consumption thus appears as a factor of production.

In society, however, the relation, of the producer to his product, as soon as it is completed, is an outward one and the return of the product to the individual depends on his relations to other individuals. He does not take immediate possession of it. Nor does the direct appropriation of the product constitute his purpose, when he produces in society. Between the producer and the product distribution steps in, which determines by social laws his share in the world of products; that is to say, distribution steps in between production and consumption.

Does distribution form an independent sphere standing side by side with and outside of production?

b. Production and Distribution. In perusing the common treatises on economics one cannot help being struck with the fact that everything is treated there twice; e.g., under distribution, there figure rent, wages, interest, and profit; while under production we find land, labor, and capital as agents of production. As re gards capital, it is at once clear that it is counted twice: first, as an agent of production; second, as a source of income; as determining factors and definite forms of distribution, interest and profit figure as such also in production, since they are forms, in which capital increases and grows, and are consequently factors of its own production. Interest and profit, as forms of distribution, imply the existence of capital as an agent of production. They are forms of distribution which have for their prerequisite capital as an agent of production. They are also forms of reproduction of capital.

In the same manner, wages is wage-labor when considered under another head; the definite character which labor has in one case as an agent of production, appears in the other as a form of distribution. If labor were not fixed as wage-labor, its manner of participation in distribution would not appear as wages, as is the case, e.g., under slavery. Finally, rent—to take at once the most developed form of distribution—by means of which landed property receives its share of the products, implies the existence of large landed property (properly speaking, agriculture on a large scale) as an agent of production, and not simply land, no more than wages represents simply labor. The relations and methods of distribution appear, therefore, merely as the reverse sides of the agents of production. An individual who participates in production as a wage laborer, receives his share of the products, i.e. of the results of production, in the form of wages. The subdivisions and organization of distribution are determined by the subdivisions and organization of production. Distribution is itself a product of production, not only in so far as the material goods are concerned, since only the results of production can be distributed; but also as regards its form, since the definite manner of participation in production determines the particular form of distribution, the form under which participation in distribution takes place. It is quite an illusion to place land under production, rent under distribution, etc.

Economists, like Ricardo, who are accused above all of having paid exclusive attention to production, define distribution, therefore, as the exclusive subject of political economy, because they instinctively regard the forms of distribution as the clearest forms in which the agents of production find expression in a given society.

To the single individual distribution naturally appears as a law established by society determining his position in the sphere of production, within which be produces, and thus antedating production. At the outset the individual has no capital, no landed property. From his birth he is assigned to wage-labor by the social process of distribution. But this very condition of being assigned to wage-labor is the result of the existence of capital and landed property as independent agents of production.

From the point of view of society as a whole, distribution seems to antedate and to determine production in another way as well, as a pre-economic fact, so to say. A conquering people divides the land among the conquerors, establishing thereby a certain division and form of landed property and determining the character of production; or, it turns the conquered people into slaves and thus makes slave labor the basis of production. Or, a nation, by revolution, breaks up large estates into small parcels of land and by this new distribution imparts to production a new character. Or, legislation perpetuates land ownership in large families or distributes labor as an hereditary privilege and thus fixes it in castes.

In all of these cases, and they are all historic, it is not distribution that seems to be organized and determined by production, but on the contrary, production by distribution.

In the most shallow conception of distribution, the latter appears as a distribution of products and to that extent as further removed from and quasi-independent of production. But before distribution means distribution of products, it is first, a distribution of the means of production, and second, what is practically another wording of the same fact, it is a distribution of the members of society among the various kinds of production (the subjection of individuals to certain conditions of production). The distribution of products is manifestly a result of this distribution, which is bound up with the process of production and determines the very organization of the latter. To treat of production apart from the distribution which is comprised in it, is plainly an idle abstraction. Conversely, we know the character of the distribution of products the moment we are given the nature of that other distribution which forms originally a factor of production. Ricardo, who was concerned with the analysis of production as it is organized in modern society and who was the economist of production *par excellence*, for that very reason declares not production but distribution as the subject proper of modern economics. We have here another evidence of the insipidity of the economists who treat production as an eternal truth, and banish history to the domain of distribution.

What relation to production this distribution, which has a determining influence on production itself, assumes, is plainly a question which falls within the province of production. Should it be maintained that at least to the extent that production depends on a certain distribution of the instruments of production, distribution in that sense precedes production and constitutes its prerequisite; it may be replied that production has in fact its prerequisite conditions, which form factors of it. These may appear at first to have a natural origin. By the very process of production they are changed from natural to historical, and if they appear during one period as a natural prerequisite of production, they formed at other periods its historical result. Within the sphere of production itself they are undergoing a constant change. E.g., the application of machinery produces a change in the distribution of the instruments of production as well as in that of products, and modern land ownership on a large scale is as much the result of modern trade and modern industry, as that of the application of the latter to agriculture.

All of these questions resolve themselves in the last instance to this: How do general historical conditions affect production and what part does it play at all in the course of history? It is evident that this question can be taken up only in connection with the discussion and analysis of production.

Yet in the trivial form in which these questions are raised above, they can be answered just as briefly. In the case of all conquests three ways lie open. The conquering people may impose its own methods of production upon the conquered (e.g., the English in Ireland in the nineteenth century, partly also in India); or, it may allow everything to remain as it was contenting itself with tribute (e.g., the Turks and the Romans); or, the two systems by mutually modifying each other may result in something new, a synthesis (which partly resulted from the Germanic conquests). In all of these conquests the method of production, be it of the conquerors, the conquered, or the one resulting from a combination of both, determines the nature of the new distribution which comes into play. Although the latter appears now as the prerequisite condition of the new period of production, it is in itself but a product of production, not of production belonging to history in general, but of production relating to a definite historical period. The Mongols with their devastations in Russia, e.g., acted in accordance with their system of production, for which sufficient pastures on large uninhabited stretches of country are the main prerequisite. The Germanic barbarians, with whom agriculture carried on with the aid of serfs was the traditional system of production and who were accustomed to lonely life in the country, could introduce the same conditions in the Roman provinces so much easier since the concentration of landed property which had taken place there, did away completely with the older systems of agriculture. There is a prevalent tradition that in certain periods robbery constituted the only source of living. But in order to be able to plunder, there must be something to plunder, i.e. there must be production. And even the method of plunder is determined by the method of production. A stockjobbing nation, e.g., cannot be robbed in the same manner as a nation of shepherds.

In the case of the slave the instrument of production is robbed directly. But then the production of the country in whose interest he is robbed, must be so organized as to admit of slave labor, or (as in South America, etc.) a system of production must be introduced adapted to slavery.

Laws may perpetuate an instrument of production, e.g., land, in certain families. These laws assume an economic importance if large landed property is in harmony with the system of production prevailing in society, as is the case, e.g., in England. In France agriculture had been carried on on a small scale in spite of the large estates, and the latter were, therefore, broken up by the Revolution. But how about the legislative attempt to perpetuate the minute subdivision of the land? In spite of these laws land ownership is concentrating again. The effect of legislation on the maintenance of a system of distribution and its resultant influence on production are to be determined elsewhere.

c. Exchange and Circulation. Circulation is but a certain aspect of exchange, or it may be defined as exchange considered as a whole. Since *exchange* is an intermediary factor between production and its dependent, distribution, on the one hand, and consumption, on the other; and since the latter appears but as a constituent of production, exchange is manifestly also a constituent part of production.

In the first place, it is clear that the exchange of activities and abilities which takes place in the sphere of production falls directly within the latter and constitutes one of its essential elements. In the second place, the same is true of the exchange of products, in so far as it is a means of completing a certain product, designed for immediate consumption. To that extent exchange constitutes an act included in production. Thirdly, the so-called exchange between dealers and dealers is by virtue of its organization determined by production, and is itself a species of productive activity. Exchange appears to be independent of and indifferent to production only in the last stage when products are exchanged directly for consumption. But in the first place, there is no exchange without a division of labor, whether natural or as a result of historical development; secondly, private exchange implies the existence of private production;

thirdly, the intensity of exchange, as well as its extent and character are determined by the degree of development and organization of production, as, e.g., exchange between city and country, exchange in the country, in the city, etc. Exchange thus appears in all its aspects to be directly included in or determined by production.

The result we arrive at is not that production, distribution, exchange, and consumption are identical, but that they are all members of one entity, different sides of one unit. Production predominates not only over production itself in the opposite sense of that term, but over the other elements as well. With it the process constantly starts over again. That exchange and consumption cannot be the predominating elements is self-evident. The same is true of distribution in the narrow sense of distribution of products; as for distribution in the sense of distribution of the agents of production, it is itself but a factor of production. A definite [form of] production thus determines the [forms of] consumption, distribution, exchange, and also the *mutual relations between these various elements*. Of course, production *in its one-sided form* is in its turn influenced by other elements; e.g., with the expansion of the market, i.e., of the sphere of exchange, production grows in volume and is subdivided to a greater extent.

With a change in distribution, production undergoes a change; as, e.g., in the case of concentration of capital, of a change in the distribution of population in city and country, etc. Finally, the demands of consumption also influence production. A mutual interaction takes place between the various elements. Such is the case with every organic body.

3. THE METHOD OF POLITICAL ECONOMY

When we consider a given country from a politico-economic standpoint, we begin with its population, then analyze the latter according to its subdivision into classes, location in city, country, or by the sea, occupation in different branches of production; then we study its exports and imports, annual production and consumption, prices of commodities, etc. It seems to be the correct procedure to commence with the real and concrete aspect of conditions as they are; in the case of political economy, to commence with population which is the basis and the author of the entire productive activity of society. Yet, on closer consideration it proves to be wrong. Population is an abstraction, if we leave out, e.g., the classes of which it consists. These classes, again, are but an empty word, unless we know what are the elements on which they are based, such as wage-labor, capital, etc. These imply, in their turn, exchange, division of labor, prices, etc. Capital, e.g., does not mean anything without wage-labor, value, money, price, etc. If we start out, therefore, with population, we do so with a chaotic conception of the whole, and by closer analysis we will gradually arrive at simpler ideas; thus we shall proceed from the imaginary concrete to less and less complex abstractions, until we get at the simplest conception. This once attained, we might start on our return journey until we would finally come back to population, but this time not as a chaotic notion of an integral whole, but as a rich aggregate of many conceptions and relations. The former method is the one which political economy had adopted in the past at its inception. The economists of the seventeenth century, e.g., always started out with the living aggregate: population, nation, state, several states, etc., but in the end they invariably arrived, by means of analysis, at certain leading, abstract general principles, such as division of labor, money, value, etc. As soon as these separate elements had been more or less established by abstract reasoning, there arose the systems of political economy which start from simple conceptions, such as labor, division of labor, demand, exchange value, and conclude with state, international exchange and world market. The latter is manifestly the scientifically correct method. The concrete is concrete, because it is a combination of many objects with different destinations, i.e. a unity of diverse elements. In our thought, it therefore appears as a process of synthesis, as a result, and not as a starting point, although it is the real starting point and, therefore, also the starting point of observation and conception. By the former method the complete conception passes into an abstract definition; by the latter, the abstract definitions lead to the reproduction of the concrete subject in the course of reasoning. Hegel fell into the error, therefore, of considering the real as the result of self-coordinating, self-absorbed, and spontaneously operating thought, while the method of advancing from the abstract to the concrete is but a way of thinking by which the concrete is grasped and is reproduced in our mind as a concrete. It is by no means, however, the process which itself generates the concrete. The simplest economic category, say, exchange value, implies the existence of population, population that is engaged in production under certain conditions; it also implies the existence of certain types of family, clan, or state, etc. It can have no other existence except as an abstract one-sided relation of an already given concrete and living aggregate.

As a category, however, exchange value leads an antediluvian existence. And since our philosophic consciousness is so arranged that only the image of the man that it conceives appears to it as the real man and the world as it conceives it, as the real world; it mistakes the movement of categories for the real act of production (which unfortunately (?) receives only its impetus from outside) whose result is the world; that is true—here we have, however, again a tautology—in so far as the concrete aggregate is a thought aggregate, in so far as the concrete subject of our thought is in fact a product of thought, of comprehension; not, however, in the sense of a product of a self-emanating conception which works outside of and stands above observation and imagination, but of a mental consummation of observation and imagination. The whole, as it appears in our heads as a thought-aggregate, is the product of a thinking mind which grasps the world in the only way open to it, a way which differs from the one employed by the artistic, religious, or practical mind. The concrete subject continues to lead an independent existence after it has been grasped, as it did before, outside of the head, so long as the head contemplates it only speculatively, theoretically. So that in the employment of the theoretical method [in political economy], the subject, society, must constantly be kept in mind as the premise from which we start.

But have these simple categories no independent historical or natural existence antedating the more concrete ones? *Ça depend.* For instance, in his *Philosophy of Law* Hegel rightly starts out with possession, as the simplest legal relation of individuals. But there is no such thing as possession before the family or the relations of lord and serf, which are a great deal more concrete relations, have come into existence. On the other hand, one would be right in saying that there are families and clans which only *possess*, but do not *own* things. The simpler category thus appears as a relation of simple family and clan communities with respect to property. In earlier society the category appears as a simple relation of a developed organism, but the concrete substratum from which springs the relation of possession, is always implied. One can imagine an isolated ravage in possession of things. But in that case possession is no legal relation. It is not true that the family came as the result of the historical evolution of possession. On the contrary, the latter always implies the existence of this "more concrete category of law." Yet so much may be said, that the simple categories are the expression of relations in which the less developed concrete entity may have been realized without entering into the manifold relations and bearings which are mentally expressed in the concrete category; but when the concrete entity attains fuller development it will retain the same category as a subordinate relation.

Money may exist and actually had existed in history before capital, or banks, or wage-labor came into existence. With that in mind, it may be said that the more simple category can serve as an expres-

sion of the predominant relations of an undeveloped whole or of the
subordinate relations of a more developed whole, [relations] which
had historically existed before the whole developed in the direction
expressed in the more concrete category. In so far, the laws of
abstract reasoning which ascends from the most simple to the complex, correspond to the actual process of history.

On the other hand, it may be said that there are highly developed
but historically unripe forms of society in which the highest economic forms are to be found, such as co-operation, advanced division of labor., etc., and yet there is no money in existence, e.g., Peru.

In Slavic communities also, money, as well as exchange to
which it owes its existence, does not appear at all or very little
within the separate communities, but it appears on their boundaries
in their inter-communal traffic; in general, it is erroneous to consider
exchange as a constituent element originating within the community.
It appears at first more in the mutual relations between different
communities, than in those between the members of the same community. Furthermore, although money begins to play its part everywhere at an early stage, it plays in antiquity the part of a predominant element only in one-sidedly developed nations, viz. trading
nations, and even in most cultured antiquity, in Greece and Rome, it
attains its full development, which constitutes the prerequisite of
modern bourgeois society, only in the period of their decay. Thus,
this quite simple category attained its culmination in the past only at
the most advanced stages of society. Even then it did not pervade (?)
all economic relations; in Rome, e.g., at the time of its highest development taxes and payments in kind remained the basis. As a matter
of fact, the money system was fully developed there only so far as
the army was concerned; it never came to dominate the entire system
of labor.

Thus, although the simple category may have existed historically before the more concrete one, it can attain its complete internal
and external development only in complex (?) forms of society,
while the more concrete category has reached its full development
in a less advanced form of society.

Labor is quite a simple category. The idea of labor in that sense,
as labor in general, is also very old. Yet, "labor" thus simply defined
by political economy is as much a modern category, as the conditions which have given rise to this simple abstraction. The monetary
system, e.g., defines wealth quite objectively, as a thing (?) in
money. Compared with this point of view, it was a great step forward, when the industrial or commercial system came to see the
source of wealth not in the object but in the activity of persons, viz.
in commercial and industrial labor. But even the latter was thus con-

sidered only in the limited sense of a money-producing activity. The physiocratic system [marks still further progress] in that it considers a certain form of labor, viz. agriculture, as the source of wealth, and wealth itself not in the disguise of money, but as a product in general, as the general result of labor. But corresponding to the limitations of the activity, this product is still only a natural product. Agriculture is productive, land is the source of production *par excellence*. It was a tremendous advance on the part of Adam Smith to throw aside all limitations which mark wealth-producing activity and [to define it] as labor in general, neither industrial, nor commercial, nor agricultural, or one as much as the other. Along with the universal character of wealth-creating activity we have now the universal character of the object defined as wealth, viz. product in general, or labor in general, but as past incorporated labor. How difficult and great was the transition, is evident from the way Adam Smith himelf falls back from time to time into the physiocratic system. Now, it might seem as though this amounted simply to finding an abstract expression for the simplest relation into which men have been mutually entering as producers from times of yore, no matter under what form of society. In one sense this is true. In another it is not.

The indifference as to the particular kind of labor implies the existence of a highly developed aggregate of different species of concrete labor, none of which is any longer the predominant one. So do the most general abstractions commonly arise only where there is the highest concrete development, where one feature appears to be jointly possessed by many, and to be common to all. Then it cannot be thought of any longer in one particular form. On the other hand, this abstraction of labor is but the result of a concrete aggregate of different kinds of labor. The indifference to the particular kind of labor corresponds to a form of society in which individuals pass with ease from one kind of work to another, which makes it immaterial to them what particular kind of work may fall to their share. Labor has become here, not only categorically but really, a means of creating wealth in general and is no longer grown together with the individual into one particular destination. This state of affairs has found its highest development in the most modern of bourgeois societies, the United States. It is only here that the abstraction of the category "labor," "labor in general," labor *sans phrase*, the starting point of modern political economy, becomes realized in practice. Thus, the simplest abstraction which modern political economy sets up as its starting point, and which expresses a relation dating back to antiquity and prevalent under all forms of society, appears in this abstraction truly realized only as a category of the most modern society. It might be said that what appears in the United States as an historical product,—viz. the indifference as to the particular kind of labor— appears among the Russians, e.g., as a natural disposition. But it makes all the difference in the world whether barbarians have a nat- ural predisposition which makes them applicable alike to every- thing, or whether civilized people apply themselves to everything. And, besides, this indifference of the Russians as to the kind of work they do, corresponds to their traditional practice of remaining in the rut of a quite definite occupation until they are thrown out of it by external influences.

This example of labor strikingly shows how even the most abstract categories, in spite of their applicability to all epochs—just because of their abstract character—are by the very definiteness of the abstraction a product of historical conditions as well, and are fully applicable only to and under those conditions.

The bourgeois society is the most highly developed and most highly differentiated historical organization of production. The cate- gories which serve as the expression of its conditions and the com- prehension of its own organization enable it at the same time to gain an insight into the organization and the conditions of production which had prevailed under all the past forms of society, on the ruins and constituent elements of which it has arisen, and of which it still drags along some unsurmounted remnants, while what had formerly been mere intimation has now developed to complete significance. The anatomy of the human being is the key to the anatomy of the ape. But the intimations of a higher animal in lower ones can be understood only if the animal of the higher order is already known. The bourgeois economy furnishes a key to ancient economy, etc. This is, however, by no means true of the method of those econo- mists who blot out all historical differences and see the bourgeois form in all forms of society. One can understand the nature of tribute, tithes, etc., after one has learned the nature of rent. But they must not be considered identical.

Since, furthermore, bourgeois society is but a form resulting from the development of antagonistic elements, some relations belonging to earlier forms of society are frequently to be found in it but in a crippled state or as a travesty of their former self, as e.g., communal property. While it may be said, therefore, that the cate- gories of bourgeois economy contain what is true of all other forms of society, the statement is to be taken *cum grano salis*. They may contain these in a developed, or crippled, or caricatured form, but always essentially different. The so-called historical development amounts in the last analysis to this, that the last form considers its predecessors as stages leading up to itself and perceives them always one-sidedly, since it is very seldom and only under certain conditions that it is capable of self-criticism; of course, we do not speak here of such historical periods which appear to their own contemporaries as periods of decay. The Christian religion became capable to assist us to an objective view of past mythologies as soon as it was ready for self-criticism to a certain extent, *dynamei* so-to-say. In the same way bourgeois political economy first came to understand the feudal, the ancient, and the oriental societies as soon as the self-criticism of the bourgeois society had commenced. So far as bourgeois political economy has not gone into the mythology of purely (?) identifying the bourgeois system with the past, its criticism of the feudal system against which it still had to wage war resembled Christian criticism of the heathen religions or Protestant criticism of Catholicism.

In the study of economic categories, as in the case of every historical and social science, it must be borne in mind that as in reality so in our mind the subject, in this case modern bourgeois society, is given and that the categories are therefore but forms of expression, manifestations of existence, and frequently but one-sided aspects of this subject, this definite society; and that, therefore, the origin of [political economy] *as a science* does not by any means date from the time to which it is referred *as such*. This is to be firmly held in mind because it has an immediate and important bearing on the matter of the subdivisions of the science.

For instance, nothing seems more natural than to start with rent, with landed property, since it is bound up with land, the source of all production and all existence, and with the first form of production in all more or less settled communities, viz. agriculture. But nothing would be more erroneous. Under all forms of society there is a certain industry which predominates over all the rest and whose condition therefore determines the rank and influence of all the rest.

It is the universal light with which all the other colors are tinged and are modified through its peculiarity. It is a special ether which determines the specific gravity of everything that appears in it.

Let us take for example pastoral nations (mere hunting and fishing tribes are not as yet at the point from which real development commences). They engage in a certain form of agriculture, sporadically. The nature of land-ownership is determined thereby. It is held in common and retains this form more or less according to the extent to which these nations hold on to traditions; such, e.g., is land-ownership among the Slavs. Among nations, whose agriculture is carried on by a settled population—the settled state constituting a great advance—where agriculture is the predominant industry, such as in ancient and feudal societies, even the manufacturing industry and its organization, as well as the forms of property which pertain to it, have more or less the characteristic features of the prevailing system of land ownership; [society] is then either entirely dependent upon agriculture, as in the case of ancient Rome, or, as in the Middle Ages, it imitates in its city relations the forms of organization prevailing in the country. Even capital, with the exception of pure money capital, has, in the form of the traditional working tool, the characteristics of land ownership in the Middle Ages.

The reverse is true of bourgeois society. Agriculture comes to be more and more merely a branch of industry and is completely dominated by capital. The same is true of rent. In all the forms of society in which land ownership is the prevalent form, the influence of the natural element is the predominant one. In those where capital predominates the prevailing element is the one historically created by society. Rent cannot be understood without capital, nor can capital, without rent. Capital is the all-dominating economic power of bourgeois society. It must form the starting point as well as the end and be developed before land-ownership is. After each has been considered separately, their mutual relation must be analyzed.

It would thus be impractical and wrong to arrange the economic categories in the order in which they were the determining factors in the course of history. Their order of sequence is rather determined by the relation which they bear to one another in modern bourgeois society, and which is the exact opposite of what seems to be their natural order or the order of their historical development. What we are interested in is not the place which economic relations occupy in the historical succession of different forms of society. Still less are we interested in the order of their succession "in idea" (*Proudhon*), which is but a hazy (?) conception of the course of history. We are interested in their organic connection within modern bourgeois society.

The sharp line of demarkation (abstract precision) which so clearly distinguished the trading nations of antiquity, such as the Phoenicians and the Carthaginians, was due to that very predominance of agriculture. Capital as trading or money capital appears in that abstraction, where capital does not constitute as yet the predominating element of society. The Lombardians and the Jews occupied the same position among the agricultural nations of the Middle Ages.

As a further illustration of the fact that the same category plays different parts at different stages of society, we may mention the following: one of the latest forms of bourgeois society, viz. stock companies, appear also at its beginning in the form of the great chartered monopolistic trading companies.

The conception of national wealth which is imperceptibly

formed in the minds of the economists of the seventeenth century, and which partly continues to be entertained by those of the eighteenth century, is that wealth is produced solely for the state, but that the power of the latter is proportional to that wealth. It was as yet an unconsciously hypocritical way in which wealth announced itself and its own production as the aim of modern states considering the latter merely as a means to the production of wealth.

The order of treatment must manifestly be as follows: first, the general abstract definitions which are more or less applicable to all forms of society, but in the sense indicated above. Second, the categories which go to make up the inner organization of bourgeois society and constitute the foundations of the principal classes; capital, wage-labor, landed property; their mutual relations; city and country; the three great social classes, the exchange between them; circulation, credit (private). Third, the organization of bourgeois society in the form of a state, considered in relation to itself; the "unproductive" classes; taxes; public debts; public credit; population; colonies; emigration. Fourth, the international organization of production; international division of labor; international exchange; import and export; rate of exchange. Fifth, the world market and crises.

Karl Marx
and
Friedrich Engels

THE GERMAN IDEOLOGY

Volume 1

CRITIQUE
OF MODERN GERMAN PHILOSOPHY
ACCORDING TO ITS REPRESENTATIVES
FEUERBACH, B. BAUER AND STIRNER

PREFACE

Hitherto men have always formed wrong ideas about themselves, about what they are and what they ought to be. They have arranged their relations according to their ideas of God, of normal man, etc. The products of their brains have got out of their hands. They, the creators, have bowed down before their creations. Let us liberate them from the chimeras, the ideas, dogmas, imaginary beings under the yoke of which they are pining away. Let us revolt against this rule of concepts. Let us teach men, says one,[a] how to exchange these imaginations for thoughts which correspond to the essence of man; says another,[b] how to take up a critical attitude to them; says the third,[c] how to get them out of their heads; and existing reality will collapse.

These innocent and childlike fancies are the kernel of the modern Young-Hegelian philosophy, which not only is received by the German public with horror and awe, but is announced by our *philosophic heroes* with the solemn consciousness of its world-shattering danger and criminal ruthlessness. The first volume of the present publication has the aim of uncloaking these sheep, who take themselves and are taken for wolves; of showing that their bleating merely imitates in a philosophic form the conceptions of the German middle class; that the boasting of these philosophic commentators only mirrors the wretchedness of the real conditions in Germany. It is its aim to ridicule and discredit the philosophic struggle with the shadows of reality, which appeals to the dreamy and muddled German nation.

---

[a] Ludwig Feuerbach.— *Ed.*
[b] Bruno Bauer.— *Ed.*
[c] Max Stirner.— *Ed.*

Once upon a time a valiant fellow had the idea that men were drowned in water only because they were possessed with the *idea of gravity*. If they were to get this notion out of their heads, say by avowing it to be a superstitious, a religious concept, they would be sublimely proof against any danger from water. His whole life long he fought against the illusion of gravity, of whose harmful consequences all statistics brought him new and manifold evidence. This valiant fellow was the type of the new revolutionary philosophers in Germany.*

---

* [The following passage is crossed out in the manuscript:] There is no specific difference between German idealism and the ideology of all the other nations. The latter too regards the world as dominated by ideas, ideas and concepts as the determining principles, and certain notions as the mystery of the material world accessible to the philosophers.

Hegel completed positive idealism. He not only turned the whole material world into a world of ideas and the whole of history into a history of ideas. He was not content with recording thought entities, he also sought to describe the act of creation.

Roused from their world of fancy, the German philosophers protest against the world of ideas to which they [...] the conception of the real, material [...].

All the German philosophical critics assert that the real world of men has hitherto been dominated and determined by ideas, images, concepts, and that the real world is a product of the world of ideas. This has been the case up to now, but it ought to be changed. They differ from each other in the manner in which they intend to deliver mankind, which in their opinion is groaning under the weight of its own fixed ideas; they differ in respect of what they proclaim to be fixed ideas; they agree in their belief in the hegemony of ideas, they agree in the belief that the action of their critical reason must bring about the destruction of the existing order of things: whether they consider their isolated rational activity sufficient or want to conquer universal consciousness.

The belief that the real world is the product of the ideal world, that the world of ideas [...].

Having lost their faith in the Hegelian world of ideas, the German philosophers protest against the domination of thoughts, ideas and concepts which, according to their opinion, i.e., according to *Hegel's illusion*, have hitherto produced, determined and dominated the real world. They make their protest and expire [...].

According to the Hegelian system ideas, thoughts and concepts have produced, determined, dominated the real life of men, their material world, their actual relations. His rebellious disciples take this [...].

First page of the Preface to *The German Ideology*
in Marx's handwriting
(*Reduced*)

I

FEUERBACH

OPPOSITION OF THE MATERIALIST AND IDEALIST OUTLOOKS[2]

[I]

[sh.1] According to German ideologists, Germany has in the last few years gone through an unparalleled revolution. The decomposition of the Hegelian system, which began with Strauss,[3] has developed into a universal ferment into which all the "powers of the past" are swept. In the general chaos mighty empires have arisen only to meet with immediate doom, heroes have emerged momentarily to be again hurled into obscurity by bolder and stronger rivals. It was a revolution beside which the French Revolution was child's play, a world struggle beside which the struggles of the Diadochi[4] appear insignificant. Principles ousted one another, intellectual heroes overthrew each other with unheard-of rapidity, and in the three years 1842-45 more was cleared away in Germany than at other times in three centuries.

All this is supposed to have taken place in the realm of pure thought.

Certainly it is an interesting event we are dealing with: the putrescence of the absolute spirit. When the last spark of its life had failed, the various components of this *caput mortuum*[a] began to decompose, entered into new combinations and formed new substances. The industrialists of philosophy, who till then had lived on the exploitation of the absolute spirit, now seized upon the new combinations. Each with all possible zeal set about retailing his apportioned share. This was bound to give rise to competition, which, to start with, was carried on in moderately civil and staid fashion. Later, when the German market was glutted, and the commodity in spite of all efforts was not favourably received in the world market, the business was spoiled in the usual German manner by cheap and spurious production, deterioration in quality, adulteration of the raw

---

[a] Literally: dead head; a term used in chemistry for the residuum left after distillation; here: remainder, residue.— *Ed.*

materials, falsification of labels, fictitious purchases, bill-jobbing and a credit system devoid of any real basis. The competition turned into a bitter struggle, which is now being extolled and interpreted to us as an upheaval of world significance, the begetter of the most prodigious results and achievements.

If we wish to rate at its true value this philosophic charlatanry, which awakens even in the breast of the righteous German citizen a glow of patriotic feeling, if we wish to bring out clearly the pettiness, the parochial narrowness of this whole Young-Hegelian movement and in particular the tragi-comic contrast between the illusions of these heroes about their achievements and the actual achievements themselves, we must look at the whole spectacle from a standpoint beyond the frontiers of Germany.*

[1.] IDEOLOGY IN GENERAL, GERMAN IDEOLOGY IN PARTICULAR

|sh.2| German criticism has, right up to its latest efforts, never left the realm of philosophy. It by no means examines its general philosophic premises, but in fact all its problems originate in a definite philosophical system, that of Hegel. Not only in its answers, even in its questions there was a mystification. This dependence on Hegel is the reason why not one of these modern critics has even attempted a comprehensive criticism of the Hegelian system, however much each

*[In the first version of the clean copy there follows a passage, which is crossed out:]

|p. 2| We preface therefore the specific criticism of individual representatives of this movement with a few general observations, elucidating the ideological premises common to all of them. These remarks will suffice to indicate the standpoint of our criticism insofar as it is required for the understanding and the motivation of the subsequent individual criticisms. We oppose these remarks |p. 3| to *Feuerbach* in particular because he is the only one who has at least made some progress and whose works can be examined *de bonne foi.*

1. Ideology in General, and Especially German Philosophy

A. We know only a single science, the science of history. One can look at history from two sides and divide it into the history of nature and the history of men. The two sides are, however, inseparable; the history of nature and the history of men are dependent on each other so long as men exist. The history of nature, called natural science, does not concern us here; but we will have to examine the history of men, since almost the whole ideology amounts either to a distorted conception of this history or to a complete abstraction from it. Ideology is itself only one of the aspects of this history.

[There follows a passage dealing with the premises of the materialist conception of history. It is not crossed out and in this volume it is reproduced as Section 2; see pp. 36-37.]

professes to have advanced beyond Hegel. Their polemics
against Hegel and against one another are confined to
this — each takes one aspect of the Hegelian system and turns
this against the whole system as well as against the aspects
chosen by the others. To begin with they took pure, unfalsified
Hegelian categories such as "substance" and "self-consciousness",[a] later they secularised these categories by giving them
more profane names such as "species", "the unique", "man",[b]
etc.

The entire body of German philosophical criticism from
Strauss to Stirner is confined to criticism of *religious* conceptions.* The critics started from real religion and theology
proper. What religious consciousness and religious conception
are was subsequently defined in various ways. The advance
consisted in including the allegedly dominant metaphysical,
political, juridical, moral and other conceptions under the
category of religious or theological conceptions; and similarly in
declaring that political, juridical, moral consciousness was
religious or theological consciousness, and that the political,
juridical, moral man — "Man" in the last resort — was religious.
The dominance of religion was presupposed. Gradually
every dominant relationship was declared to be a religious
relationship and transformed into a cult, a cult of law, a cult of
the state, etc. It was throughout merely a question of dogmas
and belief in dogmas. The world was sanctified to an
ever-increasing extent till at last the venerable Saint Max[c] was
able to canonise it *en bloc* and thus dispose of it once for all.

The Old Hegelians had *understood* everything as soon as it
was reduced to a Hegelian logical category. The Young
Hegelians *criticised* everything by ascribing religious conceptions to it or by declaring that it is a theological matter.The
Young Hegelians are in agreement with the Old Hegelians in
their belief in the rule of religion, of concepts, of a universal
principle in the existing world. Except that the one party attacks
this rule as usurpation, while the other extols it as
legitimate.

Since the Young Hegelians consider conceptions, thoughts,
ideas, in fact all the products of consciousness, to which they

* [The following passage is crossed out in the manuscript:] claiming to be
the absolute redeemer of the world from all evil. Religion was continually
regarded and treated as the arch-enemy, as the ultimate cause of all relations
repugnant to these philosophers.

[a] The basic categories of David Friedrich Strauss and Bruno Bauer.— *Ed*.
[b] The basic categories of Ludwig Feuerbach and Max Stirner.— *Ed*.
[c] Max Stirner.— *Ed*.

attribute an independent existence, as the real chains of men (just as the Old Hegelians declare them the true bonds of human society), it is evident that the Young Hegelians have to fight only against these illusions of consciousness. Since, according to their fantasy, the relations of men, all their doings, their fetters and their limitations are products of their consciousness, the Young Hegelians logically put to men the moral postulate of exchanging their present consciousness for human, critical or egoistic consciousness,[a] and thus of removing their limitations. This demand to change consciousness amounts to a demand to interpret the existing world in a different way, i.e., to recognise it by means of a different interpretation. The Young-Hegelian ideologists, in spite of their allegedly "world-shattering"[b] phrases, are the staunchest conservatives. The most recent of them have found the correct expression for their activity when they declare they are only fighting against "*phrases*". They forget, however, that they themselves are opposing nothing but phrases to these phrases, and that they are in no way combating the real existing world when they are combating solely the phrases of this world. The only results which this philosophic criticism was able to achieve were a few (and at that one-sided) elucidations of Christianity from the point of view of religious history; all the rest of their assertions are only further embellishments of their claim to have furnished, in these unimportant elucidations, discoveries of world-historic importance.

It has not occurred to any one of these philosophers to inquire into the connection of German philosophy with German reality, the connection of their criticism with their own material surroundings.[c]

[2. PREMISES OF THE MATERIALIST CONCEPTION OF HISTORY[d]]

|p. 3| The premises from which we begin are not arbitrary ones, not dogmas, but real premises from which abstraction can only be made in the imagination. They are the real individuals,

---

[a] A reference to Ludwig Feuerbach, Bruno Bauer and Max Stirner, whose basic categories were, respectively, "man", "criticism" and "ego".— *Ed.*

[b] Cf. "Ueber das Recht des Freigesprochenen..." published anonymously in *Wigand's Vierteljahrsschrift*, 1845, Bd. IV.— *Ed.*

[c] The rest of this page of the manuscript is left blank. The text following on the next page of the manuscript is reproduced in this volume as Section 3; see pp. 38-41.— *Ed.*

[d] The text of the following section has been taken from the first version of the clean copy.— *Ed.*

their activity and the material conditions of their life, both those which they find already existing and those produced by their activity. These premises can thus be |p.4| verified in a purely empirical way.

The first premise of all human history is, of course, the existence of living human individuals.* Thus the first fact to be established is the physical organisation of these individuals and their consequent relation to the rest of nature. Of course, we cannot here go either into the actual physical nature of man, or into the natural conditions in which man finds himself—geological, oro-hydrographical, climatic and so on.** All historical writing must set out from these natural bases and their modification in the course of history through the action of men.

Men can be distinguished from animals by consciousness, by religion or anything else you like. They themselves begin to distinguish themselves from animals as soon as they begin to *produce* their means of subsistence, a step which is conditioned by their physical organisation. By producing their means of subsistence men are indirectly producing their material life.

The way in which men produce their means of subsistence depends first of all on the nature of the means of subsistence they actually find in existence and have to reproduce.

|p. 5| This mode of production must not be considered simply as being the reproduction of the physical existence of the individuals. Rather it is a definite form of activity of these individuals, a definite form of expressing their life, a definite *mode of life* on their part. As individuals express their life, so they are. What they are, therefore, coincides with their production, both with *what* they produce and with *how* they produce. Hence what individuals are depends on the material conditions of their production.

This production only makes its appearance with the *increase of population.* In its turn this presupposes the *intercourse* [*Verkehr*] [5] of individuals with one another. The form of this intercourse is again determined by production.

---

* [The following passage is crossed out in the manuscript:] The first *historical* act of these individuals distinguishing them from animals is not that they think, but that they begin *to produce their means of subsistence.*

** [The following passage is crossed out in the manuscript:] These conditions determine not only the original, spontaneous organisation of men, especially racial differences, but also the entire further development, or lack of development, of men up to the present time.

[3. PRODUCTION AND INTERCOURSE. DIVISION OF LABOUR AND
FORMS OF PROPERTY—TRIBAL, ANCIENT, FEUDAL]

|sh. 3| The relations of different nations among themselves
depend upon the extent to which each has developed its
productive forces, the division of labour and internal intercourse. This proposition is generally recognised. But not only
the relation of one nation to others, but also the whole internal
structure of the nation itself depends on the stage of
development reached by its production and its internal and
external intercourse. How far the productive forces of a nation
are developed is shown most manifestly by the degree to which
the division of labour has been carried. Each new productive
force, insofar as it is not merely a quantitative extension of
productive forces already known (for instance, the bringing into
cultivation of fresh land), causes a further development of the
division of labour.

The division of labour inside a nation leads at first to the
separation of industrial and commercial from agricultural
labour, and hence to the separation of *town* and *country* and to
the conflict of their interests. Its further development leads to
the separation of commercial from industrial labour. At the
same time through the division of labour inside these various
branches there develop various divisions among the individuals
co-operating in definite kinds of labour. The relative position
of these individual groups is determined by the way work is
organised in agriculture, industry and commerce (patriarchal-
ism, slavery, estates, classes). These same conditions are to be
seen (given a more developed intercourse) in the relations of
different nations to one another.

The various stages of development in the division of labour
are just so many different forms of property, i.e., the existing
stage in the division of labour determines also the relations of
individuals to one another with reference to the material,
instrument and product of labour.

The first form of property is tribal property [*Stammeigen-
tum*] [6] It corresponds to the undeveloped stage of production, at
which a people lives by hunting and fishing, by cattle-raising or,
at most, by agriculture. In the latter case it presupposes a great
mass of uncultivated stretches of land. The division of labour is
at this stage still very elementary and is confined to a further
extension of the natural division of labour existing in the family.
The social structure is, therefore, limited to an extension of the
family: patriarchal chieftains, below them the members of the
tribe, finally slaves. The slavery latent in the family only

develops gradually with the increase of population, the growth of wants, and with the extension of external intercourse, both of war and of barter.

The second form is the ancient communal and state property, which proceeds especially from the union of several tribes into a *city* by agreement or by conquest, and which is still accompanied by slavery. Beside communal property we already find movable, and later also immovable, private property developing, but as an abnormal form subordinate to communal property. The citizens hold power over their labouring slaves only in their community, and even on this account alone they are bound to the form of communal property. It constitutes the communal private property of the active citizens who, in relation to their slaves, are compelled to remain in this spontaneously derived form of association. For this reason the whole structure of society based on this communal property, and with it the power of the people, decays in the same measure in which immovable private property evolves. The division of labour is already more developed. We already find the opposition of town and country; later the opposition between those states which represent town interests and those which represent country interests, and inside the towns themselves the opposition between industry and maritime commerce. The class relations between citizens and slaves are now completely developed.

With the development of private property, we find here for the first time the same relations which we shall find again, only on a more extensive scale, with modern private property. On the one hand, the concentration of private property, which began very early in Rome (as the Licinian agrarian law proves) and proceeded very rapidly from the time of the civil wars and especially under the emperors[7]; on the other hand, coupled with this, the transformation of the plebeian small peasantry into a proletariat, which, however, owing to its intermediate position between propertied citizens and slaves, never achieved an independent development.

The third form is feudal or estate property. If antiquity started out from the *town* and its small territory, the Middle Ages started out from the *country*. This different starting-point was determined by the sparseness of the population at that time, which was scattered over a large area and which received no large increases from the conquerors. In contrast to Greece and Rome, feudal development, therefore, begins over a much wider territory, prepared by the Roman conquests and the spread of agriculture at first associated with them. The last centuries of the declining Roman Empire and its conquest by the barbarians destroyed a considerable part of the productive forces; agriculture had declined, industry had decayed for want of a market, trade had died out or been violently interrupted, the rural and urban population had decreased. These conditions and the mode of organisation of the conquest determined by them, together with the influence of the Germanic military constitution, led to the development of feudal property. Like tribal and communal property, it is also based on a community; but the directly producing class standing over against it is not, as in the case of the ancient community, the slaves, but the enserfed small peasantry. As soon as feudalism is fully developed, there also arises antagonism to the towns. The hierarchical structure of landownership, and the armed bodies of retainers associated with it, gave the nobility power over the serfs. This feudal organisation was, just as much as the ancient communal property, an association against a subjected producing class; but the form of association and the relation to the direct producers were different because of the different conditions of production.

This feudal structure of landownership had its counterpart in the *towns* in the shape of corporative property, the feudal organisation of trades. Here property consisted |sh. 4| chiefly in the labour of each individual. The necessity for associating against the association of the robber-nobility, the need for communal covered markets in an age when the industrialist was at the same time a merchant, the growing competition of the escaped serfs swarming into the rising towns, the feudal structure of the whole country: these combined to bring about the *guilds*. The gradually accumulated small capital of individual craftsmen and their stable numbers, as against the growing population, evolved the relation of journeyman and apprentice, which brought into being in the towns a hierarchy similar to that in the country.

Thus property during the feudal epoch primarily consisted on the one hand of landed property with serf labour chained to it, and on the other of the personal labour of the individual who with his small capital commands the labour of journeymen. The organisation of both was determined by the restricted conditions of production[a]—the scanty and primitive cultivation of the land, and the craft type of industry. There was little division of labour in the heyday of feudalism. Each country bore in itself

---

[a] In the German original *Produktionsverhältnisse.— Ed.*

the antithesis of town and country; the division into estates was certainly strongly marked; but apart from the differentiation of princes, nobility, clergy and peasants in the country, and masters, journeymen, apprentices and soon also the rabble of casual labourers in the towns, there was no important division. In agriculture it was rendered difficult by the strip-system, beside which the cottage industry of the peasants themselves emerged. In industry, in the individual trades themselves, there was no division of labour at all and very little between them. The separation of industry and commerce was found already in existence in older towns; in the newer it only developed later, when the towns entered into mutual relations.

The grouping of larger territories into feudal kingdoms was a necessity for the landed nobility as for the towns. The organisation of the ruling class, the nobility, had, therefore, everywhere a monarch at its head.[a]

[4. THE ESSENCE OF THE MATERIALIST CONCEPTION OF HISTORY. SOCIAL BEING AND SOCIAL CONSCIOUSNESS]

|sh. 5| The fact is, therefore, that definite individuals who are productively active in a definite way* enter into these definite social and political relations. Empirical observation must in each separate instance bring out empirically, and without any mystification and speculation, the connection of the social and political structure with production. The social structure and the state are continually evolving out of the life-process of definite individuals, however, of these individuals, not as they may appear in their own or other people's imagination, but as they *actually* are, i.e., as they act, produce materially, and hence as they work under definite material limits, presuppositions and conditions independent of their will.**

* [The manuscript originally had:] definite individuals under definite conditions of production.

** [The following passage is crossed out in the manuscript:] The ideas which these individuals form are ideas either about their relation to nature or about their mutual relations or about their own nature. It is evident that in all these cases their ideas are the conscious expression — real or illusory — of their real relations and activities, of their production, of their intercourse, of their social and political conduct. The opposite assumption is only possible if in addition to the spirit of the real, materially evolved individuals a separate spirit is presupposed. If the conscious expression of the real relations of these individuals is illusory, if in their imagination they turn reality upside-down, then this in its turn is the result of their limited material mode of activity and their limited social relations arising from it.

---

[a] The rest of this page of the manuscript is left blank. The next page begins with a summary of the materialist conception of history. The main stages of the development of the fourth, the bourgeois, form of property are dealt with in Part IV of this chapter. Sections 2-4; see pp. 72-82.— *Ed.*

The production of ideas, of conceptions, of consciousness, is at first directly interwoven with the material activity and the material intercourse of men — the language of real life. Conceiving, thinking, the mental intercourse of men at this stage still appear as the direct efflux of their material behaviour. The same applies to mental production as expressed in the language of the politics, laws, morality, religion, metaphysics, etc., of a people. Men are the producers of their conceptions, ideas, etc., that is, real, active men, as they are conditioned by a definite development of their productive forces and of the intercourse corresponding to these, up to its furthest forms.* Consciousness [*das Bewusstsein*] can never be anything else than conscious being [*das bewusste Sein*], and the being of men is their actual life-process. If in all ideology men and their relations appear upside-down as in a *camera obscura*, this phenomenon arises just as much from their historical life-process as the inversion of objects on the retina does from their physical life-process.

In direct contrast to German philosophy which descends from heaven to earth, here it is a matter of ascending from earth to heaven. That is to say, not of setting out from what men say, imagine, conceive, nor from men as narrated, thought of, imagined, conceived, in order to arrive at men in the flesh; but setting out from real, active men, and on the basis of their real life-process demonstrating the development of the ideological reflexes and echoes of this life-process. The phantoms formed in the brains of men are also, necessarily, sublimates of their material life-process, which is empirically verifiable and bound to material premises. Morality, religion, metaphysics, and all the rest of ideology as well as the forms of consciousness corresponding to these, thus no longer retain the semblance of independence. They have no history, no development; but men, developing their material production and their material intercourse, alter, along with this their actual world, also their thinking and the products of their thinking. It is not consciousness that determines life, but life that determines consciousness. For the first manner of approach the starting-point is consciousness taken as the living individual; for the second manner of approach, which conforms to real life, it is the real

---

* [The manuscript originally had:] Men are the producers of their conceptions, ideas, etc., and precisely men conditioned by the mode of production of their material life, by their material intercourse and its further development in the social and political structure.

living individuals themselves, and consciousness is considered solely as *their* consciousness.

This manner of approach is not devoid of premises. It starts out from the real premises and does not abandon them for a moment. Its premises are men, not in any fantastic isolation and fixity, but in their actual, empirically perceptible process of development under definite conditions. As soon as this active life-process is described, history ceases to be a collection of dead facts, as it is with the empiricists (themselves still abstract), or an imagined activity of imagined subjects, as with the idealists.

Where speculation ends, where real life starts, there consequently begins real, positive science, the expounding of the practical activity, of the practical process of development of men. Empty phrases about consciousness end, and real knowledge has to take their place. When the reality is described, a self-sufficient philosophy [*die selbständige Philosophie*] loses its medium of existence. At the best its place can only be taken by a summing-up of the most general results, abstractions which are derived from the observation of the historical development of men. These abstractions in themselves, divorced from real history, have no value whatsoever. They can only serve to facilitate the arrangement of historical material, to indicate the sequence of its separate strata. But they by no means afford a recipe or schema, as does philosophy, for neatly trimming the epochs of history. On the contrary, the difficulties begin only when one sets about the examination and arrangement of the material—whether of a past epoch or of the present—and its actual presentation. The removal of these difficulties is governed by premises which certainly cannot be stated here, but which only the study of the actual life-process and the activity of the individuals of each epoch will make evident. We shall select here some of these abstractions, which we use in contradistinction to ideology, and shall illustrate them by historical examples.[a]

[II]

[1. PRECONDITIONS OF THE REAL LIBERATION OF MAN]

[1] We shall, of course, not take the trouble to explain to our wise philosophers that the "liberation" of "man" is not advanced a single step by reducing philosophy, theology, substance and all the rubbish to "self-consciousness" and by

---

[a] The clean copy ends here. The text that follows in this edition are the three parts of the rough copy of the manuscript.— *Ed.*

liberating "man" from the domination of these phrases, which have never held him in thrall.* Nor shall we explain to them that it is possible to achieve real liberation only in the real world and by real means, that slavery cannot be abolished without the steam-engine and the mule jenny, serfdom cannot be abolished without improved agriculture, and that, in general, people cannot be liberated as long as they are unable to obtain food and drink, housing and clothing in adequate quality and quantity. "Liberation" is a historical and not a mental act, and it is brought about by historical conditions, the [level] of industry, com[merce], [agri]culture, [intercourse...]ᵃ |2| then subsequently, in accordance with the different stages of their development, [they make up] the nonsense of substance, subject, self-consciousness and pure criticism, as well as religious and theological nonsense, and later they get rid of it again when their development is sufficiently advanced.** In Germany, a country where only a trivial historical development is taking place, these mental developments, these glorified and ineffective trivialities, naturally serve as a substitute for the lack of historical development, and they take root and have to be combated. But this fight is of *local* importance.***

[2. FEUERBACH'S CONTEMPLATIVE AND INCONSISTENT MATERIALISM]

[...]ᵇ |8| in reality and for the *practical* materialist, i.e., the *Communist*, it is a question of revolutionising the existing world, of practically coming to grips with and changing the things found in existence. When occasionally we find such views with Feuerbach, they are never more than isolated surmises and have much too little influence on his general outlook to be considered here as anything but embryos capable of development. Feuerbach's "conception" of the sensuous world is confined on the one hand to mere contemplation of it, and on the other to mere feeling; he posits "Man" instead of "real historical man".⁸

---

* [Marginal notes by Marx:] Philosophic liberation and real liberation.— *Man*. The *unique*. The *individual*.—Geological, hydrographical, etc., conditions. The human body. Needs and labour.

** [Marginal note by Marx:] Phrases and real movement. The importance of phrases in Germany.

*** [Marginal note by Marx:] Language is the language of re[ality].

ᵃ The manuscript is damaged here: the lower part of the sheet is torn off; one line of the text is missing.— *Ed.*

ᵇ Five pages of the manuscript are missing.— *Ed.*

"Man" is really "the German". In the first case, the *contempla-tion* of the sensuous world, he necessarily lights on things which contradict his consciousness and feeling, which disturb the harmony he presupposes, the harmony of all parts of the sensuous world and especially of man and nature.* To remove this disturbance, he must take refuge in a double perception, a profane one which perceives "only the flatly obvious" and a higher, philosophical, one which perceives the "true essence" of things. He does not see that the sensuous world around him is not a thing given direct from all eternity, remaining ever the same, but the product of industry and of the state of society; and, indeed, [a product] in the sense that it is an historical product, the result of the activity of a whole succession of generations, each standing on the shoulders of the preceding one, developing its industry and its intercourse, and modifying its social system according to the changed needs. Even the objects of the simplest "sensuous certainty" are only given him through social development, industry and commercial inter-course. The cherry-tree, like almost all fruit-trees, was, as is well known, only a few centuries ago transplanted by *commerce* into our zone, and therefore only |9| *by* this action of a definite society in a definite age has it become "sensuous certainty" for Feuerbach.

Incidentally, when things are seen in this way, as they really are and happened, every profound philosophical problem is resolved, as will be seen even more clearly later, quite simply into an empirical fact. For instance, the important question of the relation of man to nature (Bruno goes so far as to speak of "the antitheses in nature and history" (p. 110),[a] as though these were two separate "things" and man did not always have before him an historical nature and a natural history), which gave rise to all the "unfathomably lofty works"[b] on "substance" and "self-consciousness", crumbles of itself when we understand that the celebrated "unity of man with nature" has always existed in industry and has existed in varying forms in every epoch according to the lesser or greater development of industry, and so has the "struggle" of man with nature, right up to the development of his productive forces on a corresponding

* NB. F[euerbach's] error is not that he subordinates the flatly obvious, the sensuous *appearance*, to the sensuous reality established by detailed investigation of the sensuous facts, but that he cannot in the last resort cope with the sensuous world except by looking at it with the "eyes", i.e., through the "spectacles", of the *philosopher*.

[a] Bruno Bauer, "Charakteristik Ludwig Feuerbachs" — *Ed.*
[b] Paraphrase of a line from Goethe's *Faust,* "Prolog im Himmel". — *Ed.*

basis. Industry and commerce, production and the exchange of the necessities of life in their turn determine distribution, the structure of the different social classes and are, in turn, determined by it as to the mode in which they are carried on; and so it happens that in Manchester, for instance, Feuerbach sees only factories and machines, where a hundred years ago only spinning-wheels and weaving-looms were to be seen, or in the Campagna di Roma he finds only pasture lands and swamps, where in the time of Augustus he would have found nothing but the vineyards and villas of Roman capitalists. Feuerbach speaks in particular of the perception of natural science; he mentions secrets which are disclosed only to the eye of the physicist and chemist; but where would natural science be without industry and commerce? Even this "pure" natural science is provided with an aim, as with its material, only through trade and industry, through the sensuous activity of men. So much is this activity, this unceasing sensuous labour and creation, this production, the foundation of the whole sensuous world as it now exists that, were it interrupted only for a year, Feuerbach would not only find an enormous change in the natural world, but would very soon find that the whole world of men and his own perceptive faculty, nay his own esistence, were missing. Of course, in all this the priority of external nature remains unassailed, and all this has no |10| application to the original men produced by *generatio aequivoca*[a]; but this differentiation has meaning only insofar as man is considered to be distinct from nature. For that matter, nature, the nature that preceded human history, is not by any means the nature in which Feuerbach lives, it is nature which today no longer exists anywhere (except perhaps on a few Australian coral islands of recent origin) and which, therefore, does not exist for Feuerbach either.

|9| Certainly Feuerbach has |10| a great advantage over the "pure" materialists since he realises that man too is an "object of the senses". But apart from the fact that he only conceives him as an "object of the senses", not as "sensuous activity", because he still remains in the realm of theory and conceives of men not in their given social connection, not under their existing conditions of life, which have made them *what* they are, he never arrives at the actually existing, active men, but stops at the abstraction "man", and gets no further than recognising "the actual, individual, corporeal man" emotionally, i.e., he knows no other "human relations" "of man to man" than love and

---

[a] Spontaneous generation.— *Ed.*

friendship, and even then idealised. He gives no criticism of the present conditions of life. Thus he never manages to conceive the sensuous world as the total living sensuous *activity* of the individuals composing it; therefore when, for example, he sees instead of healthy men a crowd of scrofulous, overworked and consumptive starvelings, he is compelled to take refuge in the "higher perception" and in the ideal "compensation in the species", and thus to relapse into idealism at the very point where the communist materialist sees the necessity, and at the same time the condition, of a transformation both of industry and of the social structure.

As far as Feuerbach is a materialist he does not deal with history, and as far as he considers history he is not a materialist. With him materialism and history diverge completely, a fact which incidentally already follows from what has been said.*

[3. PRIMARY HISTORICAL RELATIONS, OR THE BASIC ASPECTS OF SOCIAL ACTIVITY: PRODUCTION OF THE MEANS OF SUBSISTENCE, PRODUCTION OF NEW NEEDS, REPRODUCTION OF MEN (THE FAMILY), SOCIAL INTERCOURSE, CONSCIOUSNESS]

|11|** Since we are dealing with the Germans, who are devoid of premises, we must begin by stating the first premise of all human existence and, therefore, of all history, the premise, namely, that men must be in a position to live in order to be able to "make history".[a] But life involves before everything else eating and drinking, housing, clothing and various other things.*** The first historical act is thus the production of the means to satisfy these needs, the production of material life itself. And indeed this is an historical act, a fundamental condition of all history, which today, as thousands of years ago, must daily and hourly be fulfilled merely in order to sustain human life. Even when the sensuous world is reduced to a minimum, to a stick[b] as with Saint Bruno, it presupposes the action of pro-

---

* [The following passage is crossed out in the manuscript:] The reason why we nevertheless discuss history here in greater detail is that the words "history" and "historical" usually mean everything possible to the Germans except reality, a brilliant example of this is in particular Saint Bruno with his "pulpit eloquence".

** [Marginal note by Marx:] *History.*

*** [Marginal note by Marx:] *Hegel.* Geological, hydrographical, etc., conditions.[9] Human bodies. Needs, labour.

---

[a] See this volume, pp.64-65.— *Ed.*

[b] See Bruno Bauer's article "Charakteristik Ludwig Feuerbachs". Cf. this volume, pp. 103 and 113-14.— *Ed.*

ducing this stick. Therefore in any conception of history one has first of all to observe this fundamental fact in all its significance and all its implications and to accord it its due importance. It is well known that the Germans have never done this, and they have never, therefore, had an *earthly* basis for history and consequently never a historian. The French and the English, even if they have conceived the relation of this fact with so-called history only in an extremely one-sided fashion, especially since they remained in the toils of political ideology, have nevertheless made the first attempts to give the writing of history a materialistic basis by being the first to write histories of civil society, of commerce and industry.[10]

The second point is [12] that the satisfaction of the first need, the action of satisfying and the instrument of satisfaction which has been acquired, leads to new needs; and this creation of new needs is the first historical act. Here we recognise immediately the spiritual ancestry of the great historical wisdom of the Germans who, when they run out of positive material and when they can serve up neither theological nor political nor literary rubbish, assert that this is not history at all, but the "prehistoric age". They do not, however, enlighten us as to how we proceed from this nonsensical "prehistory" to history proper; although, on the other hand, in their historical speculation they seize upon this "prehistory" with especial eagerness because they imagine themselves safe there from interference on the part of "crude facts", and, at the same time, because there they can give full rein to their speculative impulse and set up and knock down hypotheses by the thousand.

The third circumstance which, from the very outset, enters into historical development, is that men, who daily re-create their own life, begin to make other men, to propagate their kind: the relation between man and woman, parents and children, the *family*. The family, which to begin with is the only social relation, becomes later, when increased needs create new social relations and the increased population new needs, a subordinate one (except in Germany), and must then be treated and analysed according to the existing empirical data, not according to "the concept of the family", as is the custom in Germany.

These three aspects of social activity are not of course to be taken as three different stages, but just as three aspects or, to make it clear to the Germans, three "moments", which have existed simultaneously since the dawn of history and the first men, and which still assert themselves in history today.

The production of life, both of one's own in labour and of

fresh life in procreation, now appears as a twofold |13|
relation: on the one hand as a natural, on the other as a
social relation — social in the sense that it denotes the
co-operation of several individuals, no matter under what
conditions, in what manner and to what end. It follows from this
that a certain mode of production, or industrial stage, is always
combined with a certain mode of co-operation, or social stage,
and this mode of co-operation is itself a "productive force".
Further, that the aggregate of productive forces accessible to
men determines the condition of society, hence, the "history of
humanity" must always be studied and treated in relation to the
history of industry and exchange. But it is also clear that in
Germany it is impossible to write this sort of history, because
the Germans lack not only the necessary power of comprehension and the material but also the "sensuous certainty", for
across the Rhine one cannot have any experience of these things
since there history has stopped happening. Thus it is quite
obvious from the start that there exists a materialist
connection of men with one another, which is determined by
their needs and their mode of production, and which is as old as
men themselves. This connection is ever taking on new forms,
and thus presents a "history" irrespective of the existence of
any political or religious nonsense which would especially hold
men together.

Only now, after having considered four moments, four
aspects of primary historical relations, do we find that
man also possesses "consciousness".* But even from the
outset this is not "pure" consciousness. The "mind" is from the
outset afflicted with |14| the curse of being "burdened" with
matter, which here makes its appearance in the form of agitated
layers of air, sounds, in short, of language. Language is as old as
consciousness, language *is* practical, real consciousness that
exists for other men as well, and only therefore does it also
exist for me; language, like consciousness, only arises from the
need, the necessity of intercourse with other men.** Where
there exists a relationship, it exists for me; the animal does not
"*relate*" itself to anything, it does not "*relate*" itself at all. For
the animal its relation to others does not exist as a relation.
Consciousness is, therefore, from the very beginning a

---

* [Marginal note by Marx:] Men have history because they must *produce*
their life, and because they must produce it moreover in a *certain* way: this is
determined by their physical organisation; their consciousness is determined in
just the same way.
** [The following words are crossed out in the manuscript:] My relation to
my surroundings is my consciousness.

social product, and remains so as long as men exist at all. Consciousness is at first, of course, merely consciousness concerning the *immediate* sensuous environment and consciousness of the limited connection with other persons and things outside the individual who is growing self-conscious. At the same time it is consciousness of nature, which first confronts men as a completely alien, all-powerful and unassailable force, with which men's relations are purely animal and by which they are overawed like beasts; it is thus a purely animal consciousness of nature (natural religion) precisely because nature is as yet hardly altered by history — on the other hand, it is man's consciousness of the necessity of associating with the individuals around him, the beginning of the consciousness that he is living in society at all. This beginning is as animal as social life itself at this stage. It is mere herd-consciousness, and at this point man is distinguished from sheep only by the fact that with him consciousness takes the place of instinct or that his instinct is a conscious one.* This sheep-like or tribal consciousness receives its further development and extension through increased productivity, the increase of needs, and, what is fundamental to both of these, |15| the increase of population. With these there develops the division of labour, which was originally nothing but the division of labour in the sexual act, then the division of labour which develops spontaneously or "naturally" by virtue of natural predisposition (e. g., physical strength), needs, accidents, etc., etc.** Division of labour only becomes truly such from the moment when a division of material and mental labour appears.*** From this moment onwards consciousness *can* really flatter itself that it is something other than consciousness of existing practice, that it *really* represents something without representing something real; from now on consciousness is in a position to emancipate itself from the world and to proceed to the formation of "pure" theory, theology, philosophy, morality, etc. But even if this theory, theology, philosophy, morality, etc., come into con-

---

* [Marginal note by Marx:] We see here immediately: this natural religion or this particular attitude to nature is determined by the form of society and vice versa. Here, as everywhere, the identity of nature and man also appears in such a way that the restricted attitude of men to nature determines their restricted relation to one another, and their restricted attitude to one another determines men's restricted relation to nature.

** [Marginal note by Marx, which is crossed out in the manuscript:] Men's consciousness develops in the course of actual historical development.

*** [Marginal note by Marx:] The first form of ideologists, *priests,* is coincident.

tradiction with the existing relations, this can only occur because existing social relations have come into contradiction with existing productive forces; moreover, in a particular national sphere of relations this can also occur through the contradiction, arising not within the national orbit, but between this national consciousness and the practice of other nations,* i.e., between the national and the general consciousness of a nation (as is happening now in Germany); but since this contradiction appears to exist only as a contradiction within the national consciousness, it seems to this nation that the struggle too is confined to this |16| national muck, precisely because this nation represents this muck as such.

Incidentally, it is quite immaterial what consciousness starts to do on its own: out of all this trash we get only the one inference that these three moments, the productive forces, the state of society and consciousness, can and must come into contradiction with one another, because the *division of labour* implies the possibility, nay the fact, that intellectual and material activity,** that enjoyment and labour, production and consumption, devolve on different individuals, and that the only possibility of their not coming into contradiction lies in negating in its turn the division of labour. It is self-evident, moreover, that "spectres", "bonds", "the higher being", "concept", "scruple", are merely idealist, speculative, mental expressions, the concepts apparently of the isolated individual, the mere images of very empirical fetters and limitations, within which move the mode of production of life, and the form of intercourse coupled with it.***

[4. SOCIAL DIVISION OF LABOUR AND ITS CONSEQUENCES: PRIVATE PROPERTY, THE STATE, "ESTRANGEMENT" OF SOCIAL ACTIVITY]

The division of labour in which all these contradictions are implicit, and which in its turn is based on the natural division of labour in the family and the separation of society into individual families opposed to one another, simultane-

---

* [Marginal note by Marx:] *Religions.* The Germans and *ideology* as such.
** [Marginal note by Marx, which is crossed out in the manuscript:] activity and thinking, i.e., action without thought and thought without action.
*** [The following sentence is crossed out in the manuscript:] This idealist expression of actually present economic limitations exists not only purely theoretically but also in the practical consciousness, i.e., consciousness which emancipates itself and comes into contradiction with the existing mode of production devises not only religions and philosophies but also states.

ously implies the *distribution*, and indeed the *unequal* distribution, both quantitative and qualitative, of labour and its products, hence property, |17| the nucleus, the first form of which lies in the family, where wife and children are the slaves of the husband. This latent slavery in the family, though still very crude, is the first form of property, but even at this stage it corresponds perfectly to the definition of modern economists, who call it the power of disposing of the labour-power of others. Division of labour and private property are, after all, identical expressions: in the one the same thing is affirmed with reference to activity as is affirmed in the other with reference to the product of the activity.

Further, the division of labour also implies the contradiction between the interest of the separate individual or the individual family and the common interest of all individuals who have intercourse with one another. And indeed, this common interest does not exist merely in the imagination, as the "general interest", but first of all in reality, as the mutual interdependence of the individuals among whom the labour is divided.[a]

Out of this very contradiction between the particular and the common interests, the common interest assumes an independent form as the *state,* which is divorced from the real individual and collective interests, and at the same time as an illusory community, always based, however, on the real ties existing in every family conglomeration and tribal conglomeration — such as flesh and blood, language, division of labour on a larger scale, and other interests — and especially, as we shall show later, on the classes, already implied by the division of labour, which in every such mass of men separate out, and one of which dominates all the others. It follows from this that all struggles within the state, the struggle between democracy, aristocracy, and monarchy, the struggle for the franchise, etc., etc., are merely the illusory forms — altogether the general interest is the illusory form of common interests — in which the real struggles of the different classes are fought out among one another (of this the German theoreticians have not the faintest inkling, although they have received a sufficient initiation into the subject in the *Deutsch-Französische Jahrbücher*[11] and *Die heilige Familie*). Further, it follows that every class which is aiming at domination, even when its domination, as is the case with the proletariat, leads to the abolition of the old form of society in its entirety and of domination in general, must first con-

---

[a] The following two paragraphs are written in the margin: the first by Engels and the second by Marx.— *Ed.*

quer political power in order to represent its interest in turn as the general interest, which in the first moment it is forced to do.

Just because individuals seek *only* their particular interest, which for them does not coincide with their common interest, the latter is asserted as an interest "alien" ["*fremd*"] to them, and |18| "independent" of them, as in its turn a particular and distinctive "general" interest; or they themselves must remain within this discord, as in democracy. On the other hand, too, the *practical* struggle of these particular interests, which *actually* constantly run counter to the common and illusory common interests, necessitates *practical* intervention and restraint by the illusory "general" interest in the form of the state.

|17| And finally, the division of labour offers us the first example of the fact that, as long as man remains in naturally evolved society, that is, as long as a cleavage exists between the particular and the common interest, as long, therefore, as activity is not voluntarily, but naturally, divided, man's own deed becomes an alien power opposed to him, which enslaves him instead of being controlled by him. For as soon as the division of labour comes into being, each man has a particular, exclusive sphere of activity, which is forced upon him and from which he cannot escape. He is a hunter, a fisherman, a shepherd, or a critical critic, and must remain so if he does not want to lose his means of livelihood; whereas in communist society, where nobody has one exclusive sphere of activity but each can become accomplished in any branch he wishes, society regulates the general production and thus makes it possible for me to do one thing today and another tomorrow, to hunt in the morning, fish in the afternoon, rear cattle in the evening, criticise after dinner, just as I have a mind, without ever becoming hunter, fisherman, shepherd or critic.

|18| This fixation of social activity, this consolidation of what we ourselves produce into a material power above us, growing out of our control, thwarting our expectations, bringing to naught our calculations, is one of the chief factors in historical development up till now.[a] The social power, i.e., the multiplied productive force, which arises through the co-operation of different individuals as it is caused by the division of labour, appears to these individuals, since their co-operation is not voluntary but has come about naturally, not as their own united power, but as an alien force existing outside them, of the origin and goal of which they are ignorant, which they thus are no

---

[a] Here Marx added a passage in the margin which is given in this edition as the first two paragraphs of Section 5.— *Ed.*

longer able to control, which on the contrary passes through a peculiar series of phases and stages independent of the will and the action [12] of man, nay even being the prime governor of these. How otherwise could for instance property have had a history at all, have taken on different forms, and landed property, for example, according to the different premises given, have proceeded in France from parcellation to centralisation in the hands of a few, in England from centralisation in the hands of a few to parcellation, as is actually the case today? Or how does it happen that trade, which after all is nothing more than the exchange of products of various individuals and countries, rules the whole world through the relation of supply and demand — a relation which, as an English economist says, hovers over the earth like the fate of the ancients, and with invisible hand allots fortune and misfortune to men, sets up empires |19| and wrecks empires, causes nations to rise and to disappear — whereas with the abolition of the basis, private property, with the communistic regulation of production (and, implicit in this, the abolition of the alien attitude [*Fremdheit*] of men to their own product), the power of the relation of supply and demand is dissolved into nothing, and men once more gain control of exchange, production and the way they behave to one another?

[5. DEVELOPMENT OF THE PRODUCTIVE FORCES AS A MATERIAL PREMISE OF COMMUNISM]

|18| This "*estrangement*" ["*Entfremdung*"] (to use a term which will be comprehensible to the philosophers) can, of course, only be abolished given two *practical* premises. In order to become an "unendurable" power, i.e., a power against which men make a revolution, it must necessarily have rendered the great mass of humanity "propertyless", and moreover in contradiction to an existing world of wealth and culture; both these premises presuppose a great increase in productive power, a high degree of its development. And, on the other hand, this development of productive forces (which at the same time implies the actual empirical existence of men in their *world-historical*, instead of local, being) is an absolutely necessary practical premise, because without it privation, *want* is merely made general, and with *want* the struggle for necessities would begin again, and all the old filthy business would necessarily be restored; and furthermore, because only with this universal development of productive forces is a *universal* intercourse between men established, which on the one side produces in *all* nations simultaneously the phenomenon

A page of the manuscript of *The German Ideology.*
From the chapter "Feuerbach"
(*Reduced*)

of the "propertyless" mass (universal competition), making each nation dependent on the revolutions of the others, and finally puts *world-historical*, empirically universal individuals in place of local ones. Without this, 1) communism could only exist as a local phenomenon; 2) the *forces* of intercourse themselves could not have developed as *universal*, hence unendurable powers: they would have remained home-bred "conditions" surrounded by superstition; and 3) each extension of intercourse would abolish local communism. Empirically, communism is only possible as the act of the dominant peoples "all at once" and simultaneously,[13] which presupposes the universal development of productive forces and the world intercourse bound up with them.*

|19| Moreover, the mass of workers who are *nothing but workers*—labour-power on a mass scale cut off from capital or from even a limited satisfaction [of their needs] and, hence, as a result of competition their utterly precarious position, the no longer merely temporary loss of work as a secure source of life—presupposes the *world market*. The proletariat can thus only exist *world-historically*, just as communism, its activity can only have a "world-historical" existence. World-historical existence of individuals, i. e., existence of individuals which is directly linked up with world history.

|18| Communism is for us not a *state of affairs* which is to be established, an *ideal* to which reality [will] have to adjust itself. We call communism the *real* movement which abolishes the present state of things. The conditions of this movement result from the now existing premise.[a]

*   *   *

|19| The form of intercourse determined by the existing productive forces at all previous historical stages, and in its turn determining these, is *civil society*. The latter, as is clear from what we have said above, has as its premise and basis the simple family and the multiple, called the tribe, and the more precise definition of this society is given in our remarks above. Already here we see that this civil society is the true focus and theatre of all history, and how absurd is the conception of history held hitherto, which neglects the real

---

* [Above the continuation of this passage, which follows on the next page of the manuscript, Marx wrote:] *Communism.*

[a] In the manuscript this paragraph was written down by Marx in a free space above the paragraph starting with the words: This "*estrangement*".— *Ed.*

relations and confines itself to spectacular historical events.[14]

In the main we have so far considered only one aspect of human activity, the *reshaping of nature* by men. The other aspect, the *reshaping of men by men*....*

Origin of the state and the relation of the state to civil society.[a]

[6. CONCLUSIONS FROM THE MATERIALIST CONCEPTION OF HISTORY: HISTORY AS A CONTINUOUS PROCESS, HISTORY AS BECOMING WORLD HISTORY, THE NECESSITY OF COMMUNIST REVOLUTION]

|20| History is nothing but the succession of the separate generations, each of which uses the materials, the capital funds, the productive forces handed down to it by all preceding generations, and thus, on the one hand, continues the traditional activity in completely changed circumstances and, on the other, modifies the old circumstances with a completely changed activity. This can be speculatively distorted so that later history is made the goal of earlier history, e. g., the goal ascribed to the discovery of America is to further the eruption of the French Revolution. Thereby history receives its own special goals and becomes "a person ranking with other persons" (to wit: "self-consciousness, criticism, the unique", etc.), while what is designated with the words "destiny", "goal", "germ", or "idea" of earlier history is nothing more than an abstraction from later history, from the active influence which earlier history exercises on later history.

The further the separate spheres, which act on one another, extend in the course of this development and the more the original isolation of the separate nationalities is destroyed by the advanced mode of production, by intercourse and by the natural division of labour between various nations arising as a result, the more history becomes world history. Thus, for instance, if in England a machine is invented which deprives countless workers of bread in India and China, and overturns the whole form of existence of these empires, this invention becomes a world-historical fact. Or again, take the case of sugar and coffee, which have proved their world-historical importance in the nineteenth century by the fact that the lack of these products, occasioned by the Napoleonic Continental System,[15] caused the Germans |21| to rise against Napoleon, and thus

---

* [Marginal note by Marx:] Intercourse and productive power.

[a] The end of this page of the manuscript is left blank. The next page begins with an exposition of the conclusions from the materialist conception of history.— *Ed.*

became the real basis of the glorious Wars of Liberation of 1813. From this it follows that this transformation of history into world history is by no means a mere abstract act on the part of "self-consciousness", the world spirit, or of any other metaphysical spectre, but a quite material, empirically verifiable act, an act the proof of which every individual furnishes as he comes and goes, eats, drinks and clothes himself.

In history up to the present it is certainly likewise an empirical fact that separate individuals have, with the broadening of their activity into world-historical activity, become more and more enslaved under a power alien to them (a pressure which they have conceived of as a dirty trick on the part of the so-called world spirit, etc.), a power which has become more and more enormous and, in the last instance, turns out to be the *world market*. But it is just as empirically established that, by the overthrow of the existing state of society by the communist revolution (of which more below) and the abolition of private property, which is identical with it, this power, which so baffles the German theoreticians, will be dissolved; and that then the liberation of each single individual will be accomplished in the measure in which history becomes wholly transformed into world history.* From the above it is clear that the real intellectual wealth of the individual depends entirely on the wealth of his real connections. Only this will liberate the separate individuals from the various national and local barriers, bring them into practical connection with the production (including intellectual production) of the whole world and make it possible for them to acquire the capacity to enjoy this all-sided production of the whole earth (the creations of man). *All-round* dependence, this primary natural form of the *world-historical* co-operation of individuals, will be transformed by |22| this communist revolution into the control and conscious mastery of these powers, which, born of the action of men on one another, have till now overawed and ruled men as powers completely alien to them. Now this view can be expressed again in a speculative-idealistic, i.e., fantastic, way as "self-generation of the species" ("society as the subject"), and thereby the consecutive series of interrelated individuals can be regarded as a single individual, which accomplishes the mystery of generating itself. In this context it is evident that individuals undoubtedly make *one another*, physically and mentally, but do not make themselves, either in the nonsense of Saint Bruno, or in the sense of the "unique", of the "made" man.

* [Marginal note by Marx:] *On the production of consciousness.*

Finally, from the conception of history set forth by us we obtain these further conclusions: 1) In the development of productive forces there comes a stage when productive forces and means of intercourse are brought into being which, under the existing relations, only cause mischief, and are no longer productive but destructive forces (machinery and money); and connected with this a class is called forth which has to bear all the burdens of society without enjoying its advantages, which is ousted from society and |23| forced into the sharpest contradiction to all other classes; a class which forms the majority of all members of society, and from which emanates the consciousness of the necessity of a fundamental revolution, the communist consciousness, which may, of course, arise among the other classes too through the contemplation of the situation of this class. 2) The conditions under which definite productive forces can be applied are the conditions of the rule of a definite class of society, whose social power, deriving from its property, has its *practical*-idealistic expression in each case in the form of the state and, therefore, every revolutionary struggle is directed against a class which till then has been in power.* 3) In all previous revolutions the mode of activity always remained unchanged and it was only a question of a different distribution of this activity, a new distribution of labour to other persons, whilst the communist revolution is directed against the hitherto existing *mode* of activity, does away with *labour*,** and abolishes the rule of all classes with the classes themselves, because it is carried through by the class which no longer counts as a class in society, which is not recognised as a class, and is in itself the expression of the dissolution of all classes, nationalities, etc., within present society; and 4) Both for the production on a mass scale of this communist consciousness, and for the success of the cause itself, the alteration of men on a mass scale is necessary, an alteration which can only take place in a practical movement, a *revolution*; the revolution is necessary, therefore, not only because the *ruling* class cannot be overthrown in any other way, but also because the class *overthrowing* it can only in a revolution succeed in ridding itself of all the muck of ages and become fitted to found society anew.***

* [Marginal note by Marx:] These men are interested in maintaining the present state of production.

** [The following words are crossed out in the manuscript:] the modern form of activity under the rule of [...].

*** [The following passage is crossed out in the manuscript:] Whereas all communists in France as well as in England and Germany have long since

[7. SUMMARY OF THE MATERIALIST CONCEPTION OF HISTORY]

[24] This conception of history thus relies on expounding the real process of production—starting from the material production of life itself—and comprehending the form of intercourse connected with and created by this mode of production, i.e., civil society in its various stages, as the basis of all history; describing it in its action as the state, and also explaining how all the different theoretical products and forms of consciousness, religion, philosophy, morality, etc., etc., arise from it, and tracing the process of their formation from that basis; thus the whole thing can, of course, be depicted in its totality (and therefore, too, the reciprocal action of these various sides on one another). It has not, like the idealist view of history, to look for a category in every period, but remains constantly on the real *ground* of history; it does not explain practice from the idea but explains the formation of ideas from material practice, and accordingly it comes to the conclusion that all forms and products of consciousness cannot be dissolved by mental criticism, by resolution into "self-consciousness" or transformation into "apparitions", "spectres", "whimsies", [b] etc., but only by the practical overthrow of the actual social relations which gave rise to this idealistic humbug; that not criticism but revolution is the driving force of history, also of religion, of philosophy and all other kinds of theory. It shows that history

agreed on the necessity of the revolution, Saint Bruno quietly continues to dream, opining that "real humanism", i.e., communism, is to take "the place of spiritualism" (which has no place) only in order that it may gain respect. Then, he continues in his dream, "salvation" would indeed "be attained, the earth becoming heaven, and heaven earth". (The theologian is still unable to forget heaven.) "Then joy and bliss will resound in celestial harmonies to all eternity" (p. 140).[a] The holy father of the church will be greatly surprised when judgment day overtakes him, the day when all this is to come to pass—a day when the reflection in the sky of burning cities will mark the dawn, when together with the "celestial harmonies" the tunes of the *Marseillaise* and *Carmagnole* will echo in his ears accompanied by the requisite roar of cannon, with the guillotine beating time; when the infamous "masses" will shout *ça ira, ça ira* and suspend "self-consciousness" by means of the lamp-post.[16] Saint Bruno has no reason at all to draw and edifying picture "of joy and bliss to all eternity". We forego the pleasure of a priori forecasting Saint Bruno's conduct on judgment day. Moreover, it is really difficult to decide whether the *prolétaires en révolution* have to be conceived as "substance", as "mass", desiring to overthrow criticism, or as an "emanation" of the spirit which is, however, still lacking the consistency necessary to digest Bauer's ideas.

---

[a] Bruno Bauer, "Charakteristik Ludwig Feuerbachs".— *Ed.*

[b] These terms are used by Max Stirner in *Der Einzige und sein Eigenthum.* Cf. pp. 169-76 of this volume.— *Ed.*

does not end by being resolved into "self-consciousness" as "spirit of the spirit", [a] but that each stage contains a material result, a sum of productive forces, a historically created relation to nature and of individuals to one another, which is handed down to each generation from its predecessor; a mass of productive forces, capital funds and circumstances, which on the one hand is indeed modified by the new generation, but on the other also prescribes for it its conditions of life and gives it a definite development, a special character. It shows that circumstances make |25| men just as much as men make circumstances.

This sum of productive forces, capital funds and social forms of intercourse, which every individual and every generation finds in existence as something given, is the real basis of what the philosophers have conceived as "substance" and "essence of man", and what they have deified and attacked: a real basis which is not in the least disturbed, in its effect and influence on the development of men, by the fact that these philosophers revolt against it as "self-consciousness" and the "unique". These conditions of life, which different generations find in existence, determine also whether or not the revolutionary convulsion periodically recurring in history will be strong enough to overthrow the basis of everything that exists. And if these material elements of a complete revolution are not present — namely, on the one hand the existing productive forces, on the other the formation of a revolutionary mass, which revolts not only against separate conditions of the existing society, but against the existing "production of life" itself, the "total activity" on which it was based — then it is absolutely immaterial for practical development whether the *idea* of this revolution has been expressed a hundred times already, as the history of communism proves.

[8. THE INCONSISTENCY OF THE IDEALIST CONCEPTION OF HISTORY IN GENERAL AND OF GERMAN POST-HEGELIAN PHILOSOPHY IN PARTICULAR

In the whole conception of history up to the present this real basis of history has either been totally disregarded or else considered as a minor matter quite irrelevant to the course of history. History must, therefore, always be written according to an extraneous standard; the real production of life appears as

_____

[a] The terms are used by Bruno Bauer in "Charakteristik Ludwig Feuerbachs".— *Ed.*

non-historical, while the historical appears as something separated from ordinary life, something extra-superterrestrial. With this the relation of man to nature is excluded from history and hence the antithesis of nature and history is created. The exponents of this conception of history have consequently only been able to see in history the spectacular political events and religious and other theoretical struggles, and in particular with regard to each historical epoch they were compelled to *share the illusion of that epoch.* For instance, if an epoch imagines itself to be actuated by purely "political" or "religious" motives, although "religion" and "politics" are only forms of its true motives, the historian accepts this opinion. The "fancy", the "conception" of the people in question about their real practice is transformed into the sole determining and effective force, which dominates and determines their practice. When the crude form of the division of labour which is to be found among the Indians and Egyptians calls forth the caste-system in their state and religion, the historian believes that the caste-system |26| is the power which has produced this crude social form.

While the French and the English at least stick to the political illusion, which is after all closer to reality, the Germans move in the realm of the "pure spirit", and make religious illusion the driving force of history. The Hegelian philosophy of history is the last consequence, reduced to its "clearest expression", of all this German historiography, for which it is not a question of real, nor even of political, interests, but of pure thoughts, which must therefore appear to Saint Bruno as a series of "thoughts" that devour one another and are finally swallowed up in "self-consciousness"*; and even more consistently the course of history must appear to Saint Max Stirner, who knows not a thing about real history, as a mere "tale of knights, robbers and ghosts",[18] from whose visions he can, of course, only save himself by "unholiness". This conception is truly religious: it postulates religious man as the primitive man, the starting-point of history, and in its imagination puts the religious production of fancies in the place of the real production of the means of subsistence and of life itself.

This whole conception of history, together with its dissolution and the scruples and qualms resulting from it, is a purely *national* affair of the Germans and has merely *local* interest for Germany, as for instance the important question which has been

* [Marginal note by Marx:] So-called *objective* historiography[17] consists precisely in treating the historical relations separately from activity. Reactionary character.

under discussion in recent times: how exactly one "passes from the realm of God to the realm of Man" [a] — as if this "realm of God" had ever existed anywhere save in the imagination, and the learned gentlemen, without being aware of it, were not constantly living in the "realm of Man" to which they are now seeking the way; and as if the learned pastime (for it is nothing more) of explaining the mystery of this theoretical bubble-blowing did not on the contrary lie in demonstrating its origin in actual earthly relations. For these Germans, it is altogether simply a matter of resolving the ready-made nonsense they find into [27] some other freak, i.e., of presupposing that all this nonsense has a special *sense* which can be discovered; while really it is only a question of explaining these theoretical phrases from the actually existing relations. The real, practical dissolution of these phrases, the removal of these notions from the consciousness of men, will, as we have already said, be effected by altered circumstances, not by theoretical deductions. For the mass of men, i.e., the proletariat, these theoretical notions do not exist and hence do not require to be dissolved, and if this mass ever had any theoretical notions, e.g., religion, these have now long been dissolved by circumstances.

The purely national character of these questions and solutions is moreover shown by the fact that these theorists believe in all seriousness that chimeras like "the God-Man", "Man", etc., have presided over individual epochs of history (Saint Bruno even goes so far as to assert that only "criticism and critics have made history" [b], and when they themselves construct historical systems, they skip over all earlier periods in the greatest haste and pass immediately from "Mongolism" [c] to history "with meaningful content", that is to say, to the history of the *Hallische* and *Deutsche Jahrbücher* and the dissolution of the Hegelian school into a general squabble. They forget all other nations, all real events, and the *theatrum mundi* is confined to the Leipzig book fair and the mutual quarrels of "criticism", "man", and "the unique". [d] If for once these theorists treat really historical subjects, as for instance the eighteenth century, they merely give a history of ideas, separated from the facts and the practical development

---

[a] Ludwig Feuerbach, "Ueber das *Wesen des Christenthums...*". — *Ed.*

[b] Bruno Bauer, "Charakteristik Ludwig Feuerbachs". — *Ed.*

[c] Max Stirner, *Der Einzige und sein Eigenthum.* Cf. this volume, pp. 141-47 and 176-83. — *Ed.*

[d] I.e., Bruno Bauer, Ludwig Feuerbach and Max Stirner. — *Ed.*

underlying them; and even that merely in order to represent that period as an imperfect preliminary stage, the as yet limited predecessor of the truly historical age, i.e., the period of the German philosophic struggle from 1840 to 1844. As might be expected when the history of an earlier period is written with the aim of accentuating the brilliance of an unhistoric person and his fantasies, all the really historic events, even the really historic interventions of politics in history, receive no mention. Instead we get a narrative based not on research but on arbitrary constructions and literary gossip, such as Saint Bruno provided in his now forgotten history of the eighteenth century.[a] These pompous and arrogant hucksters of ideas, who imagine themselves infinitely exalted above all national prejudices, are thus in practice far more national than the beer-swilling philistines who dream of a united Germany. They do not recognise the deeds of other nations as historical; they live in Germany, within Germany |28| and for Germany; they turn the Rhine-song[19] into a religious hymn and conquer Alsace and Lorraine by robbing French philosophy instead of the French state, by Germanising French ideas instead of French provinces. Herr Venedey is a cosmopolitan compared with the Saints Bruno and Max, who, in the universal dominance of theory, proclaim the universal dominance of Germany.

[9. IDEALIST CONCEPTION OF HISTORY AND FEUERBACH'S QUASI-COMMUNISM]

It is also clear from these arguments how grossly Feuerbach is deceiving himself when (*Wigand's Vierteljahrsschrift*, 1845, Band 2) by virtue of the qualification "common man" he declares himself a communist,[20] transforms the latter into a predicate of "Man", and thinks that it is thus possible to change the word "communist", which in the real world means the follower of a definite revolutionary party, into a mere category. Feuerbach's whole deduction with regard to the relation of men to one another is only aimed at proving that men need and *always have needed* each other. He wants to establish consciousness of this fact, that is to say, like the other theorists, he merely wants to produce a correct consciousness about an *existing* fact; whereas for the real communist it is a question of overthrowing the existing state of things. We fully appreciate,

---

[a] Bruno Bauer, *Geschichte der Politik, Cultur und Aufklärung des achtzehnten Jahrhunderts.—Ed.*

however, that Feuerbach, in endeavouring to produce consciousness of just *this* fact, is going as far as a theorist possibly can, without ceasing to be a theorist and philosopher. It is characteristic, however, that Saint Bruno and Saint Max immediately put in place of the real communist Feuerbach's conception of the communist; they do this partly in order to be able to combat communism too as "spirit of the spirit", as a philosophical category, as an equal opponent and, in the case of Saint Bruno, also for pragmatic reasons.

As an example of Feuerbach's acceptance and at the same time misunderstanding of existing reality, which he still shares with our opponents, we recall the passage in the *Philosophie der Zukunft* where he develops the view that the being of a thing or a man is at the same time its or his essence,[a] that the determinate conditions of existence, the mode of life and activity of an animal or human individual are those in which its "essence" feels itself satisfied. Here every exception is expressly conceived as an unhappy chance, as an abnormality which cannot be altered. Thus if millions of proletarians feel by no means contented with their living conditions, if their "being" |29| does not in the least correspond to their "essence", then, according to the passage quoted, this is an unavoidable misfortune, which must be borne quietly. These millions of proletarians or communists, however, think quite differently and will prove this in time, when they bring their "being" into harmony with their "essence" in a practical way, by means of a revolution. Feuerbach, therefore, never speaks of the world of man in such cases, but always takes refuge in external nature, and moreover in *nature* which has not yet been subdued by men. But every new invention, every advance made by industry, detaches another piece from this domain, so that the ground which produces examples illustrating such Feuerbachian propositions is steadily shrinking. The "essence" of the fish is its "being", water — to go no further than this one proposition. The "essence" of the freshwater fish is the water of a river. But the latter ceases to be the "essence" of the fish and is no longer a suitable medium of existence as soon as the river is made to serve industry, as soon as it is polluted by dyes and other waste products and navigated by steamboats, or as soon as its water is diverted into canals where simple drainage can deprive the fish of its medium of existence. The explanation that all such contradictions are inevitable

---

[a] Cf. this volume, p. 625.— *Ed.*

abnormalities does not essentially differ from the consolation which Saint Max Stirner offers to the discontented, saying that this contradiction is their own contradiction and this predicament their own predicament, whereupon they should either set their minds at ease, keep their disgust to themselves, or revolt against it in some fantastic way. It differs just as little from Saint Bruno's allegation that these unfortunate circumstances are due to the fact that those concerned are stuck in the muck of "substance", have not advanced to "absolute self-consciousness", and do not realise that these adverse conditions are spirit of their spirit.[a]

[III]

[1. THE RULING CLASS AND THE RULING IDEAS. HOW THE HEGELIAN CONCEPTION OF THE DOMINATION OF THE SPIRIT IN HISTORY AROSE]

[30] The ideas of the ruling class are in every epoch the ruling ideas: i. e., the class which is the ruling *material* force of society is at the same time its ruling *intellectual* force. The class which has the means of material production at its disposal, consequently also controls the means of mental production, so that the ideas of those who lack the means of mental production are on the whole subject to it. The ruling ideas are nothing more than the ideal expression of the dominant material relations, the dominant material relations grasped as ideas; hence of the relations which make the one class the ruling one, therefore, the ideas of its dominance. The individuals composing the ruling class possess among other things consciousness, and therefore think. Insofar, therefore, as they rule as a class and determine the extent and compass of an historical epoch, it is self-evident that they do this in its whole range, hence among other things rule also as thinkers, as producers of ideas, and regulate the production and distribution of the ideas of their age: thus their ideas are the ruling ideas of the epoch. For instance, in an age and in a country where royal power, aristocracy and bourgeoisie are contending for domination and where, therefore, domination is shared, the doctrine of the separation of powers proves to be the dominant idea and is expressed as an "eternal law".

The division of labour, which we already saw above (pp. [15-18])[b] as one of the chief forces of history up till now,

---

[a] Bruno Bauer, "Charakteristik Ludwig Feuerbachs".— *Ed.*

[b] See this volume, pp. 50-54.— *Ed.*

manifests itself also in the ruling class as the division of mental and |3||material labour, so that inside this class one part appears as the thinkers of the class (its active, conceptive ideologists, who make the formation of the illusions of the class about itself their chief source of livelihood), while the others' attitude to these ideas and illusions is more passive and receptive, because they are in reality the active members of this class and have less time to make up illusions and ideas about themselves.Within this class this cleavage can even develop into a certain opposition and hostility between the two parts, but whenever a practical collision occurs in which the class itself is endangered they automatically vanish, in which case there also vanishes the appearance of the ruling ideas being not the ideas of the ruling class and having a power distinct from the power of this class. The existence of revolutionary ideas in a particular period presupposes the existence of a revolutionary class; about the premises of the latter sufficient has already been said above (pp. [18-19, 22-23]).[a]

If now in considering the course of history we detach the ideas of the ruling class from the ruling class itself and attribute to them an independent existence, if we confine ourselves to saying that these or those ideas were dominant at a given time, without bothering ourselves about the conditions of production and the producers of these ideas, if we thus ignore the individuals and world conditions which are the source of the ideas, then we can say, for instance, that during the time the aristocracy was dominant, the concepts honour, loyalty, etc., were dominant, during the dominance of the bourgeoisie the concepts freedom, equality, etc. The ruling class itself on the whole imagines this to be so. This conception of history, which is common to all historians, particularly since the eighteenth century, will necessarily come up against |32| the phenomenon that ever more abstract ideas hold sway, i.e., ideas which increasingly take on the form of universality. For each new class which puts itself in the place of one ruling before it is compelled, merely in order to carry through its aim, to present its interest as the common interest of all the members of society, that is, expressed in ideal form: it has to give its ideas the form of universality, and present them as the only rational, universally valid ones. The class making a revolution comes forward from the very start, if only because it is opposed to a *class*, not as a class but as the representative of the whole of

---

[a] See this volume, pp. 54-57 and 59-60.— *Ed.*

society, as the whole mass of society confronting the one ruling class.* It can do this because initially its interest really is as yet mostly connected with the common interest of all other non-ruling classes, because under the pressure of hitherto existing conditions its interest has not yet been able to develop as the particular interest of a particular class. Its victory, therefore, benefits also many individuals of other classes which are not winning a dominant position, but only insofar as it now enables these individuals to raise themselves into the ruling class. When the French bourgeoisie overthrew the rule of the aristocracy, it thereby made it possible for many proletarians to raise themselves above the proletariat, but only insofar as they became bourgeois. Every new class, therefore, achieves domination only on a broader basis than that of the class ruling previously; on the other hand the opposition of the non-ruling class to the new ruling class then develops all the more sharply and profoundly. Both these things determine the fact that the struggle to be waged against this new ruling class, in its turn, has as its aim a more decisive and more radical negation of the previous conditions of society than |33| all previous classes which sought to rule could have.

This whole appearance, that the rule of a certain class is only the rule of certain ideas, comes to a natural end, of course, as soon as class rule in general ceases to be the form in which society is organised, that is to say, as soon as it is no longer necessary to represent a particular interest as general or the "general interest" as ruling.

Once the ruling ideas have been separated from the ruling individuals and, above all, from the relations which result from a given stage of the mode of production, and in this way the conclusion has been reached that history is always under the sway of ideas, it is very easy to abstract from these various ideas "the Idea", the thought, etc., as the dominant force in history, and thus to consider all these separate ideas and concepts as "forms of self-determination" of the Concept developing in history. It follows then naturally, too, that all the relations of men can be derived from the concept of man, man as conceived, the essence of man, Man. This has been done by speculative philosophy. Hegel himself confesses at the end of

* [Marginal note by Marx:] (Universality corresponds to 1) the class versus the estate, 2) the competition, world intercourse, etc., 3) the great numerical strength of the ruling class, 4) the illusion of the *common* interests, in the beginning this illusion is true, 5) the delusion of the ideologists and the division of labour.)

the *Geschichtsphilosophie*[a] that he "has considered the progress of *the concept* only" and has represented in history the "true *theodicy*" (p. 446). Now one can go back again to the producers of "the concept", to the theorists, ideologists and philosophers, and one comes then to the conclusion that the philosophers, the thinkers as such, have at all times been dominant in history: a conclusion, as we see,[21] already expressed by Hegel.

The whole trick of proving the hegemony of the spirit in history (hierarchy Stirner calls it) is thus confined to the following three attempts.

|34| No. 1. One must separate the ideas of those ruling for empirical reasons, under empirical conditions and as corporeal individuals, from these rulers, and thus recognise the rule of ideas or illusions in history.

No. 2. One must bring an order into this rule of ideas, prove a mystical connection among the successive ruling ideas, which is managed by regarding them as "forms of self-determination of the concept" (this is possible because by virtue of their empirical basis these ideas are really connected with one another and because, conceived as *mere* ideas, they become self-distinctions, distinctions made by thought).

No. 3. To remove the mystical appearance of this "self-determining concept" it is changed into a person — "self-consciousness" — or, to appear thoroughly materialistic, into a series of persons, who represent the "concept" in history, into the "thinkers", the "philosophers", the ideologists, who again are understood as the manufacturers of history, as the "council of guardians", as the rulers.* Thus the whole body of materialistic elements has been eliminated from history and now full rein can be given to the speculative steed.

This historical method which reigned in Germany, and especially the reason why, must be explained from its connection with the illusion of ideologists in general, e. g., the illusions of the jurists, politicians (including the practical statesmen), from the dogmatic dreamings and distortions of these fellows; this is explained perfectly easily from their practical position in life, their job, and the division of labour.

[35] Whilst in ordinary life every shopkeeper[b] is very well able to distinguish between what somebody professes to be and what

---

*[Marginal note by Marx:] Man=the "thinking human spirit".

[a] G. W. F. Hegel, *Vorlesungen über die Philosophie der Geschichte.— Ed.*
[b] This word is the English in the manuscript.— *Ed.*

he really is, our historiography has not yet won this trivial insight. It takes every epoch at its word and believes that everything it says and imagines about itself is true.

[IV]
[1. INSTRUMENTS OF PRODUCTION AND FORMS OF PROPERTY]

[...][a] [40] From the first point, there follows the premise of a highly developed division of labour and an extensive commerce; from the second, the locality. In the first case the individuals must have been brought together, in the second they are instruments of production alongside the given instrument of production.

Here, therefore, emerges the difference between natural instruments of production and those created by civilisation. The *field* (water, etc.) can be regarded as a natural instrument of production. In the first case, that of the natural instrument of production, individuals are subservient to nature; in the second, to a product of labour. In the first case, therefore, property (landed property) appears as direct natural domination, in the second, as domination of labour, particularly of accumulated labour, capital. The first case presupposes that the individuals are united by some bond: family, tribe, the land itself, etc.; the second, that they are independent of one another and are only held together by exchange. In the first case, what is involved is chiefly an exchange between men and nature in which the labour of the former is exchanged for the products of the latter; in the second, it is predominantly an exchange of men among themselves. In the first case, average human common sense is adequate—physical activity and mental activity are not yet separated; in the second, the division between physical and mental labour must already have been effected in practice. In the first case, the domination of the proprietor over the propertyless may be based on personal relations, on a kind of community; in the second, it must have taken on a material shape in a third party—money. In the first case, small-scale industry exists, but determined by the utilisation of the natural instrument of production and therefore without the distribution of labour among various individuals; in the second, industry exists only in and through the division of labour.

|41| Our investigation hitherto started from the instruments of production, and it has already shown that private property was a

---

[a] Four pages of the manuscript are missing.— *Ed.*

necessity for certain industrial stages. In *industrie extractive*[22] private property still coincides with labour; in small-scale industry and all agriculture up till now property is the necessary consequence of the existing instruments of production; the contradiction between the instrument of production and private property is only the product of large-scale industry, which, moreover, must be highly developed to produce this contradiction. Thus only with large-scale industry does the abolition of private property become possible.

[2. THE DIVISION OF MATERIAL AND MENTAL LABOUR. SEPARATION OF TOWN AND COUNTRY. THE GUILD-SYSTEM]

The most important division of material and mental labour is the separation of town and country. The contradiction between town and country begins with the transition from barbarism to civilisation, from tribe to state, from locality to nation, and runs through the whole history of civilisation to the present day (the Anti-Corn Law League[23]).

The advent of the town implies, at the same time, the necessity of administration, police, taxes, etc., in short, of the municipality [*des Gemeindewesens*], and thus of politics in general. Here first became manifest the division of the population into two great classes, which is directly based on the division of labour and on the instruments of production. The town is in actual fact already the concentration of the population, of the instruments of production, of capital, of pleasures, of needs, while the country demonstrates just the opposite fact, isolation and separation. The contradiction between town and country can only exist within the framework of private property. It is the most crass expression of the subjection of the individual under the division of labour, under a definite activity forced upon him—a subjection which makes one man into a restricted town-animal, another into a restricted country-animal, and daily creates anew the conflict between their interests. Labour is here again the chief thing, power *over* individuals, and as long as this power exists, private property must exist. The abolition of the contradiction between town and country is one of the first conditions |42| of communal life, a condition which again depends on a mass of material premises and which cannot be fulfilled by the mere will, as anyone can see at the first glance. (These conditions have still to be set forth.) The separation of town and country can also be understood as the separation of capital and landed property, as the beginning of the existence and development of capital independent of landed property—the beginning of property having its basis only in labour and exchange.

In the towns which, in the Middle Ages, did not derive ready-made from an earlier period but were formed anew by the serfs who had become free, the particular labour of each man was his only property apart from the small capital he brought with him, consisting almost solely of the most necessary tools of his craft. The competition of serfs constantly escaping into the town, the constant war of the country against the towns and thus the necessity of an organised municipal military force, the bond of common ownership in a particular kind of labour, the necessity of common buildings for the sale of their wares at a time when craftsmen were also traders, and the consequent exclusion of the unauthorised from these buildings, the conflict among the interests of the various crafts, the necessity of protecting their laboriously acquired skill, and the feudal organisation of the whole of the country: these were the causes of the union of the workers of each craft in guilds. In this context we do not have to go further into the manifold modifications of the guild-system, which arise through later historical developments. The flight of the serfs into the towns went on without interruption right through the Middle Ages. These serfs, persecuted by their lords in the country, came separately into the towns, where they found an organised community, against which they were powerless and in which they had to subject themselves to the station assigned to them by the demand for their labour and the interest of their organised urban competitors. These workers, entering separately, were never able to attain to any power, since, if their labour was of the guild type which had to be learned, the guildmasters bent them to their will and organised them according to their interest; or if their labour was not such as had to be learned, and therefore not of the guild type, they were day-labourers, never managed to organise, but remained an unorganised rabble. The need for day-labourers in the towns created the rabble.

These towns were true "unions",[24] called forth by the direct |43| need of providing for the protection of property, and of multiplying the means of production and defence of the separate members. The rabble of these towns was devoid of any power, composed as it was of individuals strange to one another who had entered separately, and who stood unorganised over against an organised power, armed for war, and jealously watching over them. The journeymen and apprentices were organised in each craft as it best suited the interest of the masters. The patriarchal relations existing between them and their masters gave the latter a double power — on the one hand because of the direct influence they exerted on the whole life of the journeymen, and on the other because, for the journeymen who worked with the same master, it was a real bond which held them together against the journeymen of other masters and separated them from these. And finally, the journeymen were bound to the existing order even by their interest in becoming masters themselves. While, therefore, the rabble at least carried out revolts against the whole municipal order, revolts which remained completely ineffective because of its powerlessness, the journeymen never got further than small acts of insubordination within separate guilds, such as belong to the very nature of the guild-system. The great risings of the Middle Ages all radiated from the country, but equally remained totally ineffective because of the isolation and consequent crudity of the peasants.[25]—

Capital in these towns was a naturally evolved capital, consisting of a house, the tools of the craft, and the natural, hereditary customers; and not being realisable, on account of the backwardness of intercourse and the lack of circulation, it had to be handed down from father to son. Unlike modern capital, which can be assessed in money and which may be indifferently invested in this thing or that, this capital was directly connected with the particular work of the owner, inseparable from it and to this extent *estate* capital.—

In the towns, the division of labour between the |44| individual guilds was as yet very little developed and, in the guilds themselves, it did not exist at all between the individual workers. Every workman had to be versed in a whole round of tasks, had to be able to make everything that was to be made with his tools. The limited intercourse and the weak ties between the individual towns, the lack of population and the narrow needs did not allow of a more advanced division of labour, and therefore every man who wished to become a master had to be proficient in the whole of his craft. Medieval craftsmen therefore had an interest in their special work and in proficiency in it, which was capable of rising to a limited artistic sense. For this very reason, however, every medieval craftsman was completely absorbed in his work, to which he had a complacent servile relationship, and in which he was involved to a far greater extent than the modern worker, whose work is a matter of indifference to him.—

[3. FURTHER DIVISION OF LABOUR. SEPARATION OF COMMERCE AND INDUSTRY. DIVISION OF LABOUR BETWEEN THE VARIOUS TOWNS. MANUFACTURE]

The next extension of the division of labour was the separation of production and intercourse, the formation of a special class of merchants; a separation which, in the towns bequeathed by a former period, had been handed down (among other things with the Jews) and which very soon appeared in the newly formed ones. With this there was given the possibility of commercial communications transcending the immediate neighbourhood, a possibility the realisation of which depended on the existing means of communication, the state of public safety in the countryside, which was determined by political conditions (during the whole of the Middle Ages, as is well known, the merchants travelled in armed caravans), and on the cruder or more advanced needs (determined by the stage of culture attained) of the region accessible to intercourse.

With intercourse vested in a particular class, with the extension of trade through the merchants beyond the immediate surroundings of the town, there immediately appears a reciprocal action between production and intercourse. The towns enter into relations *with one another*, new tools are brought from one town into the other, and the separation between production and intercourse soon calls forth a new division of production between |45| the individual towns, each of which is soon exploiting a predominant branch of industry. The local restrictions of earlier times begin gradually to be broken down.—

It depends purely on the extension of intercourse whether the productive forces evolved in a locality, especially inventions, are lost for later development or not. As long as there exists no intercourse transcending the immediate neighbourhood, every invention must be made separately in each locality, and mere chances such as irruptions of barbaric peoples, even ordinary wars, are sufficient to cause a country with advanced productive forces and needs to have to start right over again from the beginning. In primitive history every invention had to be made daily anew and in each locality independently. That even with a relatively very extensive commerce, highly developed productive forces are not safe from complete destruction, is proved by the Phoenicians, whose inventions were for the most part lost for a long time to come through the ousting of this nation from commerce, its conquest by Alexander and its consequent decline. Likewise, for instance, glass-staining in the Middle Ages. Only when intercourse has become world intercourse and has as its basis large-scale industry, when all nations are drawn into the competitive struggle, is the permanence of the acquired productive forces assured.—

The immediate consequence of the division of labour between the various towns was the rise of manufactures, branches of production which had outgrown the guild-system. Intercourse with foreign nations was the historical premise for the first flourishing of manufactures, in Italy and later in Flanders. In other countries, England and France for example, manufactures were at first confined to the home market. Besides the premises already mentioned manufactures presuppose an already advanced concentration of population, particularly in the countryside, and of capital, which began to accumulate in the hands of individuals, partly in the guilds in spite of the guild regulations, partly among the merchants.

|46| The kind of labour which from the first presupposed machines, even of the crudest sort, soon showed itself the most capable of development. Weaving, earlier carried on in the country by the peasants as a secondary occupation to procure their clothing, was the first labour to receive an impetus and a further development through the extension of intercourse. Weaving was the first and remained the principal manufacture. The rising demand for clothing materials, consequent on the growth of population, the growing accumulation and mobilisation of natural capital through accelerated circulation, and the demand for luxuries called forth by this and favoured generally by the gradual extension of intercourse, gave weaving a quantitative and qualitative stimulus, which wrenched it out of the form of production hitherto existing. Alongside the peasants weaving for their own use, who continued, and still continue, with this sort of work, there emerged a new class of weavers in the towns, whose fabrics were destined for the whole home market and usually for foreign markets too.

Weaving, an occupation demanding in most cases little skill and soon splitting up into countless branches, by its whole nature resisted the trammels of the guild. Weaving was, therefore, carried on mostly in villages and market centres, without guild organisation, which gradually became towns, and indeed the most flourishing towns in each land.

With guild-free manufacture, property relations also quickly changed. The first advance beyond naturally derived estate capital was provided by the rise of merchants, whose capital was from the beginning movable, capital in the modern sense as far as one can speak of it, given the circumstances of those times. The second advance came with manufacture, which again mobilised a mass of natural capital, and altogether increased the mass of movable capital as against that of natural capital.

At the same time, manufacture became a refuge of the peasants from the guilds which excluded them or paid them badly, just as earlier the guild-towns had served the peasants as a refuge |47| from the landlords.—

Simultaneously with the beginning of manufactures there was a period of vagabondage caused by the abolition of the feudal bodies of retainers, the disbanding of the armies consisting of a motley crowd that served the kings against their vassals, the improvement of agriculture, and the transformation of large strips of tillage into pasture land. From this alone it is clear that this vagabondage is strictly connected with the disintegration of the feudal system. As early as the thirteenth century we find isolated epochs of this kind, but only at the end of the fifteenth and beginning of the sixteenth does this vagabondage make a general and permanent appearance. These vagabonds, who were so numerous that, for instance, Henry VIII of England had 72,000 of them hanged,[26] were only prevailed upon to work with the greatest difficulty and through the most extreme necessity, and then only after long resistance. The rapid rise of manufactures, particularly in England, absorbed them gradually.—

With the advent of manufacture the various nations entered into competitive relations, a commercial struggle, which was fought out in wars, protective duties and prohibitions, whereas earlier the nations, insofar as they were connected at all, had carried on an inoffensive exchange with each other. Trade had from now on a political significance.

With the advent of manufacture the relations between worker and employer changed. In the guilds the patriarchal relations between journeyman and master continued to exist; in manufacture their place was taken by the monetary relations between worker and capitalist—relations which in the countryside and in small towns retained a patriarchal tinge, but in the larger, the real manufacturing towns, quite early lost almost all patriarchal complexion.

Manufacture and the movement of production in general received an enormous impetus through the extension of intercourse which came with the discovery of America and the sea-route to the East Indies. The new products imported thence, particularly the masses of gold and silver which came into circulation, had totally changed the position of the classes towards one another, dealing a hard blow to feudal landed property and to the workers; the expeditions of adventurers, colonisation, and above all the extension of markets into a world market, which had now become possible and was daily becoming more and more a fact, called forth a new phase |48| of historical development, into which in general we need not here enter further. Through the colonisation of the newly discovered countries the commercial struggle of the nations against one another was given new fuel and accordingly greater extension and animosity.

The expansion of commerce and manufacture accelerated the accumulation of movable capital, while in the guilds, which were not stimulated to extend their production, natural capital remained stationary or even declined. Commerce and manufacture created the big bourgeoisie; in the guilds was concentrated the petty bourgeoisie, which no longer was dominant in the towns as formerly, but had to bow to the might of the great merchants and manufacturers.* Hence the decline of the guilds, as soon as they came into contact with manufacture.

The relations between nations in their intercourse took on two different forms in the epoch of which we have been speaking. At first the small quantity of gold and silver in circulation occasioned the ban on the export of these metals; and industry, made necessary by the need for employing the growing urban population and for the most part imported from abroad, could not do without privileges which could be granted not only, of course, against home competition, but chiefly against foreign. The local guild privilege was in these original prohibitions extended over the whole nation. Customs duties originated from the tributes which the feudal lords exacted from merchants passing through their territories as protection money against robbery, tributes later imposed likewise by the towns, and which, with the rise of the modern states, were the Treasury's most obvious means of raising money.

The appearance of American gold and silver on the European markets, the gradual development of industry, the rapid expansion of trade and the consequent rise of the non-guild

---

* [Marginal note by Marx:] Petty bourgeoisie — Middle class — Big bourgeoisie.

bourgeoisie and the increasing importance of money, gave these measures another significance. The state, which was daily less and less able to do without money, now retained the ban on the export of gold and silver out of fiscal considerations; the bourgeois, for whom these quantities of money which were hurled on to the market became the chief object of speculative buying, were thoroughly content with this; privileges established earlier became a source of income for the government and were sold for money; in the customs legislation there appeared export duties which, since they only hampered industry, |49| had a purely fiscal aim.—

The second period began in the middle of the seventeenth century and lasted almost to the end of the eighteenth. Commerce and navigation had expanded more rapidly than manufacture, which played a secondary role; the colonies were becoming considerable consumers; and after long struggles the various nations shared out the opening world market among themselves. This period begins with the Navigation Laws [27] and colonial monopolies. The competition of the nations among themselves was excluded as far as possible by tariffs, prohibitions and treaties; and in the last resort the competitive struggle was carried on and decided by wars (especially naval wars). The mightiest maritime nation, the English, retained preponderance in commerce and manufacture. Here, already, we find concentration in one country.

Manufacture was all the time sheltered by protective duties in the home market, by monopolies in the colonial market, and abroad as much as possible by differential duties. The working-up of home-produced material was encouraged (wool and linen in England, silk in France), the export of home-produced raw material forbidden (wool in England), and the [working-up] of imported raw material neglected or suppressed (cotton in England). The nation dominant in maritime trade and colonial power naturally secured for itself also the greatest quantitative and qualitative expansion of manufacture. Manufacture could not be carried on without protection, since, if the slightest change takes place in other countries, it can lose its market and be ruined; under reasonably favourable conditions it may easily be introduced into a country, but for this very reason can easily be destroyed. At the same time through the mode in which it is carried on, particularly in the eighteenth century in the countryside, it is to such an extent interwoven with the conditions of life of a great mass of individuals, that no country dare jeopardise their existence by permitting free competition.

Consequently, insofar as manufacture manages to export, it depends entirely on the extension or restriction of commerce, and exercises a relatively very small reaction [on the latter]. Hence its secondary [role] and the influence of [the merchants] in the eighteenth century. |50| It was the merchants and especially the shipowners who more than anybody else pressed for state protection and monopolies; the manufacturers also demanded and indeed received protection, but all the time were inferior in political importance to the merchants. The commercial towns, particularly the maritime towns, became to some extent civilised and acquired the outlook of the big bourgeoisie, but in the factory towns an extreme petty-bourgeois outlook persisted. Cf. Aikin, etc.[a] The eighteenth century was the century of trade. Pinto says this expressly: *"Le commerce fait la marotte du siècle"*[b]; and: *"Depuis quelque temps il n'est plus question que de commerce, de navigation et de marine."*[c]

The movement of capital, although considerably accelerated, still remained, however, relatively slow. The splitting-up of the world market into separate parts, each of which was exploited by a particular nation, the prevention of competition between the different nations, the clumsiness of production and the fact that finance was only evolving from its early stages, greatly impeded circulation. The consequence of this was a haggling, mean and niggardly spirit which still clung to all merchants and to the whole mode of carrying on trade. Compared with the manufacturers, and above all with the craftsmen, they were certainly big bourgeois; compared with the merchants and industrialists of the next period they remain petty bourgeois. Cf. Adam Smith.[d]—

This period is also characterised by the cessation of the bans on the export of gold and silver and the beginning of money trade, banks, national debts, paper money, speculation in stocks and shares, stockjobbing in all articles and the development of finance in general. Again capital lost a great part of the natural character which had still clung to it.

---

[a] John Aikin, *A Description of the Country from Thirty to Forty Miles round Manchester.— Ed.*

[b] "Commerce is the rage of the century". Isaac Pinto, "Lettre sur la jalousie du commerce" (published in Pinto's book *Traité de la Circulation et du Crédit*).— *Ed.*

[c] "For some time now people have been talking only about commerce, navigation and the navy" (ibid.).— *Ed.*

[d] Adam Smith, *An Inquiry into the Nature and Causes of the Wealth of Nations.— Ed.*

[4. MOST EXTENSIVE DIVISION OF LABOUR. LARGE-SCALE INDUSTRY]

The concentration of trade and manufacture in one country, England, developing irresistibly in the seventeenth century, gradually created for this country a relative world market, and thus a demand for the manufactured products of this country which could no longer be met by the industrial productive forces hitherto existing. This demand, outgrowing the productive forces, was the motive power which, by producing large-scale industry — the application of elemental forces to industrial ends, machinery and the most extensive division of labour — called into existence the third |51| period of private property since the Middle Ages. There already existed in England the other preconditions of this new phase: freedom of competition inside the nation, the development of theoretical mechanics, etc. (indeed, mechanics, perfected by Newton, was altogether the most popular science in France and England in the eighteenth century). (Free competition inside the nation itself had everywhere to be won by a revolution — 1640 and 1688 in England, 1789 in France.)

Competition soon compelled every country that wished to retain its historical role to protect its manufactures by renewed customs regulations (the old duties were no longer any good against large-scale industry) and soon after to introduce large-scale industry under protective duties. In spite of these protective measures large-scale industry universalised competition (it is practical free trade; the protective duty is only a palliative, a measure of defence *within* free trade), established means of communication and the modern world market, subordinated trade to itself, transformed all capital into industrial capital, and thus produced the rapid circulation (development of the financial system) and the centralisation of capital. By universal competition it forced all individuals to strain their energy to the utmost. It destroyed as far as possible ideology, religion, morality, etc., and, where it could not do this, made them into a palpable lie. It produced world history for the first time, insofar as it made all civilised nations and every individual member of them dependent for the satisfaction of their wants on the whole world, thus destroying the former natural exclusiveness of separate nations. It made natural science subservient to capital and took from the division of labour the last semblance of its natural character. It altogether destroyed the natural character, as far as this is possible with regard to labour, and resolved all natural relations into money relations. In the place of naturally grown towns it created the modern, large industrial cities which have sprung up overnight. It destroyed the crafts and all earlier stages of industry wherever it gained mastery. It completed the victory of the town over the country. Its [basis] is the automatic system. It produced a mass of productive forces, for which private property became just as much a fetter [52] as the guild had been for manufacture and the small, rural workshop for the developing handicrafts. These productive forces receive under the system of private property a one-sided development only, and for the majority they become destructive forces; moreover, a great many of these forces can find no application at all within the system of private property. Generally speaking, large-scale industry created everywhere the same relations between the classes of society, and thus destroyed the peculiar features of the various nationalities. And finally, while the bourgeoisie of each nation still retained separate national interests, large-scale industry created a class which in all nations has the same interest and for which nationality is already dead; a class which is really rid of all the old world and at the same time stands pitted against it. For the worker it makes not only his relation to the capitalist, but labour itself, unbearable.

It is evident that large-scale industry does not reach the same level of development in all districts of a country. This does not, however, retard the class movement of the proletariat, because the proletarians created by large-scale industry assume leadership of this movement and carry the whole mass along with them, and because the workers excluded from large-scale industry are placed by it in a still worse situation than the workers in large-scale industry itself. The countries in which large-scale industry is developed act in a similar manner upon the more or less non-industrial countries, insofar as the latter are swept by world intercourse into the universal competitive struggle.

*   *   *

These different forms [of production] are just so many forms of the organisation of labour, and hence of property. In each period a unification of the existing productive forces takes place, insofar as this has been rendered necessary by needs.

[5. THE CONTRADICTION BETWEEN THE PRODUCTIVE FORCES AND THE FORM OF INTERCOURSE AS THE BASIS OF SOCIAL REVOLUTION]

The contradiction between the productive forces and the form of intercourse, which, as we saw, has occurred several times in past history, without, however, endangering its basis, necessarily on each occasion burst out in a revolution, taking on at the same time various subsidiary forms, such as all-embracing collisions, collisions of various classes, contradictions of consciousness, battle of ideas, political struggle, etc. From a narrow point of view one may isolate one of these subsidiary forms and consider it as the basis of these revolutions; and this is all the more easy as the individuals who started the revolutions had illusions about their own activity according to their degree of culture and the stage of historical development.

Thus all collisions in history have their origin, according to our view, in the contradiction between the productive forces and the form [53] of intercourse. Incidentally, to lead to collisions in a country, this contradiction need not necessarily have reached its extreme limit in that particular country. The competition with industrially more advanced countries, brought about by the expansion of international intercourse, is sufficient to produce a similar contradiction in countries with a less advanced industry (e.g., the latent proletariat in Germany brought into more prominence by the competition of English industry).

[6. COMPETITION OF INDIVIDUALS AND THE FORMATION OF CLASSES. CONTRADICTION BETWEEN INDIVIDUALS AND THEIR CONDITIONS OF LIFE. THE ILLUSORY COMMUNITY OF INDIVIDUALS IN BOURGEOIS SOCIETY AND THE REAL UNION OF INDIVIDUALS UNDER COMMUNISM. SUBORDINATION OF THE SOCIAL CONDITIONS OF LIFE TO THE POWER OF THE UNITED INDIVIDUALS]

Competition separates individuals from one another, not only the bourgeois but still more the workers, in spite of the fact that it brings them together. Hence it is a long time before these individuals can unite, apart from the fact that for the purpose of this union — if it is not to be merely local — the necessary means, the big industrial cities and cheap and quick communications, have first to be produced by large-scale industry. Hence every organised power standing over against these isolated individuals, who live in conditions daily reproducing this isolation, can only be overcome after long struggles. To demand the opposite would be tantamount to demanding that competition should not exist in this definite epoch of history, or that the individuals should banish from their minds conditions over which in their isolation they have no control.

The building of houses. With savages each family has as a matter of course its own cave or hut like the separate family tent of the nomads. This separate domestic economy is made only the more necessary by the further development of private property. With the agricultural peoples a communal domestic economy is just as impossible as a communal cultivation of the soil. A great advance was the building of towns. In all previous periods, however, the abolition [*Aufhebung*] [a] of individual economy, which is inseparable from the abolition of private property, was impossible for the simple reason that the material conditions required were not present. The setting-up of a communal domestic economy presupposes the development of machinery, the use of natural forces and of many other productive forces — e.g., of water-supplies, [54] gas-lighting, steam-heating, etc., the supersession [Aufhebung] [a] of town and country. Without these conditions a communal economy would not in itself form a new productive force; it would lack material basis and rest on a purely theoretical foundation, in other words, it would be a mere freak and would amount to nothing more than a monastic economy. — What was possible can be seen in the towns brought into existence by concentration and in the construction of communal buildings for various definite purposes (prisons, barracks, etc.). That the supersession of individual economy is inseparable from the supersession of the family is self-evident.

(The statement which frequently occurs with Saint Sancho that each man is all that he is through the state [b] is fundamentally

---

[a] *Aufhebung*—a term used by Hegel to denote the negation of an old form while preserving its positive content in the new, which supersedes it.— *Ed.*

[b] Max Stirner, *Der Einzige und sein Eigenthum.*— *Ed.*

the same as the statement that the bourgeois is only a specimen of the bourgeois species; a statement which presupposes that the bourgeois *class* existed before the individuals constituting it.*)

In the Middle Ages the citizens in each town were compelled to unite against the landed nobility to defend themselves. The extension of trade, the establishment of communications, led separate towns to establish contacts with other towns, which had asserted the same interests in the struggle with the same antagonist. Out of the many local communities of citizens in the various towns there arose only gradually the middle *class*. The conditions of life of the individual citizens became, on account of their contradiction to the existing relations and of the mode of labour determined by these, conditions which were common to them all and independent of each individual. The citizens created these conditions insofar as they had torn themselves free from feudal ties, and were in their turn created by them insofar as they were determined by their antagonism to the feudal system which they found in existence. With the setting up of intercommunications between the individual towns, these common conditions developed into class conditions. The same conditions, the same contradiction, the same interests were bound to call forth on the whole similar customs everywhere. The bourgeoisie itself develops only gradually together with its conditions, splits according to the division of labour into various sections and finally absorbs all propertied classes it finds in existence** (while it develops the majority of the earlier propertyless and a part of the hitherto propertied classes into a new class, the proletariat) in the measure to which all property found in existence is transformed into industrial or commercial capital.

The separate individuals form a class only insofar as |55| they have to carry on a common battle against another class; in other respects they are on hostile terms with each other as competitors. On the other hand, the class in its turn assumes an independent existence as against the individuals, so that the latter find their conditions of life predetermined, and have their position in life and hence their personal development assigned to them by their class, thus becoming subsumed under

---

* [Marginal note by Marx:] With the philosophers *pre-existence* of the class.
** [Marginal note by Marx:] To begin with, it absorbs the branches of labour directly belonging to the state and then all ± [more or less] ideological professions.

it. This is the same phenomenon as the subjection of the separate individuals to the division of labour and can only be removed by the abolition of private property and of labour[a] itself. We have already indicated several times that this subsuming of individuals under the class brings with it their subjection to all kinds of ideas, etc.

If this development of individuals, which proceeds within the common conditions of existence of estates and classes, historically following one another, and the general conceptions thereby forced upon them — if this development is considered from a *philosophical* point of view, it is certainly very easy to imagine that in these individuals the species, or man, has evolved, or that they evolved man — and in this way one can give history some hard clouts on the ear. One can then conceive these various estates and classes to be specific terms of the general expression, subordinate varieties of the species, or evolutionary phases of man.

This subsuming of individuals under definite classes cannot be abolished until a class has evolved which has no longer any particular class interest to assert against a ruling class.

The transformation, through the division of labour, of personal powers (relations) into material powers, cannot be dispelled by dismissing the general idea of it from one's mind, but can only be abolished by the individuals again subjecting these material powers to themselves and abolishing the division of labour.* This is not possible without the community. Only within the community has each individual |56| the means of cultivating his gifts in all directions; hence personal freedom becomes possible only within the community. In the previous substitutes for the community, in the state, etc., personal freedom has existed only for the individuals who developed under the conditions of the ruling class, and only insofar as they were individuals of this class. The illusory community in which individuals have up till now combined always took on an independent existence in relation to them, and since it was the combination of one class over against

* [Marginal note by Engels:] (Feuerbach: being and essence). [Cf. this volume, pp. 66-67.— *Ed.*]

---

[a] Regarding the meaning of "abolition of labour" (*Aufhebung der Arbeit*) see this volume, pp. 59-60, 87-89, 94-98.— *Ed.*

another, it was at the same time for the oppressed class not only a completely illusory community, but a new fetter as well. In the real community the individuals obtain their freedom in and through their association.

Individuals have always proceeded from themselves, but of course from themselves within their given historical conditions and relations, not from the "pure" individual in the sense of the ideologists. But in the course of historical development, and precisely through the fact that within the division of labour social relations inevitably take on an independent existence, there appears a cleavage in the life of each individual, insofar as it is personal and insofar as it is determined by some branch of labour and the conditions pertaining to it. (We do not mean it to be understood from this that, for example, the rentier, the capitalist, etc., cease to be persons; but their personality is conditioned and determined by quite definite class relations, and the cleavage appears only in their opposition to another class and, for themselves, only when they go bankrupt.) In the estate (and even more in the tribe) this is as yet concealed: for instance, a nobleman always remains a nobleman, a commoner always a commoner, a quality inseparable from his individuality irrespective of his other relations. The difference between the private individual and the class individual, the accidental nature of the conditions of life for the individual, appears only with the emergence of the class, which is itself a product of the bourgeoisie. This accidental character as such is only engendered and developed |57| by competition and the struggle of individuals among themselves. Thus, in imagination, individuals seem freer under the dominance of the bourgeoisie than before, because their conditions of life seem accidental; in reality, of course, they are less free, because they are to a greater extent governed by material forces. The difference from the estate comes out particularly in the antagonism between the bourgeoisie and the proletariat. When the estate of the urban burghers, the corporations, etc., emerged in opposition to the landed nobility, their condition of existence — movable property and craft labour, which had already existed latently before their separation from the feudal institutions — appeared as something positive, which was asserted against feudal landed property, and, therefore, in its own way at first took on a feudal form. Certainly the fugitive serfs treated their previous servitude as something extraneous to their personality. But here they only were doing what every class that is freeing itself from a fetter does; and they did not free themselves as a class but individually. Moreover, they did not break loose from the system of estates, but only formed a new estate, retaining their previous mode of labour even in their new situation, and developing it further by freeing it from its earlier fetters, which no longer corresponded to the development already attained.

For the proletarians, on the other hand, the condition of their life, labour, and with it all the conditions of existence of modern society, have become something extraneous, something over which they, as separate individuals, have no control, and over which no *social* organisation can give them control. The contradiction between the individuality of each separate proletarian and labour, the condition of life forced upon him, becomes evident to him, for he is sacrificed from youth onwards and, within his own class, has no chance of arriving at the conditions which would place him in the other class.—

|58| NB. It must not be forgotten that the serf's very need of existing and the impossibility of a large-scale economy involved the distribution of allotments [a] among the serfs and very soon reduced the services of the serfs to their lord to an average of payments in kind and labour-services. This made it possible for the serf to accumulate movable property and hence facilitated his escape from his lord and gave him the prospect of making his way as a townsman; it also created gradations among the serfs, so that the runaway serfs were already half burghers. It is likewise obvious that the serfs who were versed in a craft had the best chance of acquiring movable property.—

Thus, while the fugitive serfs only wished to have full scope to develop and assert those conditions of existence which were already there, and hence, in the end, only arrived at free labour, the proletarians, if they are to assert themselves as individuals, have to abolish the hitherto prevailing condition of their existence (which has, moreover, been that of all society up to then), namely, labour. Thus they find themselves directly opposed to the form in which, hitherto, the individuals, of which society consists, have given themselves collective expression, that is, the state; in order, therefore, to assert themselves as individuals, they must overthrow the state.

---

[a] This word is in English in the manuscript.— *Ed.*

It follows from all we have been saying up till now that* the communal relation into which the individuals of a class entered, and which was determined by their common interests as against a third party, was always a community to which these individuals belonged only as average individuals, only insofar as they lived within the conditions of existence of their class — a relation in which they participated not as individuals but as members of a class. With the community of revolutionary proletarians, on the other hand, who take their conditions |59| of existence and those of all members of society under their control, it is just the reverse; it is as individuals that the individuals participate in it. For it is the association of individuals (assuming the advanced stage of modern productive forces, of course) which puts the conditions of the free development and movement of individuals under their control — conditions which were previously left to chance and had acquired an independent existence over against the separate individuals precisely because of their separation as individuals and because their inevitable association, which was determined by the division of labour, had, as a result of their separation, become for them an alien bond. Up till now association (by no means an arbitrary one, such as is expounded for example in the *Contrat social*,[a] but a necessary one) was simply an agreement about those conditions, within which the individuals were free to enjoy the freaks of fortune (compare, e.g., the formation of the North American state and the South American republics). This right to the undisturbed enjoyment, within certain conditions, of fortuity and chance has up till now been called personal freedom.— These conditions of existence are, of course, only the productive forces and forms of intercourse at any particular time.

Communism differs from all previous movements in that it overturns the basis of all earlier relations of production and intercourse, and for the first time consciously treats all naturally evolved premises as the creations of hitherto existing men, strips them of their natural character and subjugates them to the

---

*[The following is crossed out in the manuscript:] the individuals who freed themselves in any historical epoch merely developed further the conditions of existence which were already present and which they found in existence.

---

[a] Jean Jacques Rousseau, *Du Contrat social.—Ed.*

power of the united individuals. Its organisation is, therefore, essentially economic, the material production of the conditions of this unity; it turns existing conditions into conditions of unity. The reality which communism creates is precisely the true basis for rendering it impossible that anything should exist independently of individuals, insofar as reality is nevertheless only a product of the preceding intercourse of individuals. Thus the communists in practice treat the conditions created up to now by production and intercourse as inorganic conditions, without, however, imagining that it was the plan or the destiny of previous generations to give them material, and without believing that these conditions were inorganic for the individuals creating them.

[7. CONTRADICTION BETWEEN INDIVIDUALS AND THEIR CONDITIONS OF LIFE AS CONTRADICTION BETWEEN THE PRODUCTIVE FORCES AND THE FORM OF INTERCOURSE. DEVELOPMENT OF THE PRODUCTIVE FORCES AND THE CHANGING FORMS OF INTERCOURSE]

[60] The difference between the individual as a person and whatever is extraneous to him is not a conceptual difference but a historical fact. This distinction has a different significance at different times — e.g., the estate as something extraneous to the individual in the eighteenth century, and so too, more or less, the family. It is not a distinction that we have to make for each age, but one which each age itself makes from among the different elements which it finds in existence, and indeed not according to any idea, but compelled by material collisions in life.

What appears accidental to a later age as opposed to an earlier — and this applies also to the elements handed down by an earlier age — is a form of intercourse which corresponded to a definite stage of development of the productive forces. The relation of the productive forces to the form of intercourse is the relation of the form of intercourse to the occupation or activity of the individuals. (The fundamental form of this activity is, of course, material, on which depend all other forms — mental, political, religious, etc. The different forms of material life are, of course, in every case dependent on the needs which are already developed, and the production, as well as the satisfaction, of these needs is an historical process, which is not found in the case of a sheep or a dog (Stirner's refractory principal argument [a] *adversus hominem*), although

---

[a] Cf. Max Stirner, "Recensenten Stirners", and also this volume, pp. 104-105.— *Ed.*

sheep and dogs in their present form certainly, but in spite of themselves, are products of an historical process. The conditions under which individuals have intercourse with each other, so long as this contradiction is absent, are conditions appertaining to their individuality, in no way external to them; conditions under which alone these definite individuals, living under definite relations, can produce their material life and what is connected with it, are thus the conditions of their self-activity and are produced by this self-activity.* The definite condition under which they produce thus corresponds, as long as |61| the contradiction has not yet appeared, to the reality of their conditioned nature, their one-sided existence, the one-sidedness of which only becomes evident when the contradiction enters on the scene and thus exists solely for those who live later. Then this condition appears as an accidental fetter, and the consciousness that it is a fetter is imputed to the earlier age as well.

These various conditions, which appear first as conditions of self-activity, later as fetters upon it, form in the whole development of history a coherent series of forms of intercourse, the coherence of which consists in this: an earlier form of intercourse, which has become a fetter, is replaced by a new one corresponding to the more developed productive forces and, hence, to the advanced mode of the self-activity of individuals — a form which in its turn becomes a fetter and is then replaced by another. Since these conditions correspond at every stage to the simultaneous development of the productive forces, their history is at the same time the history of the evolving productive forces taken over by each new generation, and is therefore the history of the development of the forces of the individuals themselves.

Since this development takes place spontaneously, i.e., is not subordinated to a general plan of freely combined individuals, it proceeds from various localities, tribes, nations, branches of labour, etc., each of which to start with develops independently of the others and only gradually enters into relation with the others. Furthermore, this development proceeds only very slowly; the various stages and interests are never completely overcome, but only subordinated to the prevailing interest and trail along beside the latter for centuries afterwards. It follows from this that even within a nation the individuals, even apart from their pecuniary circumstances, have quite diverse de-

---

* [Marginal note by Marx:] Production of the form of intercourse itself.

velopments, and that an earlier interest, the peculiar form of intercourse of which has already been ousted by that belonging to a later interest, remains for a long time afterwards in possession of a traditional power in the illusory community (state, law), which has won an existence independent of the individuals; a power which in the last resort can only be broken by a revolution. This explains why, with reference to individual points |62| which allow of a more general summing-up, consciousness can sometimes appear further advanced than the contemporary empirical conditions, so that in the struggles of a later epoch one can refer to earlier theoreticians as authorities.

On the other hand, in countries like North America, which start from scratch in an already advanced historical epoch, the development proceeds very rapidly. Such countries have no other natural premises than the individuals who have settled there and were led to do so because the forms of intercourse of the old countries did not correspond to their requirements. Thus they begin with the most advanced individuals of the old countries, and, therefore, with the correspondingly most advanced form of intercourse, even before this form of intercourse has been able to establish itself in the old countries. This is the case with all colonies, insofar as they are not mere military or trading stations. Carthage, the Greek colonies, and Iceland in the eleventh and twelfth centuries, provide examples of this. A similar relationship issues from conquest, when a form of intercourse which has evolved on another soil is brought over complete to the conquered country: whereas in its home it was still encumbered with interests and relations left over from earlier periods, here it can and must be established completely and without hindrance, if only to assure the conquerors' lasting power. (England and Naples after the Norman conquest,[28] when they received the most perfect form of feudal organisation.)

[8. THE ROLE OF VIOLENCE (CONQUEST) IN HISTORY]

This whole conception of history appears to be contradicted by the fact of conquest. Up till now violence, war, pillage, murder and robbery, etc., have been accepted as the driving force of history. Here we must limit ourselves to the chief points and take, therefore, only the most striking example — the destruction of an old civilisation by a barbarous people and the resulting formation of an entirely new organisation of society. (Rome and the barbarians; feudalism and Gaul; the Byzantine Empire and the Turks.)

|63| With the conquering barbarian people war itself is still, as indicated above,[a] a regular form of intercourse, which is the more eagerly exploited as the increase in population together with the traditional and, for it, the only possible crude mode of production gives rise to the need for new means of production. In Italy, on the other hand, the concentration of landed property (caused not only by buying-up and indebtedness but also by inheritance, since loose living being rife and marriage rare, the old families gradually died out and their possessions fell into the hands of a few) and its conversion into grazing-land (caused not only by the usual economic factors still operative today but by the importation of plundered and tribute corn and the resultant lack of demand for Italian corn) brought about the almost total disappearance of the free population; the slaves died out again and again, and had constantly to be replaced by new ones. Slavery remained the basis of the entire production process. The plebeians, midway between freemen and slaves, never succeeded in becoming more than a proletarian rabble. Rome indeed never became more than a city; its connection with the provinces was almost exclusively political and could, therefore, easily be broken again by political events.

Nothing is more common than the notion that in history up till now it has only been a question of *taking.* The barbarians *take* the Roman Empire, and this fact of taking is made to explain the transition from the old world to the feudal system. In this taking by barbarians, however, the question is whether the nation which is conquered has evolved industrial productive forces, as is the case with modern peoples, or whether its productive forces are based for the most part merely on their concentration and on the community. Taking is further determined by the object taken. A banker's fortune, consisting of paper, cannot be taken at all without the taker's submitting to the conditions of production and intercourse of the country

---

[a] Probably a reference to one of the missing pages of the manuscript (see this volume, pp. 70-71). A similar idea is expressed in the clean copy; see this volume, pp. 38-39.— *Ed.*

taken. Similarly the total industrial capital of a modern industrial country. And finally, everywhere there is very soon an end to taking, and when there is nothing more to take, you have to set about producing. From this necessity of producing, which very soon asserts itself, it follows |64| that the form of community adopted by the settling conquerors must correspond to the stage of development of the productive forces they find in existence; or, if this is not the case from the start, it must change according to the productive forces. This, too, explains the fact, which people profess to have noticed everywhere in the period following the migration of the peoples, namely that the servant was master, and that the conquerors very soon took over language, culture and manners from the conquered.

The feudal system was by no means brought complete from Germany, but had its origin, as far as the conquerors were concerned, in the martial organisation of the army during the actual conquest, and this evolved only after the conquest into the feudal system proper through the action of the productive forces found in the conquered countries. To what an extent this form was determined by the productive forces is shown by the abortive attempts to realise other forms derived from reminiscences of ancient Rome (Charlemagne, etc.).

To be continued.—

[9. CONTRADICTION BETWEEN THE PRODUCTIVE FORCES AND THE FORM OF INTERCOURSE UNDER THE CONDITIONS OF LARGE-SCALE INDUSTRY AND FREE COMPETITION. CONTRADICTION BETWEEN LABOUR AND CAPITAL]

In large-scale industry and competition the whole mass of conditions of existence, limitations, biases of individuals, are fused together into the two simplest forms: private property and labour. With money every form of intercourse, and intercourse itself, becomes fortuitous for the individuals. Thus money implies that all intercourse up till now was only intercourse of individuals under particular conditions, not of individuals as individuals. These conditions are reduced to two: accumulated labour or private property, and actual labour. If both or one of these ceases, then intercourse comes to a standstill. The modern economists themselves, e.g., Sismondi, Cherbuliez, etc., oppose *association des individus* to *association des capitaux*.[a] On

---

[a] Antoine-Elysée Cherbuliez, *Riche ou Pauvre.—Ed.*

the other hand, the individuals themselves are entirely subordinated to the division of labour and hence are brought into the
most complete dependence on one another. Private property,
insofar as within labour it confronts labour, evolves out of the
necessity of accumulation, and is in the beginning still mainly a
communal form but in its further development it approaches
more and more the modern form of private property. The
division of labour implies from the outset the division of the
conditions of labour, of tools and materials, and thus the
fragmentation of accumulated capital among different owners,
and thus, also, the fragmentation between capital and labour,
and the different forms of property itself. The more the division
of labour develops |65| and accumulation grows, the further
fragmentation develops. Labour itself can only exist on the
premise of this fragmentation.

(Personal energy of the individuals of various nations — Germans and Americans — energy even as a result of miscegenation — hence the cretinism of the Germans; in France. England,
etc., foreign peoples transplanted to an already developed soil,
in America to an entirely new soil; in Germany the indigenous
population quietly stayed where it was.)

Thus two facts are here revealed.* First the productive forces
appear as a world for themselves, quite independent of and
divorced from the individuals, alongside the individuals; the
reason for this is that the individuals, whose forces they are,
exist split up and in opposition to one another, whilst, on the
other hand, these forces are only real forces in the intercourse
and association of these individuals. Thus, on the one hand, we
have a totality of productive forces, which have, as it were,
taken on a material form and are for the individuals themselves
no longer the forces of the individuals but of private property,
and hence of the individuals only insofar as they are owners of
private property. Never, in any earlier period, have the
productive forces taken on a form so indifferent to the
intercourse of individuals *as* individuals, because their intercourse itself was still a restricted one. On the other hand,

* [Marginal note by Engels:] Sismondi.

standing against these productive forces, we have the majority of the individuals from whom these forces have been wrested away, and who, robbed thus of all real life-content, have become abstract individuals, who are, however, by this very fact put into a position to enter into relation with one another *as individuals*.

Labour, the only connection which still links them with the productive forces and with their own existence, has lost all semblance of self-activity and only sustains their |66| life by stunting it. While in the earlier periods self-activity and the production of material life were separated since they devolved on different persons, and while, on account of the narrowness of the individuals themselves, the production of material life was considered a subordinate mode of self-activity, they now diverge to such an extent that material life appears as the end, and what produces this material life, labour (which is now the only possible but, as we see, negative form of self-activity), as the means.

[10. THE NECESSITY, PRECONDITIONS AND CONSEQUENCES OF THE ABOLITION OF PRIVATE PROPERTY]

Thus things have now come to such a pass that the individuals must appropriate the existing totality of productive forces, not only to achieve self-activity, but, also, merely to safeguard their very existence.

This appropriation is first determined by the object to be appropriated, the productive forces, which have been developed to a totality and which only exist within a universal intercourse. Even from this aspect alone, therefore, this appropriation must have a universal character corresponding to the productive forces and the intercourse. The appropriation of these forces is itself nothing more than the development of the individual capacities corresponding to the material instruments of production. The appropriation of a totality of instruments of production is, for this very reason, the development of a totality of capacities in the individuals themselves.

This appropriation is further determined by the persons appropriating. Only the proletarians of the present day, who are completely shut off from all self-activity, are in a position to achieve a complete and no longer restricted self-activity, which consists in the appropriation of a totality of productive forces and in the development of a totality of capacities entailed by this. All earlier revolutionary appropriations were restricted; individuals, whose self-activity was restricted by a crude instrument of production and a limited intercourse, appropriated this crude instrument |67| of production, and hence merely achieved a new state of limitation. Their instrument of production became their property, but they themselves remained subordinate to the division of labour and their own instrument of production. In all appropriations up to now, a mass of individuals remained subservient to a single instrument of production; in the appropriation by the proletarians, a mass of instruments of production must be made subject to each individual, and property to all. Modern universal intercourse cannot be controlled by individuals, unless it is controlled by all.

This appropriation is further determined by the manner in which it must be effected. It can only be effected through a union, which by the character of the proletariat itself can again only be a universal one, and through a revolution, in which, on the one hand, the power of the earlier mode of production and intercourse and social organisation is overthrown, and, on the other hand, there develops the universal character and the energy of the proletariat, which are required to accomplish the appropriation, and the proletariat moreover rids itself of everything that still clings to it from its previous position in society.

Only at this stage does self-activity coincide with material life, which corresponds to the development of individuals into complete individuals and the casting-off of all natural limitations. The transformation of labour into self-activity corresponds to the transformation of the previously limited intercourse into the intercourse of individuals as such. With the appropriation of the total productive forces by the united individuals, private property comes to an end. Whilst previously in history a particular condition always appeared as accidental, now the isolation of individuals and each person's particular way of gaining his livelihood have themselves become accidental.

The individuals, who are no longer |68| subject to the division of labour, have been conceived by the philosophers as an ideal, under the name "man", and the whole process which we have outlined has been regarded by them as the evolutionary process of "man", so that at every historical stage "man" was substituted for the individuals existing hitherto and shown as the motive force of history. The whole process was thus conceived as a process of the self-estrangement [*Selbstentfrem-dungsprozess*] of "man",* and this was essentially due to the fact that the average individual of the later stage was always foisted on to the earlier stage, and the consciousness of a later age on to the individuals of an earlier. Through this inversion, which from the first disregards the actual conditions, it was possible to transform the whole of history into an evolutionary process of consciousness.

$$\times \quad * \quad *$$

Civil society embraces the whole material intercourse of individuals within a definite stage of the development of productive forces. It embraces the whole commercial and industrial life of a given stage and, insofar, transcends the state and the nation, though, on the other hand again, it must assert itself in its external relations as nationality and internally must organise itself as state. The term "civil society"[29] emerged in the eighteenth century, when property relations had already extricated themselves from the ancient and medieval community. Civil society as such only develops with the bourgeoisie; the social organisation evolving directly out of production and intercourse, which in all ages forms the basis of the state and of the rest of the idealistic[a] superstructure, has, however, always been designated by the same name.

[11.] THE RELATION OF STATE AND LAW TO PROPERTY

The first form of property, in the ancient world as in the Middle Ages, is tribal property, determined with the Romans chiefly by war, with the [69] Germans by the rearing of cattle. In the case of the ancient peoples, since several tribes live together in one city, tribal property appears as state property, and the right of the individual to it as mere "possession" which, however, like tribal property as a whole, is confined to landed property only. Real private property began with the ancients, as with modern nations, with movable property. (Slavery and community) (*dominium ex jure Quiritum*[b]).— In the case of the nations which grew out of the

---

* [Marginal note by Marx:] Self-estrangement.

---

[a] I.e., ideal, ideological.— *Ed.*
[b] Ownership in accordance with the law applying to full Roman citizens.— *Ed.*

Middle Ages, tribal property evolved through various stages — feudal landed property, corporative movable property, capital invested in manufacture — to modern capital, determined by large-scale industry and universal competition, i.e., pure private property, which has cast off all semblance of a communal institution and has shut out the state from any influence on the development of property. To this modern private property corresponds the modern state, which, purchased gradually by the owners of property by means of taxation, has fallen entirely into their hands through the national debt, and its existence has become wholly dependent on the commercial credit which the owners of property, the bourgeois, extend to it, as reflected in the rise and fall of government securities on the stock exchange. By the mere fact that it is a *class* and no longer an *estate*, the bourgeoisie is forced to organise itself no longer locally, but nationally, and to give a general form to its average interests. Through the emancipation of private property from the community, the state has become a separate entity, alongside and outside civil society; but it is nothing more than the form of organisation which the bourgeois are compelled to adopt, both for internal and external purposes, for the mutual guarantee of their property and interests. The independence of the state is only found nowadays in those countries where the estates have not yet completely developed into classes, where the estates, done away with in more advanced countries, still play a part and there exists a mixture, where consequently no section of the population can achieve dominance over the others. This is the case particularly in Germany. The most perfect example of the modern state is North [70] America. The modern French, English and American writers all express the opinion that the state exists only for the sake of private property, so that this view has also been generally accepted by the average man.

Since the state is the form in which the individuals of a ruling class assert their common interests, and in which the whole civil society of an epoch is epitomised, it follows that all common institutions are set up with the help of the state and are given a political form. Hence the illusion that law is based on the will, and indeed on the will divorced from its real basis — on *free* will. Similarly, justice is in its turn reduced to statute law.

Civil law develops simultaneously with private property out of the disintegration of the natural community. With the Romans the development of private property and civil law had no further industrial and commercial consequences, because their whole mode of production did not alter.* With modern peoples, where the feudal community was disintegrated by industry and trade, there began with the rise of private property and civil law a new phase, which was capable of further development. The very first town which carried on an extensive maritime trade in the Middle Ages, Amalfi, also developed maritime law.[30] As soon as industry and trade developed private property further, first in Italy and later in other countries, the highly developed Roman civil law was immediately adopted again and raised to authority. When later the bourgeoisie had acquired so much power that the princes took up its interests in order to overthrow the feudal nobility by means of the bourgeoisie, there began in all countries — in France in the sixteenth century — the real development of law, which in all [71] countries except England proceeded on the basis of the Roman code of laws. In England, too, Roman legal principles had to be introduced to further the development of civil law (especially in the case of movable property). (It must not be forgotten that law has just as little an independent history as religion.)

In civil law the existing property relations are declared to be the result of the general will. The *jus utendi et abutendi*[a] itself asserts on the one hand the fact that private property has become entirely independent of the community, and on the other the illusion that private property itself is based solely on the private will, the arbitrary disposal of the thing. In practice, the *abuti* has very definite economic limitations for the owner of private property, if he does not wish to see his property and hence his *jus abutendi* pass into other hands, since actually the thing, considered merely with reference to his will, is not a thing at all, but only becomes a thing, true property, in intercourse, and independently of the law (*a relationship*, which the philosophers call an idea**). This juridical illusion, which reduces law to the mere will, necessarily leads, in the further development of property relations, to the position that a man may have a legal title to a thing without really having the thing. If, for instance, the income from a piece of land disappears owing to competition, then the proprietor has

* [Marginal note by Engels:] (Usury!)

** [Marginal note by Marx:] For the *philosophers relationship=idea.* They only know the relation of "Man" to himself and hence for them all real relations become ideas.

---

[a] The right of use and of disposal.— *Ed.*

certainly his legal title to it along with the *jus utendi et abutendi*. But he can do nothing with it: he owns nothing as a landed proprietor if he has not enough capital elsewhere to cultivate his land. This illusion of the jurists also explains the fact that for them, as for every code, it is altogether fortuitous that individuals enter into relations among themselves (e.g., contracts); it explains why they consider that these relations [can] be entered into or not at will, [72] and that their content [rests] purely on the individual free will of the contracting parties.

Whenever, through the development of industry and commerce, new forms of intercourse have been evolved (e.g., insurance companies, etc.), the law has always been compelled to admit them among the modes of acquiring property.[a]

[12. FORMS OF SOCIAL CONSCIOUSNESS]

The influence of the division of labour on science.

The role of *repression* with regard to the state, law, morality, etc.

It is precisely because the bourgeoisie rules as a class that in the law it must give itself a general expression.

Natural science and history.

There is no history of politics, law, science, etc., of art, religion, etc.*

Why the ideologists turn everything upside-down.

Clerics, jurists, politicians.

Jurists, politicians (statesmen in general), moralists, clerics.

For this ideological subdivision within a class: 1) *The occupation assumes an independent existence owing to division of labour.* Everyone believes his craft to be the true one. Illusions regarding the connection between their craft and reality are the more likely to be cherished by them because of the very nature of the craft. In consciousness—in jurisprudence, politics, etc.—relations become concepts; since they do

---

* [Marginal note by Marx:] To the "community" as it appears in the ancient state, in feudalism and in the absolute monarchy, to this bond correspond especially the religious conceptions.

---

[a] The following notes, written by Marx, were intended for further elaboration.— *Ed.*

not go beyond these relations, the concepts of the relations also become fixed concepts in their mind. The judge, for example, applies the code, he therefore regards legislation as the real, active driving force. Respect for their goods, because their craft deals with general matters.

Idea of law. Idea of state. The matter is turned upside-down in *ordinary* consciousness.

Religion is from the outset *consciousness of the transcendental* arising from *actually existing* forces.

This more popularly.

Tradition, with regard to law, religion, etc.

*   *   *

[73][a] Individuals always proceeded, and always proceed, from themselves. Their relations are the relations of their real life-process. How does it happen that their relations assume an independent existence over against them? and that the forces of their own life become superior to them?

In short: *division of labour*, the level of which depends on the development of the productive power at any particular time.

Landed property. Communal property. Feudal. Modern. Estate property. Manufacturing property. Industrial capital.

---

[a] This, the last, page is not numbered in the manuscript. It contains notes relating to the beginning of the authors' exposition of the materialist conception of history. The ideas outlined here are set forth in the clean copy, Section 3 (see this volume, pp. 39-42).— *Ed.*

THE LEIPZIG COUNCIL [31]

In the third volume of the *Wigand'sche Vierteljahrsschrift* for 1845 the battle of the Huns, prophetically portrayed by Kaulbach,[32] actually takes place. The spirits of the slain, whose fury is not appeased even in death, raise a hue and cry, which sounds like the thunder of battles and war-cries, the clatter of swords, shields and iron waggons. But it is not a battle over earthly things. The holy war is being waged not over protective tariffs, the constitution, potato blight,[33] banking affairs and railways, but in the name of the most sacred interests of the spirit, in the name of "substance", "self-consciousness", "criticism", the "unique" and the "true man". We are attending a council of church fathers. As these church fathers are the last specimens of their kind, and as here, it is to be hoped, the cause of the Most High, alias the Absolute, is being pleaded for the last time, it is worth while taking a verbatim report of the proceedings.

Here, first of all, is *Saint Bruno*, who is easily recognised by his *stick* ("become sensuousness, become a *stick*", *Wigand.* p. 130).[a] His head is crowned with a halo of "pure criticism" and, full of contempt for the world, he wraps himself in his "self-consciousness". He has "*smashed* religion in its entirety and the state in its manifestations" (p. 138), by violating the concept of "substance" in the name of the Most High

---

[a] Bruno Bauer, "Charakteristik Ludwig Feuerbachs".—*Ed.*

self-consciousness. The ruins of the church and "debris" of the state lie at his feet, while his glance "strikes down" the "masses" into the dust. He is like God, he has neither father nor mother, he is "his own creation, his own product". (P. 136.) In short, he is the "Napoleon" of the spirit, in spirit he is "Napoleon". His spiritual exercises consist in constantly "examining himself, and in this self-examination he finds the impulse to self-determination" (p. 136); as a result of such wearisome self-recording he has obviously become emaciated. Besides "examining" himself — from time to time he "examines" also, as we shall see, the *Westphälische Dampfboot*.[a]

Opposite him stands *Saint Max*, whose services to the Kingdom of God consist in asserting that he has established and proved — on approximately 600 printed pages[b] — his identity, that he is not just anyone, not some "Tom, Dick or Harry", but precisely Saint Max and no other. About his halo and other marks of distinction only one thing can be said: that they are "his object and thereby his property", that they are "unique" and "incomparable" and that they are "inexpressible". (P. 148.)[c] He is simultaneously the "phrase" and the "owner of the phrase", simultaneously Sancho Panza and Don Quixote. His ascetic exercises consist of sour thoughts about thoughtlessness, of considerations throughout many pages about inconsiderateness and of the sanctification of unholiness. Incidentally, there is no need for us to elaborate on his virtues, for concerning all the qualities ascribed to him — even if there were more of them than the names of God among the Muslims — he is in the habit of saying: I am all this and something more, I am the all of this nothing and the nothing of this all. He is favourably distinguished from his gloomy rival in possessing a certain solemn "*light-heartedness*" and from time to time he interrupts his serious ponderings with a "*critical hurrah*".

These two grand masters of the Holy Inquisition summon the heretic Feuerbach, who has to defend himself against the grave

---

[a] See this volume, pp. 121-23.— *Ed.*
[b] Max Stirner, *Der Einzige und sein Eigenthum.*— *Ed.*
[c] See Max Stirner, "Recensenten Stirners".— *Ed.*

charge of gnosticism. The heretic Feuerbach, "thunders" Saint Bruno, is in possession of *hyle*,[a] substance, and refuses to hand it over lest my infinite self-consciousness be reflected in it. Self-consciousness has to wander like a ghost until it has taken back into itself all things which arise from it and flow into it. It has already swallowed the whole world, except for this *hyle*, substance, which the gnostic Feuerbach keeps under lock and key and refuses to hand over.

Saint Max accuses the gnostic of doubting the dogma revealed by the mouth of Saint Max himself, the dogma that "every goose, every dog, every horse" is "the perfect, or, if one prefers the superlative degree, the most perfect, man". (*Wigand*, p. 187: "The aforesaid does not lack a tittle of what makes man a man. Indeed, the *same* applies also to every goose, every dog, every horse".)

Besides the hearing of these important indictments, sentence is also pronounced in the case brought by the two saints against Moses Hess and in the case brought by Saint Bruno against the authors of *Die heilige Familie*. But as these accused have been busying themselves with "worldly affairs" and, therefore, have failed to appear before the Santa Casa,[34] they are sentenced in their absence to eternal banishment from the realm of the spirit for the term of their natural life.

Finally, the two grand masters are again starting some strange intrigues among themselves and against each other.*

---

* [The following passage is crossed out in the manuscript:] On the plea that he is an "unusually cunning and politic mind" (*Wigand*, p. 192) *Dottore Graziano*, alias Arnold Ruge, appears in the background.[b]

---

[a] Matter.— *Ed.*

[b] This seems to indicate that originally a chapter on Ruge was also planned.— *Ed.*

II

SAINT BRUNO

1. "CAMPAIGN" AGAINST FEUERBACH

Before turning to the solemn discussion which Bauer's self-consciousness has with itself and the world, we should reveal one secret. Saint Bruno uttered the battle-cry and kindled the war only because he had to "safeguard" himself and his stale, soured criticism against the ungrateful forgetfulness of the public, only because he had to show that, in the changed conditions of 1845, criticism always remained itself and unchanged. He wrote the second volume of the "good cause and his own cause"[a]; he stands his ground, he fights *pro aris et focis*.[b] In the true theological manner, however, he conceals this aim of his by an appearance of wishing to "characterise" Feuerbach. Poor Bruno was quite forgotten, as was best proved by the polemic between Feuerbach and Stirner,[c] in which no notice at all was taken of him. For just this reason he seized on this polemic in order to be able to proclaim himself, as the antithesis of the antagonists, their higher unity, the Holy Spirit.

Saint Bruno opens his "campaign" with a burst of artillery fire against Feuerbach, that is to say, with a revised and enlarged reprint of an article which had already appeared in the *Norddeutsche Blätter*.[d] Feuerbach is made into a knight of "*substance*" in order that Bauer's "*self-consciousness*" shall stand out in stronger relief. In this transubstantiation of

---

[a] Bruno Bauer's article "Charakteristik Ludwig Feuerbachs" is here ironically called the second volume of Bauer's book *Die gute Sache der Freiheit und meine eigene Angelegenheit* (The Good Cause of Freedom and My Own Cause).— *Ed.*

[b] Literally: for altars and hearths, used in the sense of: for house and home — that is, pleading his own cause.— *Ed.*

[c] Feuerbach, "Ueber das *Wesen des Christenthums* in Beziehung auf den *Einzigen und sein Eigenthum*".— *Ed.*

[d] I.e., Bruno Bauer's article "Ludwig Feuerbach".— *Ed.*

Feuerbach, which is supposed to be proved by all the writings of the latter, our holy man jumps at once from Feuerbach's writings on Leibnitz and Bayle[a] to the *Wesen des Christen-thums*, leaving out the article against the "positive philosophers"[35] in the *Hallische Jahrbücher.*[b] This "oversight" is "in place". For there Feuerbach revealed the whole wisdom of "self-consciousness" as against the positive representatives of "substance", at a time when Saint Bruno was still indulging in speculation on the immaculate conception.

It is hardly necessary to mention that Saint Bruno still continues to prance about on his old-Hegelian war horse. Listen to the first passage in his latest revelations from the Kingdom of God:

"Hegel combined into one Spinoza's substance and Fichte's ego; the unity of both, the combination of these opposing spheres, etc., constitutes the peculiar interest but, at the same time, the weakness of Hegel's philosophy. [...] This contradiction in which Hegel's system was entangled had to be resolved and destroyed. But he could only do this by making it impossible for all time to put the question: what is the relation of *self-consciousness* to the *absolute spirit....* This was possible in two ways. Either self-consciousness had to be burned again in the flames of substance, i. e., the pure substantiality relation had to be firmly established and maintained, or it had to be shown that personality is the creator of its own attributes and essence, that it belongs to the *concept* of personality *in general* to posit itself" (the "concept" or the "personality"?) "as limited, and again to abolish this limitation which it posits by its *universal essence,* for precisely this essence is *only the result* of its — *inner self-distinction,* of its activity." (*Wigand,* pp. 86, 87, 88.)[c]

In *Die heilige Familie* (p. 220)[d] Hegelian philosophy was represented as a union of Spinoza and Fichte and at the same time the contradiction involved in this was emphasised. The specific peculiarity of Saint Bruno is that, unlike the authors of *Die heilige Familie,* he does not regard the question of the relation of self-consciousness to substance as "a point of controversy *within* Hegelian speculation", but as a world-historic, even an absolute question. This is the sole form in which he is capable of expressing the conflicts of the present day. He really believes that the triumph of self-consciousness over substance has a most essential influence not only on

---

[a] The reference is to the following works of Feuerbach: *Geschichte der neuern Philosophie. Darstellung, Entwicklung und Kritik der Leibnitz'schen Philosophie* and *Pierre Bayle.— Ed.*

[b] Ludwig Feuerbach, "Zur Kritik der 'positiven Philosophie' ".— *Ed.*

[c] Bruno Bauer, "Charakteristik Ludwig Feuerbachs".— *Ed.*

[d] See Karl Marx and Frederick Engels, *Collected Works,* Vol. 4, p. 139.— *Ed.*

European equilibrium but also on the whole future development of the Oregon problem. As to the extent to which the abolition of the Corn Laws in England depends on it, very little has so far transpired.[36]

The abstract and nebulous expression into which a real collision is distorted by Hegel is held by this "critical" mind to be the real collision itself. Bruno accepts the *speculative* contradiction and upholds one part of it against the other. A philosophical *phrase* about a real question is for him the real question itself. Consequently, on the one hand, instead of real people and their real consciousness of their social relations, which apparently confront them as something independent, he has the mere abstract expression: *self-consciousness*, just as, instead of real production, he has the *activity of this self-consciousness, which has become independent*. On the other hand, instead of real nature and the actually existing social relations, he has the philosophical summing-up of all the philosophical categories or names of these relations in the expression: *substance*; for Bruno, along with all philosophers and ideologists, erroneously regards thoughts and ideas — the independent intellectual expression of the existing world — as the basis of this existing world. It is obvious that with these two abstractions, which have become senseless and empty, he can perform all kinds of tricks without knowing anything at all about real people and their relations. (See, in addition, what is said about substance in connection with Feuerbach and concerning "humane liberalism"[a] and the "Holy" in connection with Saint Max.) Hence, he does not forsake the speculative basis in order to solve the contradictions of speculation; he manoeuvres while remaining on that basis, and he *himself* still stands so much on the specifically Hegelian basis that the relation of "self-consciousness" to the "absolute spirit" still gives him no peace. In short, we are confronted with the *philosophy of self-consciousness* that was announced in the *Kritik der Synoptiker*, carried out in *Das entdeckte Christenthum* and which, unfortunately, was long ago anticipated in Hegel's *Phänomenologie*. This new philosophy of Bauer's was completely disposed of in *Die heilige Familie* on pages 220 et seq. and on pages 304-07.[b] Here, however, Saint Bruno even contrives to caricature himself by smuggling in "personality", in order to be able, with

---

[a] See this volume, pp. 46, 61, 249-57 and 298-318.— *Ed.*

[b] See Karl Marx and Frederick Engels, *Collected Works*, Vol. 4, pp. 139 et seq. and 191-93.— *Ed.*

Stirner, to portray the single individual as "his own product", and *Stirner* as *Bruno's product*. This step forward deserves a brief notice.

First of all, let the reader compare this caricature with the original, the explanation given of self-consciousness in *Das entdeckte Christenthum*, page 113, and then let him compare this explanation with its prototype, with Hegel's *Phänomenologie*, pages 575, 583 and so on. (Both these passages are reproduced in *Die heilige Familie*, pages 221, 223, 224. a) But now let us turn to the caricature! "Personality in general"! "Concept"! "Universal essence"! "To posit itself as limited and again to abolish the limitation"! "Inner self-distinction"! What tremendous "results"! "Personality in general" is either nonsense "in general" or the abstract concept of personality. Therefore, it is part of the "concept" of the concept of personality to "posit itself as limited". This limitation, which belongs to the "concept" of its concept, personality directly afterwards posits "by its universal essence". And after it has again abolished this limitation, it turns out that "precisely this essence" is "the *result* of its inner self-distinction". The entire grandiose result of this intricate tautology amounts, therefore, to Hegel's familiar trick of the self-distinction of man in thought, a self-distinction which the unfortunate Bruno stubbornly proclaims to be the sole activity of "personality in general". A fairly long time ago it was pointed out to Saint Bruno that there is nothing to be got from a "personality" whose activity is restricted to these, by now trivial, logical leaps. At the same time the passage quoted contains the naïve admission that the essence of Bauer's "personality" is the concept of a concept, the abstraction of an abstraction.

Bruno's criticism of Feuerbach, insofar as it is new, is restricted to hypocritically representing Stirner's reproaches against Feuerbach *and Bauer* as Bauer's reproaches against Feuerbach. Thus, for example, the assertions that the "essence of man is essence in general and something holy", that "man is the God of man", that the human species is "the Absolute", that Feuerbach splits man "into an essential and an unessential ego" (although Bruno always declares that the abstract is the essential and, in his antithesis of criticism and the mass, conceives this split as far more monstrous than Feuerbach does), that a struggle must be waged against the "predicates of

---

a See Karl Marx and Frederick Engels, *Collected Works*, Vol. 4, pp. 139-41.— *Ed.*

God", etc. On the question of selfish and selfless love, Bruno, polemising with Feuerbach, copies Stirner almost word for word for three pages (pp. 133-35) just as he very clumsily copies Stirner's phrases: "every man is his own creation", "truth is a ghost", and so on. In addition, in Bruno the "creation" is transformed into a "product". We shall return to this exploitation of Stirner by Saint Bruno.

Thus, the first thing that we discovered in Saint Bruno was his continual dependence on Hegel. We shall not, of course, dwell further on the remarks he has copied from Hegel, but shall only put together a few more passages which show how firmly he believes in the power of the philosophers and how he shares their illusion that a modified consciousness, a new turn given to the interpretation of existing relations, could overturn the whole hitherto existing world. Imbued with this faith, Saint Bruno also has one of his pupils certify — in issue IV of Wigand's quarterly, p. 327 — that his phrases on personality given above, which were proclaimed by him in issue III, were "world-shattering ideas".[a]

Saint Bruno says (*Wigand*, p. 95)[b]:

"Philosophy has never been anything but theology reduced to its most general form and given its most rational expression."

This passage, aimed *against* Feuerbach, is copied almost word for word from Feuerbach's *Philosophie der Zukunft* (p. 2):

"Speculative philosophy is true, consistent, *rational* theology."

Bruno continues:

"Philosophy, in alliance with religion, has always striven for the absolute dependence of the individual and has *actually achieved this* by demanding and causing the absorption of the individual life in universal life, of the accident in substance, of man in the absolute spirit."

As if Bruno's "philosophy", "in alliance with" Hegel's, and his still continuing forbidden association with theology, did not "demand", if not "cause", the "absorption of man" in the idea of one of his "accidents", that of self-consciousness, as "substance"! Moreover, one sees from this whole passage with what joy the church father with his "pulpit eloquence" continues to proclaim his "world-shattering" faith in the mysterious power of the holy theologians and philosophers. Of course, in the

---

[a] "Ueber das Recht des Freigesprochenen...".— *Ed.*

[b] Bruno Bauer, "Charakteristik Ludwig Feuerbachs".— *Ed.*

interests of the "good cause of freedom and his own cause".[a]
On page 105 our godfearing man has the insolence to reproach
Feuerbach:

"Feuerbach *made* of the individual, of the depersonalised man of
Christianity, not a man, not a true" (!) "real" (!!) "personal" (!!!) "man" (these
predicates owe their origin to *Die heilige Familie* and Stirner), "but an
emasculated man, a slave"—

and thereby utters, *inter alia*, the nonsense that he, Saint Bruno,
can *make* people by means of the *mind*.

Further on in the same passage he says:

"According to Feuerbach the individual has to subordinate himself to the
species, serve it. The species of which Feuerbach speaks is Hegel's Absolute,
and it, too, exists nowhere."

Here, as in all the other passages, Saint Bruno does not
deprive himself of the glory of making the actual relations of
individuals dependent on the philosophical interpretation of
these relations. He has not the slightest inkling of the
correlation which exists between the concepts of Hegel's
"absolute spirit" and Feuerbach's "species" on the one hand
and the existing world on the other.

On page 104 the holy father is mightily shocked by the heresy
with which Feuerbach transforms the holy trinity of reason,
love and will into something that "is *in* individuals and *over*
individuals", as though, in our day, every inclination, every
impulse, every need did not assert itself as a force "in the
individual and *over* the individual", whenever circumstances
hinder their satisfaction. If the holy father Bruno experiences
hunger, for example, without the means of appeasing it, then
even his stomach will become a force "*in* him and *over* him".
Feuerbach's mistake is not that he stated this fact but that in
idealistic fashion he endowed it with independence instead of
regarding it as the product of a definite and surmountable stage
of historical development.

Page 111: "Feuerbach is a slave and his servile nature does not allow him to
fulfil the work of a *man*, to recognise the essence of religion" (what a fine "work
of a man"!).... "He does not perceive the essence of religion because he does
not know the *bridge* over which he can make his way to the *source* of
religion."

Saint Bruno still seriously believes that religion has its own
"essence". As for the "bridge", "*over which*" one makes one's
way to the "*source* of religion", this asses' bridge[b] must

---

[a] An ironical allusion to Bauer's book *Die gute Sache der Freiheit und meine
eigene Angelegenheit.— Ed.*

[b] A pun in the original: *Eselsbrücke* (asses' bridge)—an expedient used by
dull or lazy people to understand a difficult problem.— *Ed.*

certainly be an *aqueduct*. At the same time Saint Bruno establishes himself as a curiously modernised Charon who has been retired owing to the building of the bridge, becoming a tollkeeper[a] who demands a halfpenny[a] from every person crossing the bridge to the spectral realm of religion.

On page 120 the saint remarks:

"How could Feuerbach exist if there were no *truth* and truth were only a *spectre*" (Stirner, help![b]) "of which hitherto man has been afraid?"

The "man" who fears the "spectre" of "truth" is no other than the worthy Bruno himself. Ten pages earlier, on p. 110, he had already let out the following world-shattering cry of terror at the sight of the "spectre" of truth:

"Truth which is never of itself encountered as a ready-made object and which develops *itself* and reaches unity only in the unfolding of personalitv."

Thus, we have here not only truth, this spectre, transformed into a person which develops itself and reaches unity, but in addition this trick is accomplished in a third personality outside it, after the manner of the tapeworm. Concerning the holy man's former love affair with truth, when he was still young and the lusts of the flesh still strong in him — see *Die heilige Familie*, p. 115 et seq.[c]

How purified of all fleshly lusts and earthly desires our holy man now appears is shown by his vehement polemic against Feuerbach's *sensuousness*. Bruno by no means attacks the highly restricted way in which Feuerbach recognises *sensuousness*. He regards Feuerbach's unsuccessful attempt, since it is an attempt to escape ideology, as — a *sin*. Of course! Sensuousness is lust of the eye, lust of the flesh and arrogance[d]—horror and abomination[e] in the eyes of the Lord! Do you not know that to be fleshly minded is death, but to be spiritually minded is life and peace; for to be fleshly minded is hostility to criticism, and everything of the flesh is of this world. And do you not know that it is written: the works of the flesh are manifest, they are adultery, fornication, uncleanness, obscenity, idolatry, witch-

---

[a] This word is in English in the manuscript.— *Ed.*

[b] A paraphrase of the expression "Samuel, hilf!" (Samuel, help!), from Carl Maria von Weber's opera *Der Freischütz* (libretto by Friedrich Kind), Act II, Scene 6.— *Ed.*

[c] See Karl Marx and Frederick Engels, *Collected Works*, Vol. 4, p. 79 et seq.— *Ed.*

[d] Cf. 1 John 2:16.— *Ed.*

[e] Cf. Ezekiel 11:18.— *Ed.*

craft, enmity, strife, envy, anger, quarrelsomeness, discord, sinful gangs, hatred, murder, drunkenness, gluttony and the like.[a] I prophesy to you, as I prophesied before, that those who do such works will not inherit the kingdom of criticism; but woe to them for in their thirst for delights they are following the path of Cain and are falling into the error of Balaam, and will perish in a rebellion, like that of Korah. These lewd ones feast shamelessly on your alms, and fatten themselves. They are clouds without water driven by the wind; bare, barren trees, twice dead and uprooted; wild ocean waves frothing their own shame; errant stars condemned to the gloom of darkness for ever.[b] For we have read that in the last days there will be terrible times, people will appear who think much of themselves, lewd vilifiers who love voluptuousness[c] more than criticism, makers of sinful gangs, in short, slaves of the flesh. Such people are shunned by Saint Bruno, who is spiritually minded and loathes the stained covering of the flesh[d] and for this reason he condemns Feuerbach, whom he regards as the Korah of the gang, to remain outside together with the dogs, the magicians, the debauched and the assassins.[e] "Sensuousness"—ugh! Not only does it throw the saintly church father into the most violent convulsions, but it even makes him sing, and on page 121 he chants the "song of the end and the end of the song". Sensuousness — do you know, unfortunate one, what sensuousness is? Sensuousness is — a "stick". (P. 130.) Seized with convulsions, Saint Bruno even wrestles on one occasion with one of his own theses, just as Jacob of blessed memory wrestled with God, with the one difference that God twisted Jacob's thigh, while our saintly epileptic twists all the limbs and ties of his own thesis, and so, by a number of striking examples, makes clear the identity of subject and object:

"Feuerbach may say what he likes ... all the same he *destroys*" (!) "*man* ... for he transforms the *word* man into a mere *phrase* ... for he *does not wholly make*" (!) "*and create*" (!) "*man, but* raises the whole of mankind to the absolute, for *in addition* he declares *not* mankind, *but rather* the senses to be the organ of the absolute, and stamps the sensuous — the object of the senses, of perception, of sensation — as the absolute, the indubitable and the immediately certain." Whereby Feuerbach — such is Saint Bruno's opinion — "can undoubtedly shake layers of the air, but he cannot *smash the phenomena of human essence,* because

---

[a] Cf. Galatians 5:19-21.— *Ed.*
[b] Cf. Jude 11-13.— *Ed.*
[c] Cf. 2 Timothy 3:1-4.— *Ed.*
[d] Cf. Jude 23.— *Ed.*
[e] Cf. Revelation 22:15.— *Ed.*

his *innermost*" (!) "essence and his vitalising spirit [...] already destroys the *external*" (!) "sound *and* makes it empty *and* jarring". (P. 121.)

Saint Bruno himself gives us mysterious but decisive disclosures about the causes of his nonsensical attitude:

"As though my ego does not also possess just this particular *sex, u n i q u e, compared with all others,* and these particular, unique sex organs." (Besides his "unique sex organs", this noble-minded man also possesses a special "unique sex"!)

This unique sex is explained on page 121 in the sense that:

"sensuousness, like a vampire, sucks all the marrow and blood from the *life* of man; it is the insurmountable barrier against which man has to deal himself a mortal *blow*".

But even the saintliest man is not pure! They are all sinners and lack the glory that they should have before "self-consciousness". Saint Bruno, who in his lonely cell at midnight struggles with "substance", had his attention drawn by the frivolous writings of the heretic Feuerbach to women and female beauty. Suddenly his sight becomes less keen; his pure self-consciousness is besmirched, and a reprehensible, sensuous fantasy plays about the frightened critic with lascivious images. The spirit is willing but the flesh is weak.[a] Bruno stumbles, he falls, he forgets that he is the power that "with its strength binds, frees and dominates the world",[b] he forgets that these products of his imagination are "spirit of his spirit", he loses all "self-control" and, intoxicated, stammers a dithyramb to female beauty, to its "tenderness, softness, womanliness", to the "full and rounded limbs" and the "surging, undulating, seething, rushing and hissing, wave-like structure of the body"[c] of woman. Innocence, however, always reveals itself — even where it sins. Who does not know that a "*surging, undulating, wave-like s t r u c t u r e* of the body" is something that no eye has ever seen, or ear heard? Therefore — hush, sweet soul, the spirit will soon prevail over the rebellious flesh and set an insurmountable "barrier" to the overflowing, seething lusts, "against which" they will soon deal themselves a "mortal blow".

"Feuerbach" — the saint finally arrives at this through a critical understanding of *Die heilige Familie* — "is a materialist tempered with and corrupted by

---

[a] Cf. Matthew 26:41.— *Ed.*

[b] Cf. ibid.. 16:19.— *Ed.*

[c] Marx and Engels have inserted the words "seething, rushing and hissing"— which occur in Schiller's poem "Der Taucher" ("The Diver")— into the passage they quote from Bruno Bauer's article "Charakteristik Ludwig Feuerbachs".— *Ed.*

humanism, i. e., a materialist who is unable to endure the earth and its being"
(Saint Bruno knows the being of the earth as distinct from the earth itself, and
knows how one should behave in order to "*endure the being* of the earth"!) "but
wants to spiritualise himself and rise into heaven; and at the same time he is a
humanist who cannot think and build a spiritual world, but one who is
impregnated with materialism", and so on. (P. 123.)

Just as for Saint Bruno humanism, according to this, consists
of "thinking" and of "building a spiritual world", so materialism
consists of the following:

"The materialist recognises only the existing, actual being, *matter*" (as
though man with all his attributes, including thought, were not an "*existing,
actual being*"), "and recognises *it* as actively extending and realising *itself* in
multiplicity, *nature*," (P. 123).

First, *matter* is an existing, actual being, but only in itself,
concealed; only when it "actively extends and realises itself in
multiplicity" (an "existing, *actual* being" "*realises* itself"!!),
only then does it become *nature*. First there exists the *concept*
of matter, an abstraction, an idea, and this latter realises itself in
actual nature. Word for word the Hegelian theory of the
pre-existence of the creative categories. From this point of view
it is understandable that Saint Bruno mistakes the philosophical
phrases of the materialists concerning matter for the actual
kernel and content of their world outlook.

2. SAINT BRUNO'S VIEWS ON THE STRUGGLE BETWEEN FEUERBACH AND STIRNER

Having thus admonished Feuerbach with a few weighty
words, Saint Bruno takes a look at the struggle between
Feuerbach and the unique. The first evidence of his interest in
this struggle is a methodical, triple smile.

"The critic pursues his path irresistibly, confident of victory, and victorious.
He is slandered — he *smiles*. He is called a heretic — he *smiles*. The old world
starts a crusade against him — he *smiles*."

Saint Bruno — this is thus established — pursues his path but
he does not pursue it like other people, he follows a critical
course, he accomplishes this important action with a *smile*.

"He does smile his face into more lines than are in the new map, with the
augmentation of the Indies. I know my lady will strike him: if she do, he'll
smile and take't for a great art" [a] — like Shakespeare's Malvolio.

---

[a] Shakespeare, *Twelfth Night*, Act III, Scene 2. Marx and Engels quote
these lines from the German translation by August Wilhelm von Schlegel. But
they have substituted the word "*Kunst*" (art) for the word "*Gunst*"
(favour).— *Ed.*

Saint Bruno himself does not lift a finger to refute his two opponents, he knows a better way of ridding himself of them, he leaves them—*divide et impera*—to their own quarrel. He confronts Stirner with Feuerbach's man (p. 124), and Feuerbach with Stirner's unique (p. 126 et seq.); he knows that they are as incensed against each other as the two Kilkenny cats in Ireland, which so completely devoured each other that finally only their tails remained.[37] And Saint Bruno passes sentence on these tails, declaring that they are "*substance*" and, consequently, condemned to eternal damnation.

In confronting Feuerbach with Stirner he repeats what Hegel said of Spinoza and Fichte, where, as we know, the punctiform ego is represented as one, and moreover the most stable, aspect of substance. However much Bruno formerly raged against egoism, which he even considered the *odor specificus* of the masses, on page 129 he accepts egoism from Stirner—only this should be "not that of Max Stirner", but, of course, that of Bruno Bauer. He brands Stirner's egoism as having the moral defect "that his ego for the support of its egoism requires hypocrisy, deception, external violence". For the rest, he believes (see p. 124) in the critical miracles of Saint Max and sees in the latter's struggle (p. 126) "a real effort to radically destroy substance". Instead of dealing with Stirner's criticism of Bauer's "pure criticism", he asserts on p. 124 that Stirner's criticism could affect him just as little as any other, "*because he himself is the critic*".

Finally Saint Bruno refutes both of them, Saint Max and Feuerbach, applying almost literally to Feuerbach and Stirner the antithesis drawn by Stirner between the critic Bruno Bauer and the dogmatist.

Wigand, p. 138: "Feuerbach puts himself in opposition to, and *thereby*" (!) "*stands in opposition to*, the unique. He is a *communist* and wants to be one. The unique is an *egoist* and has to be one; he is the *holy one*, the other the *profane one*, he is the *good one*, the other the *evil one*, he is God, the other is man. Both are *dogmatists*."

The point is, therefore, that he accuses both of dogmatism.

Der Einzige und sein Eigenthum, p. 194: "The critic is afraid of becoming dogmatic or of putting forward dogmas. Obviously, he would then become the opposite of a critic, a dogmatist; he who as a critic was *good*, would now become *evil*, or from being *unselfish*" (a communist) "would become an *egoist*, etc. Not a single dogma!—that is his dogma."

3. SAINT BRUNO VERSUS THE AUTHORS OF *DIE HEILIGE FAMILIE*

Saint Bruno, who has disposed of Feuerbach and Stirner in the manner indicated and who has "cut the unique off from all progress", now turns against the apparent "consequences of Feuerbach", the German communists and, especially, the authors of *Die heilige Familie*. The expression "real humanism", which he found in the preface to this polemic treatise,[a] provides the main basis of his hypothesis. He will recall a passage from the Bible:

"And I, brethren, could not speak unto you as unto spiritual, but as unto carnal" (in our case it was just the opposite), "even as unto babes in Christ. I have fed you with milk, and not with meat: for hitherto ye were not able to bear it." (1 Corinthians 3:1-2.)

The first impression that *Die heilige Familie* made on the worthy church father was one of profound distress and serious, respectable sorrow. The one good side of the book is that it

"showed what Feuerbach *had* to become, and the position his philosophy *can* adopt, if it *desires* to fight against criticism" (p. 138),

that, consequently, it combined in an easy-going way "desiring" with "what can be" and "what must be", but this good side does not outweigh its many distressing sides. Feuerbach's philosophy, which strangely enough is presupposed here,

"*dare not* and *cannot* understand the critic, *dare not* and *cannot* know and perceive criticism in its development, *dare not* and *cannot* know that, in relation to all that is transcendental, criticism is a constant struggle and victory, a continual destruction and creation, the *sole*"(!) "creative and productive principle. It *dare not* and *cannot* know how the critic has worked, and still works, to posit and to *make*" (!) "the transcendental forces, which up to now have suppressed mankind and not allowed it to breathe and live, into what they *really are*, the spirit of the spirit, the innermost of the innermost, a native thing" (!) "out of and in the native soil, products and creations of self-consciousness. It *dare not* and *cannot* know that the critic and only the critic has smashed religion in its entirety, and the state in its various manifestations, etc." (Pp. 138, 139.)

Is this not an exact copy of the ancient Jehovah, who runs after his errant people who found greater delight in the cheerful pagan gods, and cries out:

"Hear me, Israel, and close not your ear, Judah! Am I not the Lord your God, who led you out of the land of Egypt into the land flowing with milk and honey, and behold, from your earliest youth you have done evil in my sight and angered me with the work of my hands and turned your back unto me and not

---

[a] See Karl Marx and Frederick Engels, *Collected Works*, Vol. 4, p. 7.— *Ed.*

your face towards me, though I invariably tutored you; and you have brought abominations into my house to defile it, and built the high places of Baal in the valley of the son of Himmon, which I did not command, and it never entered my head that you should do such abominations; and I have sent to you my servant Jeremiah, to whom I did address my word, beginning with the thirteenth year of the reign of King Josiah, son of Amon, unto this day — and for twenty-three years now he has been zealously preaching to you, but ye have not harkened. Therefore says the Lord God: Who has ever heard the like of the virgin of Israel doing such an abomination. For rain water does not disappear so quickly as my people forgets me. O earth, earth, earth, hear the word of the Lord!"[a]

Thus, in a lengthy speech on "to dare" and "to be able", Saint Bruno asserts that his communist opponents have misunderstood him. The way in which he describes criticism in this recent speech, the way in which he transforms the former forces that suppressed "the life of mankind" into "transcendental forces", and these transcendental forces into the "spirit of the spirit", and the way in which he presents "criticism" as the sole branch of production, proves that the apparent misconception is nothing but a disagreeable conception. We proved that Bauer's criticism is beneath all criticism, owing to which we have inevitably become dogmatists. He even in all seriousness reproaches us for our insolent disbelief in his ancient phrases. The whole mythology of independent concepts, with Zeus the Thunderer — self-consciousness — at the head, is paraded here once again to the "jingling of hackneyed phrases of a whole janissary band of current categories" (*Literatur-Zeitung*, cf. *Die heilige Familie*, p. 234[b]). First of all, of course, the myth of the creation of the world, i. e., of the hard "*labour*" of the critic, which is "the sole creative and productive principle, a constant struggle and victory, a continual destruction and creation", "working" and "having worked". Indeed, the reverend father even reproaches *Die heilige Familie* for understanding "criticism" in the same way as he understands it himself in the present rejoinder. After taking back "substance" "into the land of its birth, self-consciousness, the criticising and" (since *Die heilige Familie* also) "the criticised man, and *discarding* it" (self-consciousness here seems to take the place of an ideological lumber-room), he continues:

"It" (the alleged philosophy of Feuerbach) "dare not know that criticism *and* the critics, as long as they have existed" (!), "have guided and made history, that

---

[a] Cf. Jeremiah 2:6, 32:22, 30, 33-35, 25:3, 19:3, 18:13, 14, 22:29.— *Ed.*
[b] The passage from "Correspondenz aus der Provinz" published in the *Allgemeine Literatur-Zeitung* was quoted in *The Holy Family* (see Karl Marx and Frederick Engels, *Collected Works*, Vol. 4, p. 148).— *Ed.*

even their opponents and all the movements and agitations of the present time are their creation, that it is they alone who hold *power in their hands, because strength is in their consciousness*, and because they derive power *from themselves*, from their deeds, *from criticism*, from their opponents, from their creations; that only by the act of criticism is man freed, and thereby men also, and man is *created*" (!) "and thereby mankind as well."

Thus, criticism *and* the critics are first of all two wholly different subjects, existing and operating apart from each other. The critic is a subject different from criticism, and criticism is a subject different from the critic. This personified criticism, criticism as a subject, is precisely that "critical criticism" against which *Die heilige Familie* was directed. "Criticism and the critics, as long as they have existed, have guided and made history." It is clear that they could not do so "as long as they" did not "exist", and it is equally clear that "as long as they have existed" they "made history" in their own fashion. Finally, Saint Bruno goes so far as to "dare and be able" to give us one of the most profound explanations about the state-shattering power of criticism, namely, that "criticism and the critics hold *power in their hands*, because" (a fine "because"!) "*strength is in their consciousness*", and, secondly, that these great manufacturers of history "hold power in their hands", because they "derive power from themselves and from criticism" (i. e., again from themselves)—whereby it is still, unfortunately, not proven that it is possible to "derive" anything at all from there, from "themselves", from "criticism". On the basis of criticism's own words, one should at least believe that it must be difficult to "derive" from there anything more than the category of "substance" "discarded" there. Finally, criticism also "derives" "from criticism" "power" for a highly monstrous oracular dictum. For it reveals to us a secret that was hidden[a] from our fathers and unknown to our grandfathers, the secret that "only by the act of criticism is man created, and thereby mankind as well" — whereas, up to now, criticism was erroneously regarded as an act of people who existed prior to it owing to quite different acts. Hence it seems that Saint Bruno himself came "into the world, from the world, and to the world" through "criticism", i. e., by *generatio aequivoca*.[b] All this is, perhaps, merely another interpretation of the following passage from the Book of Genesis: And Adam *knew*, i. e., criticised, Eve his wife; and she conceived,[c] etc.

---

[a] Cf. Colossians 1:26.— *Ed*.
[b] Spontaneous generation.— *Ed*.
[c] Cf. Genesis 4:1.— *Ed*.

Thus we see here the whole familiar critical criticism, which was already sufficiently characterised in *Die heilige Familie,* confronting us again with all its trickery as though nothing had happened. There is no need to be surprised at this, for the saint himself complains, on page 140, that *Die heilige Familie* "cuts criticism off from all progress". With the greatest indignation Saint Bruno reproaches the authors of *Die heilige Familie* because, by means of a chemical process, they evaporated Bauer's criticism from its "*fluid*" state into a "*crystalline*" state.

It follows that "institutions of mendicancy", the "baptismal certificate of adulthood", the "regions of pathos and thunder-like aspects", the "Mussulman conceptual affliction" (*Die heilige Familie,* pp. 2, 3, 4[a] according to the critical *Literatur-Zeitung*) — all this is nonsense only if it is understood in the "crystalline" manner. And the twenty-eight historical howlers of which criticism was proved guilty in its excursion on "Englische Tagesfragen"[b] — are they not errors when looked at from the "fluid" point of view? Does criticism insist that, from the fluid point of view, it prophesied a priori the Nauwerck conflict[38] — long after this had taken place before its eyes — and did not construct it *post festum*?[c] Does it still insist that the word *maréchal* could mean "*farrier*" from the "crystalline" point of view, but from the "fluid" point of view at any rate must mean "*marshal*"? Or that although in the "crystalline" conception "*un fait physique*" may mean "a physical fact", the true "fluid" translation should be "a fact of physics"? Or that "*la malveillance de nos bourgeois juste-milieux*"[d] in the "fluid" state still means "the carefreeness of our good burghers"? Does it insist that, from the "fluid" point of view, "a child that does not, in its turn, become a father or mother is *essentially a daughter*"? That someone can have the task "of representing, as it were, the last tear of grief shed by the past"? That the various concierges, lions, grisettes, marquises, scoundrels and wooden doors in Paris in their "fluid" form are nothing but phases of the mystery

---

[a] The expressions quoted are from Carl Reichardt's reviews, published in the *Allgemeine Literatur-Zeitung,* of the following books: Karl Heinrich Brüggemann, *Preussens Beruf in der deutschen Staats-Entwicklung...,* and Daniel Benda, *Katechismus für wahlberechtigte Bürger in Preussen.* They are also quoted in *The Holy Family* (see Karl Marx and Frederick Engels, *Collected Works,* Vol. 4, p. 10).— *Ed.*

[b] An article by Julius Faucher.— *Ed.*

[c] An allusion to the article by [E.] J[ungnitz] "Herr Nauwerck und die philosophische Facultät" published in *Allgemeine Literatur-Zeitung.— Ed.*

[d] The ill will of our middle-of-the-road bourgeois.— *Ed.*

"in whose concept in general it belongs to posit itself as limited and again to abolish this limitation which is posited by its universal essence, for precisely this essence is only the result of its inner self-distinction, its activity"[a]? That critical criticism in the "fluid" sense "pursues its path irresistibly, victorious and confident of victory", when in dealing with a question it first asserts that it has revealed its "true and general significance" and then admits that it "had neither the will nor the right to go beyond criticism", and finally admits that "it had still to take one step but that step was impossible because — it was impossible" (*Die heilige Familie*, 184[b])? That from the "fluid" point of view "the future is still the work" of criticism, although "fate may *decide* as it will"[c]? That from the fluid point of view criticism achieved nothing superhuman when it "came into *contradiction* with its *true elements* — a *contradiction* which had *already* found its *solution* in *these same elements*" [d]?

The authors of *Die heilige Familie* have indeed committed the frivolity of conceiving these and hundreds of other statements as statements expressing firm, "crystalline" *nonsense* — but the synoptic gospels should be read in a "fluid" way, i. e., according to the sense of their authors, and on no account in a "crystalline" way, i. e., according to their actual nonsense, in order to arrive at true faith and to admire the harmony of the critical household.

"Engels and Marx, therefore, know only the criticism of the *Literatur-Zeitung*"[e]

— a deliberate lie, proving how "fluidly" our saint has read a book in which his latest works are depicted merely as the culmination of all the "work he has done". But the church father lacked the calm to read in a crystalline way, for he fears his opponents as rivals who contest his canonisation and "want to deprive him of his sanctity, in order to make *themselves* sanctified".

Let us, incidentally, note the fact that, according to Saint Bruno's present statement, his *Literatur-Zeitung* by no means aimed at founding "social society" or at "representing, as it were, the last tear of grief" shed by German ideology, nor did it

---

[a] Bruno Bauer, "Charakteristik Ludwig Feuerbachs".— *Ed.*

[b] See Karl Marx and Frederick Engels, *Collected Works*, Vol. 4, p. 118.— *Ed.*

[c] Bruno Bauer, "Neueste Schriften über die Judenfrage".— *Ed.*

[d] Bruno Bauer, "Was ist jetzt der Gegenstand der Kritik?"— *Ed.*

[e] Bruno Bauer, "Charakteristik Ludwig Feuerbachs".— *Ed.*

aim at putting mind in the sharpest opposition to the mass and developing critical criticism in all its purity, but only—at "depicting the liberalism and radicalism of 1842 and their echoes in their half-heartedness and phrase-mongering", hence at combating the "echoes" of what has long disappeared. *Tant de bruit pour une omelette!*[a] Incidentally, it is just here that the conception of history peculiar to German theory is again shown in its "purest" light. The year 1842 is held to be the period of the greatest brilliance of German liberalism, because at that time philosophy took part in politics. Liberalism vanishes for the critic with the cessation of the *Deutsche Jahrbücher* and the *Rheinische Zeitung*, the organs of liberal and radical theory. After that, apparently, there remain only the "echoes"—whereas in actual fact only now, when the German bourgeoisie feels a real need for political power, a need produced by economic relations, and is striving to satisfy it, has liberalism in Germany an actual existence and thereby the chance of some success.

Saint Bruno's profound distress over *Die heilige Familie* did not allow him to criticise this work "out of himself, through himself and with himself". To be able to master his pain he had first to obtain the work in a "fluid" form. He found this fluid form in a confused review, teeming with misunderstandings, in the *Westphälische Dampfboot*, May issue, pp. 206-14. All his quotations are taken from passages quoted in the *Westphälische Dampfboot* and he quotes nothing that is not quoted there.

The language of the saintly critic is likewise determined by the language of the Westphalian critic. In the first place, all the statements from the Foreword which are quoted by the Westphalian (*Dampfboot*, p. 206) are transferred to the *Wigand'sche Vierteljahrsschrift*. (Pp. 140, 141.) This transference forms the chief part of Bauer's criticism, according to the old principle already recommended by Hegel:

"To trust common sense and, moreover, in order to keep up with the times and advance with philosophy, to read *reviews* of philosophical works, perhaps even their *prefaces* and introductory paragraphs; for the latter give the general principles on which everything turns, while the former give, along with the historical information, also an appraisal which, because it is an appraisal, even goes beyond that which is appraised. This beaten track can be followed in one's dressing-gown; but the elevated feeling of the eternal, the sacred, the infinite,

---

[a] Much ado about an omelette! An exclamation which Jacques Vallée, Sieur des Barreaux, is supposed to have made when a thunderstorm occurred while he was eating an omelette on a fast-day.— *Ed.*

pursues its path in the vestments of a high priest, a path" which, as we have seen, Saint Bruno also knows how to "pursue" while "striking down". (Hegel, *Phänomenologie*, p. 54.)

The *Westphalian* critic, after giving a few quotations from the preface, continues:

"Thus the Foreword itself leads to the *battlefield* of the book", etc. (P. 206.)

The *saintly* critic, having transferred these quotations into the *Wigand'sche Vierteljahrsschrift*, makes a more subtle distinction and says:

"Such is the *terrain* and the *enemy* which Engels and Marx have created for *battle*."

From the discussion of the critical proposition: "the worker creates nothing", the *Westphalian* critic gives only the summarising *conclusion*.

The *saintly* critic actually believes that this is all that was said about the proposition, copies out the Westphalian quotation on page 141 and rejoices at the discovery that only "assertions" have been put forward in opposition to criticism.

Of the examination of the critical outpourings about love, the *Westphalian* critic on page 209 first writes out the *corpus delicti* in part and then a few disconnected sentences from the refutation, which he desires to use as an authority for his nebulous, sickly-sweet sentimentality.

On pages 141-42 the *saintly* critic copies him out word for word, sentence by sentence, in the same order as his predecessor quotes.

The *Westphalian* critic exclaims over the corpse of Herr Julius Faucher: "Such is the fate of the beautiful on earth!"[a]

The *saintly* critic cannot finish his "hard work" without appropriating this exclamation to use irrelevantly on page 142.

The *Westphalian* critic on page 212 gives a would-be summary of the arguments which are aimed against Saint Bruno himself in *Die heilige Familie*.

The *saintly* critic cheerfully and literally copies out all this stuff together with all the Westphalian exclamations. He has not the slightest idea that *nowhere* in the whole of this polemic discourse does anyone reproach him for "transforming the problem of political emancipation into that of human emancipation", for "wanting to kill the Jews", for "transforming the Jews into theologians", for "transforming Hegel into Herr Hinrichs", etc. Credulously, the *saintly* critic repeats the *Westphalian*

---

[a] Schiller, *Wallenstein's Tod*, Act IV, Scene 12.— *Ed.*

critic's allegation that in *Die heilige Familie, Marx* volunteers to provide some sort of scholastic little treatise "in reply to Bauer's *silly self-apotheosis*". Yet the words "silly self-apotheosis", which Saint Bruno gives as a *quotation,* are nowhere to be found in the whole of *Die heilige Familie,* but they do occur with the Westphalian critic. Nor is the little treatise offered as a reply to the "*self-apology*" of criticism on pages 150-63 of *Die heilige Familie,* but only in the following section on page 165,[a] in connection with the world-historic question: "Why did Herr Bauer *have to* engage in politics?"

Finally on page 143 Saint Bruno presents *Marx* as an "*amusing comedian*", here again following his Westphalian model, who resolved the "world-historic drama of critical criticism", on page 213, into a "*most amusing comedy*".

Thus one sees how the opponents of critical criticism "dare and can" "know *how the critic has worked and still works*"!

4. OBITUARY FOR "M. HESS"

"What Engels and Marx could *not yet* do, M. Hess has accomplished."

Such is the great, divine transition which — owing to the relative "can" and "cannot" be done of the evangelists — has taken so firm a hold of the holy man's fingers that it has to find a place, relevantly or irrelevantly, in every article of the church father.

"What Engels and Marx could not yet do, M. Hess has accomplished." But what is this "what" that "Engels and Marx could not yet do"? Nothing more nor less, indeed, than — to criticise Stirner. And why was it that Engels and Marx "could *not yet*" criticise Stirner? For the sufficient reason that — Stirner's book *had not yet appeared* when they wrote *Die heilige Familie.*

This speculative trick — of joining together everything and bringing the most diverse things into an apparent causal relation — has truly taken possession not only of the head of our saint but also of his fingers. With him it has become devoid of any contents and degenerates into a burlesque manner of uttering tautologies with an important mien. For example, already in the *Allgemeine Literatur-Zeitung* (1, 5) we read:

---

[a] See Karl Marx and Frederick Engels, *Collected Works,* Vol. 4, pp. 99-106 and 107.— *Ed.*

"The difference between my work and the pages which, for example, a Philippson covers with writing" (that is, the *empty* pages on which, "for example, a Philippson" writes) *"must, therefore, be so constituted as in fact it is"*!!! [a]

"M. Hess", for whose writings Engels and Marx take absolutely no responsibility, seems such a strange phenomenon to the saintly critic that he is only capable of copying long excerpts from *Die letzten Philosophen* and passing the judgment that "on some points this criticism has not understood Feuerbach *or also*" (oh, theology!) "the vessel wishes to rebel against the potter". Cf. Epistle to the Romans, 9: 20-21. Having once more performed the "hard work" of quoting, our saintly critic finally arrives at the conclusion that Hess copies from *Hegel*, since he uses the two words "united" and "development". Saint Bruno, of course, had in a round-about way to try to turn against Feuerbach the proof given in *Die heilige Familie* of his own complete dependence on Hegel.

"See, that is how Bauer had to end! He fought as best he could against all the Hegelian categories", with the exception of self-consciousness — particularly in the glorious struggle of the *Literatur-Zeitung* against Herr Hinrichs. How he fought and conquered them we have already seen. For good measure, let us quote *Wigand*, page 110, where he asserts that

the "true" (1) *"solution"* (2) *"of contradictions"* (3) "in nature and history" (4), the *"true unity"* (5) "of separate relations" (6), the "genuine" (7) "basis" (8) "and abyss" (9) "of religion, the truly *infinite*" (10), "irresistible, self-creative" (11) "personality" (12) "has not yet been found".

These three lines contain not two doubtful Hegelian categories, as in the case of Hess, but a round dozen of "true, infinite, irresistible" Hegelian categories which reveal themselves as such by "the true unity of separate relations" — "see, that is how Bauer had to end!" And if the holy man thinks that in Hess he has discovered a Christian believer, not because Hess "hopes" — as Bruno says — but because he does *not* hope and because he talks of the "resurrection", then our great church father enables us, on the basis of this same page 110, to demonstrate his very pronounced *Judaism*. He declares there

"that the *true, living man in the flesh has not yet been born*"!!! (a new elucidation about the determination of the "unique sex") "and the mongrel produced" (*Bruno Bauer*?!?) "is not yet able to master all *dogmatic formulas*", etc.

---

[a] Bruno Bauer, "Neueste Schriften über die Judenfrage".— *Ed.*

That is to say, the *Messiah* is not yet born, the *son of man* has first to come into the world and this world, being the world of the Old Testament, is still under the rod of the *law*, of "dogmatic formulas".

Just as Saint Bruno, as shown above, made use of "Engels and Marx" for a transition to Hess, so now the latter serves him to bring Feuerbach finally into causal connection with his excursions on Stirner, *Die heilige Familie* and *Die letzten Philosophen*.

> "See, that is how Feuerbach had to end!" "Philosophy had to end *piously*", etc. (*Wigand,* p. 145.)

The true causal connection, however, is that this exclamation is an imitation of a passage from Hess' *Die letzten Philosophen* aimed against Bauer, among others (Preface, p. 4):

> "Thus [...] and in no other way had the last offspring of the Christian ascetics [...] to take farewell of the world."

Saint Bruno ends his speech for the prosecution against Feuerbach and his alleged accomplices with the reproach to Feuerbach that all he can do is to "trumpet", to "blow blasts on a trumpet", whereas Monsieur B. Bauer or Madame la critique, the "mongrel produced", to say nothing of the continual "destruction", *"drives forth in his triumphal chariot and gathers new triumphs"* (p. 125), "hurls down from the throne" (p. 119), "slays" (p. 111), "strikes down like thunder" (p. 115), "destroys once and for all" (p. 120), "shatters" (p. 121), allows nature merely to "vegetate" (p. 120), builds "stricter" (!) "prisons" (p. 104) and, finally, with "crushing" pulpit eloquence expatiates, on p. 105, in a brisk, pious, cheerful and free[a] fashion on the "stably-strongly-firmly-existing", hurling "rock-like matter and rocks" at Feuerbach's head (p. 110) and, in conclusion, by a side thrust vanquishes Saint Max as well, by adding "the most abstract abstractness" and "the hardest hardness" (on p. 124) to "critical criticism", "social society" and "rock-like matter and rocks".

All this Saint Bruno accomplished "through himself, in himself and with himself", because he is "He himself"; indeed, he is "himself always the greatest and can always be the

---

[a] "Brisk, pious, cheerful and free" (*frisch, fromm, fröhlich und frei*)—the initial words of a students' saying, which were turned by Ludwig Jahn into the motto of the sport movement he initiated.— *Ed.*

greatest" (*is* and *can* be!) "through himself, in himself and with himself". (P. 136.) That's that.

Saint Bruno would undoubtedly be dangerous to the female sex, for he is an "irresistible personality", if "in the same measure on the other hand" he did not fear "sensuousness as the barrier against which man has to deal himself a mortal *blow*". Therefore, "through himself, in himself and with himself" he will hardly pluck any flowers but rather allow them to wither in infinite longing and hysterical yearning for the "irresistible personality", who "possesses this unique sex and these unique, particular sex organs".*

---

* [The following passage is crossed out in the manuscript:]
5. Saint Bruno in His "Triumphal Chariot"
Before leaving our church father "victorious confident of victory", let us for a moment mingle with the gaping crowd that comes up running just as eagerly when he "drives forth in his triumphal chariot and gathers new triumphs" as when General Tom Thumb with his four ponies provides a diversion. It is not surprising that we hear the humming of street-songs, for to be welcomed with street-songs "belongs after all to the concept" of triumph "in general".

III

SAINT MAX[39]

"Was jehen mir die jrinen Beeme an?"[a]

Saint Max exploits, "employs" or "uses" the Council to deliver a long apologetic commentary on "*the book*", which is none other than "*the* book", the book as such, the book pure and simple, i.e., the perfect book, the Holy Book, the book as something holy, the book as the holy of holies, the book in heaven, viz., *Der Einzige und sein Eigenthum*. "The book", as we know, *fell* from the heavens towards the end of 1844 and took on the shape of a servant with O. Wigand in Leipzig.[40] It was, therefore, at the mercy of the vicissitudes of terrestrial life and was attacked by three "unique ones", viz., the mysterious personality of *Szeliga,* the gnostic *Feuerbach* and *Hess.*[b] However much at every moment Saint Max as creator towers over himself as a creation, as he does over his other creations, he nevertheless took pity on his weakly offspring and, in order to defend it and ensure its safety, let out a loud "critical hurrah". In order to fathom in all their significance both this "critical hurrah" and *Szeliga's* mysterious personality, we must here, to some extent, deal with church history and look more closely at "the book". Or, to use the language of Saint Max: we "shall episodically put" "into this passage" a church-historical "meditation" on *Der Einzige und sein Eigenthum* "simply because" "it seems to us that it could contribute to the elucidation of the rest".

---

[a] "What are the green trees to me?" — a paraphrase (in the Berlin dialect) of a sentence from Heine's work *Reisebilder,* Dritter Teil, "Die Bäder von Lucca", Kapitel IV.— *Ed.*

[b] Szeliga, "*Der Einzige und sein Eigenthum*"; Feuerbach, "Ueber das *Wesen des Christenthums* in Beziehung auf den *Einzigen und sein Eigenthum*"; Hess, *Die letzten Philosophen.— Ed.*

"Lift up your heads, O ye gates; and be ye lift up, ye everlasting doors; and the King of Glory shall come in.

"Who is this King of Glory? The War-Lord strong and mighty, the War-Lord mighty in battle.

"Lift up your heads, O ye gates; even lift them up, ye everlasting doors; and the King of Glory shall come in.

"Who is this King of Glory? The Lord Unique,[a] he is the King of Glory." (Psalms, 24:7-10.)

---

[a] In the Bible "The Lord of Hosts".— *Ed.*

1. THE UNIQUE AND HIS PROPERTY

The man who "has based his cause on nothing"[a] begins his lengthy "critical hurrah" like a good German, straightway with a jeremiad: "Is there anything that is not to be my cause?" (p. 5 of the "book"). And he continues lamenting heart-rendingly that "everything is to be his cause", that "God's cause, the cause of mankind, of truth and freedom, and in addition the cause of his people, of his lord", and thousands of other good causes, are imposed on him. Poor fellow! The French and English bourgeois complain about lack of markets, trade crises, panic on the stock exchange, the political situation prevailing at the moment, etc.; the German petty bourgeois, whose active participation in the bourgeois movement has been merely an ideal one, and who for the rest exposed only himself to risk, sees his own cause simply as the "good cause", the "cause of freedom, truth, mankind", etc.

Our German school-teacher simply believes this illusion of the German petty bourgeois and on three pages he provisionally discusses all these good causes.

He investigates "God's cause", "the cause of mankind" (pp. 6 and 7) and finds these are "purely egoistical causes", that both "God" and "mankind" worry only about what is *theirs*, that "truth, freedom, humanity, justice" are "only interested in themselves and not in us, only in their own well-being and not in ours" — from which he concludes that all these persons "are

---

[a] Here and below Marx and Engels paraphrase the first lines of Goethe's poem "Vanitas! Vanitatum vanitas!": "Ich hab' mein' Sach' auf Nichts gestellt." ("I have based my cause on nothing.") "Ich hab' mein' Sach' auf Nichts gestellt" is the heading of Stirner's preface to his book.— *Ed.*

thereby exceptionally well-off". He goes so far as to transform these idealistic phrases — God, truth, etc. — into prosperous burghers who "are exceptionally well-off" and enjoy a "*profitable* egoism". But this vexes the holy egoist: "And I?" he exclaims.

"I, for my part, draw the lesson from this and, instead of continuing to serve these great egoists, I should rather be an egoist myself!" (P. 7.)

Thus we see what holy motives guide Saint Max in his transition to egoism. It is not the good things of this world, not treasures which moth and rust corrupt, not the capital belonging to his fellow unique ones, but heavenly treasure, the capital which belongs to God, truth, freedom, mankind, etc., that gives him no peace.

If it had not been expected of him that he should serve numerous good causes, he would never have made the discovery that he also has his "own" cause, and therefore he would never have based this cause of his "on nothing" (i.e., "the book").

If Saint Max had looked a little more closely at these various "causes" and the "owners" of these causes, e.g., God, mankind, truth, he would have arrived at the opposite conclusion: that egoism based on the egoistic mode of action of these persons must be just as imaginary as these persons themselves.

Instead of this, our saint decides to enter into competition with "God" and "truth" and to base his cause on himself —

"on myself, on the I that is, just as much as God, the nothing of everything else, the I that is everything for me, the I that is the unique.... I am nothing in the sense of void, *but* the creative nothing, the nothing from which I myself, as creator, create everything."

The holy church father could also have expressed this last proposition as follows: I am everything in the void of nonsense, "*but*" I am the nugatory creator, the all, from which I myself, as creator, create nothing.

Which of these two readings is the correct one will become evident later. So much for the preface.

"The book" itself is divided like the book "of old", into the Old and New Testament — namely, into the unique history of man (The Law and the Prophets) and the inhuman history of the unique (The Gospel of the Kingdom of God). The former is history in the framework of logic, the logos confined in the past; the latter is logic in history, the emancipated logos, which struggles against the present and triumphantly overcomes it.

THE OLD TESTAMENT: MAN[41]

1. THE BOOK OF GENESIS, I.E., A MAN'S LIFE

Saint Max pretends here that he is writing the *biography* of his mortal enemy, "*man*", and not of a "*unique*" or "real individual". This ties him up in delightful contradictions.

As becomes every normal genesis "a man's life" begins *ab ovo*, with the "child". As revealed to us on page 13, the child

"from the outset lives a life of struggle against the entire world, it resists everything and everything resists it". "Both remain enemies" but "with awe and respect" and "are constantly on the watch, *looking for* each other's *weaknesses*".

This is further amplified, on page 14:

"we", as children, "try to find out the *basis of things* or what lies behind them; *therefore*" (so no longer out of enmity) "we *are trying to discover* everybody's *weaknesses*". (Here the finger of *Szeliga*, the mystery-monger, is evident.[a])

Thus, the *child* immediately becomes a *metaphysician*, trying to find out the "*basis* of things".

This *speculating* child, for whom "the nature of things" lies closer to his heart than his toys, "sometimes", in the long run, succeeds in coping with the "world of things", conquers it and then enters a new phase, the *age of youth*, when he has to face a new "arduous struggle of life", the struggle against reason, for the "*spirit means the first self-discovery*" and: "We are above the world, we are spirit". (P. 15.) The point of view of the *youth* is a "heavenly one"; the child merely "*learned*", "he did not dwell on purely logical or theological problems" — *just as* (the child) "Pilate" hurriedly passed over the question: "What is truth?"[b] (P. 17.) The youth "tries to master thoughts", he "understands ideas, the *spirit*" and "seeks ideas"; he "is engrossed in thought" (p. 16), he has "absolute thoughts, i.e., *nothing but thoughts*, logical thoughts". The youth who thus "deports himself", instead of chasing after young women and other earthly things, is no other than the young "Stirner", the studious Berlin youth, busy with Hegel's logic and gazing with amazement at the great Michelet. Of *this* youth it is rightly said on page 17:

"to bring to light *pure thought*, to devote oneself to it — in this is the *joy of youth*, and all the bright images of the world of thought — truth, freedom, mankind, *Man*, etc. — illumine and inspire the youthful soul".

[a] An allusion to Szeliga's article "Eugen Sue: Die Geheimnisse von Paris. Kritik". See Karl Marx and Frederick Engels, *Collected Works*, Vol. 4, p. 54.— *Ed.*

[b] John 18:38.— *Ed.*

This youth then "throws aside" the "object" as well and "occupies himself" exclusively "with his thoughts";

"he includes all that is not spiritual under the contemptuous name of *external things*, and if, all the same, he does cling to such external things as, for example, students' customs, etc., it happens only when and because he *discovers* spirit in them, i.e., when they become *symbols* for him". (Who will not "*discover*" "Szeliga" here?)

Virtuous Berlin youth! The beer-drinking ritual of the students' association was for him only a "symbol" and only for the sake of the "symbol" was he after a drinking bout many a time found under the table, where he probably also wished to "discover spirit"! — How virtuous is this good youth, whom old *Ewald,* who wrote two volumes on the "virtuous youth",[a] could have taken as a model, is seen also from the fact that it was "made known" to him (p. 15): "Father and mother should be abandoned, all natural authority should be considered broken." For him, "the rational man, the family as a natural authority does not exist; there follows a renunciation of parents, brothers and sisters, etc." — But they are all "re-born as *spiritual, rational* authority", thanks to which the good youth reconciles obedience and fear of one's parents with his speculating conscience, and everything remains as before. Likewise "it is said" (p. 15): "We ought to obey God rather than men."[b] Indeed, the good youth reaches the highest peak of morality on page 16, where "it is said": "One should obey one's conscience rather than God." This moral exultation raises him even above the "revengeful Eumenides" and even above the "anger of Poseidon" — he is afraid of nothing so much as his "conscience".

Having discovered that "the spirit is the essential" he no longer even fears the following perilous conclusions:

"If, *however*, the spirit is recognised as the essential, *nevertheless* it makes a difference *whether* the spirit is poor or rich, and *therefore*" (!) "*one* strives to become rich in spirit; the *spirit* wishes to expand, to establish its realm, a realm not of this world, which has just been overcome. *In this way,* the spirit strives to become all in all"[c] (*what way* is this?), "i.e., *although* I am spirit, *nevertheless* I am not perfect spirit *and must*" (?) "first seek the perfect spirit." (P. 17.)

"Nevertheless *it* makes a difference".—"*It*", what is this? What is the "It" that makes the difference? We shall very often

[a] Johann Ludwig Ewald, *Der gute Jüngling, gute Gatte und Vater, oder Mittel, um es zu werden.— Ed.*

[b] The Acts of the Apostles 5:29.— *Ed.*

[c] 1 Corinthians 15:28.— *Ed.*

come across this mysterious "It" in our holy man, and it will then turn out that it is the unique from the standpoint of *substance*, the beginning of "unique" logic, and as such the true identity of Hegel's "being" and "nothing". Hence, for everything that this "It" does, says or performs, we shall lay the responsibility on our saint, whose relation to it is that of its creator. First of all, this "It", as we have seen, makes a difference between poor and rich. And why? Because "the spirit is recognised as the essential". Poor "It", which without this recognition would never have arrived at the difference between poor and rich! "And therefore *one* strives", etc. "*One*"! We have here the second impersonal person which, together with the "It", is in Stirner's service and must perform the heaviest menial work for him. How these two are accustomed to support each other is clearly seen here. Since "It" makes a difference whether the spirit is poor or rich, "one" (could anyone but Stirner's faithful servant[a] have had this idea!) — "*one, therefore, strives to become rich in spirit*". "It" gives the signal and immediately "one" joins in at the top of its voice. The division of labour is classically carried out.

Since "one strives to become *rich in spirit, the spirit* wishes to expand, to establish *its realm*", etc. "If however" a connection is present here "it still makes a difference" whether "one" wants to become "*rich in spirit*" or whether "*the spirit* wants to establish its realm". Up to now "*the spirit*" has *not* wanted *anything*, "*the spirit*" has not yet figured as a *person* — it was only a matter of the spirit of the "youth", and not of "*the spirit*" as such, of the spirit as *subject*. But our holy writer now needs a spirit different from that of the youth, in order to place it in opposition to the latter as a foreign, and in the last resort, as a holy spirit. *Conjuring trick* No. 1.

"In this way the spirit strives to become all in all", a somewhat obscure statement, which is then explained as follows:

"Although I am spirit, nevertheless I am not perfect spirit *and must first seek the perfect spirit*."

But if Saint Max is the "imperfect spirit", "nevertheless it makes a difference" whether he has to "*perfect*" *his* spirit or seek "*the perfect* spirit". A few lines earlier he was in fact dealing only with the "*poor*" and "*rich*" spirit — a quantitative,

---

[a] An ironical allusion to Franz Szeliga. See this volume, p. 161.— *Ed.*

profane distinction—and now there suddenly appears the "*imperfect*" and "*perfect*" spirit—a qualitative, mysterious distinction. The striving towards the development of one's own spirit can now be transformed into the hunt of the "imperfect spirit" for "*the* perfect spirit". The holy spirit wanders about like a ghost. *Conjuring trick* No. 2.

The holy author continues:

"But thereby" (i.e., by the transformation of the striving towards "perfection" of *my* spirit into search for "*the* perfect spirit") "I, who have only just found myself as spirit, at once lose myself again, in that I bow down before the perfect spirit, as a spirit which is not my own, but a spirit of the *beyond*, and I feel my emptiness." (P. 18.)

This is nothing but a further development of conjuring trick No. 2. After the "perfect spirit" has been *assumed* as an *existing being* and opposed to the "imperfect spirit", it becomes obvious that the "imperfect spirit", the youth, painfully feels his "emptiness" to the depths of his soul. Let us go on!

"True, it is all a matter of spirit, *but* is every spirit the right spirit? The right and true spirit is the ideal of the spirit, the 'holy spirit'. It is not my or your spirit but *precisely*" (!)—"an ideal spirit, a spirit of the beyond—'God'. 'God is spirit[a] ' ". (P. 18.)

Here the "perfect spirit" has been suddenly transformed into the "right" spirit, and immediately afterwards into the "right and true spirit". The latter is more closely defined as the "ideal of the spirit, the holy spirit" and this is proved by the fact that it is "not my or your spirit but *precisely* a spirit of the beyond, an ideal spirit —God". The true spirit is the *ideal* of the spirit, "precisely" because it is *ideal!* It is the holy spirit "precisely" because it is —God! What "virtuosity of thought"! We note also in passing that up to now nothing was said about "your" spirit. Conjuring trick No. 3.

Thus, if I seek to train myself as a mathematician, or, as Saint Max puts it, to "perfect" myself as a mathematician, then I am seeking the "perfect" mathematician, i.e., the "right and true" mathematician, the "ideal" of the mathematician, the "holy" mathematician, who is distinct from me and you (although in my eyes you may be a perfect mathematician, just as for the Berlin youth his professor of philosophy is the perfect spirit); but a mathematician who is "precisely ideal, of the beyond", the mathematician in the heavens, "God". God is a mathematician.

---

[a] John 4:24.— *Ed.*

Saint Max arrives at all these great results because "it makes a difference whether the spirit is rich or poor", i.e., in plain language, it makes a difference whether anyone is rich or poor in spirit, and because his "youth" has discovered this remarkable fact.

On page 18 Saint Max continues:

"*It* divides the *man* from the youth that the former takes the world as it is", etc.

Consequently, we do not learn how the youth arrives at the point where he suddenly takes the world "as it is", nor do we see our holy dialectician making the transition from youth to man, we merely learn that "*It*" has to perform this service and "*divide*" the youth from the man. But even this "It" by itself does not suffice to bring the cumbersome waggonload of unique thoughts into motion. For after "*It*" has "divided the man from the youth", the man all the same relapses again into the youth, begins to occupy himself afresh "exclusively with the spirit" and does not get going until "one" hurries to his assistance with a change of horses. "Only when *one* has grown fond of oneself *corporeally,* etc." (p. 18), "only then" everything goes forward smoothly again, the man discovers that he has a personal interest, and arrives at "the *second self-discovery*", in that he not only "finds himself as spirit", like the youth, "and then at once loses himself again in the universal spirit", but finds himself "as *corporeal* spirit". (P. 19.) This "corporeal spirit" finally arrives at having an "interest not only in its own spirit" (like the youth), "but in total satisfaction, in the satisfaction of the whole fellow" (an interest in the satisfaction of the whole fellow!)—he arrives at the point where "he is pleased with himself exactly as he is". Being a German, Stirner's "man" arrives at everything very late. He could see, sauntering along the Paris boulevards or in London's Regent Street, hundreds of "young men", fops and dandies who have not yet found themselves as "corporeal spirits" and are nevertheless "pleased with themselves exactly as they are", and whose main interest lies in the "satisfaction of the whole fellow".

This second "self-discovery" fills our holy dialectician with such enthusiasm that he suddenly forgets his role and begins to speak not of the *man*, but of *himself*, and reveals that he himself, he the unique, is "the man", and that "the man"="the unique". A new conjuring trick.

"How I find myself" (it should read: "how the youth finds himself") "behind the *things,* and indeed as *spirit,* so subsequently, too, I must find myself". (it should read: "the man must find himself") "behind the *thoughts*, i.e., as their creator and owner. In the period of spirits, thoughts outgrew me" (the youth), "although they were the offspring of my brain; like delirious fantasies they floated around me and agitated me greatly, a dreadful power. The thoughts became themselves *corporeal*, they were spectres like God, the Emperor, the Pope, the Fatherland, etc.; by destroying their corporeality, I take them back into my own corporeality and *announce:* I alone am corporeal. And now I take the world as it is for me, as *my* world, as my property: I relate everything to myself."

Thus, the man, identified here with the "unique", having first given thoughts corporeality, i.e., having transformed them into spectres, now destroys this corporeality again, by taking them back into his own body, which he thus makes into a body of spectres. The fact that he arrives at his own corporeality only through the negation of the spectres, shows the nature of this constructed corporeality of the man, which he has first to "announce" to "himself", in order to believe in it. But what he "announces to himself" he does not even "announce" correctly. The fact that apart from his "unique" body there are not also to be found in his head all kinds of independent bodies, spermatozoa, he transforms into the *"fable"* [a]: I *alone* am corporeal. Another conjuring trick.

Further, the man who, as a youth, stuffed his head with all kinds of nonsense about existing powers and relations such as the Emperor, the Fatherland, the state, etc., and knew them only as his own "delirious fantasies", in the form of his conceptions — this man, *according to Saint Max, actually destroys all these powers* by getting out of his head his false opinion of them. On the contrary: now that he no longer looks at the world through the spectacles of his fantasy, he has to think of the practical interrelations of the world, to get to know them and to act in accordance with them. By destroying the *fantastic* corporeality which the world had for him, he finds its real corporeality outside his fantasy. With the disappearance of the *spectral* corporeality of the Emperor, what disappears for him is not the corporeality, but the *spectral character* of the Emperor, the actual power of whom he can now at last appreciate in all its scope. Conjuring trick No. 3 [a].

The youth as a man does not even react critically towards ideas which are valid also for others and are current as categories, but is critical only of those ideas that are the "mere offspring of his brain", i.e., general concepts about existing

---

[a] In German a play on words: "Ich sage"— I say, I announce — and "die Sage"— fable, myth, saga.— *Ed.*

conditions reproduced in his brain. Thus, for example, he does not even resolve the *category* "Fatherland", but only his personal opinion of this category, after which the *generally valid* category still remains, and even in the sphere of "philosophical thought" the work is only just beginning. He wants, however, to make us believe that he has destroyed the category itself because he has destroyed his emotional personal relation to it — exactly as he has wanted to make us believe that he has destroyed the power of the Emperor by giving up his fantastic conception of the Emperor. Conjuring trick No. 4.

"*And now*," continues Saint Max, "I take the world as it is for me, as my world, as my property."

He takes the world as it is for him, i.e., *as he is compelled to take it*, and thereby he has *appropriated* the world for himself, has made it his property — a mode of acquisition which, indeed, is not mentioned by any of the economists, but the method and success of which will be the more brilliantly disclosed in "the book". Basically, however, he "takes" not the "world", but only his "delirious fantasy" about the world as his own, and makes it his property. He takes the world as his conception of the world, and the world as his conception is his imagined property, the property of his conception, his conception as property, his property as conception, his own peculiar conception, or his conception of property; and all this he expresses in the incomparable phrase: "I relate everything to myself."

After the man has recognised, as the saint himself admits, that the world was only populated by spectres, because the youth saw spectres, after the *illusory world* of the youth has disappeared for the man, the latter finds himself in a *real* world, independent of youthful fancies.

And so, it should therefore read, I take the world as it is *independently of myself*, in the form in which it *belongs to itself* ("the man takes" — see page 18 — "the world as it is", and not as he would like it to be), in the first place as my non-property (hitherto it was my property only as a spectre); I relate myself to everything and only to that extent do I relate everything to myself.

"If I as spirit rejected the world with the deepest contempt for it, then I as proprietor reject the spectres or ideas into their emptiness. They no longer have power over me, just as no 'earthly force' has power over the spirit." (P. 20.)

We see here that the proprietor, Stirner's man, at once enters into possession, *sine beneficio deliberandi atque inventarii*,[a] of the inheritance of the youth which, according to his own statement, consists only of "delirious fantasies" and "spectres". He believes that in the process of changing from a child into a youth he had truly coped with the world of things, and in the process of changing from a youth into a man he had truly coped with the world of the spirit, that now, as a man, he has the whole world in his pocket and has nothing more to trouble him. If, according to the words of the youth which he repeats, no earthly force outside him has any power over the spirit, and hence the spirit is the supreme power on earth—and he, the man, has forced this omnipotent spirit into subjection to himself—is he not then completely omnipotent? He forgets that he has only destroyed the fantastic and spectral form assumed by the idea of "Fatherland", etc., in the brain of the "youth", but that he has still *not touched* these ideas, insofar as they express *actual* relations. Far from having become the master of ideas—he is only now capable of arriving at "ideas".

"Now, let us say in conclusion, it can be clearly seen" (p. 199) that the holy man has brought his interpretation of the different stages of life to the desired and predestined goal. He informs us of the result achieved in a thesis that is a spectral shade which we shall now confront with its lost body.

Unique thesis, p. 20.	Owner of the accompanying liberated shade.
"The child was *realistic*, in thrall to the *things of this world*, until little by little he succeeded in penetrating *behind these very things*. The youth was *idealistic*, inspired by thoughts, until he worked his way up to become a man, the egoistic man, who deals with things and thoughts as he pleases and puts his personal interest above everything. Finally, the old man? It will be time enough to speak of this when I become one."	The child was *actually* in thrall *to the world of his things*, until *little by little* (a borrowed conjuring trick standing for development) he succeeded in leaving *these very things behind him*. The youth was *fanciful* and was made thoughtless by his enthusiasm, until he was brought down by the man, the egoistic *burgher*, with whom things and thoughts deal as they please, because his personal interest puts everything above him. Finally, the old man?—"Woman, what have I to do with thee?"[b]

---

[a] Without the advantage of deliberation and inventory—the right of deliberation and inventory is an old principle of the law of inheritance, which grants the heir time to decide whether he wants to accept or to reject a legacy.—*Ed.*

[b] John 2:4.—*Ed.*

The entire history of "a man's life" amounts, therefore, "let us say in conclusion", to the following:

1. Stirner regards the various stages of life only as "self-discoveries" of the individual, and these "self-discoveries" are moreover always reduced to a definite relation of consciousness. Thus the variety of *consciousness* is here the life of the individual. The physical and social changes which take place in the individuals and produce an altered consciousness are, of course, of no concern to Stirner. In Stirner's work, therefore, child, youth and man always find the world ready-made, just as they merely "find" "themselves"; absolutely nothing is done to ensure that there should be something which can in fact be found. But even the relation of *consciousness* is not correctly understood either, but only in its speculative distortion. Hence, too, all these figures have a philosophical attitude to the world — "the child is *realistic*", "the youth is *idealistic*", the man is the negative unity of the two, absolute negativity, as is evident from the above-quoted final proposition. Here the secret of "a man's life" is revealed, here it becomes clear that the "*child*" was only a disguise of "*realism*", the "*youth*" a disguise of "*idealism*", the "*man*" of an attempted *solution* of this *philosophical antithesis.* This solution, this "*absolute negativity*", is arrived at — it is now seen — only thanks to the man blindly taking on trust the illusions both of the child and of the youth, *believing* thus to have overcome the world of things and the world of the spirit.

2. Since Saint Max pays no attention to the physical and social "life" of the individual, and says nothing at all about "life", he quite consistently abstracts from historical epochs, nationalities, classes, etc., or, which is the *same thing*, he inflates the *consciousness* predominant in the class nearest to him in his immediate environment into the normal consciousness of "a man's life". In order to rise above this local and pedantic narrow-mindedness he has only to confront "his" youth with the first young clerk he encounters, a young English factory worker or young Yankee, not to mention the young Kirghiz-Kazakhs.

3. Our saint's enormous gullibility — the true spirit of his book — is not content with causing his youth to believe in his child, and his man to believe in his youth. The illusions which some "youths", "men", etc., have or claim to have about themselves, are without any examination accepted by Stirner himself and confused with the "*life*", with the *reality*, of these highly ambiguous youths and men.

4. The prototype of the entire structure of the stages of life has already been depicted in the third part of Hegel's *Encyclopädie*[a] and "in various transformations" in other passages in Hegel as well. Saint Max, pursuing "his own" purposes, had, of course, to undertake certain "transformations" here also. Whereas Hegel, for example, is still to such an extent guided by the empirical world that he portrays the German burgher as the servant of the world around him, Stirner has to make him the master of this world, which he is not even in imagination. Similarly, Saint Max pretends that he does not speak of the old man for empirical reasons; he wishes to wait until he becomes one himself (here, therefore, "a man's life" = his unique life). Hegel briskly sets about constructing the four stages of the human life because, in the real world, the negation is posited twice, i.e., as moon and as comet (cf. Hegel's *Naturphilosophie*[b]), and therefore the quaternity here takes the place of the trinity. Stirner finds his own uniqueness in making moon and comet coincide and so abolishes the unfortunate old man from "a man's life". The reason for this conjuring trick becomes evident as soon as we examine the construction of the unique history of man.

2. THE ECONOMY OF THE OLD TESTAMENT

We must here, for a moment, jump from the "Law" to the "Prophets", since at this point already we reveal the secret of unique domestic economy in heaven and on earth. In the Old Testament, too — where the law, man, still is a school-master of the unique (Galatians 3:24) — the history of the kingdom of the unique follows a wise plan fixed from eternity. Everything has been foreseen and preordained in order that the unique could appear in the world, when the time had come[c] to redeem holy people from their holiness.

The first book, "A Man's Life", is also called the "Book of Genesis", because it contains in embryo the entire domestic economy of the unique, because it gives us a prototype of the whole subsequent development up to the moment when the time comes for the end of the world. The entire unique history

---

[a] G.W.F. Hegel, *Encyclopädie der philosophischen Wissenschaften im Grundrisse. C. Die Philosophie des Geistes.— Ed.*

[b] G.W.F. Hegel, *Vorlesungen über die Naturphilosophie.— Ed.*

[c] Galatians 4:4:— *Ed.*

revolves round three stages: child, youth and man, who return "in various transformations" and in ever widening circles until, finally, the entire history of the world of things and the world of the spirit is reduced to "child, youth and man". Everywhere we shall find nothing but disguised "child, youth and man", just as we already discovered in them three disguised categories.

We spoke above of the German philosophical conception of history. Here, in Saint Max, we find a brilliant example of it. The speculative idea, the abstract conception, is made the driving force of history, and history is thereby turned into the mere history of philosophy. But even the latter is not conceived as, according to existing sources, it actually took place — not to mention how it evolved under the influence of real historical relations — but as it was understood and described by recent German philosophers, in particular Hegel and Feuerbach. And from these descriptions again only that was selected which could be adapted to the given end, and which came into the hands of our saint by tradition. Thus, history becomes a mere history of illusory ideas, a history of spirits and ghosts, while the real, empirical history that forms the basis of this ghostly history is only utilised to provide bodies for these ghosts; from it are borrowed the names required to clothe these ghosts with the appearance of reality. In making this experiment our saint frequently forgets his role and writes an undisguised ghost-story.

In his case we find this method of making history in its most naive, most classic simplicity. Three simple categories — realism, idealism and absolute negativity (here named "*egoism*") as the unity of the two — which we have already encountered in the shape of the child, youth and man, are made the basis of all history and are embellished with various historical signboards; together with their modest suite of auxiliary categories they form the content of all the allegedly historical phases which are trotted out. Saint Max once again reveals here his boundless faith by pushing to greater extremes than any of his predecessors faith in the speculative content of history dished up by German philosophers. In this solemn and tedious construction of history, therefore, all that matters is to find a pompous series of resounding names for three categories that are so hackneyed that they no longer dare to show themselves publicly under their own names. Our anointed author could perfectly well have passed from the "man" (p. 20) immediately to the "ego" (p. 201) or better still to the "unique" (p. 485); but that would have been too simple. Moreover, the strong competition among the

German speculative philosophers makes it the duty of each new competitor to offer an ear-splitting historical advertisement for his commodity.

"The force of true development", to use *Dottore Graziano*'s words, "proceeds most forcibly" in the following "transformations":

Basis:

    I. Realism.

    II. Idealism.

    III. The negative unity of the two. "*One*". (P. 485.)

First nomenclature:

    I. *Child,* dependent on things (realism).

    II. *Youth,* dependent on ideas (idealism).

    III. *Man*—(as the negative unity)

        expressed positively:

          the owner of ideas and things, ⎫

        expressed negatively: ⎬ (egoism)

          free from ideas and things   ⎪

Second, h i s t o r i c a l nomenclature: ⎭

    I. *Negro* (realism, child).

    II. *Mongol* (idealism, youth).

    III. *Caucasian* (negative unity of realism and idealism, man).

Third, most general nomenclature:

    I. Realistic egoist (egoist in the ordinary sense) — child, Negro.

    II. Idealist egoist (devotee) — youth, Mongol.

    III. True egoist (the unique) — man, Caucasian.

Fourth, historical nomenclature. Repetition of the preceding stages within the category of the Caucasian.

    I. The *Ancients.* Negroid Caucasians — childish men — pagans — dependent on things — realists — the world.

    Transition (child penetrating behind the "things of this world"): Sophists, Sceptics, etc.

    II. The *Moderns.* Mongoloid Caucasians — youthful men — Christians — dependent on ideas — idealists — spirit.

    1. Pure history of spirits,[a] Christianity as spirit. "The spirit."

    2. Impure history of spirits. Spirit in relation to others. "The Possessed".

---

[a] In the German original "*Geistergeschichte*", that is, "ghost-story" (*Geister*—ghosts or spirits; *Geschichte*—story or history). In this volume, however, it has usually been rendered as "history of spirits" to bring out more clearly the connection with the words that precede or follow it.— *Ed.*

A. Purely impure history of spirits.
a) *The apparition*, the ghost, the spirit in the Negroid state, as thing-like spirit and spiritual thing—objective being for the Christian, spirit as child.
b) *The whimsy*, the fixed idea, the spirit in the Mongolian condition, as spiritual in the spirit, determination in consciousness, conceptual being in the Christian—spirit as youth.
B. Impurely impure (historical) history of spirits.
a) Catholicism—Middle Ages (the Negro, child, realism, etc.).
b) Protestantism—modern times in modern times—(Mongol, youth, idealism, etc.).
Within Protestantism it is possible to make further subdivisions, for example:
   α) English philosophy—realism, child, Negro.
   ß) German philosophy—idealism, youth, Mongol.
3. *The Hierarchy*—negative unity of the two within the Mongoloid-Caucasian point of view. Such unity appears where historical relations are changed into actually existing relations or where opposites are presented as existing side by side. Here, therefore, we have two co-existing stages:
A. *The "uneducated"*[a] (evil ones, bourgeois, egoists in the the ordinary sense)=Negros, children, Catholics, realists, etc.
B. *The "educated"* (good ones, *citoyens*, devotees, priests, etc.)=Mongols, youths, Protestants, idealists.
These two stages exist side by side and hence it follows "easily" that the "educated" rule over the "uneducated"—this is the *hierarchy*. In the further course of historical development there arises then
the non-Hegelian from the "uneducated",
the Hegelian from the "educated",*
from which it follows that the Hegelians rule over the non-Hegelians. In this way Stirner converts the speculative notion of the domination of the speculative idea in history into the notion of the domination of the speculative philosophers themselves. The view of history hitherto held by him—the domination of the idea—becomes in the hierarchy a relation actually existing at

* "The shaman and the speculative philosopher denote the lowest and the highest point in the scale of the *inner* man, the Mongol." (P. 453.)

[a] Here and later the authors ironically use Berlin dialect words for uneducated (*unjebildet*) and educated (*jebildet*).— *Ed.*

present; it becomes the world domination of ideologists. This shows how deeply Stirner has plunged into speculation. This domination of the speculative philosophers and ideologists is finally developing, "for the time has come" for it, into the following, concluding nomenclature:

a) *Political liberalism*, dependent on things, independent of persons — realism, child, Negro, the ancient, apparition, Catholicism, the "uneducated", masterless.

b) Social liberalism, independent of things, dependent on the spirit, without object — idealism, youth, Mongol, the modern, whimsy, Protestantism, the "educated", propertyless.

c) *Humane liberalism*, masterless and propertyless, that is godless, for God is simultaneously the supreme master and the supreme possession, hierarchy — negative unity in the sphere of liberalism and, as such, domination over the world of things and thoughts; at the same time the perfect egoist in the abolition of egoism — the perfect hierarchy. At the same time, it forms the

Transition (youth penetrating behind the world of thoughts) to

III. the "*ego*" — i.e., the perfect Christian, the perfect man, the Caucasian Caucasian and true egoist, who — just as the Christian became spirit through the supersession of the ancient world — becomes a corporeal being[a] through the dissolution of the realm of spirits, by entering, *sine beneficio deliberandi et inventarii*, into the inheritance of idealism, the youth, the Mongol, the modern, the Christian, the possessed, the whimsical, the Protestant, the "educated", the Hegelian and the humane liberal.

NB. 1. "At times" Feuerbachian and other categories, such as reason, the heart, etc., may be also "included episodically", should a suitable occasion arise, to heighten the colour of the picture and to produce new effects. It goes without saying that these, too, are only new disguises of the ever-present idealism and realism.

2. The rather pious Saint Max, *Jacques le bonhomme*, has nothing real and mundane to say about real mundane history, except that under the name of "nature", the "world of things", the "world of the child", etc., he always opposes it to consciousness, as an object of speculation of the latter, as a

---

[a] In German a pun on *"der Leibhaftige"*, which can mean corporeal being or the devil.— *Ed.*

world which, in spite of its continual annihilation, continues to exist in a mystical darkness, in order to reappear on every convenient occasion — probably because children and Negroes continue to exist, and hence also their world, the so-called world of things, "easily" continues to exist. Concerning such historical and non-historical constructions, good old *Hegel* wrote with regard to Schelling — the model for all constructors — that one can say the following in this context:

> "It is no more difficult to handle the instrument of this monotonous formalism than a painter's palette which has only two colours, say black" (realistic, childish, Negroid, etc.) "and yellow" [a] (idealist, youthful, Mongolian, etc.), "in order to use the former to paint a surface when something historical" (the "world of things") "is required, and the latter when a landscape" ("heaven", spirit, holiness, etc.) "is needed." (*Phänomenologie,* p. 39.)

"Ordinary consciousness" has even more pointedly ridiculed constructions of this kind in the following song:

> The master sent out John
> And told him to cut the hay;
> But John did not cut the hay
> Nor did he come back home.
>
> Then the master sent out the dog
> And told him to bite John;
> But the dog did not bite John,
> John did not cut the hay
> And they did not come back home.
>
> Then the master sent out the stick
> And told it to beat the dog;
> But the stick did not beat the dog,
> The dog did not bite John,
> John did not cut the hay
> And they did not come back home.
>
> Then the master sent out fire
> And told it to burn the stick;
> But the fire did not burn the stick,
> The stick did not beat the dog,
> The dog did not bite John,
> John did not cut the hay
> And they did not come back home.
>
> Then the master sent out water
> And told it to put out the fire;
> But the water did not put out the fire,
> The fire did not burn the stick,
> The stick did not beat the dog,
> The dog did not bite John,
> John did not cut the hay
> And they did not come back home.

---

[a] Hegel mentions red and green as examples.— *Ed.*

Then the master sent out the ox
And told it to drink the water;
But the ox did not drink the water,
The water did not put out the fire,
The fire did not burn the stick,
The stick did not beat the dog,
The dog did not bite John,
John did not cut the hay
And they did not come back home.

Then the master sent out the butcher
And told him to slaughter the ox;
But the butcher did not slaughter the ox,
The ox did not drink the water,
The water did not put out the fire,
The fire did not burn the stick,
The stick did not beat the dog,
The dog did not bite John,
John did not cut the hay
And they did not come back home.

Then the master sent out the hangman
And told him to hang the butcher;
The hangman did hang the butcher,
The butcher slaughtered the ox,
The ox drank the water,
The water put out the fire,
The fire burnt the stick,
The stick beat the dog,
The dog bit John,
John cut the hay,
And they all came back home.[a]

We shall now see with what "virtuosity of thought" and with what schoolboyish material Jacques le bonhomme elaborates on this scheme.

3. THE ANCIENTS

Properly speaking we ought to begin here with the Negroes; but Saint Max, who undoubtedly sits in the "Council of Guardians", in his unfathomable wisdom introduces the Negroes only later, and even then "without any claim to thoroughness and authenticity". If, therefore, we make Greek philosophy precede the Negro era, i.e., the campaigns of Sesostris and Napoleon's expedition to Egypt,[42] it is because we are confident that our holy author has arranged everything wisely.

---

[a] A German nursery rhyme.—*Ed.*

"Let us, therefore, take a look at the activities which tempt" Stirner's ancients.

" 'For the ancients, the world was a truth,' says Feuerbach; but he forgets to make the important addition: a truth, the untruth of which they sought to penetrate and, finally, did indeed ᵨenetrate." (P. 22.)

"For the ancients", *their* "world" (not *the* world) "was a truth"—whereby, of course, no truth about the ancient world is stated, but only that the ancients did not have a Christian attitude to their world. As soon as *untruth* penetrated their world (i.e., as soon as this world itself disintegrated in consequence of practical conflicts—and to demonstrate this materialistic development empirically would be the only thing of interest), the ancient philosophers sought to penetrate the world of truth or the truth of their world and then, of course, they found that it had become untrue. Their very search was itself a symptom of the internal collapse of this world. Jacques le bonhomme transforms the idealist symptom into the material cause of the collapse and, as a German church father, makes antiquity itself seek its own negation, Christianity. For him this position of antiquity is inevitable because the ancients are "*children*" who seek to penetrate the "world of things". "And that is fairly easy too": by transforming the ancient world into the later consciousness regarding the ancient world, Jacques le bonhomme can, of course, jump in a single leap from the materialistic ancient world to the world of religion, to Christianity. Now the "word of God" immediately emerges in opposition to the real world of antiquity; the Christian conceived as the modern sceptic emerges in opposition to the ancient man conceived as philosopher. His Christian "is never convinced of the vanity of the word of God" and, in consequence of this lack of conviction, he "believes" "in its eternal and invincible truth". (P. 22.) Just as Stirner's ancient is ancient because he is a non-Christian, not yet a Christian or a hidden Christian, so his primitive Christian is a Christian because he is a non-atheist, not yet an atheist or a hidden atheist. Stirner, therefore, causes Christianity to be negated by the ancients and modern atheism by the primitive Christians, instead of the reverse. Jacques le bonhomme, like all other speculative philosophers, seizes everything by its philosophical tail. A few more examples of this childlike gullibility immediately follow.

"The Christian must consider himself a 'stranger on the earth' (Epistle to the Hebrews 11:13)." (P. 23.)

On the contrary, the strangers on earth (arising from extremely natural causes, e.g., the colossal concentration of wealth in the whole Roman world, etc., etc.) had to consider themselves Christians. It was not their Christianity that made them vagrants, but their vagrancy that made them Christians.

On the same page the holy father jumps straight from Sophocles' *Antigone* and the sacredness of the burial ceremonial connected with it to the Gospel of Matthew 8:22 (let the dead bury their dead), while Hegel, at any rate in the *Phänomenologie*, gradually passes from the *Antigone*, etc., to the Romans. With equal right Saint Max could have passed at once to the Middle Ages and, together with Hegel, have advanced this biblical statement against the crusaders or even, in order to be quite original, have contrasted the burial of Polynices by Antigone with the transfer of the ashes of Napoleon from St. Helena to Paris. It is stated further:

"In Christianity the inviolable truth of family ties" (which on page 22 is noted as one of the "truths" of the ancients) "is depicted as an untruth which should be got rid of as quickly as possible (Mark, 10:29) and so in everything." (P. 23.)

This proposition, in which reality is again turned upside-down, should be put the right way up as follows: the actual untruth of family ties (concerning which, *inter alia,* the still existing documents of pre-Christian Roman legislation should be examined) is depicted in Christianity as an inviolable truth, "and so in everything".

From these examples, therefore, it is superabundantly evident how Jacques le bonhomme, who strives to "get rid as quickly as possible" of empirical history, stands facts on their heads, causes material history to be produced by ideal history, "and so in everything". At the outset we learn only the alleged attitude of the ancients to their world; as dogmatists they are put in opposition to the ancient world, their own world, instead of appearing as its creators; it is a question only of the relation of consciousness to the object, to truth; it is a question, therefore, only of the philosophical relation of the ancients to their world — ancient history is replaced by the history of ancient philosophy, and this only in the form in which Saint Max imagines it according to Hegel and Feuerbach.

Thus the history of Greece, from the time of Pericles inclusively, is reduced to a struggle of abstractions: reason, spirit, heart, worldliness, etc. These are the Greek parties. In this ghostly world, which is presented as the Greek world, allegorical persons such as Madame Purity of Heart "machinate" and mythical figures like Pilate (who must never be missing where there are children) find a place quite seriously side by side with Timon of Phlius.

After presenting us with some astounding revelations about the Sophists and Socrates, Saint Max immediately jumps to the Sceptics. He discovers that they completed the work which Socrates began. Hence the positive philosophy of the Greeks that followed immediately after the Sophists and Socrates, especially Aristotle's encyclopaedic learning, does not exist at all for Jacques le bonhomme. He strives "to get rid as quickly as possible" of the past and hurries to the transition to the "moderns", finding this transition in the Sceptics, Stoics and Epicureans. Let us see what our holy father has to reveal about them.

> "The Stoics wish to realise the ideal of the wise man ... the man who knows how to live ... they find this ideal in contempt for the world, in a life without living development [...] without friendly intercourse with the world, i.e., in a life of isolation [...] not in a life in common with others; the Stoic alone lives, for him everything else is dead. The Epicureans, on the other hand, demand an active life." (P. 30.)

We refer Jacques le bonhomme — the man who wants to realise himself and who knows how to live — to, *inter alia*, Diogenes Laertius: there he will discover that the wise man, the *sophos*, is nothing but the idealised Stoic, not the Stoic the realised wise man; he will discover that the *sophos* is by no means only a Stoic but is met with just as much among the Epicureans, the Neo-academists and the Sceptics. Incidentally, the *sophos* is the first form in which the Greek *philosophos* confronts us; he appears mythologically in the seven wise men, in practice in Socrates, and as an ideal among the Stoics, Epicureans, Neo-academists[43] and Sceptics. Each of these schools, of course, has its own σοφός,[a] just as Saint Bruno has his own "unique sex". Indeed, Saint Max can find "*le sage*" again in the eighteenth century in the philosophy of Enlightenment, and even in Jean Paul in the shape of the "wise men" like Emanuel,[b] etc. The Stoical wise man by no means has in mind "life without living development", but an *absolutely active* life, as is evident even from his concept of nature, which is Heraclitean, dynamic, developing and living, while for the Epicureans the principle of the concept of nature is the *mors immortalis*,[c] as Lucretius says, the atom, and, in opposition to

---

[a] Wise man.— *Ed.*

[b] Jean Paul, *Hesperus oder 45 Hundsposttage.*— *Ed.*

[c] Immortal death. Lucretius, *De rerum natura libri sex*, Book 3, Verse 882.— *Ed.*

Aristotle's divine energy, divine leisure is put forward as the ideal of life instead of "active life".

"The ethics of the Stoics (their only science, for they were unable to say anything about the spirit except what its relation to the world should be; and about nature — physics — they could say only that the wise man has to assert himself against it) is not a doctrine of the spirit, but merely a doctrine of rejection of the world and of self-assertion against the world." (P. 31.)

The Stoics were able to "say about nature" that physics is one of the most important sciences for the philosopher and consequently they even went to the trouble of further developing the physics of Heraclitus; they were "further able to say" that the ὥρα, masculine beauty, is the highest that the individual could represent, and glorified life in tune with nature, although they fell into contradictions in so doing. According to the Stoics, philosophy is divided into three doctrines: "physics, ethics, logic".

"They compare philosophy to the animal and to the egg, logic — to the bones and sinews of the animal, and to the outer shell of the egg, ethics — to the flesh of the animal and to the albumen of the egg, and physics — to the *soul* of the animal and to the yolk of the egg." (Diogenes Laertius, *Zeno*.)

From this alone it is evident how little true it is to say that "ethics is the only science of the Stoics". It should be added also that, apart from Aristotle, they were the chief founders of formal logic and systematics in general.

That the "Stoics were unable to say anything about the spirit" is so little true that even *seeing spirits* originated from them, on account of which Epicurus opposes them, as an Enlightener, and ridicules them as "old women", while precisely the Neo-Platonists borrowed part of their tales about spirits from the Stoics. This spirit-seeing of the Stoics arises, on the one hand, from the impossibility of achieving a dynamic concept of nature without the material furnished by empirical natural science, and, on the other hand, from their effort to interpret the ancient Greek world and even religion in a speculative manner and make them analogous to the thinking spirit.

"The ethics of the Stoics" is so much a "doctrine of world rejection and of self-assertion against the world" that, for example, it was counted a Stoical virtue to "have a sound fatherland, a worthy friend", that "the beautiful alone" is declared to be "the good", and that the Stoical wise man is allowed to mingle with the world in every way, for example, to commit incest, etc., etc. The Stoical wise man is to such an extent caught up "in a life of isolation and not in a life in common with others" that it is said of him in *Zeno*:

"Let not the wise man wonder at anything that seems wonderful—but neither will the worthy man live in *solitude*, for he is *social* by nature and *active in practice*." (Diogenes Laertius, Book VII, 1.)

Incidentally, it would be asking too much to demand that, for the sake of refuting this schoolboyish wisdom of Jacques le bonhomme, one should set forth the very complicated and contradictory ethics of the Stoics.

In connection with the Stoics, Jacques le bonhomme has to note the existence of the *Romans* also (p. 31), of whom, of course, he is unable to say anything, since they have no philosophy. The only thing we hear of them is that *Horace* (!) "did not go beyond the Stoics' worldly wisdom". (P. 32.) *Integer vitae, scelerisque purus!* [a]

In connection with the Stoics, *Democritus* is also mentioned in the following way: a muddled passage of Diogenes Laertius (*Democritus*, Book IX, 7, 45), which in addition has been inaccurately translated, is copied out from some textbook, and made the basis for a lengthy diatribe about Democritus. This diatribe has the distinguishing feature of being in direct contradiction to its basis, i.e., to the above-mentioned muddled and inaccurately translated passage, and converts "peace of mind" (Stirner's translation of εὐθυμία , in Low German *Wellmuth*) into "rejection of the world". The fact is that Stirner imagines that Democritus was a Stoic, and indeed of the sort that the unique and the ordinary schoolboyish conscious-ness conceive a Stoic to be. Stirner thinks that "his whole activity amounts to an endeavour to detach himself from the world", "hence to a rejection of the world", and that in the person of Democritus he can refute the Stoics. That the eventful life of Democritus, who had wandered through the world a great deal, flagrantly contradicts this notion of Saint Max's; that the real source from which to learn about the philosophy of Democritus is Aristotle and not a couple of anecdotes from Diogenes Laertius; that Democritus, far from rejecting the world, was, on the contrary, an empirical natural scientist and the first encyclopaedic mind among the Greeks; that his almost unknown ethics was limited to a few remarks which he is *alleged* to have made when he was an old, much-travelled man; that his writings on natural science can be called philosophy only *per abusum*,[b] because for him, in contrast to Epicurus, the atom was only a physical hypothesis, an expedient for explaining

---

[a] He of life without flaw, pure from sin. Horace, *The Odes*, Book 1—Ode XXII, Verse 1.—*Ed.*

[b] By abuse, i.e., improperly, wrongly.—*Ed.*

facts, just as it is in the proportional combinations of modern chemistry (Dalton and others)—all this does not suit the purpose of Jacques le bonhomme. Democritus must be understood in the "unique" fashion, Democritus speaks of euthymia, hence of peace of mind, hence of withdrawal into oneself, hence of rejection of the world. Democritus is a Stoic, and he differs from the Indian fakir mumbling "Brahma" (the word should have been "Om"),[44] only as the comparative differs from the superlative, i.e., "only *in degree*".

Of the Epicureans our friend knows exactly as much as he does of the Stoics, viz., the unavoidable schoolboy's minimum. He contrasts the Epicurean "hedone"[a] with the "ataraxia"[b] of the Stoics and Sceptics, not knowing that this "ataraxia" is also to be found in Epicurus and, moreover, as something placed higher than the "hedone" — in consequence of which his whole contrast falls to the ground. He tells us that the Epicureans "teach *only a different attitude* to the world" from that of the Stoics; but let him show us the (non-Stoic) philosopher of "ancient or modern times" who does not do "only" the same. Finally, Saint Max enriches us with a new dictum of the Epicureans: "the world must be deceived, for it is my enemy". Hitherto it was only known that the Epicureans made statements in the sense that the world must be *disillusioned*, and especially freed from fear of gods, for the world is my *friend*.

To give our saint some indication of the real base on which the philosophy of Epicurus rests, it is sufficient to mention that the idea that the state rests on the mutual agreement of people, on a *contrat social* (συνθήχη [c]), is found for the first time in Epicurus.

The extent to which Saint Max's disclosures about the Sceptics follow the same line is already evident from the fact that he considers their philosophy more radical than that of Epicurus. The Sceptics reduced the theoretical relation of people to things to *appearance*, and in practice they left everything as of old, being guided by this appearance just as much as others are guided by actuality; they merely gave it another name. Epicurus, on the other hand, was the true radical Enlightener of antiquity; he openly attacked the ancient religion, and it was from him, too, that the atheism of the Romans, insofar as it existed, was derived. For this reason, too,

---

[a] Pleasure.— *Ed.*

[b] Equanimity, imperturbability, intrepidity.— *Ed.*

[c] Contract (see Karl Marx and Frederick Engels, *Collected Works*, Vol. 1, pp. 409-10).— *Ed.*

Lucretius praised Epicurus as the hero who was the first to overthrow the gods and trample religion underfoot; for this reason among all church fathers, from Plutarch to Luther, Epicurus has always had the reputation of being the atheist philosopher *par excellence*, and was called a swine; for which reason, too, Clement of Alexandria says that when Paul takes up arms against philosophy he has in mind Epicurean philosophy alone. (*Stromatum*, Book I [chap. XI], p. 295, Cologne edition, 1688.)[a] Hence we see how "cunning, perfidious" and "clever" was the attitude of this open atheist to the world in directly attacking its religion, while the Stoics adapted the ancient religion in their own speculative fashion, and the Sceptics used their concept of "appearance" as the excuse for being able to accompany all their judgments with a *reservatio mentalis*.

Thus, according to Stirner, the Stoics finally arrive at "contempt for the world" (p. 30), the Epicureans at "the same worldly wisdom as the Stoics" (p. 32), and the Sceptics at the point where they "let the world alone and do not worry about it at all". Hence, according to Stirner, all three end in an attitude of indifference to the world, of "contempt for the world". (P. 485.) Long before him, Hegel expressed it in this way: Stoicism, Scepticism, Epicureanism "aimed at making the mind indifferent towards everything that actuality has to offer". (*Philosophie der Geschichte,*[b] p. 327.)

"The ancients," writes Saint Max, summing up his criticism of the ancient world of ideas, "it is true, had ideas, but they did not know *the idea.*" (P. 30.) In this connection, "one should recall what was said earlier about our childhood ideas" (ibid.).

The history of ancient philosophy has to conform to Stirner's design. In order that the Greeks should retain their role of children, Aristotle ought not to have lived and his thought in and for itself (ἡ νόησις ἡ καθ' αὐτήν), his self-thinking reason (αὐτόν δὲ νοεῖ ὁ νοῦς) and his self-thinking intellect (ἡ νόησις τῆς νοήσεως) should never have occurred; and in general his *Metaphysics* and the third book of his *Psychology*[c] ought not to have existed.

With just as much right as Saint Max here recalls "what was said earlier about our childhood", when he discussed "our childhood" he could have said: let the reader look up what will

---

[a] See Karl Marx and Frederick Engels, *Collected Works*, Vol. 1, p. 488.— *Ed.*

[b] G. W. F. Hegel, *Vorlesungen über die Philosophie der Geschichte.*— *Ed.*

[c] Aristoteles. *De anima.*— *Ed.*

be *said* below about the ancients and the Negroes and will *not* be said about Aristotle.

In order to appreciate the true meaning of the last ancient philosophies during the dissolution of the ancient world, Jacques le bonhomme had only to look at the real situation in life of their adherents under the world dominion of Rome. He could have found, *inter alia*, in Lucian a detailed description of how the people regarded them as public buffoons, and how the Roman capitalists, proconsuls, etc., hired them as court jesters for their entertainment, so that after squabbling at the table with slaves for a few bones and a crust of bread and after being given a special sour wine, they would amuse the master of the house and his guests with delightful words like "ataraxia", "aphasia",[a] "hedone", etc.*

Incidentally, if our good man wanted to make the history of ancient philosophy into a history of antiquity, then as a matter of course he ought to have merged the Stoics, Epicureans and Sceptics in the Neo-Platonists, whose philosophy is nothing but a fantastic combination of the Stoic, Epicurean and Sceptical doctrine with the content of the philosophy of Plato and Aristotle. Instead of that, he merges these doctrines directly in Christianity.**

It is not "Stirner" that has left Greek philosophy "behind him", but Greek philosophy that has "Stirner" behind *it*. (Cf. *Wigand*, p. 186.[b]) Instead of telling us *how* "antiquity" arrives at a world of things and "copes" with it, this ignorant school-master causes antiquity blissfully to vanish by means of a quotation from Timon; whereby antiquity the more naturally "arrives at its final goal" since, according to Saint Max, the ancients "found themselves placed by *nature*" in the ancient "communality", which, "let us say in conclusion", "can be understood" the more easily because this communality, the

* [The following passage is crossed out in the manuscript:] ... just as after the Revolution the French aristocrats became the dancing instructors of the whole of Europe, and the English lords will soon find their true place in the civilised world as stable-hands and kennel-men.

** [The following passage is crossed out in the manuscript:] On the contrary, Stirner should have shown us that Hellenism even after its disintegration still continued to exist for a long time; that next to it the Romans gained world domination, what they really did in the world, how the Roman world developed and declined, and finally how the Hellenic and Roman world perished, spiritually in Christianity and materially in the migration of the peoples.

---

[a] Refusal to express any definite opinion.— *Ed.*
[b] M. Stirner, "Recensenten Stirners".— *Ed.*

family, etc., are dubbed "the so-called *natural* ties". (P. 33.) By means of nature the ancient "world of things" is created, and by means of Timon and Pilate (p. 32) it is destroyed. Instead of describing the "world of things" which provides the material basis of Christianity, he causes this "world of things" to be annihilated in the world of the spirit, in Christianity.

The German philosophers are accustomed to counterpose antiquity, as the epoch of realism, to Christianity and modern times, as the epoch of idealism, whereas the French and English economists, historians and scientists are accustomed to regard antiquity as the period of idealism in contrast to the materialism and empiricism of modern times. In the same way antiquity can be considered to be idealistic insofar as in history the ancients represent the "*citoyen*", the idealist politician, while in the final analysis the moderns turn into the "bourgeois", the realist *ami du commerce*[a]— or again it can be considered to be realistic, because for the ancients the communality was a "truth", whereas for the moderns it is an idealist "lie". All these abstract counterposings and historical constructions are of very little use.

The "unique thing" we learn from this whole portrayal of the ancients is that, whereas Stirner "knows" very few "things" about the ancient world, he has all the "better seen through" them. (Cf. *Wigand*, p. 191.)

Stirner is truly that same "man child" of whom it is prophesied in the Revelation of St. John, 12:5, that he "was to rule all nations with a rod of iron". We have seen how he sets about the unfortunate heathen with the iron rod of his ignorance. The "moderns" will fare no better.

4. THE MODERNS

"Therefore if any man be in Christ, he is a new creature; old things are passed away; behold, all things are become new." (2 Corinthians 5:17.) (P. 33.)

By means of this biblical saying the ancient world has now indeed "passed away" or, as Saint Max really wanted to say, "all gone",[b] and with one leap [c] we have jumped over to the new, Christian, youthful, Mongoloid "world of the spirit". We shall see that this, too, will have "all gone" in a very short space of time.

[a] An expression of Fourier (see Ch. Fourier, *Des trois unités externes*).— *Ed.*
[b] Here the authors ironically use the Berlin dialect words *alle jeworden.—Ed.*
[c] In German a pun on the word *Satz*, which means a leap, a jump and also a sentence, a proposition.— *Ed.*

"Whereas it was stated above 'for the ancients, the world was a truth', we must say here 'for the moderns the spirit was a truth', but in neither case should we forget the important addition: 'a truth, the untruth of which they sought to penetrate and, finally, did indeed penetrate'." (P. 33.)

While we do not wish to devise any Stirner-like constructions, "we must say here": for the moderns truth was a spirit, namely the holy spirit. Jacques le bonhomme again takes the moderns not in their actual historical connection with the "world of things" — which, despite being "all gone", nevertheless continues to exist — but in their theoretical, and indeed religious, attitude. For him the history of the Middle Ages and modern times again exists only as the history of religion and philosophy; he devoutly believes all the illusions of these epochs and the philosophical illusions about these illusions. Thus, having given the history of the moderns the same turn as he gave that of the ancients, Saint Max can then easily "demonstrate" in it a "similar course to that taken by antiquity", and pass from the Christian religion to modern German philosophy as rapidly as he passed from ancient philosophy to the Christian religion. On page 37 he himself gives a characterisation of his historical illusions, by making the discovery that "the ancients have nothing to offer but *worldly wisdom*" and that "the moderns have never gone, and do not go, beyond *theology*", and he solemnly asks: "What did the *moderns* seek to penetrate?" The ancients and moderns alike do nothing else in history but "seek to penetrate something"—the ancients try to find out what is behind the world of things, the moderns behind the world of the spirit. In the end the ancients are left "without a world" and the moderns "without a spirit"; the ancients wanted to become idealists, the moderns to become realists (p. 485), but both of them were only occupied with the divine (p. 488)— "history up to now" is only the "history of the spiritual man" (what faith!) (p. 442)— in short we have again the child and the youth, the Negro and the Mongol, and all the rest of the terminology of the "various transformations".

At the same time we see a faithful imitation of the speculative manner, by which children beget their father, and what is earlier is brought about by what is later. From the very outset Christians must "seek to penetrate the untruthfulness of their truth", they must immediately be hidden atheists and critics, as was already indicated concerning the ancients. But not satisfied with this, Saint Max gives one more brilliant example of his "virtuosity in" (speculative) "thought" (p. 230):

> "Now, *after* liberalism has acclaimed *man, one* can state that thereby *only the last consequence* of Christianity *has been drawn* and that Christianity *originally set itself no other task* than that of ... realising *man*."

Since allegedly the last consequence of Christianity has been drawn, *"one"* can state that it has been drawn. As soon as the later ones have transformed what was earlier *"one* can state" that the earlier ones "originally", namely *"in truth"*, in essence, in heaven, as hidden Jews, "set themselves no other task" than that of being transformed by the later ones. *Christianity*, for Jacques le bonhomme, is a self-positing subject, the absolute spirit, which "originally" posits its end as its beginning. Cf. Hegel's *Encyclopädie*, etc.

> "Hence" (namely because one can attribute an imaginary task to Christianity) "there follows the delusion" (of course, before Feuerbach it was impossible to know what task Christianity "had originally set itself") "that Christianity attaches infinite value to the ego, as revealed, for example, in the theory of immortality and pastoral work. No, it attaches this value to *man* alone, *man* alone is immortal, and only because I am a *man*, am I also immortal."

If, then, from the whole of Stirner's scheme and formulation of tasks it emerges, already sufficiently clearly, that Christianity can lend immortality only to Feuerbach's "man", we learn here in addition that this comes about also because Christianity does not ascribe this immortality — to *animals* as well.

Let us now also draw up a scheme *à la* Saint Max.

"Now, after" modern large-scale landownership, which has arisen from the process of parcellation, has actually *"proclaimed"* primogeniture, *"one can state that thereby only the last consequence"* of the parcellation of landed property *"has been drawn" "and that"* parcellation *"in truth originally set itself no other task than that of realising"* primogeniture, true primogeniture. *"Hence there follows the delusion"* that parcellation *"attaches infinite value"* to equal rights of members of the family, *"as revealed, for example"*, in the laws of inheritance of the *Code Napoléon. "No, it attaches this value solely"* to the eldest son; *"only"* the eldest son, the future owner of the entailed estate, will become a large landowner, *"and only because I am"* the eldest son, *"I will also be"* a large landowner.

In this way it is infinitely easy to give history "unique" turns, as one has only to describe its very latest result as the "task" which "in truth originally it set itself". Thereby earlier times acquire a bizarre and hitherto unprecedented appearance. It produces a striking impression, and does not require great production costs. As, for instance, if one says that the real "task" which the institution of landed property "originally set itself" was to replace people by sheep — a consequence which has recently become manifest in Scotland, etc., or that the proclamation of the Capet dynasty[45] "originally in truth set itself the task" of sending Louis XVI to the guillotine and M. Guizot into the government. The important thing is to do it in a solemn, pious, priestly way, to draw a deep breath, and then suddenly to burst out: "Now, at last, *one* can state it."

What Saint Max says about the moderns in the above section (pp. 33-37) is only the prologue to the spirit history which is in store for us. Here, too, we see how he tries "to rid himself as quickly as possible" of empirical facts and parades before us the same categories as in the case of the ancients — *reason, heart, spirit*, etc.— only they are given different names. The Sophists become sophistical scholastics, "humanists, Machiavellism (the art of printing, the New World", etc.; cf. Hegel's *Geschichte der Philosophie*,[a] III, p. 128) who represent reason; Socrates is transformed into Luther, who extols the heart (Hegel, l.c., p. 227), and of the post-Reformation period we learn that during that time it was a matter of "empty cordiality" (which in the section about the ancients was called "purity of heart", cf. Hegel, l.c., p. 241). All this on page 34. In this way Saint Max "proves" that "Christianity takes a course similar to that of antiquity". After Luther he no longer even troubles to provide names for his categories; he hurries in seven-league boots to modern German philosophy. Four appositions ("until nothing remains but empty cordiality, all the universal love of mankind, love of *man*, consciousness of freedom, 'self-consciousness'", p. 34; Hegel, l.c., pp. 228, 229), four words fill the gulf between Luther and Hegel and "only thus is Christianity completed". This whole argument is achieved in one masterly sentence, with the help of such levers as "at last" — "and from that time"—"since *one*"—"also"—"from day to day"—"until finally", etc., a sentence which the reader can verify for himself on the classic page 34 already mentioned.

Finally Saint Max gives us a few more examples of his faith, showing that he is so little ashamed of the Gospel that he asserts: "We really are nothing but spirit", and maintains that at the end of the ancient world "after long efforts" the "spirit" has really "rid itself of the world". And immediately afterwards he once more betrays the secret of his scheme, by declaring of the Christian spirit that "*like a youth* it entertains plans for improving or saving the world". All this on page 36.

---

[a] G.W.F. Hegel, *Vorlesungen über die Geschichte der Philosophie.—Ed.*

"So he carried me away in the spirit into the wilderness: and I saw a woman sit upon a scarlet-coloured beast, full of names of blasphemy.... And upon her forehead was a name written, Mystery, Babylon the Great ... and I saw the woman drunken with the blood of the saints", etc. (Revelation of St. John, 17, Verses 3, 5, 6.)

The apocalyptic prophet did not prophesy accurately this time. Now at last, after Stirner has acclaimed *man*, one can state that he ought to have said: So he carried me into the wilderness of the spirit. And I saw a man sit upon a scarlet-coloured beast, full of blasphemy of names ... and upon his forehead was a name written, Mystery, the unique ... and I saw the man drunken with the blood of the holy, etc.

So we now enter the wilderness of the spirit.

A. The Spirit (Pure History of Spirits)

The first thing we learn about the "spirit" is that it is not the spirit but "the *realm* of spirits" that "is immensely large". Saint Max has nothing to say immediately of the spirit except that "an immensely large realm of spirits" exists — just as all he knows of the Middle Ages is that this period lasted for "a long time". Having presupposed that this "realm of spirits" exists, he subsequently proves its existence with the help of ten theses.

1. The spirit is not a free spirit until it is not occupied *w i t h itself alone*, until it is not "solely concerned" *w i t h its own* world, the "spiritual" world (first with itself alone and then with its own world).
2. "It is a *free* spirit only *in* a world of its own."
3. "Only *b y m e a n s o f* a spiritual world is the spirit really spirit."
4. "Before the spirit has created its world of spirits, it is not spirit."...
5. "Its creations make it spirit."...
6. "Its creations are its world."...
7. "The spirit is the creator of a spiritual world." ...
8. "The spirit exists only when it creates the spiritual."...
9. "Only together with the spiritual, which is its creation, is it real."...
10. "*But* the works or offspring of the spirit are nothing but—spirits." (Pp. 38-39.)

In thesis 1 the "spiritual world" is again immediately presupposed as existing, instead of being deduced, and this thesis 1 is again preached to us in theses 2-9 in eight new transformations. At the end of thesis 9 we find ourselves exactly where we were at the end of thesis 1 — and then in thesis 10 a "*but*" suddenly introduces us to "*spirits*", about whom so far nothing has been said.

"*Since* the spirit exists only by creating the spiritual, *we look* around for its first creations." (P.41.)

According to theses 3, 4, 5, 8, and 9, however, the spirit is its own creation. This is now expressed thus, the spirit, i.e., the first creation of the spirit, "must arise out of nothing" ... "it must first create itself" ... "its first creation is itself, the spirit". (Ibid.) "When it has accomplished this creative act there follows from then on a natural reproduction of creations *just as, according to the myth*, only the first human beings had to be created and the rest of the human race was reproduced of itself." (Ibid.)

"However mystical this may sound, we nevertheless experience this daily. Are you a thinking person before you think? In creating your *first thought*, you create *yourself, the thinker*, for you do not think until you think, i.e.,"—i.e.,—"*have* some thought. Is it not your singing alone that makes you a singer, your speech that makes you a speaking person? Well, in the same way only the creation of the spiritual makes you spirit."

Our saintly conjurer assumes that the spirit creates the spiritual in order to draw the conclusion that the spirit creates itself *as spirit*; on the other hand, he assumes it *as spirit* in order to allow it to arrive at its spiritual creations (which, "according to the myth, are reproduced of themselves" and become spirits). So far we have the long-familiar orthodox-Hegelian phrases. The genuinely "unique" exposition of what Saint Max wants to say only begins with the example he gives. That is to say, if Jacques le bonhomme cannot get any further, if even "One" and "It" are unable to float his stranded ship, "Stirner" calls his third serf to his assistance, the "You", who never leaves him in the lurch and on whom he can rely in extremity. This "You" is an individual whom we are not encountering for the first time, a pious and faithful servant,[a] whom we have seen going through fire and water, a worker in the vineyard of his lord, a man who does not allow anything to terrify him, in a word he is: Szeliga.* When "Stirner" is in the utmost plight in his exposition he cries out: Szeliga, help![c]— and trusty Eckart Szeliga immediately puts his shoulder to the wheel to get the cart out of the mire. We shall have more to say later about Saint Max's relation to Szeliga.

It is a question of spirit which creates *itself* out of *nothing*, hence it is a question of *nothing*, which *out of nothing* makes itself *spirit*. From this Saint Max derives the creation of Szeliga's spirit from Szeliga. And who else if not Szeliga could "Stirner" count on allowing himself to be put in the place of nothing in the manner indicated above? Who could be taken in by such a trick but Szeliga, who feels highly flattered at being

* Cf. *Die heilige Familie, oder Kritik der kritischen Kritik*, where the earlier exploits of this man of God have already been set forth.[b]

[a] Matthew 25:21.— *Ed.*
[b] See Karl Marx and Frederick Engels, *Collected Works*, Vol. 4, pp. 55-77.— *Ed.*
[c] A paraphrase of the expression "Samuel, hilf!" (Samuel, help!) from Carl Maria von Weber's opera *Der Freischütz* (libretto by Friedrich Kind), Act II, Scene 6.— *Ed.*

allowed to appear at all as one of the *dramatis personae*? What
Saint Max had to prove was not that a given "you", i.e., the
given Szeliga, becomes a thinker, speaker, singer from the
moment when he begins to think, speak, sing—but that the
thinker creates *himself out of nothing* by beginning to think, that
the *singer* creates *himself out of nothing* by beginning to sing,
etc., and it is not even the thinker and the singer, but the *thought*
and the *singing* as subjects that create *themselves out of nothing*
by beginning to think and to sing. For the rest, "Stirner makes
only the extremely simple reflection" and states only the
"extremely popular" proposition (cf. *Wigand*, p. 156) that
Szeliga develops one of his qualities by developing it. There is,
of course, absolutely nothing "to be wondered at" in the fact
that Saint Max does not even "make" correctly "such simple
reflections", but expresses them incorrectly in order thereby to
prove a still much more incorrect proposition with the aid of the
most incorrect logic in the world.

Far from it being true that "out of nothing" I make myself, for
example, a "speaker", the nothing which forms the basis here is
a very manifold something, the real individual, his speech
organs, a definite stage of physical development, an existing
language and dialects, ears capable of hearing and a human
environment from which it is possible to hear something, etc.,
etc. Therefore, in the development of a property something is
created by something out of something, and by no means
comes, as in Hegel's *Logik*, from nothing, through nothing to
nothing.[a]

Now that Saint Max has his faithful Szeliga close at hand,
everything goes forward smoothly again. We shall see how, by
means of his "you", he again transforms the spirit into the
youth, exactly as he earlier transformed the youth into the
spirit; here we shall again find the whole history of the youth
repeated almost word for word, only with a few camouflaging
alterations—just as the "immensely large realm of spirits"
mentioned on page 37 was nothing but the "realm of the spirit",
to found and enlarge which was the "aim" of the spirit of the
youth. (P.17.)

"*Just as* you, however, distinguish yourself from the thinker, singer,
speaker, *so* you distinguish yourself no less from the spirit and are well aware
that you are something else as well as spirit. However, *just as* in the enthusiasm
of thinking it may *easily* happen that sight and hearing fail the thinking ego, *so*
the enthusiasm of the spirit has seized you *too, and* you *now* aspire with all your
might to become wholly spirit and merged in spirit. The spirit is your ideal,
something unattained, something of the beyond: spirit means your— God, 'God

---

[a] Cf. G.W.F. Hegel, *Wissenschaft der Logik*, Th. I, Abt. 2.— *Ed.*

is spirit'[a].... You inveigh against yourself, you who cannot get rid of a relie of the non-spiritual. Instead of saying: I am more than spirit, *you say* contritely: I am less than spirit, and I can only envisage spirit, pure spirit, or the spirit which is nothing but spirit, but I am not it, *and since I am not it, then it is an other*, it exists as an other, whom I call 'God'."

After previously for a long time occupying ourselves with the trick of making something out of nothing, we now suddenly, perfectly "naturally", come to an individual who is something else as well as spirit, consequently is something, and wants to become pure spirit, i.e., nothing. This much easier problem, i.e., to turn something into nothing, once again poses the whole story of the youth, who "has yet to seek the perfect spirit", and one needs merely to repeat the old phrases from pages 17-18 to be extricated from all difficulties. Particularly, when one has such an obedient and gullible servant as Szeliga, on whom "Stirner" can impose the idea that *just as* "in the enthusiasm of thinking it may *easily*"(!) "happen that sight and hearing fail" him, "Stirner", *so* he, Szeliga, has also been "seized with the enthusiasm of the spirit" and he, Szeliga, "is now aspiring with all his might to *become* spirit", instead of acquiring spirit, that is to say, he now has to play the role of the youth as presented on page 18. Szeliga believes it and in fear and trembling he obeys; he obeys when Saint Max thunders at him: The spirit is your ideal—your God. You do this for me, you do that for me. Now you "inveigh", now "you say", now "you *can* envisage", etc. When "Stirner" imposes on him the idea that "the pure spirit is an other, for he" (Szeliga) "is *not* it", then in truth, it is only Szeliga who is capable of believing him and who gabbles the entire nonsense after him, word for word. Incidentally, the method by which Jacques le bonhomme makes up this nonsense was already exhaustively analysed when dealing with the youth. Since you are well aware that you are something else as well as a mathematician, you aspire to become wholly a mathematician, to become merged in mathematics, the mathematician is your ideal, mathematician means your—God. You say contritely: I am less than a mathematician and I can only envisage the mathematician, and since I am not him, then he is an other, he exists as an other, whom I call "God". Someone else in Szeliga's place would say—Arago.

"Now, at last, after" we have proved Stirner's thesis to be a repetition of the "youth", "one can state" that he "in truth originally set himself no other task" than to identify the spirit of Christian asceticism with spirit in general, and to identify the

[a] John 4:24.— *Ed.*

frivolous esprit, for example, of the eighteenth century with Christian spiritlessness.

It follows, therefore, that the necessity of spirit dwelling in the beyond, i.e., being God, is not to be explained, as Stirner asserts, "because ego and spirit are different names for different things, because ego is not spirit and spirit is not ego". (P. 42.) The explanation lies in the "enthusiasm of the spirit" which is ascribed without any grounds to Szeliga and which makes him an ascetic, i.e., a man who wishes to become God (pure spirit), and because he is not able to do this posits God outside himself. But it was a matter of the spirit having first to create *itself* out of nothing and then having to create *spirits* out of itself. Instead of this, Szeliga now produces God (the unique spirit that makes its appearance here) not because he, Szeliga, is the *spirit*, but because he is Szeliga, i.e., imperfect spirit, unspiritual spirit, and therefore at the same time non-spirit. But Saint Max does not say a word about how the Christian conception of spirit as God arises, although this is now no longer such a clever feat; he assumes the existence of this conception in order to explain it.

The history of the creation of the spirit "has in truth originally set itself no other task" than to put Stirner's stomach among the stars.

"Precisely because we are not the *spirit* which dwells within us, for that very reason we had to	Precisely because we are not the *stomach* which dwells within us, for that very reason we had to

put it outside of ourselves; it was not us, and therefore we could not conceive it as existing except outside of ourselves, beyond us, in the *beyond*." (P. 43.)

It was a matter of the spirit having first to create itself and then having to create something other than itself out of itself; the question was: What is this something else? No answer is given to this question, but after the above-mentioned "various transformations" and twists, it becomes distorted into the following new question:

"The spirit is *something other* than the ego. But what is this something other?" (P. 45.)

Now, therefore, the question arises: What is the spirit other than the ego? whereas the original question was: What is the spirit, owing to its creation out of nothing, other than itself? With this Saint Max jumps to the next "transformation".

B. The Possessed (Impure History of Spirits)

Without realising it, Saint Max has so far done no more than give instruction in the art of spirit-seeing, by regarding the ancient and modern world only as the "pseudo-body of a spirit", as a spectral phenomenon, and seeing in it only struggles of spirits. Now, however, he consciously and *ex professo* gives instruction in the art of ghost-seeing.

Instructions in the art of seeing spirits. First of all one must become transformed into a complete fool, i.e., imagine oneself to be Szeliga, and then say to oneself, as Saint Max does to this Szeliga: "Look around you in the world and say for yourself whether a spirit is not looking at you from everywhere!" If one can bring oneself to imagine this, then the spirits will come "easily", of themselves; in a "flower" one sees only the "creator", in the mountains — a "spirit of loftiness", in water — a "spirit of longing" or the longing of the spirit, and one hears "millions of spirits speak through the mouths of people". If one has achieved this level, if one can exclaim with Stirner: "*Yes*, ghosts are teeming in the whole world," then "it is not difficult to advance to the point" (p. 93) where one makes the further exclamation: "Only *in* it? *No*, the world itself is an apparition" (let your communication be, Yea, yea; Nay, nay: for whatsoever is more than these cometh of evil,[a] i.e., a logical transition), "it is the wandering pseudo-body of a spirit, it is an apparition." Then cheerfully "look near at hand or into the distance, you are surrounded by a ghostly world.... You see spirits". If you are an ordinary person you can be satisfied with that, but if you are thinking of ranking yourself with Szeliga, then you can also look into yourself and then "you should not be surprised" if, in these circumstances and from the heights of Szeligality, you discover also that "your spirit is a ghost haunting your body", that you yourself are a ghost which "awaits salvation, that is, a spirit". Thereby you will have arrived at the point where you are capable of seeing "spirits" and "ghosts" in "all" people, and therewith spirit-seeing "reaches its final goal". (Pp. 46, 47.)

The basis of this instruction, only much more correctly expressed, is to be found in Hegel, *inter alia*, in the *Geschichte der Philosophie*, III, pp. 124, 125.

Saint Max has such faith in his own instruction that as a result he himself becomes Szeliga and asserts that

"ever since the world was made flesh,[b] the world *is* spiritualised, bewitched, a ghost". (P. 47.)

"Stirner" "sees spirits".

Saint Max intends to give us a phenomenology of the Christian spirit and in his usual way seizes on only one aspect.

[a] Matthew 5:37.—*Ed.*
[b] John 1:14.— *Ed.*

For the Christian the world was only spiritualised but equally *de*spiritualised as, for example, Hegel quite correctly admits in the passage mentioned, where he brings the two aspects into relation with each other, which Saint Max should also have done if he wanted to proceed historically. As against the world's despiritualisation in the Christian consciousness, the ancients, "who saw gods everywhere", can with equal justification be regarded as the spiritualisers of the world — a conception which our saintly dialectician rejects with the well-meaning warning: "Gods, my dear modern man, are not spirits." P. 47.) Pious Max recognises only the *holy* spirit as spirit.

But even if he had given us this phenomenology (which after Hegel is moreover superfluous), he would all the same have given us nothing. The standpoint at which people are content with such tales about spirits is itself a religious one, because for people who adopt it religion is a satisfactory answer, they regard religion as *causa sui*[a] (for both "self-consciousness" and "man" are still religious) instead of explaining it from the empirical conditions and showing how definite relations of industry and intercourse are necessarily connected with a definite form of society, hence, with a definite form of state and hence, with a definite form of religious consciousness. If Stirner had looked at the real history of the Middle Ages, he could have found why the Christian's notion of the world took precisely this form in the Middle Ages, and how it happened that it subsequently passed into a different one; he could have found that *"Christianity" has no history whatever* and that all the different forms in which it was visualised at various times were not "self-determinations" and "further developments" "of the religious spirit", but were brought about by wholly empirical causes in no way dependent on any influence of the religious spirit.

Since Stirner "does not stick to the rules" (p. 45), it is possible, before dealing in more detail with spirit-seeing, to say here and now that the various "transformations" of Stirner's people and their world consist merely in the transformation of the entire history of the world into the body of Hegel's philosophy; into ghosts, which only apparently are an "other being" of the thoughts of the Berlin professor. In the *Phänomenologie*, the Hegelian bible, "the book", individuals are first of all transformed into "consciousness" [and the] world

---

[a] Its own cause.— *Ed.*

into "object", whereby the manifold variety of forms of life and history is reduced to a different attitude of "consciousness" to the "object". This different attitude is reduced, in turn, to three cardinal relations: 1) the relation of consciousness to the object as to truth, or to truth as mere object (for example, sensual consciousness, natural religion, Ionic philosophy, Catholicism, the authoritarian state, etc.); 2) the relation of consciousness as *the true* to the object (reason, spiritual religion, Socrates, Protestantism, the French Revolution); 3) the true relation of consciousness to truth as object, or to the object as truth (logical thinking, speculative philosophy, the spirit as existing for the spirit). In Hegel, too, the first relation is defined as God the Father, the second as Christ, the third as the Holy Spirit, etc. Stirner already used these transformations when speaking of child and youth, of ancient and modern, and he repeats them later in regard to Catholicism and Protestantism, the Negro and the Mongol, etc., and then accepts this series of camouflages of a thought in all good faith as the world against which he has to assert and maintain himself as a "corporeal individual".

Second set of instructions in spirit-seeing. How to transform the world into the spectre of truth, and oneself into something made holy or spectral. A conversation between Saint Max and his servant Szeliga. (Pp. 47, 48.)

Saint Max: "You have spirit, for you have thoughts. What are your thoughts?"

Szeliga: "Spiritual entities."

Saint Max: "Hence they are not things?"

Szeliga: "No, but they are the spirit of things, the important element in all things, their innermost essence, their idea."

Saint Max: "What do you think is, therefore, not merely your thought?"

Szeliga: "On the contrary, it is the most real, genuinely true thing in the world: it is truth itself; when I but truly think, I think the truth. I can admittedly be mistaken about the truth and *fail to perceive* it, but when I truly *perceive,* then the object of my perception is the truth."

Saint Max: "Thus, you endeavour all the time to perceive the truth?"

Szeliga: "For me the truth is sacred [a] .... *The truth* I cannot abolish; in the truth I believe, and therefore I investigate into its nature; there is nothing higher than it, it is eternal. The truth is sacred, eternal, it is the holy, the eternal."

Saint Max (indignantly): "But you, by allowing yourself to become filled with this holiness, become yourself holy."

Thus, when Szeliga truly perceives some object, the object ceases to be an object and becomes "the truth". This is the first manufacture of spectres on a large scale.— It is now no longer a

---

[a] Here and in the following passages the German word *heilig* and its derivatives are used, which can mean: holy, pious, sacred, sacredness, saintly, saint, to consecrate, etc.— *Ed.*

matter of perceiving objects, but of perceiving the truth; first he perceives objects truly, which he defines as the truth of perception, and he transforms this into perception of the truth. But after Szeliga has thus allowed truth as a spectre to be imposed on him by the threatening saint, his stern master strikes home with a question of conscience, whether he is filled "all the time" with longing for the truth, whereupon the thoroughly confused Szeliga blurts out somewhat prematurely: "For me the truth is sacred." But he immediately notices his error and tries to correct it, by shamefacedly transforming objects no longer into the truth, but into a number of truths, and abstracting "the truth" as the truth of these truths, "the truth" which he can now no longer abolish after he has *distinguished* it from truths which are capable of being abolished. Thereby it becomes "eternal". But not satisfied with giving it predicates such as "sacred, eternal", he transforms it into the holy, the eternal, as subject. After this, of course, Saint Max can explain to him that having become "filled" with this holiness, he "himself becomes holy" and "should not be surprised" if he now "finds nothing but a spectre" in himself. Then our saint begins a sermon:

"The holy, moreover, is not for your senses" and quite consistently appends by means of the conjunction "*and*": "never will you, as a sensuous being, discover its traces"; that is to say, after sensuous objects are "all gone" and "the truth", "the sacred truth", "the holy" has taken their place. "But" — obviously! — "for your faith or more exactly for your spirit" (for your lack of spirit), "for it is itself *something* spiritual" (*per appositionem*[a]), "*a spirit*" (again *per appos.*), "is *spirit for the spirit*".

Such is the art of transforming the ordinary world, "objects", by means of an arithmetical series of *appositions*, into "spirit for the spirit". Here we can only admire this dialectical method of appositions — later we shall have occasion to explore it and present it in all its classical beauty.[b]

The method of appositions can also be reversed — for example here, after we have once produced "the holy" it does not receive further appositions, but is made the apposition of a new definition; this is combining progression with equation. Thus, as a result of some dialectical process "there remains the idea of another entity" which "I should serve more than myself" (*per appos.*), "which for me should be more important than everything else" (*per appos.*), "in short — a something *in which I should seek my true salvation*" (and finally *per appos.* the return to the first series), and which becomes "something 'holy'". (P.

---

[a] By means of an apposition.— *Ed.*

[b] See this volume, pp. 290-91 *et seqq.*—*Ed.*

48.) We have here two progressions which are equated to each other and can thus provide the opportunity for a great variety of equations. We shall deal with this later. By this method too, "the sacred", which hitherto we have been acquainted with only as a purely theoretical designation of purely theoretical relations, has acquired a new practical meaning as "something in which I should seek my true salvation", which makes it possible to make the holy the opposite of the egoist. Incidentally we need hardly mention that this entire dialogue with the sermon that follows is nothing but another repetition of the story of the youth already met with three or four times before.

Here, having arrived at the "egoist", we need not stick to Stirner's "rules" either, because, firstly, we have to present his argument in all its purity, free from any intervening intermezzos, and, secondly, because in any case these intermezzi (on the analogy of "*a* Lazaroni"—*Wigand*, p. 159, the word should be Lazzarone—Sancho would say intermezzi's) will occur again in other parts of the book, for Stirner, far from obeying his own requirement "always to draw back into himself", on the contrary expresses himself again and again. We shall only just mention that the question raised on page 45: What is this something distinct from the "ego" that is the spirit? is now answered to the effect that it is the holy, i.e., that which is foreign to the "ego", and that everything that is foreign to the "ego" is — thanks to some unstated appositions, appositions "in themselves"— accordingly without more ado regarded as spirit. Spirit, the holy, the foreign are identical ideas, on which he declares war, in the same way almost word for word as he did at the very outset in regard to the youth and the man. We have, therefore, still not advanced a step further than we had on page 20.

a) The Apparition

Saint Max now begins to deal seriously with the "spirits" that are "offspring of the spirit" (p. 39), with the ghostliness of everything. (P. 47.) At any rate, he imagines so. Actually, however, he only substitutes a new name for his former conception of history according to which people were from the outset the representatives of general concepts. These general concepts appear here first of all in the Negroid form as objective spirits having for people the character of objects, and at this level are called spectres or — *apparitions*. The chief spectre is, of course, "man" himself, because, according to what has been previously said, people only exist for one another as representatives of a universal — essence, concept, the holy, the foreign, the spirit — i.e., only as spectral persons, spectres, and because, according to Hegel's *Phänomenologie*, page 255 and elsewhere, the spirit, insofar as for man it has the "form of thinghood", is another man (see below about "the *man*").

Thus, we see here the skies opening and the various kinds of spectres passing before us one after the other. Jacques le bonhomme forgets only that he has already caused ancient and modern times to parade before us like gigantic spectres, compared with which all the harmless fancies about God, etc., are sheer trifles.

Spectre No. 1: the *supreme being,* God. (P. 53.) As was to be expected from what has preceded, Jacques le bonhomme, whose faith moves all the mountains[a] of world history, believes that "for thousands of years people have set themselves the *task*", "have tired themselves out struggling with the awful impossibility, the endless Danaidean labour" — "to prove the existence of God". We need not waste any more words on this incredible belief.

Spectre No. 2: *essence.* What our good man says about essence is limited — apart from what has been copied out of Hegel — to "pompous words and miserable thoughts". (P. 53.) "The advance from" essence "to" world essence "is not difficult", and this world essence is, of course,

Spectre No. 3: the *vanity of the world.* There is nothing to say about this except that from it "easily" arises

Spectre No. 4: *good and evil beings.* Something, indeed, could be said about this but is not said — and one passes at once to the next:

Spectre No. 5: the *essence and its realm.* We should not be at all surprised that we find here essence for the second time in our honest author, for he is fully aware of his "clumsiness" (*Wigand*, p. 166), and therefore repeats everything several times in order not to be misunderstood. Essence is here in the first place defined as the proprietor of a "realm" and then it is said of it that it is "essence" (p. 54), after which it is swiftly transformed into

Spectre No. 6: *"essences".* To perceive and to recognise them, and them alone, is religion. "Their realm" (of essences) "is — a realm of essences." (P. 54.) Here there suddenly appears for no apparent reason

---

[a] Cf. 1 Corinthians 13:2.— *Ed.*

Spectre No. 7: the *God-Man*, Christ. Of him Stirner is able to say that he was "*corpulent*". If Saint Max does not believe in Christ, he at least believes in his "actual corpus". According to Stirner, Christ introduced great distress into history, and our sentimental saint relates with tears in his eyes "how the strongest Christians have racked their brains in order to comprehend him"—indeed,

"there has never been a spectre that caused such mental anguish, and no shaman, spurring himself into wild frenzy and nerve-racking convulsions, can have suffered such agony as Christians have suffered on account of this most incomprehensible spectre".

Saint Max sheds a sympathetic tear at the grave of the victims of Christ and then passes on to the "horrible being",

Spectre No. 8, *man*. Here our bold writer is seized with immediate "horror"—"he is terrified of himself", he sees in every man a "frightful spectre", a "sinister spectre" in which something "stalks". (Pp. 55, 56.) He feels highly uncomfortable. The split between phenomenon and essence gives him no peace. He is like Nabal, Abigail's husband, of whom it is written that his essence too was separated from his phenomenal appearance: "And there was a man in Maon, *whose possessions[a] were in Carmel.*" (1 Samuel 25:2.) But in the nick of time, before the "mental anguish" causes Saint Max in desperation to put a bullet through his head, he suddenly remembers the ancients who "took no notice of anything of the kind in their slaves". This leads him to

Spectre No. 9, *the national spirit* (p. 56), about which too Saint Max, who can no longer be restrained, indulges in "frightful" fantasies, in order to transform

Spectre No. 10, "*everything*", into an apparition and, finally, where all enumeration ends, to hurl together in the class of spectres the "holy spirit", truth, justice, law, the good cause (which he still cannot forget) and half a dozen other things completely foreign to one another.

Apart from this there is nothing remarkable in the whole chapter except that Saint Max's faith moves an historical mountain. That is to say, he utters the opinion (p. 56):

"Only for the sake of a supreme being has anyone ever been worshipped, only as a spectre has he been regarded as a sanctified, i.e." (*that is!*) "protected and recognised person."

---

[a] In German a pun on the word *Wesen* (essence)—in Luther's Bible translation *Wesen* is used in its old meaning: "possession".— *Ed.*

If we shift this mountain, moved by faith alone, back into its proper place, then "it will read": Only for the sake of persons who are protected, i.e., who protect themselves, and who are privileged, i.e., who seize privileges for themselves, have supreme beings been worshipped and spectres sanctified. Saint Max imagines, for example, that in antiquity, when each people was held together by material relations and interests, e.g., by the hostility of the various tribes, etc., when owing to a shortage of productive forces each had either to be a slave or to possess slaves, etc., etc., when, therefore, belonging to a particular people was a matter of "the most natural interest" (*Wigand*, p. [162])—that then, it was only the concept people, or "nationality" that gave birth to these interests from itself; he imagines also that in modern times, when free competition and world trade gave birth to hypocritical, bourgeois cosmopolitanism and the notion of man—that here, on the contrary, the later philosophical construction of man brought about those relations as its "revelations". (P. 51.) It is the same with religion, with the realm of essences, which he considers the unique realm, but concerning the essence of which he knows nothing, for otherwise he must have known that religion *as such* has neither essence, nor realm. In religion people make their empirical world into an entity that is only conceived, imagined, that confronts them as something foreign. This again is by no means to be explained from other concepts, from "self-consciousness" and similar nonsense, but from the entire hitherto existing mode of production and intercourse, which is just as independent of the pure concept as the invention of the self-acting mule[a] and the use of railways are independent of Hegelian philosophy. If he wants to speak of an "essence" of religion, i.e., of a material basis of this inessentiality,[b] then he should look for it neither in the "essence of man", nor in the predicates of God, but in the material world which each stage of religious development finds in existence. (Cf. above *Feuerbach*.)[c]

All the "spectres" which have filed before us were concepts. These concepts—leaving aside their real basis (which Stirner in any case leaves aside)—understood as concepts inside consciousness, as thoughts in people's heads, transferred from

---

[a] The English term is used in the original.— *Ed.*

[b] In German a pun on the words *Wesen*—essence, substance, being—and *Unwesen*—literally inessence. *Unwesen* can be rendered in English as disorder, nuisance, confusion or, in a different context, monster.— *Ed.*

[c] See this volume, pp. 61-62.— *Ed.*

their objectivity back into the subject, elevated from substance into self-consciousness, are — *whimsies* or *fixed ideas.*

Concerning the origin of Saint Max's history of ghosts, see Feuerbach in *Anekdota* II, p. 66,[a] where it is stated:

> "Theology is *belief in ghosts.* Ordinary theology, however, has its ghosts in the sensuous imagination, speculative theology has them in non-sensuous abstraction."

And since Saint Max shares the belief of all critical speculative philosophers of modern times that thoughts, which have become independent, objectified thoughts — ghosts — have ruled the world and continue to rule it, and that all history up to now was the history of theology, nothing could be easier for him than to transform history into a history of ghosts. Sancho's history of ghosts, therefore, rests on the traditional belief in ghosts of the speculative philosophers.

b) W h i m s y

"Man, there are spectres in your head!... You have a fixed idea!" thunders Saint Max at his slave Szeliga. "Don't think I am joking," he threatens him. Don't dare to think that the solemn "Max Stirner" is capable of joking.

The man of God is again in need of his faithful Szeliga in order to pass from the object to the subject, from the apparition to the whimsy.

Whimsy is the hierarchy in the single individual, the domination of thought "in him over him". After the world has confronted the fantasy-making youth (of page 20) as a world of his "feverish fantasies", as a world of ghosts, "the offsprings of his own head" inside his head begin to dominate him. The world of his feverish fantasies — this is the step forward he has made — now exists as the world of his deranged mind. Saint Max — the man who is confronted by "the world of the moderns" in the form of the fantasy-making youth — has necessarily to declare that "almost the whole of mankind consists of veritable fools, inmates of a mad-house". (P. 57.)

The whimsy which Saint Max discovers in the heads of people is nothing but his own whimsy — the whimsy of the

---

[a] Ludwig Feuerbach, "Vorläufige Thesen zur Reformation der Philosophie".— *Ed.*

"saint" who views the world *sub specie aeterni*[a] and who takes both the hypocritical phrases of people and their illusions for the true motives of their actions; that is why our naïve, pious man confidently pronounces the great proposition: "Almost all mankind clings to something higher." (P. 57.)

"Whimsy" is "a fixed idea", i. e., "an idea which has subordinated man to itself" or — as is said later in more popular form — all kinds of absurdities which people "*have stuffed into their heads*". With the utmost ease, Saint Max arrives at the conclusion that everything that has subordinated people to itself — for example, the need to produce in order to live, and the relations dependent on this — is such an "absurdity" or "*fixed idea*". Since the child's world is the only "world of things", as we learned in the myth of "a man's life", everything that does not exist "for the child" (at times also for the animal) is in any case an "idea" and "easily also" a "fixed idea". We are still a long way from getting rid of the youth and the child.

The chapter on whimsy aims merely at establishing the existence of the category of whimsy in the history of "man". The actual struggle against whimsy is waged throughout the entire "book" and particularly in the second part. Hence a few examples of whimsy can suffice us here.

On page 59, Jacques le bonhomme believes that

"our newspapers are full of politics, because they are in the grip of the delusion that man was created in order to become a *zoon politikon*".[b]

Hence, according to Jacques le bonhomme, people engage in politics because our newspapers are full of them! If a church father were to glance at the stock exchange reports of our newspapers, he could not judge differently from Saint Max and would have to say: these newspapers are full of stock exchange reports because they are in the grip of the delusion that man was created in order to engage in financial speculation. Thus, it is not the newspapers that possess whimsies, but whimsies that possess "Stirner".

Stirner explains the condemnation of incest and the institutions of monogamy from "the holy", "they are the holy". If among the Persians incest is not condemned, and if the institution of polygamy occurs among the Turks, then in those

---

[a] Under the aspect of eternity (see Benedictus Spinoza, *Ethica*, Pars quinta).— *Ed.*

[b] Political animal — thus Aristotle defines man at the beginning of *De republica*, Book I.— *Ed.*

places incest and polygamy are "the holy". It is not possible to see any difference between these two "holies" other than that the nonsense with which the Persians and Turks have "stuffed their heads" is different from that with which the Christian Germanic peoples have stuffed their heads.— Such is the church father's manner of "detaching himself" from history "in good time".— Jacques le bonhomme has so little inkling of the real, materialist causes for the condemnation of polygamy and incest in certain social conditions that he considers this condemnation to be merely the dogma of a creed and in common with every philistine imagines that when a man is imprisoned for a crime of this kind, it means that "moral purity" is confining him in a "house of moral correction" (p. 60)— just as jails in general seem to him to be houses for moral correction— in this respect he is at a lower level than the educated bourgeois, who has a better understanding of the matter — cf. the literature on prisons. "Stirner's" "jails" are the most trite illusions of the Berlin burgher which for him, however, hardly deserve to be called a "house of moral correction".

After Stirner, with the help of an "episodically included" "historical reflection", has discovered that

"it had to come to pass that the whole man with all his abilities would prove to be religious" (p. 64) "so, too, in point of fact" "it is not surprising" — "for we are now so thoroughly religious"—"that" the *oath* "of the *members of the jury* condemns us to death and that by means of the '*official oath*' the police constable, as a good Christian, has us put in the clink".

When a gendarme stops him for smoking in the Tiergarten,[46] the cigar is knocked out of his mouth not by the royal Prussian gendarme who is paid to do so and shares in the money from fines, but by the "official oath". In precisely the same way the power of the bourgeois in the jury court becomes transformed for Stirner— owing to the pseudo-holy appearance which the *amis du commerce* assume here — into the power of making a vow, the power of the oath, into the "*holy*". "Verily, I say unto you: I have not found so great faith, no, not in Israel." (Matthew 8:10.)

"For some persons a thought becomes a maxim, so that it is not the person who possesses the maxim, but rather the latter that possesses him, and with the maxim he again acquires a firm standpoint." But "it is not of him that willeth, nor of him that runneth, but of God that sheweth mercy". (Romans 9:16.)

Therefore Saint Max has on the same page to receive several thorns in the flesh[a] and must give us a number of maxims:

---

[a] 2 Corinthians 12:7.— *Ed.*

firstly, *the* maxim [to recognise] no maxims, with which goes, secondly, the maxim not to have any firm standpoint; thirdly, the maxim "although we *should* possess spirit, spirit *should* not possess us"; and fourthly, the maxim that one should also be aware of one's flesh, "for only by being aware of his flesh is man fully aware of himself, and only by being fully aware of *himself*, is he aware or rational".

C. THE IMPURELY IMPURE HISTORY OF SPIRITS

a) Negroes and Mongols

We now go back to the beginning of the "unique" historical scheme and nomenclature. The child becomes the Negro, the youth — the Mongol. See "The Economy of the Old Testament".

"The historical reflection on our Mongolhood, which I *shall include episodically* at this point, I present *without any claim* to thoroughness *or even* to authenticity, *but solely because it seems to me that it can contribute* to clarifying the rest." (P. 87.)

Saint Max tries to "clarify" for himself his phrases about the child and the youth by giving them world-embracing names, and he tries to "clarify" these world-embracing names by replacing them with his phrases about the child and the youth. "The *Negroid character* represents *antiquity*, dependence on *things*" (*child*); "the *Mongoloid character* — the period of dependence on *thoughts*, the *Christian* epoch" (the *youth*). (Cf. "The Economy of the Old Testament".) "The following words are reserved for the future: I am owner of the *world of things,* and I am owner of the *world of thoughts.*" (Pp. 87, 88.) This "future" has already happened once, on page 20, in connection with the *man*, and it will occur again later, beginning with page 226.

First "*historical reflection* without claim to thoroughness or even to authenticity": Since Egypt is part of Africa where Negroes live, it follows that "included" "in the Negro era" (p. 88) are the "campaigns of Sesostris", which never took place, and the "significance of Egypt" (the significance it had also at the time of the Ptolemies, Napoleon's expedition to Egypt, Mohammed Ali, the Eastern question, the pamphlets of

Duvergier de Haurannes, etc.), "and of North Africa in general" (and therefore of Carthage, Hannibal's campaign against Rome, and "easily also", the significance of Syracuse and Spain, the Vandals, Tertullian, the Moors, Al Hussein Abu Ali Ben Abdallah Ibn Sina, piratical states, the French in Algeria, Abd-el-Kader, Père Enfantin[47] and the four new toads of the *Charivari*). (P. 88.) Consequently, Stirner clarifies the campaigns of Sesostris, etc., by transferring them to the Negro era, and he clarifies the Negro era by "episodically including" it as a historical illustration of his unique thoughts "about our childhood years".

Second "historical reflection": "To the Mongoloid era belong the campaigns of the Huns and Mongols up to the Russians" (and *Wasserpolacken*[48]); thus here again the campaigns of the Huns and Mongols, together with the Russians, are "clarified" by their inclusion in the "Mongoloid era", and the "Mongoloid era" — by pointing out that it is the era of the phrase "dependence on thoughts", which we have already encountered in connection with the *youth*.

Third "historical reflection":

> In the Mongoloid era the "value of my ego cannot possibly be put at a high level because the *hard* diamond of the *non-ego* is too high in price, because it is still too gritty and impregnable for it to be absorbed and consumed by my ego. On the contrary, people are simply exceptionally busy crawling about on this static world, this substance, like parasitic animalcules on a body from whose juices they extract nourishment, but nevertheless do not devour the body. It is the bustling activity of noxious insects, the industriousness of Mongols. Among the Chinese *indeed* everything remains as of old, etc.... *Therefore*" (because among the Chinese everything remains as of old) "in our Mongol era every change has only been reformatory and corrective, and not destructive, devouring or annihilating. The substance, the object remains. All our industriousness is only the activity of ants and the jumping of fleas ... juggling on the tightrope of the objective", etc. (P. 88, cf. Hegel, *Philosophie der Geschichte*, pp. 113, 118, 119 (unsoftened substance), p. 140, etc., where China is understood as "substantiality".)

We learn here, therefore, that in the *true* Caucasian era people will be guided by the maxim that the earth, "substance", the "object", the "static" has to be devoured, "consumed", "annihilated", "absorbed", "destroyed", and along with the earth the solar system that is inseparable from it. World-devouring "Stirner" has already introduced us to the "reformatory or corrective activity" of the Mongols as the youth's and Christian's "plans for the salvation and *correction* of the world" on page 36. Thus we have still not advanced a step. It is characteristic of the entire "unique" conception of history that the highest stage of this Mongol activity earns the title of "*scientific*" — from which already now the conclusion can be drawn, which Saint Max later tells us, that the culmination of the Mongolian heaven is the Hegelian kingdom of spirits.

Fourth "*historical reflection*". The world on which the Mongols crawl about is now transformed by means of a "flea jump" into the "positive", this into the "precept", and, with the help of a paragraph on page 89, the precept becomes "morality". "Morality appears in its first form as custom" — hence it comes forward as a *person*, but in a trice it becomes transformed into a sphere:

> "To act in accordance with the morals and customs of one's country means *here*" (i. e., in the sphere of morality) "to be moral." "Therefore" (because this occurs in the sphere of morality as a custom) "*pure, moral behaviour in the most straightforward form* is practised in ... *China!*"

Saint Max is unfortunate in his examples. On page 116 in just the same way he attributes to the North Americans the "religion of honesty". He regards the two most rascally nations on earth, the patriarchal swindlers — the Chinese, and the civilised swindlers — the Yankees, as "straightforward", "moral" and "honest". If he had looked up his crib he could have found the North Americans classed as swindlers on page 81 of the *Philosophie der Geschichte* and the Chinese ditto on page 130.

"One" — that friend of the saintly worthy man — now helps him to arrive at *innovation*, and from this an "*and*" brings him back to *custom*, and thus the material is prepared for achieving a master stroke in the

Fifth historical reflection: "There is in fact no doubt that by means of custom man protects himself against the importunity of things, of the world" — for example, from hunger;

"*and*" — as quite naturally follows from this —

"*founds a world of his own*" — which "Stirner" has need of now —

"*in which alone he feels in his native element and at home*",— "*alone*", after he has first by "custom" made himself "at home" in the existing "world" —

"*i. e., builds himself a heaven*" — because China is called the Celestial Empire.

"*For indeed heaven has no other significance than that of being the real homeland of man*" — in this context, however, it signifies the imagined unreality of the real homeland —

"*where nothing alien any longer prevails upon him*", i. e., where what is his own prevails upon him as something alien, and all the rest of the old story. "Or rather", to use Saint Bruno's words, or "it is easily possible", to use Saint Max's words, that this proposition should read as follows:

Stirner's proposition without claim to thoroughness or even to authenticity	Clarified proposition
"There is in fact no doubt that by means of custom man protects himself against the importunity of things, of the world, and founds a world of his own, in which alone he feels in his native element and at home, i. e., builds himself a *heaven*. For indeed 'heaven' has no other significance than that of being the real homeland of man, where nothing alien any longer prevails upon him and rules over him, no earthly influence any longer estranges him from himself, in short, where earthly dross is thrown aside and the struggle against the world has come to an end, where, therefore, nothing is forbidden him any more." (P. 89.)	"There is in fact no doubt" that because China is called the Celestial Empire, because "Stirner" happens to be speaking of China, and as he is "accustomed" by means of ignorance "to protect himself against the importunity of things, of the world, and to found a world of his own, in which alone he feels in his native element and at home"—therefore he "builds himself a heaven" out of the Chinese Celestial Empire. "For indeed" the importunity of the world, of things, "has no other significance than that of being the real" hell of the unique, "in which" everything "prevails upon him and rules over him" as something "alien", but which he is able to transform into a "heaven" by "estranging himself" from all "earthly influences", historical facts and connections, and hence no longer thinks them strange; "in short", it is a sphere "where the earthly", the historical "dross is thrown aside", and where Stirner "does not find" in the "end" "of the world" any more "struggle"—and thereby everything has been said.

Sixth "historical reflection". On page 90, Stirner imagines that

"in China *everything is provided for;* no matter what happens, the Chinese *always knows* how he should behave, and he has no need to decide according *to circumstances; no unforeseen event* will overthrow his celestial calm".

Nor any British bombardment either — he knew exactly "how he should behave", particularly in regard to the unfamiliar steamships and shrapnel-bombs.[49]

Saint Max extracted that from Hegel's *Philosophie der Geschichte*, pages 118 and 127, to which, of course, he had to add something unique, in order to achieve his reflection as given above.

"*Consequently*," continues Saint Max, "*mankind* climbs the first rung of the ladder of education by means of custom, *and since it imagines* that by gaining culture, it has gained heaven, the realm of culture or second nature, it *actually* mounts the first rung of the heavenly ladder." (P. 90.)

"Consequently", i. e., because Hegel begins history with China, and because "the Chinese does not lose his equanimity", "Stirner" transforms mankind into a person who "mounts the first rung of the ladder of culture" and indeed does so "by means of custom", because China has no other meaning for Stirner than that of being the embodiment of "custom". Now it is only a question for our zealot against the holy of transforming the "ladder" into a "heavenly ladder", since China is also called the *Celestial* Empire. "Since mankind imagines" ("where from" does Stirner "know everything that" mankind imagines, see *Wigand*, page 189) — and this ought to have been proved by Stirner — firstly that it transforms "culture" into the "heaven of culture", and secondly that it transforms the "heaven of culture" into the "culture of heaven" — (an alleged notion on the part of mankind which appears on page 91 as a notion of Stirner's and thereby receives its correct expression) —"so it *actually* mounts the first rung of the heavenly ladder". Since it *imagines* that it mounts the first rung of the heavenly ladder — so — it mounts it *actually!* "*Since*" the "youth" "imagines" that he becomes pure spirit, he does actually become such! See the "youth" and the "Christian" on the transition from the world of things to the world of the spirit where the simple formula for this heavenly ladder of "unique" ideas already occurs.

Seventh historical reflection, page 90. "If Mongolism" (it follows immediately after the heavenly ladder, whereby "Stirner", through the alleged notion on the part of mankind, was able to ascertain the existence of a spiritual essence [*Wesen*]), "if Mongolism has established the existence of spiritual beings [*Wesen*]" (rather — if "Stirner" has established his fancy about the spiritual essence of the Mongols), "*then* the Caucasians have fought for thousands of years against these spiritual beings, in order to get to the bottom of them". (The youth, who becomes a man and "tries all the time" "to penetrate behind thoughts", the Christian, who "tries all the time" "to explore the depths of divinity".) Since the Chinese have noted the existence of God knows what spiritual beings ("Stirner" does not note a single one, apart from his heavenly ladder) — so for thousands of years the Caucasians have to wrangle with "these" Chinese "spiritual beings"; moreover, two lines below Stirner puts on record that they actually "stormed the *Mongolian* heaven, the *tien*", and continues: "When will they destroy this heaven, when will they finally become *actual Caucasians* and *find themselves?*"

Here we have the negative unity, already seen earlier as

man, now appearing as the "actual Caucasian", i.e., not Negroid, not Mongolian, but as the *Caucasian Caucasian.* This latter, therefore, as a concept, as essence, is here separated from the actual Caucasians, is counterposed to them as the "ideal of the Caucasian", as a "vocation" in which they should "find themselves", as a "destiny", a "task", as "the holy", as "the holy" Caucasian, "the perfect" Caucasian, "who indeed" is the Caucasian "in heaven— *God".*

"In the sedulous struggle of the Mongolian race, men *had built* a heaven"— so "Stirner" believes (p. 91), forgetting that actual Mongols are much more occupied with sheep than with heaven [a]— "when the people of the Caucasian stock, so long as they ... *have* to do with heaven ... *undertook* the business of storming heaven." *Had built* a heaven, when ... so long as they *have* ... [they] *undertook.* The unassuming "historical reflection" is here expressed in a *consecutio temporum* [b] which also does not "lay claim" to classic form "or even" to grammatical correctness; the construction of the sentences corresponds to the construction of history. "Stirner's" "claims" "are restricted to this" and "thereby achieve their final goal".

Eighth historical reflection, which is the reflection of reflections, the alpha and omega of the whole of Stirner's history: Jacques le bonhomme, as we have pointed out from the beginning, sees in all the movement of nations that has so far taken place merely a sequence of heavens (p. 91), which can also be expressed as follows: successive generations of the Caucasian race up to the present day did nothing but squabble about the concept of morality (p. 92) and "their activity has been restricted to this". (P. 91.) If they had got out of their heads this unfortunate morality, this apparition, they would have achieved something; as it was, they achieved nothing, absolutely nothing, and have to allow Saint Max to set them a task as if they were schoolboys. It is completely in accordance with his view of history that at the end (p. 92) he conjures up speculative philosophy so that "in it this heavenly kingdom, the kingdom of spirits and spectres, should find its proper order"— and that in a later passage speculative philosophy should be conceived as the "perfect kingdom of spirits".

---

[a] In German a pun on the words *die Hämmel*—the sheep, and *die Himmel*—the heavens.— *Ed.*

[b] Sequence of tenses.— *Ed.*

Why it is that for those who regard history in the Hegelian manner the result of all preceding history was finally bound to be the kingdom of spirits perfected and brought into order in speculative philosophy—the solution of this secret "Stirner" could have very simply found by recourse to Hegel himself. To arrive at this result "the concept of spirit must be taken as the basis and *then* it must be shown that history is the process of the spirit itself". (*Geschichte der Philosophie,* III, p. 91.) After the "concept of spirit" has been imposed on history as its basis, it is very easy, of course, to "show" that it is to be discovered everywhere, and then to make this as a process "find its proper order".

After making everything "find its proper order", Saint Max can now exclaim with enthusiasm: "To desire to win freedom for the spirit, that is Mongolism", etc. (cf. p. 17: "To bring to light pure thought, etc.— that is the joy of the youth", etc.), and can declare hypocritically: "*Hence it is obvious* that Mongolism ... represents non-sensuousness and unnaturalness", etc.— when he ought to have said: it is obvious that the Mongol is only the disguised youth who, being the negation of the world of things, can also be called "unnaturalness", "non-sensuousness", etc.

We have again reached the point where the "youth" can pass into the "man": "But who will transform the spirit into its nothing? *He,* who by means of the spirit represented nature as the futile, the finite, the transitory" (i. e., imagined it as such—and, according to page 16 et seq., this was done by the youth, later the Christian, then the Mongol, then the Mongoloid Caucasian, but properly speaking only by idealism), "he alone can also degrade the spirit" (namely in his imagination) "to the same futility" (therefore the Christian, etc.? No, exclaims "Stirner" resorting to a similar trick as on pages 19-20 in the case of the man). "I can do it, each of you can do it who operates and creates" (in his imagination) "as the unrestricted ego", "in a word, the *egoist* can do it" (p. 93), i. e., the man, the Caucasian Caucasian, who therefore is the perfect Christian, the true Christian, the holy one, the *embodiment* of the holy.

Before dealing with the further nomenclature, we also "should like at this point to include an historical reflection" on the origin of Stirner's "historical reflection about our Mongolism"; our reflection differs, however, from Stirner's in that it definitely "lays claim to thoroughness and authenticity". His whole historical reflection, just as that on the "ancients", is a concoction out of Hegel.

The Negroid state is conceived as "the child" because Hegel says on page 89 of his *Philosophie der Geschichte*:

"Africa is the *country of the childhood* of history." "In defining the African" (Negroid) "spirit we must entirely discard the *category of universality*" (p. 90) — i.e., although the child or the Negro has ideas, he still does not have *the* idea. "Among the Negroes consciousness has not yet reached a firm objective existence, as for example *God, law*, in which man would have the *perception of his essence*" ... "thanks to which, knowledge of an *absolute being* is totally absent. The Negro represents *natural man* in all his lack of restraint." (P. 90.) "Although they must be conscious of their dependence on the natural" (on things, as "Stirner" says), "this, however, does not lead them to the consciousness of something higher." (P. 91.)

Here we meet again all Stirner's determinations of the child and the Negro — dependence on things, independence of ideas and especially of "the idea", "the essence", "the absolute" (holy) "being", etc.

He found that in Hegel the Mongols and, in particular, the Chinese appear as the beginning of history and since for Hegel, too, history is a history of spirits (but not in such a childish way as with "Stirner"), it goes without saying that the Mongols brought the spirit into history and are the original representatives of everything "sacred". In particular, on page 110, Hegel describes the "*Mongolian* kingdom" (of the Dalai-Lama) as the "*ecclesiastical*" realm, the "kingdom of theocratic rule", a "spiritual, religious kingdom" — in contrast to the worldly empire of the Chinese. "Stirner", of course, has to identify China with the Mongols. In Hegel, on page 140, there even occurs the "*Mongolian principle*" from which "Stirner" derived his "*Mongolism*". Incidentally, if he really wanted to reduce the Mongols to the category of "idealism", he could have "found established" in the Dalai-Lama system and Buddhism quite different "spiritual beings" from his fragile "heavenly ladder". But he did not even have time to look properly at Hegel's *Philosophie der Geschichte*. The peculiarity and uniqueness of Stirner's attitude to history consists in the egoist being transformed into a "clumsy" copier of Hegel.

b) Catholicism and Protestantism
(Cf. "The Economy of the Old Testament")

What we here call Catholicism, "Stirner" calls the "Middle Ages", but as he confuses (as "in everything") the pious, religious character of the Middle Ages, the religion of the Middle Ages, with the actual, profane Middle Ages in flesh and blood, we prefer to give the matter its right name at once.

"The Middle Ages" were a *"lengthy period*, in which people were content with the illusion of having the truth" (they did not desire or do anything else), "without seriously thinking about whether one must be true oneself in order to possess the truth." — "In the Middle Ages *people*" (that is, the whole of the Middle Ages) "mortified the *flesh*, in order to become capable of assimilating the holy." (P. 108.)

Hegel defines the attitude to the divine in the Catholic church by saying

"that people's attitude to the absolute was as to something purely external" (Christianity in the form of externality) (*Geschichte der Philosophie*, III, p. 148, and elsewhere). Of course, the individual has to be purified in order to assimilate the truth, but "this also occurs in an external way, through redemptions, fasts, self-flagellations, visits to holy places, pilgrimages". (Ibid., p. 140.)

"Stirner" makes this transition by saying:

"In the same way, *too, as people* strain their eyes in order to see a distant object ... so they mortified the flesh, etc."

Since in "Stirner's" "book" the Middle Ages are identified with Catholicism, they naturally end with *Luther*. (P. 108.) Luther himself is reduced to the following definition, which has already cropped up in connection with the youth, in the conversation with Szeliga and elsewhere:

"Man, if he wants to attain *truth, must become as true* as truth itself. Only he who already has truth in *faith* can participate in it."

Concerning Lutheranism, Hegel says:

"The *truth* of the gospel exists only in the *true attitude* to it.... The essential attitude of the spirit exists only for the spirit.... Hence the *attitude* of the spirit to the content is that although the content is essential, it is equally essential that the holy and consecrating spirit should stand in relation to this content." (*Geschichte der Philosophie*, III, p. 234.) "This then is the Lutheran faith—his" (i.e., man's) "*faith* is required of him and *it alone can truly be taken into account*." (Ibid., p. 230.) "Luther ... affirms that the divine is divine only insofar as it is apprehended in this subjective spirituality of *faith*." (Ibid., p. 138.) "The doctrine of the" (Catholic) "church is truth as *existent truth*." (*Philosophie der Religion*,[a] II, p. 331.)

"Stirner" continues:

"Accordingly, with Luther the knowledge arises that truth, because it is thought, exists only for the thinking man, and this means that with regard to his object — thought — man must adopt a totally different standpoint, a pious" (*per appos.*), "scientific standpoint, or that of thinking." (P. 110.)

Apart from the repetition which "Stirner" again "includes" here, only the transition from faith to thinking deserves attention. Hegel makes the transition in the following way:

---

[a] G.W.F. Hegel, *Vorlesungen über die Philosophie der Religion.—Ed.*

"But this spirit" (namely, the holy and consecrating spirit) "is, secondly, essentially also thinking spirit. Thinking as such must also have its development in it", etc. ([*Geschichte der Philosophie*,] p. 234.)

"Stirner" continues:

"This thought" ("that I am *spirit*, spirit alone") "pervades the history of the Reformation down to the present day." (P. 111.)

From the sixteenth century onwards, no other history exists for "Stirner" than the history of the Reformation — and the latter only in the interpretation in which Hegel presents it.

Saint Max has again displayed his gigantic faith. He has again taken as literal truth all the illusions of German speculative philosophy; indeed, he has made them still more speculative, still more abstract. For him there exists only the history of religion and philosophy — and this exists for him only through the medium of Hegel, who with the passage of time has become the universal crib, the reference source for all the latest German speculators about principles and manufacturers of systems.

Catholicism=attitude to truth as thing, child, Negro, the "ancient".

Protestantism=attitude to truth in the spirit, youth, Mongol, the "modern".

The whole scheme was superfluous, since all this was already present in the section on "spirit".

As already mentioned in "The Economy of the Old Testament", it is now possible to make the child and the youth appear again in new "transformations" within Protestantism, as "Stirner" actually does on page 112, where he conceives English, empirical philosophy as the child, in contrast to German, speculative philosophy as the youth. Here again he copies out *Hegel*, who here, as elsewhere in the "book", frequently appears as "*one*".

"One" — i. e., Hegel — "expelled Bacon from the realm of philosophy." "And, indeed, what is called English philosophy does not seem to have got any farther than the discoveries made by so-called clear intellects such as Bacon and Hume." (P. 112.)

Hegel expresses this as follows:

"Bacon is in fact the real leader and representative of what is called philosophy in England and beyond which the English have by no means gone as yet." (*Geschichte der Philosophie*, III, p. 254.)

The people whom "Stirner" calls "clear intellects" Hegel (ibid., p. 255) calls "educated men of the world" — Saint Max on one occasion even transforms them into the "simplicity of childish nature", for the English philosophers have to represent the *child*. On the same childish grounds Bacon is not allowed to have "concerned himself with theological problems and cardinal propositions", regardless of what may be said in his writings (particularly *De Augmentis Scientiarum,*[a] *Novum Organum* and the *Essays*[b]). On the other hand, "German thought ... sees life only in cognition itself" (p. 112), for it is the *youth*. *Ecce iterum Crispinus!*[c]

How Stirner transforms Descartes into a German philosopher, the reader can see for himself in "the book", p. 112.

D. Hierarchy

In the foregoing presentation Jacques le bonhomme conceives history merely as the product of abstract thoughts — or, rather, of his notions of abstract thoughts — as governed by these notions, which, in the final analysis, are all resolved into the "holy". This domination of the "holy", of thought, of the Hegelian absolute idea over the empirical world he further portrays as a historical relation existing at the present time, as the domination of the holy ones, the ideologists, over the vulgar world — as a *hierarchy*. In this hierarchy, what previously appeared *consecutively* exists *side by side*, so that one of the two co-existing forms of development rules over the other. Thus, the youth rules over the child, the Mongol over the Negro, the modern over the ancient, the selfless egoist (*citoyen*) over the egoist in the usual sense of the word (*bourgeois*), etc.— see "The Economy of the Old Testament". The "destruction" of the "world of things" by the "world of the spirit" appears here as the "domination" of the "world of thoughts" over the "world of things". The outcome, of course, is bound to be that the domination which the "world of thoughts" exercises from the outset in history is at the end of the latter also presented as the real, actually existing domination of the thinkers — and, as we shall see, in the final analysis, as the domination of the speculative philosophers — over the world of things, so that Saint Max has only to fight against thoughts and ideas of the ideologists and to overcome them, in order to make himself "possessor of the world of things and the world of thoughts".

---

[a] Francis Bacon, *De Dignitate et Augmentis Scientiarum.*— *Ed.*
[b] Francis Bacon, *The Essays or Councels. Civill and Morall.*— *Ed.*
[c] And there is Crispinus again — the opening words of Juvenal's fourth satire.— *Ed.*

"*Hierarchy is the domination of thought*, the domination of the spirit. We are still hierarchical to this day, we are under the yoke of those who rely on thoughts, and thoughts" — who has failed to notice it long ago? — "are the *holy*." (P. 97.) (Stirner has tried to safeguard himself against the reproach that in his whole book he has only been producing "thoughts", i.e., the "holy", by in fact nowhere producing any thoughts in it. Although in the Wigand periodical he ascribes to himself "virtuosity in thinking", i. e., according to his interpretation, virtuosity in the fabrication of the "holy"—and this we shall concede him.)—"Hierarchy is the *supreme domination of spirit*." (P. 467.)—"The *medieval* hierarchy was only a weak hierarchy, for it was forced to allow all kinds of profane barbarism to exist unrestricted alongside it" ("how Stirner knows so much about what the hierarchy was forced to do", we shall soon see), "and only the Reformation steeled the power of the hierarchy." (P. 110.) "Stirner" indeed thinks that "the domination of spirits was never before so all-embracing and omnipotent" as after the Reformation; he thinks that this domination of spirits "instead of divorcing the religious principle from art, state and science, on the contrary, raised these wholly from actuality into the kingdom of the spirit and made them religious".

This view of modern history merely dilates upon speculative philosophy's old illusion of the domination of spirit in history. Indeed, this passage even shows how pious Jacques le bonhomme in all good faith continually takes the world outlook derived from Hegel, and which has become traditional for him, as the *real world*, and "manoeuvres" on that basis. What may appear as "his own" and "unique" in this passage is the conception of this domination of the spirit as a *hierarchy*—and here, again, we will "include" a brief "historical reflection" on the origin of Stirner's "hierarchy".

Hegel speaks of the philosophy of hierarchy in the following "transformations":

"We have seen in Plato's *Republic* the idea that philosophers should govern; now" (in the Catholic Middle Ages) "the time has come when it is affirmed that the *spiritual should dominate*; but the spiritual has acquired the meaning that the *clerical*, the *clergy*, should dominate. Thus, the spiritual is made a special being, the individual." (*Geschichte der Philosophie*, III, p. 132.) — "Thereby actuality, the mundane, *is forsaken by God* ... a few individual persons are *holy*, the others *unholy*." (Ibid., p. 136.) "Godforsakenness" is more closely defined thus: "All these forms" (family, work, political life, etc.) "are considered nugatory, *unholy*." (*Philosophie der Religion*, II, p. 343.) — "It is a union with worldliness which is unreconciled, *worldiness* which is *crude in itself*" (for this Hegel elsewhere also uses the word "barbarism"; cf., for example, *Geschichte der Philosophie*, III, p. 136) "and, being crude in itself, is simply subjected to domination." (*Philosophie der Religion*, II, pp. 342, 343.) — "This domination" (the hierarchy of the Catholic church) "is, therefore, a domination of passion, although it should be the domination of the spiritual." (*Geschichte der Philosophie*, III, p. 134.) — "*The true domination of the spirit, however,* cannot be domination of the spirit in the sense that what opposes it should be something subordinate." (Ibid., p. 131.) — "The true meaning is that the *spiritual as such*" (according to "Stirner" the "holy") "should be *the determining factor, and this has been so until our times; thus, we see in the French Revolution*" (*following in the wake* of Hegel, "Stirner" sees it) "that the *abstract idea should dominate*: state constitutions and laws should be determined by it, it should constitute the bond between people, and people should be conscious that *that which they hold as valid are abstract ideas*, liberty and equality, etc." (*Geschichte der Philosophie*, III, p. 132.) The true domination of spirit as brought about by Protestantism, in contrast to its imperfect form in the Catholic hierarchy, is defined further in the sense that "the *earthly is made spiritual in itself*" (*Geschichte der Philosophie*, III, p. 185); "that the divine is realised in the sphere of actuality" (the Catholic Godforsakenness of actuality, therefore, ceases to exist—*Philosophie der Religion*, II, p. 344); that the "contradiction" between holiness and worldliness "is resolved in *morality*" (*Philosophie der Religion*, II, p. 343); that "*moral institutions*" (marriage, the family, the state, earning one's livelihood, etc.) are "*divine, holy*". (*Philosophie der Religion*, II, p. 344.)

Hegel expresses this true domination of spirit in two forms:

"*State, government, law, property, civic order*" (and, as we know from his other works, art, science, etc., as well), "all this is *the religious*... emerging in the form of the finite." (*Geschichte der Philosophie*, III, p. 185.)

And, finally, this domination of the religious, the spiritual, etc., is expressed as the domination of philosophy:

"Consciousness of the spiritual is now" (in the eighteenth century) "essentially the foundation, and *thereby domination has passed to philosophy.*" (*Philosophie der Geschichte*, p. 440.)

Hegel, therefore, ascribes to the Catholic hierarchy of the Middle Ages the intention of wanting "to be the domination of spirit" and thereupon regards it as a restricted, imperfect form of this domination of spirit, the culmination of which he sees in Protestantism and its alleged further development. However unhistorical this may be, nevertheless, Hegel is sufficiently historically-minded not to extend the use of the *name* "hierarchy" beyond the bounds of the Middle Ages. But Saint Max knows from this same Hegel that the later epoch is the "truth" of the preceding one; hence the epoch of the perfect domination of spirit is the truth of that epoch in which the domination of spirit was as yet imperfect, so that Protestantism is the truth of hierarchy and therefore *true hierarchy*. Since, however, only *true* hierarchy deserves to be called hierarchy, it is clear that the hierarchy of the Middle Ages had to be "weakly", and it is all the easier for Stirner to prove this since in the passages given above and in hundreds of other passages from Hegel the imperfection of the domination of spirit in the Middle Ages is portrayed. He only needed to copy these out, the whole of his "*own*" work consisting in substituting the word "hierarchy" for "domination of spirit". There was no need for him even to formulate the simple argument by means of which domination of spirit as such is transformed by him into hierarchy, since it has become the fashion among German theoreticians to give the name of the cause to the effect and, for example, to put back into the category of theology everything that has arisen out of theology and has not yet fully attained the height of the principles of these theoreticians—e. g., Hegelian speculation, Straussian pantheism, etc.— a trick especially prevalent in 1842. From the above-quoted passages it also follows that Hegel: 1) appraises the French Revolution as a new and more perfect phase of this domination of spirit; 2) regards philosophers as the rulers of the world of the nineteenth century; 3) maintains that now only abstract ideas have validity among people; 4) that he already regards marriage, the family, the state, earning one's livelihood, civic order, property, etc., as "divine and holy", as the *"religious principle"* and 5) that *morality* as worldly sanctity or as sanctified worldliness is represented as the highest and ultimate form of the domination of spirit over the world—all these things are repeated *word for word* in "Stirner".

Accordingly there is no need to say or prove anything more concerning Stirner's hierarchy, apart from why Saint Max copied out Hegel—a fact, however, for the explanation of which further material data are necessary, and which, therefore, is only explicable for those who are acquainted with the Berlin atmosphere. It is another question how the Hegelian idea of the domination of spirit arose, and about this see what has been said above.[a]

Saint Max's adoption of Hegel's world domination of the philosophers and his transformation of it into a hierarchy are due to the extremely uncritical credulity of our saint and to a "holy" or unholy ignorance which is content with "seeing through" history (i. e., with glancing *through* Hegel's historical writings) without troubling to "know" many "things" about it. In general, he was bound to be afraid that as soon as he "learned" he would no longer be able to "abolish and dissolve" (p. 96), and, therefore, remain stuck in the "bustling activity of noxious insects"— a sufficient reason not to "proceed" to the "abolition and dissolution" of his own ignorance.

If, like Hegel, one designs such a system for the first time, a system embracing the whole of history and the present-day world in all its scope, one cannot possibly do so without comprehensive, positive knowledge, without great energy and

---

[a] See this volume, pp. 67-71.— *Ed.*

keen insight and without dealing at least in some passages with empirical history. On the other hand, if one is satisfied with exploiting an already existing pattern, transforming it for one's own purposes and demonstrating this conception of one's "own" by means of isolated examples (e. g., Negroes and Mongols, Catholics and Protestants, the French Revolution, etc.)—and this is precisely what our warrior against the holy does—then absolutely no knowledge of history is necessary. The result of all this exploitation inevitably becomes comic; most of all comic when a jump is made from the past into the immediate present, examples of which we saw already in connection with "whimsy".[a]

As for the actual hierarchy of the Middle Ages, we shall merely note here that it did not exist for the people, for the great mass of human beings. For the great mass only feudalism existed, and hierarchy only existed insofar as it was itself either feudal or anti-feudal (within the framework of feudalism). Feudalism itself had entirely empirical relations as its basis. Hierarchy and its struggle against feudalism (the struggle of the ideologists of a class against the class itself) are only the ideological expression of feudalism and of the struggles developing within feudalism itself—which include also the struggles of the feudally organised nations among themselves. Hierarchy is the ideal form of feudalism; feudalism is the political form of the medieval relations of production and intercourse. Consequently, the struggle of feudalism against hierarchy can only be explained by elucidating these practical material relations. This elucidation of itself puts an end to the previous conception of history which took the illusions of the Middle Ages on trust, in particular those illusions which the Emperor and the Pope brought to bear in their struggle against each other.

Since Saint Max merely reduces the Hegelian abstractions about the Middle Ages and hierarchy to "pompous words and paltry thoughts", there is no need to examine in more detail the actual, historical hierarchy.

From the above it is now clear that the trick can also be reversed and Catholicism regarded not just as a preliminary stage, but also as the negation of the real hierarchy; in which case Catholicism=negation of spirit, non-spirit, sensuousness, and then one gets the great proposition of Jacques le

---

[a] See this volume, pp. 173-76.— *Ed.*

bonhomme — that the *Jesuits* "saved us from the *decay* and *destruction* of sensuousness." (P. 118.) What would have happened to "us" if the "destruction" of sensuousness had come to pass, we do not learn. The whole material movement since the sixteenth century, which did not save "us" from the "decay" of sensuousness, but, on the contrary, developed "sensuousness" to a much wider extent, does not exist for "Stirner" — it is the Jesuits who brought about all that. Compare, incidentally, Hegel's *Philosophie der Geschichte*, p. 425.

By carrying over the old domination of the clerics to modern times, Saint Max interprets modern times as *"clericalism"*; and then by regarding this domination of the clerics carried over to modern times as something distinct from the old medieval clerical domination, he depicts it as domination of the ideologists, as *"scholasticism"*. Thus clericalism=hierarchy as the domination of the spirit, scholasticism=the domination of the spirit as hierarchy.

"Stirner" achieves this simple transition to clericalism — which is no transition at all — by means of three weighty transformations.

Firstly, he "has" the "concept of clericalism" in anyone "who lives for a great idea, for a good cause" (still the good cause!), "for a doctrine, etc."

Secondly, in his world of illusion Stirner "comes up against" the "age-old illusion of a world that has not yet learned to dispense with clericalism", namely — "to live and create for the sake of an *idea*, etc."

Thirdly, "it is the domination of the idea, i. e., clericalism", that is: "Robespierre, for example" (for example!), "Saint-Just, and so on" (and so on!) "were out-and-out priests", etc. All three transformations in which clericalism is "discovered", "encountered" and "called upon" (all this on p. 100), therefore, express nothing more than what Saint Max has already repeatedly told us, namely, the domination of spirit, of the idea, of the holy, over "life" (ibid.).

After the "domination of the idea, i. e., clericalism" has thus been foisted upon history, Saint Max can, of course, without difficulty find this "clericalism" again in the whole of preceding history, and thus depict "Robespierre, for example, Saint-Just, and so on" as priests and identify them with Innocent III and Gregory VII, and so all uniqueness vanishes in the face of *the unique*. All of them, properly speaking, are merely different *names*, different disguises for *one* person, "clericalism", which made all history from the beginning of Christianity. As to how, with this sort of conception of history, "all cats become grey", since all historical differences are "abolished" and "resolved" in the "notion of clericalism" — as to this, Saint Max at once gives us a striking example in his "Robespierre, for example, Saint-Just, and so on". Here we are first given Robespierre as an "example" of Saint-Just, and Saint-Just — as an "and-so-on" of Robespierre. It is then said:

"These representatives of holy interests are confronted by a world of innumerable 'personal', earthly interests."

By whom were they confronted? By the Girondists and Thermidorians, who (see "for example" R. Levasseur's *Mémoires*, "and so on", "i. e.", Nougaret, *Histoire des prisons*; Barère; *"Deux amis de la liberté"* [50] (*et du commerce*)[a]; Montgaillard, *Histoire de France*; Madame Roland, *Appel à la postérité*; J. B. Louvet's *Mémoires* and even the disgusting *Essais historiques* by Beaulieu, etc., etc., as well as all the proceedings before the revolutionary tribunal, "and so on") constantly reproached them, the real representatives of revolutionary power, i. e., of the class which *alone* was truly revolutionary, the "innumerable" masses, for violating "sacred interests", the constitution, freedom, equality, the rights of man, republicanism, law, *sainte propriété*,[b] "for example" the division of powers, humanity, morality, moderation, "and so on". They were opposed by all the *priests*, who accused them of violating all the main and secondary items of the religious and moral catechism (see "for example" *Histoire du clergé de France pendant la révolution*, by M. R.,[c] Paris, libraire catholique, 1828, "and so on"). The historical comment of the bourgeois that during the *règne de la terreur* "Robespierre, for example, Saint-Just, and so on" cut off the heads of *honnêtes gens*[d] (see the numerous writings of the simpleton Monsieur *Peltier*, "for example", *La conspiration de Robespierre* by *Montjoie*, "and so on") is expressed by Saint Max in the following transformation:

"Because the revolutionary priests and school-masters served *Man*, they cut the throats of *men*."

This, of course, saves Saint Max the trouble of wasting even one "unique" little word about the actual, empirical grounds for

---

[a] Two friends of freedom (and of commerce).— *Ed.*
[b] Sacred property.— *Ed.*
[c] Hippolyte Régnier d'Estourbet.— *Ed.*
[d] Respectable people.— *Ed.*

the cutting off of heads—grounds which were based on extremely worldly interests, though not, of course, of the stockjobbers, but of the "innumerable" masses. An earlier "priest", *Spinoza*, already in the seventeenth century had the brazen audacity to act the "strict school-master" of Saint Max, by saying: "Ignorance is no argument."[a] Consequently Saint Max loathes the priest Spinoza to such an extent that he accepts his anti-cleric, the priest *Leibniz*, and for all such astonishing phenomena as the terror, "for example", the cutting off of heads, "and so on", produces "sufficient grounds", viz., that "the ecclesiastics stuffed their heads with something of the kind". (P. 98.)

Blessed Max, who has found sufficient grounds for everything ("I have now found the ground into which my anchor is eternally fastened",[b] in the idea, "for example", in the "clericalism", "and so on" of "Robespierre, for example, Saint-Just, and so on", George Sand, Proudhon, the chaste Berlin seamstress,[c] etc.)—this blessed Max "does not blame the class of the bourgeoisie for having asked its egoism how far it should give way to the revolutionary idea *as such*". For Saint Max "the revolutionary idea" which inspired the *habits bleus*[51] and *honnêtes gens* of 1789 is the same "idea" as that of the sansculottes of 1793, *the same* idea concerning which people deliberate whether to "give way" to it—but no further "space can be given"[d] to any "idea" about this point.

We now come to present-day hierarchy, to the domination of the idea in ordinary life. The whole of the second part of "the book" is filled with struggle against this "hierarchy". Therefore we shall deal with it in detail when we come to this second part. But since Saint Max, as in the section on "whimsy", takes delight in anticipating his ideas here and repeats what comes later in the beginning, as he repeats the beginning in what comes later, we are compelled already at this point to note a few examples of his hierarchy. His method of writing a book is the unique "egoism" which we find in the whole book. His self-delight stands in inverse proportion to the delight experienced by the reader.

Since the middle class demand love for *their* kingdom, their

---

[a] Benedictus Spinoza, *Ethica*, Pars prima, Appendix.— *Ed.*
[b] The words are from a Protestant hymn.— *Ed.*
[c] Marie Wilhelmine Dähnhardt.— *Ed.*
[d] In German a pun: *Raum geben*—to give way, to yield to, and to give space to something.— *Ed.*

regime, they want, according to Jacques le bonhomme, to "establish the kingdom of love on earth". (P. 98.) Since they demand respect for their domination and for the conditions in which it is exercised, and therefore want to usurp domination over respect, they demand, according to this worthy man, the domination of *respect* as such, their attitude towards respect is the same as towards the holy spirit dwelling within them. (P. 95.) Jacques le bonhomme, with his faith that can move mountains, takes as the actual, earthly basis of the bourgeois world the distorted form in which the sanctimonious and hypocritical ideology of the bourgeoisie voices their particular interests as universal interests. Why this ideological delusion assumes precisely this form for our saint, we shall see in connection with "political liberalism".[a]

Saint Max gives us a new example on page 115, speaking of the family. He declares that, although it is very easy to become emancipated from the domination of one's own family, nevertheless, "refusal of allegiance easily arouses pangs of conscience", and so people retain family affection, the concept of the family, and therefore have the "holy conception of the family", the "holy". (P. 116.)

Here again our good man perceives the domination of the holy where entirely empirical relations dominate. The attitude of the bourgeois to the institutions of his regime is like that of the Jew to the law; he evades them whenever it is possible to do so in each individual case, but he wants everyone else to observe them. If the entire bourgeoisie, in a mass and at one time, were to evade bourgeois institutions, it would cease to be bourgeois — a conduct which, of course, never occurs to the bourgeois and by no means depends on their willing or running.[52] The dissolute bourgeois evades marriage and secretly commits adultery; the merchant evades the institution of property by depriving others of property by speculation, bankruptcy, etc.; the young bourgeois makes himself independent of his own family, if he can by in fact abolishing the family as far as he is concerned. But marriage, property, the family remain untouched in theory, because they are the practical basis on which the bourgeoisie has erected its domination, and because in their bourgeois form they are the conditions which make the bourgeois a bourgeois, just as the constantly evaded law makes the religious Jew a religious Jew. This attitude of the

---

[a] See this volume, pp. 208-13.— *Ed.*

bourgeois to the conditions of his existence acquires one of its universal forms in bourgeois morality. One cannot speak at all of the family "*as such*". Historically, the bourgeois gives the family the character of the bourgeois family, in which boredom and money are the binding link, and which also includes the bourgeois dissolution of the family, which does not prevent the family itself from always continuing to exist. Its dirty existence has its counterpart in the holy concept of it in official phraseology and universal hypocrisy. Where the family is *actually* abolished, as with the proletariat, just the opposite of what "Stirner" thinks takes place. There the concept of the family does not exist at all, but here and there family affection based on extremely real relations is certainly to be found. In the eighteenth century the concept of the family was abolished by the philosophers, because the actual family was already in process of dissolution at the highest pinnacles of civilisation. The internal family bond, the separate components constituting the concept of the family were dissolved, for example, obedience, piety, fidelity in marriage, etc.; but the real body of the family, the property relation, the exclusive attitude in relation to other families, forced cohabitation — relations determined by the existence of children, the structure of modern towns, the formation of capital, etc.— all these were preserved, although with numerous violations, because the existence of the family is made necessary by its connection with the mode of production, which exists independently of the will of bourgeois society. That it was impossible to do without it was demonstrated in the most striking way during the French Revolution, when for a moment the family was as good as legally abolished. The family continues to exist even in the nineteenth century, only the process of its dissolution has become more general, not on account of the concept, but because of the higher development of industry and competition; the family still exists although its dissolution was long ago proclaimed by French and English Socialists and this has at last penetrated also to the German church fathers, by way of French novels.

One other example of the domination of the idea in everyday life. Since school-masters may be told to find consolation for their scanty pay in the holiness of the cause they serve (which could only occur in Germany), Jacques le bonhomme actually believes that such talk is the reason for their low salaries. (P. 100.) He believes that "the holy" in the present-day bourgeois world has an actual money value, he believes that the meagre funds of the Prussian state (see, *inter alia*, Browning on this subject[a]) would be so increased by the abolition of "the holy" that every village school-master could suddenly be paid a ministerial salary.

This is the hierarchy of nonsense.

The "keystone of the magnificent cathedral"—as the great Michelet[b] puts it—of hierarchy is "sometimes" the work of "One".

"*One sometimes* divides people into two classes, the educated and the uneducated." (One sometimes divides apes into two classes, the tailed and the tailless.) "The former, insofar as they were worthy of their name, occupied themselves with thoughts, with the spirit." They "dominated in the post-Christian epoch and for their thoughts they demanded ... respect". The uneducated (the animal, the child, the Negro) are "powerless" against thoughts and "are dominated by them. That is the meaning of hierarchy."

The "educated" (the youth, the Mongol, the modern) are, therefore, again only occupied with "spirit", pure thought, etc.; they are metaphysicians by profession, in the final analysis Hegelians. "Hence" the "uneducated" are the non-Hegelians.[c] Hegel was indubitably "the most educated" Hegelian and therefore in his case it must "become apparent what a longing for things particularly the most educated man possesses". The point is that the "educated" and "uneducated" are within themselves in conflict with each other; indeed, in every man the "uneducated" is in conflict with the "educated". And since the greatest longing for things, i.e., for that which belongs to the "uneducated", becomes apparent in Hegel, it also becomes apparent here that "the most educated" man is at the same time "the most uneducated".

"There" (in Hegel) "reality should be completely in accordance with thought and no concept be without reality."

This should read: there the ordinary idea of reality should receive its complete philosophical expression, while Hegel imagines, on the contrary, that "consequently" every philosophical expression creates the reality that is in accordance with it. Jacques le bonhomme takes Hegel's illusion about his own philosophy for the genuine coin of Hegelian philosophy.

---

[a] G. Browning, *The domestic and financial Condition of Great Britain; preceded by a Brief Sketch of her Foreign Policy; and of the Statistics and Politics of France, Russia, Austria, and Prussia.—Ed.*

[b] Carl Ludwig Michelet, *Geschichte der letzten Systeme der Philosophie in Deutschland von Kant bis Hegel.—Ed.*

[c] Here the authors ironically use Berlin dialect words for educated, uneducated and most educated (*Jebildete, Unjebildete, Allerjebildetste*).— *Ed.*

The Hegelian philosophy, which in the form of the domination of the Hegelians over the non-Hegelians appears as the
crown of the hierarchy, now conquers the last world empire.

"Hegel's system was the supreme *despotism* and *autocracy* of thought, the
omnipotence and *almightiness* of the spirit." (P. 97.)

Here, therefore, we find ourselves in the realm of spirits of
Hegelian philosophy, which stretches from Berlin to Halle and
Tübingen, the realm of spirits whose history was written by
Herr Bayrhoffer [a] and for which the great Michelet collected the
statistical data.

The preparation for this realm of spirits was the French
Revolution which "*did nothing* but transform *things* into *ideas
about things*" (p. 115; cf. above Hegel on the revolution, p.
[...[b]]).

"So people remained citizens" (in "Stirner", this occurs
earlier, but "what Stirner says is not what he has in mind, and
what he has in mind cannot be said", *Wigand*, p. 149) and "lived
in *reflection*, they had their *eye* on an object, before which" (*per
appos.*) "they felt reverence and fear". "Stirner" says in a
passage on page 98: "The road to hell is paved with good
intentions." But we say: the road to the unique is paved with
bad concluding clauses [c], with appositions, which are his
"heavenly ladder" borrowed from the Chinese, and his "rope of
the objective" (p. 88) on which he makes his "flea-jumps". In
accordance with this, for "modern philosophy *or* modern
times"— since the emergence of the realm of spirits modern
times *are* indeed nothing but modern philosophy — it is an easy
matter to "transform the existing objects into notional objects,
i.e., into concepts", page 114, a work which Saint Max
continues.

We have already seen our knight of the rueful countenance
even "before the mountains were brought forth",[d] which he
later moved by his faith, right at the beginning of his book,
galloping headlong towards the great result of his "magnificent
cathedral". His "donkey", apposition, could not jump swiftly
enough for him; now, at last, on page 114, he has reached his
goal and by means of a mighty "or" has transformed *modern
times* into *modern philosophy.*

---

[a] Karl Theodor Bayrhoffer, *Die Idee und Geschichte der Philosophie.*— Ed.
[b] See this volume, pp. 187-89.— Ed.
[c] In German a pun: *Vorsätze*—intentions, and *Nachsätze*—concluding
clauses, conclusions.— Ed.
[d] Psalms 90:2.— Ed.

Thereby ancient times (i. e., the ancient and modern, Negroid and Mongolian but, properly speaking, only pre-Stirnerian times) "reached their final goal". We can now reveal why Saint Max gave the title "*Man*" to the whole of the first part of his book and made out his entire history of miracles, ghosts and knights to be the history of "*man*". The ideas and thoughts of people were, of course, ideas and thoughts about themselves and their relationships, their consciousness of *themselves* and of people *in general*—for it was the consciousness not merely of a single individual but of the individual in his interconnection with the whole of society and about the whole of the society in which they lived. The conditions, independent of them, in which they produced their life, the necessary forms of intercourse connected herewith, and the personal and social relations thereby given, had to take the form — insofar as they were expressed in thoughts — of ideal conditions and necessary relations, i. e., they had to be expressed in consciousness as determinations arising from the concept of man *as such*, from human essence, from the nature of man, from man *as such*. What people were, what their relations were, appeared in consciousness as ideas of man *as such*, of his modes of existence or of his immediate conceptual determinations. So, after the ideologists had assumed that ideas and thoughts had dominated history up to now, that the history of these ideas and thoughts constitutes all history up to now, after they had imagined that real conditions had conformed to man *as such* and his ideal conditions, i. e., to conceptual determinations, after they had made the history of people's consciousness of themselves the basis of their actual history, after all this, nothing was easier than to call the history of consciousness, of ideas, of the holy, of established concepts — the history of "man" and to put it in the place of real history. The only distinction between Saint Max and all his predecessors is that he knows *nothing* about these concepts — even in their arbitrary isolation from real life, whose products they were — and his trivial creative work in his copy of Hegelian ideology is restricted to establishing his ignorance even of what he copies.— It is already evident from this how he can counterpose the history of the real individual in the form of *the unique* to his fantasy about the history of man.

The unique history takes place at the beginning in the Stoa in Athens, later almost wholly in Germany, and finally at the Kupfergraben [53] in Berlin, where the despot of "modern philosophy or modern times" set up his imperial residence. That already shows how exclusively national and local is the matter dealt with. Instead of world history, Saint Max gives a few and, what is more, extremely meagre and biased comments on the history of *German* theology and philosophy. If on occasion we appear to go outside Germany, it is only in order to cause the deeds and thoughts of other peoples, e. g., the French Revolution, to "reach their final goal" in Germany, namely, at the Kupfergraben. Only national-German facts are given, they are dealt with and interpreted in a national-German manner, and the result remains a national-German one. But even that is not enough. The views and education of our saint are not only German, but of a Berlin nature through and through. The role allotted to Hegelian philosophy is that which it plays in Berlin, and Stirner confuses Berlin with the world and world history. The "youth" is a Berliner; the good citizens that we encounter throughout the book are Berlin beer-drinking philistines. With such premises for the starting-point, it is natural that the result arrived at is merely one confined within the national and local framework. "Stirner" and his whole philosophical fraternity, among whom he is the weakest and most ignorant member, afford a practical commentary to the valiant lines of the valiant Hoffmann von Fallersleben:

> In Germany alone, in Germany alone,
> Would I for ever live.[a]

The local Berlin conclusion of our valiant saint—that in Hegelian philosophy the world has "all gone"—enables him now without much expense to arrive at a universal empire of his "own". The Hegelian philosophy transformed everything into thought, into the holy, into apparition, into spirit, into spirits, into spectres. "Stirner" will fight against them, he will conquer them in his imagination and will erect on their dead bodies his "own" "unique", "corporeal" empire, the empire of the "fine fellow".

"For we *wrestle not against flesh and blood*, but against principalities, against powers, against the *rulers* of the darkness *of this world*, against *spiritual wickedness* in high places." (Ephesians 6:12.)

Now "Stirner" has his "feet shod with the preparation" for waging the fight against thoughts. He has no need first to "take the shield of faith", for he has never laid it down. Armed with the "helmet" of disaster and the "sword" of spiritlessness (see ibid.[b]), he goes into battle. "And it was given unto him to make

---

[a] From the poem "Auf der Wanderung" by Hoffmann von Fallersleben.— *Ed.*

[b] Ephesians 6:15, 16, 17 (paraphrased).— *Ed.*

war with the holy" but not "to overcome" it. (Revelation of St. John 13:7.)

5. "STIRNER" DELIGHTED IN HIS CONSTRUCTION

We now find ourselves again exactly where we were on page 19 in connection with the youth, who became the man, and on page 90 in connection with the Mongoloid Caucasian, who was transformed into the Caucasian Caucasian and "found himself". We are, therefore, at the third self-finding of the mysterious individual whose "arduous life struggle" Saint Max depicts for us. Only the whole story is now behind us, and, in view of the extensive material we have worked through, we must take a retrospective look at the gigantic corpse of the ruined man.

Though on a later page, where he has long ago forgotten his history, Saint Max asserts that "genius has long since been regarded as the creator of new world-historic productions" (p. 214), we have already seen that even his bitterest enemies cannot revile *his* history on that score, at any rate, for in it no individuals, let alone geniuses, make their appearance, but only ossified, crippled thoughts and Hegelian changelings.

Repetitio est mater studiorum.[a] Saint Max, who expounded his whole history of "philosophy or time" only in order to find an opportunity for a few hurried studies of Hegel, finally repeats once again his whole unique history. However, he does it with a turn towards natural history, offering us important information about "unique" natural science, the reason being that for him, whenever the "world" has to play an important role, it immediately becomes transformed into *nature.* "Unique" natural science begins at once with the admission of its impotence. It does not examine the actual relation of man to nature, determined by industry and natural science, but proclaims a fantastic relation of man to nature.

"How little can man conquer! He has to allow the sun to trace its course, the sea to roll its waves, the mountains to tower to the sky." (P. 122.)

Saint Max who, like all saints, loves miracles, but can only perform a logical miracle, is annoyed because he cannot make the sun dance the cancan, he grieves because he cannot still the ocean, he is indignant because he must allow the mountains to tower to the sky. Although on page 124 the world already becomes "prosaic" at the end of antiquity, it is still, for our

---

[a] Repetition is the mother of learning.— *Ed.*

saint, highly unprosaic. For him it still is the "sun" and not the earth that traces its course, and to his sorrow he cannot *à la* Joshua command "sun, stand thou still".[a] On page 123, Stirner discovers that

at the end of the ancient world, "spirit" "again foamed and frothed over irresistibly because *gases*" (spirits) "developed within it and, after the *mechanical impact* from outside became ineffective, *chemical tensions*, which stimulate in the interior, began to come into wonderful play".

This sentence contains the most important data of the "unique" philosophy of nature, which on the previous page had already arrived at the conclusion that for man nature is the "unconquerable". Earthly physics knows nothing about a mechanical impact which becomes ineffective — *unique* physics alone has the merit of this discovery. Earthly chemistry knows no "gases" which stimulate "chemical tensions" and, what is more, "in the interior". Gases which enter into new combinations, into new chemical relations, do not stimulate any "tensions", but at most lead to a fall of tension, insofar as they pass into a liquid state of aggregation and thereby their volume decreases to something less than one-thousandth of their former volume. If Saint Max feels "tensions" "in" his own "interior" due to "gases", these are highly "mechanical impacts", and by no means "chemical tensions". They are produced by a chemical transformation, determined by physiological causes, of certain mixtures into others, whereby part of the constituents of the former mixture becomes gaseous, therefore, occupies a larger volume and, in the absence of space for it, causes a "mechanical impact" or pressure towards the outside. [That] these non-existent "chemical tensions" "come" into extremely "wonderful play" in Saint Max's "interior", namely, this time in his *head*, "we see" from the role they play in "unique" natural science. Incidentally, it is to be desired that Saint Max would no longer withhold from the profane natural scientists what nonsense he has in mind with the crazy expression "chemical tensions", which moreover "stimulate in the interior" (as though a "mechanical impact" on the stomach does not "stimulate it in the interior" as well).

Saint Max wrote his "unique" natural science only because on this occasion he was unable to touch on the ancients in decent fashion without at the same time letting fall a few words about the "world of things", about nature.

At the end of the ancient world the ancients, we are assured here, are all transformed into Stoics, "whom *no* collapse of the

---

[a] Joshua 10:12.—*Ed.*

world" (how many times is it supposed to have collapsed?) "could put out of countenance". (P. 123.) Thus, the ancients become Chinese, who also "cannot be thrown down from the heavens of their tranquillity by any unforeseen event" (or idea [a]). (P. 90.) Indeed, Jacques le bonhomme seriously believes that against the last of the ancients "the mechanical impact from outside became ineffective". How far this corresponds to the actual situation of the Romans and Greeks at the end of the ancient world, to their complete lack of stability and confidence, which could hardly oppose any remnant of *vis inertiae* to the "mechanical impact"—on this point compare, *inter alia*, Lucian. The powerful mechanical shocks which the Roman Empire received as a result of its division among several Caesars and their wars against one another, as a result of the colossal concentration of property, particularly landed property, in Rome, and the decrease in Italy's population caused by this, and as a result of the [pressure of the] Huns and Teutons—these shocks, in the opinion of our saintly historian, "became ineffective"; only the "chemical tensions", only the "gases" which Christianity "stimulated in the interior" over-threw the Roman Empire. The great earthquakes [in the West] and in the East, and other "mechanical impacts" which buried hundreds of thousands of people under the [ruins] of their towns and [which by no] means left the consciousness of people unchanged, were presumably, according to "Stirner", also "ineffective" or were chemical tensions. And *"in fact"* (!) "ancient history ends in this, that I have made the world my property"—which is proved by means of the biblical saying: "All things are delivered unto me" (i. e., Christ) "of my Father." [b] Here, therefore, I=Christ. In this connection, Jacques le bonhomme cannot refrain from believing the Christian that he could move mountains, etc., if he "only wanted to". As a Christian he proclaims himself the lord of the world, but he is this only *as a Christian*; he proclaims himself the "owner of the world". "Thereby egoism won its first full victory, since I elevated myself to be the owner of the world." (P. 124.) In order to rise to the level of the perfect Christian, Stirner's ego had only to carry through the struggle to become *poor in spirit* as well (which he succeeded in doing even before the mountains arose). "Blessed are the poor in spirit: for theirs

---

[a] In the German original a pun: *Fall*—event—and *Einfall*, which can mean idea, brainwave, invasion or collapse.— *Ed.*

[b] Matthew 11:27.— *Ed.*

is the kingdom of heaven."[a] Saint Max has reached perfection as regards poverty of spirit and even boasts of it in his great rejoicing before the Lord.

Saint Max, poor in spirit, believes in the fantastic gas formations of the Christians arising from the decomposition of the ancient world. The ancient Christian owned nothing in this world and was, therefore, satisfied with his imaginary heavenly property and his divine right to ownership. Instead of making the world the possession of the people, he proclaimed himself and his ragged fraternity to be "God's own possession" (1 Peter, 2:9). According to "Stirner", the Christian idea of the world is the world into which the ancient world is actually dissolved, although this is at most [a world] of fantasy into which the world of ancient ideas has [been transformed] and in which the Christian [by faith] can move mountains, can feel [all-powerful] and press forward to a position where the "mechanical impact is ineffective". Since for "Stirner" people are no longer determined by the [external] world, are no longer driven forward by the mechanical impact of the need to produce, since, in general, the mechanical impact, and with it the sexual act as well, has ceased to operate, it is only by a miracle that they have been able to continue to exist. Of course, for German prigs and school-masters with a gaseous content like that of "Stirner", it is far easier to be satisfied with the Christian fantasy about property — which is truly nothing but the property of Christian fantasy — than to describe the transformation of the real property relations and production relations of the ancient world.

That same primitive Christian who, in the imagination of Jacques le bonhomme, was the owner of the ancient world, actually belonged for the most part to the world of owners; he was a slave and could be sold on the market. But "Stirner", delighted in his construction, irrepressibly continues his rejoicing.

"The first property, the first splendour has been won!" (P. 124.)

In the same way, Stirner's egoism continues to gain property and splendour and to achieve "complete victories". The theological attitude of the primitive Christian to the ancient world is the perfect prototype of all his property and all his splendour.

The following are the grounds given for this property of the Christian:

---

[a] Matthew 5:3.— Ed.

"The world has lost its divine character ... it has become prosaic, it is my property, which I dispose of as I (viz., the spirit) choose." (P. 124.)

This means: the world has lost its divine character, therefore, it is freed from my fantasies for my own consciousness; it has become prosaic, consequently its relation to me is prosaic and it disposes of me in the prosaic way it favours, by no means to please me. Apart from the fact that "Stirner" here actually thinks that in ancient times the prosaic world did not exist and the divine principle held sway in the world, he even falsifies the Christian concept, which continually bemoans its impotence in relation to the world, and itself depicts its victory over the world *in* its fantasy as merely an ideal one, by transferring it to the day of judgment. Only when a great secular power took possession of Christianity and exploited it, whereupon, of course, it ceased to be unworldly, could Christianity imagine itself to be the owner of the world. Saint Max ascribes to the Christian the same false relation to the ancient world as he ascribes to the youth with regard to the "world of the child"; he puts the egoist in the same relation to the world of the Christian as he puts the man to the world of the youth.

The Christian has now nothing more to do than to become poor in spirit as quickly as possible and perceive the world of spirit in all its vanity — just as he did with the world of things — in order to be able to "dispose as he chooses" of the world of spirit also, whereby he becomes a perfect Christian, an egoist. The attitude of the Christian to the ancient world serves, therefore, as the standard for the attitude of the egoist to the modern world. The preparation for this spiritual poverty was the content of "almost two thousand years" of life — a life whose main epochs, of course, took place only in Germany.

"*After various transformations* the holy spirit *in the course of time* became the absolute idea, which again in *manifold refractions* split up into the various ideas of love of mankind, civic virtue, rationality, etc." (Pp. 125, 126.)

The German stay-at-home again turns the thing upside-down. The ideas of love of mankind, etc.— coins whose impressions had already been totally worn away, particularly owing to their great circulation in the eighteenth century — were recast by Hegel in the sublimate of the absolute idea, but after this reminting they were just as little successful in retaining their value abroad as Prussian paper money.

The consistent conclusion — which has already appeared again and again — of Stirner's view of history is as follows:

"Concepts should play the decisive role everywhere, concepts should regulate life, concepts should rule. That is the religious world to which Hegel gave systematic expression" (p. 126), and which our good-natured philistine so much mistakes for the real world that on the following page (p. 127) he can say:

"Now nothing but spirit rules in the world."

Stuck fast in this world of illusion, he can (on p. 128) build first of all an "altar" and then "erect a church" "round this altar", a church whose "walls" have legs for making progress and "move ever farther forward". "Soon this church embraces the whole earth." He, the unique, and Szeliga, his servant, stand outside, they "wander round these walls, and are driven out to the very edge". "Howling with agonising hunger", Saint Max calls to his servant: "One step more and the world of the holy has conquered." But Szeliga suddenly *sinks* into the outermost abyss", which lies above him — a literary miracle! For, since the earth is a sphere, the abyss can only lie above Szeliga as soon as the church embraces the whole earth. So he reverses the laws of gravity, ascends backwards into heaven and thereby reflects honour on "unique" natural science, which is all the easier for him since, according to page 126, "the nature of the thing and the concept of relation" are a matter of indifference to "Stirner", "do not guide him in his treatment or conclusion", and the "relationship into which" Szeliga "entered" with gravity "is itself unique" by virtue of Szeliga's "uniqueness", and by no means "depends" on the nature of gravity or on how "others", for instance, natural scientists, "classify it". "Stirner" moreover objects to Szeliga's "action being separated from the real" Szeliga and "assessed according to human standards".

Having thus arranged for decent accommodation in heaven for his faithful servant, Saint Max passes on to the subject of his own passion. On page 95 he discovers that even the "gallows" has the "colour of the holy"; "people loathe coming into contact with it, there is something uncanny, i. e., unfamiliar, strange about it". In order to transcend this strangeness of the gallows, he transforms it into his own gallows, which he can only do by hanging himself on it. The lion of Judah makes also this last sacrifice to egoism.[a] The holy Christian allows himself to be nailed to the cross, not to redeem the cross, but to redeem people from their impiety; the unholy Christian hangs himself on the gallows in order to redeem the gallows from holiness or to redeem himself from the strangeness of the gallows.

---

[a] Cf. Revelation of St. John 5:5.—*Ed.*

"The first splendour, the first property has been won, the first complete victory achieved!" The holy warrior has now conquered history, he has transformed it into thoughts, pure thoughts, which are nothing but thoughts — and at the end of time only a host of thoughts confront him. And so Saint Max, having taken his "gallows" on his back, just like an ass that carries a cross, and his servant Szeliga, who was welcomed in heaven with kicks and has returned to his master with his head hanging, set out to fight against this host of thoughts or, rather, against the mere halo of these thoughts. This time it is Sancho Panza, full of moral sayings, maxims and proverbs, who takes on himself the struggle against the holy, and Don Quixote plays the role of his pious and faithful servant. The honest Sancho fights just as bravely as the *caballero Manchego*[a] did in the old days, and like him does not fail several times to mistake a herd of Mongolian sheep for a swarm of spectres. The plump Maritornes "in the course of time, after various transformations in manifold refractions", is transformed into a chaste Berlin seamstress,[b] dying of anaemia, a subject on which Saint Sancho composes an elegy, one which causes all young graduates and Guards lieutenants to remember Rabelais' statement that the world-liberating "soldier's prime weapon is the flap of his trousers".[c]

Sancho Panza achieves his heroic feats by *perceiving* the entire opposing host of thoughts in its nullity and vanity. All his great deed is confined to mere perception which in the end leaves everything existing as it was, changing only his conception, and that not even of things, but of philosophical phrases about things.

Thus, after the ancients have been presented realistically as child, Negro, Negroid Caucasians, animal, Catholics, English philosophy, the uneducated, non-Hegelians, and the world of things, and the moderns have been presented idealistically as youth, Mongol, Mongoloid Caucasians, man, Protestants, German philosophy, the educated, Hegelians, and the world of thoughts — after everything has happened that was from time immemorial decided in the Council of Guardians, the time has at last arrived. The negative unity of the ancient and the modern,

---

[a] Knight of La Mancha, i.e., Don Quixote.— *Ed*.
[b] Marie Wilhelmine Dähnhardt.— *Ed*.
[c] Cf. the heading of Chapter 8, Book 3 of Rabelais' *Gargantua and Pantagruel*.— *Ed*.

which has already figured as the man, the Caucasian, the
Caucasian Caucasian, the perfect Christian, in servant's
clothing, seen "through a glass darkly" (1 Corinthians 13:12),
can now, after the passion and death of Stirner on the gallows
and Szeliga's ascent to heaven in full glory, return to the
simplest nomenclature and appear in the clouds of heaven
endowed with great power and majesty.[a] "And so it is said":
what was previously "One" (see "Economy of the Old
Testament") has become "*ego*" — the negative unity of realism
and idealism, of the world of things and the world of spirit.
Schelling calls this unity of realism and idealism "indifference"
or, rendered in the Berlin dialect, *Jleichjiltigkeit*; in Hegel it
becomes the negative unity in which the two moments are
transcended. Saint Max who, being a proper German speculative philosopher, is still tormented by the "unity of opposites",
is not satisfied with this; he wants this unity to be visible to him
in the form of a "corporeal individual", in a "fine fellow", and
he is encouraged in this by Feuerbach's views expressed in the
Anekdota[b] and in the *Philosophie der Zukunft*. This "ego" of
Stirner's which is the final outcome of the hitherto existing
world is, therefore, not a "corporeal individual", but a category
constructed on the Hegelian method and supported by appositions, the further "flea-jumps" of which we shall trace in the
New Testament. Here we shall merely add that in the final
analysis this ego comes into existence because it has the same
illusions about the world of the Christian as the Christian has
about the world of things. Just as the Christian takes possession
of the world of things by "getting into his head" fantastic
nonsense about them, so the "ego" takes possession of the
Christian world, the world of thoughts, by means of a series of
fantastic ideas about it. What the Christian imagines about his
own relation to the world, "Stirner" accepts in good faith, finds
excellent, and good-naturedly repeats after him.

"Therefore we conclude that a man is *justified by faith without the deeds*."
(Epistle to the Romans 3:28.)

Hegel, for whom the modern world was also resolved into the
world of abstract ideas, defines the task of the modern
philosopher, in contrast to that of the ancient, as consisting in
the following: instead of, like the ancients, freeing himself from
"natural consciousness" and "purging the individual of the

---

[a] Cf. Matthew 24:30.— *Ed.*
[b] Ludwig Feuerbach, "Vorläufige Thesen zur Reformation der
Philosophie".— *Ed.*

immediate, sensuous method and making him into conceived and thinking substance" (into spirit), the modern philosopher should "abolish firm, definite, fixed ideas". This, he adds, is accomplished by "dialectics". (*Phänomenologie*, pp. 26, 27.) The difference between "Stirner" and Hegel is that the former achieves the same thing without the help of dialectics.

6. THE FREE ONES

What role "the free ones" have to play here is stated in the economy of the Old Testament. We cannot help it that the ego, which we had approached so closely, now recedes from us again into the nebulous distance. It is not at all our fault that we did not pass at once to the ego from page 20 of "the book".

A. Political Liberalism

The key to the criticism of liberalism advanced by Saint Max and his predecessors is the history of the German bourgeoisie. We shall call special attention to some aspects of this history since the French Revolution.

The state of affairs in Germany at the end of the last century is fully reflected in Kant's *Critik der practischen Vernunft*. While the French bourgeoisie, by means of the most colossal revolution that history has ever known, was achieving domination and conquering the Continent of Europe, while the already politically emancipated English bourgeoisie was revolutionising industry and subjugating India politically, and all the rest of the world commercially, the impotent German burghers did not get any further than "good will". Kant was satisfied with "good will" alone, even if it remained entirely without result, and he transferred the *realisation* of this good will, the harmony between it and the needs and impulses of individuals, to *the world beyond*. Kant's good will fully corresponds to the impotence, depression and wretchedness of the German burghers, whose petty interests were never capable of developing into the common, national interests of a class and who were, therefore, constantly exploited by the bourgeois of all other nations. These petty, local interests had as their counterpart, on the one hand, the truly local and provincial narrow-mindedness of the German burghers and, on the other hand, their cosmopolitan swollen-headedness. In general, from the time of the Reformation German development has borne a completely petty-bourgeois character. The old feudal aristocracy was, for the most part, annihilated in the peasant wars; what remained of it were either imperial petty princes who gradually achieved a certain independence and aped the absolute monarchy on a minute, provincial scale, or lesser landowners who partly squandered their little bit of property at the tiny courts, and then gained their livelihood from petty positions in the small armies and government offices—or, finally, Junkers from the backwoods, who lived a life of which even the most modest English squire[a] or French *gentilhomme de province* would have been ashamed. Agriculture was carried on by a method which was neither parcellation nor large-scale production, and which, despite the preservation of feudal dependence and corvées, never drove the peasants to seek emancipation, both because this method of farming did not allow the emergence of any active revolutionary class and because of the absence of the revolutionary bourgeoisie corresponding to such a peasant class.

As regards the middle class, we can only emphasise here a few significant factors. It is significant that linen manufacture, i. e., an industry based on the spinning-wheel and the hand-loom, came to be of some importance in Germany at the very time when in England those cumbersome tools were already being ousted by machines. Most characteristic of all is the position of the German middle class in relation to *Holland*. Holland, the only part of the Hanseatic League[54] that became commercially important, tore itself free, cut Germany off from world trade except for two ports (Hamburg and Bremen) and since then dominated the whole of German trade. The German middle class was too impotent to set limits to exploitation by the Dutch. The bourgeoisie of little Holland, with its well-developed class interests, was more powerful than the far more numerous German middle class with its indifference and its divided petty interests. The fragmentation of interests was matched by the fragmentation of political organisation, the division into small principalities and free imperial cities. How could *political* concentration arise in a country which lacked all the *economic* conditions for it? The impotence of each separate sphere of life (one can speak here neither of estates nor of classes, but at most of former estates and classes not yet born) did not allow any one of them to gain exclusive domination. The inevitable consequence was that during the epoch of absolute monarchy, which assumed here its most stunted, semi-

---

[a] Marx and Engels use the English word.— *Ed.*

patriarchal form, the special sphere which, owing to division of labour, was responsible for the administration of public interests acquired an abnormal independence, which became still greater in the bureaucracy of modern times. Thus, the state built itself up into an apparently independent force, and this position, which in other countries was only transitory — a transition stage — it has maintained in Germany until the present day. This position of the state explains both the conscientiousness of the civil servant, which is found nowhere else, and all the illusions about the state which are current in Germany, as well as the apparent independence of German theoreticians in relation to the middle class — the seeming contradiction between the form in which these theoreticians express the interests of the middle class and these interests themselves.

The characteristic form which French liberalism, based on real class interests, assumed in Germany we find again in Kant. Neither he, nor the German middle class, whose whitewashing spokesman he was, noticed that these theoretical ideas of the bourgeoisie had as their basis material interests and a *will* that was conditioned and determined by the material relations of production. Kant, therefore, separated this theoretical expression from the interests which it expressed; he made the materially motivated determinations of the will of the French bourgeois into *pure* self-determinations of *"free will"*, of the will in and for itself, of the human will, and so converted it into purely ideological conceptual determinations and moral postulates. Hence the German petty bourgeois recoiled in horror from the practice of this energetic bourgeois liberalism as soon as this practice showed itself, both in the Reign of Terror and in shameless bourgeois profit-making.

Under the rule of Napoleon, the German middle class pushed its petty trade and its great illusions still further. As regards the petty-trading spirit which predominated in Germany at that time, Saint Sancho can, *inter alia*, compare Jean Paul, to mention only works of fiction, since they are the only source open to him. The German citizens, who railed against Napoleon for compelling them to drink chicory [55] and for disturbing their peace with military billeting and recruiting of conscripts, reserved all their moral indignation for Napoleon and all their admiration for England; yet Napoleon rendered them the greatest services by cleaning out Germany's Augean stables and establishing civilised means of communication, whereas the English only waited for the opportunity to exploit them *à tort et à travers.*[a] In the same petty-bourgeois spirit the German princes imagined they were fighting for the principle of legitimism and against revolution, whereas they were only the paid mercenaries of the English bourgeoisie. In the atmosphere of these universal illusions it was quite in the order of things that the estates privileged to cherish illusions — ideologists, schoolmasters, students, members of the *Tugendbund*[56] — should talk big and give a suitable high-flown expression to the universal mood of fantasy and indifference.

The political forms corresponding to a developed bourgeoisie were passed on to the Germans from outside by the July revolution[b] — as we mention only a few main points we omit the intermediary period. Since German economic relations had by no means reached the stage of development to which these political forms corresponded, the middle class accepted them merely as abstract ideas, principles valid in and for themselves, pious wishes and phrases, Kantian self-determinations of the will and of human beings as they ought to be. Consequently their attitude to these forms was far more moral and disinterested than that of other nations, i. e., they exhibited a highly peculiar narrow-mindedness and remained unsuccessful in all their endeavours.

Finally the ever more powerful foreign competition and world intercourse — from which it became less and less possible for Germany to stand aside — compelled the diverse local interests in Germany to adopt some sort of common attitude. Particularly since 1840, the German middle class began to think about safeguarding these common interests; its attitude became national and liberal and it demanded protective tariffs and constitutions. Thus it has now got almost as far as the French bourgeoisie in 1789.

If, like the Berlin ideologists, one judges liberalism and the state within the framework of local German impressions, or limits oneself merely to criticism of German-bourgeois illusions about liberalism, instead of seeing the correlation of liberalism with the real interests from which it originated and without which it cannot really exist — then, of course, one arrives at the most banal conclusions. This German liberalism, in the form in which it expressed itself up to the most recent period, is, as we have seen, even in its popular form, empty enthusiasm, ideological reflections about *real* liberalism. How easy it is,

---

[a] At random, recklessly.— *Ed.*

[b] Of 1830.— *Ed.*

therefore, to transform its content wholly into philosophy, into pure conceptual determinations, into "rational cognition"! Hence if one is so unfortunate as to know even this bourgeoisified liberalism only in the sublimated form given it by Hegel and the school-masters who depend on him, then one will arrive at conclusions belonging exclusively to the sphere of the holy. Sancho will provide us with a pitiful example of this.

"Recently" in active circles "so much has been said" about the rule of the bourgeois, "that it is not surprising that news of it", if only through the medium of L. Blanc (translated by the Berliner Buhl),[a] etc., "has even penetrated to Berlin" and there attracted the attention of easy-going school-masters. (*Wigand*, p. 190.) It cannot, however, be said that "Stirner" in his method of appropriating current ideas has "adopted a particularly fruitful and profitable style" (*Wigand*, ibid.) — as was already evident from his exploitation of Hegel and will now be further exemplified.

It has not escaped our school-master that in recent times the liberals have been identified with the bourgeois. Since Saint Max identifies the bourgeois with the good burghers, with the petty German burghers, he does not grasp what has been transmitted to him as it is in fact and as it is expressed by all competent authors — viz., that the liberal phrases are the idealistic expression of the real interests of the bourgeoisie — but, on the contrary, as meaning that the final goal of the bourgeois is to become a perfect liberal, a citizen of the state. For Saint Max the bourgeois is not the truth of the *citoyen*, but the *citoyen* the truth of the bourgeois. This conception, which is as holy as it is German, goes to such lengths that, on page 130, "the middle class" (it should read: the domination of the bourgeoisie) is transformed into a "*thought, nothing but* a thought" and "the state" comes forward as the "true man", who in the "Rights of Man" confers the rights of "Man", the true solemnisation on each individual bourgeois. And all this occurs after the illusions about the state and the rights of man had already been adequately exposed in the *Deutsch-Französische Jahrbücher*,* a fact which Saint Max

* In the *Deutsch-Französische Jahrbücher* this was done, in view of the context, only in relation to the rights of man proclaimed by the French Revolution. [Cf. Karl Marx, "Zur Judenfrage" (see Karl Marx and Frederick Engels, *Collected Works*, Vol 3, pp. 161-65).— *Ed.*] Incidentally, this whole conception of competition as "the rights of man" can already be found

[a] The reference is to Louis Blanc, *Histoire de dix ans 1830-1840*, which appeared in Berlin in 1844-45 in Ludwig Buhl's translation under the title *Geschichte der Zehn Jahre.— Ed.*

notices at last in his "Apologetical Commentary" anno 1845. Hence he can transform the bourgeois — having separated the bourgeois as a liberal from the empirical bourgeois — into a holy liberal, just as he transforms the state into the "holy", and the relation of the bourgeois to the modern state into a holy relation, into a *cult* (p. 131) — and with this, in effect, he concludes his criticism of political liberalism. He has transformed it into the "holy".*

We wish to give here a few examples of how Saint Max embellishes this property of his with historical arabesques. For this purpose he uses the French Revolution, concerning which a small contract to supply him with a few data has been negotiated by his history-broker, Saint Bruno.

On the basis of a few words from Bailly, obtained moreover through the intermediary of Saint Bruno's *Denkwürdigkeiten*,[a] the statement is made that through the convening of the States General "those who hitherto were subjects arrive at the consciousness that they are proprietors". (P. 132.) On the contrary, *mon brave!* By the convening of the States General, those who hitherto were proprietors show their consciousness of being no longer subjects — a consciousness which was long ago arrived at, for example in the Physiocrats, and — in polemical form against the bourgeoisie — in Linguet (*Théorie des lois civiles*, 1767), Mercier, Mably, and, in general, in the writings against the Physiocrats. This meaning was also immediately understood at the beginning of the revolution — for example by Brissot, Fauchet, Marat, in the *Cercle social*[57] and by all the democratic opponents of Lafayette. If Saint Max had understood the matter as it took place independently of his history-broker, he would not have been surprised that "Bailly's words certainly *sound* [as if each man were now a proprietor..." and that the bourgeois ... express ... the rule of the proprietors ... that now the proprietors have become the bourgeoisie *par excellence*.[58]]

among representatives of the bourgeoisie a century earlier (John Hampden. Petty, Boisguillebert, Child, etc.). On the relation of the theoretical liberals to the bourgeois compare what has been said [above] on the relation of the ideologists of a class to the class itself. [See this volume, p. 190.— *Ed.*]

* [The following passage is crossed out in the manuscript:] For him thereby criticism as a whole "achieves its final goal" and all cats turn grey, thereby he also admits his ignorance of the *real* basis and the real content of the rule of the bourgeoisie.

---

[a] A reference to Edgar Bauer's essay "Bailly und die ersten Tage der Französischen Revolution" in *Denkwürdigkeiten zur Geschichte der neuen Zeit seit der Revolution*, by Bruno and Edgar Bauer.— *Ed.*

[...] "As early as July 8 the statement of the Bishop of Autun[a] and Barère [destroyed] the illusion that [each man], the individual, was of importance in the legislature; it [showed] the utter impotence of the constituents. The majority of the deputies has become master." [Stirner, op. cit., p. 132 f.]

The "*statement* of the Bishop of Autun and Barère" is a *motion* tabled by the former on July 4 (not 8), with which Barère had nothing to do except that together with many others he supported it on July 8. It was carried on July 9, hence it is not at all clear why Saint Max speaks of "July 8". This motion by no means "destroyed" "the illusion that *each man, the individual,* was of importance", etc.; but it destroyed the binding force of the *Cahiers* given to the deputies, that is, the influence and the "importance", not of "each man, the individual", but of the feudal 177 *bailliages* and 431 *divisions des ordres.* By carrying the motion, the Assembly discarded the characteristic features of the old, feudal *États généraux.*[59] Moreover, it was at that time by no means a question of the correct theory of popular representation, but of highly practical, essential problems. Broglie's army held Paris at bay and drew nearer every day; the capital was in a state of utmost agitation; hardly a fortnight had passed since the *jeu de paume* and the *lit de justice*[60]; the court was plotting with the bulk of the aristocracy and the clergy against the National Assembly; lastly, owing to the still existing feudal provincial tariff barriers, and as a result of the feudal agrarian system as a whole, most of the provinces were in the grip of famine and there was a great scarcity of money. At that moment it was a question of an *assemblée essentiellement active,* as Talleyrand himself put it, while the *Cahiers* of [the] aristocratic and other reactionary groups provided the court with an opportunity to declare [the] decision of the Assembly [void by referring] to the wishes of the constituents. The Assembly proclaimed its independence by carrying Talleyrand's motion and seized the power it required, which in the political sphere could, of course, only be done within the framework of political form and by making use of the existing theories of Rousseau, etc. (Cf. *Le point du jour*, par Barère de Vieuzac, 1789, Nos. 15 and 17.) The National Assembly had to take this step because it was being urged forward by the immense mass of the people that stood behind it. By so doing, therefore, it did not at all transform itself into an "utterly egoistical chamber, completely cut off from the umbilical cord and ruthless"

---

[a] I. e., Talleyrand, who was Bishop of Autun from 1788 to 1791.— *Ed.*

[p. 147]; on the contrary it actually transformed itself thereby into the *true organ* of the vast majority of Frenchmen, who would otherwise have crushed it, as they later crushed "utterly egoistical" deputies who "completely cut themselves off from the umbilical cord". But Saint Max, with the help of his history-broker, sees here merely the solution of a theoretical question; he takes the Constituent Assembly, six days before the storming of the Bastille, for a council of *church fathers* debating a point of dogma! The question regarding the "importance of each man, the individual", can, moreover, only arise in a democratically elected representative body, and during the revolution it only came up for discussion in the Convention, and for as empirical reasons as earlier the question of the *Cahiers.* A problem which the Constituent Assembly decided *also* theoretically was the distinction between the representative body of a ruling *class* and that of the ruling *estates*; and this political rule of the bourgeois *class* was determined by each individual's position, since it was determined by the relations of production prevailing at the time. The representative system is a very specific product of modern bourgeois society which is as inseparable from the latter as is the isolated individual of modern times.

Just as here Saint Max takes the 177 *bailliages* and 431 *divisions des ordres* for "individuals", so he later sees in the absolute monarch and his *car tel est notre plaisir*[a] the rule of the "individual" as against the constitutional monarch, the "rule of the apparition ["] (p. 141), and in the aristocrat and the guild-member he again sees the "individual" in contrast to the citizen. (P. 137.)

> "The Revolution was not directed against *reality,* but against this reality, against this *definite existence.*" (P. 145.)

Hence, not against the really existing system of landowner-ship, of taxes, of customs duties which hampered commerce at every turn, and the [...]

[...][b] "Stirner" thinks] it makes no difference ["to 'the good burghers' who defends them] and their principles, whether an absolute or a constitutional king, a republic, etc." — For the "good burghers" who quietly drink their beer in a Berlin beer-cellar this undoubtedly "makes no difference"; but for the historical bourgeois it is by no means a matter of indifference.

---

[a] For this is our will — the concluding words of royal edicts.— *Ed.*

[b] A gap in the manuscript.— *Ed.*

The "good burgher" "Stirner" here again imagines — as he does throughout this section — that the French, American and English bourgeois are good Berlin beer-drinking philistines. If one translates the sentence above from the language of political illusion into plain language, it means: "it makes no difference" to the bourgeoisie whether it rules unrestrictedly or whether its political and economic power is counterbalanced by other classes. Saint Max believes that an absolute king, or someone else, *could* defend the bourgeoisie just as successfully as it defends itself. And even "its principles", which consist in subordinating state power to "*chacun pour soi, chacun chez soi*"[a] and exploiting it for that purpose — an "absolute monarch" is supposed to be able to do that! Let Saint Max name any country with developed trade and industry and strong competition where the bourgeoisie entrusts its defence to an "absolute monarch".

After this transformation of the historical bourgeois into German philistines devoid of history, "Stirner", of course, does not need to know any other bourgeois than "comfortable burghers and loyal officials" (!!) — two spectres who only dare to show themselves on "holy" German soil — and can lump together the whole class as "obedient servants" (p. 138). Let him just take a look at these obedient servants on the stock exchanges of London, Manchester, New York and Paris. Since Saint Max is well under way, he can now go the whole hog[b] and, believing one of the narrow-minded theoreticians of the *Einundzwanzig Bogen* who says that "liberalism is rational cognition applied to our existing conditions"[c], can declare that "the liberals are fighters for reason". It is evident from these [...] phrases how little the Germans have recovered [from] their original illusions about liberalism. Abraham "against hope believed in hope" ... and his faith "was imputed to him for righteousness" (Romans 4:18 and 22).

"The state pays well, so that its good citizens can without danger pay poorly; it provides itself by means of good payment with servants from whom it forms a force — the police — for the protection of good citizens and the good citizens willingly pay high taxes to the state in order to pay so much lower amounts to their workers." (P. 152.)

---

[a] Each for himself and the devil take the hindmost.— *Ed.*

[b] The words "the whole hog" are in English in the manuscript.— *Ed.*

[c] From the article "Preussen seit der Einsetzung Arndt's bis zur Absetzung Bauer's" published anonymously in the *Einundzwanzig Bogen aus der Schweiz.— Ed.*

This should read: the bourgeois pay their state well and make the nation pay for it so that without risk they should be able to pay poorly; by good payment they ensure that the state servants are a force available for their protection — the police; they willingly pay, and force the nation to pay high taxes so as to be able without danger to shift the sums they pay on to the workers as a levy (as a deduction from wages). "Stirner" here makes the new economic discovery that wages are a levy, a tax, paid by the bourgeois to the proletarian; whereas the other, mundane economists regard taxes as a tribute which the proletarian pays to the bourgeois.

Our holy church father now passes from the holy middle class to the Stirnerian "unique" proletariat. (P. 148.) The latter consists of "rogues, prostitutes, thieves, robbers and murderers, gamblers, propertyless people with no occupation and frivolous individuals". (Ibid.) They form the "dangerous proletariat" and for a moment are reduced by "Stirner" to "individual shouters", and then, finally, to "vagabonds", who find their perfect expression in the "*spiritual* vagabonds" who do not "keep within the bounds of a moderate way of thinking"....

"*So wide a meaning* has the so-called proletariat or" (*per appos.*) "pauperism!" (P. 149.)

On page 151 ["on the other hand,] the state sucks the life-blood" of the proletariat. Hence the entire proletariat consists of ruined bourgeois and ruined proletarians, of a collection of *ragamuffins*, who have existed in every epoch and whose existence *on a mass scale* after the decline of the Middle Ages preceded the mass formation of the ordinary proletariat, as Saint Max can ascertain by a perusal of English and French legislation and literature. Our saint has exactly the same notion of the proletariat as the "good comfortable burghers" and, particularly, the "loyal officials". He is consistent also in identifying the proletariat with pauperism, whereas pauperism is the position only of the ruined proletariat, the lowest level to which the proletarian sinks who has become incapable of resisting the pressure of the bourgeoisie, and it is only the proletarian whose whole energy has been sapped who becomes a pauper. Compare Sismondi,[a] Wade,[b] etc. "Stirner" and his

---

[a] Simonde de Sismondi, *Nouveaux principes d'économie politique.— Ed.*
[b] John Wade, *History of the Middle and Working Classes.— Ed.*

fraternity, for example, can in the eyes of the proletarians, in certain circumstances count as paupers but never as proletarians.

Such are Saint Max's "own" ideas about the bourgeoisie and the proletariat. But since with these imaginations about liberalism, good burghers and vagabonds he, of course, gets nowhere, he finds himself compelled in order to make the transition to communism to bring in the actual, ordinary bourgeois and proletarians insofar as he knows about them from hearsay. This occurs on pages 151 and 152, where the lumpen-proletariat becomes transformed into "workers", into ordinary proletarians, while the bourgeois "in course of time" undergoes "occasionally" a series of "various transformations" and "manifold refractions". In one line we read: "*The propertied rule*", i.e., the profane bourgeois; six lines later we read: "The citizen is what he is by the grace of the state", i.e., the holy bourgeois; yet another six lines later: "The state is the *status* of the middle class", i.e., the profane bourgeois; this is then explained by saying that "the state gives the propertied" "their property in feudal possession" and that the "money and property" of the "capitalists", i.e., the holy bourgeois, is such "state property" transferred by the state to "feudal possession". Finally, this omnipotent state is again transformed into the "state of the propertied", i.e., of the profane bourgeois, which is in accord with a later passage: "Owing to the revolution the *bourgeoisie became o m n i p o t e n t*" (p. 156). Even Saint Max would never have been able to achieve these "heartrending" and "horrible" contradictions—at any rate, he would never have dared to promulgate them—had he not had the assistance of the German word *Bürger* [citizen], which he can interpret at will as "*citoyen*" or as "*bourgeois*" or as the German "good burgher".

Before going further, we must take note of two more great politico-economic discoveries which our simpleton "brings into being" "in the depths of his heart" and which have in common with the "joy of youth" of page 17 the feature of being also "pure thoughts".

On page 150 all the evil of the existing social relations is reduced to the fact that "burghers and workers believe in the 'truth' of money". Jacques le bonhomme imagines that it is in the power of the "burghers" and "workers", who are scattered among all civilised states of the world, suddenly, one fine day, to put on record their "disbelief" in the "truth of money"; he even believes that if this nonsense were possible, something would be achieved by it. He believes that any Berlin writer could abolish the "truth of money" with the same ease as he abolishes in his mind the "truth" of God or of Hegelian philosophy. That money is a necessary product of definite relations of production and intercourse and remains a "truth" so long as these relations exist — this, of course, is of no concern to a holy man like Saint Max, who raises his eyes towards heaven and turns his profane backside to the profane world.

The second discovery is made on page 152 and amounts to this, that "the worker cannot turn his labour to account" because he "falls into the hands" of "those who" have received "some kind of state property" "in feudal possession". This is merely a further explanation of the sentence on page 151 already quoted above where the state sucks the life-blood of the worker. And here everyone will immediately "put forward" "the simple reflection"—that "Stirner" does not do so is not "surprising"—how does it come about that the state has not given the "workers" also some sort of "state property" in "feudal possession". If Saint Max had asked himself this question he would probably have managed to do without his construction of the "holy" burghers, because he would have been bound to see the relation in which the propertied stand to the modern state.

By means of the opposition of the bourgeoisie and proletariat — as even "Stirner" knows — one arrives at communism. But *how* one arrives at it, *only* "Stirner" knows.

"The workers have the most tremendous power in their hands ... they have *only* to cease work and to *regard* what they have produced by their labour as their property and to enjoy it. This is the meaning of the workers' disturbances which flare up *here and there*." (P. 153.)

Workers' disturbances, which even under the Byzantine Emperor Zeno led to the promulgation of a law (Zeno, *de novis operibus constitutio*[a]), which "flared up" in the fourteenth century in the form of the Jacquerie and Wat Tyler's rebellion, in 1518 on the Evil May Day[b] in London, and in 1549 in the great uprising of the tanner Kett,[61] and later gave rise to Act 15 of the second and third year of the reign of Edward VI, and a series of similar Acts of Parliament; the disturbances which soon afterwards, in 1640 and 1659 (eight uprisings in one year), took place in Paris and which already since the fourteenth century

---

[a] Zeno, Decree on New Works.— *Ed.*
[b] The words "Evil May Day" are in English in the original.— *Ed.*

must have been frequent in France and England, judging by the legislation of the time; the constant war which since 1770 in England and since the revolution in France has been waged with might and cunning by the workers against the bourgeoisie — all this exists for Saint Max only "here and there", in Silesia, Poznan, Magdeburg and Berlin, "according to German newspaper reports".

What is produced by labour, according to Jacques le bonhomme's imagination, would continue to exist and be reproduced, as an object to be "regarded" and "enjoyed", even if the producers "ceased work".

As he did earlier in the case of money, now again our good burgher transforms "the workers", who are scattered throughout the civilised world, into a private club which has only to adopt a decision in order to get rid of all difficulties. Saint Max does not know, of course, that at least fifty attempts have been made in England since 1830, and at the present moment yet another is being made, to gather all the English workers into a single association and that highly empirical causes have frustrated the success of all these projects. He does not know that even a minority of workers who combine and go on strike very soon find themselves compelled to act in a revolutionary way — a fact he could have learned from the 1842 uprising in England and from the earlier Welsh uprising of 1839, in which year the revolutionary excitement among the workers first found comprehensive expression in the "sacred month", which was proclaimed simultaneously with a general arming of the people.[62] Here again we see how Saint Max constantly tries to pass off his nonsense as "*the* meaning" of historical facts (in which he is successful at best in relation to *his* "One") — historical facts "on which he foists his own meaning, which are thus bound to lead to nonsense". (*Wigand*, p. 194.) Incidentally, it would never enter the head of any proletarian to turn to Saint Max for advice about the "meaning" of the proletarian movements or what should be undertaken at the present time against the bourgeoisie.

After this great campaign, our Saint Sancho returns to his Maritornes with the following fanfare:

> "The state rests on the *slavery of labour*. If *labour* were to become *free*, the state would be lost." (P. 153)

The *modern* state, the rule of the bourgeoisie, is based on *freedom of labour*. The idea that along with freedom of religion, state, thought, etc., and hence "occasionally" "also" "perhaps" with freedom of *labour*, not I become free, but only one of my enslavers — this idea was borrowed by Saint Max himself, many times, though in a very distorted form, from the *Deutsch-Französische Jahrbücher*.[a] Freedom of labour is free competition of the workers among themselves. Saint Max is very unfortunate in political economy as in *all other* spheres. Labour *is* free in all civilised countries; it is not a matter of freeing labour but of abolishing it.

B. Communism

Saint Max calls communism "social liberalism", because he is well aware how great is the disrepute of the word liberalism among the radicals of 1842 and the most advanced Berlin "free-thinkers".[63] This transformation gives him at the same time the opportunity and courage to put into the mouths of the "social liberals" all sorts of things which had never been uttered before "Stirner" and the refutation of which is intended to serve also as a refutation of *communism*.

Communism is overcome by means of a series of partly logical and partly historical constructions.

First logical construction.

Because "we have seen ourselves made into servants of egoists", "we should" not ourselves "become egoists ... but should rather see to it that egoists become impossible. We want to turn them all into ragamuffins, we want no one to possess anything, in order that 'all' should be possessors.— So say the social [liberals].— Who is this person whom you call 'all'? It is 'society'". (P. 153.)

With the aid of a few quotation marks Sancho here transforms "all" into a person, society as a person, as a subject=holy society, the holy. Now our saint knows what he is about and can let loose the whole torrent of his flaming anger against "the holy", as the result of which, of course, communism is annihilated.

That Saint Max here again puts *his* nonsense into the mouth of the "social [liberals]", as being the meaning of *their* words, is not "surprising". He identifies first of all "owning" as a private property-owner with "owning" in general. Instead of examining the definite relations between private property and production, instead of examining "owning" as a landed proprietor, as a rentier, as a merchant, as a factory-owner, as a worker — where "owning" would be found to be a quite distinct kind of owning,

---

[a] Cf. Karl Marx and Frederick Engels, *Collected Works*, Vol. 3, p. 152.— *Ed.*

control over other people's labour — he transforms all these relations into "owning as such".[a]

[...] political liberalism, which made the "nation" the supreme owner. Hence communism has no longer to "abolish" any "personal property" but, at most, has to equalise the distribution of "feudal possessions", to introduce *égalité* there.

On society as "supreme owner" and on the "ragamuffin", Saint Max should compare, *inter alia, L'Égalitaire* for 1840:

"Social property is a contradiction, but social wealth is a consequence of communism. Fourier, in contradistinction to the modest bourgeois moralists, repeats a hundred times that it is not a social evil that some have too much but that all have too little", and therefore draws attention also to the "poverty of the rich", in *La fausse industrie*, Paris, 1835, p. 410.

Similarly as far back as 1839 — hence before Weitling's *Garantien*[b] — it is stated in the German communist magazine *Die Stimme des Volks* (second issue, p. 14) published in Paris:

"Private property, the much praised, industrious, comfortable, innocent 'private gain', does obvious harm to the wealth of life."[c]

Saint Sancho here takes as communism the ideas of a few liberals tending towards communism, and the mode of expression of some communists who, for very practical reasons, express themselves in a political form.

After "Stirner" has transferred property to "society", all the members of this society in his eyes at once become paupers and ragamuffins, although — even according to *his* idea of the communist order of things — they "own" the "supreme owner". — His benevolent proposal to the communists — "to transform the word 'Lump'[d] into an honourable form of address, just as the revolution did with the word 'citizen'" — is a striking example of how he confuses communism with something which long ago passed away. The revolution even "transformed" the word sansculotte "into an honourable form of address", as against "*honnêtes gens*", which he translates very inadequately as good citizens. Saint Sancho does this in order that there may be fulfilled the words in the book of the

---

[a] Four pages of the manuscript are missing here which contained the end of the "*first logical construction*" and the beginning of the "*second logical construction*". — *Ed.*

[b] Wilhelm Weitling, *Garantien der Harmonie und Freiheit.* — *Ed.*

[c] This seems to be a quotation from the article "Politischer und Socialer Umschwung" published in *Blätter der Zukunft*, 1846, No. 5. *Die Stimme des Volks* was probably mentioned by mistake. — *Ed.*

[d] Ragamuffin. — *Ed.*

prophet Merlin about the three thousand and three hundred slaps which the man who is to come will have to give himself:

> Es menester que Sancho tu escudero
> Se dé tres mil azotes, y trecientos
> En *ambas sus valientes posaderas*
> Al aire descubiertas, y de modo
> Que le escuezan, le amarguen y le enfaden.

(Don Quijote, tomo II, cap. 35.).[a]

Saint Sancho notes that the "elevation of society to supreme owner" is a "second *robbery* of the personal element in the interests of humanity", while communism is only the completed robbery of the "robbery of the personal element". "Since he unquestionably regards robbery as detestable", Saint Sancho "therefore believes for example" that he "has branded" communism "already by the" above "proposition" ("the book", p. 102). "Once" "Stirner" has "detected" "even robbery" in communism, "how could he fail to feel 'profound disgust' at it and 'just indignation'"! (*Wigand*, p. 156.) We now challenge "Stirner" to name a bourgeois who has written about communism (or Chartism) and has not put forward the same absurdity with great emphasis. Communism will certainly carry out "robbery" of what the bourgeois regards as "personal".

First corollary.

Page 349: "Liberalism at once came forward with the statement that it is an essential feature of man to be not *property*, but *property-owner*. Since it was a question here of man, and not of an individual, the question of how much, which was precisely what constituted the particular interest of individuals, was left to their discretion. *Therefore*, the egoism of individuals had the widest scope as regards this how much and carried on tireless competition."

That is to say: liberalism, i.e., liberal private property-owners, at the beginning of the French Revolution gave private property a liberal appearance by declaring it one of the rights of man. They were forced to do so if only because of their position as a revolutionising party; they were even compelled not only to give the mass of the French [rural] population the right to property, [but also] to let them *seize actual* property, and they could do all this because thereby their own "how much", which

---

[a] Needful it is that your squire, Sancho Panza,
Shall deal himself three thousand and three hundred
Lashes upon his two *most ample buttocks,*
Both to the air exposed, and in such sort
That they shall smart, and sting and vex him sorely.
(Don Quixote, Vol. II, Ch. 35.)—*Ed.*

was what chiefly interested them, remained intact and was even made safe.

We find here further that Saint Max makes competition arise from liberalism, a slap that he gives history in revenge for the slaps which he had to give himself above. A "more exact explanation" of the manifesto with which he makes liberalism "*at once* come forward" can be found in Hegel, who in 1820 expressed himself as follows:

"In respect of external things it is rational" (i.e., it becomes me as reason, as a man) "that I should possess property... what and *how much* I possess is, therefore, legally a matter of chance." (*Rechtsphilosophie*,[a] § 49.)

It is characteristic of Hegel that he turns the phrase of the bourgeois into the true concept, into the essence of property, and "Stirner" faithfully imitates him. On the basis of the above analysis, Saint Max now makes the further statement, that

communism "raised the question as to *how much* property, and answered it in the sense that man should have as much as he needs. Can my egoism be satisfied with that?... No. I must rather have as much as I am capable of appropriating." (P. 349.)

First of all it should be remarked here that communism has by no means originated from § 49 of Hegel's *Rechtsphilosophie* and its "what and how much". Secondly, "communism" does not dream of wanting to give anything to "man", for "communism" is not at all of the opinion that "man" "needs" anything apart from a brief critical elucidation. Thirdly, Stirner foists on to communism the conception of "need" held by the present-day bourgeois; hence he introduces a distinction which, on account of its paltriness, can be of importance only in present-day society and its ideal copy — Stirner's union of "individual shouters" and free seamstresses. "Stirner" has again achieved great "penetration" into the essence of communism. Finally, in his demand to have as much as he is capable of appropriating (if this is not the usual bourgeois phrase that everyone should have as much as his ability[b] permits him, that everyone should have the right of free gain), Saint Sancho assumes communism as having already been achieved in order to be able freely to develop his "ability" and put it into operation, which by no means depends solely on him, any more than his fortune itself,

---

[a] G.W.F. Hegel, *Grundlinien der Philosophie des Rechts*. The preface to this work is dated June 25, 1820.— *Ed.*

[b] The German word *Vermögen* used several times in this passage means not only ability, capability but also wealth, fortune, means, property; the authors here play on the various meanings of the word.— *Ed.*

but depends also on the relations of production and intercourse in which he lives. (Cf. the chapter on the "Union".[a]) Incidentally, even Saint Max himself does not behave according to his doctrine, for throughout his "book" he "needs" things and uses things which he was not "capable of appropriating".

Second corollary.

"But the social reformers preach a social law to us. The individual thus becomes the slave of society." (P. 246.) "In the opinion of the communists, everyone should enjoy the eternal rights of man." (P. 238.)

Concerning the expressions "law", "labour", etc., how they are used by proletarian writers and what should be the attitude of criticism towards them, we shall speak in connection with "true socialism" (see Volume II). As far as law is concerned, we with many others have stressed the opposition of communism to law, both political and private, as also in its most general form as the rights of man. See the *Deutsch-Französische Jahrbücher*, where privilege, the special right, is considered as something corresponding to private property inseparable from social classes, and law as something corresponding to the state of competition, of free private property (p. 206 and elsewhere); equally, the rights of man themselves are considered as privilege, and private property as monopoly. Further, criticism of law is brought into connection with German philosophy and presented as the consequence of criticism of religion (p. 72); further, it is expressly stated that the legal axioms that are supposed to lead to communism are axioms of private property, and the right of common ownership is an imaginary premise of the right of private property. (Pp. 98, 99.)[b] Incidentally, even in the works of German Communists passages appeared very early — e.g., in the writings of Hess, *Einundzwanzig Bogen aus der Schweiz*, 1843, p. 326[c] and elsewhere — which could be appropriated and distorted by Stirner in his criticism of law.

Incidentally, the idea of using the phrase quoted above against Babeuf, of regarding him as the theoretical representa-

---

[a] See this volume, pp. 415-18.— *Ed.*

[b] Cf. "Outlines of a Critique of Political Economy" by Engels and "Contribution to the Critique of Hegel's Philosophy of Law. Introduction" and "On the Jewish Question" by Marx (see Karl Marx and Frederick Engels, *Collected Works*, Vol. 3, pp. 408, 175, 146).— *Ed.*

[c] This refers to Moses Hess' article "Philosophie der That", which was published in *Einundzwanzig Bogen aus der Schweiz.— Ed.*

tive of communism could only occur to a Berlin school-master. "Stirner", however, has the effrontery to assert on page 247 that

communism, which assumes "that all people by nature have equal rights, refutes its own thesis and asserts that people by nature have no rights at all. For it does not want, for example, to admit that parents have rights in relation to their children; it abolishes the family. In general, this whole revolutionary or Babouvist principle (compare *Die Kommunisten in der Schweiz, Kommissional-bericht*,[a] p. 3) is based on a religious, i.e., false, outlook".

A Yankee comes to England, where he is prevented by a Justice of the Peace from flogging his slave, and he exclaims indignantly: "Do you call this a land of liberty, where a man can't larrup his nigger?"[b]

Saint Sancho here makes himself doubly ridiculous. Firstly, he sees an abolition of the "equal rights of man" in the recognition of the "equal rights by nature" of children in relation to parents, in the granting of *the same* rights of man to children as well as to parents. Secondly, two pages previously Jacques le bonhomme tells us that the state does not interfere when a father beats his son, because it recognises family rights. Thus, what he presents, on the one hand, as a particular right (family right), he includes, on the other hand, among the "equal rights of man by nature". Finally, he admits that he knows Babeuf only from the Bluntschli report, while this report (p. 3), in turn, admits that its wisdom is derived from the worthy L. Stein,[c] Doctor of Law. Saint Sancho's thorough knowledge of communism is evident from this quotation. Just as Saint Bruno is his broker as regards revolution, so Saint Bluntschli is his broker as regards communists. With such a state of affairs we ought not to be surprised that a few lines lower down our rustic word of God[d] reduces the *fraternité* of the Revolution to "equality of the children of God" (in what Christian dogma is there any talk of *égalité*?).

Third corollary.

Page 414: Because the principle of community culminates in communism, therefore, communism = "apotheosis of the state founded on love".

---

[a] Johann Caspar Bluntschli, *Die Kommunisten in der Schweiz nach den bei Weitling vorgefundenen Papieren.— Ed.*

[b] This sentence is in English in the original.— *Ed.*

[c] Lorenz von Stein, *Der Socialismus und Communismus des heutigen Frankreichs.— Ed.*

[d] Cf. August Friedrich Ernst Langbein's poem "Der Landprediger".— *Ed.*

From the state founded on love, which is Saint Max's own fabrication, he here derives communism, which then, of course, remains an exclusively Stirnerian communism. Saint Sancho knows only egoism on the one hand or the claim to the loving services, pity and alms of people on the other hand. Outside and above this dilemma nothing exists for him at all.

Third logical construction.

"Since the most oppressive evils are to be observed in society, it is especially" (!) "the oppressed" (!) who "think that the blame is to be found in society and set themselves the task of discovering the right society". (P. 155.)

On the contrary, it is "Stirner" who "sets himself the task" of discovering the "society" which is "right" for *him*, the holy society, the society as the incarnation of the holy. Those who are "oppressed" nowadays "in society", "think" only about how to achieve the society which is *right for them*, and this consists primarily in abolishing the present society on the basis of the existing productive forces. If, e.g., "oppressive evils are to be observed" in a machine, if, for example, it refuses to work, and those who need the machine (for example, in order to make money) find the fault in the machine and try to alter it, etc.— then, in Saint Sancho's opinion, they are setting themselves the task not of putting the machine *right*, but of discovering the *right* machine, the holy machine, the machine as the incarnation of the holy, the holy as a machine, the machine in the heavens. "Stirner" advises them to seek the blame "*in themselves*". Is it not their fault that, for example, they need a hoe and a plough? Could they not use their bare hands to plant potatoes and to extract them from the soil afterwards? The saint, on page 156, preaches to them as follows:

"It is merely an ancient phenomenon that one seeks first of all to lay the blame anywhere but on oneself — and therefore on the state, on the selfishness of the rich, for which, however, we ourselves are to blame."

The "oppressed" who seeks to lay the "blame" for pauperism on the "state" is, as we have noted above, no other than Jacques le bonhomme himself. Secondly, the "oppressed" who comforts himself by causing the "blame" to be laid on the "selfishness of the rich" is again no other than Jacques le bonhomme. He could have learned something better about the other oppressed from the *Facts and Fictions* of John Watts,[a]

---

[a] John Watts, *The Facts and Fictions of Political Economists.*— *Ed.*

tailor and doctor of philosophy, from Hobson's *Poor Man's Companion*, etc. And, thirdly, who is the person that should bear the "blame"? Is it, perhaps, the proletarian child who comes into the world tainted with scrofula, who is reared with the help of opium and is sent into the factory when seven years old — or is it, perhaps, the individual worker who is here expected to "revolt" by himself against the world market — or is it, perhaps, the girl who must either starve or become a prostitute? No, not these but only he who seeks "all the blame", i.e., the "blame" for everything in the present state of the world, "in himself", viz., once again no other than Jacques le bonhomme himself. "This is merely the ancient phenomenon" of Christian heart-searching and doing penitence in a German-speculative form, with its idealist phraseology, according to which I, the actual man, do not have to change actuality, which I can only change together with others, but have to change myself in myself. "It is the internal struggle of the writer with himself." (*Die heilige Familie*, p. 122, cf. pp. 73, 121 and 306.[a])

According to Saint Sancho, therefore, those oppressed by society seek the right society. If he were consistent, he should make those who "seek to lay the blame on the state" — and according to him they are *the very same* people — also seek the *right state*. But he cannot do this, because he has heard that the Communists want to abolish the state. He has now to construct this abolition of the state, and our Saint Sancho once more achieves this with the aid of his "ass", the apposition, in a way that "looks very simple":

"Since the workers are in a *state of distress*" [*Notsand*], "the existing *state of affairs*" [*Stand der Dinge*], "i.e., the *state*" [*Staat*] (*status*=state or estate) "must be abolished". (Ibid.)

Thus:

the state of distress	=	the existing state of affairs
the existing state of affairs	=	state or estate
state, estate	=	*status*
status	=	the State

Conclusion: the state of distress=the State

[a] See Karl Marx and Frederick Engels, *Collected Works*, Vol. 4, pp. 83, 53, 82, 192.— *Ed.*

What could "look simpler"? "It is only surprising" that the English bourgeois in 1688 and the French in 1789 did not "put forward" the same "simple reflections" and equations, since in those times it was much more the case that estate=status = the state. It follows from this that wherever a "state of distress" exists, "the state", which is, of course, the same in Prussia and North America, must be abolished.

As is his custom, Saint Sancho now presents us with a few proverbs of Solomon.

Proverb of Solomon No. 1.

Page 163: "That society is no ego, which could give, etc., but an instrument from which we can derive benefit; that we have no social duties, but only interests; that we do not owe any sacrifices to society, but if we do sacrifice something we sacrifice it for ourselves — all this is disregarded by the social [liberals], because they are in thrall to the religious principle and are zealously striving for a — holy society."

The following "penetrations" into the essence of communism result from this:

1. Saint Sancho has quite forgotten that it was he himself who transformed "society" into an "ego" and that consequently he finds himself only in his own "society".

2. He believes that the Communists are only waiting for "society" to "give" them something, whereas at most they want to give themselves a society.

3. He transforms society, even before it exists, into an instrument from which he wants to derive benefit, without him and other people by their mutual social relations creating a society, and hence this "instrument".

4. He believes that in communist society there can be a question of "duties" and "interests", of two complementary aspects of an antithesis which exists only in bourgeois society (under the guise of interest the reflecting bourgeois always inserts a third thing between himself and his mode of action — a habit seen in truly classic form in Bentham, whose nose had to have some interest before it would decide to smell anything. Compare "the book" on the *right* to one's nose, page 247).

5. Saint Max believes that the Communists want to "make sacrifices" for "society", when they want at most to sacrifice existing society; in this case he should describe their consciousness that their struggle is the common cause of all people who have outgrown the bourgeois system as a sacrifice that they make to themselves.

6. That the social [liberals] are in thrall to the religious principle and

7. that they are striving for a holy society — these points have already been dealt with above. How "zealously" Saint Sancho "strives" for a "holy society", so as to be able to refute communism by means of it, we have already seen.
Proverb of Solomon No. 2.

Page 277: "If interest in the social problem were less passionate and blind, then *one* ... would understand that a society cannot be turned into a new one so long as those of whom it consists *and* who constitute it, remain as of old."

"Stirner" believes that the communist proletarians who revolutionise society and put the relations of production and the form of intercourse on a new basis — i.e., on themselves as new people, on their new mode of life — that these proletarians remain "as of old". The tireless propaganda carried on by these proletarians, their daily discussions among themselves, sufficiently prove how little they themselves want to remain "as of old", and how little they want people to remain "as of old". They would only remain "as of old" if, with Saint Sancho, they "sought the blame in themselves"; but they know too well that only under changed circumstances will they cease to be "as of old", and therefore they are determined to change these circumstances at the first opportunity. In revolutionary activity the changing of oneself coincides with the changing of circumstances. — This great saying is explained by means of an equally great example which, of course, is again taken from the world of "the holy".

"If, for example, the Jewish people was to give rise to a *society* which spread a new faith throughout the world, then *these apostles* could not remain Pharisees."

The first Christians	= a society for spreading faith (founded *anno* 1).
	= *Congregatio de propaganda fide*[64] (founded *anno* 1640).
Anno 1	= *Anno* 1640.
This society which should arise	= These apostles.
These apostles	= Non-Jews.
The Jewish people	= Pharisees.
Christians	= Non-Pharisees.
	= Not the Jewish people.

What can look simpler?

Reinforced by these equations, Saint Max calmly utters the great historic words[a]:

"Human beings, by no means intending to achieve their own development, *have always wanted* to form a society."

Human beings, by no means wanting to form a society, have, nevertheless, only achieved the development of society, because they have always wanted to develop only as isolated individuals and therefore achieved their own development only in and through society. Incidentally it would only occur to a saint of the type of our Sancho to separate the development of "human beings" from the development of the "society" in which they live, and then let his fantasy roam on this fantastic basis. Incidentally he has forgotten his own proposition, inspired by Saint Bruno, in which just previously he set people the moral demand of changing themselves and thereby changing their society — a proposition, therefore, in which he identifies the development of people with the development of their society.

Fourth logical construction.

On page 156 he makes the Communists say, in opposition to the citizens:

"Our essence" (!) "does not consist in all of us being equal children of the state" (!), "but in that we all exist for one another. We are all equal in that we all exist for one another, that each works for the other, that each of us is a worker." He then regards "to exist as a worker" as equivalent to "each of us exists *only* through the other", so that the other, "for example, works to clothe me, and I to satisfy his need of entertainment, he for my food and I for his instruction. Hence participation in labour is our dignity and our equality.

"What advantage do we derive from citizenship? Burdens. And what value is put on our labour? The lowest possible.... What can you put against us? Again, only labour!" "Only for labour do we owe you a recompense"; "only for what you do that is useful to us" "have you any claim on us". "We want to be only worth so much to you as we perform for you; but you should be valued by us in just the same way." "Deeds which are of some value to us, i.e., work beneficial to the community, determine value.... He who does something useful takes second place to no one, or — all workers (beneficial to the community) are equal. Since however the worker is worthy of his wage,[b] then let the wage also be equal." (Pp. 157, 158.)

With "Stirner", "communism" begins with searchings for "*essence*"; being a good "youth" he wants again only to "penetrate behind things". That communism is a highly practical

---

[a] Paraphrase of a line from Goethe's *Iphigenie auf Tauris* , Act I, Scene 3.— *Ed.*

[b] Cf. Luke 10:7.— *Ed.*

movement, pursuing practical aims by practical means, and that only perhaps in Germany, in opposing the German philosophers, can it spare a moment for the problem of "essence"—this, of course, is of no concern to our saint. This Stirnerian "communism", which yearns so much for "essence", arrives, therefore, only at a philosophical category, i.e., "being-for-one-another", which then by means of a few arbitrary equations:

Being-for-one-another =to exist *only* through another
=to exist as a worker
=universal community of workers

is brought somewhat closer to the empirical world. We would, moreover, challenge Saint Sancho to indicate, for example, in *Owen* (who, after all, as a representative of English communism can serve as an example of "communism" just as well as, for example, the non-communist Proudhon,* from whom the greater part of the above propositions were abstracted and then rearranged) a passage containing anything of these propositions about "essence", universal community of workers, etc. Incidentally we do not even have to go so far back. The third issue of *Die Stimme des Volks*, the German communist magazine already quoted above, says:

"What is today called labour is only a miserably small part of the vast, mighty process of production; for *religion* and *morality* honour with the name of *labour* only the kind of production that is repulsive and dangerous, and in addition they venture to embellish such labour with all kinds of maxims — as it were words of blessing (or witchcraft) — 'labour in the sweat of thy brow' as a test imposed by God; 'labour sweetens life' for encouragement, etc. The morality of the world in which we live takes very good care not to apply the term work to the pleasing and free aspects of human intercourse. These aspects are reviled by morality, although they too constitute production. Morality eagerly

* Proudhon, who was as early as 1841 strongly criticised by the communist workers' journal *La Fraternité* for advocating equal wages, community of workers in general and also the other economic prejudices which can be found in the works of this outstanding writer; Proudhon, from whom the Communists have accepted nothing but his criticism of property.... [The note was left unfinished.]

reviles them as vanity, vain pleasure, sensuality. Communism has exposed this hypocritical preaching, this miserable morality." [a]

As universal community of workers, Saint Max reduces the whole of communism to equal wages — a discovery which is then repeated in the following three "refractions": on page 351, "Against competition there rises the principle of the society of ragamuffins — *distribution*. Is it possible then that I, who am very resourceful[b] should have no advantage over one who is resourceless?" Further, on page 363, he speaks of a "universal tax on human activity in communist society". And, finally, on page 350, he ascribes to the Communists the view that "labour" is "the only resource" of man. Thus, Saint Max re-introduces into communism private property in its dual form — as distribution and wage-labour. As before in connection with "robbery", Saint Max here again displays the most ordinary and narrow-minded bourgeois views as "his own" "penetrations" into the essence of communism. He shows himself fully worthy of the honour of having been taught by Bluntschli. As a real petty bourgeois, he is then afraid that he, "who is very resourceful", "should have no advantage over one who is resourceless"— although he should fear nothing so much as being left to his own "resources".

Incidentally, he "who is very resourceful" imagines that citizenship is a matter of indifference to the proletarians, after he has first assumed that they *have* it. This is just as he imagined above that for the bourgeoisie the form of government is a matter of indifference. The workers attach so much importance to citizenship, i.e., to *active* citizenship, that where they *have* it, for instance in America, they "make good use" of it, and where they do not have it, they strive to obtain it. Compare the proceedings of the North American workers at innumerable meetings, the whole history of English Chartism, and of French communism and reformism.[65]

---

[a] This seems to be a quotation from the article "Politischer und Socialer Umschwung" published in *Blätter der Zukunft*, 1846, No. 5. *Die Stimme des Volks* was probably mentioned by mistake.— *Ed.*

[b] In this section the authors play on the different meanings of the word "*Vermögen*" and its derivatives *vielvermögend, unvermögend*, etc. "*Der Vielvermögende*" can denote a person who is able, capable, wealthy, powerful, resourceful, a man of property, etc.; der "*Unvermögende*", on the other hand, can mean unable, incapable, inept, powerless, impecunious, resourceless, etc. — *Ed.*

First corollary.

"The worker, being conscious that the essential thing about him is that he is a worker, keeps himself away from egoism and subordinates himself to the supremacy of a society of workers, just as the bourgeois adhered with devotion" (!) "to the state based on competition." (P. 162.)

The worker is at most conscious that for the bourgeois the essential thing about him is that he is a worker, who, therefore, can assert himself against the bourgeois as such. Both these discoveries of Saint Sancho, the "devotion of the bourgeois" and the "*state* based on competition", can be recorded only as fresh proofs of the "resourcefulness" of the "very resourceful" man.

Second corollary.

"The aim of communism *is supposed to be* the 'well-being of all'. *This indeed really looks* as though in this way no one need be in an inferior position. But what sort of well-being will this be? Have all one and the same well-being? Do all people feel equally well in one and the same circumstances?... If that is so, then it is a matter of 'true well-being'. Do we not thereby arrive precisely at the point where the tyranny of religion begins?... Society has decreed that a particular sort of well-being is 'true well-being', and if this well-being were, for example, *honestly earned enjoyment*, but you preferred enjoyable idleness, then society ... would prudently refrain from making provision for what is for you the rule of the holy, hierarchy][a] well-being. By proclaiming the well-being of all, communism destroys the well-being of those who up to now have lived as rentiers", etc. (Pp. 411, 412.)

"If that is so", the following equations result from it:

The well-being of all	= Communism
	= If that is so
	= One and the same well-being of all
	= Equal well-being of all in one and the same circumstances
	= True well-being
	= [Holy well-being, the holy,
	= Tyranny of religion.
Communism	= Tyranny of religion.

"This indeed really looks as though" "Stirner" has said the same thing about communism as he has said previously about everything else.

How deeply our saint has "penetrated" into the essence of communism is evident also from the fact that he ascribes to communism the desire to bring about "true well-being" in the

---

[a] This passage is enclosed in square brackets in the manuscript.— *Ed.*

shape of "honestly earned enjoyment". Who, except "Stirner" and a few Berlin cobblers and tailors, thinks of "honestly earned enjoyment"! * And, what is more, to put this into the mouth of communists, for whom the basis of this whole opposition between work and enjoyment disappears. Let our highly moral saint put his mind at rest on this score. "Honest earning" will be left to him and those whom, unknown to himself, he represents — his petty handicraftsmen who have been ruined by industrial freedom and are morally "indignant". "Enjoyable idleness", too, belongs wholly to the most trivial bourgeois outlook. But the crowning point of the whole statement is the artful bourgeois scruple that he raises against the communists: that they want to abolish the "well-being" of the rentier and yet talk about the "well-being of all". Consequently, he believes that in communist society there will still be rentiers, whose "well-being" would have to be abolished. He asserts that "well-being" *as rentier* is inherent in the individuals who are at present rentiers, that it is inseparable from their individuality, and he imagines that for these individuals there can exist no other "well-being" than that which is determined by their position as rentiers. He believes further that a society which has still to wage a struggle against rentiers and the like, is already organised in a communist way.** The communists, at any rate, will have no scruples about overthrowing the rule of the bourgeoisie and abolishing its "well-being", as soon as they are strong enough to do so.*** It does not matter to them at all

---

* [The following passage is crossed out in the manuscript:] Who, except Stirner, is able to attribute such moral absurdities to the immoral revolutionary proletarians, who, as the whole civilised world knows (Berlin, being merely "educated" [*jebildet*], of course does not belong to the civilised world), have the wicked intention not "honestly to earn" their "enjoyment" but to take it by conquest!

** [The following passage is crossed out in the manuscript:] And finally he makes the moral demand that the communists should quietly allow themselves to be exploited to all eternity by rentiers, merchants, factory-owners, etc., because they cannot abolish this exploitation without at the same time destroying the "well-being" of these gentlemen. Jacques le bonhomme, who poses here as the champion of the *gros*-bourgeois, can save himself the trouble of preaching moralising sermons to the communists, who can every day hear much better ones from his "good burghers".

*** [The following passage is crossed out in the manuscript:] ... and they will have no scruples about it precisely because for them the "well-being of all" regarded as "corporeal individuals" is more important that the "well-being" of the hitherto existing social classes. The "well-being" which the rentier enjoys as *rentier* is not the "well-being" of the individual as such, but of the rentier, not an individual well-being but a well-being that is general within the framework of the class.

whether this "well-being" common to their enemies and determined by class relations also appeals as personal "well-being" to a sentimentality which is narrow-mindedly presumed to exist.

Third corollary.
On page 190, in communist society

"worry arises again in the form of labour".

The good citizen "Stirner", who is already rejoicing that he will again find his beloved "worry" in communism, has nevertheless miscalculated this time. "Worry" is nothing but the mood of oppression and anxiety which in the middle class is the necessary companion of labour, of beggarly activity for securing scanty earnings. "Worry" flourishes in its purest form among the good German burghers, where it is chronic and "always identical with itself", miserable and contemptible, whereas the poverty of the proletarian assumes an acute, sharp form, drives him into a life-and-death struggle, makes him a revolutionary, and therefore engenders not "worry", but passion. If then communism wants to abolish both the "worry" of the burgher and the poverty of the proletarian, it goes without saying that it cannot do this without abolishing the cause of both, i.e., "labour".

We now come to the *historical constructions* of communism.
First historical construction.

"So long as faith was sufficient for the honour and dignity of man, no objection could be raised against any, even the most arduous labour."... "The oppressed classes could tolerate their misery only so long as they were Christians" (the most that can be said is that they were Christians so long as they tolerated their miserable position), "for Christianity" (which stands behind them with a stick) "keeps their grumbling and indignation in check." (P. 158.)

"How 'Stirner' knows so well" what the oppressed classes could do, we learn from the first issue of the *Allgemeine Literatur-Zeitung*, where "criticism in the form of a master-bookbinder" quotes the following passage from an unimportant book [a]:

---

[a] The passage is from August Theodor Woeniger's book *Publicistische Abhandlungen*, quoted by Carl Ernst Reichardt —"the master-bookbinder"— in his article "Schriften über den Pauperismus" (cf. Karl Marx and Frederick Engels, *The Holy Family*, in the *Collected Works* by Karl Marx and Frederick Engels, Vol. 4, pp. 9-11).— *Ed.*

"Modern pauperism has assumed a political character; whereas formerly the beggar bore his fate *submissively* and regarded it as *God's will*, the modern *ragamuffin* asks whether he is forced to drag out his life in poverty just because he chanced to be born in rags."

It was due to this power of Christianity that during the liberation of the feudal serfs the most bloody and embittered struggles were precisely those against the *spiritual* feudal lords, and it was carried through despite all the grumbling and indignation of Christianity as embodied in the priests (cf. Eden, *History of the Poor,* Book I[a]; Guizot, *Histoire de la civilisation en France*; Monteil, *Histoire des Français des divers états*, etc.), while, on the other hand, the minor priests, particularly at the beginning of the Middle Ages, incited the feudal serfs to "grumbling" and "indignation" against the temporal feudal lords (cf., *inter alia*, even the well-known capitulary of Charlemagne[66]). Compare also what was written above in connection with the "workers' disturbances which flare up here and there", about the "oppressed classes" and their revolts in the fourteenth century.[b]

The earlier forms of workers' uprisings were connected with the degree of development of labour in each case and the resulting form of property; direct or indirect communist uprisings were connected with large-scale industry. Instead of going into this extensive history, Saint Max accomplishes a holy transition from the *patient* oppressed classes to the *impatient* oppressed classes:

"Now, when everyone *ought to* develop *into a man*" ("how", for example, do the Catalonian workers[67] "know" that "everyone ought to develop into a man"?), "the confining of man to machine labour amounts to slavery." (P. 158.)

Hence, prior to Spartacus and the uprising of the slaves, it was Christianity that prevented the "confining of man to machine labour" from "amounting to slavery"; and in the days of Spartacus it was only the concept of "man" that removed this relation and brought about slavery. "Or did Stirner perhaps" "even" hear something about the connection between modern labour unrest and machine production and wanted here to give an intimation of this? In that case it was not the introduction of machine labour that transformed the workers into rebels, but the introduction of the concept of "man" that transformed machine labour into slavery.— "If that is so" then "it indeed

---

[a] Frederic Morton Eden, *The State of the Poor: or, an History of the Labouring Classes in England.— Ed.*
[b] See this volume, pp. 219-20.— *Ed.*

really looks as though" we have here a "unique" history of the workers' movements.

Second historical construction.

"The bourgeoisie has preached the gospel of material enjoyment and is now surprised that this doctrine finds supporters among us proletarians." (P. 159.)

Just now the workers wanted to realise the concept of "man", the holy; now it is "material enjoyment", the worldly; above it was a question of the "drudgery" of labour, now it is only the labour of enjoyment. Saint Sancho strikes himself here on *ambas sus valientes posaderas* [a]— first of all on material history, and then on Stirner's, holy history. According to material history, it was the aristocracy that first put the gospel of worldly enjoyment in the place of enjoyment of the gospel; it was at first for the aristocracy that the sober bourgeoisie applied itself to work and it very cunningly left to the aristocracy the enjoyment from which it was debarred by its own laws (whereby the power of the aristocracy passed in the form of money into the pockets of the bourgeoisie).

According to Stirner's history, the bourgeoisie was satisfied to seek "the holy", to pursue the cult of the state and to "transform all existing objects into imaginary ones", and it required the Jesuits to "save sensuousness from complete decay". According to this same Stirnerian history, the bourgeoisie usurped all power by means of revolution, consequently also its gospel, that of material enjoyment, although according to the same Stirnerian history we have now reached the point where "ideas alone rule the world". Stirner's hierarchy thus finds itself "*entre ambas posaderas*".

Third historical construction.

Page 159: "After the bourgeois had given freedom from the commands and arbitrariness of individuals, there remained the arbitrariness which arises from the conjuncture of conditions and which can be called the fortuitousness of circumstances. There remained—luck and those favoured by luck."

Saint Sancho then makes the communists "find a law and a new order which puts an end to these fluctuations" (the thingumbob), about which order he knows this much, that the communists should now proclaim: "Let this order henceforth be holy!" (whereas he ought now rather to have proclaimed: Let the disorder of my fantasies be the holy order of the communists). "Here is wisdom" (Revelation of St. John, 13:18). "Let him that hath understanding count the number" of

---

[a] His two most ample buttocks.— *Ed.*

absurdities which Stirner — usually so verbose and always repeating himself — [here] squeezes into a few [lines].

In its most general form the first proposition reads: after the bourgeoisie had abolished feudalism, the bourgeoisie remained. Or: after the domination of individuals had been abolished in "Stirner's" imagination, precisely the opposite remained to be done. "It indeed really looks as though" one could bring the two most distant historical epochs into a relationship which is the holy relationship, the relationship as the holy, the relationship in heaven.

Incidentally, this proposition of Saint Sancho's is not satisfied with the above-mentioned *mode simple* of absurdity, it has to bring it to the *mode composé* and *bicomposé*[a] of absurdity. For, firstly, Saint Max believes the bourgeoisie which liberates *itself* that, by liberating *itself* from the commands and arbitrariness of individuals, it has liberated the mass of society as a whole from the commands and arbitrariness of individuals. Secondly, in reality it liberated itself not from the "commands and arbitrariness of individuals", but from the domination of the corporation, the guild, the estates, and hence was now for the first time, as *actual* individual bourgeois, in a position to impose "commands and arbitrariness" on the workers. Thirdly, it only abolished the more or less idealistic appearance of the former commands and former arbitrariness of individuals, in order to establish instead these commands and this arbitrariness in their material crudity. He, the bourgeois, wanted his "commands and arbitrariness" to be no longer restricted by the hitherto existing "commands and arbitrariness" of political power concentrated in the monarch, the nobility and the corporations, but at most restricted only by the general interests of the whole bourgeois class, as expressed in bourgeois legislation. He did nothing more than abolish the commands and arbitrariness *over* the commands and arbitrariness of the individual bourgeois (see "Political Liberalism").

Instead of making a real analysis of the conjuncture of conditions, which with the rule of the bourgeoisie became a totally different conjuncture of totally different conditions, Saint Sancho leaves it in the form of the general category "conjuncture, etc.", and bestows on it the still more indefinite name of "fortuitousness of circumstances", as though the "commands and arbitrariness of individuals" are not themselves

---

[a] These terms were used by Charles Fourier (see Ch. Fourier, *Théorie de l'unité universelle*).— *Ed.*

a "conjuncture of conditions". Having thus done away with the real basis of communism, i.e., the *definite* conjuncture of conditions, under the bourgeois regime, he can now also transform this airy communism into his holy communism. "It indeed really looks" as though "Stirner" is a "man with only ideal", imagined, historical "wealth"—the *"perfect ragamuffin"*. See "the book", p. 362.

This great construction or, rather, its major proposition is once more and with great emphasis repeated on page 189 in the following form:

> "Political liberalism abolished the inequality of master and servant; it made people *masterless*, anarchic" (!); "the master was then separated from the individual, from the egoist, to become a *spectre*, the law or the state."

Domination of spectres = (hierarchy) = absence of domination, equivalent to the domination of the "omnipotent" bourgeois. As we see, this domination of spectres is, on the contrary, the domination of the *many* actual masters; hence with equal justification communism could be regarded as liberation from this domination of the many. This, however, Saint Sancho could not do, for then not only his logical constructions of communism but also the whole construction of "the free ones" would be overthrown. But this is how it is throughout "the book". A single conclusion from our saint's own premises, a single historical fact, overthrows the entire series of penetrations and results.

Fourth historical construction. On page 350, Saint Sancho derives communism directly from the abolition of serfdom.

I. *Major proposition*:

> "Extremely much was gained when people succeeded in being *regarded*" (!) "as property-owners. Thereby serfdom was abolished and everyone who until then had himself been *property* henceforth became a *master*."

(According to the *mode simple* of absurdity this means: serfdom was abolished as soon as it was abolished.) The *mode composé* of this absurdity is that Saint Sancho believes that people became "property-owners" by means of holy contemplation, by means of "regarding" and "being regarded", whereas the difficulty consisted in becoming a "property-owner", and consideration came later of itself. The *mode bicomposé* of the absurdity is that when the abolition of serfdom, which at first was still partial, had begun to develop its consequences and thereby became universal, people ceased to be able to "succeed" in being "regarded" as *worth* owning (for the property-owners those they owned had become too expensive);

consequently the vast mass "who until then had themselves been property", i.e., unfree workers, became as a result not "masters", but free workers.

II. *Minor historical proposition,* which embraces about eight centuries, although one "will of course not perceive how momentous" it is. (Cf. *Wigand,* p. 194.)

"However, *henceforth* your having [*Dein Haben*] and what you have [*Deine Habe*] *no longer* suffices, and is *no longer* recognised; *on the other hand,* your working and your work increases in value. We *now* respect your *mastery* of things as *previously*" (?) "we respected your possession of them. Your labour is your wealth. You are now the master or possessor of what you have obtained by work and not by inheritance." (Ibid.)

"Henceforth"—"no   longer"—"on   the   other   hand"— "now"—"as   previously"—"now"—"or"—"not"— such   is   the content of this proposition.

Although "Stirner" has "now" arrived at this, that you (viz., Szeliga) are the master of what you have obtained by work and not by inheritance, it "now" occurs to him that just the opposite is the case at present — and so he causes communism to be born as a monster from these two distorted propositions.

III. *Communist conclusion.*

"Since, *however,* NOW everything is inherited and every farthing you possess bears not the stamp of work, but of inheritance" (the culminating absurdity), "SO everything must be remoulded."

On this basis Szeliga is able to imagine that he has arrived at both the rise and fall of the medieval communes, and the communism of the nineteenth century. And thereby Saint Max, despite everything "inherited" and "obtained by work", does not arrive at any "mastery of things", but at most at "having" nonsense.

Lovers of constructions can now see in addition on page 421 how Saint Max, after constructing communism from serfdom, then constructs it again in the form of serfdom *under* a liege lord — society — on the same model as he already, above, transformed the means by which we earn something into the "holy", by "grace" of which something is given to us. Now, in conclusion, we shall deal in addition only with a few "penetrations" into the essence of communism, which follow from the premises given above.

First of all, "Stirner" gives a new *theory of exploitation* which consists in this:

"the worker in a pin factory performs only one piece of work, only plays into the hand of another and is used, exploited by that other". (P. 158.)

Thus, here "Stirner" makes the discovery that the workers in a factory exploit one another, since they "play into the hands" of one another; whereas the factory-owner, whose hands do not work at all, cannot, therefore, exploit the workers. "Stirner" here gives a striking example of the lamentable position in which communism has put the German theoreticians. Now they have to concern themselves also with mundane things like pin factories, etc., in relation to which they behave like real barbarians, like Ojibbeway Indians and New Zealanders. Stirnerian communism "on the contrary says" (ibid.):

"All work should have the aim of satisfying 'man'. Therefore, he" ("Man") "must become *master* of it, i.e., *be able* to perform it as a totality."

"Man" must become a master!—"Man" remains a maker of pin-heads, but he has the consolation of knowing that the pin-head is part of the pin and that he *is able* to make the whole pin. The fatigue and disgust caused by the eternally repeated making of pin-heads is transformed, by this knowledge, into the "satisfaction of man". O Proudhon!

A further penetration:

"Since communists declare that only *free activity* is the essence" (*iterum Crispinus*)[a] "of man, they, like every *workaday mode of thought*, need a *Sunday*, a time of exaltation and devotion, in addition to their *dull labour*."

Apart from the "essence of man" that is dragged in here, the unfortunate Sancho is forced to convert "free activity", which is for the communists the creative manifestation of life arising from the free development of all abilities of the "whole fellow" (in order to make it comprehensible to "Stirner"), into "dull labour", for our Berliner notices that the question here is not one of the "hard work of thought". By this simple transformation the communists can now also be transposed into the "workaday mode of thought". Then, of course, together with the work-day of the middle class its Sunday also is to be found again in communism.

Page 161: "The Sunday aspect of communism consists in the communist seeing in you the man, the brother."

Thus, the communist appears here as "man" and as "worker". This Saint Sancho calls (loc. cit.) "a dual *employment* of man by the communists — an office of material earning and one of spiritual earning".

Here, therefore, he brings back even "earning" and bureaucracy into communism which, of course, thereby "attains its final

---

[a] Crispinus again.— *Ed.*

goal" and ceases to be communism. Incidentally he has to do this, because in his "union", which he will construct later, each also is given a "dual position"—as man and as the "unique". For the present, he legitimises this dualism by foisting it on communism, a method we shall find again in his theory of feudalism and of utilisation.

On page 344 "Stirner" believes that the "communists" want to "settle the question of property amicably", and on page 413 he even makes them appeal to the self-sacrifice of people [and to] the self-denying disposition of the capitalists!* The few non-revolutionary communist *bourgeois* who made their appearance since the time of Babeuf were a rare occurrence; the vast majority of the communists in all countries are revolutionary. All communists in France reproach the followers of Saint-Simon and Fourier with their peaceableness and differ from the latter chiefly in their having abandoned all hope of an "amicable settlement", just as in Britain it is the same criterion which chiefly distinguishes the Chartists from the socialists. Saint Max could discover the communist view of the "self-denying disposition of the rich" and the "self-sacrifice of people" from a few passages of Cabet, the very communist who most of all could give the impression that he appeals for *dévoûment*, self-sacrifice. These passages are aimed against the republicans and especially against the attacks on communism made by Monsieur Buchez, who still commands the following of a very small number of workers in Paris:

"The same thing applies to self-sacrifice (*dévoûment*); it is the doctrine of Monsieur Buchez, this time divested of its Catholic form, for Monsieur Buchez undoubtedly fears that his Catholicism is repugnant to the mass of the workers, and drives them away. 'In order to fulfil their *duty* (*devoir*) worthily'—says Buchez—'*self-sacrifice* (*dévoûment*) is needed.'—Let those who can understand the difference between *devoir* and *dévoûment*.—'We require self-sacrifice from everyone, both for great national unity and for the workers' association ... it is necessary for us to be united, always devoted (*dévoués*) to one another.'—It is necessary, it is necessary—that is easy to say, and people have been saying it for a long time and they will go on saying it for a very long time yet without any more success, if they cannot devise other means! Buchez complains of the self-seeking of the rich; but what is the use of such complaints? All who are unwilling to sacrifice themselves Buchez declares to be enemies.

" 'If,' he says, 'impelled by egoism, a man refuses to sacrifice himself for others, what is to be done?... We have not a moment's hesitation in answering:

---

* [The following passage is crossed out in the manuscript:] Here Saint Max again ascribes to himself the wisdom of seizing and striking, as though his whole harangue about the rebellious proletariat were not an unsuccessful travesty of Weitling and his thieving proletariat,—Weitling is one of the few communists whom he knows by the grace of Bluntschli.

society always has the *right* to take from us what our own duty bids us sacrifice to it.... Self-sacrifice is the only means of fulfilling one's duty. Each one of us must sacrifice himself, always and everywhere. He who out of egoism refuses to fulfil his duty of self-sacrifice must be *compelled* to do it.'— Thus Buchez cries out to all: sacrifice yourselves, sacrifice yourselves! Think only of sacrificing yourselves! Does this not mean to misunderstand human nature and trample it underfoot? Is not this a false view? We might almost say — a *childish, silly* view." (Cabet, *Réfutation des doctrines de l'Atelier*, pp. 19, 20.)

Cabet, further, on page 22, demonstrates to the republican Buchez that he inevitably arrives at an "aristocracy of self-sacrifice" with various ranks, and then asks ironically:

"What then becomes of *dévoûment*? What remains of *dévoûment* if people sacrifice themselves only in order to reach the highest pinnacles of *hierarchy*?... Such a system might originate in the mind of a man who would like to become Pope or Cardinal — but in the minds of workers!!!"—"M. Buchez does not want labour to become a *pleasant diversion*, nor that man should work for his own well-being and create new pleasures for himself. He asserts ... 'that man exists on earth only to fulfil a *calling*, a *duty (une fonction, un devoir)*'. 'No,' he preaches to the communists, 'man, this great force, has not been created for himself (*n'a point été fait pour lui-même*).... That is a crude idea. Man is a worker (*ouvrier*) in the world, he must accomplish the work (*œuvre*) which morality imposes on his activity, that is his duty.... Let us never lose sight of the fact that we have to fulfil a *high calling (une haute fonction)* — a calling that began with the first day of man's existence and will come to an end only at the same time as humanity.'— But who revealed all these fine things to [M.]Buchez? (*Mais qui a révélé toutes ces belles choses à M. Buchez lui-même*"— which Stirner would have translated: How is it that Buchez knows so well what man should do?) — "*Du reste, comprenne qui pourra.*[a]— Buchez continues: 'What! Man had to wait thousands of centuries in order to learn from you communists that he was created for himself and has no other aim than to live in all possible pleasures.... But one must not fall into such an error. One must not forget that *we are created in order to labour (faits pour travailler)*, to labour *always*, and that the only thing we can demand is what is *necessary for life (la suffisante vie)*, i.e., the well-being that suffices for us to carry out our calling properly. Everything that is beyond this boundary is *absurd* and *dangerous*.'— But just prove it, prove it! And do not be satisfied merely with delivering oracles like a prophet! At the very outset you speak of *thousands of centuries*! And then, who asserts that people have been waiting for us down *all* the centuries? But have people perhaps been waiting for you with all your theories about *dévoûment, devoir, nationalité française, association ouvriere*? 'In conclusion,' says Buchez, 'we ask you not to take offence at what we have said.'— We also are polite Frenchmen and we, too, ask you not to take offence." (P. 31).—"'*Believe us*,' says Buchez, 'there exists a *communauté* which was created long ago and of which you too are members.'— Believe us, Buchez," concludes Cabet, "become a communist!"

"Self-sacrifice", "duty", "social obligation", "the right of society", "the calling, the destiny of man", "to be a worker the calling of man", "moral cause", "workers' association", "crea-

---

[a] "However, let him who can understand it." — *Ed.*

tion of what is indispensable for life"— are not these the same things for which Saint Sancho reproaches the communists, and for the *absence* of which the communists are reproached by M. Buchez, whose solemn reproaches are ridiculed by Cabet? Do we not find here even Stirner's "hierarchy"?

Finally, Saint Sancho deals communism the *coup de grâce* on page 169, by uttering the following proposition:

"By taking away also *property*" (!) "the socialists do not take into account that its continuance is safeguarded by the peculiarities of human beings. Are only money and goods property, or is not every opinion also something that is mine, that belongs to me? *Hence*, every opinion must be abolished or made impersonal."

Or does Saint Sancho's opinion, insofar as it does not become the opinion of others as well, give him command over anything, even over another's opinion? By bringing into play against communism the capital of his opinion, Saint Max again does nothing but advance against it the oldest and most trivial bourgeois objections, and he thinks he has said something new because for him, the "educated" Berliner, these hackneyed ideas are new. Destutt de Tracy among, and after, many others said the same thing much better approximately thirty years ago, and also later, in the book quoted below. For example:

"Formal proceedings were instituted against property, and arguments were brought forward for and against it, as though it depended on us to decide whether property should or should not exist in the world; but this is based on a complete misunderstanding of our nature." (*Traité de la volonté*, Paris, 1826, p. 18.)

And then M. Destutt de Tracy undertakes to prove that *propriété, individualité* and *personnalité* are identical, that the "ego" [*moi*] also includes "mine" [*mien*], and he finds as a natural basis for private property that

"nature has endowed man with an inevitable and inalienable property, property in the form of his own individuality". (P. 17.) — The individual "clearly sees that this *ego* is the exclusive owner of the body which it animates, the organs which it sets in motion, all their capacities, all their forces, all the effects they produce, all their passions and actions; for all this ends and begins with this ego, exists only through it, is set in motion through its action; and no other person can make use of these same instruments or be affected in the same way by them". (P. 16.) "Property exists, if not precisely everywhere that a sentient individual exists, at least wherever there is a conative individual." (P. 19.)

Having thus made private property and personality identical, Destutt de Tracy with a play on the words *propriété* and *propre*,[a]

---

[a] One's own.— *Ed.*

like "Stirner" with his play on the words *Mein*[a] and *Meinung*,[b] *Eigentum*[c] and *Eigenheit*,[d] arrives at the following conclusion:

> "It is, therefore, quite futile to argue about whether it would not be better for each of us to have nothing of our own (*de discuter s'il ne vaudrait pas mieux que rien ne fût propre à chacun de nous*) ... in any case it is equivalent to asking whether it would not be desirable for us to be quite different from what we are, and even to examining whether it would not be better for us not to exist at all." (P. 22.)

"These are extremely popular", now already traditional objections to communism, and for that very reason "it is not surprising that Stirner" repeats them.

When the narrow-minded bourgeois says to the communists: by abolishing property, i.e., my existence as a capitalist, as a landed proprietor, as a factory-owner, and your existence as workers, you abolish my individuality and your own; by making it impossible for me to exploit you, the workers, to rake in my profit, interest or rent, you make it impossible for me to exist as an individual.— When, therefore, the bourgeois tells the communists: by abolishing my existence *as a bourgeois*, you abolish my existence *as an individual*; when thus he identifies himself as a bourgeois with himself as an individual, one must, at least, recognise his frankness and shamelessness. For the bourgeois it is actually the case, he believes himself to be an individual only insofar as he is a bourgeois.

But when the theoreticians of the bourgeoisie come forward and give a general expression to this assertion, when they equate the bourgeois's property with individuality in theory as well and want to give a logical justification for this equation, then this nonsense begins to become solemn and holy.

Above "Stirner" refuted the communist abolition of private property by first transforming private property into "having" and then declaring the verb "to have" an indispensable word, an eternal truth, because even in communist society it could happen that Stirner will "have" a stomach-ache. In exactly the same way here his arguments regarding the impossibility of abolishing private property depend on his transforming private property into the concept of property, on exploiting the etymological connection between the words *Eigentum* and

---

[a] My, mine.— *Ed.*
[b] Opinion, view.— *Ed.*
[c] Property.— *Ed.*
[d] Peculiarity.— *Ed.*

eigen[a] and declaring the word *eigen* an eternal truth, because even under the communist system it could happen that a stomach-ache will be *eigen* to him. All this theoretical nonsense, which seeks refuge in etymology, would be impossible if the actual private property that the communists want to abolish had not been transformed into the abstract notion of "property". This transformation, on the one hand, saves one the trouble of having to say anything, or even merely to know anything, about actual private property and, on the other hand, makes it easy to discover a contradiction in communism, since *after* the abolition of *(actual)* property it is, of course, easy to discover all sorts of things in communism which can be included in the concept "property". In reality, of course, the situation is just the reverse.* In reality I possess private property only insofar as I have something vendible, whereas what is peculiar to me [*meine Eigenheit*] may not be vendible at all. My frock-coat is private property for me only so long as I can barter, pawn or sell it, so long [as it] is [marketable]. If it loses that feature, if it becomes tattered, it can still have a number of features which make it valuable *for me*, it may even become a feature of me and turn me into a tatterdemalion. But no economist would think of classing it as my private property, since it does not enable me to command any, even the smallest, amount of other people's labour. A lawyer, an ideologist of private property, could perhaps still indulge in such twaddle. Private property alienates [*entfremdet*] the individuality not only of people but also of things. Land has nothing to do with rent of land, the machine has nothing to do with profit. For the landed proprietor, land has the significance only of rent of land; he leases his plots of land and receives rent; this is a feature which land can lose without losing a single one of its inherent features, without, for example, losing any part of its fertility; it is a feature the extent and even the existence of which depends on social relations which are created and destroyed without the assistance of individual landed proprietors. It is the same with machines. How little connection there is between money, the most general form of property, and personal peculiarity, how much they are

---

* [The following passage is crossed out in the manuscript:] Actual private property is something extremely general which has nothing at all to do with individuality, which indeed directly nullifies individuality. Insofar as I am regarded as a property-owner I am not regarded as an individual—a statement which is corroborated every day by the marriages for money.

---

[a] Own, peculiar.— *Ed.*

directly opposed to each other was already known to Shakespeare better than to our theorising petty bourgeois:

> Thus much of this will make black, white; foul, fair;
> Wrong, right; base, noble; old, young; coward, valiant.
> This yellow slave...
> Will make the hoar leprosy adored...
> This it is
> That makes the wappened widow wed again;
> She, whom the spital-house and ulcerous sores
> Would cast the gorge at, this embalms and spices
> To th' April day again...
> Thou visible god,
> That solder'st close impossibilities,
> And makest them kiss![a]

In a word, rent of land, profit, etc., these actual forms of
existence of private property, are *social relations* corresponding
to a definite stage of production, and they are "*individual*" only
so long as they have not become fetters on the existing
productive forces.

According to Destutt de Tracy, the majority of people, the
proletarians, must have lost all individuality long ago, although
nowadays it looks as if it was precisely among them that
individuality is most developed. For the bourgeois it is all the
easier to prove on the basis of his language the identity of
commercial and individual, or even universal, human relations,
as this language itself is a product of the bourgeoisie, and
therefore both in actuality and in language the relations of
buying and selling have been made the basis of all others. For
example, *propriété*—property [*Eigentum*] and characteristic
feature [*Eigenschaft*]; property—possession [*Eigentum*] and
peculiarity [*Eigentümlichkeit*]; "*eigen*" ["one's own"]—in the
commercial and in the individual sense; *valeur*, value, *Wert*[b];
commerce, *Verkehr*[c]; *échange*, exchange, *Austausch*,[d] etc., all
of which are used both for commercial relations and for
characteristic features and mutual relations of individuals as
such. In the other modern languages this is equally the case. If
Saint Max seriously applies himself to exploit this ambiguity, he
may easily succeed in making a brilliant series of new economic
discoveries, without knowing anything about political economy;
for, indeed, his new economic facts, which we shall take note of
later, lie wholly within this sphere of synonymy.

---

[a] William Shakespeare, *Timon of Athens*, Act IV, Scene 3.— *Ed.*
[b] Worth, value.— *Ed.*
[c] Intercourse, traffic, commerce, communication.— *Ed.*
[d] Exchange, barter, interchange.— *Ed.*

Our kindly, credulous Jacques takes the bourgeois play on the words *Eigentum* [property] and *Eigenschaft* [characteristic feature] so literally, in such holy earnest, that he even endeavours to behave like a private property-owner in relation to his own features, as we shall see later on.

Finally, on page 421, "Stirner" instructs communism that

"*actually* it" (viz., communism) "does not attack property, but the alienation of property".

In this new revelation of his, Saint Max merely repeats an old witticism already used repeatedly by, for example, the Saint-Simonists. Cf., for example, *Leçons sur l'industrie et les finances*, Paris, 1832,[a] where, *inter alia*, it is stated:

"Property will not be abolished, but its form will be changed ... it will for the first time become *true personification* ... it will for the first time acquire its real. individual character." (Pp. 42, 43.)

Since this phrase, introduced by the French and particularly enlarged on by Pierre Leroux, was seized on with great pleasure by the German speculative socialists and used for further speculation, and finally gave occasion for reactionary intrigues and sharp practices — we shall not deal with it here where it says nothing, but later on, in connection with true socialism.[b]

Saint Sancho, [following the] example of Woeniger, whom Reichardt [used], takes delight in turning the proletarians, [and hence] also the communists, into "*ragamuffins*". He defines his "ragamuffin" on page 362 as a "man possessing only ideal wealth". If Stirner's "ragamuffins" ever set up a vagabond kingdom, as the Paris beggars did in the fifteenth century, then Saint Sancho will be the vagabond king, for he is the "perfect" ragamuffin, a man possessing not even ideal wealth and therefore living on the interest from the capital of his opinion.

C. Humane Liberalism

After Saint Max has interpreted liberalism and communism as imperfect modes of existence of philosophical "man", and thereby also of modern German philosophy in general (which he was justified in doing, since in Germany not only liberalism but communism as well was given a petty-bourgeois and at the same time highflown ideological form), after this, it is easy for him to depict the latest forms of German philosophy, what he has called "humane liberalism", as perfect liberalism and communism, and, at the same time, as criticism of both of them.

---

[a] The author of these lectures is Isaac Pereire.— *Ed.*

[b] See this volume, pp. 495-96.— *Ed.*

With the aid of this holy construction we now get the following three delightful transformations (cf. also "The Economy of the Old Testament"):

1. The individual *is* not man, therefore he is of no value — absence of personal will, ordinance —"whose name will be named": "masterless"— political liberalism, which we have already dealt with above.

2. The individual *has* nothing human, therefore no validity attaches to mine and thine or property: "propertyless"— communism, which we have also already dealt with.

3. In criticism the individual should give place to Man, now found for the first time: "godless" =identity of "masterless" and "propertyless" — humane liberalism. (Pp. 180-81.)— In a more detailed exposition of this last negative unity, the unshakable orthodoxy of Jacques reaches the following climax (p. 189):

"The egoism of property loses its last possession if even the words 'my God' become meaningless, *for*" (a grand "for"!) "God only exists if he has at heart the salvation of each individual, just as the latter seeks his salvation in God."

According to this, the French bourgeois would only "lose" his "last" "property" if the word *adieu* were banished from the language. In complete accord with the preceding construction, property in God, holy property in heaven, the property of fantasy, the fantasy of property, are here declared to be supreme property and the last sheet-anchor of property.

From these three illusions about liberalism, communism and German philosophy, he now concocts his new — and, thanks be to the "holy", this time the last — transition to the "*ego*". Before following him in this, let us once more glance at his last "arduous life struggle" with "humane liberalism".

After our worthy Sancho in his new role of *caballero andante*,[a] and in fact as *caballero de la tristisima figura*,[b] has traversed the whole of history, everywhere battling and "blowing down" spirits and spectres, "dragons and ostriches, satyrs and hobgoblins, wild beasts of the desert and vultures, bitterns and hedgehogs" (cf. Isaiah 34:11-14), how happy he must now be, after his wanderings through all these different lands, to come at last to his island of Barataria,[68] to "the land" as such, where "man" goes about in *puris naturalibus*[c]! Let us once more recall his great thesis, the dogma imposed on him, on which his whole construction of history rests, to the effect that:

[a] Knight-errant.— *Ed.*
[b] Knight of the most rueful countenance.— *Ed.*
[c] In the pure natural state.— *Ed.*

"the truths which arise from the concept of *man* are revered as revelations of precisely this concept and regarded as holy"; "the revelations of this holy concept", even "with the abolition of many a truth manifested by means of this concept, are not deprived of their holiness". (P. 51.)

We need hardly repeat what we have already proved to our holy author in respect of all his examples, namely, that empirical relations, created by real people in their real intercourse and not at all by the holy concept of man, are afterwards interpreted, portrayed, imagined, consolidated and justified by people as a revelation of the concept "man". One may also recall his hierarchy. And now on to humane liberalism.

On page 44, where Saint Max "in brief" "contrasts Feuerbach's [theological] view with our view", at first nothing but phrases are advanced against Feuerbach. As we already saw in regard to the manufacture of spirits, where "Stirner" places his stomach among the stars (the third Dioscuros, a patron saint and protector against seasickness [69]), because he and his stomach are "different names for totally different things" (p. 42), so, here, too, essence [*Wesen*][a] appears first of all as an existing thing, and "so it is now said" (p. 44):

"The supreme being *is*, indeed, the essence of man, but precisely because it is his *essence*, and not man himself, it *makes absolutely no difference* whether we see this essence outside man and perceive it as 'God' or find it in man and call it the 'essence of man' or 'man'. *I* am neither God nor man, neither the supreme being nor my essence—and, therefore, in the main, it makes no difference whether I *think* of this essence as inside me or outside me."

Hence, the "essence of man" is presupposed here as an existing thing, it *is* the "supreme being", it *is* not the "ego", and, instead of saying something about "essence", Saint Max restricts himself to the simple statement that it makes "no difference" "whether I *think* of it as inside me or outside me", in this locality or in that. That this indifference to essence is no mere carelessness of style is already evident from the fact that he himself makes the distinction between essential and inessential and that with him even the "*noble essence of* egoism" finds a place. (P. 71.) Incidentally everything the German theoreticians have said so far about essence and non-essence is to be found already far better said by Hegel in his *Logik*.

We found the boundless orthodoxy of "Stirner" with regard to the illusions of German philosophy expressed in concentrated form in the fact that he constantly foists "man" on history as the sole *dramatis persona* and believes that "man" has made history. Now we shall find the same thing recurring in

---

[a] *Wesen* can mean either essence or being.— *Ed.*

connection with Feuerbach, whose illusions "Stirner" faithfully
accepts in order to build further on their foundation.

Page 77: "In general Feuerbach *only transposes subject and predicate*, giving
preference to the latter. But since he says himself: 'Love is not holy because it is
a predicate of God (nor have people ever held it to be holy for that reason) but it
is a predicate of God because it is divine by and for itself', he was able to
conclude that the struggle had to be begun against the predicates themselves,
against love and everything holy. How could he hope to turn people away from
God, once he had left them the *divine*? And if, as Feuerbach says, the main thing
for people has never been God, but only his predicates, he could after all have
allowed them to keep this tinsel, since the puppet, the real kernel, still
remained."

Since, therefore, Feuerbach *"himself"* says this, it is reason
enough for Jacques le bonhomme to *believe* him that people
have esteemed love because it is "divine by and for itself". If
precisely the *opposite* of what Feuerbach says took
place — and we "make bold to say this" (*Wigand*, p. 157) — if
neither God nor his predicates have ever been the main thing for
people, if this itself is only a religious illusion of German
theory — it means that the very same thing has happened to our
Sancho as happened to him before in Cervantes, when four
stumps were put under his saddle while he slept and his ass was
led away from under him.

Relying on these statements of Feuerbach, Sancho starts a
battle which was likewise already anticipated by Cervantes in
the nineteenth chapter, where the *ingenioso hidalgo* fights
against the predicates, the mummers, while they are carrying
the corpse of the world to the grave and who, entangled in their
robes and shrouds, are unable to move and so make it easy for
our hidalgo to overturn them with his lance and give them a
thorough thrashing. The last attempt to exploit further the
criticism of religion as an independent sphere (a criticism which
has been flogged to the point of exhaustion), to remain within
the premises of German theory and yet to appear to be going
beyond them, and to cook from this bone, gnawed away to the
last fibres, a thin Rumford beggar's broth[70] [for "the]
book"— this last attempt consisted in attacking material relations, not in their actual form, and not even in the form of
the mundane illusions of those who are practically involved in
the present-day world, but in the heavenly extract of their
mundane form as predicates, as emanations from God, as
angels. Thus, the heavenly kingdom was now repopulated and
abundant new material created for the old method of exploitation of this heavenly kingdom. Thus, the struggle against
religious illusions, against God, was again substituted for the
real struggle. Saint Bruno, who earns his bread by theology, in

his "arduous life struggle" against substance makes the same attempt *pro aris et focis*[a] as a theologian to go beyond the limits of theology. His "substance" is nothing but the predicates of God united under one name; with the exception of personality, which he reserves for himself—these predicates of God are again nothing but deified names for the ideas of people about their definite, empirical relations, ideas which subsequently they hypocritically retain because of practical considerations. With the theoretical equipment inherited from Hegel it is, of course, not possible even to understand the empirical, material attitude of these people. Owing to the fact that Feuerbach showed the religious world as an illusion of the earthly world—a world which in his writing appears merely as a *phrase*—German theory too was confronted with the question which he left unanswered: how did it come about that people "got" these illusions "into their heads"? Even for the German theoreticians this question paved the way to the materialistic view of the world, a view which is *not without premises*, but which empirically observes the actual material premises as such and for that reason is, for the first time, *actually* a critical view of the world. This path was already indicated in the *Deutsch-Französische Jahrbücher*—in the *Einleitung zur Kritik der Hegelschen Rechtsphilosophie* and *Zur Judenfrage*.[b] But since at that time this was done in philosophical phraseology, the traditionally occurring philosophical expressions such as "human essence", "species", etc., gave the German theoreticians the desired reason for misunderstanding the real trend of thought and believing that here again it was a question merely of giving a new turn to their worn-out theoretical garment—just as Dr. Arnold Ruge, the *Dottore Graziano* of German philosophy, imagined that he could continue as before to wave his clumsy arms about and display his pedantic-farcical mask. One has to "leave philosophy aside" (*Wigand*, p. 187, cf. Hess, *Die letzten Philosophen*, p. 8), one has to leap out of it and devote oneself like an ordinary man to the study of actuality, for which there exists also an enormous amount of literary material, unknown, of course, to the philosophers. When, after that, one again encounters people like *Krummacher* or "*Stirner*", one finds that one has long ago left them "behind" and below. Philosophy and the study of the actual world have the same relation to one another as onanism

---

[a] For home and hearth.— *Ed.*
[b] See Karl Marx and Frederick Engels, *Collected Works*, Vol. 3, pp. 146-87.— *Ed.*

and sexual love. Saint Sancho, who in spite of his absence of thought—which was noted by us patiently and by him emphatically—remains within the world of pure thoughts, can, of course, save himself from it only by means of a moral postulate, the postulate of "*thoughtlessness*" (p. 196 of "the book"). He is a bourgeois who saves himself in the face of commerce by the *banqueroute cochonne*,[71] whereby, of course, he becomes not a proletarian, but an impecunious, bankrupt bourgeois. He does not become a man of the world, but a bankrupt philosopher without thoughts.

The predicates of God handed down from Feuerbach as real forces over people, as hierarchs, are the monstrosity which is substituted for the empirical world and which "Stirner" finds in existence. So heavily does Stirner's entire "peculiarity" depend merely on "prompting". If "Stirner" (see also p. 63) reproaches Feuerbach for reaching no result because he turns the predicate into the subject and vice versa, he himself is far less capable of arriving at anything, [for] he faithfully accepts these Feuer-bachian predicates, transformed into subjects, as real personalities ruling [the world], he faithfully accepts these phrases about relations as actual relations, attaching the predicate "holy" to them, *transforming this predicate into a subject*, the "holy", i.e., doing exactly the same as that for which he reproaches Feuerbach. And so, after he has thus completely got rid of the definite content that was the matter at issue, he begins his struggle—i.e., his "antipathy"—against this "holy", which, of course, always remains the same. Feuerbach has still the consciousness "that for him it is 'only a matter of destroying an illusion' "—and it is this with which Saint Max reproaches him (p. 77 of "the book")—although Feuerbach still attaches much too great importance to the struggle against this illusion. In "Stirner" even this consciousness has "all gone", he actually believes in the domination of the abstract ideas of ideology in the modern world; he believes that in his struggle against "predicates", against concepts, he is no longer attacking an illusion, but the real forces that rule the world. Hence his manner of turning everything upside down, hence the immense credulity with which he takes at their face value all the sanctimonious illusions, all the hypocritical asseverations of the bourgeoisie. How little, incidentally, the "puppet" is the "real kernel" of the "tinsel", and how lame this beautiful analogy is, can best be seen from "Stirner's" own "puppet"—"the book", which contains no "kernel", whether "real" or not "real", and where even the little that there is in its 491 pages scarcely deserves the name "tinsel".— If, however, we must find some sort of "kernel" in it, then that kernel is the *German petty bourgeois.*

Incidentally, as regards the source of Saint Max's hatred of "predicates", he himself gives an extremely naïve disclosure in the "Apologetic Commentary". He quotes the following passage from *Das Wesen des Christenthums* (p. 31): "A true atheist is only one for whom the *predicates* of the divine being, e.g., love, wisdom, justice, are nothing, but not one for whom only the *subject* of these predicates is nothing"— and then he exclaims triumphantly: "*Does this not hold good for Stirner?*"—"Here is wisdom." In the above passage Saint Max found a hint as to how one should start in order to go "*farthest of all*". He believes Feuerbach that the above passage reveals the "essence" of the "*true atheist*", and lets Feuerbach set him the "task" of becoming a "true atheist". The "unique" is "the *true atheist*".

Even more credulously than in relation to Feuerbach does he "handle" matters in relation to Saint Bruno or "criticism". We shall gradually see all the things that he allows "criticism" to impose on him, how he puts himself under its police surveillance, how it dictates his mode of life, his "calling". For the time being it suffices to mention as an example of his faith in criticism that on page 186 he treats "criticism" and the "mass" as two persons fighting against each other and "striving to free themselves from egoism", and on page 187 he "accepts" both "for what *they ... give themselves out to be*".

With the struggle against humane liberalism, the long struggle of the Old Testament, when man was a school-master of the unique, comes to an end; the time is fulfilled, and the gospel of grace and joy is ushered in for sinful humanity.

The struggle over "man" is the fulfilment of the word, as written in the twenty-first chapter of Cervantes, which deals with "the high adventure and rich prize of Mambrino's helmet". Our Sancho, who in everything imitates his former lord and present servant, "has sworn to win Mambrino's helmet"— man — for himself. After having during his various "campaigns" [a] sought in vain to find the longed-for helmet among the ancients and moderns, liberals and communists, "he caught sight of a man on a horse carrying something on his head

---

[a] In the German original the word *Auszüge* is used, which can mean departures, campaigns or extracts, abstracts.— *Ed.*

which shone like gold". And he said to Don Quixote-Szeliga: "If I am not mistaken, there is someone approaching us bearing on his head that helmet of Mambrino, about which I swore the oath you know of." "Take good care of what you say, your worship, and even greater care of what you do," replied Don Quixote, who by now has become wiser. "Tell me, can you not see that knight coming towards us on a dapple-grey steed with a gold helmet on his head?"—"What I see and perceive," replies Don Quixote, "is nothing but a man on a grey ass like yours with something glittering on his head."—"Why, that is Mambrino's helmet," says Sancho.

Meanwhile, at a gentle trot there approaches them *Bruno*, the holy barber, on his small ass, Criticism, with his barber's basin on his head; Saint Sancho sets on him lance in hand, Saint Bruno jumps from his ass, drops the basin (for which reason we saw him here at the Council without the basin) and rushes off across country, "for he is the Critic himself". Saint Sancho with great joy picks up the helmet of Mambrino, and to Don Quixote's remark that it looks exactly like a barber's basin he replies: "This famous, enchanted helmet, which has become 'ghostly', undoubtedly fell into the hands of a man who was unable to appreciate its worth, and so he melted down one half of it and hammered out the other half in such a way that, as you say, it appears to be a barber's basin; in any case, whatever it may look like to the vulgar eye, for me, since I know its value, that is a matter of indifference."

"The second splendour, the second property, has now been won!"

Now that he has gained his helmet, "man", he puts himself in opposition to him, behaves towards him as towards his "most irreconcilable enemy" and declares outright to him (why, we shall see later) that he (Saint Sancho) is not "man", but an "unhuman being, the inhuman". In the guise of this "inhuman", he now moves to Sierra-Morena, in order to prepare himself by acts of penitence for the splendour of the New Testament. There he strips himself "stark naked" (p. 184) in order to achieve his peculiarity and surpass what his predecessor in Cervantes does in chapter twenty-five:

> "And hurriedly stripping off his breeches, he stood in his skin and his shirt. And then, without more ado, he took two goat leaps into the air turning head over heels, thereby revealing such things as caused his trusty armour-bearer to turn Rosinante aside, so as not to see them."

The "inhuman" far surpasses its mundane prototype. It "*resolutely turns its back on itself* and thus also turns away from the disquieting critic", and "leaves him behind". The "*inhuman*" then enters into an argument with criticism that has been "left behind"; it "despises itself", it "conceives itself in comparison with another", it "commands God", it "seeks its better self outside itself", it does penance for not yet being unique, it declares itself to be the unique, "the egoistical and the *unique*"—although it was hardly necessary for it to state this after having resolutely turned its back *on itself.* The "inhuman" has accomplished all this by its own efforts (see Pfister, *Geschichte der Teutschen*) and now, purified and triumphant, it rides on its ass into the kingdom of the unique.

End of the Old Testament

THE NEW TESTAMENT: "EGO" [72]

1. THE ECONOMY OF THE NEW TESTAMENT

Whereas in the Old Testament the object of our edification was "unique" logic in the framework of the *past,* we are now confronted by the *present time* in the framework of "unique" logic. We have already thrown sufficient light on the "unique" in his manifold antediluvian "refractions"—as man, Caucasian Caucasian, perfect Christian, truth of humane liberalism, negative unity of realism and idealism, etc., etc. Along with the historical construction of the "ego", the "ego" itself also collapses. This "ego", the end of the historical construction, is no "corporeal" ego, carnally procreated by man and woman, which needs no construction in order to exist; it is an "ego" spiritually created by two categories, "idealism" and "realism", a merely conceptual existence.

The New Testament, which has already been dissolved together with its premise, the Old Testament, possesses a domestic economy that is literally as wisely designed as that of the Old, namely the same "with various transformations", as can be seen from the following table:

I. *Peculiarity*—the ancients, child, Negro, etc., in their *truth,* i.e., development from the "world of things" to one's "own" outlook and taking possession of this world. Among the ancients this led to riddance of the world, among the moderns—riddance of spirit, among the liberals—riddance of the individual, among the communists—riddance of property, among the humane [liberals]—riddance of God; hence it led in general to the category of riddance (freedom) as the goal. The negated category of *riddance* is *peculiarity,* which of course has no other content than this riddance.

Peculiarity is the philosophically constructed quality of all the qualities of Stirner's individual.

II. The *owner*—as such Stirner has penetrated beyond the *untruthfulness* of the world of things and the world of spirit; hence the *moderns*, the phase of Christianity within the logical development: youth, Mongol.—Just as the moderns divide into the triply determined free ones, so the owner falls into three further determinations:

1. *My power*, corresponding to *political liberalism*, where the *truth of right* is brought to light and right as the power of "man" is resolved in power as the right of the "ego". The struggle against the *state as such*.

2. *My intercourse*, corresponding to *communism*, whereby the *truth of society* is brought to light and society (in its forms of prison society, family, state, burgeois society, etc.) as intercourse mediated by "man" is resolved in the intercourse of the "ego".

3. *My self-enjoyment*, corresponding to critical, *humane liberalism*, in which the *truth of criticism*, the consumption, dissolution and truth of absolute self-consciousness, comes to light as self-consumption, and criticism as dissolution in the interests of man is transformed into dissolution in the interests of the "ego".

The peculiarity of the individuals was resolved, as we have seen, in the universal category of peculiarity, which was the negation of riddance, of freedom in general. A description of the special qualities of the individual, therefore, can again only consist in the negation of this "freedom" in its three "refractions"; each of these negative freedoms is now converted by its negation into a positive quality. Obviously, just as in the Old Testament riddance of the world of things and the world of thoughts was already regarded as the acquisition of both these worlds, so here also it is a matter of course that this peculiarity or acquisition of things and thoughts is in its turn represented as perfect riddance.

The "ego" with its property, its world, consisting of the qualities just "pointed out", is *owner*. As self-enjoying and self-consuming, it is the "ego" raised to the second power, the owners of the owner, it being as much rid of the owner as the owner belongs to it; the result is "absolute negativity" in its dual determination as indifference, "unconcern"[a] and negative relation to itself, the owner. Its property in respect of the

---

[a] In the manuscript the Berlin dialect form *Jleichjültigkeit* (unconcern) is used.— *Ed.*

world and its riddance of the world is now transformed into this negative relation to itself, into this self-dissolution and self-ownership of the owner. The ego thus determined, is —

III. *The unique*, who again, therefore, has no other content than that of owner plus the philosophical determination of the "negative relation to himself". The profound Jacques pretends that there is nothing to say about this unique, because it is a corporeal, not constructed individual. But the matter here is rather the same as in the case of Hegel's absolute idea at the end of the *Logik* and of absolute personality at the end of the *Encyclopädie*, about which there is likewise nothing to say because the construction contains everything that can be said about such constructed personalities. Hegel knows this and does not mind admitting it, whereas Stirner hypocritically maintains that his "unique" is also something different from the constructed unique alone, but something that cannot be expressed, viz., a corporeal individual. This hypocritical appearance vanishes if the thing is reversed, if the unique is defined as owner, and it is said of the owner that he has the universal category of peculiarity as his universal determination. This not only says everything that is "*sayable*" about the unique, but also what he *is* in general—minus the fantasy of Jacques le bonhomme about him.

"O the depth of the riches both of the wisdom and knowledge of the unique! How incomprehensible are his thoughts, and his ways past finding out!"[a]

"Lo, these are parts of his ways: but how little a portion is heard of him!" (Job 26:14.)

2. THE PHENOMENOLOGY OF THE EGOIST IN AGREEMENT WITH HIMSELF, OR THE THEORY OF JUSTIFICATION

As we have already seen in "The Economy of the Old Testament" and afterwards, Saint Sancho's true egoist in agreement with himself must on no account be confused with the trivial, everyday egoist, the "*egoist in the ordinary sense*". Rather he has as his presupposition both this latter (the one in thrall to the world of things, child, Negro, ancient, etc.) and the selfless egoist (the one in thrall to the world of thoughts, youth, Mongol, modern, etc.). It is, however, part of the nature of the secrets of the unique that this antithesis and the negative unity which follows from it — the "*egoist in agreement with himself*"— can be examined only now in the New Testament.

Since Saint Max wishes to present the "true egoist" as something quite new, as the goal of all preceding history, he

---

[a] Romans 11:33 (paraphrased).— *Ed.*

must, on the one hand, prove to the selfless, the advocates of *dévoûment*, that they are egoists against their will, and he must prove to the egoists in the ordinary sense that they are selfless, that they are not true, holy, egoists.—Let us begin with the first, with the selfless.

We have already seen countless times that in the world of Jacques le bonhomme everyone is obsessed by the holy. "Nevertheless it makes a difference" whether "one is educated or uneducated". The educated, who are occupied with pure thought, confront us here as "obsessed" by the holy *par excellence*. They are the "selfless" in their practical guise.

"Who then is selfless? Completely" (!) "most" (!!) "likely" (!!!) "he who stakes everything else on *one thing*, one aim, one purpose, one passion.... He is ruled by a passion to which he sacrifices all others. And are these selfless not selfish, perhaps? Since they *possess* only a single ruling passion, they are concerned only with a single satisfaction, but the more ardently on that account. All their deeds and actions are egoistic, but it is a *one-sided, concealed, narrow egoism*; it is—obsession." (P. 99.)

Hence, according to Saint Sancho, they *possess* only a *single* ruling passion; ought they to be concerned also with the passions which not *they* but *others possess*, in order to rise to an all-round, unconcealed, unrestricted egoism, in order to correspond to this *alien* scale of "holy" egoism?

In this passage are incidentally introduced also the "miser" and the "*pleasure-seeker*" (probably because Stirner thinks that he seeks "*pleasure*" as such, holy pleasure, and not all sorts of real pleasures), as also "Robespierre, for example, Saint-Just, and so on" (p. 100) as examples of "selfless, obsessed egoists". "From a certain moral point of view it is argued" (i.e., our holy "egoist in agreement with himself" argues from his own point of view in extreme disagreement with himself) "approximately as follows":

"But if I sacrifice other passions to one passion, I still do not thereby sacrifice *myself* to this passion, and I do not sacrifice anything thanks to which I am *truly* I myself." (P. 386.)

Saint Max is compelled by these two propositions "in disagreement with each other" to make the "paltry" distinction that one may well sacrifice six "for example", or seven, "and so on", passions to a single other passion without ceasing to be "truly I myself", but by no means ten passions, or a still greater number. Of course, neither Robespierre nor Saint-Just was "*truly* I myself", just as neither was truly "man", but they were *truly* Robespierre and Saint-Just, those unique, incomparable individuals.

The trick of proving to the "selfless" that they are egoists is an old dodge, sufficiently exploited already by Helvétius and Bentham. Saint Sancho's "own" trick consists in the transformation of "egoists in the ordinary sense", the bourgeois, into non-egoists. Helvétius and Bentham, at any rate, prove to the bourgeois that by their narrow-mindedness they *in practice* harm themselves, but Saint Max's "own" trick consists in proving that they do not correspond to the "ideal", the "concept", the "essence", the "calling", etc., of the egoist and that their attitude towards themselves is not that of absolute negation. Here again he has in mind only his German petty bourgeois. Let us point out, incidentally, that whereas on page 99 our saint makes the "miser" figure as a "selfless egoist", on page 78, on the other hand, the "avaricious one" is included among "egoists in the ordinary sense", among the "impure, unholy".

This second class of the hitherto existing egoists is defined on page 99 as follows:

"These people" (the bourgeois) "are therefore not selfless, not inspired, not ideal, not consistent, not enthusiasts; they are *egoists in the ordinary sense*, selfish people, thinking of their own advantage, sober, calculating, etc."

Since "the book" is not all of a piece, we have already had occasion, in connection with "whimsy" and "political liberalism", to see how Stirner achieves the trick of transforming the bourgeois into non-egoists, chiefly owing to his great ignorance of real people and conditions. This same ignorance serves him here as a lever.

"This" (i.e., Stirner's fantasy about unselfishness) "is repugnant to the stubborn brain of worldly man but for thousands of years he at least succumbed so far that he had to bend his obstinate neck and worship higher powers." (P. 104.) The egoists in the ordinary sense "behave half clerically and half in a worldly way, they serve both God and Mammon". (P. 105.)

We learn on page 78: "The Mammon of heaven and the God of the world both demand precisely the *same* degree of *self-denial*", hence it is impossible to understand how self-denial for Mammon and self-denial for God can be opposed to each other as "worldly" and "clerical".

On page 105-106, Jacques le bonhomme asks himself:

"How does it happen, then, that the egoism of those who assert their personal interest nevertheless constantly succumbs to a clerical or school-masterly, i.e., an ideal, interest?"

(Here, one must in passing "point out" that in this passage the bourgeois are depicted as representatives of *personal* interests.) It happens because:

"Their personality seems to them too small, too unimportant — as indeed it is — to lay claim to everything and be able to assert itself fully. A sure sign of this is the fact that they divide themselves into two persons, an eternal and a temporal; on Sundays they take care of the eternal aspect and on weekdays the temporal. They have the priest within them, therefore they cannot get rid of him."

Sancho experiences some scruples here; he asks anxiously whether "the same thing will happen" to peculiarity, the egoism in the extraordinary sense.

We shall see that it is not without grounds that this anxious question is asked. Before the cock has crowed twice, Saint Jacob (Jacques le bonhomme) will have "*denied*" himself thrice.[a]

He discovers to his great displeasure that the two sides prominently appearing in history, the private interest of individuals and the so-called general interest, always accompany each other. As usual, he discovers this in a false form, in its holy form, from the aspect of ideal interests, of the holy, of illusion. He asks: how is it that the ordinary egoists, the representatives of personal interests, are at the same time dominated by general interests, by school-masters, by the hierarchy? His reply to the question is to the effect that the bourgeois, etc., "seem to themselves too small", and he discovers a "sure sign" of this in the fact that they behave in a religious way, i.e., that their personality is divided into a temporal and an eternal one, that is to say, he explains their religious behaviour by their religious behaviour, after first transforming the struggle between general and personal interests into a mirror image of the struggle, into a simple reflection inside religious fantasy.

How the matter stands as regards the domination of the ideal, see above in the section on hierarchy.

If Sancho's question is translated from its highflown form into everyday language, then "it now reads":

How is it that personal interests always develop, against the will of individuals, into class interests, into common interests which acquire independent existence in relation to the individual persons, and in their independence assume the form of *general* interests? How is it that as such they come into contradiction with the actual individuals and in this contradiction, by which they are defined as *general* interests, they can be conceived by consciousness as *ideal* and even as religious, holy interests? How is it that in this process of private interests acquiring independent existence as class interests the personal behaviour of the individual is bound to be objectified [*sich versachlichen*], estranged [*sich entfremden*], and at the same

---

[a] Cf. Mark 14:30.— *Ed.*

time exists as a power independent of him and without him, created by intercourse, and is transformed into social relations, into a series of powers which determine and subordinate the individual, and which, therefore, appear in the imagination as "holy" powers? Had Sancho understood the fact that within the framework of definite *modes of production,* which, of course, are not dependent on the will, alien [*fremde*] practical forces, which are independent not only of isolated individuals but even of all of them together, always come to stand above people — then he could be fairly indifferent as to whether this fact is presented in a religious form or distorted in the fancy of the egoist, above whom everything is placed in imagination, in such a way that he places nothing above himself. Sancho would then have descended from the realm of speculation into the realm of reality, from what people fancy to what they actually are, from what they imagine to how they act and are bound to act in definite circumstances. What seems to him a product of *thought,* he would have understood to be a product of *life.* He would not then have arrived at the absurdity worthy of him — of explaining the division between personal and general interests by saying that people imagine this division *also* in a religious way and *seem* to themselves to be such and such, which is, however, only another word for "imagining".

Incidentally, even in the banal, petty-bourgeois German form in which Sancho perceives the contradiction of personal and general interests, he should have realised that individuals have always started out from themselves, and could not do otherwise, and that therefore the two aspects he noted are aspects of the personal development of individuals; both are equally engendered by the empirical conditions under which the individuals live, both are only expressions of *one and the same* personal development of people and are therefore only in *seeming* contradiction to each other. As regards the position — determined by the special circumstances of development and by division of labour — which falls to the lot of the given individual, whether he represents to a greater extent one or the other aspect of the antithesis, whether he appears more as an egoist or more as selfless — that was a quite subordinate question, which could only acquire any interest at all if it were raised in definite epochs of history in relation to definite individuals. Otherwise this question could only lead to morally false, charlatan phrases. But as a dogmatist Sancho falls into error here and finds no other way out than by declaring that the Sancho Panzas and Don Quixotes are born such, and that then the Don Quixotes stuff all kinds of nonsense into the heads of the Sanchos; as a dogmatist he seizes on one aspect, conceived in a school-masterly manner, declares it to be characteristic of individuals as such, and expresses his aversion to the other aspect. Therefore, too, as a dogmatist, the other aspect appears to him partly as a mere *state of mind, dévoûment*, partly as a mere "*principle*", and not as a relation necessarily arising from the preceding natural mode of life of individuals. One has, therefore, only to "get this principle out of one's head", although, according to Sancho's ideology, it creates all kinds of empirical things. Thus, for example, on page 180 "social life, all sociability, all fraternity and all that ... was created by the life principle [a] or social principle". It is better the other way round: life created the principle.

Communism is quite incomprehensible to our saint because the communists do not oppose egoism to selflessness or selflessness to egoism, nor do they express this contradiction theoretically either in its sentimental or in its highflown ideological form; they rather demonstrate its material source, with which it disappears of itself. The communists do not preach *morality* at all, as Stirner does so extensively. They do not put to people the moral demand: love one another, do not be egoists, etc.; on the contrary, they are very well aware that egoism, just as much as selflessness, *is* in definite circumstances a necessary form of the self-assertion of individuals. Hence, the communists by no means want, as Saint Max believes, and as his loyal *Dottore Graziano* (Arnold Ruge) repeats after him (for which Saint Max calls him "an unusually cunning and politic mind", *Wigand*, p. 192), to do away with the "private individual" for the sake of the "general", selfless man. That is a figment of the imagination concerning which both of them could already have found the necessary explanation in the *Deutsch-Französische Jahrbücher*. Communist theoreticians, the only communists who have time to devote to the study of history, are distinguished precisely by the fact that they alone have *discovered* that throughout history the "general interest" is created by individuals who are defined as "private persons". They know that this contradiction is only a *seeming* one because one side of it, what is called the "general interest", is constantly being produced by the other side, private interest, and in relation to the latter it is by no means an independent force with an independent history — so that this contradiction is in practice constantly destroyed and reproduced. Hence it is not

---

[a] Stirner has "love principle".— *Ed.*

a question of the Hegelian "negative unity" of two sides of a contradiction, but of the materially determined destruction of the preceding materially determined mode of life of individuals, with the disappearance of which this contradiction together with its unity also disappears.

Thus we see how the "egoist in agreement with himself" as opposed to the "egoist in the ordinary sense" and the "selfless egoist", is based from the outset on an illusion about both of these and about the real relations of real people. The representative of personal interests is merely an "egoist in the ordinary sense" because of his necessary contradiction to communal interests which, within the existing mode of production and intercourse, are given an independent existence as general interests and are conceived and vindicated in the form of ideal interests. The representative of the interests of the community is merely "selfless" because of his opposition to personal interests, fixed as private interests, and because the interests of the community are defined as general and ideal interests.

Both the "selfless egoist" and the "egoist in the ordinary sense" coincide, in the final analysis, in *self-denial*.

Page 78: "Thus, self-denial is common to both the holy and unholy, the pure and impure: the impure *denies* all better feelings, all shame, even natural timidity, and follows only the desire which rules him. The pure renounces his natural relation to the world.... Impelled by the thirst for money, the avaricious person denies all promptings of conscience, all sense of honour, all soft-heartedness and pity; he is blind to all consideration, his desire drives him on. The holy person acts similarly: he makes himself a laughing-stock in the eyes of the world, he is 'hard-hearted' and 'severely just', for he is carried away by his longing."

The "avaricious man", shown here as an impure, unholy egoist, hence as an egoist in the ordinary sense, is nothing but a figure on whom moral readers for children and novels dilate, but that actually occurs only as an exception, and is by no means the representative of the avaricious bourgeois. The latter, on the contrary, have no need to deny the "promptings of conscience", "the sense of honour", etc., or to restrict themselves to the one passion of avarice alone. On the contrary, their avarice engenders a series of other passions — political, etc.— the satisfaction of which the bourgeois on no account sacrifice. Without going more deeply into this matter, let us at once turn to Stirner's "self-denial".

For the self which denies itself, Saint Max here substitutes a different self which exists only in Saint Max's imagination. He makes the "impure" sacrifice general qualities such as "better feelings", "shame", "timidity", "sense of honour", etc., and does not at all ask whether the impure actually possesses these properties. As if the "impure" is necessarily bound to possess all these qualities! But even if the "impure" did possess all of them, the sacrifice of these qualities would still be no *self*-denial, but only confirm the fact—which has to be justified even in morality "in agreement with itself"—that for the sake of one passion several others are sacrificed. And, finally, according to this theory, everything that Sancho does or does not do is "self-denial". He may or may not act in a particular manner [...].*

Although** on page 420 Saint Max now says:

* [There is a gap here. An extant page, which has been crossed out and greatly damaged, contains the following:] he is an egoist, his own self-denial. If he pursues an interest he denies the indifference to this interest, if he does something he denies idleness. Nothing is easier [...] for Sancho than to prove to the *"egoist in the ordinary sense"* — his stumbling-block—that he always denies himself, because he always denies the opposite of what he does, and never denies his real interest.

In accordance with his theory of self-denial Sancho can exclaim on page 80: "Is perhaps unselfishness unreal and non-existent? On the contrary, nothing is more common!"

We are really very happy [about the "unselfishness"] of the consciousness of the German petty [bourgeois]....

He immediately gives a good example of this unselfishness by [adducing] Orphanage-F[rancke,[73] O'Connell, Saint Boniface, Robespierre, Theodor Körner...].

O'Connell, [...], every [child] in Britain knows this. Only in Germany, and particularly in Berlin, is it still possible to believe that O'Connell is "unselfish". O'Connell, who "tirelessly works" to place his illegitimate children and to enlarge his fortune, who has not for love exchanged his lucrative legal practice (£10,000 per annum) for the even more lucrative job of an agitator (£20,000-30,000 per annum) (especially lucrative in Ireland, where he has no competition); O'Connell who, acting as middleman,[a] "hard-heartedly" exploits the Irish peasants making them live with their pigs while he, King Dan, holds court in princely style in his palace in Merrion Square and at the same time laments continually over the misery of these peasants, "for he is carried away by his longing"; O'Connell, who always pushes the movement just as far as is necesarry to secure his national tribute[b] and his position as chief, and who every year after collecting the tribute gives up all agitation in order to pamper himself on his estate at Derrynane. Because of his legal charlatanism carried on over many years and his exceedingly brazen exploitation of every movement in which he participated, O'Connell is regarded with contempt even by the English bourgeoisie, despite his usefulness.

It is moreover obvious that Saint Max, the discoverer of true egoism, is strongly interested in proving that unselfishness has hitherto ruled the world. Therefore he puts forward the great proposition (*Wigand,* p. 165) that the world was "not egoistic for millennia". At most he admits that from time to time the "egoist" appeared as Stirner's forerunner and "ruined nations".

** [Marx made the following note at the beginning of this page:] *III. Consciousness.*

---

    a The word is in English in the original.— *Ed.*
    b These two words are in English in the manuscript.— *Ed.*

"Over the portals of our [epoch] are written not the words ... 'know thyself', [but] 'turn yourself to account]' " [*Verwerte Dich*]

(here our school-master again transforms the actual turning to account which he finds in existence into a moral precept about turning to account), nevertheless [for the] "egoist in the ordinary [sense" instead of for] the former "selfless egoist", "the [Apollonic" maxim [74] should read:

"]Only *know yourselves* [, only know what] you [are in reality and give up your foolish endeavour to be something different from what you are!" "For": "This leads to the phenomenon of *deceived* egoism, in which I satisfy not myself, but] only one [of my desires, e.] g., the [thirst for] happiness. [— All] your deeds and [actions are secret], concealed ... [egoism,] *unconscious egoism*, [but] *for that very reason* not egoism, but slavery, service, self-denial. *You are egoists and at the same time not egoists, inasmuch as you deny egoism.*" (P. 217.)

"No sheep, no dog, endeavours to become a real" egoist (p. 443); "no animal" calls to the others: "Only know yourselves, only know what you are in reality".— "It is your nature to be" egoistical, "you are" egoistical "natures, i.e.", egoists. "But precisely because you are that already, you have no need to become so." (Ibid.) To what you are belongs also your consciousness, and since you are egoists you possess also the consciousness corresponding to your egoism, and therefore there is no reason at all for paying the slightest heed to Stirner's moral preaching to look into your heart and do penance.

Here again Stirner exploits the old philosophical device to which we shall return later. The philosopher does not say directly: You are not people. [He says:] You have always been people, but you were not *conscious* of what you were, and for that very reason you were not in reality True People. Therefore your appearance was not appropriate to your essence. You were people and you were not people.

In a roundabout way the philosopher here admits that a definite consciousness is appropriate to definite people and definite circumstances. But at the same time he imagines that his moral demand to people — the demand that they should change their consciousness — will bring about this altered consciousness, and in people who have changed owing to changed empirical conditions and who, of course, now also possess a different consciousness, he sees nothing but a changed [consciousness].— It is just the same [with the consciousness for which you are secretly] longing; [in regard to this] you are [secret, unconscious] egoists — i.e., you are really egoists, insofar as you are *unconscious* but you are non-egoists, insofar as you are *conscious*. Or: at the root of your present [consciousness lies] a definite being, which is not the [being] which I demand; your consciousness is the consciousness of the egoist such as he should not [be], and therefore it shows that you yourselves are egoists such as egoists should not be — or it shows that you *should be* different from what you *really are.* This entire separation of consciousness from the individuals who are its basis and from their actual conditions, this notion that the egoist of present-day bourgeois society does not possess the consciousness corresponding to his egoism, is merely an old philosophical fad that Jacques le bonhomme here credulously accepts and copies.* Let us deal with Stirner's "touching example" of the avaricious person. He wants to persuade this avaricious person, who is not an "avaricious person" in general, but the avaricious "Tom or Dick"; a quite individually defined, "unique" avaricious person, whose avarice is not the category of "avarice" (an abstraction of Saint Max's from his all-embracing, complex, "unique" manifestation of life) and "does not depend on the heading under which other people" (for example, Saint Max) "classify it"—he wants to persuade this avaricious person by moral exhortations that he "is satisfying not himself but one of his desires". But "you are you only for a [moment], only as a momentary being are you real. What [is separated from you,] from the momentary being" is something absolutely higher, [e.g., money. But whether] "for you" money is "rather" [a higher pleasure], whether it is for you [something "absolutely higher" or] not [...]ᵃ perhaps ["deny"] myself [? — He] finds that I am possessed [by avarice] day and night, [but] this is so only in his reflection. It is he who makes "day and night" out of the many moments in which I am always the momentary being, always myself, always real, just as he alone embraces in one moral judgment the different moments of my manifestation of life and asserts that they are the satisfaction of avarice. When Saint Max announces that I am satisfying only one of my desires, and not myself, he puts me as a complete and whole being in opposition to me myself. "And in what does this complete and whole being consist? It is certainly

* [The following passage is crossed out in the manuscript:] This fad becomes most ridiculous in history, where the consciousness of a later epoch regarding an earlier epoch naturally differs from the consciousness the latter has of itself, e.g., the Greeks saw themselves through the eyes of the Greeks and not as we see them now; to blame them for not seeing themselves with our eyes — that is, "not being conscious of themselves as they really were"— amounts to blaming them for being Greeks.

ᵃ The following passage is damaged.— *Ed.*

not your momentary being, not what you are at the present moment"—hence, according to Saint Max himself, it consists in the holy "being". (*Wigand,* p. 171.) When "Stirner" says that I must change my consciousness, then I know for my part that my momentary consciousness also belongs to my momentary being, and Saint Max, by disputing that I have this consciousness, attacks as a covert moralist my whole mode of life.* And then—"do you exist only when you think about yourself, do you exist only owing to self-consciousness?" (*Wigand,* pp. 157-58.) How can I be anything but an egoist? How can Stirner, for example, be anything but an egoist—whether he denies egoism or not? "You are egoists and you are not egoists, inasmuch as you deny egoism"—that is what you preach.

Innocent, "deceived", "unavowed" school-master! Things are just the reverse. We egoists in the ordinary sense, we bourgeois, know quite well: *Charité bien ordonnée commence par soi-même,*a and we have long had the motto: love thy neighbour as thyself,b interpreted in the sense that each is a neighbour to himself. But we deny that we are heartless egoists, exploiters, ordinary egoists, whose hearts cannot be lifted up to the exalted feeling of making the interests of their fellow-men their own—which, between ourselves, only means that we declare our interests to be the interests of our fellow-men. [You] deny the "ordinary" [egoism of the] unique egoist [only because] you ["deny]" your ["natural] relations to the [world]". Hence you do not understand why we bring practical egoism to perfection precisely by denying the phraseology of egoism—we who are concerned with realising real egoistical interests, not the holy interest of egoism. Incidentally, it could be foreseen—and here the bourgeois coolly turns his back on Saint Max—that you German school-masters, if you once took up the defence of egoism, would proclaim not real, "mundane and plainly evident" egoism ("the book", p. 455), that is to say, "not what is called" egoism, but egoism in the extraordinary, school-masterly sense, philosophical or vagabond egoism.

The egoist in the extraordinary sense, therefore, is "only now discovered". "Let us examine this new discovery more closely." (P. 11.)

From what has been just said it is already clear that the egoists who existed till now have only to change their

* [Here Marx repeats the remark:] III (Consciousness).

---

a Charity begins at home.— *Ed.*
b Galatians 5:14.— *Ed.*

consciousness in order to become egoists in the extraordinary sense, hence that the egoist in agreement with himself is distinguished from the previous type only by consciousness, i.e., only as a learned man, as a philosopher. It further follows from the whole historical outlook of Saint Max that, because the former egoists were ruled only by the "holy", the true egoist has to fight only against the "holy". "Unique" history has shown us how Saint Max transformed historical conditions into ideas, and then the egoist into a sinner against these ideas; how every egoistic manifestation was transformed into a sin [against these] ideas, [the power of] the privileged into a sin [against the idea] of equality, into the sin of despotism. [Concerning the] idea of freedom [of competition,] therefore, it could be [said in "the book"] that [private property is regarded] by him [(p. 155) as"] the personal" [...] great, [...] [selfless] egoists [...] essential and invincible [...] only to be fought by transforming them into something holy and then asserting that he abolishes the holiness in them, i.e., his holy idea about them, [i.e.,] abolishes them only insofar as they exist in him as *a holy one*.[a]

Page 50 *: "How you are *at each moment* you are as your creation, and it is precisely in this *creation* that you do not want to lose yourself, the *creator*. You yourself are a higher being than yourself, i.e., you are not merely a creation, but likewise a creator; and it is this that you fail to recognise as an involuntary egoist, and for that reason the higher being is something foreign to you."

In a somewhat different variation, this same wisdom is stated on page 239 of "the book":

"The species is *nothing*" (later it becomes all sorts of things, see "Self-Enjoyment"), "and when the individual rises above the limitations of his individuality, it is precisely here that he himself appears as an individual; he exists only by raising himself, he exists only by not remaining what he is, otherwise he would be done for, dead."

In relation to these propositions, to his "creation", Stirner at once begins to behave as "creator", "by no means losing himself in them":

"You are you only *for a moment*, only as a momentary being are you real.... At each moment I am wholly what I am ... what is separated from you, the momentary being", is "something absolutely higher" ... (*Wigand*, p. 170); and on page 171 (ibid.), "your being" is defined as "your momentary being".

Whereas in "the book" Saint Max says that besides a momentary being he has also another, higher being, in the "Apologetical Commentary" "the momentary being" [of his] individual is equated with his "complete [and whole] being", and

---

* [Marx wrote at the top of this page:] II (Creator and Creation).

[a] This paragraph is damaged.— *Ed.*

every [being] as a "momentary being" is transformed [into an] "absolutely higher being". In "the book" therefore he is, at every moment, a higher being than what he is at that moment, whereas in the "Commentary", everything that he is not directly at a given moment is defined as an "absolutely higher being", a holy being.— And in contrast to all this division we read on page 200 of "the book":

"I know nothing about a division into an '*imperfect*' and a '*perfect*' ego."

"The egoist in agreement with himself" needs no longer sacrifice himself to something higher, since in his own eyes he is himself this higher being, and he transfers this schism between a "higher" and a "lower being" into himself. So, in fact (Saint Sancho contra Feuerbach, "the book", p. 243), "the highest being has undergone nothing but a metamorphosis". The true egoism of Saint Max consists in an egoistic attitude to real egoism, to himself, as he is "at each moment". This egoistic attitude to egoism is selflessness. From this aspect Saint Max as a creation is an egoist in the ordinary sense; as creator he is a selfless egoist. We shall also become acquainted with the opposite aspect, for both these aspects prove to be genuine determinations of reflection since they undergo absolute dialectics in which each of them is the opposite of itself.

Before entering more deeply into this mystery in its esoteric form, one has to observe some of [its arduous] life battles.

[On pages 82, 83, Stirner achieves the feat of] bringing the most general quality, [the egoist,] [into agreement] with himself as creator, [from the standpoint of the world] of spirit:

["Christianity aimed] at [delivering us from natural determination (determination through nature), from desires as a driving force, it consequently wished that man should not allow himself to be] determined [by his desires. This does not mean that] he [should *have*] no [desires], but that [desires] should not possess [him,] that [they] should not become fixed, unconquerable, ineradicable. *Could we not* apply these machinations of Christianity against desires to its own precept, that we should be determined by the spirit ...? ... Then *this* would signify the dissolution of spirit, the dissolution of all thoughts. As one ought to have said there ... so one would have to say now: We should indeed possess spirit, but spirit should not possess us."

"And they that are Christ's have crucified the flesh with the affections and lusts" (Galatians 5:24)— thus, according to Stirner, they deal with their crucified affections and lusts like true owners. He accepts Christianity in instalments, but will not let matters rest at the crucified flesh alone, wanting to crucify his spirit as well, consequently, the "whole fellow".

The only reason why Christianity wanted to free us from the domination of the flesh and "desires as a driving force" was because it regarded our flesh, our desires as something foreign to us; it wanted to free us from determination by nature only because it regarded our own nature as not belonging to us. For if I myself am not nature, if my natural desires, my whole natural character, do not belong to myself — and this is the doctrine of Christianity — then all determination by nature — whether due to my own natural character or to what is known as external nature — seems to me a determination by something foreign, a fetter, compulsion used against me, *heteronomy as opposed to autonomy of the spirit.* Stirner accepts this Christian dialectic without examining it and then applies it to our spirit. Incidentally, Christianity has indeed never succeeded in freeing us from the domination of desires, even in that *juste milieu* sense foisted on it by Saint Max; it does not go beyond mere moral injunctions, which remain ineffective in real life. Stirner takes moral injunctions for real deeds and supplements them with the further categorical imperative: "We should indeed possess spirit, but spirit should not possess us" — and consequently all his egoism in agreement with itself is reduced "on closer examination", as Hegel would say, to a moral philosophy that is as delightful as it is edifying and contemplative.

Whether a desire becomes fixed or not, i.e., whether it obtains exclusive [power over us] — which, however, does [not] exclude [further progress] — depends on whether material circumstances, "bad" mundane conditions permit the normal satisfaction of this desire and, on the other hand, the development of a totality of desires. This latter depends, in turn, on whether we live in circumstances that allow all-round activity and thereby the full development of all our potentialities. On the actual conditions, and the possibility of development they give each individual, depends also whether thoughts become fixed or not — just as, for example, the fixed ideas of the German philosophers, these "victims of society", *qui nous font pitié,*[a] are inseparable from the German conditions. Incidentally, in Stirner the domination of desires is a mere phrase, the imprint of the absolute saint. Thus, still keeping to the "touching example" of the avaricious person, we read:

> "An avaricious person is not an owner, but a servant, and he can do nothing for his own sake without at the same time doing it for the sake of his master." (P. 400.)

No one can do anything without at the same time doing it for the sake of one or other of his needs and for the sake of the organ of this need — for Stirner this means that this need and its

---

[a] For whom we feel pity.— *Ed.*

organ are made into a master over him, just as earlier he made the *means* for satisfying a need (cf. the sections on political liberalism and communism) into a master over him. Stirner cannot eat without at the same time eating for the sake of his stomach. If the worldly conditions prevent him from satisfying his stomach, then his stomach becomes a master over him, the desire to eat becomes a fixed desire, and the thought of eating becomes a fixed idea — which at the same time gives him an example of the influence of world conditions in fixing his desires and ideas. Sancho's "revolt" against the fixation of desires and thoughts is thus reduced to an impotent moral injunction about self-control and provides new evidence that he merely gives an ideologically high-sounding expression to the most trivial sentiments of the petty bourgeois.*

* [The following passage is crossed out in the manuscript]: Since they attack the material basis on which the hitherto inevitable fixedness of desires and ideas depended, the communists are the only people through whose historical activity the liquefaction of the fixed desires and ideas is in fact brought about and ceases to be an impotent moral injunction, as it was up to now with all moralists "down to" Stirner. Communist organisation has a twofold effect on the desires produced in the individual by present-day relations; some of these desires — namely desires which exist under all relations, and only change their form and direction under different social relations — are merely altered by the communist social system, for they are given the opportunity to develop normally; but others — namely those originating solely in a particular society, under particular conditions of [production] and intercourse — are totally deprived of their conditions of existence. Which [of the desires] will be merely changed and [which eliminated] in a communist [society] can [only be determined in a practical] way, by [changing the real], actual ["desires", and not by making comparisons with earlier historical conditions.]

The two expressions: ["fixed" and "desires"], which we [have just used in order to be able] to disprove [this "unique" fact of] Stirner's, [are of course] quite inappropriate. The fact that one desire of an individual in modern society can be satisfied at the expense of all others, and that this "ought not to be" and that this is more or less the case with all individuals in the world today and that thereby the free development of the individual as a whole is made impossible — this fact is expressed by Stirner thus: "the desires become fixed" in the egoist in disagreement with himself, for Stirner knows nothing of the empirical connection of this fact with the world as it is today. A desire is already by its mere existence something "fixed", and it can occur only to Saint Max and his like not to allow his sex instinct, for instance, to become "fixed"; it is that already and will cease to be fixed only as the result of castration or impotence. Each need, which forms the basis of a "desire", is likewise something "fixed", and try as he may Saint Max cannot abolish this "fixedness" and for example contrive to free himself from the necessity of eating within "fixed" periods of time. The communists have no intention of abolishing the fixedness of their desires and needs, an intention which Stirner, immersed in his world of fancy, ascribes to them and to all other men; they only strive to achieve an organisation of production and intercourse which will make possible the normal satisfaction of all needs, i.e., a satisfaction which is limited only by the needs themselves.

Thus, in this first example he fights, on the one hand, against his carnal desires, and on the other against his spiritual thoughts—on the one hand against his flesh, on the other against his spirit—when they, his creations, want to become independent of him, their creator. How our saint conducts this struggle, how he behaves as creator towards his creation, we shall now see.

In the Christian "in the ordinary sense", in the *chrétien "simple"*, to use Fourier's expression,

"*spirit* has undivided power and pays no heed to any persuasion of the '*flesh*'. However, only through the '*flesh*' can I break the tyranny of the *spirit*; for only when man perceives also his *flesh* does he perceive himself wholly, and only when he perceives himself *wholly* does he become perceptive or rational.... But as soon as the *flesh* speaks and — as cannot be otherwise — in a passionate tone ... then he" (the *chrétien simple*) "believes he hears devil voices, voices against the *spirit* ... and with good reason comes out passionately against them. He would not be a Christian if he were prepared to tolerate them." (P. 83.)

Hence, when his spirit wishes to acquire independence in relation to him, Saint Max calls his flesh to his aid, and when his flesh becomes rebellious, he remembers that he is also spirit. What the Christian does in one direction, Saint Max does in both. He is the *chrétien "composé"*, he once again reveals himself as the perfect Christian.

Here, in this example, Saint Max, as spirit, does not appear as the creator of his flesh, and vice versa; he finds his flesh and his spirit both present, and only when one side rebels does he remember that he has also the other, and asserts this other side, as his true ego, against it. Here, therefore, Saint Max is creator only insofar as he is one who is "*also-otherwise-determined*", insofar as he possesses yet another quality besides that which it just suits him to subsume under the category of "creation". His entire creative activity consists here in the good resolution to perceive himself, and indeed to perceive himself *entirely* or be *rational*,* to perceive himself as a "complete, entire being", as a being different from "his momentary being", and even in direct contradiction to the kind of being he is "momentarily".

[Let us now turn to one of the "arduous] life battles" [of our saint]:

[Pages 80, 81: "My zeal] need not [be less than the] most fanatical, [but at the

---

* Here, therefore, Saint Max completely justifies Feuerbach's "touching example" of the hetaera and the beloved. In the first case, a man "perceives" *only his flesh* or only her flesh, in the second he perceives *himself entirely* or her *entirely*. See *Wigand*, pp. 170, 171.

same] time [I remain] towards [it cold as ice, sceptical], and its [most irreconcilable enemy;] I remain [its *judge*, for I am its] owner."

[If one desires to] give [meaning] to what Saint [Sancho] says about himself, then it amounts to this: his creative activity here is limited to the fact that in his zeal he preserves the consciousness of his zeal, that he reflects on it, that he adopts the attitude of the reflecting ego to himself as the real ego. It is to consciousness that he arbitrarily gives the name "creator". He is "creator" only insofar as he possesses *consciousness*.

"Thereupon, you forget yourself in sweet self-oblivion.... But do you exist only when you think of yourself, and *do you vanish when you forget yourself?* Who does not forget himself at every instant, who does not lose sight of himself *a thousand times an hour?*" (*Wigand*, pp. 157, 158.)

This, of course, Sancho cannot forgive his "self-oblivion" and therefore "remains at the same time its most irreconcilable enemy".

Saint Max, the creation, burns with immense zeal at the very time when Saint Max, the creator, has already risen above his zeal by means of reflection; or the real Saint Max burns with zeal, and the reflecting Saint Max imagines that he has risen above this zeal. This rising in reflection above what he actually is, is now amusingly and adventurously described in the phrases of a novel to the effect that he allows his zeal to remain in existence, i.e., he does not draw any serious consequences from his hostility to it, but his attitude towards it is "cold as ice", "sceptical" and that of its "most irreconcilable enemy".

Insofar as Saint Max burns with zeal, i.e., insofar as zeal is his true quality, his attitude to it is not that of creator; and insofar as his attitude is that of creator, he does not really burn with zeal, zeal is foreign to him, not a quality of him. So long as he burns with zeal he is not the owner of zeal, and as soon as he becomes the owner, he ceases to burn with zeal. As an aggregate complex, he is at every instant, in the capacity of creator and owner, the sum total of all his qualities, with the exception of the one quality which he puts in opposition to himself, the embodiment of all the others, as creation and property — so that precisely *that* quality which he stresses as *his own* is always *foreign* to him.

No matter how extravagant Saint Max's true story of his heroic exploits within himself, in his own consciousness, may sound, it is nevertheless an acknowledged fact that there do exist reflecting individuals, who imagine that in and through reflection they have risen above everything,* because in actual fact they never go beyond reflection.

This trick — of declaring oneself against some definite quality as being someone who is also-otherwise-determined, namely, in the present example as being the *possessor of reflection directed towards the opposite* — this trick can be applied with the necessary variations to any quality you choose. For example, my indifference need be no less than that of the most *blasé* person; but at the same time I remain towards it extremely ardent, sceptical and its most irreconcilable enemy, etc.

[It should] not be forgotten that [the aggregate] complex of all his [qualities, the owner] — in which capacity [Saint] Sancho [by reflecting opposes one particular] quality — is in this [case nothing but Sancho's] simple [reflection about this] one quality, [which he has] transformed [into his ego by] putting forward, instead of the whole [complex. one] merely reflecting [quality and] putting forward in opposition to each of his qualities [and to] the series [merely the one] quality of reflection, an ego, and himself as the imagined ego.

Now he himself gives expression to this hostile attitude to himself, this solemn parody of Bentham's bookkeeping [75] of his own interests and qualities.

Page 188: "An interest, no matter towards what end it may be directed, acquires a slave in the shape of myself, if I am unable to rid myself of it; it is no longer my property, but I am its property. Let us, therefore, accept the directive of criticism that we should feel happy only in dissolution."

"We"! — Who are "We"? It never occurs to "us" to "accept" the "directive of criticism". — Thus Saint Max, who for the moment is under the police surveillance of "criticism", here demands "the same well-being for all", "equal well-being for all in one and the same [respect]", "the direct tyrannical domination of *religion*".

His interestedness in the extraordinary sense is here revealed as a heavenly disinterestedness.

* [The following passage is crossed out in the manuscript:] All this is in fact merely a highflown description of the bourgeois. who controls each of his emotions so that he should not sustain any loss, and on the other hand boasts about numerous qualities, i. e., philanthropic zeal, towards which he must remain "cold as ice, sceptical and an irreconcilable enemy", in order not to lose himself as owner in his philanthropic zeal but to remain the owner of philanthropy. Whereas the bourgeois sacrifices his inclinations and desires always for a definite *real* interest, Saint Max sacrifices the quality towards which he adopts the attitude of the "most irreconcilable enemy" for the sake of his reflecting ego. his reflection.

Incidentally, there is no need here to deal at length with the fact that in existing society it does not at all depend on Saint Sancho whether an "interest" "acquires a slave in the shape of himself" and whether "he is unable to rid himself of it". The fixation of interests through division of labour and class relations is far more obvious than the fixation of "desires" and "thoughts".

In order to outbid critical criticism, our saint should at least have gone as far as the dissolution of dissolution, for otherwise dissolution becomes an interest which he cannot get rid of, which in him acquires a slave. Dissolution is no longer his property, but he is the property of dissolution. Had he wanted to be consistent in the example just given, [he should] [have treated his zeal against his] own "zeal" as [an "interest"] and [behaved] towards it [as an "irreconcilable] enemy". [But he should have] also considered his ["ice-cold" disinterestedness] in relation to his ["ice-cold" zeal] and become [just as wholly "ice-cold"]— and thereby, [obviously, he would have spared] his original ["interest"] and hence himself the "temptation" to turn [in a circle] on the [heel] of speculation.— Instead, he cheerfully continues (ibid.):

"I shall only take care to safeguard my own property for myself" (i.e., to safeguard myself from my property) "and, in order to safeguard it, I take it back into myself at any time, I destroy in it any inclination towards independence and absorb it before it becomes fixed and can become a fixed idea or passion."

How does Stirner "absorb" the persons who are his property!

Stirner has just allowed himself to be given a "vocation" by "criticism". He asserts that he at once absorbs this "vocation" again, by saying on page 189:

"I do this, however, not for the sake of my human vocation, but because I call on myself to do so."

If I do not call on myself to do so, I am, as we have just heard, a slave, not an owner, not a true egoist, I do not behave to myself as creator, as I should do as a true egoist; therefore, insofar as a person wants to be a true egoist, he must call himself to this vocation given him by "criticism". Thus, it is a universal vocation, a vocation for all, not merely *his* vocation, but also his *vocation*.

On the other hand, the true egoist appears here as an ideal which is unattainable by the majority of individuals, for (p. 434) "innately limited intellects unquestionably form the most numerous class of mankind"—and how could these "limited intellects" be able to penetrate the mystery of unlimited absorption of oneself and the world.

Incidentally, all these terrible expressions—to destroy, to absorb, etc.—are merely a new variation of the above-mentioned "ice-cold, most irreconcilable enemy".

Now, at last, we are put in a position to obtain an insight into Stirner's objections to communism. They were nothing but a preliminary, concealed legitimisation of his egoism in agreement with itself, in which these objections are resurrected in the flesh. The "*equal well-being of all in one and the same respect*" is resurrected in the demand that "*we* should [only] feel happy in [dissolution]". "*Care*]" is resurrected [in the form of the unique "care]" to secure [one's ego] [as one's property]; [but "with the passage of time]" ["care"] again arises as to "how" [one can arrive] at a [unity—] viz., unity [of creator and creation.] And, finally, humanism re[-appears, which in the form of the true] egoist confronts empirical individuals as an unattainable ideal. Hence page 117 of "the book" should read as follows: Egoism in agreement with itself really endeavours to transform every man into a "secret police state". The spy and sleuth "reflection" keeps a strict eye on every impulse of spirit and body, and every deed and thought, every manifestation of life is, for him, a matter of reflection, i.e., a police matter. It is this dismemberment of man into "natural instinct" and "reflection" (the inner plebeian—creation, and the internal police—creator) which constitutes the egoist in agreement with himself.*

Hess (*Die letzten Philosophen*, p. 26) reproached our saint:

"He is constantly under the secret police surveillance of his critical conscience .... He has not forgotten the 'directive of criticism ... to feel happy only in dissolution'.... The egoist—his critical conscience is always reminding him—should never become so interested in anything as to devote himself entirely to his subject", and so on.

Saint Max "empowers himself" to answer as follows:

When "Hess says of Stirner that he is constantly, etc.— what does this mean except that when he criticises he wants to criticise not at random" (i.e., by the way: in the unique fashion), "not talking twaddle, but criticising properly" (i.e., like a human being)?

"What it means", when Hess speaks of the secret police, etc., is so clear from the passage by Hess quoted above that even

* [The following passage is crossed out in the manuscript:] Incidentally, if Saint Max makes "a Prussian officer of high rank" say: "Every Prussian carries his gendarme in his heart", it ought to read: the king's gendarme, for only the "egoist in agreement with himself" carries *his own* gendarme in his heart.

Saint Max's "unique" understanding of it can only be explained as a deliberate misunderstanding. His "virtuosity of thought" is transformed here into a virtuosity in lying, for which we do not reproach him since it was his only way out, but which is hardly in keeping with the subtle little distinctions on the right to lie which he sets out elsewhere in "the book". Incidentally, we have already demonstrated — at greater length than he deserves — that "when he criticises", Sancho by no means "criticises properly", but "criticises at random" and "talks twaddle".

Thus, the attitude of the true egoist as creator towards himself as creation was first of all defined in the sense that in opposition to a definition in which he became fixed as a creation — for example, as against himself as thinker, as spirit — he asserts himself as a person also-otherwise-determined, as flesh. Later, he no longer asserts himself as *really* also-otherwise-determined, but as the *mere idea of being also-otherwise-determined* in general — hence, in the above example as someone who also-does-not-think, who is thoughtless or indifferent to thought, an idea which he abandons again as soon as its nonsensicalness becomes evident. See above on turning round on the heel of speculation.[a] Hence the creative activity consisted here in the reflection that this single determination, in the present case thought, could also be indifferent for him, i.e., it consisted in reflecting in general; as a result, of course, he creates only reflective definitions, if he creates anything at all (e.g., the idea of antithesis, the simple essence of which is concealed by all kinds of fiery arabesques).

As for the *content* of himself as a creation, we have seen that nowhere does he create this content, these definite qualities, e.g., his thought, his zeal, etc., but only the reflective definition of this content as creation, the idea that these definite qualities are his creations. All his qualities are present in him and whence they come is all the same to him. He, therefore, needs neither to develop them — for example, to learn to dance, in order to have mastery over his feet, or to exercise his thought on material which is not given to everyone, and is not procurable by everyone, in order to become the owner of his thought — nor does he need to worry about the conditions in the world, which in reality determine the extent to which an individual can develop.

---

[a] See this volume, pp. 276-77.— *Ed.*

Stirner actually only rids himself of one quality by means of another (i.e., the suppression of his remaining qualities by this "other"). In reality, however, [as we] have [already shown,] he does this only insofar as this quality has not only achieved free development, i.e., has not remained merely potential, but also insofar as conditions in the world have permitted him to develop in an equal measure a *totality* of qualities, [that is to say,] thanks to the division of [labour,][a] thus making possible the [predominant pursuit] of a [single passion, e.]g., that of [writing] books. [In general], it is an [absurdity to] assume, as Saint [Max does], that one could satisfy one [passion] apart from all others, that one could satisfy it without at the same time satisfying *oneself*, the entire living individual. If this passion assumes an abstract, isolated character, if it confronts me as an alien power, if, therefore, the satisfaction of the individual appears as the one-sided satisfaction of a single passion — this by no means depends on consciousness or "good will" and least of all on lack of reflection on the concept of this quality, as Saint Max imagines.

It depends not on *consciousness*, but on *being*; not on thought, but on life; it depends on the individual's empirical development and manifestation of life, which in turn depends on the conditions obtaining in the world. If the circumstances in which the individual lives allow him only the [one]-sided development of one quality at the expense of all the rest, [if] they give him the material and time to develop only that one quality, then this individual achieves only a one-sided, crippled development. No moral preaching avails here. And the manner in which this one, pre-eminently favoured quality develops depends again, on the one hand, on the material available for its development and, on the other hand, on the degree and manner in which the other qualities are suppressed. Precisely because thought, for example, is the thought of a particular, definite individual, it remains *his* definite thought, determined by his individuality and the conditions in which he lives. The thinking individual therefore has no need to resort to prolonged reflection about thought as such in order to declare that his thought is his own thought, his property; from the outset it is his own, peculiarly determined thought and it was precisely his peculiarity which [in the case of Saint] Sancho [was found to be] the "opposite" of this, a peculiarity which is peculiarity "*as such*". In the case of an individual, for example, whose life

---

[a] See this volume, pp. 271-73.— *Ed.*

embraces a wide circle of varied activities and practical relations to the world, and who, therefore, lives a many-sided life, thought has the same character of universality as every other manifestation of his life. Consequently, it neither becomes fixed in the form of abstract thought nor does it need complicated tricks of reflection when the individual passes from thought to some other manifestation of life. From the outset it is always a factor in the total life of the individual, one which disappears and is reproduced as *required*.

In the case of a parochial Berlin school-master or author, however, whose activity is restricted to arduous work on the one hand and the pleasure of thought on the other, whose world extends from Moabit to Köpenick and ends behind the Hamburger Tor,[76] whose relations to this world are reduced to a minimum by his pitiful position in life, when such an individual experiences the need to think, it is indeed inevitable that his thought becomes just as abstract as he himself and his life, and that thought confronts him, who is quite incapable of resistance, in the form of a fixed power, whose activity offers the individual the possibility of a momentary escape from his "bad world", of a momentary pleasure. In the case of such an individual the few remaining desires, which arise not so much from intercourse with the world as from the constitution of the human body, express themselves only through *repercussion*, i.e., they assume in their narrow development the same one-sided and crude character as does his thought, they appear only at long intervals, stimulated by the excessive development of the predominant desire (fortified by immediate physical causes, e.g., [stomach] spasm) and are manifested turbulently and forcibly, with the most brutal suppression of the ordinary, [natural] desire [—this leads to further] domination over [thought.] As a matter of course, the school-master's [thinking reflects on and speculates about] this empirical [fact in a school]-masterly fashion. [But the mere announcement] that Stirner in general "creates" [his qualities] does not [explain] even their particular form of development. The extent to which these qualities develop on the universal or local scale, the extent to which they transcend local narrow-mindedness or remain within its confines, depends not on Stirner, but on the development of world intercourse and on the part which he and the locality where he lives play in it. That under favourable circumstances some individuals are able to rid themselves of their local narrow-mindedness is by no means due to individuals imagining that they have got rid of, or intend to get rid of their local narrow-mindedness, but is only due to the fact that in their real empirical life individuals, actuated by empirical needs, have been able to bring about world intercourse.*

The only thing our saint achieves with the aid of his arduous reflection about his qualities and passions is that by his constant crotchetiness and scuffling with them he poisons the enjoyment and satisfaction of them.

Saint Max creates, as already said, only himself as a creation, i.e., he is satisfied with placing himself in this category of created entity. His activity [as] creator consists in regarding himself as a creation, and he does not even go on to resolve this division of himself into [creator and] creation, which is his own [product]. The division [into the "essential" and] the "inessential" becomes [for him a] permanent life process, [hence mere appearance,] i.e., his real life exists only [in "pure"] reflection, is [not] even actual existence; [for since this latter is at every] instant outside [him and his reflection], he tries [in vain to] present [reflection as] essential.

> "But [since] this enemy" (viz., the true egoist as a creation) "begets himself in his defeat, since consciousness, by becoming fixed on him, does not free itself from him, but instead always dwells on him and always sees itself besmirched, and since this content of his endeavour is at the same time the very lowest, we find only an individual restricted to himself and his petty activity" (inactivity), "and *brooding over himself, as unhappy* as he is *wretched.*" (Hegel.)[a]

What we have said so far about the division of Sancho into creator and creation, he himself now finally expresses in a logical form: the creator and the creation are transformed into the presupposing and the presupposed ego, or (inasmuch as his presupposition [of his ego] is a *positing*) into the positing and the posited ego:

> "I for my part start from a certain presupposition since I *presuppose* myself; but my presupposition does not strive for its perfection" (rather does Saint Max

---

* [The following passage is crossed out in the manuscript:] This specifically revolutionary attitude of the communists to the hitherto existing conditions of the life of the individuals has already been described above [see this volume, pp. 261, 272-74]. In a later profane passage Saint Max admits that the ego receives an "impulse" (in Fichte's sense) from the world. That the communists intend to gain control over this "impulse"—which indeed becomes an extremely complex and multifariously determined "impulse" if one is not content with the mere phrase—is, of course, for Saint Max much too daring an idea to discuss.

---

[a] G. W. F. Hegel, *Phänomenologie des Geistes*. B. Selbstbewusstsein. 3. Das unglückliche Bewusstsein.— *Ed.*

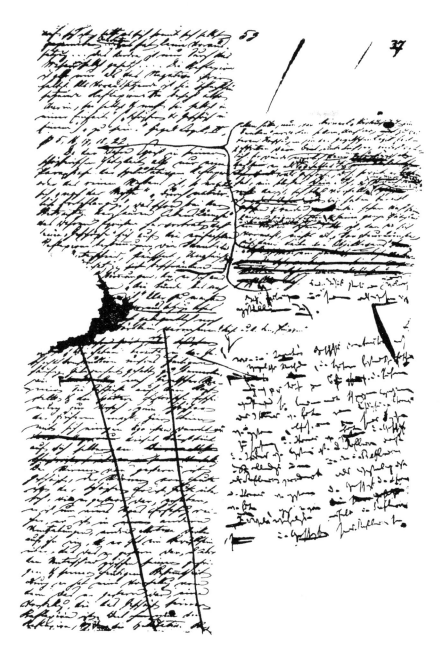

A page of the manuscript of *The German Ideology*.
From the chapter "Saint Max"
(*Reduced*)

strive for its abasement), "on the contrary, it serves me merely as something to enjoy and consume" (an enviable enjoyment!). "I am nourished by my presupposition alone and exist only by consuming it. But *for that reason*" (a grand "for that reason"!) "the presupposition in question is no presupposition at all; *for since*" (a grand "for since"!) "I am the unique" (it should read: the true egoist in agreement with himself), "I know nothing about the duality of a presupposing and presupposed ego (of an 'imperfect' and 'perfect' ego or man)"—it should read: the perfection of my ego consists in this alone, that at every instant I know myself as an imperfect ego, as a creation—"*but*" (a magnificent "but"!) "the fact that I consume myself signifies merely that I am." (It should read: The fact that I am signifies here merely that in me I consume in imagination the category of the presupposed.) "I do not presuppose myself, because I really only posit or create myself perpetually (viz., I posit and create myself as the presupposed, posited or created) "and I am I only because I am not presupposed, but posited" (it should read: and I exist only because I am antecedent to my positing) "and, again, I am posited only at the moment when I posit myself, i.e., I am creator and creation in one."

Stirner is a "posited man",[a] since he is always a posited ego, and his ego is "*also a man*". (*Wigand*, p. 183.) "*For that reason*" he is a posited man; "*for since*" he is never driven by his passions to excesses, "*therefore*", he is what burghers call a sedate man, "*but*" the fact that he is a sedate man "signifies merely" that he always keeps an account of his own transformations and refractions.

What was so far only "for us"—to use for once, as Stirner does, the language of Hegel—viz., that his whole creative activity had no other content than general definitions of reflection, is now "posited" by Stirner himself. Saint Max's struggle against "*essence*" here attains its "final goal" in that he identifies himself with essence, and indeed with pure, speculative essence. The relation of creator and creation is transformed into an explication of *self-presupposition*, i.e., [Stirner transforms] into an extremely "clumsy" and confused [idea] what Hegel [says] about reflection in "the [Doctrine of Essence]". [Since] Saint Max takes out *one* [element of his] reflection, [viz., positing reflection, his fantasies become] "negative", [because he] transforms himself, etc., into "self-[presupposition", in] contradistinction to [himself as the positing] and himself as the posited, [and] transforms reflection into the mystical antithesis of creator and creation. It should be pointed out, by the way, that in this section of his *Logik* Hegel analyses the "machinations" of the "creative nothing", which explains also why Saint Max already on page 8 had to "posit" himself as this "creative nothing".

---

[a] In the German original this is a pun: *gesetzter Mann* can mean "sedate man" or "posited man".—*Ed.*

We shall now "episodically insert" a few passages from Hegel's explanation of self-presupposition for comparison with Saint Max's explanation. But as Hegel does not write so incoherently and "at random" as our Jacques le bonhomme, we shall have to collect these passages from various pages of the *Logik* in order to bring them into correspondence with Sancho's great thesis.

"Essence presupposes itself and is itself the transcendence of this presupposition. Since it is the repulsion of itself from itself or indifference towards itself, negative relation to itself, it thereby posits itself against itself ... positing has no presupposition ... the other is only posited through essence itself.... Thus, reflection is only the negative of itself. Reflection insofar as it presupposes is simply positing reflection. It consists therefore in this, that it is itself and not itself in a unity" ("creator and creation in one"). (Hegel, *Logik*, II, pp. 5, 16, 17, 18, 22.)

One might have expected from Stirner's "virtuosity of thought" that he would have gone on to further researches into Hegel's *Logik*. However, he wisely refrained from doing so. For, if he had done so, he would have found that he, as mere "posited" ego, as creation, i.e., insofar as he possesses *existence*, is merely a *seeming* ego, and he is *"essence"*, *creator*, only insofar as he does *not* exist, but only imagines himself. We have already seen, and shall see again further on, that all his qualities, his whole activity, and his whole attitude to the world, are a mere appearance which he creates for himself, nothing but "juggling tricks on the tightrope of the objective". His ego is always a dumb, hidden "ego", hidden in his *ego* imagined as *essence*.

Since the true egoist in his creative activity is, therefore, only a paraphrase of speculative reflection or pure essence, it follows, "according to the myth", "by natural reproduction", as was already revealed when examining the "arduous life battles" of the true egoist, that his "creations" are limited to the simplest determinations of reflection, such as identity, difference, equality, inequality, [opposition,] etc.— determinations [of reflection] which he [tries] to make clear for himself in ["himself"], concerning whom "the tidings have [gone] as far as [Berlin]". [Concerning] his *presuppositionless* [ego] we [shall] have occasion to "hear [a little] word" later on. See, *inter alia*, "The Unique".[a]

As in *Sancho*'s construction of history the later historical phenomenon is transformed, by Hegel's method, into the cause, the creator, of an earlier phenomenon, so in the case of the

---

[a] See this volume, pp. 458-59.—*Ed.*

egoist in agreement with himself the Stirner of today is transformed into the creator of the Stirner of yesterday, although, to use his language, the Stirner of today is the creation of the Stirner of yesterday. Reflection, indeed, reverses all this, and in reflection the Stirner of yesterday is the creation of the Stirner of today, as a product of reflection, as an idea — just as in reflection the conditions of the external world are *creations* of his reflection.

Page 216: "Do not *seek* in 'self-denial' the freedom that actually deprives you of yourselves, but *seek* yourselves" (i.e., seek yourselves in self-denial), "*become egoists*, each of you should become an *all-powerful* ego!"

After the foregoing, we should not be surprised if later on Saint Max's attitude to this proposition is again that of creator and most irreconcilable enemy and he "dissolves" his lofty moral postulate: "Become an *all-powerful* ego" into this, that each, in any case, does what he can, and that he can do what he does, and therefore, of course, for Saint Max, he is "all-powerful".

Incidentally, the nonsense of the egoist in agreement with himself is summarised in the proposition quoted above. First comes the moral injunction to seek and, moreover, to seek oneself. This is defined in the sense that man should become something that he so far is not, namely, an egoist, and this egoist is defined as being an "all-powerful ego", in whom the peculiar ability has become resolved from actual ability into the ego, into omnipotence, into the fantastic idea of ability. To seek oneself means, therefore, to become something different from what one is and, indeed, to become *all-powerful*, i.e., nothing, a non-thing, a phantasmagoria.

We have now progressed so far that one of the profoundest mysteries of the unique, and at the same time a problem that has long kept the civilised world in a state of anxious suspense, can be disclosed and solved.

Who is Szeliga? Since the appearance of the critical *Literatur-Zeitung* (see *Die heilige Familie*, etc.) this question has been put by everyone who has followed the development of German philosophy. Who is Szeliga? Everyone asks, everyone listens attentively when he hears the barbaric sound of this name — but no one replies.

Who is Szeliga? Saint Max gives us the key to this "secret of secrets".

Szeliga is Stirner as a creation, Stirner is Szeliga as creator.
Stirner is the "I", Szeliga the "you", in "the book". Hence
Stirner, the creator, behaves towards Szeliga, his creation, as
towards his "most irreconcilable enemy". As soon as Szeliga
wishes to acquire independence in relation to Stirner — he made
a hapless attempt in this direction in the *Norddeutsche
Blätter*[a] — Saint Max "takes him back into himself", an
experiment which was carried out against this attempt of
Szeliga's on pages 176-79 of the "Apologetic Commentary" in
Wigand. The struggle of the creator against the creation, of
Stirner against Szeliga, is, however, only a seeming one: [Now]
Szeliga advances against his creator the phrases of this [creator
himself] — for example, the assertion "that [the mere,] bare
body is [absence of] thought". (*Wigand*, p. 148.) Saint [Max,] as
we have seen, [was thinking] only of [the bare flesh], the body
before its [formation], and in [this connection] he gave the body
the [determination] of being "the other of thought", non-thought
and the non-thinking being, hence absence of thought; and
indeed in a later passage he bluntly declares that *only* absence of
thought (as previously *only* the flesh — thus the two concepts
are treated as identical) saves him from thoughts. (P. 196.)
    We find a still more striking proof of this mysterious
connection in *Wigand*. We have already seen on page 7 of "the
book" that the "ego", i.e., Stirner, is "the unique". On page 153
of the "Commentary" he addresses his "you": "*You*"... "are the
content of the phrase", viz., the content of the "unique", and on
the same page it is stated: "he overlooks the fact that *he himself,
Szeliga, is the content of the phrase*". "The unique" is a phrase,
as Saint Max says in so many words. Considered as the "*ego*",
i.e., as *creator*, he is the *owner of the phrase* — this is *Saint
Max*. Considered as "*you*", i.e., as *creation*, he is the *content of
the phrase* — this is *Szeliga*, as we have just been told. Szeliga
the creation appears as a selfless egoist, as a degenerate Don
Quixote; Stirner the creator appears as an egoist in the ordinary
sense, as Saint Sancho Panza.
    Here, therefore, the other aspect of the antithesis of creator
and creation makes its appearance, each of the two aspects
containing its opposite in itself. Here Sancho Panza Stirner, the
egoist in the ordinary sense, is victorious over Don Quixote
Szeliga, the selfless and illusory egoist, is victorious over him
precisely *as* Don Quixote by his faith in the world domination of
the holy. Who indeed was Stirner's egoist in the [ordinary]

---

[a] Szeliga, "*Der Einzige und sein Eigenthum*. Von Max Stirner".— *Ed.*

sense if not Sancho [Panza,] and who his self-sacrificing egoist [if not] Don Quixote, and what was [their mutual] relation in the [form in which it has so far existed if] not the relation of [Sancho Panza Stirner] to Don Quixote [Szeliga? Now as] Sancho Panza [Stirner belongs to himself as] Sancho only [in order to make Szeliga as] Don Quixote [believe that] he surpasses him in Don [quixotry,] and [in accordance with this role, as] the presupposed universal Don [quixotry,] he takes [no steps] against the [Don quixotry of his] former master (Don quixotry, by which he swears with all the firm faith of a servant), and at the same time he displays the cunning already described by Cervantes. In actual content he is, therefore, the defender of the practical petty bourgeois, but he combats the consciousness that corresponds to the petty bourgeois, a consciousness which in the final analysis reduces itself to the idealising ideas of the petty bourgeois about the bourgeoisie to whom he cannot attain.

Thus, Don Quixote now, as Szeliga, performs menial services for his former armour-bearer.

How greatly Sancho in his new "transformation" has retained his old habits, he shows on every page. "Swallowing" and "consuming" still constitute one of his chief qualities, his "natural timidity" has still such mastery over him that the King of Prussia and Prince Heinrich LXXII become transformed for him into the "Emperor of China" or the "Sultan" and he ventures to speak only about the "G .....[a] chambers"; he still strews around him proverbs and moral sayings from his knapsack, he continues to be afraid of "spectres" and even asserts that they alone are to be feared; the only difference is that whereas Sancho in his unholiness was bamboozled by the peasants in the tavern, now in a state of saintliness he continually bamboozles himself.

But let us return to Szeliga. Who has not long ago discovered the hand of Szeliga in all the "phrases" which Saint Sancho put into the mouth of his "you"? And it is always possible to discover traces of Szeliga not only in the phrases of this "you", but also in the phrases in which Szeliga appears as creator, i.e., as *Stirner*. But because Szeliga is a creation, he could only figure in *Die heilige Familie* as a "*mystery*". The revelation of this mystery was the task of Stirner the creator. We surmised, of course, that some great, holy adventure was at the root of this. Nor were we deceived. The unique adventure really has

---

[a] German.— *Ed.*

never been seen or heard of and surpasses the adventure with the fulling mills in Cervantes's twentieth chapter.

3. THE REVELATION OF JOHN THE DIVINE, OR "THE LOGIC OF THE NEW WISDOM"

In the beginning was the word, the logos. In it was life, and the life was the light of men. And the light shone in darkness and the darkness *did not comprehend* it. That was the true light, it was in the world, and the world did not know it. He came into *his own*, and his own received him not. But as many as received him, to them gave he power to become owners, who believe in the name of the unique. [But who] has ever [seen] the unique [?] [a]

[Let] us now [examine] this "light of the [world" in "the] logic of the new wisdom [", for Saint] Sancho does not rest content with his previous [destructions].

[In the case of our] "unique" author, it is a matter [of course that] the basis of his [genius lies] in the brilliant [series of personal] advantages [which constitute] his special [virtuosity] of thought. [Since] all these advantages have already been extensively demonstrated, it suffices here to give a brief summary of the most important of them: carelessness of thought — confusion — incoherence — admitted clumsiness — endless repetitions — constant contradiction with himself — unequalled comparisons — attempts to intimidate the reader — systematic legacy-hunting in the realm of thoughts by means of the levers "you", "it", "one", etc., and crude abuse of the conjunctions for, therefore, for that reason, because, accordingly, but, etc.— ignorance — clumsy assertions — solemn frivolity — revolutionary phrases and peaceful thoughts — bluster — bombastic vulgarity and coquetting with cheap indecency — elevation of Nante the loafer [77] to the rank of an absolute concept — dependence on Hegelian traditions and current Berlin phrases — in short, sheer manufacture of a thin beggar's broth (491 pages of it) in the Rumford manner.

Drifting like bones in this beggar's broth are a whole series of *transitions*, a few specimens of which we shall now give for the amusement of the German public depressed as it is:

"Could we not — now, however — one sometimes shares — one can then — to the efficacy of ... belongs especially that which one frequently ... hears called — and that is to say — to conclude, it can now be clear — in the

---

[a] John 1:1, 4-5, 9-12, 18 (paraphrased).— *Ed.*

meantime—thus it can, incidentally, be thought here—were it not for—or if, perhaps, it were not—progress from ... to the point that ... is not difficult—from a certain point of view it is argued approximately thus—for example, *and so on*", etc., and "it is to that" in all possible "transformations".

We can at once mention here a [logical] trick about which [it is impossible] to decide whether it owes [its] existence to the [lauded] efficiency of Sancho [or to] the inefficiency of his [thinking]. This [trick consists] in seizing on [*one* aspect] treating it as if it were the sole [and only] aspect so far known of an idea [or] concept which [has several well]-defined aspects, foisting this aspect [on the concept as] its *sole characteristic* and then setting [against it every other] aspect under a [new name, as] something original. This is how the concepts of freedom and peculiarity are dealt with, [as] we shall see later.[a]

Among the categories which owe their origin not so much to the personality of Sancho, as to the universal distress in which the German theoreticians find themselves at the present time, the first place is taken by *trashy distinction*, the extreme of trashiness. Since our saint immerses himself in such "soul-torturing" antitheses as singular and universal, private interest and universal interest, ordinary egoism and selflessness, etc., in the final analysis one arrives at the trashiest mutual concessions and dealings between the two aspects, which again rest on the most subtle distinctions — distinctions whose existence side by side is expressed by *"also"* and whose separation from each other is then maintained by means of a miserable *"insofar as"*. Such trashy distinctions, for instance, are: how people *exploit* one another, but none does so *at the expense of another*; the extent to which something in me is *inherent* or *suggested*; the construction of *human* and of *unique* work, existing side by side; what is indispensable for *human* life and what is indispensable for *unique* life; what belongs to personality in its pure form and what is essentially fortuitous, to decide which Saint Max, from his point of view, has no criterion at all; what belongs to the *rags and tatters* and what to the *skin* of the individual; what by means of denial he *gets rid of* altogether or *appropriates*, to what extent he sacrifices merely his freedom or merely his peculiarity, in which case he also makes a sacrifice but only insofar as, properly speaking, he does not make a sacrifice; what brings me into relation with others as a link or as a personal relation. Some of these distinctions are absolutely trashy, others — in the case of Sancho at least — lose all

---

[a] See this volume, pp. 324-27.— *Ed.*

meaning and foundation. One can regard as the peak of these trashy distinctions that between the *creation of the world* by the individual and the *impulse* which the individual receives from the world. If, for example, he had gone more deeply here into this impulse, into the whole extent and multifarious character of its influence on him, he would in the end have discovered the contradiction that he is as *blindly* [*dependent*] on the world as he [egoistically] and ideologically *creates* [it]. (See: "My Self-Enjoyment".[a]) He [would not then have put] side by side [his"] *also*" and "*insofar as*", [any more than] "human" work [and] "unique" work; he would not have opposed one to the other, therefore one would [not have] attacked the other [in the rear,] and the "egoist *in agreement* [with himself"] would not be completely [subordinated to himself] but we [know] that the latter did not need to be [presupposed] because from the outset this was the point of departure.

This trashy play with distinctions occurs throughout "the book"; it is a main lever also for the other logical tricks and particularly takes the form of a moral casuistry that is as self-satisfied as it is ridiculously cheap. Thus, it is made clear to us by means of examples how far the true egoist has the right to tell lies and how far he has not; to what extent the betrayal of confidence is "despicable" and to what extent it is not; to what extent the Emperor Sigismund and the French King Francis I had the right to break their oath [78] and how far their behaviour in this respect was "disgraceful", and other subtle historical illustrations of the same sort. Against these painstaking distinctions and petty questions there stands out in strong relief the indifference of our Sancho for whom it is all the same and who ignores all actual, practical and conceptual differences. In general we can already say now that his ability to distinguish is far inferior to his ability not to distinguish, to regard all cats as black in the darkness of the holy, and to reduce everything to anything — an art which finds its adequate expression in the use of the *apposition*.

Embrace your "ass", Sancho, you have found him again here. He gallops merrily to meet you, taking no notice of the kicks he has been given, and greets you with his ringing voice. Kneel before him, embrace his neck and fulfil the calling laid down for you by Cervantes in Chapter XXX.

The *appositionis* Saint Sancho's ass, his logical and historical locomotive, the driving force of "the book", reduced to its

---

[a] See this volume, pp. 446-47.— *Ed.*

briefest and simplest expression. In order to transform one idea into another, or to prove the identity of two quite different things, a few intermediate links are sought which partly by their meaning, partly by their etymology and partly by their mere sound can be used to establish an apparent connection between the two basic ideas. These links are then appended to the first idea in the form of an apposition, and in such a way that one gets farther and farther away from the starting-point and nearer and nearer to the point one wants to reach. If the chain of appositions has got so far that one can draw a conclusion without any danger, the final idea is likewise fastened on in the form of an apposition by means of a dash, and the trick is done. This is a highly recommendable method of insinuating thoughts, which is the more effective the more it is made to serve as the lever for the main arguments. When this trick has been successfully performed several times, one can, following Saint Sancho's procedure, gradually omit some of the intermediate links and finally reduce the series of appositions to a few absolutely essential hooks.

The apposition, as we have seen above, can also be reversed and thus lead to new, even more complicated tricks and more astounding results. We have seen there, too, that the apposition is the logical form of the infinite series of mathematics.[a]

Saint Sancho employs the apposition in two ways: on the one hand, purely logically, in the canonisation of the world, where it enables him to transform any earthly thing into "the holy", and, on the other hand, historically, in disquisitions on the connection of various epochs and in summing them up, each historical stage being reduced to a single word, and the final result is that the last link of the historical series has not got us an inch farther than the first, and in the end all the epochs of the series are combined in a single abstract category like idealism, dependence on thoughts, etc. If the historical series of appositions is to be given the appearance of progress, this is achieved by regarding the concluding phrase as the completion of the first epoch of the series, and the intermediate links as ascending stages of development leading to the final, culminating phrase.

Alongside the apposition we have *synonymy*, which Saint Sancho exploits in every way. If two words are etymologically linked or are merely similar in sound, they are made responsible for each other, or if one word has different meanings, then, according to need, it is used sometimes in one sense and

---

[a] See this volume, p. 168.— *Ed.*

sometimes in the other, while Saint Sancho makes it appear that he is speaking of one and the same thing in different "refractions". Further, a special branch of synonymy consists of *translation*, where a French or Latin expression is supplemented by a German one which only half-expresses it, and in addition denotes something totally different; as we saw above, for example, when the word "*respektieren*" was translated "to experience reverence and fear", and so on. One recalls the words *Staat, Status, Stand, Notstand*, etc.[a] In the section on communism we have already had the opportunity of observing numerous examples of this use of ambiguous expressions. Let us briefly examine an example of etymological synonymy.

> "The word '*Gesellschaft*'[b] is derived from the word '*Sal*'. If there are many people in a *Saal*,[c] then the *Saal* brings it about that they are in society. They *are* in society and they constitute at most a *salon society*, since they talk in conventional *salon phrases*. If real *intercourse* takes place, it should be regarded as independent of society." (P. 286.)

Since the "word '*Gesellschaft*' is derived from '*Sal*' " (which, incidentally, is not true, for the *original* roots of all words are *verbs*) then "*Sal*" must be equivalent to "*Saal*". But "*Sal*" in old High-German means a *building*; *Kisello, Geselle*—from which *Gesellschaft* is derived—means a *house companion*; hence "*Saal*" is dragged in here quite arbitrarily. But that does not matter; "*Saal*" is immediately transformed into "salon", as though there was not a gap of about a thousand years and a great many miles between the old High-German "*Sal*" and the modern French "*salon*". Thus society is transformed into a salon society, in which, according to the German philistine idea, an intercourse consisting only of phrases takes place and all real intercourse is excluded.—Incidentally since Saint Max only aimed at transforming society into "the holy", he could have arrived at this by a much shorter route if he had made a somewhat more accurate study of etymology and consulted any dictionary of word roots. What a find it would have been for him to discover there the etymological connection between the words "*Gesellschaft*" and "*selig*"; *Gesellschaft—selig—heilig—das Heilige*[d]—what could look simpler?

If "Stirner's" etymological synonymy is correct, then the communists are seeking the true earldom, the earldom as the

---

    [a] See this volume, p. 233.— *Ed.*
    [b] Society.— *Ed.*
    [c] Hall, room.— *Ed.*
    [d] Society — blessed — holy — the holy.—*Ed.*

holy. As *Gesellschaft* comes from *Sal*, a building, so *Graf*[a] (Gothic *garâvjo*) comes from the Gothic *râvo*, house. *Sal*, building= *râvo*, house; consequently *Gesellschaft= Grafschaft*[b]. The prefixes and suffixes are the same in both words, the root syllables have the same meaning — hence the holy society of the communists is the holy earldom, the earldom as the holy — what could look simpler? Saint Sancho had an inkling of this, when he saw in communism the perfection of the feudal system, i.e., the system of earldoms.

Synonymy serves our saint, on the one hand, to transform empirical relations into speculative relations, by using in its speculative meaning a word that occurs both in practical life and in philosophical speculation, uttering a few phrases about this speculative meaning and then making out that he has thereby also criticised the actual relations which this word denotes as well. He does this with the word *speculation.* On page 406, "speculation" "appears" showing two sides as *one* essence that possesses a "dual manifestation" — O Szeliga! He rages against *philosophical* speculation and thinks he has thereby also settled accounts with *commercial* speculation, about [which] he knows nothing. On the other hand, this synonymy enables him, a concealed petty bourgeois, to transform bourgeois relations (see what was said above in dealing with "communism" about the connection between language and bourgeois relations[c]) into personal, individual relations, which one cannot attack without attacking the individuality, "peculiarity" and "uniqueness" of the individual. Thus, for example, Sancho exploits the etymological connection between *Geld*[d] and *Geltung*[e], *Vermögen*[f] and *vermögen*[g], etc.

Synonymy, combined with the apposition, provides the main lever for his *conjuring tricks*, which we have already exposed on countless occasions. To give an example how easy this art is, let us also perform a conjuring trick *à la* Sancho.

Wechsel[h], as *change*, is the law of phenomena, says Hegel. *This is the reason*, "Stirner" could continue, for the phenomenon of the strictness of the law against false *bills of exchange*;

---

[a] Earl.— *Ed.*
[b] Earldom.— *Ed.*
[c] See this volume, p. 248.— *Ed.*
[d] Money.— *Ed.*
[e] Worth, value, validity.— *Ed.*
[f] Wealth, property, ability, capability.— *Ed.*
[g] To be able, capable.— *Ed.*
[h] Change, bill of exchange.— *Ed.*

for we see here the law raised above phenomena, the law as such, holy law, the law as the holy, the holy itself, against which sin is committed and which is avenged in the punishment. Or in other words: *Wechsel* "in its dual manifestation", as a bill of exchange (*lettre de change*) and as change (*changement*), leads to *Verfall*[a] (*échéance* and *décadence*). *Decline* as a result of *change* is observed in history, *inter alia*, in the fall of the Roman Empire, feudalism, the German Empire and the domination of Napoleon. The "transition from" these great *historical crises* "to" the *commercial crises* of our day "is not difficult", and this explains also why these commercial crises are always determined by the *expiry of bills of exchange*.

Or he could also, as in the case of "*Vermögen*" and "*Geld*", justify the "*Wechsel*" etymologically and "from a certain point of view argue approximately as follows". The communists want, among others things, to abolish the *Wechsel (bill of exchange)*. But does not the main pleasure of the world lie precisely in *Wechsel* (change)? They want, therefore, the dead, the immobile, *China*—that is to say, the perfect Chinese is a communist. "Hence" communist declamations against *Wechsel*-briefe and *Wechsler*. As though every letter were not a *Wechsel*brief, a letter that notes a *change*, and every man not a *Wechselnder*, a *Wechsler!*[b]

To give the simplicity of his construction and logical tricks the appearance of great variety, Saint Sancho needs the *episode*. From time to time he "*episodically*" inserts a passage which belongs to another part of the book, or which could quite well have been left out altogether, and thus still further breaks the thread of his so-called argument, which has already been repeatedly broken without that. This is accompanied by the naïve statement that "we" "do not stick to the rules", and after numerous repetitions causes in the reader a certain insensitiveness to even the greatest incoherence. When one reads "the book", one becomes accustomed to everything and finally one readily submits even to the worst. Incidentally, these episodes (as was only [to be] expected from Saint Sancho) are themselves only imaginary and mere repetitions under [other guises] of phrases encountered hundreds of times [already].

After Saint Max has [thus displayed] his personal qualities,

---

[a] Expiry, falling due (of bill); decline, decay.— *Ed.*
[b] Here and above the authors play on the different meanings of the words *Wechsel* (change, bill of exchange), *Wechselbrief* (bill of exchange), *Wechsler* (money-changer) and *Wechselnder* (a changing person).— *Ed.*

and then revealed himself as ["*appearance*" and] as "*essence*"
in the distinction, [in] synonymy and in the episode, [we] come
[to the] true culmination and completion of logic, the "*concept*".

[The] concept is the "ego" (see Hegel's *Logik*, Part 3), logic
[as the ego]. This is the pure relation [of the] ego to the world, a
relation [divested] of all the real relations that exist for it; [a
formula] for all the equations to [which the holy] man reduces
mundane [concepts]. It was already [revealed] above that by
applying this formula to all sorts of things Sancho merely makes
an unsuccessful "attempt" to understand the various pure
determinations of reflection, such as identity, antithesis, etc.

Let us begin at once with a definite example, e.g., the relation
between the "ego" and the people.

I am not the people.

The people = non-I

I = the non-people.

Hence, I am the negation of the people, the people is
dissolved in me.

The second equation can be expressed also by an auxiliary
equation:

The people's ego is non-existent,

or:

The ego of the people is the negation of my ego.

The whole trick, therefore, consists in: 1) that the negation
which at the outset belonged to the copula is attached first to the
subject and then to the predicate; and 2) that the negation, the
"not", is, according to convenience, regarded as an expression
of dissimilarity, difference, antithesis or direct dissolution. In
the present example it is regarded as absolute dissolution, as
complete negation; we shall find that — at Saint Max's convenience — it is used also in the other meanings. Thus the
tautological proposition that I am not the people is transformed
into the tremendous new discovery that I am the dissolution of
the people.

For the equations given above, it was not even necessary for
Saint Sancho to have any idea of the people; it was enough for
him to know that I and the people are "totally different names
for totally different things"; it was sufficient that the two words
do not have a single letter in common. If now there is to be
further speculation about the people from the standpoint of
egoistical logic, it suffices to attach any kind of trivial
determination to the people and to "I" from outside, from
day-to-day experience, thus giving rise to new equations. At the
same time it is made to appear that different determinations are

being criticised in different ways. We shall now proceed to speculate in this manner about freedom, happiness and wealth:

Basic equations: The people = non-I.

Equation No. 1: Freedom of the people = Not my freedom.
Freedom of the people = My non-freedom.
Freedom of the people = My lack of freedom.

(This can also be reversed, resulting in the grand proposition: My lack of freedom = slavery is the freedom of the people.)

Equation No. 2: Happiness of the people = Not my happiness.
Happiness of the people = My non-happiness.
Happiness of the people = My unhappiness.

(Reversed equation: My unhappiness, my distress, is the happiness of the people.)

Equation No. 3: Wealth of the people = Not my wealth.
Wealth of the people = My non-wealth.
Wealth of the people = My poverty.

(Reversed equation: My poverty is the wealth of the people.) This can be continued *ad libitum* and extended to other determinations.

For the formation of such equations all that is required, apart from a very general acquaintance with such ideas as Stirner can combine in one notion with "people", is to know the positive expression for the result obtained in the negative form, e.g., "poverty"—for "non-wealth", etc. That is to say, as much knowledge of the language as one acquires in everyday life is quite sufficient to arrive in this way at the most surprising discoveries.

The entire trick here, therefore, consisted in transforming not-my-wealth, not-my-happiness, not-my-freedom into my non-wealth, my non-happiness, my non-freedom. The "not", which in the first equation is a general negation that can express all possible forms of difference, e.g., it may merely mean that it is our common, and not exclusively my, wealth—this "not" is transformed in the [second] equation into the negation of my wealth, [my] happiness, etc., and ascribes to me [non-happiness], unhappiness, slavery. [Since] I am denied some definite form of wealth, [the people's] wealth, but by no means [wealth] in general, [Sancho believes poverty] must be ascribed to me. [But] this is also [brought about] by expressing my non-freedom in a positive way and so transforming it into my ["lack of freedom"]. But [my non-freedom] can, of course, also mean hundreds [of other] things—e.g., my ["lack of freedom"], my non-freedom from [my] body, etc.

We started out just now from the second equation: the people=non-I. We could also have taken the third equation as our starting-point: I=the non-people, and then, in the case of wealth for example, according to the same method, it would be proved in the end that "my wealth is the poverty of the people". Here, however, Saint Sancho would not proceed in this way, but would dissolve altogether the property relations of the people and the people itself, and then arrive at the following result: my wealth is the destruction not only of the people's wealth but of the people itself. This shows how arbitrarily Saint Sancho acted when he transformed non-wealth into poverty. Our saint applies these different methods higgledy-piggledy and exploits negation sometimes in one meaning and sometimes in another. Even "anyone who has not read Stirner's book" "sees at once" (*Wigand*, p. 191) what confusions this is liable to produce.

In just the same way the "ego" "operates" against the state.

I am not the state.

State=non-I.

I="Negation" of the state.

Nothing of the state=I.

Or in other words: I am the "creative nothing" in which the state is swallowed up.

This simple melody can be used to ring the changes with any subject.

The great proposition that forms the basis of all these equations is: I am not non-I. This non-I is given various names, which, on the one hand, can be purely logical, e.g., being-in-itself, other-being, or, on the other hand, the names of concrete ideas such as the people, state, etc. In this way the appearance of a development can be produced by taking these names as the starting-point and gradually reducing them—with the aid of equations, or a series of appositions—again to the non-ego, which was their basis at the outset. Since the real relations thus introduced figure only as different modifications of the non-ego, and only nominally different modifications at that—nothing at all need be said about these real relations themselves. This is all the more ludicrous since [the real] relations are the relations [of the individuals] themselves, and declaring them to be relations [of the non]-ego only proves that one knows nothing about them. The matter is thereby so greatly simplified that even "the great majority consisting of innately limited intellects" can learn the trick in ten minutes at most. At the same time, this gives us a criterion of the "uniqueness" of Saint Sancho.

Saint Sancho further defines the non-ego opposed to the ego as being that which is *alien* to the ego, that which is the alien. The relation of the non-ego to the ego is "therefore" that of alienation [*Entfremdung*]. We have just given the logical formula by which Saint Sancho presents any object or relation whatsoever as that which is alien to the ego, as the alienation of the ego; on the other hand, Saint Sancho can, as we shall see, also present any object or relation as something created by the ego *and belonging to it*. Apart, first of all, from the arbitrary way in which he presents, or does not present, any relation as a relation of alienation (for everything can be made to fit in the above equations), we see already here that his only concern is to present all actual relations, [and also] actual individuals, [as alienated] (to retain this philosophical [expression] for the time being), to [transform] them into the wholly [abstract] phrase of alienation. Thus [instead] of the task of describing [actual] individuals in their [actual] alienation and in the empirical relations of this alienation, [purely empirical] relations, the same happens here — the setting forth is replaced by the [mere idea] of alienation, of [*the* alien], of *the* holy. [The] substitution of the *category* of alienation (this is again a determination of reflection which can be considered as antithesis, difference, non-identity, etc.) finds its final and highest expression in "the alien" being transformed again into "*the holy*", and alienation into the relation of the ego to anything whatever as the holy. We prefer to elucidate the logical process on the basis of Saint Sancho's relation to the holy, since this is the predominant formula, and in passing we note that "the alien" is considered also as "the *existing*" (*per appos.*), that which exists apart from me, that which exists independently of me, *per appos.*, that which is regarded as independent owing to my non-independence, so that Saint Sancho can depict as the holy everything that exists independently of him, e.g., the Blocksberg.[79]

Because the holy is something alien, everything alien is transformed into the holy; and because everything holy is a bond, a fetter, all bonds and all fetters are transformed into the holy. By this means Saint Sancho has already achieved the result that everything alien becomes for him a mere *appearance*, a mere *idea*, from which he frees himself by simply protesting against it and declaring that he does not have this idea. Just as we saw in the case of the egoist not in agreement with himself[a]:

---

[a] See this volume, pp. 267-70.— *Ed.*

people have only to change their consciousness to make everything in the world all right.[a]

Our whole exposition has shown that Saint Sancho criticises all actual conditions by declaring them "the holy", and combats them by combating his holy idea of them. This simple trick of transforming everything into the holy was achieved, as we have already seen in detail above, by Jacques le bonhomme accepting in good faith the illusions of philosophy, the ideological, speculative expression of reality divorced from its empirical basis, for reality, just as he mistook the illusions of the petty [bourgeois concerning] the bourgeoisie for the "[holy essence" of the] bourgeoisie, and could therefore imagine that he was only dealing with thoughts and ideas. With equal ease people were transformed into the "holy", for after their thoughts had been divorced from them themselves and from their empirical relations, it became possible to consider people as mere vehicles for these thoughts and thus, for example, the bourgeois was made into the holy liberal.

The positive relation of [Sancho]—who is in the final analysis [pious]—to the holy (a relation [he] calls *respect*) figures also [under the] name of "love". "Love" [is a] relation that approves of "[Man"], the holy, the ideal, the supreme being, or such a human, holy, ideal, essential relation. Anything that was elsewhere designated as the existence of the *holy*, e.g., the state, prisons, torture, police, trade and traffic, etc., can also be regarded by Sancho as "another example" of "*love*". This new nomenclature enables him to write new chapters about what he has already utterly rejected under the trade mark of the holy and respect. It is the old story of the goats of the shepherdess Torralva, in a holy form. And as at one time, with the aid of this story, he led his master by the nose, so now he leads himself and the public by the nose throughout the book without, however, being able to break off his story as wittily as he did in those earlier times when he was still a secular armour-bearer. In general, since his canonisation Sancho has lost all his original mother wit.

The first difficulty appears to arise because this holy is in itself very diverse, so that when criticising some definite holy thing one ought to leave the holiness out of account and criticise the definite content itself. Saint Sancho avoids this rock by presenting everything definite as merely an "*example*" of the holy; just as in Hegel's *Logik* it is immaterial whether atom or

---

[a] The words "all right" are in English in the original.—*Ed.*

personality is adduced to explain "being-for-itself", or the solar system, magnetism or sexual love as an example of attraction. It is, therefore, by no means an accident that "the book" teems with *examples*, but is rooted in the innermost essence of the method of exposition employed in it. This is the "unique" possibility which Saint Sancho has of producing an appearance of some sort of content, the prototype of which is already to be found in Cervantes, since Sancho also speaks all the time in examples. Thus Sancho is able to say: "Another example of *the* holy" (the uninteresting) "is labour". He could have continued: another example is the state, another is the family, another is rent of land, another is Saint Jacob (Saint-Jacques, le bonhomme), another is Saint Ursula and her eleven thousand virgins.[80] Indeed, in his imagination, all these things have this in common: that they are the "holy". But at the same time they are totally different things, and it is just this that constitutes their specific nature. Insofar as one speaks of their specific nature, one does not speak of them as "the holy".

[Labour is] not rent of land, and [rent of land] is not the state; [the main] thing, therefore, is to define [what] the state, land rent and labour are [apart from] their imagined holiness, [and Saint] Max achieves this in the following way. [He pretends to] be speaking about the state, [labour,] etc., and then calls ["the" state] the reality of some [sort of idea] — of love, of [being]-for-one-another, of the existing, of power over [individuals], and — by means [of a] dash — of "the holy", but [he could] have said [that at the] outset. Or [he says] of labour that it is regarded as a life task, [a vocation, a] destiny —"the holy". That is to say, the state and labour are first of all brought under a particular *kind* of the holy which has been previously prepared in the same way, and this *particular* holy is then again dissolved in the *universal* "holy"; all of which can take place without saying anything about labour and the state. The same stale cud can then be chewed over again on any convenient occasion, because everything that is apparently the object of criticism serves our Sancho merely as an excuse for declaring that the abstract ideas and the predicates transformed into subjects (which are nothing but suitably assorted holies, a sufficient store of which is always kept in reserve) are what they were made to be at the outset, viz., *the holy*. He has in fact reduced everything to its exhaustive, classic expression, by saying of it that it is "another example of the holy". The definitions which he has picked up by hearsay, and which are supposed to relate to content, are altogether superfluous, and on closer examination it is found.

too, that they introduce neither definition nor content and amount to no more than ignorant banalities. This cheap "virtuosity of thought" which polishes off any subject-matter whatever even before knowing anything about it, can of course be acquired by anyone and not in ten minutes, as previously [stated],[a] but even in five. In the "Commentary" Saint Sancho threatens us with *"treatises"* about Feuerbach, socialism, bourgeois society, and only the holy knows what else. Provisionally we can already here reduce these treatises to their simplest expression as follows:

First treatise: Another example of the holy is *Feuerbach*.

Second treatise: Another example of the holy is *socialism*.

Third treatise: Another example of the holy is *bourgeois society*.

Fourth treatise: Another example of the holy is the "treatise" in the Stirner manner.

Etc., *in infinitum*.

A little reflection shows that the second rock against which Saint Sancho was bound to suffer shipwreck was his own assertion that every individual is totally different from every other, is unique. Since every individual is an altogether different being, hence an other-being, it is by no means necessary that what is alien, holy, for one individual should be so for another individual; it even *cannot* be so. And the common name used, such as state, religion, morality, etc., should not mislead us, for these names are only abstractions from the actual attitude of separate individuals, and these objects, in consequence of the totally different attitude towards them of the unique individuals, become for each of the latter *unique* objects, hence totally different objects, which have only their name in common. Consequently, Saint Sancho could at most have said: for me, Saint Sancho, the state, religion, etc., are the alien, the holy. Instead of this he has to make them the absolutely holy, the holy for all individuals — how else could he have fabricated his constructed ego, his egoist in agreement with himself, etc., how else could he at all have written his whole "book"? How little it occurs to him to make each "unique" the measure of his own "uniqueness", how much he uses his own "uniqueness" as a measure, as a moral norm, to be applied to all other individuals, like a true moralist forcing them into his Procrustean bed, is already evident, *inter alia*, from his judgment on the departed and forgotten Klopstock, whom he opposes with the moral

---

[a] See this volume, p. 297.— *Ed.*

maxim that he ought to have adopted an "attitude to religion altogether *his own*", in that case he would have arrived not at a *religion of his own,* which would be the correct conclusion (a conclusion that "Stirner" himself draws innumerable times, e.g., in regard to money), but at a "dissolution and swallowing up of religion" (p. 85), a universal result instead of an individual, unique result. As though Klopstock had not arrived at a "dissolution and swallowing up of religion", and indeed at a quite individual, unique dissolution, such as only this unique Klopstock could have "achieved", a dissolution whose uniqueness "Stirner" could have easily seen even from the many unsuccessful imitations. Klopstock's attitude to religion is supposed to be not his "own", although it was altogether peculiar to him, and indeed was a relation to religion which made Klopstock Klopstock. His attitude to religion would have been "peculiar" [a] only if he had behaved towards it not like Klopstock but like a modern German philosopher.

The "egoist in the ordinary sense", who is not so docile as Szeliga and who has already above put forward all sorts of objections, here makes the following retort to our saint: here in the actual world, as I know very well, I am concerned with my own advantage and nothing else, *rien pour la gloire.* [b] Besides this, I enjoy thinking that I am immortal and can have advantages also in heaven. Ought I to sacrifice this egoistical conception for the sake of the mere consciousness of egoism in agreement with itself, which will not bring me in a farthing? The philosophers tell me: that is inhuman. What do I care? Am I not a human being? Is not everything I do human, and human because I do it, and is it any concern of mine how "others" "classify" my actions? You, Sancho, who indeed are also a philosopher, but a bankrupt one — and because of your philosophy you deserve no financial credit, and because of your bankruptcy you deserve no intellectual credit — you tell me that my attitude to religion is not one peculiar to me. What you say, therefore, is the same as what the other philosophers tell me, but in your case, as usual, it loses all meaning since you call "peculiar" what they call "human". Could you speak of any other peculiarity than your own and transform your own relation again into a universal one? In my own way, my attitude to religion, if you like, is also a critical one. Firstly, I have no

---

[a] A play on the word *eigen* which can mean one's own, belonging to oneself or peculiar, strange, etc.— *Ed.*

[b] Mere honour is worth nothing.— *Ed.*

hesitation in sacrificing it, as soon as it attempts to interfere in my commerce; secondly, in my business affairs it is useful for me to be regarded as religious (as it is useful for my proletarian, if the pie that I eat here he eats at least in heaven); and, finally, I turn heaven into my property. It is *une propriété ajoutée à la propriété*,[a] although already Montesquieu, who was of course a quite different type of man from you, tried to make me believe that it is *une terreur ajoutée à la terreur*.[b] My attitude to heaven is not like that of any other person, and by virtue of the unique attitude that I adopt towards it, it is a unique object, a unique heaven. At most, therefore, you are criticising your idea of my heaven, but not my heaven. And now immortality! Here you become simply ridiculous. I deny my egoism — as you assert to please the philosophers — because I immortalise it and declare the laws of nature and thought null and void, as soon as they want to give my existence a determination which is not produced by me myself and is highly unpleasant for me, namely, death. You call immortality "tedious stability"—as though I could not always live an "eventful" life so long as trade is flourishing in this or the other world and I can do business in other things than your "book". And what can be "more stable" than death, which against my will puts an end to my movement and submerges me in the universal, nature, the species, the holy? And now the state, law, police! For many an "ego" they may appear to be alien powers; but I know that they are my own powers. Incidentally — and at this point the bourgeois, this time with a gracious nod of the head, again turns his back on our saint — as far as I am concerned, go on blustering against religion, heaven, God and so on. I know all the same that in everything that interests me — private property, value, price, money, purchase and sale — you always perceive something "peculiar".

We have just seen how individuals differ from one another. But every individual again is diverse in himself. Thus, by reflecting himself in one of these qualities, i.e., by regarding, *defining* his "ego" through one of these determinations, Saint Sancho can define the object of the other qualities and these other qualities themselves as the alien, the holy; and so in turn with all his qualities. Thus, for example, that which is object for his flesh is the holy for his spirit, or that which is object for his need of rest is the holy for his need of movement. His

---

[a] Property added to property.— *Ed.*

[b] Terror added to terror.— *Ed.*

transformation, described above, of all action and inaction into self-denial is based on this trick. Moreover, his ego is no *real* ego, but only the ego of the equations given above, the same ego that in formal logic, in the theory of propositions, figures as *Caius*.[81]

"Another example", namely, a more general example of the canonisation of the world, is the transformation of real collisions, i.e., collisions between individuals and their actual conditions of life, into ideal collisions, i.e., into collisions between these individuals and the ideas which they form or get into their heads. This trick, too, is extremely simple. As Saint Sancho earlier made the thoughts of individuals into something existing independently, so here he separates the ideal reflection of real collisions from these collisions and turns this reflection into something existing independently. The real contradictions in which the individual finds himself are transformed into contradictions of the individual with his idea or, as Saint Sancho also expresses it more simply, into contradictions with the idea *as such*, with the Holy. Thus he manages to transform the real collision, the prototype of its ideal copy, into the consequence of this ideological pretence. Thus he arrives at the result that it is not a question of the practical abolition of the practical collision, but only of *renouncing the idea of this collision*, a renunciation which he, as a good moralist, insistently urges people to carry out.

After Saint Sancho has thus transformed all the contradictions and collisions in which the individual finds himself into mere contradictions and collisions of the individual with one or other of his ideas, an idea which has become independent of him and has subordinated him to itself, and, therefore, is "easily" transformed into the idea *as such*, the holy idea, the Holy—after this there remains only one thing for the individual to do: to commit the sin against the Holy Spirit, to abstract from this idea and declare the holy to be a spectre. This logical swindle, which the individual performs on himself, our saint regards as one of the greatest efforts of the egoist. On the other hand, however, anyone can see how easy it is in this way to declare that from the egoistical point of view all historically ocurring conflicts and movements are subsidiary, without knowing anything about them. To do this one has only to extract a few of the phrases usually adopted in such cases, to transform them, in the manner indicated, into "the holy", to depict the individuals as being subordinated to this holy, and to put oneself forward as one who despises "the holy as such".

A further offshoot of this logical trick, and indeed our saint's favourite manoeuvre, is the exploitation of the words designation, vocation, task, etc., thereby immensely facilitating the transformation of whatever he likes into the holy. For, in vocation, designation, task, etc., the individual appears in his own imagination as something different from what he actually is, as the alien, hence as the holy, and in opposition to his real being he asserts his idea of what he ought to be as the rightful, the ideal, the holy. Thus, when it is necessary for him, Saint Sancho can transform everything into the holy by means of the following series of appositions: to designate oneself, i.e., to choose a designation (insert here any content you like) for oneself; to choose the designation *as such*; to choose a holy designation, to choose a designation as the holy, i.e., to choose the holy as designation. Or: to be designated, i.e., to have a designation, to have *the* designation, the holy designation, designation as the holy, the holy as designation, the holy for designation, the designation of the holy.

And now, of course, it only remains for him strongly to admonish people to select for themselves the designation of absence of any designation, the vocation of absence of any vocation, the task of absence of any task — although throughout "the book", "up to and including" the "Commentary", he does nothing but select designations for people, set people tasks and, like a prophet in the wilderness, call them to the gospel of true egoism, about whom, of course, it is said: many are called but only one — *O'Connell*— is chosen.[a]

We have already seen above how Saint Sancho separates the ideas of individuals from the conditions of their life, from their practical collisions and contradictions, in order then to transform them into the holy. Now these ideas appear in the form of *designation, vocation, task.* For Saint Sancho vocation has a double form; firstly as the vocation which others choose for me — examples of which we have already had above in the case of the newspapers that are full of politics and the prisons that our saint mistook for houses of moral correction.*[b] Afterward

* [The following passage is crossed out in the manuscript:] We have already earlier discussed at length this kind of vocation where one of the conditions of the life of a class is singled out by the individuals constituting this class and put forward as a general demand to all men, where the bourgeois makes politics and morals, the existence of which is indispensable to him, the vocation of all men.

---

[a] Cf. Matthew 20:16 ("for many be called, but few chosen"). See also this volume, p. 272-73.— *Ed.*

[b] See this volume, pp. 174-76.— *Ed.*

vocation appears also as a vocation in which the individual himself believes. If the ego is divorced from all its empirical conditions of life, its activity, the conditions of its existence, if it is separated from the world that forms its basis and from its own body, then, of course, it has no other vocation and no other designation than that of representing the Caius of the logical proposition and to assist Saint Sancho in arriving at the equations given above. In the real world, on the other hand, where individuals have needs, they thereby already have a *vocation* and *task*; and at the outset it is still immaterial whether they make this their vocation in their imagination as well. It is clear, however, that because the individuals possess consciousness they form an idea of this vocation which their empirical existence has given them and, thus, furnish Saint Sancho with the opportunity of seizing on the word vocation, that is, on the mental expression of their actual conditions of life, and of leaving out of account these conditions of life themselves. The proletarian, for example, who like every human being has the vocation of satisfying his needs and who is not in a position to satisfy even the needs that he has in common with all human beings, the proletarian whom the necessity to work a 14-hour day debases to the level of a beast of burden, whom competition degrades to a mere thing, an article of trade, who from his position as a mere productive force, the sole position left to him, is squeezed out by other, more powerful productive forces—this proletarian is, if only for these reasons, confronted with the real task of revolutionising his conditions. He can, of course, imagine this to be his "vocation", he can also, if he likes to engage in propaganda, express his "vocation" by saying that to do this or that is the human vocation of the proletarian, the more so since his position does not even allow him to satisfy the needs arising directly from his human nature. Saint Sancho does not concern himself with the reality underlying this idea, with the practical aim of this proletarian—he clings to the word "vocation" and declares it to be the holy, and the proletarian to be a servant of the holy—the easiest way of considering himself superior and "proceeding further".

Particularly in the relations that have existed hitherto, when one class always ruled, when the conditions of life of an individual always coincided with the conditions of life of a class, when, therefore, the practical task of each newly emerging class was bound to appear to each of its members as a *universal* task, and when each class could actually overthrow its predecessor only by liberating the individuals of *all* classes from certain chains which had hitherto fettered them — under these circumstances it was essential that the task of the individual members of a class striving for domination should be described as a universal human task.

Incidentally, when for example the bourgeois tells the proletarian that his, the proletarian's, human task is to work fourteen hours a day, the proletarian is quite justified in replying in the same language that on the contrary his task is to overthrow the entire bourgeois system.

We have already repeatedly seen how Saint Sancho puts forward a whole series of tasks all of which resolve themselves into the final task, which exists for all people, that of true egoism. But even where he does not reflect, and does not see himself as creator and creation, he manages to arrive at a task by means of the following trashy distinction.

Page 466: "Whether you want to continue to occupy yourself with thinking depends on you. *If you* wish to achieve anything substantial in thinking, then" (the conditions and designations begin for you) "then ... anyone who wishes to think, therefore, certainly has a task, which by having that wish *he* sets himself, *consciously* or *unconsciously*; but no one has the task of thinking."

First of all, apart from any other content of this proposition, it is incorrect even from Saint Sancho's own viewpoint, since the egoist in agreement with himself, whether he wishes it or not, certainly has the "task" of thinking. He must think, on the one hand, to keep in check the flesh, which can be tamed only through the spirit, through thought, and, on the other hand, to be able to fulfil his reflective determination as creator and creation. Consequently he sets the whole world of deceived egoists the "task" of knowing themselves — a "task" which, of course, cannot be accomplished without thought.

In order to change this proposition from the form of trashy distinction into a logical form, one must first of all get rid of the term "substantial". For each person the "substantial" that he wishes to achieve in thought is something different, depending on his degree of education, the conditions of his life and his aim at the time. Saint Max, therefore, does not give us here any firm criterion for determining *when* the task begins which one sets oneself by thinking and how far one can go in thought without setting oneself any task—he limits himself to the relative expression "substantial". But for me everything is "substantial" that induces me to think, everything about which I think is "substantial". Therefore instead of: "if you want to achieve anything substantial in thinking", it should read: "if you want *to think* at all". This depends, however, not at all on your wishing or not wishing, since you possess consciousness and can satisfy your needs only by an activity in which you have to use your consciousness *as well*. Further, the hypothetical form must be got rid of. "*If* you *want* to think"— then from the outset you are setting yourself the "task" of thinking; Saint Sancho had no need to proclaim this tautological statement with such pomposity. The whole proposition was only clothed in this form of trashy distinction and pompous tautology in order to conceal the content: as a *definite* person, an actual person, you have a *designation*, a task, whether you are conscious of it or not.* It arises from your need and the connection of the latter with the existing world. Sancho's real wisdom lies in his assertion that it depends on your will whether you think, live, etc., whether in general you possess any sort of determinateness. He is afraid that otherwise determination would cease to be your self-determination. When you equate your self with your reflection or, according to need, with your will, then it is obvious that in this abstraction everything that is not posited by your reflection or your will is not self-determination—therefore also, for example, your breathing, your blood circulation, thought, life, etc. For Saint Sancho, however, self-determination does not even consist in will but, as we saw already in regard to the true egoist,[a] in the *reservatio mentalis* of indifference to any kind of determinateness—an indifference which reappears here as absence of determination. In his "own" series of appositions this would assume the following form: as opposed to all real determination, he chooses absence of determination as his determination, at each moment he distinguishes between himself and the undeterminated, thus at each moment he is also some other than he is, a third person, and indeed the other pure and simple, the holy other, the other counterposed to all uniqueness, the undeterminated, the universal, the ordinary—the ragamuffin.

If Saint Sancho saves himself from determination by his leap

* [The following passage is crossed out in the manuscript:] You cannot live, eat, sleep, you cannot move or do anything at all without at the same time setting yourself a task, without designation—this is a theory, therefore, which, instead of getting away from the setting of tasks, from vocations, etc., as it pretends to do, is even more intent on transforming every manifestation of life, and even life itself, into a "task".

---

[a] See this volume, pp. 278-80.— *Ed.*

into absence of determination (which is itself a determination and indeed the worst of all), then the practical, moral content of this whole trick, apart from what was said above in connection with the true egoist, is merely an apology for the vocation forced on every individual in the world as it has existed so far. If, for example, the workers assert in their communist propaganda that the vocation, designation, task of every person is to achieve all-round development of all his abilities, including, for example, the ability to think, Saint Sancho sees in this only the vocation to something alien, the assertion of "the holy". He seeks to free them from this by defending the individual who has been crippled by the division of labour at the expense of his abilities and relegated to a one-sided vocation against his *own* need to become different, a need which has been *stated to be* his vocation by others. What is here asserted in the form of a vocation, a designation, is precisely the negation of the vocation that has hitherto resulted in practice from the division of labour, i.e., the only actually existing vocation— hence, the negation of vocation altogether. The all-round realisation of the individual will only cease to be conceived as an ideal, a vocation, etc., when the impact of the world which stimulates the real development of the abilities of the individual is under the control of the individuals themselves, as the communists desire.

Finally, in the egoistical logic all the twaddle about vocation has moreover the purpose of making it possible to introduce the holy into things and to enable us to destroy them without having to touch them. Thus, for example, one person or another regards work, business affairs, etc., as his vocation. Thereby these become holy work, holy business affairs, the holy. The true egoist does not regard them as vocation; thereby he has dissolved holy work and holy business affairs. So they remain what they are and he remains what he was. It does not occur to him to investigate whether work, business affairs, etc., these modes of existence of individuals, by their real content and process of development necessarily lead to those ideological notions which he combats as independent beings, or, to use his expression, which he canonises.

Just as Saint Sancho canonises communism in order later, in connection with the union, the better to palm off his holy idea of it as his "own" invention, so, in exactly the same way, he blusters against "vocation, designation, task" merely in order to reproduce them throughout his book as the *categorical imperative*. Wherever difficulties arise, Sancho hacks his way through them by means of a categorical imperative such as "turn yourself to account", "recognise yourself", "let each become an all-powerful ego", etc. On the categorical imperative, see the section on the "union"; on "vocation", etc., see the section on "self-enjoyment".

We have now revealed the chief logical tricks Saint Sancho uses to canonise the existing world and thereby to criticise and consume it. Actually, however, he consumes only the holy in the world, without even touching the world itself. Hence it is obvious that he has to remain wholly conservative in practice. If he wanted to criticise, then earthly criticism would begin just where any possible halo ends. The more the normal form of intercourse of society, and with it the conditions of the ruling class, develop their contradiction to the advanced productive forces, and the greater the consequent discord within the ruling class itself as well as between it and the class ruled by it, the more fictitious, of course, becomes the consciousness which originally corresponded to this form of intercourse (i.e., it ceases to be the consciousness corresponding to this form of intercourse), and the more do the old traditional ideas of these relations of intercourse, in which actual private interests, etc., etc., are expressed as universal interests, descend to the level of mere idealising phrases, conscious illusion, deliberate hypocrisy. But the more their falsity is exposed by life, and the less meaning they have for consciousness itself, the more resolutely are they asserted, the more hypocritical, moral and holy becomes the language of this normal society. The more hypocritical this society becomes, the easier it is for such a credulous man as Sancho to discover everywhere the idea of the holy, the ideal. From the universal hypocrisy of society he, the credulous, can deduce universal faith in the holy, the domination of the holy, and can even mistake this holy for the pedestal of existing society. He is the dupe of this hypocrisy, from which he should have drawn exactly the opposite conclusion.

The world of the holy is in the final analysis epitomised in "man". As we have already seen throughout the Old Testament, Sancho regards "man" as the active subject on which the whole of previous history is based; in the New Testament he extends this domination of "man" to the whole of the existing, contemporary physical and spiritual world, and also to the properties of the individuals at present existing. Everything belongs to "man" and thus the world is transformed into the "world of man". The holy as a person is "man", which for Sancho is only another name for the concept, the idea. The conceptions and ideas of people, separated from actual things, are bound, of course, to have as their basis not actual individuals, but the individual of the philosophical conception, the individual separated from his actuality and existing only in thought, "man" as such, the concept of man. With this, his faith in philosophy reaches its culmination.

Now that everything has been transformed into "the holy" or into what belongs to "man", our saint is enabled to proceed further to *appropriation*, by renouncing the idea of "the holy" or of "man" as a power standing above him. Owing to the alien having been transformed into the holy, into a mere idea, this idea of the alien, which he mistakes for the actually existing alien, is of course his property. The basic formulas for appropriation of the world of man (the way in which the ego gains possession of the world when it no longer has any respect for the holy) are already contained in the equations given above.

As we have seen, Saint Sancho is already master of his qualities as the egoist in agreement with himself. In order to become master of the world, all he has to do is to make it one of his qualities. The simplest way of doing so is for Sancho to proclaim the quality of "man", with all the nonsense contained in this, directly as *his* quality. Thus he claims for himself, for example, as a quality of the ego, the nonsense of *universal love of mankind* by asserting that he loves "*everyone*" (p. 387) and indeed with the consciousness of egoism, for "love makes him happy". A person who has such a happy nature, indubitably belongs to those of whom it is said: Woe unto you if you offend even *one of these little ones!*[a]

The second method is that Saint Sancho tries to preserve something as a *quality of his*, while he transforms it — when it seems necessary to him as a *relation* — into a relation, a mode of existence, of "man", a *holy relation*, and thereby repudiates it. Saint Sancho does this even when the quality, separated from the relation through which it is realised, becomes pure nonsense. Thus, for example, on page 322 he wants to preserve national pride by declaring that "nationality is one of *his qualities* and the nation *his owner* and master". He could have continued: *religiousness* is a quality of mine, I have no intention of renouncing it as one of my qualities — religion is my master, the holy. Family love is a quality of mine, the family is my

---

[a] Cf. Luke 17:1-2.— *Ed.*

master. Justice is a quality of mine, the law is my master; to engage in politics is a quality of mine, the state is my master.

The third method of appropriation is employed when some alien power whose force he experiences in practice is regarded by him as holy and spurned altogether without being appropriated. In this case he sees his own powerlessness in the alien power and recognises this powerlessness as his property, his creation, above which he always stands as creator. This, for example, is the case with the state. Here, too, he fortunately arrives at the point at which he has to deal not with something alien, but only with a quality of his own, against which he needs only to set himself as creator in order to overcome it. In an emergency, therefore, the lack of a quality is also taken by him as a quality of his. When Saint Sancho is starving to death it is not due to lack of food, but to his own hungriness, his own quality of starving. If he falls out of a window and breaks his neck, it happens not because the force of gravity plunges him downwards, but because absence of wings, inability to fly, is a quality of his own.

The fourth method, which he employs with the most brilliant success, consists in declaring that everything that is the object of one of his qualities, is, since it is his object, his property, because he has a relation to it by virtue of one of his qualities, irrespective of the character of this relation. Thus, what has up to now been called seeing, hearing, feeling, etc., Sancho, this inoffensive acquisitor, calls: acquiring property. The shop at which I am looking is, as something seen by me, the object of my eye, and its reflection on my retina is the possession of my eye. And now the shop, besides its relation to the eye, becomes his possession and not merely the possession of his eye—his possession, which is as much upside-down as the image of the shop on his retina. When the shopkeeper lets down the shutters (or, as Szeliga puts it, the "blinds and curtains" a), his property disappears and, like a bankrupt bourgeois, he retains only the painful memory of vanished brilliance. If "Stirner" passes by the royal kitchen he will undoubtedly acquire possession of the smell of the pheasants roasting there, but he will not even see the pheasants themselves. The only persisting possession that falls to his share is a more or less vociferous rumbling in his stomach. Incidentally, what and how much he can see depends

---

a The words are from Szeliga's article "Eugen Sue: 'Die Geheimnisse von Paris' ".—*Ed.*

not only on the existing state of affairs in the world, a state of affairs by no means created by him, but also on his purse and on the position in life which falls to his lot owing to division of labour, which perhaps shuts away very much from him, although he may have very acquisitive eyes and ears.

If Saint Sancho had said simply and frankly that everything that is the object of his imagination, as an object imagined by him, i.e., as his idea of an object, is his idea, i.e., his possession (and the same thing holds with looking at something, etc.), one would only have marvelled at the childish naïveté of a man who believes that such a triviality is a discovery and a fortune. But the fact that he passes off this conjectural property as property in general was bound, of course, to have a magical attraction for the propertyless German ideologists.

Every other person in his sphere of action, too, is his object, and "as his object—his property", his creature. Each ego says to the other (see p. 184):

"For me you are only what you are for me" (for example, my *exploiteur*), "namely, my object and, because *my* object, my property".

Hence also my creature, which at any moment as creator I can swallow up and take back into myself. Thus, each ego regards the other not as a property-owner, but as his property; not as "ego" (see [p. 184)] but as being-for-him, as object; not as belonging to himself, but as belonging to *him*, to another, as alienated *from himself.* "Let us take both for what they give themselves out to be" (p. 187), for property-owners, for something belonging to themselves, "and for what they take each other to be", for property, for something belonging to the alien. They are property-owners and they are not property-owners (cf. p. 187). What is important for Saint Sancho, however, in all relations to others, is not to take the real relation, but how each can see himself in his *imagination*, in his reflection.

Since everything that is *object* for the "ego" is, through the medium of one or other of his properties, also *his* object and, therefore, *his property*—thus, for example, the beatings he receives as the object of *his* members, *his* feelings and *his* mind, are *his* object and, therefore, his property—hi is able to proclaim himself the owner of every object that exists for him. By this means he can proclaim that the world surrounding him is his property, and that he is its owner—no matter how much it maltreats him and debases him to the level of a "man having only ideal wealth, a ragamuffin". On the other hand, since every object for the "ego" is not only *my* object, but also my *object*, it is possible, with the same indifference towards the content, to declare that every *object* is not-my-own, alien, holy. One and the same object and one and the same relation can, therefore, with equal ease and with equal success be declared to be the holy and my property. Everything depends on whether stress is laid on the word "*my*" or on the word "*object*". The methods of appropriation and canonisation are merely two different "refractions" of one "transformation".

All these methods are merely positive expressions for negating what was posited as alien to the ego in the above equations; except that the negation is again, as above, taken in various determinations. Negation can, firstly, be determined in a purely formal way, so that it does not at all affect the content — as we saw above in the case of love of mankind and in all cases when its whole alteration is limited to introducing consciousness of indifference. Or the whole sphere of the object or predicate, the whole content, can be negated, as in the case of religion and the state. Or, thirdly, the copula alone, my hitherto alien relation to the predicate, can be negated and the stress laid on the word "*my*" so that my attitude to what is mine is that of property-owner — in the case of money, for instance, which becomes coin of my own coining. In this last case both the quality of Man and his relation can lose all meaning. Every one of the qualities of Man, by being taken back into myself, is extinguished in my individuality. It is no longer possible to say what the quality is. It remains only nominally what it was. As "*mine*", as determinateness dissolved in me, it no longer has any determinateness whether in relation to others or in relation to me, it is only posited by me, an *illusory* quality. Thus, for example, my thought. Just as with my qualities, so with the things which stand in a relation to me and which, as we have seen above, are basically also only my qualities — as, for example, in the case of the shop I am looking at. Insofar [therefore,] as thought in me is totally [different] from all [other] qualities, just as, for example, a jeweller's shop is totally different from a sausage shop, etc.— the [difference] emerges again as a difference of appearance, and reasserts itself externally too in my manifestation for others. Thereby this annihilated determinateness is fortunately restored and, insofar as it is at all possible to express it in words, must also be reproduced in the old expressions. (Incidentally, we shall be hearing a little more yet concerning Saint Sancho's non-etymological illusions about language.)

The simple equation encountered above is here replaced by the *antithesis*. In its simplest form it is expressed, for example, as follows:

Man's thought — my thought, egoistical thought,

where the word "*my*" means only that he can also be without thoughts, so that the word *my* abolishes *thought*. The antithesis already becomes more complicated in the following example:

Money as man's ⎫ ___ ⎧Money of my own coining as the
means of exchange ⎰   ⎩egoist's means of exchange,

where the absurdity stands revealed.

The antithesis becomes still more complicated when Saint Max introduces a determination and wants to create the appearance of a far-reaching development. Here the single antithesis becomes a series of antitheses. First of all, for example, it is stated:

Right in general as ⎫ ___ ⎧ Right is what is
the right of man ⎰   ⎩ right for me,

where, instead of right, he might equally well have put any other word, since admittedly it no longer has any meaning. Although this nonsense continues to crop up all the time, in order to proceed further he has to introduce another, *well-known* determination of right which can be used both in the purely personal and in the ideological sense — for example, *might* as the basis of right. Only now, where the right mentioned in the first thesis has acquired yet another determination, which is retained in the antithesis, can this antithesis produce some content. Now we get:

Right — might of Man⎫ ___ ⎧Might — my right

which then again simply becomes reduced to:

Might as my right=My might.

These antitheses are no more than positive reversals of the above-mentioned negative equations, in which antitheses continually proved to be contained in the conclusion. They even surpass those equations in simple grandeur and great simple-mindedness.

Just as previously Saint Sancho could regard everything as *alien*, as existing independently of him, as holy, so now with equal ease he can regard everything as his own product, as only existing thanks to him, as his property. Indeed, since he transforms everything into his qualities, it only remains for him to behave towards them as he behaves towards his original qualities, in the capacity of the egoist in agreement with himself, a procedure we do not need to repeat here. In this way our Berlin school-master becomes the absolute master of the world—"this, of course, is also the case with every goose, every dog, every horse". (*Wigand*, p. 187.)

The real logical experiment, on which all these forms of appropriation are based, is a mere form of *speech*, namely a *paraphrase*, expressing one relation as a manifestation, as a mode of existence of another. Just as we have seen that every relation can be depicted as an example of the relation of property, in exactly the same way it can be depicted as the relation of love, might, exploitation, etc. Saint Sancho found this manner of paraphrase ready-made in philosophical speculation where it plays a very important part. See below on the "theory of exploitation".[a]

The various categories of appropriation become *emotional* categories as soon as the appearance of practice is introduced and appropriation is to be taken seriously. The emotional form of assertion of the ego against the alien, the holy, the world of "Man", is *bragging*. Refusal to revere the holy is proclaimed (reverence, respect, etc.—these emotional categories serve to express his relation to the holy or to some third thing as the holy), and this permanent refusal is entitled a deed, a deed that appears all the more comic because all the time Sancho is battling only against the spectre of his own sanctifying conception. On the other hand, since the world, despite his refusal to revere the holy, treats him in the most ungodly fashion, he enjoys the inner satisfaction of declaring to the world that he has only to attain power over it in order to treat it without any reverence. This threat with its world-shattering *reservatio mentalis* completes the comedy. To the first form of bragging belongs Saint Sancho's statement on page 16 that he "is not afraid of the anger of *Poseidon*, nor of the vengeful *Eumenides*", "does not fear the curse" (p. 58), "desires no forgiveness" (p. 242), etc., and his final assurance that

---

[a] See this volume, pp. 434-38.— *Ed.*

he commits "the most boundless desecration" of the holy. To the second form belongs his threat against the moon (p. 218):

"If only I could seize you, I would in truth seize you, and if only I could find a means to get to you, you would in no way terrify me.... I do not surrender to you, but am only biding my time. Even if for the present I refrain from having designs on you, I still have a grudge against you" —

an apostrophe in which our saint sinks below the level of Pfeffel's pug-dog in the ditch.[82] And likewise on page 425, where he "does not renounce power over life and death", etc.

Finally, the practice of bragging [can] again become mere [practice] within the sphere of theory [by] our holy man [asserting] in the [most] pompous language that he has performed actions that he has never performed, and [at the same time] endeavouring by means of high-sounding phrases to smuggle in traditional trivialities [as] his original creations. Actually this is characteristic of the *entire book*, particularly his construction of history—which is foisted on us as an exposition of his thought but is only a bad piece of copying out—then the assurance that "the book" "appears to be written against man" (*Wigand*, p. 168), and a multitude of separate assertions, such as: "With one puff of the living ego I blow down whole peoples" (p. 219 of "the book"), "I recklessly attack" (p. 254), "the people is dead" (p. 285), further the assurance that he "delves into the bowels of right" (p. 275), and, finally, the challenging call, embelished with quotations and aphorisms, for "a flesh-and-blood opponent" (p. 280).

Bragging is already in itself sentimental. But, in addition, *sentimentality* occurs in "the book" as a particular category, which plays a definite part especially in positive appropriation that is no longer mere assertion against the alien. However simple the methods of appropriation so far examined, with a more detailed exposition the appearance has to be given that the ego thereby acquires also property "in the ordinary sense", and this can only be achieved by a forcible puffing-up of this ego, by enveloping himself and others in a sentimental charm. Sentimentality cannot be avoided since, without previous examination, he claims the predicates of "Man" as his own — he asserts, for example, that he "loves" "*everyone*" "out of egoism"—and thus gives his qualities an exuberant turgidity. Thus, on page 351, he declares that the "smile of the infant" is "his property" and in the same passage the stage of civilisation at which old men are no longer killed off is depicted with the most touching expressions as the deed of these old men themselves, etc. His attitude to Maritornes also belongs wholly to this same sentimentality.

The unity of sentimentality and bragging is *rebellion*. Directed outwards, against others, it is bragging; directed inwards, as grumbling-in-oneself, it is sentimentality. It is the specific expression of the impotent dissatisfaction of the philistine. He waxes indignant at the thought of atheism, terrorism, communism, regicide, etc. The object against which Saint Sancho rebels is *the holy*; therefore rebellion, which indeed is also characterised as a *crime*, becomes, in the final analysis, a *sin*. It is therefore by no means necessary for rebellion to take the form of an *action*, as it is only the "sin" against "the holy". Saint Sancho, therefore, is satisfied with "getting" "holiness" or the "spirit of alienation" "out of his head" and accomplishing his ideological appropriation. But just as present and future are altogether confused in his head, and just as he sometimes asserts that he has already appropriated everything and sometimes that it has still to be acquired, so in connection with rebellion also at times it occurs to him quite accidentally that he is still confronted by the *actually existing* alien even after he has finished with the halo of the alien. In this case, or rather in the case of this sudden idea, rebellion is transformed into an imaginary act, and the ego into "we". We shall examine this in more detail later. (See "*Rebellion*".[a])

The true egoist, who from the description given so far has proved to be the greatest conservative, finally collects up the fragments of the "world of man", twelve basketfuls; for "far be it that anything should be lost!" Since his whole activity is limited to trying a few hackneyed, casuistical tricks on the world of thoughts handed down to him by philosophical tradition, it is a matter of course that the real world does not exist for him at all and, therefore, too, remains in existence as before. The content of the New Testament will furnish us with detailed proof of this.

Thus, "we appear at the *bar of majority* and are declared of age".

(P. 86.)

---

[a] See this volume, p. 406.— *Ed.*

4. PECULIARITY

"To create for oneself one's *own world*, that means building a heaven for oneself." (P. 89 of "the book".)*

We have already "penetrated" into the innermost sanctuary of this heaven; now we shall try to learn "more things" about it. In the New Testament, however, we shall rediscover the same hypocrisy that permeated the Old Testament. Just as in the latter the historical data were only names for a few simple categories, so here in the New Testament, too, all worldly relations are only disguises, different designations, for the meagre content which we have assembled in the "Phenomenology" and "Logic". Under the appearance of speaking about the actual world, Saint Sancho always speaks only about these meagre categories.

"You do not want the *freedom* to have all these fine things.... You want to have them in actuality ... to possess them as *your property*.... You ought to be not only a *free person*, but also an *owner*." (P. 205.)

One of the oldest formulas arrived at by the early social movement—the opposition between socialism in its most miserable form and liberalism—is here exalted into an utterance of the "egoist in agreement with himself". How old this opposition is even for Berlin, our holy man could have seen if only from the fact that it is mentioned with terror already in Ranke's *Historisch-politische Zeitschrift*, Berlin, 1831.[a]

"How I utilise it" (freedom) "depends on my peculiarity." (P. 205.)

The great dialectician can also reverse this and say: "How I utilise my peculiarity depends on my freedom."—Then he continues:

"Free—from what?"

* [The following passage is crossed out in the manuscript:] Up to now freedom has been defined by philosophers in two ways; on the one hand, as power, as domination over the circumstances and conditions in which an individual lives—by all materialists; on the other hand, as self-determination, riddance of the real world, as merely imaginary freedom of the spirit—this definition was given by all idealists, especially the German idealists.

Having seen in the "Phenomenology" above how Saint Max's true egoist seeks his egoism in dissolution, in achieving riddance, the idealist freedom, it seems strange that in the chapter on "Peculiarity" he puts forward against "riddance" the opposite definition, i.e., power over the circumstances which determine him, materialist freedom.

[a] Leopold Ranke's "Einleitung" in *Historisch-politische Zeitschrift*, I. Band, Hamburg, 1832 (the place and date of publication are cited incorrectly in the text).— *Ed.*

Here, therefore, by means of a dash freedom is already transformed into freedom *from something* and, *per appos.*, from "everything". This time, however, the apposition is given in the form of a proposition that apparently provides a closer definition. Having thus achieved this great result, Sancho becomes sentimental.

"Oh, how much can be shaken off!" First, the "yoke of serfdom", then a whole series of other yokes, leading imperceptibly to the result that "the most perfect self-denial is nothing but freedom, freedom ... from one's own ego, and the urge towards freedom as something absolute ... has deprived us of our *peculiarity*."

By means of an extremely artless series of yokes, liberation from serfdom, which was the assertion of the individuality of the serfs and at the same time the abolition of a definite empirical barrier, is here equated with the much earlier Christian-idealist freedom of the Epistles to the Romans and Corinthians, thereby transforming freedom in general into self-denial. At this point we have already finished with freedom, since it is now indisputably the "holy". Saint Max transforms a definite historical act of self-liberation into the abstract category of "freedom", and this category is then defined more closely by means of a totally different historical phenomenon which can likewise be included under the general conception of "freedom". This is the whole trick by which the throwing off of the yoke of serfdom is transformed into self-denial.

To make his theory of freedom as clear as noonday to the German citizen, *Sancho* now begins to declaim in the burgher's own language, particularly that of the Berlin burgher:

"But the freer I become, the larger does compulsion loom before my eyes, and the more powerless do I feel. The unfree son of the wilds is not yet aware of all the limitations that trouble an 'educated' man, he imagines himself freer than the latter. In proportion as I achieve freedom for myself I create new limits and new tasks for myself; no sooner have I invented railways than I again feel myself weak because I still cannot sail through the air like a bird, and I have no sooner solved a problem that was perplexing my mind than countless others await me", etc. (Pp. 205, 206.)

O "clumsy" story-writer for townsman and villager!

Not the "unfree sons of the wilds" but "educated people" "imagine" the savage freer than the educated man. That the "son of the wilds" (whom F. Halm brought on the stage)[a] is ignorant of the limitations of the educated man because he cannot experience them is just as clear as that the "educated" citizen of Berlin, who only knows the "son of the wilds" from

---

[a] Friedrich Halm. *Der Sohn der Wildniss.— Ed.*

the theatre, knows nothing of the limitations of the savage. The simple fact is this: the limitations of the savage are not those of the civilised man. The comparison that our saint draws between them is the fantastic comparison of an "educated" Berliner whose education consists of knowing nothing about either of them. That he knows nothing of the limitations of the savage is explicable, although after the large number of new travel books, it is certainly easy enough to know something about them; but that he is also ignorant of the limitations of the educated man, is proved by his example of railways and flying. The inactive petty bourgeois, for whom railways dropped from the sky and who for that very reason imagines that he invented them himself, begins to indulge in fantasies about aerial flight after having once travelled by railway. Actually, the balloon came *first* and then the railways. Saint Sancho had to reverse this, for otherwise everyone would have seen that when the balloon was invented the demand for railways was still a long way off, whereas the opposite is easy to imagine. In general, Sancho turns empirical relations upside down. When hackney carriages and carts no longer sufficed for the growing requirements of communication, when, *inter alia*, the centralisation of production due to large-scale industry necessitated new methods to accelerate and expand the transport of its mass of products, the locomotive was invented and thus the use of railways for transport on a large scale. The inventor and shareholders were interested in their profits, and commerce in general in reducing production costs; the possibility, indeed the absolute necessity, of the invention lay in the empirical conditions. The application of the new invention in the various countries depended on the various empirical conditions; in America, for example, on the need to unite the individual states of that vast area and to link the semi-civilised districts of the interior with the sea and the markets for their products. (Compare, *inter alia*, M. Chevalier, *Lettres sur l'Amérique du Nord*.) In other countries, for example in Germany, where every new invention makes people regret that it does not complete the sum total of inventions — in such countries after stubbornly resisting these detestable railways which cannot supply them with wings, people are nevertheless compelled by competition to accept them in the end and to give up hackney carriages and carts along with the time-honoured, respectable spinning-wheel. The absence of other profitable investment of capital made railway construction the predominant branch of industry in Germany. The development of her railway construction and reverses on the world market went hand in hand. But nowhere are railways built for the sake of the category *"freedom from"*; Saint Max could have realised this even from the fact that no one builds railways in order to *free* himself *from* his money. The real kernel of the burgher's ideological contempt for railways due to his longing to fly like a bird is to be found in his preference for hackney carriages, vans and country roads. Sancho yearns for his "own world" which, as we saw above, is heaven. Therefore he wants to replace the locomotive by Elijah's fiery chariot and be carried up to heaven.

After the actual tearing down of restrictions — which is at the same time an extremely positive development of the productive forces, real energy and satisfaction of urgent requirements, and an expansion of the power of individuals — after the actual tearing down of restrictions has been transformed in the eyes of this passive and ignorant spectator into simple freedom *from* a restriction, which he can again logically make into a postulate of freedom from restriction *as such* — at the conclusion of the whole argument, we arrive at what was already presupposed at the beginning:

"To be free from something means only *to be relieved of* something, *to be rid of* something." (P. 206.)

He at once gives an extremely unfortunate example: "He is free of headache is equivalent to saying: he is rid of it"; as though this "riddance" of headache were not equivalent to a wholly positive ability to dispose of my head, equivalent to ownership of my head, while as long as I had a headache I was the property of my sick head.

"In 'riddance' — in riddance from sin, from God, from morality, etc.— we consummate the freedom that Christianity recommends." (P. 206.)

Hence our "consummate Christian", too, finds his peculiarity only in "riddance" from "thought", from "determination", from "vocation", from "law", from "constitution", etc., and invites his brothers in Christ to "feel happy only in dissolution", i.e., in accomplishing "riddance" and the "consummate", "Christian freedom".

He continues:

"Ought we, perhaps, to renounce freedom because it turns out to be a Christian ideal? No, *nothing should be lost*" (*voilà notre conservateur tout trouvé*[a]), "freedom too should not be lost, it should however become our *own,* and it cannot become our own in the form of freedom." (P. 207.)

---

[a] There's the conservative all complete.— *Ed.*

Here "our egoist" (*toujours et partout*[a]) "in agreement with himself" forgets that already in the Old Testament, thanks to the Christian ideal of freedom, i.e., thanks to the illusion of freedom, we became "owners" of the "world of things"; he forgets, likewise, that accordingly we had only to get rid of the "world of thoughts" to become "owners" of that world as well, that in this context "peculiarity" was for him a *consequence* of freedom, of riddance.

Having interpreted freedom as the state of being free *from* something, and this, in turn, as "riddance", and this as the Christian ideal of freedom, and hence as the freedom of "Man", our saint can, with the material thus prepared, carry through a practical course of his logic. The first, simplest antithesis reads:

Freedom of Man — My freedom,

where in the antithesis freedom ceases to exist "in the form of freedom". Or:

$$\left.\begin{array}{l}\text{Riddance in the interests}\\\text{of Man}\end{array}\right\} - \left\{\begin{array}{l}\text{Riddance in my}\\\text{interests.}\end{array}\right.$$

Both these antitheses, with a numerous retinue of declamations, continually appear throughout the chapter on peculiarity, but with their help alone our world-conquering Sancho would attain very little, he would not even attain the island of Barataria. Earlier, when observing the behaviour of people from his "own world", from his "heaven", he set aside two factors of actual liberation in making his abstraction of freedom. The first factor was that individuals in their self-liberation satisfy a definite need actually experienced by them. As the result of setting aside this factor, "*Man*" has been substituted for actual individuals, and striving for a fantastic ideal — for freedom as such, for the "freedom of Man"— has been substituted for the satisfaction of actual needs.

The second factor was that an ability that has hitherto existed merely as a potentiality in the individuals who are freeing themselves begins to function as a real power, or that an already existing power becomes greater by removal of some restriction. The removal of the restriction, which is merely a *consequence* of the new creation of power, can of course be considered the main thing. But this illusion arises only if one takes politics as the basis of empirical history, or if, like Hegel, one wants everywhere to demonstrate the negation of negation, or finally if, after the new power has been created, one

---

[a] Always and everywhere.— *Ed.*

reflects, as an ignorant citizen of Berlin, on this new creation.

By setting aside this second factor for his own use, Saint Sancho acquires a determinateness that he can counterpose to the remaining, abstract *caput mortuum* of "freedom". Thus he arrives at the following new antitheses:

| *Freedom*, the empty removal of alien power | — | Peculiarity, the actual possession of one's own power. |

Or, even:

| Freedom, repulsion of alien power | — | Peculiarity, possession of one's own power. |

To show the extent to which Saint Sancho has juggled his *own* "power", which he here counterposes to freedom, out of this same freedom and into himself, we do not intend to refer him to the materialists or communists, but merely to the *Dictionnaire de l'académie*, where he will find that the word *liberté* is most frequently used in the sense of *puissance*. If, however, Saint Sancho should maintain that he does not combat "*liberté*", but "*freedom*", then he ought to consult Hegel on negative and positive freedom.[a] As a German petty bourgeois, he might enjoy the concluding remark in this chapter.

The antithesis can also be expressed as follows:

| Freedom, idealistic striving for riddance and the struggle against other-being | — | Peculiarity, *actual* riddance and pleasure in one's own existence. |

Having thus, by means of a cheap *abstraction, distinguished* peculiarity from freedom, Sancho pretends that he is only now beginning to analyse this difference and exclaims:

"What a difference there is between freedom and peculiarity!" (P. 207.)

We shall see that, apart from the general antitheses, he has achieved nothing, and that peculiarity "in the ordinary sense" continues most amusingly to creep in side by side with this definition of peculiarity.

"In spite of the state of slavery, one can be inwardly free, although, again, only from *various things*, but not from *everything*; but the slave cannot be *free* from the whip, from the despotic mood, etc., of his master."

"On the other hand, peculiarity is my *whole* essence and existence, it is I myself. I am free from that which I have got *rid of*; I am the owner of that which I have in my *power* or which I have mastered. I am *my own* at all times and under

---

[a] G. W. F. Hegel, *Grundlinien der Philosophie des Rechts*. Einleitung.— *Ed.*

all circumstances, if only I *know how* to possess myself and do not abandon myself to others. I cannot truly *want* the state of being free, because I cannot ... achieve it; I can only wish for it and strive towards it, *for* it remains an ideal, a spectre. At every moment the fetters of actuality cut very deeply into my flesh. But I remain *my own*. Belonging as a feudal serf to some master, I *think* only of myself and of my own advantage; his blows, it is true, strike me: I am not *free* from them; but I e n d u r e t h e m o n l y f o r m y o w n g o o d, for example, in order to deceive him by an appearance of patience and to lull him into security or perhaps in order not to incur something worse by my defiance. But since I constantly have in mind myself and my own advantage" (while the blows retain possession of him and his back) "I seize on the first convenient opportunity" (i.e., he "wishes", he "strives" towards the first convenient opportunity, which, however, "remains an ideal, a spectre") "to crush the slave-owner. That I then become *free* from him and his whip is only a consequence of my previous egoism. It will, perhaps, be said here that even in the state of slavery I was free, namely 'in myself' or 'inwardly'; however, 'free in oneself' is not 'actually free', and 'inwardly' is not 'outwardly'. On the other hand, I was myself, *my own wholly and completely,* both inwardly and *outwardly.* Under the domination of a cruel master, my body is not 'free' from the pain of torture and the lashes of the whip; *but it is m y bones that crack under torture, m y muscles that twitch under the blows, and it is I who groan because m y body suffers. The fact that I sigh and tremble proves that I still belong to myself, that I am my own."* (Pp. 207, 208.)

Our Sancho, who here again acts the story-teller for the petty bourgeois and villagers, proves here that, despite the numerous drubbings he has already received in Cervantes, he has always remained "owner" of himself and that these blows belonged rather to his "peculiarity". He is "his own" "at all times and under all circumstances" *provided* he *knows how* to possess himself. Here, therefore, peculiarity is hypothetical and depends on his knowledge, by which term he understands a slavish casuistry. This knowledge later on becomes *thinking* as well, when he begins "to think" about himself and his "advantage"— this thinking and this imagined "advantage" being his imagined "property". It is further interpreted in the sense that he endures the blows "for his own good", where peculiarity once again consists in the *idea* of "good", and where he "endures" the bad in order not to become the "owner" of "something worse". Subsequently, knowledge is revealed also as the "owner" of the reservation about "the first convenient opportunity", hence of a mere *reservatio mentalis,* and, finally, as the "crushing" of the "slave-owner", in the anticipation of the idea, in which case he is the "owner" of this anticipation, whereas at present the slave-owner actually tramples him underfoot. While, therefore, he identifies himself here with his *consciousness,* which endeavours to calm itself by means of all kinds of maxims of worldly wisdom, in the end he identifies himself with his body, so that he is wholly "his own", outwardly as well as inwardly, so long as he still retains a spark of life, even if it is merely unconscious life. Such phenomena as the cracking of his "bones", the twitching of his muscles, etc., are phenomena which, when translated from the language of *unique* natural science into the language of pathology, can be produced with the aid of galvanism on his corpse, when freshly cut down from the gallows on which he hanged himself, as we saw above, and which can be produced even in a dead frog—these phenomena serve him here as proof that he is "wholly and completely" "both inwardly and outwardly" still "his own", that he still has control over himself. The very fact which demonstrates the power and peculiarity of the slave-owner, namely that it is precisely *he* who is flogged and not someone else, that it is precisely *his* bones that "crack", *his* muscles that twitch, without his being able to alter it—this very fact here serves our saint as proof of his own peculiarity and power. Thus, when he lies trussed up in the *spanso bocko*[83] torture of Surinam, unable to move hand or foot, or any other of his limbs, and has to put up with everything done to him, in such circumstances his power and peculiarity do not consist in his being able to make use of his limbs, but in the fact that they are *his* limbs. Here once again he has saved his peculiarity by always considering himself as otherwise-determined— sometimes as mere consciousness, sometimes as an unconscious body (see the "Phenomenology"[a]).

At any rate, Saint Sancho "endures" his portion of blows with more dignity than actual slaves do. However often, in the interests of the slave-owners, missionaries may tell the slaves that they have to "endure" the blows "for their own good", the slaves are not taken in by such twaddle. They do not coldly and timidly reflect that they would otherwise "incur something worse", nor do they imagine that they "deceive the slave-owner by an appearance of patience". On the contrary, they scoff at their torturers, they jeer at the latter's impotence even to force them to humble themselves, and they suppress every "groan" and every sigh, as long as the physical pain permits them to do so. (See Charles Comte, *Traité de législation.*) They are, therefore, neither "inwardly" nor "outwardly" their own "owners", but only the "owners" of their defiance, which could equally well be expressed by saying that they are neither "inwardly" nor "outwardly" "free", but are free only in one respect, namely that they are "inwardly" free from self-

---

[a] See this volume, p. 288-89.— *Ed.*

humiliation as they also show "outwardly". Insofar as "Stirner" suffers blows, he is the owner of the blows and thus free from being not beaten; and this freedom, this riddance, belongs to his peculiarity.

From the fact that Saint Sancho assumes that the reservation about running away at "the first convenient opportunity" is a special characteristic of peculiarity and sees in the "liberation" thus obtained "merely the consequence of his previous egoism" (*of his own* egoism, i. e., egoism in agreement with itself), it follows that he imagines that the insurgent Negroes of Haiti[84] and the fugitive Negroes of all the colonies wanted to free not *themselves*, but "Man". The slave who takes the decision to free himself must already be superior to the idea that slavery is his "peculiarity". He must be "*free*" from this "*peculiarity*". The "peculiarity" of an individual, however, can consist in his "*abandoning*" himself. For "one" to assert the opposite means to apply an "alien scale" to this individual.

In conclusion, Saint Sancho takes revenge for the blows he has received by the following address to the "owner" of his "peculiarity", the slave-owner.

"My *leg* is not 'free' from the blows of the master, but it is *my* leg, and it *cannot be taken away*. Let him tear it from me and see whether he has possession of my leg! He will find in his hands nothing but the corpse of my leg, which is as little my leg as a dead dog is a dog." (P. 208.)

But let him — Sancho, who imagines here that the slave-owner wants to have his *living* leg, probably for his own use — let him "see" what he still retains of his leg which "cannot be taken away". He retains nothing but the loss of his leg and has become the one-legged owner of his torn-out leg. If he has to labour at a tread-mill eight hours every day, then it is *he* who in the course of time becomes an idiot, and idiocy will then be *his* "peculiarity". Let the judge who sentences him to this "see" whether he has still Sancho's brain "in his hands". But that will be of little help to poor Sancho.

"The first property, the first splendour has been won!"

After our saint, by means of these examples, which are worthy of an ascetic, has revealed the difference between freedom and peculiarity, at a considerable belletristical production cost, he quite unexpectedly declares on page 209 that

"between peculiarity and freedom there lies a still *deeper* gulf than the simple verbal difference".

This "deeper gulf" consists in the fact that the above definition of freedom is repeated with "manifold transformations" and "refractions" and numerous "episodical insertions". From the definition of "freedom" as "riddance" the questions arise: from what should people be free (p. 209), etc., disputes concerning this "from what" (ibid.) (here, too, as a German petty bourgeois, he sees in the struggle of actual interests only wrangling about the definition of this "from what", in which connection, of course, it appears very strange to him that the "citizen" does not wish to be free "from citizenship", page 210). Then the proposition is repeated that the removal of a barrier is the establishment of a new barrier, in the form that "the striving for a definite freedom always includes the aim of a new rule", page 210 (in which connection we learn that in the revolution the bourgeois was not striving for his own rule but for the "rule of law"— see above concerning liberalism[a]); then follows the result that one does not wish to be rid of what "is wholly to one's liking, e. g., the irresistible glance of the beloved". (P. 211.) Further on, it turns out that freedom is a "phantom" (p. 211), a "dream" (p. 212); then we learn by the way that the "voice of nature" can sometimes also become "peculiarity" (p. 213); on the other hand the "voice of God and conscience" is to be considered "devil's work", and the author boasts: "Such godless people" (who consider it the work of the devil) "do exist; how will you deal with them?" (Pp. 213, 214.) But it is not nature that should determine me, but I who should determine my nature, says the egoist in agreement with himself. And my conscience is also a "voice of nature".

In this connection it also turns out that the animal "takes very correct steps". (P. 213.) We learn further that "freedom is silent about what should happen after I have become free". (P. 215.) (See "Solomon's Song of Songs".[b]) The exposition of the above-mentioned "deeper gulf" is closed by Saint Sancho repeating the scene with the blows and this time expressing himself somewhat more clearly about peculiarity:

"Even when unfree, even bound by a thousand fetters, I nevertheless exist, and I exist not only just in the future, and in the hope, like freedom, but even as the most abject of slaves I am present." (P. 215.)

Here, therefore, he counterposes *himself* and "*freedom*" as two persons, and peculiarity becomes mere existence, being present, and indeed the "most abject" presence. Peculiarity here is the simple registering of personal identity. Stirner, who

---

[a] See this volume, pp. 238-40.— *Ed.*
[b] See this volume, pp. 459-61.— *Ed.*

in an earlier passage has already constituted himself the "secret police state", here sets himself up as the passport department. "By no means" should "anything be lost" from "the world of human beings!" (See "Solomon's Song of Songs".)

According to page 218, one can also "give up" one's peculiarity through "submissiveness", "submission", although, according to the preceding, peculiarity cannot cease so long as one is *present* at all, even in the most "abject" or "submissive" form. And is not the "most abject" slave the "most submissive"? According to one of the earlier descriptions of peculiarity, one can only "give up" one's peculiarity by giving up one's *life*.

On page 218, peculiarity as one aspect of freedom, as power, is once again set against freedom as riddance; and among the means by which Sancho pretends to protect his peculiarity, are mentioned "hypocrisy", "deception" (means which my peculiarity employs, because it had to "submit" to the conditions of the world), etc.,

"for the means that I employ are determined by what I am".

We have already seen that among these means the *absence* of any means plays a major role, as was evident also from his proceedings against the moon (see above "Logic"[a]).Then, for a change, freedom is regarded as "*self-liberation*", "i. e., that I can only have as much freedom as I procure by my peculiarity", where the definition of freedom as *self-determination*, which occurs among all, and particularly German, ideologists, makes its appearance as peculiarity. This is then explained to us on the example of "sheep" to whom it is of no "use" at all "if they are given freedom of speech". (P. 220.) How trivial is his conception here of peculiarity as self-liberation is evident if only from his repetition of the most hackneyed phrases about granted freedom, setting free, self-liberation, etc. (Pp. 220, 221.) The antithesis between freedom as riddance and peculiarity as the negation of this riddance is now also portrayed poetically:

"Freedom arouses your wrath against everything that you are not" (it is, therefore, *wrathful* peculiarity, or have choleric natures, e. g., Guizot, in Saint Sancho's opinion, no "peculiarity"? And do I not enjoy myself in wrath against others?), "egoism calls on you to *rejoice* over yourself, to delight in yourself" (hence egoism is freedom which rejoices; incidentally, we have already become acquainted with the joy and self-enjoyment of the egoist in agreement with himself).

---

[a] See this volume, p. 316.— *Ed.*

"Freedom is and remains a longing" (as though longing were not also a peculiarity, the self-enjoyment of individuals of a particular nature, especially of Christian-German individuals — and should this longing "be lost"?). "Peculiarity is a reality which *of itself* abolishes all the non-freedom which is an impediment and blocks your own path" (in which case, then, until non-freedom is abolished my peculiarity is a *blocked* peculiarity. It is characteristic again of the German petty bourgeois that for him all barriers and obstacles disappear "of themselves", since he never lifts a finger to achieve it, and by habit he turns those barriers which do not disappear "of themselves" into his peculiarity. It may be remarked in passing that peculiarity appears here as an acting *person*, although it is later demoted to a mere *description* of its owner). (P. 215.)

The same antithesis appears again in the following form:

"As being *your own, you are in actuality rid of everything*, and what remains with you, you have yourself accepted, it is your choice and option. One who is his own is *born free*, one who is free on the other hand is only one who desires freedom."

Nevertheless Saint Sancho "admits" on page 252

"that each *is born* as a *human being*; hence in this respect the newborn children are equal".

What you as being your own have not "rid yourself of" is "your choice and option", as in the case of the beatings of the slave mentioned above.— Banal paraphrase! — Here, therefore, peculiarity is reduced to the fantastic idea that Saint Sancho has voluntarily accepted and retained everything from which he has not "rid" himself, e. g., hunger when he has no money. Apart from the many things, e. g., dialect, scrofula, haemorrhoids, poverty, one-leggedness, forced philosophising imposed on him by division of labour, etc., etc.— apart from the fact that it in no way depends on him whether he "accepts" these things or not; all the same, even if for an instant we accept his premises, he has only the choice between definite things which lie within his province and which are in no way posited by his peculiarity. As an Irish peasant, for example, he can only choose to eat potatoes or starve, and he is not always free to make even this choice. In the sentence quoted above one should note also the beautiful apposition, by which, just as in jurisprudence, "acceptance" is directly identified with "choice" and "option". Incidentally, it is impossible to say what Saint Sancho means by one who is "born free", whether in the context or outside it.

And is not a feeling instilled into him, his feeling accepted by him? And do we not learn on pages 84, 85, that "instilled" feelings are not "one's own" feelings? For the rest, it turns out here, as we have already seen in connection with Klopstock[a] (who is put forward here as an example), that "one's own" behaviour by no means coincides with individual behaviour, although for Klopstock Christianity seems to have been "quite right" and in no way to have "obstructively blocked his path".

"One who is his own does not *need to free himself*, because from the outset he rejects everything except himself.... Although he remains in the confines of childish reverence, he already *works* to '*free*' himself from this enthralment."

Since one who is his own does not *need* to free himself, already as a child he works to free himself, and all this because, as we have seen, he is one who is "*born free*". "Although he remains in the confines of childish reverence" he already reflects without any restraint, namely in his own fashion, about this his own enthralment. But this should not surprise us: we already saw at the beginning of the Old Testament what a prodigy the egoist in agreement with himself was.

"*Peculiarity works in the little egoist* and *secures* him the desired 'freedom.'"

It is not "Stirner" who lives, it is "peculiarity" that lives, "works" and "secures" *in* him. Here we learn that peculiarity is not a *description* of one who is his own, but that one who is his own is merely a *paraphrase* of peculiarity.

As we have seen, "riddance" at its climax was riddance from one's own self, self-denial. We saw also that on the other hand he put forward "peculiarity" as the assertion of self, as self-interestedness. But we have seen likewise that this self-interestedness itself was again self-denial.

For some time past we have been painfully aware that "the holy" was missing. But we rediscover it suddenly, on page 224, at the end of the section on peculiarity, where it stands quite bashfully and proves its identity by means of the following new turn of expression:

"My relation to something which I selfishly carry on" (or do not carry on at all) "is *different* from my relation to something which I unselfishly serve" (or which I carry on).

But Saint Max is not satisfied with this remarkable piece of tautology, which he "accepted" from "choice and option"; there

---

[a] See this volume, pp. 301-02.— *Ed.*

suddenly reappears the long forgotten "one", in the shape of
the night watchman who establishes the identity of the holy, and
declares that he

"could put forward the following distinguishing mark: against the former I
can *sin* or commit a *sin*" (a remarkable tautology!), "the other I can only *lose by
my folly*, push away from myself, deprive myself of it, i. e., do something
stupid" (it follows that he can lose himself by his folly, can deprive himself of
himself, can be deprived of himself — can be deprived of life). "Both these
points of view are applicable to *freedom of trade*, because it" is partly taken for
the holy and partly not so taken, or, as Sancho himself expresses it more
circumstantially, "because it is partly regarded as a freedom which can be
granted or withdrawn *depending on circumstances*, and partly as a freedom
which should be regarded as *holy under all circumstances*." (Pp. 224, 225.)

Here again Sancho reveals his "peculiar" "penetration" into
the question of freedom of trade and protective tariffs. He is
herewith given the "vocation" of pointing out just one single
case where freedom of trade was regarded as "holy" 1) *because*
it is a "*freedom*", and 2) "*under all circumstances*". The holy
comes in useful for all purposes.

After peculiarity, by means of logical antitheses and the
phenomenological "being-also-otherwise-determined", has been
constructed, as we have seen, from a "freedom" previously
trimmed up for the purpose — Saint Sancho meanwhile having
"dismissed" everything that happened to suit him (e. g.,
beatings) into peculiarity, and whatever did not suit him into
freedom — we learn finally that all this was still not true
peculiarity.

"Peculiarity," it is stated on page 225, "is not at all an *idea*, such as freedom,
etc., it is only a description — of the *owner*."

We shall see that this "description of the owner" consists in
negating freedom in the three refractions which Saint Sancho
ascribes to it — liberalism, communism and humanism — comprehending it in its *truth* and then calling this process of thought,
which is extremely simple according to advanced logic, the
description of a real ego.

The entire chapter about peculiarity boils down to the most
trivial self-embellishments by means of which the German petty
bourgeois consoles himself for his own impotence. Exactly like
Sancho, he thinks that in the struggle of bourgeois interests

against the remnants of feudalism and absolute monarchy in other countries everything turns merely on a question of principles, on the question of *from what* "Man" should free himself. (See also above on political liberalism [a].) Therefore in freedom of trade he sees only a freedom and, exactly like Sancho, expatiates with a great air of importance about whether "Man" ought to enjoy freedom of trade "under all circumstances" or not. And when, as is inevitable in such conditions, his aspirations for freedom suffer a miserable collapse, then, again like Sancho, he consoles himself that "Man", or he himself, cannot "become free from everything", that freedom is a highly indefinite concept, and that even Metternich and Charles X were able to appeal to "true freedom" (p. 210 of "the book"; and it need only be remarked here that it is precisely the reactionaries, especially the Historical School and the Romanticists[85] who — again just like Sancho — reduce true freedom to peculiarity, for instance, to the peculiarity of the Tyrolean peasants, and in general, to the peculiar development of individuals, and also of localities, provinces and estates).— The petty bourgeois also consoles himself that as a German, even if he is not free, he finds compensation for all sufferings in his own indisputable peculiarity. Again like Sancho, he does not see in freedom a power that he is able to obtain and therefore declares his own impotence to be power.

What the ordinary German petty bourgeois whispers to himself as a consolation, in the quiet depths of his mind, the Berliner trumpets out loudly as an ingenious turn of thought. He is proud of his trashy peculiarity and his peculiar trashiness.

5. THE OWNER

For the way in which the "owner" is divided into three "refractions": "my power", "my intercourse" and "my self-enjoyment", see "The Economy of the New Testament". We shall pass directly to the first of these refractions.

A. My Power

The chapter on power has in its turn a trichotomous structure in that it treats of: 1) right, 2) law, and 3) crime. In order to

---

[a] See this volume, pp. 215-17.— *Ed.*

conceal this trichotomy, Sancho resorts very frequently to the "episode". We give here the entire content in tabular form, with the necessary episodical insertions.

I. Right

A. Canonisation in General

Another example of the *holy* is *right*.
Right is not ego
    =not my right
    =alien right
    =existing right.
All existing right =alien right
    =right *of others* (not my right)   The holy
    =right given by others
    =(right which *one* gives me,
        which is meted out to me).
    (Pp. 244, 245.)

Note No. 1. The reader will wonder why the conclusion of equation No. 4 suddenly appears in equation No. 5 as the antecedent of the conclusion of equation No. 3, so that in the place of "right", "all existing right" suddenly appears as the antecedent. This is done to create the illusion that Saint Sancho is speaking of *actual*, existing right which, however, he by no means intends to do. He speaks of right only insofar as it is represented to be a holy "predicate".

Note No. 2. After right has been determined as "alien right", it can be given any names you like, such as "Sultan's right", "people's right", etc., depending on how Saint Sancho wishes to define the alien from whom he receives the right in question. This allows Sancho to go on to say that "alien right is given by nature, God, popular choice, etc." (p. 250), hence "not by me". What is naïve is only the method by which our saint through the use of synonymy tries to give some semblance of development to the above simple equations.

"If some blockhead considers me right" (what if he himself is the blockhead who considers him right?), "I begin to be mistrustful of my right" (it would be desirable in "Stirner's" interests that this were so). "But even if a wise man considers me right, this still does not mean that I am right. Whether I am right is quite independent of my being acknowledged right by fools or wise men. Nevertheless, up to now we have striven for *this right*. We seek *right* and to this end we appeal to the *court*.... But what do I seek from this court? I seek Sultan's right, not my right, I seek alien right ... before the high court of censorship I seek, therefore, the right of censorship." (Pp. 244, 245.)

One has to admire the cunning use of synonymy in this masterly proposition. Recognition of right in the ordinary conversational sense is identified with recognition of right in the juridical sense. Even more worthy of admiration is the faith capable of moving mountains in the idea that one "appeals to the court" for the sake of the pleasure of vindicating one's right — a faith which explains that courts are due to litigiousness.*

Notable, finally, is also the craftiness with which Sancho — as in the case of equation No. 5 above — smuggles in, *in advance*, the more concrete name, in this case "Sultan's right", in order to be able more confidently *later* to bring in his universal category of "alien right".

Alien right	=not my right.
My being right according to alien right	=not to be right
	=*to have no right*
	=to be *rightless*. (P. 247.)
My right	=not your right
	= *your wrong*.
Your right	=my wrong.

Note. "You desire to be in the right against others" (it should read: to be in your right). "You cannot be this, in relation to them you will always remain in the 'wrong', *for* they would not be your opponents if they were not also in 'their' right. They will always 'consider' you 'wrong'.... If you remain on the basis of right, then you remain on the basis of litigiousness." (Pp. 248, 253.)

"Let us in the meantime consider the subject from yet another aspect." Having thus given adequate evidence of his knowledge

---

* [The following passage is crossed out in the manuscript:] What idea Saint Jacques le bonhomme really has of a court can even be deduced from the fact that as an illustration he mentions the high court of censorship, which at best can only be regarded as a court according to Prussian notions; a court which can merely introduce administrative measures, but is unable either to inflict penalties or to settle civil suits. What does it matter to a saint who is always concerned with *real* individuals, that two completely different systems of production form the basis of the individuals where court and administration are separate, and where they are combined in a patriarchal way.

The above equations are now transformed into the moral injunctions "vocation", "designation", and "task", which Saint Max shouts in a thunderous voice to his faithful servant Szeliga, who has an uneasy conscience. Like a Prussian non-commissioned officer (his own "gendarme" speaks through his mouth) Saint Max addresses Szeliga in the third person: he should see to it that his right to eat remains uncurtailed, etc. The *right* of the proletarians to eat has never been "curtailed", nevertheless it happens "of itself" that they are very often unable to "exercise" it.

of right, Saint Sancho can now restrict himself to defining right once again as the holy, in this connection repeating some of the epithets previously given to the holy with the addition of the word "right".

"Is not right a *religious concept*, i. e., something *holy*?" (P. 247.)

"Who can ask about 'right' if he does not have a *religious standpoint*?" (Ibid.)

"Right '*in and for itself*'. Therefore without relation to me? '*Absolute right*!' Therefore separated from me. — Something '*being in and for itself*'! — An *Absolute*! An *eternal* right, like an eternal truth"—the *holy*. (P. 270.)

"You recoil in horror before others because you imagine you see by their side the *spectre of right*!" (P. 253.)

"You creep about in order to win the *apparition* over to your side." (Ibid.)

"Right is a *whimsy*, dispensed by an *apparition*" (the synthesis of the two propositions given above). (P. 276.)

"Right is ... *a fixed idea*." (P. 270.)

"Right is *spirit*...." (P. 244.)

"Because right can be dispensed only by a *spirit*." (P. 275.)

Saint Sancho now expounds again what he already expounded in the Old Testament, viz., what a "fixed idea" is, with the only difference that here "right" crops up everywhere as "another example" of the "fixed idea".

"Right is originally my thought, or it" [a] (!) "has its origin in me. But if it[a] has escaped from me" (in common parlance, absconded), "if the 'word' has been uttered, then it has become *flesh*" [b] (and Saint Sancho can eat his fill of it), "a *fixed idea*" — for which reason Stirner's whole book consists of "fixed ideas", which have "escaped" from him, but have been caught by us and confined in the much-praised "house for the correction of morals". "*Now* I can no longer get rid of the idea" (after the idea has got rid *of him*!); "however I twist and turn, it confronts me." (The pigtail, which hangs down behind him.[c]) "*Thus*, people have been unable to regain control of the idea of 'right' that they themselves have created. Their creature runs away with them. *That is absolute right, which is absolved*" (O synonymy!) "and *detached* from me. Since we worship it as Absolute, we cannot devour it again and it deprives us of our creative power; the creation is more than the creator, it exists in and for itself. Do not allow right to run about freely any longer...." (We shall already in this sentence follow this advice and chain it up for the time being.) (P. 270.)

Having thus dragged right through all possible ordeals of sanctification by fire and water and canonised it, Saint Sancho has thereby destroyed it.

"With absolute right, *right itself disappears*, at the same time the *domination of the concept of right*" (hierarchy) "is wiped out. *For* one should not forget that

---

[a] The German pronoun *er*, used in Stirner's book, refers to "my thought".— *Ed.*

[b] Cf. John 1:14.— *Ed.*

[c] The words are from Chamisso's poem "Tragische Geschichte". — *Ed.*

concepts, ideas, and principles have up to now ruled over us and that among these *rulers* the concept of right *or* the concept of justice has played one of the most important parts." (P. 276.)

That relations of right here once again appear as the domination of the *concept* of right and that Stirner kills right simply by declaring it a concept, and therefore the holy, is something to which we are already accustomed; on this see "Hierarchy".[a] Right [according to Stirner] does not arise from the material relations of people and the resulting antagonism of people against one another, but from their struggle against their own concept, which they should "get out of their heads". See "Logic".[b]

This last form of the canonisation of right comprises also the following three notes:

Note 1.

"So long as this *alien* right coincides with *mine*, I shall, of course, find the latter *also* in it." (P. 245.)

Saint Sancho might ponder awhile over this proposition.

Note 2.

"If once an *egoistic interest* crept in, then society was corrupted ... as is shown, for example, by the Roman society with its highly developed *civil law*." (P. 278.)

According to this, Roman society from the very outset must have been *corrupted* Roman society, since egoistic interest is manifested in the Ten Tables[86] even more sharply than in the "highly developed civil law" of the imperial epoch. In this unfortunate reminiscence from Hegel, therefore, civil *law* is considered a symptom of *egoism*, and not of the *holy*. Here, too, Saint Sancho might well reflect on the extent to which civil *law* [Privat*recht*] is linked with private *property* [Privat*eigentum*] and to what extent civil law implies a multitude of other legal relations (cf. "Private Property, State and Right"[c]) about which Saint Max has nothing to say except that they are the holy.

Note 3.

"*Although* right is derived from the *concept, nevertheless* it only comes into *existence* because it *serves* men's needs."

So says Hegel (*Rechtsphilosophie*,[d] para. 209, Addition) from whom our saint derived the hierarchy of concepts in the modern

[a] See this volume, pp. 194-95, 197-98.— *Ed.*
[b] See this volume, p. 298-99, 303-05.— *Ed.*
[c] See this volume, p. 375.— *Ed.*
[d] G.W.F. Hegel, *Grundlinien der Philosophie des Rechts.*— *Ed.*

world. Hegel, therefore, explains the *existence* of right from the empirical *needs* of individuals, and rescues the *concept* only by means of a simple assertion. One can see how infinitely more materialistically Hegel proceeds than our "corporeal ego", Saint Sancho.

B. Appropriation by Simple Antithesis

a) The right of man	—	My right.
b) Human right	—	Egoistic right.
c) Alien right=to be author-⎰ ised by others ⎱	—	⎰My right=to be ⎱authorised by myself.
d) Right is that which man⎰ considers right ⎱	—	⎰Right is that which ⎱I consider right.

"This is egoistic right, i. e., I consider it right, therefore, it is right" (*passim*; the last sentence is on p. 251).

Note 1.

"I am authorised by myself to commit murder if I do not forbid myself to do so, if I myself am not afraid of murder as a wrong." (P. 249.)

This should read: I *commit murder* if I do not forbid myself to do so, if I am not *afraid* of murder. This whole proposition is a boastful expansion of the second equation in antithesis c, where the word "authorised" has lost its meaning.

Note 2.

"I decide whether it is right *within me; outside me,* no right exists." (P. 249.)— "Are we what is *in us*? No, no more than we are what is outside us.... Precisely because we are not the spirit which dwells *in us,* for that very reason we had to transfer it *outside us* ... think of it as existing *outside us ... in the beyond.*" (P. 43.)

Thus, according to his own statement on page 43, Saint Sancho has again to transfer the right "in him" to "outside himself", and indeed "into the beyond". But if at some stage he wants to appropriate things for himself in this fashion, then he can transfer "into himself" morality, religion, everything "holy", and decide whether "in him" it is the moral, the religious, the holy — "outside him there exists no" morality, religion, holiness — in order thereupon to transfer them, according to page 43, again outside himself, into the beyond. Thereby the "restoration of all things"[a] according to the Christian model is brought about.

---

[a] Mark 9:12.— *Ed.*

Note 3.

"Outside me no right exists. If I consider it right then it is right. It is possible that it is still not on that account right for others." (P. 249.)

This should read: If I consider it right then it is right for me, but it is still not right for others. We have by now had sufficient examples of the sort of synonymical "flea-jumps" Saint Sancho makes with the word "right". The right and right, legal "right", moral "right", what he considers "right", etc. — all are used higgledy-piggledy, as it suits him. Let Saint Max attempt to translate his propositions about right into another language; his nonsense would then become fully apparent. Since this synonymy was dealt with exhaustively in "The Logic [of the New Wisdom]", we need here only refer to that section.[a]

The proposition mentioned above is also presented in the following three "transformations":

A. "Whether I am right or not, of that there can be no other judge than I myself. Others can judge and decide only whether they agree with my right and whether it exists as right also for them." (P. 246.)

B. "It is true that society wants *each person* to attain his right, but only right sanctioned by society, social right, and not actually *his* right" (it should read: "what is *his*" — "right" is a quite meaningless word here. And then he continues boastfully:) "I, however, give myself, or take for myself, right on my own authority.... Owner and creator of my right" ("creator" only insofar as he first declares right to be his thought and then asserts that he has taken this thought back into himself), "I recognise no other source of right but myself — neither God, nor the state, nor nature, nor man, neither divine nor human right." (P. 269.)

C. "Since *human* right is always something given, in reality it always amounts to the right which people *give* to, i. e., *concede*, one another." (P. 251.)

Egoistical right, on the other hand, is the right which *I give myself* or *take*.

However, "let us say in conclusion, it can be seen" that in Sancho's millennium egoistical right, about which people "*came to terms*" with each other, is not so very different from that which people "*give to*" or "*concede*" one another.

Note 4.

"In conclusion, I have now still to take back the half-and-half mode of expression which I *desired* to use only while I was delving into the bowels of right and allowed at least the *word* to remain. In point of fact, however, together with the concept the word loses its meaning. What I called *my* right, is no longer right at all." (P. 275.)

Everyone will see at a glance why Saint Sancho allowed the "*word*" right to remain in the above antitheses. For as he does

---

[a] See this volume, p. 291-94.— *Ed.*

not speak at all about the *content* of right, let alone criticise it, he can only by retaining the *word* right make it appear that he is speaking about right. If the *word* right is left out of the *anti*thesis, all that it contains is "I", "my" and the other grammatical forms of the first person pronoun. The content was always introduced only by means of examples which, however, as we have seen, were nothing but tautologies, such as: if I commit murder, then I commit murder, etc., and in which the words "right", "authorised", etc., were introduced only to conceal the simple tautology and give it some sort of connection with the antitheses. The *synonymy*, too, was intended to create the appearance of dealing with some sort of content. Incidentally, one can see at once what a rich source of *bragging* this empty chatter about right provides.

Thus, all the "delving into the bowels of right" amounted to this, that Saint Sancho "made use of a half-and-half mode of expression" and "allowed at least the *word* to remain", because he was unable to say anything about the *subject itself*. If the antithesis is to have any meaning, that is to say, if "Stirner" simply wanted to demonstrate in it his repugnance to right, then one must say rather that it was not he who "delved into the bowels of right", but that right "delved" into *his* bowels and that he merely recorded the fact that right is not to his liking. "Keep this right uncurtailed", Jacques le bonhomme!

To introduce some sort of content into this void, Saint Sancho has to undertake yet another logical manoeuvre, which with great "virtuosity" he thoroughly shuffles together with canonisation and the simple antithesis, and so completely masks with numerous episodes that the German public and German philosophers, at any rate, were unable to see through it.

C. Appropriation by Compound Antithesis

"Stirner" now has to introduce an empirical definition of right, which he can ascribe to the individual, i. e., he has to recognise something else in right besides holiness. In this connection, he could have spared himself all his clumsy machinations, since, starting with Machiavelli, Hobbes, Spinoza, Bodinus and others of modern times, not to mention earlier ones, might has been represented as the basis of right. Thereby the theoretical view of politics was freed from morality, and apart from the postulate of an independent treatment of politics nothing was accepted. Later, in the eighteenth century in France and in the nineteenth century in

England, all right was reduced to civil law (which Saint Max does not discuss) and the latter to a quite definite power, the power of the owners of private property. Moreover, the matter was by no means left at a mere phrase.

Thus Saint Sancho draws the definition of *might* from *right* and explains it as follows:

"We are in the habit of classifying states according to the various ways in which the 'supreme *power*' is divided ... hence, the supreme power! Power over whom? Over the individual.... The state uses force ... the behaviour of the state is *exercise of force*, and it calls its force *right*.... The collective as a whole ... has a power which is called rightful, i. e., which is right." (Pp. 259, 260.)

Through "our" "habit", our saint arrives at his longed-for power and can now "look after"[a] himself.

Right, the might of man — might, my right.
Intermediate equations:
> To be authorised=To be empowered.
> To authorise oneself=To empower oneself.

Antithesis:
> To be authorised by man — To be empowered by me.

First antithesis:
> Right, might of man — Might, my right

now becomes converted into:

$$Right\ of\ man\ -\ \begin{cases} Might\ of\ me, \\ My\ might, \end{cases}$$

because in the thesis right and might are identical, and in the antithesis the "half-and-half mode of expression" has to be "taken back", since right, as we have seen, has "lost all meaning".

Note 1. Examples of bombastic and boastful paraphrases of the above antitheses and equations:

"What you have the power to be, you have the right to be." "I derive all right and all authority from *myself*, I am *authorised* to do everything which I have the *power* to do."—"I do not demand any right, and therefore I need recognise none. What I can obtain for myself by force, I obtain for myself, and what I cannot obtain by force, to that I have no right either, etc.—It is a matter of indifference to me whether I am authorised or not; if only I have the *power*, then I am already *empowered* as a matter of course and do not need any other power or authority." (Pp. 248, 275.)

Note 2. Examples of the way in which Saint Sancho expounds might as the real basis of right:

---

[a] In the German original a pun on the word *pflegen*, which can mean to be in the habit, to be accustomed to and to look after, to take care of.— *Ed.*

"Thus, 'the communists' say" (how on earth does "Stirner" know what the communists say, since he has never set eyes on anything concerning them except the Bluntschli report,[a] Becker's *Volksphilosophie* and a few other things?): "Equal work gives people the right to equal enjoyment.... No, equal work does not give you this right, only equal enjoyment gives you the right to equal enjoyment. Enjoy, and you are entitled to enjoyment.... If you take enjoyment, then it is your right; if, on the other hand, you only yearn for it, without seizing it, it will remain as before the 'established right' of those who have the privilege of enjoyment. It is their right, just as it would become your right, by your seizing it." (P. 250.)

Compare what is here put into the mouth of the communists with what was previously said about "communism". Saint Sancho again presents the proletarians here as a "closed society", which has only to take the decision of "seizing" in order the next day to put a summary end to the entire hitherto existing world order. But in reality the proletarians arrive at this unity only through a long process of development in which the appeal to their right also plays a part. Incidentally, this appeal to their right is only a means of making them take shape as "they", as a revolutionary, united mass.

As for the above proposition itself, from start to finish it is a brilliant example of tautology, as is at once clear if one omits both might and right, which can be done without any harm to the content. Secondly, Saint Sancho himself distinguishes between personal and material property,[b] thereby making a distinction between enjoying and the power to enjoy. I may have great *personal* power (capacity) of enjoyment without necessarily having the corresponding *material* power (money, etc.). Thus my actual "enjoyment" still remains hypothetical.

"That the child of royalty sets himself above other children," continues our school-master, using examples suitable for a child's book, "is already his act, one which ensures his superiority, and that other children recognise and approve this act is *their* act, which makes them deserving of being subjects." (P. 250.)

In this example, the social relation in which the royal child stands to other children is regarded as the power and indeed as the *personal* power of the royal child, and as the impotence of other children. If the fact that other children allow themselves to be commanded by the royal child is regarded as the "*act*" of the other children, this proves at most that they are egoists. "Peculiarity is at work in the little egoists" and induces them to exploit the royal child, to extract an advantage from him.

---

[a] Johann Caspar Bluntschli, "Die Kommunisten in der Schweiz nach den bei Weitling vorgefundenen Papieren".— *Ed.*

[b] In the original *Vermögen*, which can mean both ability, faculty, power and means, fortune, property.— *Ed.*

"It is said" (i. e., Hegel said) "that punishment is the right of the criminal.[a] But impunity is equally his right. If he succeeds in his undertakings, he gets his right, and if he fails it equally serves him right. If someone with reckless courage puts himself in danger and is killed, we say: it serves him right, he asked for it. But if he overcomes the danger, i. e., if his *power* is victorious, it appears he is also *right*. If a child plays with a knife and cuts himself, it serves him right; if he does not cut himself, that is also all right. Therefore it serves the criminal right if he suffers the penalty he risked; why did he take the risk, knowing the possible consequences?" (P. 255.)

In the concluding words of the last sentence, where the criminal is asked why he took the risk, the school-masterish nonsense of the whole passage is latent. Whether it serves a criminal right if on burgling a house he falls down and breaks his leg, or a child who cuts himself — all these important questions, with which only a man like Saint Sancho is capable of occupying himself, yield only the result that here *chance* is declared to be my power. Thus, in the first example it was my action that was "my power", in the second example it was social relations independent of me, in the third it was chance. But we have already encountered these contradictory definitions in connection with peculiarity.

Between the above childish examples Sancho inserts the following amusing little intermezzo:

"*For otherwise* right would be a humbug. The tiger who attacks me is right and I, who kill it, am also right. I am protecting against it not my right, but myself." (P. 251.)

In the first part of this passage Saint Sancho sets himself in a relation of right to the tiger, but in the second part it occurs to him that basically no relation of right is involved at all. *For that reason* "right" appears to "be a humbug". The right of "Man" merges into the right of the "Tiger".

This concludes the criticism of right. Long after having learned from hundreds of earlier writers that right originated from force, we now learn from Saint Sancho that "right" is "the power of man". Thus he has successfully eliminated all questions about the connection between right and *real* people and their relations, and has established his antithesis. He restricts himself to abolishing right in the form in which he posits it, namely, as the holy, i. e., he restricts himself to abolishing the holy and leaving right untouched.

This criticism of right is embellished with a host of

---

[a] G.W.F. Hegel, *Grundlinien der Philosophie des Rechts*, I. Theil, 3. Abschnitt.— *Ed.*

episodes — all sorts of things which people are "in the habit" of discussing at Stehely's between two and four in the afternoon.
Episode 1. "The right of man" and *"established right".*

"When the revolution made 'equality' into a 'right', it [the revolution] fled into the *religious* sphere, into the domain of the *holy,* the *ideal. Therefore* a struggle has been waged ever since over the holy, inalienable rights of man. Quite naturally and with equal justification, the 'established right of the existing' is asserted against the eternal right of man; right against right, and of course each of these condemns the other as a wrong. Such has been the dispute over right since the revolution." (P. 248.)

Here Saint Sancho first of all repeats that the rights of man are "the holy" and that *t h e r e f o r e* a struggle over the rights of man has been waged ever since. Thereby he only proves that the material basis of this struggle is still, for him, holy, i. e., alien.

Since the "right of man" and "established right" are both "rights", they are "equally justified" and here in fact "justified" in the *historical* sense. Since both are "rights" in the *legal* sense, they are "equally justified" in the *historical* sense. In this way one can dispose of everything in the shortest space of time without knowing anything about the matter. Thus, for example, it can be said of the struggle over the Corn Laws in England: "quite naturally and with equal justification" rent, which is also profit (gain), is "asserted" against the profit (gain) [of the manufacturers], gain against gain, and "of course each of these decries the other. Such has been the struggle" over the Corn Laws in England since 1815.[87]

Incidentally, Stirner might have said from the outset: existing right is the right of man, human right. In certain circles one is also "in the habit" of calling it "established right". Where then is the difference between the "right of man" and "established right"?

We already know that alien, holy right is what is given to me by others. But since the rights of man are also called natural, innate rights, and since for Saint Sancho the name is the thing itself, it follows that they are rights which are mine by nature, i. e., by birth.

But "established rights amount to *the same thing,* namely to nature, which gives me a right, that is to birth *and, furthermore,* to inheritance", and *so* on. "I am born as a man is equivalent to saying: I am born as a king's son."

This is on pages 249, 250, where Babeuf is reproached for not having had this dialectical talent for dissolving differences. Since "under all circumstances", the "ego" is "also" man, as Saint Sancho later concedes, and therefore has the benefit "also" of what it has as man, just as the ego, for instance, as a

Berliner has the benefit of the Berlin Tiergarten,[a] so "also" the ego has the benefit of the right of man "under all circumstances". But since he is by no means born a "king's son" "under all circumstances", he by no means has the benefit of "established right" "under all circumstances". In the sphere of right, therefore, there is an essential difference between the "right of man" and "established right". If it had not been necessary for Saint Sancho to conceal his logic it "should have been said here": After I have, in my opinion, dissolved the concept of right, in the way in which I am generally "in the habit" of dissolving concepts, the struggle over these two special rights becomes a struggle within a concept which, in my opinion, has been dissolved by me, and "therefore" does not need to be touched upon any further by me.

For greater thoroughness Saint Sancho could have added the following new turn of expression: *The right of man* too is acquired, hence *well acquired*, and *well-acquired* [i. e., established] *right* is the human right possessed by men, *the right of man.*

That such concepts, if they are divorced from the empirical reality underlying them, can be turned inside-out like a glove[b] has already been thoroughly enough proved by Hegel, whose use of this method, as against the abstract ideologists, was justified. Saint Sancho, therefore, has no need to make it appear ridiculous by his own "clumsy" "machinations".

So far established right and the right of man "have amounted to *the same thing*", so that Saint Sancho could reduce to nothing a struggle that exists outside his mind, in history. Now our saint proves that he is as keen-witted in drawing distinctions as he is all-powerful in heaping everything together, in order to be able to bring about a new terrible struggle in the "creative nothing" of his head.

"I am also ready to admit" (magnanimous Sancho) "that everyone is born as a human being" (hence, according to the above-mentioned reproach against Babeuf, also as a "king's son"), "hence, the *newly born* are in this respect *equal* to one another ... only because as yet they reveal themselves and act as nothing but mere children of men, naked little human beings." On the other hand, adults are the "children of their own creation". They "possess more than merely innate rights, they have *acquired* rights".

(Does Stirner believe that the infant emerged from the mother's womb without any act of his own, an act by which he

---

[a] A park in Berlin.— *Ed.*
[b] Cf. William Shakespeare, *Twelfth Night*, Act III, Scene 1.— *Ed.*

acquired the "right" to be outside the mother's womb; and does not every child from the very beginning reveal himself and act as a "unique" child?)

"What a contradiction, what a battlefield! The old battle of innate rights and established rights!" (P. 252.)

What a battle of bearded men against babes!

Incidentally, Sancho speaks against the rights of man only because "in recent times" it has again become "customary" to speak against them. In fact he has "acquired" these innate rights of man. In connection with peculiarity we already met the man who is "born free"[a]; there Sancho made peculiarity the innate right of man, because merely by being born he revealed himself as being free and acted as such. Furthermore: "Every ego is already *from birth* a criminal against the state", whereby a crime against the state becomes an innate right of man, and the child already commits a crime against something that does not yet exist for him, but for which he exists. Finally, "Stirner" speaks further on about "*innately* limited intellects", "*born* poets", "*born* musicians", etc. Since here the power (musical, poetic *resp.* limited *ability*) is innate, and right=power, one sees how "Stirner" claims for the "ego" the innate rights of man, although this time equality does not figure among these rights.

Episode 2. Privileges and equal rights. Our Sancho first of all transforms the struggle over privilege and equal right into a struggle over the mere "*c o n c e p t s*" privileged and equal. In this way he saves himself the trouble of having to know anything about the medieval mode of production, the political expression of which was privilege, and the modern mode of production, of which *right* as such, *equal right*, is the expression, or about the relation of these two modes of production to the legal relations which correspond to them. He can even reduce the two above-mentioned "concepts" to the still simpler expression: equal and unequal, and prove that one and the same thing (e. g., other people, a dog, etc.) may, according to circumstances, be a matter of indifference — i. e., of equanimity, equality, or it may not be a matter of indifference — i. e., it may be different, unequal, preferred, etc., etc.

"Let the brother of low degree rejoice in that he is exalted." (Saint-Jacques le bonhomme 1:9.)[b]

---

[a] See this volume, p. 330.— *Ed.*
[b] James 1:9.— *Ed.*

II. Law

Here we must disclose to the reader a great secret of our saint, viz., that he begins his whole treatise about right with a general explanation of right, which "escapes" from him so long as he is speaking about right, and which he is only able to recapture when he begins to speak about something totally different, namely—law. Then the gospel called out to our saint: judge not, that ye be not judged[a]— and he opened his mouth and taught, saying:

"*Right is the spirit of society.*"(But society is the holy.) "*If* society has a will, *then* this will is *indeed* right: *society exists only* thanks to right. But *since* it *exists only thanks to the fact*" (not thanks to right, but *only* thanks to the fact) "that it exercises its *domination* over individuals, *so* right is its *dominant* will." (P. 244.)

That is to say: "*right* ... is ... has ... then ... indeed ... exists only ... since ... exists only thanks to the fact ... that ... so ... *dominant will*". This passage is Sancho in all his perfection.

This passage "escaped" at that time from our saint because it was not suitable for his theses, and has now been partially recaptured because it is now partially suitable again.

"States endure so long as there is a *dominant will* and this *dominant will* is regarded as equivalent to one's own will. The will of the ruler is law." (P. 256.)

The dominant will of society =right,
Dominant will =law —
Right =law.

"Sometimes", i. e., as the trade mark of his "treatise" about law, there will still turn out to be a distinction between right and law, a distinction which—strange to say—has almost as little to do with his "treatise" about law as the definition of right which "escaped" from him has to do with the "treatise" about "right":

"But what is *right*, what is considered legitimate in a society, is *also* given a verbal expression—in *law*." (P. 255.)

This proposition is a "clumsy" copy of Hegel:

"That which is lawful is the source of the knowledge of what is right or, properly, what is legitimate."

What Saint Sancho calls "receiving verbal expression", Hegel also calls: "posited", "known", etc., *Rechtsphilosophie*, para 211 et seq.

---

[a] Matthew 7:1.— *Ed.*

It is very easy to understand why Saint Sancho had to exclude right as the "will" or the "dominant will" of society from his "treatise" about right. Only to the extent that *right* was defined as man's *power* could he take it back into himself as *his power*. For the sake of his antithesis, therefore, he had to hold fast to the materialistic definition of "power" and let the idealistic definition of "*will*" "escape". Why, when speaking of "law", he now recaptures "will" we shall understand in connection with the antitheses about law.

In actual history, those theoreticians who regarded *might* as the basis of right were in direct contradiction to those who looked on *will* as the basis of right—a contradiction which Saint Sancho could have regarded also as that between realism (the child, the ancient, the Negro, etc.) and idealism (the youth, the modern, the Mongol, etc.). If power is taken as the basis of right, as Hobbes, etc., do, then right, law, etc, are merely the symptom, the expression of *other* relations upon which state power rests. The material life of individuals, which by no means depends merely on their "will", their mode of production and form of intercourse, which mutually determine each other — this is the real basis of the state and remains so at all the stages at which division of labour and private property are still necessary, quite independently of the *will* of individuals. These actual relations are in no way created by the state power; on the contrary they are the power creating it. The individuals who rule in these conditions—leaving aside the fact that their power must assume the form of the *state*—have to give their will, which is determined by these definite conditions, a universal expression as the will of the state, as law, an expression whose content is always determined by the relations of this class, as the civil and criminal law demonstrates in the clearest possible way. Just as the weight of their bodies does not depend on their idealistic will or on their arbitrary decision, so also the fact that they enforce their own will in the form of law, and at the same time make it independent of the personal arbitrariness of each individual among them, does not depend on their idealistic will. Their personal rule must at the same time assume the form of average rule. Their personal power is based on conditions of life which as they develop are common to many individuals, and the continuance of which they, as ruling individuals, have to maintain against others and, at the same time, to maintain that they hold good for everybody. The expression of this will, which is determined by their common interests, is the law. It is precisely because individuals who are independent of one another assert themselves and their own will, and because on this basis their attitude to one another is bound to be egoistical, that self-denial is made necessary in law and right, self-denial in the exceptional case, and self-assertion of their interests in the average case (which, therefore, not *they*, but only the "egoist in agreement with himself" regards as self-denial). The same applies to the classes which are ruled, whose will plays just as small a part in determining the existence of law and the state. For example, so long as the productive forces are still insufficiently developed to make competition superfluous, and therefore would give rise to competition over and over again, for so long the classes which are ruled would be wanting the impossible if they had the "will" to abolish competition and with it the state and the law. Incidentally, too, it is only in the imagination of the ideologist that this "will" arises before relations have developed far enough to make the emergence of such a will possible. After relations have developed sufficiently to produce it, the ideologist is able to imagine this will as being purely arbitrary and therefore as conceivable at all times and under all circumstances.

Like right, so crime, i.e., the struggle of the isolated individual against the predominant relations, is not the result of pure arbitrariness. On the contrary, it depends on the same conditions as that domination. The same visionaries who see in right and law the domination of some independently existing general will can see in crime the mere violation of right and law. Hence the state does not exist owing to the dominant will, but the state, which arises from the material mode of life of individuals, has also the form of a dominant will. If the latter loses its domination, it means that not only the will has changed but also the material existence and life of the individuals, and only for that reason has their will changed. It is possible for rights and laws to be "inherited",[a] but in that case they are no longer dominant, but nominal, of which striking examples are furnished by the history of ancient Roman law and English law. We saw earlier how a theory and history of pure thought could arise among philosophers owing to the separation of ideas from the individuals and their empirical relations which serve as the basis of these ideas. In the same way, here too one can separate right from its real basis, whereby one obtains a "dominant will"

---

[a] Paraphrase of a passage from Goethe's *Faust*, I. Teil, 2."Studierzimmer-szene", where Mephistopheles says: "Laws and rights are inherited like an eternal malady."— *Ed.*

which in different eras undergoes various modifications and has its own, independent history in its creations, the laws. On this account, political and civil history becomes ideologically merged in a history of the domination of successive laws. This is the specific illusion of lawyers and politicians, which Jacques le bonhomme adopts *sans façon*. He succumbs to the same illusion as, for example, Frederick William IV, who also regards laws as mere caprices of the dominant will and hence always finds that they come to grief against the "awkward something"[a] of the world. Hardly [one] of his quite harmless whims reaches a further stage of realisation than cabinet decrees. Let him issue an order for a twenty-five million loan, i.e., for one hundred and tenth part of the English national debt, and he will see whose will his dominant will is. Incidentally, we shall find later on, too, that Jacques le bonhomme uses the phantoms or apparitions of his sovereign and fellow-Berliner as documents out of which to weave his own theoretical whimsies about right, law, crime, etc. This should occasion us the less surprise since even the spectre of the *Vossische Zeitung* repeatedly "offers" him something, e.g., the constitutional state. The most superficial examination of legislation, e.g., poor laws in all countries, shows how far the rulers got when they imagined that they could achieve something by means of their "dominant will" alone, i.e., simply by exercising their will. Incidentally, Saint Sancho has to accept the illusion of the lawyers and politicians about the dominant will in order to let his own will be splendidly displayed in the equations and antitheses with which we shall presently delight ourselves, and in order to arrive at the result that he can get out of his head any idea which he has put into it.

"My brethren, count it all joy when ye fall into divers temptations." (Saint-Jacques le bonhomne, 1, 2.)[b]

$$Law \quad = dominant\ will\ of\ the\ state,$$
$$= state\ will.$$

Antitheses:

State will, alien will — My will, own will.
Dominant will of the state — My own will
— My self-will.

---

[a] Paraphrase of a line from Goethe's *Faust*, I. Teil, 1. "Studierzimmerszene", where Mephistopheles says: "This something, this awkward world."—*Ed.*

[b] James 1:2.—*Ed.*

| Subjects of the state, who sustain the law of the state | "Subjects of themselves (unique ones), who bear their own law in themselves". (P. 268.) |

Equations:

A)	State will	=	Not-my will.
B)	My will	=	Not-state will.
C)	Will	=	Desire
D)	My will	=	Non-desire of the state,
		=	Will against the state,
		=	Ill will towards the state.
E)	To desire the	=	Self-will.
	non-state Self-will	=	Not to desire the state.
F)	State will	=	Negation of my will,
		=	My lack of will.
G)	My lack of will	=	Existence of state will.

(We know already from the preceding that the existence of the state *will* is equal to the existence of the *state*, from which the following new equation results:)

H)	My lack of will	=	Existence of the state.
I)	The negation of my lack of will	=	Non-existence of the state.
K)	Self-will	=	Negation of the state.
L)	My will	=	Non-existence of the state.

Note 1.

According to the already quoted passage from page 256: "States endure so long as the *dominant* will is *regarded* as equivalent to one's *own* will."

Note 2.

"He who in order to exist" (the conscience of the state is appealed to) "is compelled to count on the *lack of will* of others is a *creation* of those others, just as the master is a creation of the servant." (P. 257.) (Equations F, G, H, I.)

Note 3.

"*My own will* is the *corrupter of* the state. Therefore, it is branded by the latter as *self-will*. One's own will and the state are powers that are mortal enemies, between whom eternal peace is impossible." (P. 257.) — "Therefore *it* in fact watches everybody, *it* sees an egoist in everyone (self-will), "and *it* fears the egoist." (P. 263.) "The state ... opposes the duel ... even a *scuffle* is punishable" (even if the police are not called in.)(P. 245.)

Note 4.

"For it, for the state, it is absolutely essential that no one should have *his own will*; if anyone had such a will, the state would have to expel him" (imprison, banish); "if *everyone* had it" ("who is this person whom you call 'everyone'"?) "then they would abolish the state." (P. 257.)

This can also be expressed rhetorically:

"What is the use of your laws if no one obeys them, what is the use of your orders if everybody refuses to accept any orders?" (P. 256.)*

Note 5.

The simple antithesis: "state will — my will" is given an apparent motivation in the following paragraph: "Even if *one* were to imagine a case where each individual in the nation had expressed the same will and thus a perfect *collective will*" (!) "had come into existence, things would still remain the same. Would I not today and later be bound by my will of yesterday?... My creation, that is, a definite expression of will, would have become my master; but I ... the creator, would be hampered in my course and my dissolution.... Because yesterday I possessed will, I have today no will of my own; yesterday voluntary, today involuntary." (P. 258.)

The old thesis, which has often been put forward both by revolutionaries and reactionaries, that in a democracy individuals only exercise their sovereignty for a moment and then at once relinquish their authority — this thesis Saint Sancho endeavours to appropriate here in a "clumsy" fashion by applying to it his phenomenological theory of creator and creation. But the theory of creator and creation deprives this thesis of all meaning. According to this theory of his, it is not that Saint Sancho has no will of his own today because he has changed his will of yesterday, i.e., has a differently defined will, so that the nonsense which yesterday he exalted into a law as the expression of his will, now weighs like a bond or fetter on his more enlightened will of today. On the contrary, according to his theory, his will of today *must* be the negation of his will of yesterday, because, as creator, he is in duty bound to dissolve

---

* [The following passage is crossed out in the manuscript:] Note 5. "People try to distinguish between *law* and the arbitrary command, or *ordinance*. However, a law relating to human action ... is a *declaration of will*, hence a command (ordinance)." (P. 256.) .... "Someone can, of course, declare what he is prepared to put up with and consequently forbid the opposite by a law, announcing that he will treat the transgressor as an enemy.... I am forced to put up with the fact that he treats me as his enemy, but I shall never permit him to treat me as if I were his creature and to make his reason or perhaps unreasonableness my guiding principle." (P. 256.)—Thus Sancho raises no objections here against the law when it treats the transgressor as an *enemy*. His hostility towards the law is directed only against the form, not against the content. Any repressive law which threatens him with the gallows and the wheel is acceptable to him if he can consider it as a declaration of war. Saint Sancho is satisfied if one does him the honour of regarding him as an *enemy*, and not as a *creature*. In reality he is at best the *enemy* of "Man", but the *creature* of the conditions in Berlin.

his will of yesterday. Only as "one without will" is he creator, as one actually having will he is always the creation. (See "Phenomenology"[a].) In that case, however, it by no means follows that "because yesterday he possessed will", today he is "without will", but rather that he bears *ill will* to his will of yesterday, whether the latter has assumed the form of law or not. In both cases he can abolish it as he, in general, is accustomed to do, namely *as his will.* Thereby he has done full justice to egoism in agreement with itself. It is, therefore, a matter of complete indifference here whether his will of yesterday has assumed as law the form of something existing outside his head, particularly if we recall that earlier the "word which escaped from him" behaved likewise in a rebellious way towards him. In the above-mentioned thesis, moreover, Saint Sancho desires to preserve, not indeed his self-will but his *free* will, *freedom* of will, *freedom*, which is a serious offence against the moral code of the egoist in agreement with himself. In committing this offence, Saint Sancho even goes so far as to proclaim that true peculiarity is the inner freedom that was so much condemned above, the freedom of bearing ill will.

"How is this to be changed?" cries Sancho. "Only in one way: by not recognising any duty, i.e., not binding myself and not allowing myself to be bound [....]

"However, they will bind me! *No one can bind my will, and my ill will remains free!*" (P. 258.)

"Drums and trumpets pay homage
To his youthful splendour!"[b]

Here Saint Sancho forgets "to make the simple reflection" that his "will" is indeed "bound" inasmuch as, against his will, it is *"ill* will".

The above proposition that the individual will is bound by the general will expressed through law completes, by the way, the idealistic conception of the state, according to which it is only a matter of the will, and which has led French and German writers to the most subtle philosophising.*

* [The following passage is crossed out in the manuscript:] Whether or not tomorrow the self-will of an individual will feel oppressed by the law which yesterday he helped to make, depends on whether new circumstances have arisen and whether his interests have changed to such an extent that yesterday's law no longer corresponds to his changed interests. If the new circumstances affect the interests of the ruling class as a whole, the class will alter the law; if

---

[a] See this volume, pp. 274-76.— *Ed.*
[b] From Heine's poem "Berg-Idylle."— *Ed.*

Incidentally, if it is merely a matter of "desiring" and not of "being able" and, at worse, merely of "ill will", then it is incomprehensible why Saint Sancho wants to abolish altogether an object so productive of "desiring" and "ill will" as state law.

"Law in general, etc.— that is the stage we have reached today." (P. 256.)

The things Jacques le bonhomme believes!

―――――――

The equations so far examined were purely destructive as regards state and law. The true egoist *had* to adopt a purely destructive attitude to both. We missed appropriation; on the other hand, we had the satisfaction of seeing Saint Sancho performing a great trick in which he shows how the state is destroyed by a mere change of will, a change which in turn depends, of course, only on the will. However, appropriation is not lacking here either, although it is quite secondary, and can produce results only later on "from time to time". The two antitheses given above:

State will, alien will — My will, own will,

Dominant will of the state — My own will

can also be summarised as follows:

Domination of alien will — Domination of one's own will.

In this new antithesis, which incidentally all the time formed the concealed basis of his destruction of the state through his self-will, Stirner appropriates the political illusion about the domination of arbitrariness, of ideological will. He could also have expressed this as follows:

Arbitrariness of law — Law of arbitrariness.

Saint Sancho, however, did not reach such simplicity of expression.

―――――――

they affect only a few individuals the majority will, of course, disregard their ill will.

Equipped with this freedom of the ill will, Sancho can now re-establish the restriction imposed on the will of one person by the will of the others; it is precisely this restriction which forms the basis of the above-mentioned idealist conception of the state.

"Everything would be higgledy-piggledy if everyone could do what he liked.— But who says that everyone can do everything?" ("What he likes" is here prudently omitted.)—

"Every one of you should become an omnipotent ego!" declared the egoist in agreement with himself.

"What do you exist for," he continues, "you who need not put up with everything? Defend yourself, then no one will harm you." (P. 259.) And to remove the last semblance of a difference he lets "a few million" "stand as a protection" behind the one "you", so that the whole discussion can very well serve as a "clumsy" beginning of a political theory in the spirit of Rousseau.

In antithesis III we already have a "law within him", but he appropriates the law still more directly in the following antithesis:

Law, the state's declaration ⎫ _ ⎧ Law, declaration of my will,
of will   ⎭   ⎩ my declaration of will.

"Someone can, of course, declare what he is prepared to put up with, and consequently forbid the opposite by a *law*", etc. (P. 256.)

This prohibition is necessarily accompanied by threats. The last antithesis is of importance for the section on crime.

Episodes. We are told on page 256 that there is no difference between "law" and "arbitrary command, ordinance" because both="declaration of will", consequently "command".— On pages 254, 255, 260 and 263, while pretending to speak about "the State" Stirner substitutes the *Prussian* state and deals with questions that are of the greatest importance for the *Vossische Zeitung*, such as the constitutional state, removability of officials, bureaucratic arrogance and similar nonsense. The only important thing here is the discovery that the old French parliaments insisted on their right to register royal edicts *because* they wanted "to judge according to their own right". The registration of laws by the French parliaments came into being at the same time as the bourgeoisie and hence the acquisition of absolute power by the kings, for whom in face of both the feudal nobility and foreign states it became necessary to plead an alien will on which their own will depended, and at the same time to give the bourgeois some sort of guarantee. Saint Max can learn more about this from the history of his beloved Francis I; for the rest, before speaking about the French parliaments again, he might consult the fourteen volumes of *Des États généraux et autres assemblées nationales*, Paris, 1788,[a] concerning what the French parliaments wanted or did not want and their significance. In general it would be in place here to introduce a short episode about the *erudition* of our saint who is so desirous of conquests. Apart from theoretical works, such as the writings of Feuerbach and Bruno Bauer, as well as the Hegelian tradition, which is his main source, apart from these meagre theoretical sources, our Sancho uses and quotes the following historical sources: on the French Revolution—Rutenberg's *Politische Reden* and the Bauers' *Denkwürdigkeiten*; on communism—Proudhon, Au-

---

[a] By Charles Joseph Mayer.— *Ed.*

gust Becker's *Volksphilosophie*, the *Einundzwanzig Bogen* and the Bluntschli report; on liberalism — the *Vossische Zeitung*, the *Sächsische Vaterlandsblätter*, Protocols of the Baden Chamber, the *Einundzwanzig Bogen* again and Edgar Bauer's epoch-making work[a]; in addition, here and there as historical evidence there are also quoted: the Bible, Schlosser's *18. Jahrhundert*,[b] Louis Blanc's *Histoire de dix ans*, Hinrichs' *Politische Vorlesungen*, Bettina's *Dies Buch gehört dem König*, Hess' *Triarchie*,[c] the *Deutsch-Französische Jahrbücher*, the Zurich *Anekdota*, Moriz Carrière on Cologne Cathedral, the session of the Paris Chamber of Peers of April 25, 1844, Karl Nauwerck, *Emilia Galotti*,[d] the Bible — in short, the entire Berlin reading-room together with its owner, Willibald Alexis Cabanis. After this sample of Sancho's profound studies, one can easily understand why it is that he finds in this world so very much that is alien, i.e., holy.

III. Crime

Note 1.

"If you allow yourself to be judged right by someone else, then you must equally allow yourself to be judged wrong by him. If you receive justification and reward from him, then expect also accusation and punishment from him. Right   is   accompanied   by   *wrong*,   legality   by *crime*.Who — are — you?— You — are — a — *criminal*!!" (P. 262.)

The *code civil* is accompanied by the *code pénal*, the *code pénal* by the *code de commerce*. Who are you? You are a *commerçant*!

Saint Sancho could have spared us this nerve-shattering surprise. In his case the words: "If you allow yourself to be judged right by someone else, then you must equally allow yourself to be judged wrong by him" have lost all meaning if they are intended to add a new definition; for one of his earlier equations already states: If you allow yourself to be judged right by someone else, then you allow yourself to be judged by alien right, hence *your wrong*.

---

[a] Edgar Bauer, *Die liberalen Bestrebungen in Deutschland.*— Ed.
[b] Friedrich Christoph Schlosser, *Geschichte des achtzehnten Jahrhunderts und des neunzehnten bis zum Sturz des französischen Kaiserreichs.*— Ed.
[c] Moses Hess, *Die europäische Triarchie.*— Ed.
[d] The reference is to Moriz Carrière, *Der Kölner Dom als freie deutsche Kirche*; François Guizot, *Discours dans la chambre des pairs le 25 avril 1844*; Karl Nauwerck, *Ueber die Theilnahme am Staate*; Gotthold Ephraim Lessing's drama *Emilia Galotti.*— Ed.

A. Simple Canonisation of Crime and Punishment

a. Crime

As regards crime, we have already seen that this is the name for a universal category of the egoist in agreement with himself, the negation of the holy, *sin*. In the previously given antitheses and equations concerning examples of the holy (state, right, law), the negative relation of the ego to these holies, or the copula, could also be called crime, just as about Hegelian logic, which is likewise an example of the holy, Saint Sancho can also say: I am not Hegelian logic, I am a sinner against Hegelian logic. Since he was speaking of right, state, etc., he should now have continued: another example of sin or crime are what are called *juridical* or *political* crimes. Instead of this, he again informs us in detail that these crimes are

<blockquote>
sin against the holy,
  "   "   the fixed idea,
  "   "   the spectre,
  "   "   "Man".
</blockquote>

"Criminals exist only against *something holy*." (P. 268.)
"*Only owing to the holy does the criminal code exist*." (P. 318.)
"Crimes arise from the *fixed idea*." (P. 269.)
"One sees here that it is again 'Man' who also creates the concept of crime, of sin, *and thereby* also of right." (Previously it was the reverse.) "A man in whom I do not recognise man is a sinner." (P. 268.)

Note 1.

"Can I assume that someone commits a crime against me" (this is asserted in opposition to the French people in the revolution), "without also assuming that he ought to act as I consider right? And actions of this kind I *call* the right, the good, etc., those deviating from this—a crime. Accordingly I *think* that the others ought to aim with me *at the same* goal ... as beings who should obey some sort of 'rational' law" (Vocation! Designation! Task! The holy!!!). "I *lay down* what Man is and what it means to act truly as a man, and I demand from each that this law should become for him the norm and the ideal; in the reverse case he *proves himself* a sinner and criminal...." (Pp. [267], 268.)

At the same time, he sheds an anxious tear at the grave of those "proper people" who in the epoch of terror were slaughtered by the sovereign people in the name of the holy. Further, by means of an example, he shows how the names of real crimes can be construed from this holy point of view.

"If, as in the revolution, this *spectre*, man, is understood to mean the 'good citizen', then the familiar 'political transgressions and crimes' are *brought about from* this concept of man." (He should have said: this concept, etc., *brings up* the familiar crimes.) (P. 268.)

A brilliant example of the extent to which credulity is Sancho's predominant quality in the section on crime is furnished by his transformation of the sansculottes of the revolution into "good citizens" of Berlin through a synonymical abuse of the word *citoyen*. According to Saint Max, "good citizens and loyal officials" are inseparable. Hence "Robespierre, for example, Saint-Just, and so on" would be "loyal officials", whereas Danton was responsible for a cash deficit and squandered state money. Saint Sancho has made a good start for a history of the revolution for the Prussian townsman and villager.

Note 2.

Having thus described for us political and juridical crime as an example of crime in general — namely his category of crime, sin, negation, enmity, insult, contempt for the holy, disreputable behaviour towards the holy — Saint Sancho can now confidently declare:

"In crime, the egoist has hitherto asserted himself and mocked the holy." (P. 319.)

In this passage all the crimes hitherto committed are assigned to the credit of the egoist in agreement with himself, although subsequently we shall have to transfer a few of them to the debit side. Sancho imagines that hitherto crimes have been committed only in order to mock at "the holy" and to assert oneself not against things, but against the holy *aspect* of things. Because the theft committed by a poor devil who appropriates someone else's taler can be put in the category of a crime against the law, *for that reason* the poor devil committed the theft just because of a desire to break the law. In exactly the same way as in an earlier passage Jacques le bonhomme imagined that laws are issued only for the sake of the holy, and that thieves are sent to prison only for the sake of the holy.

b. Punishment

Since we are at present concerned with juridical and political crimes we discover in this connection that such crimes "in the ordinary sense" usually involve a *punishment*, or, as it is written, "the wages of sin is death".[a] After what we have already learned about crime, it follows, of course, that punishment is the self-defence and resistance of *the holy* to those who desecrate it.

[a] Romans 6:23.— *Ed.*

Note 1.

"Punishment has sense only when it is intended as expiation for violating something holy." (P. 316.) In punishing, "we commit the folly of desiring to satisfy right, a spectre" (the holy). "The holy must" here "defend itself against man" (Saint Sancho here "commits the folly" of mistaking "Man" for "the unique ones", the "proper egos", etc.) (P. 318.)

Note 2.

"Only owing to the Holy does the criminal code exist and it disintegrates of itself when *punishment* is abandoned." (P. 318.)

What Saint Sancho really wants to say is: Punishment falls into decay of itself if the criminal code is abandoned, i.e., punishment only exists owing to the criminal code. "But is not" a criminal code that only exists owing to punishment "all nonsense, and is not" punishment that exists only owing to the criminal code "also nonsense"? (Sancho contra Hess, *Wigand*,[a] p. 186.) Sancho here mistakes the criminal code for a textbook of theological morality.

Note 3.

As an example of how crime arises from the fixed idea, there is the following:

"The *sanctity* of marriage is a *fixed idea*. From this *sanctity* it follows that infidelity is a *crime*, and therefore a *certain law on marriage*" (to the great annoyance of the "G[erman] Chambers" and of the "Emperor of all R[ussias]", not to speak of the "Emperor of Japan" and the "Emperor of China", and particularly the "Sultan") "imposes a shorter or longer term of punishment for that." (P. 269.)

Frederick William IV, who thinks he is able to promulgate laws in accordance with the holy, and therefore is always at loggerheads with the whole world, can comfort himself with the thought that in our Sancho he has found at least one man imbued with faith in the state. Let Saint Sancho just compare the Prussian marriage law, which exists only in the head of its author, with the provisions of the *Code civil*, which are operative in practice, and he will be able to discover the difference between holy and worldly marriage laws.[88] In the Prussian phantasmagoria, for reasons of state, the sanctity of marriage is supposed to be enforced both upon husband and wife; in French practice, where the wife is regarded as the private property of her husband, only the wife can be punished for adultery, and then only on the demand of the husband, who exercises his property right.

---

[a] Max Stirner, "Recensenten Stirners".— *Ed.*

B. *Appropriation of Crime and Punishment Through Antithesis*

Crime in the sense of man $\quad=\begin{cases}\text{Violation of man's law (of}\\ \quad\text{the state's declaration of}\\ \quad\text{will, of state power),}\\ \quad\text{p. 259 et seq.}\end{cases}$

$\left.\text{Crime in my sense}\quad\right\}=\begin{cases}\text{Violation of my law (of my}\\ \quad\text{declaration of will, of my}\\ \quad\text{power), p. 256 and }pas\text{-}\\ sim.\end{cases}$

These two equations are counterposed as antitheses and derive simply from the opposition of "man" and the "ego". They merely sum up what has been said already.

The holy punishes the "ego" — "I punish the 'ego'."
Crime=hostility to } — { *Hostility*=crime against my
Man's law (the Holy). law.

The criminal=the enemy or } { *Enemy* or *opponent*=crimi-
opponent of the holy (the } — { nal against the "ego",
Holy as a moral person). the corporeal.

Punishment=self-defence of
the holy against the } — { *My self-defence*=My punish-
"ego". ment of the "ego".

Punishment=satisfaction } { *Satisfaction   (vengeance)*=
(vengeance) of man in } — { My punishment of the
relation to the "ego". "ego".

In the last antithesis, satisfaction can also be called *self*-satisfaction, since it is the satisfaction of *me,* in opposition to the satisfaction of *man.*

If in the above antithetical equations only the first member is taken into account, then one obtains the following series of simple antitheses where the thesis always contains the holy, universal, alien *name*, while the *anti-* thesis always contains the worldly, personal, appropriated *name.*

Crime   — Hostility.
Criminal   — Enemy or opponent.
Punishment   — My defence.
                 Satisfaction, vengeance,
Punishment   — self-satisfaction.

In an instant we shall say a few words about these equations and antitheses which are so simple that even a "born simpleton" (p. 434) can master this "unique" method of thought in five minutes. But first a few more quotations in addition to those given earlier.

Note 1.

"In relation to me you can never be a *criminal* but only an *opponent*" (p. 268),—and "enemy" in the same sense on p. 256.—Crime as the hostility of man is illustrated on page 268 by the example of the "enemies of the Fatherland".—"*Punishment ought*" (a moral postulate) "to be replaced by *satisfaction,* which again cannot aim at satisfying right or justice, but at giving *us* satisfaction." (P. 318.)

Note 2.

While Saint Sancho attacks the halo (the windmill) of existing power, he does not even understand this power, let alone come to grips with it; he only advances the moral demand that the relation of the ego to it should be formally changed. (See "Logic".[a])

"I am forced to put up with the fact" (bombastic assurance) "that he" (viz., my enemy, who has a few million people behind him) "treats me as his enemy; but I shall never permit him to treat me as his creature or to make his reason or unreasonableness my guiding principle" (p. 256, where he allows the aforesaid Sancho a very restricted freedom, namely the choice between allowing himself to be treated as his creature or of suffering the 3,300 lashes imposed by Merlin on his *posaderas.* This freedom is allowed him by any criminal code which, it is true, does not first ask the aforesaid Sancho in what form it should declare its hostility to him).— "But even if you *impress* your opponent as a force" (being for him an "*impressive* force") "you do not on that account become a sanctified authority; unless he is a *wretch.* He is not obliged to *respect* you and *pay regard* to you even if he has to be *on his guard* against you and your power." (P. 258.)

Here Saint Sancho himself appears as a "wretch" when with the greatest seriousness he haggles[b] about the difference between "to impress" and "to be respected", "to be on one's guard" and to "have regard for"—a difference of a sixteenth part at most. When Saint Sancho is "on his guard" against someone,

"he gives himself over to *reflection,* and he has an object which he *has in view,* which he *respects* and which inspires him with reverence and fear". (P. 115.)

In the above equations, punishment, vengeance, satisfaction, etc., are depicted as coming only from me; inasmuch as Saint Sancho is the object of satisfaction, the antitheses can be turned round: then self-satisfaction is transformed into another-getting-satisfaction-with-regard-to-me or the prejudicing-of-my-satisfaction.

---

[a] See this volume, p. 303.— *Ed.*

[b] In the original a pun on the word *Schächer,* which Stirner uses in the passage quoted— *Schächer* means "wretch" or "robber", while *schachern* means to barter, to haggle.— *Ed.*

Note 3.

The very same ideologists who could imagine that right, law, state, etc., arose from a general concept, in the final analysis perhaps the concept of man, and that they were put into effect for the sake of this concept — these same ideologists can, of course, also imagine that crimes are committed purely because of a wanton attitude towards some concept, that crimes, in general. are nothing but making mockery of concepts and are only punished in order to do justice to the insulted concepts. Concerning this we have already said what was necessary in connection with right, and still earlier in connection with hierarchy, to which we refer the reader.

In the above-mentioned antitheses, the canonised definitions — crime, punishment, etc.— are confronted with the name of another definition, which Saint Sancho in his favourite fashion *extracts* from these *first* definitions and *appropriates for himself*. This new definition, which, as we have said, appears here as a mere name, being worldly is supposed to contain the direct *individual* relation and express the *factual* relations. (See "Logic".) The history of right shows that in the earliest, most primitive epochs these individual, factual relations in their crudest form directly constituted right. With the development of civil society, hence with the development of private interests into class interests, the relations of right underwent changes and acquired a civilised form. They were no longer regarded as individual, but as *universal* relations. At the same time, division of labour placed the protection of the conflicting interests of separate individuals into the hands of a few persons, whereby the barbaric enforcement of right also disappeared. Saint Sancho's entire criticism of right in the above-mentioned antitheses is limited to declaring the *civilised* form of legal relations and the civilised division of labour to be the fruit of the "fixed idea", of the holy, and, on the other hand, to claiming *for himself* the barbaric expression of relations of right and the barbaric method of settling conflicts. For him it is all *only* a matter of *names*; he does not touch on the content itself, since he does not know the real relations on which these different forms of right are based, and in the juridical expression of class relations perceives only the idealised names of those barbaric relations. Thus, in Stirner's declaration of will, we rediscover the feud; in hostility, self-defence, etc.— a copy of club-law and practice of the old feudal mode of life; in satisfaction, vengeance, etc.— the *jus talionis*, the old German *Gewere, compensatio, satisfactio* — in short, the chief elements of the *leges barbarorum* and *consuetudines feudorum*,[89] which Sancho has appropriated for himself and taken to his heart not from libraries, but from the tales of his former master about Amadis of Gaul. In the final analysis, therefore, Saint Sancho again arrives merely at an impotent moral injunction that everybody should himself obtain satisfaction and carry out punishment. He believes Don Quixote's assurance that by a mere moral injunction he can without more ado convert the material forces arising from the division of labour into personal forces. How closely juridical relations are linked with the development of these material forces due to the division of labour is already clear from the historical development of the power of the law courts and the complaints of the feudal lords about the legal development. (See, e.g., Monteil, loc. cit.,[a] XIVe, XVe *siècle*.) It was just in the epoch between the rule of the aristocracy and the rule of the bourgeoisie, when the interests of two classes came into conflict, when trade between the European nations began to be important, and hence international relations themselves assumed a *bourgeois* character, it was just at that time that the power of the courts of law began to be important, and under the rule of the bourgeoisie, when this broadly developed division of labour becomes absolutely essential, the power of these courts reaches its highest point. What the servants of the division of labour, the judges and still more the *professores juris*, imagine in this connection is a matter of the greatest indifference.

C. Crime in the Ordinary and Extraordinary Sense

We saw above that crime in the ordinary sense, by being falsified, was put to the credit of the egoist in the extraordinary sense. Now this falsification becomes obvious. The extraordinary egoist now finds that he commits only extraordinary crimes, which have to be set against the ordinary crimes. Therefore we debit the aforesaid egoist with the ordinary crimes, which have been previously entered into the credit column.

The struggle of the ordinary criminals against other people's property can also be expressed as follows (although this holds good of any competitor):

---

[a] See this volume, pp. 236-37.— *Ed.*

that they — "seek *other people's* goods" (p. 265),
        seek holy goods,
        seek *the holy*, and in this way the ordinary
criminal is transformed into a "believer". (P. 265.)

But this reproach which the egoist in the extraordinary sense levels against the criminal in the ordinary sense is only an apparent one — for it is indeed he himself who strives for the halo of the whole world. The real reproach that he levels against the criminal is not that he seeks "*the holy*", but that he seeks "*goods*".

After Saint Sancho has built himself a "world of his own, a heaven", namely this time an imaginary world of feuds and knights-errant, transferred to the modern world, after he has at the same time given documentary evidence of his difference, as a knightly criminal, from ordinary criminals, after this he once more undertakes a crusade against "dragons and ostriches, hobgoblins",[a] "ghosts, apparitions and fixed ideas". His faithful servant, Szeliga, gallops reverently after him. As they wend their way, however, there occurs the astounding adventure of the unfortunate ones who were being dragged off to some place they had no wish to go to, as described in Chapter XXII of Cervantes. For while our knight-errant and his servant Don Quixote were jogging along their path, Sancho raised his eyes and saw coming towards him some dozen men on foot manacled and bound together by a long chain, accompanied by a commissar and four gendarmes, belonging to the holy Hermandad,[90] to the Hermandad which is holy, to the holy. When they came close, Saint Sancho very politely asked the guards to be so kind as to tell him why these people were being led in chains.— They are convicts of His Majesty sent to work at Spandau,[91] you do not have to know any more.— How, cried Saint Sancho, men being forced? Is it possible that the king can use force against someone's "proper ego"? In that case I take upon myself the vocation of putting a stop to this force. "The behaviour of the state is violent action, and it calls this justice. Violent action of an individual, however, it calls crime." Thereupon Saint Sancho first of all began to admonish the prisoners, saying that they ought not to grieve, that although they were "not free", they were still their "own", and that although maybe their "bones" might "crack" under the lash of the whip and that perhaps they might even have a "leg torn off",

---

[a] Cf. Isaiah 34:13-14.— *Ed.*

yet, he said, you will triumph over all that, for "no one can bind
your will!" "And I know for certain that there is no witchcraft in
the world that could direct and compel the will, as some
simpletons imagine; for the will is our free arbitrary power and
there is no magic herb or spell that can subdue it." Yes, "your
will no one can bind and your ill will remains free!"

But since this sermon did not pacify the convicts, who began
one after the other to relate how they had been unjustly
condemned, Sancho said: "Dear brethren, from what you have
related it has become clear to me that, although you have been
punished for your crimes, yet the punishment which you are
suffering gives you little pleasure and that hence you are
reluctant to receive it and do not look forward to it. And it is
highly possible that the cause of your ruin is pusillanimity on the
rack in one case, poverty in another, lack of favour in a third
and, finally, the *judge's* unfair *judgment*, and that *you have not
been given the justice that was your due*, 'your right'. All this
compels me to show you why heaven sent me into the world.
But since the wisdom of the egoist in agreement with himself
prescribes not doing by force what can be done by agreement, I
hereby request the commissar and gendarmes to release you and
let you go your ways. Moreover, my dear gendarmes, these
unfortunates have done *you* no harm. It does not behove egoists
in agreement with themselves to become the executioners of
other unique ones who have done them no harm. Evidently,
with you 'the category of the one who has been robbed stands in
the forefront'. Why do you show such 'zeal' in your actions
'against crime'? 'Verily, verily I say unto you, you are
enthusiastic for morality, you are filled with the idea of
morality', 'you persecute all those who are hostile to
it'—'Owing to your oath as officials', you are bringing these
poor convicts 'to prison', you are the holy! Therefore release
these people voluntarily. If you do not, you will have to reckon
with me, who 'overthrows nations with one puff of the living
ego', who 'commits the most unmeasured desecration' and 'is
not afraid even of the Moon'."

"This is a fine piece of impudence indeed!" cried the
commissar. "You'd do better to put that basin straight on your
head and be on your way!"

Saint Sancho, however, infuriated by this Prussian rudeness,
couched his lance and rushed at the commissar with as much
speed as the "apposition" is capable of, so that he immediately
threw him to the ground. There ensued a general mêlée, during
which the convicts freed themselves from their chains, a
gendarme threw Szeliga Don Quixote into the *Landwehrgraben*[92]

or sheep's ditch [*Schafgraben*], and Saint Sancho performed the most heroic feats in his struggle against the holy. A few minutes later, the gendarmes were scattered, Szeliga crept out of the ditch and the holy was abolished for the time being.

Then Saint Sancho gathered round him the liberated convicts and addressed them as follows (pp. 265, 266 of "the book"):

"What is the *ordinary* criminal" (the criminal in the ordinary sense) "but a man who has committed the *fatal mistake*" (a fatal story-teller for the townsman and the villager!) "of striving after what belongs to the people instead of seeking what is *his own*? He has desired the *contemptible*" (a general muttering among the convicts at this moral judgment) "goods of *another*, he has done what *believers* do who aspire to what belongs to God" (the criminal as a noble soul). "What does the priest do who admonishes the criminal? He tells him of the great violation of right he has committed by his action in desecrating what the state has sanctified, the property of the state, which also includes the life of the state's subjects. Instead of this the priest might have done *better* to reproach the criminal with having besmirched himself" (titters among the convicts at this egoistical appropriation of banal clerical phraseology), "by not *despising the alien* but regarding it as *worthy of being robbed*" (murmuring among the convicts). "He could have done so, were he not a priest" (one of the convicts: "In the ordinary sense!"). I, however, "speak with the criminal as with an *egoist*, and he will be *ashamed*" (shameless, loud cheers from the criminals, who do not wish to be called upon to feel shame), "not because he has committed a crime against your laws and your goods, but because he considered it worth while to circumvent your laws" (this refers only to "circumvention in the ordinary sense"; elsewhere, however, "I go round a rock so long as I am unable to blow it up" and I "circumvent", for example, *even* the "censorship"), "and to desire your goods" (renewed cheers); "he will be *ashamed*...."

Gines de Passamonte, the arch-thief, who in general was not very patient, shouted: "Are we then to do nothing but feel *ashamed*, be submissive, when a priest in the extraordinary sense 'admonishes' us?"

"He will be ashamed," continues Sancho, "that he did not despise you, together with what is yours, that he was too little of an egoist." (Sancho here applies an alien measure to the egoism of the criminal. In consequence, a general bellowing breaks out among the convicts; in some confusion, Sancho gives way, turning with a rhetorical gesture to the absent "good burghers".) "But you cannot speak to him egoistically, for you have not the stature of a criminal, you ... perpetrate nothing."

Gines again interrupts: "What credulity, my good man! Our prison warders perpetrate all kinds of crimes, they embezzle, they defraud, they commit rape [...ᵃ]

ᵃ Twelve pages of the manuscript are missing here.—*Ed.*

[B. My Intercourse]

[I. Society][93]

[...] again he reveals only his credulity. The reactionaries knew already that by the constitution the bourgeoisie abolishes the naturally arisen state and establishes and *makes* its own state, that *"le pouvoir constituant, qui était dans le temps"* naturally *"passa dans la volonté humaine"*,[a] that "this *fabricated* state was like a fabricated, painted tree",[b] etc. See Fiévée's *Correspondance politique et administrative*, Paris, 1815, *Appel à la France contre la division des opinions*, *Le drapeau blanc*, by Sarran *ainé*,[c] the *Gazette de France* of the Restoration period, and the earlier works of Bonald, de Maistre, etc. The liberal bourgeois, in turn, reproach the old republicans — about whom they obviously know as little as Saint Max knows about the bourgeois state — on the grounds that their patriotism is nothing but *"une passion factice envers un être abstrait, une idée générale"* [d] (Benj. Constant, *De l'esprit de conquête*, Paris, 1814, p. 48), whereas the reactionaries accused the bourgeois on the grounds that their political ideology is nothing but *"une mystification que la classe aisée fait subir à celles qui ne le sont pas"* (*Gazette de France*, 1831, Février[e]).

On page 295, Saint Sancho declares that the state is "an institution for making the nation Christian", and all he can say about the basis of the state is that it "is held together" with the "cement" of "respect for the law", or that the holy "is held together" by respect (the holy as link) for the holy. (P. 314.) Note 4.

"If the state is holy, there must be censorship." (P. 316.) The French Government does not contest freedom of the press as a right of man, but it demands a guarantee from the individual that he is *really a human being.*" (*Quel bonhomme!*[f] Jacques le bonhomme is "called upon" to study the September Laws.[94]) (P. 380.)

---

[a] "The constitutional power which had been shaped in the course of time had permeated the human will." [Lourdoueix], "Appel à la France contre la division des opinions" (quoted from Karl Wilhelm Lancizolle's book *Ueber Ursachen, Character und Folgen der Julitage*).— *Ed.*

[b] Karl Wilhelm Lancizolle, op. cit.— *Ed.*

[c] Sarran the elder.— *Ed.*

[d] "An artificial passion directed towards something abstract, a general idea."— *Ed.*

[e] "A deception with which the wealthy class deludes those that are not wealthy." Quoted from Karl Wilhelm Lancizolle, op. cit.— *Ed.*

[f] What a simpleton!— *Ed.*

Note 5, in which we find the most profound explanations about the various forms of the state, which Jacques le bonhomme makes independent and in which he sees only different attempts to realise the true state.

"The republic is *nothing but* absolute monarchy, for it makes no difference whether the monarch is called prince or people, since both are majesties" (the holy).... "Constitutionalism is a step further than the republic, for it is the state in the process of *dissolution*."

This dissolution is explained as follows:

"In the constitutional state ... the government wants to be absolute, and the people wants to be absolute. These two absolutes" (i.e., holies) "will destroy one another." (P. 302.) "I am not the state, I am the creative negation of the state"; "thereby all questions" (about the constitution, etc.) "sink into their true nothing". (P. 310.)

He should have added that these propositions about forms of the state are merely a paraphrase of this "nothing", whose sole creation is the proposition given above: I am not the state. Saint Sancho, just like a German school-master, speaks here of "the Republic", which is, of course, far older than constitutional monarchy, e.g., the Greek republics.

That in a democratic, representative state like North America class conflicts have already reached a form which the constitutional monarchies are only just being forced to approach — about this, of course, he knows nothing. His phrases about constitutional monarchy prove that since 1842 by the Berlin calendar[95] he has learned nothing and forgotten nothing.[a]

Note 6.

"The state owes its existence only to the contempt which I have for myself", and "with the disappearance of this disdain it will fade away entirely" (it seems that it depends solely on Sancho how soon all the states on earth will "fade away". Repetition of Note 3 in the reversed equation, see "Logic"[b]): "It exists only when in is *superior to me*, only as *might* [*Macht*] and the *mighty* [*Mächtiger*]. *Or*" (a remarkable *or* which proves just the opposite of what it is intended to prove) "can you imagine a state the inhabitants of which *in all their entirety*" (a jump from "I" to "we") "*attach no importance* to it [*sich allesamt nichts aus ihm machen*]?" (P. 377.)

There is no need to dwell on the synonymy of the words "*Macht*", "*Mächtig*" and "*machen*".

---

[a] Paraphrase of the French saying: "*Ils n'ont rien appris ni rien oublié*" ("They have learned nothing and forgotten nothing"); when it was first coined, shortly after the French Revolution, it was used in relation to the royalists.— *Ed.*

[b] See this volume, pp. 297-98 — *Ed.*

From the fact that in any state there are people who attach importance to it, i. e., who, in the state and thanks to the state, *themselves* acquire importance, Sancho concludes that the state is a power standing above these people. Here again it is only a matter of getting the fixed idea about the state out of one's mind. Jacques le bonhomme continues to imagine that the state is a mere idea and he believes in the independent power of this idea of the state. He is the true "politician who believes in the state, is possessed by the state" (p. 309). Hegel idealises the conception of the state held by the political ideologists who still took separate individuals as their point of departure, even if it was merely the *will* of these individuals; Hegel transforms the common will of these individuals into the absolute will, and Jacques le bonhomme *bona fide* accepts this idealisation of ideology as the correct view of the state and, in this belief, criticises it by declaring the Absolute to be the Absolute.

5. Society as Bourgeois Society

We shall spend somewhat more time on this chapter because, not unintentionally, it is the most confused of all the confused chapters in "the book", and because at the same time it proves most strikingly how little our saint succeeds in getting to know things in their mundane shape. Instead of making them worldly, he makes them holy by "giving" the reader the "benefit" only of his own holy conception. Before coming to bourgeois society proper, we shall hear some new explanations about property in general and in its relation to the state. These explanations appear the newer because they give Saint Sancho the opportunity to put forward again his most favourite equations about right and the state and thus to give his "treatise" "more manifold transformations" and "refractions". We need, of course, only quote the last members of these equations since the reader will still have in mind their context from the chapter "My Power".

Private property or
bourgeois property   = Not my property
                           = Holy property
                           = Property of others
                           = Respected property or respect
                             for the property of others
                           = Property of *man*. (Pp. 327, 369.)

From these equations one obtains at once the following antitheses:

Property in the bourgeois⎫ ⎧Property in the egoistical sense
sense   ⎭ ⎩(p. 327).

    "Property of *man*"   —"My property".
    ("Human belongings" —My belongings). P. 324.
    Equations: Man = Right
                          = State power.

Private property or⎫
bourgeois property ⎭ = Rightful property (p. 324),
                           = mine by virtue of right (p. 332),
                           = guaranteed property,
                           = property of others,
                           = property belonging to another,
                           = property belonging to right,
                           = property by right (pp. 367, 332),
                           = a concept of right,
                           = something spiritual,
                           = universal,
                           = fiction,
                           = pure thought,
                           = fixed idea,
                           = spectre,
                           = property of the spectre. (Pp.
                              368, 324, 332, 367, 369.)
          Private property = Property of right.
                    Right = Power of the state.
          Private property = Property in the power of the
                           state,
                           = State property, or also
                 Property = State property.
          State property = My non-property.
                     State = The sole owner. (Pp. 339, 334.)

We now come to the antitheses:

        Private property⎫ ⎧*Egoistical property.*
Authorised by right (by the⎬ ⎨Empowered by me to have
state, by Man) to have   ⎭ ⎩property.
property.   (P. 339.)

    Mine by virtue of right — Mine by virtue of my power or
                            force. (P. 332.)
Property given by another —Property taken by me. (P. 339.)
Rightful property of others — Rightful property of another is
                            what I consider right (p. 339),

which can be repeated in a hundred other formulas if, for
example, one puts plenary powers instead of power, or uses
formulas already given.

Private property = alien rela-⎫ ⎧My property=property relation
tion to the property of all⎬−⎨to the property of all others.
others.   ⎭ ⎩

Or also:

Property comprising a few   Property   comprising   every-
objects   − thing. (P. 343.)

Alienation [*Entfremdung*], as the relation or link in the above equations, can be expressed also in the following antitheses:

| *Private property* — *Egoistical property.* |

"To behave towards proper-⎫   ⎧"To renounce the holy rela-
ty as towards something ho-⎪   ⎪tion towards property",
ly, a spectre",   ⎬   ⎨no longer to regard it as
"to respect it",   ⎪   ⎪alien,
                           ⎪ −⎨no longer to fear the spectre,
                           ⎪   ⎪to have no respect for prop-
"to have respect for proper-⎪   ⎪erty,
ty". (P. 324.)   ⎭   ⎩to have the property of lack
                                 of respect.
                                 (Pp. 368, 340, 343.)

The modes of appropriation contained in the above equations and antitheses will be dealt with when we come to the "union", but as for the time being we are still in the "holy society", we are here only concerned with canonisation.

Note. In the section "Hierarchy" we already dealt with the question why the ideologists can regard the property relation as a relation of "Man", the different forms of which in different epochs are determined by the individuals' conception of "Man". It suffices here to refer the reader to that analysis.[a]

Treatise 1. On the parcellation of landed property, the redemption of feudal obligations and the swallowing-up of small landed property by large landed property.

All these things are deduced from holy property and the equation: bourgeois property=respect for the holy.

1. "Property in the bourgeois sense means *holy* property, in such a way that I must *respect* your property. 'Respect for property!' *Hence* the politicians would like everyone to possess his little piece of property and by their endeavour have partly brought about an incredible parcellation." (Pp. 327, 328.)—2. "The political liberals see to it that as far as possible all feudal obligations are redeemed and that everyone is a free master on his land, even though this land has only such a quantity of ground" (the land has a *quantity of ground!*) "that it can be adequately fertilised by the manure from one person.... No matter how small it is, so long as it is one's own, i.e., a *respected property!* The more such owners there are, the more free people and good patriots has the state." (P. 328.)—3. "Political liberalism, like everything religious, counts on *respect,*

_____
[a] See this volume, pp. 197-99.— *Ed.*

humanity, the virtues òf love. Therefore it experiences constant vexation. *For in practice people respect nothing*, and every day small properties are being bought up by large landowners, and the 'free people' are turned into day-labourers. If, on the other hand, the 'small owners' had *borne in mind* that large property also belongs to them, they would not have respectfully excluded themselves from it and would not have become excluded." (P. 328.)

1. Here, therefore, first of all the whole development of parcellation, about which Saint Sancho knows only that it is the holy, is explained from a mere idea which "the politicians" "have got into their heads". *Because* "the politicians" demand "respect for property", *hence* they "would like" parcellation, which moreover was carried out everywhere by *not respecting* other people's property! "The politicians" actually have "partly brought about an incredible parcellation". It was therefore through the action of the "politicians" that in France even before the revolution, just as today in Ireland and partly in Wales, parcellation had long existed in *agriculture*, and that capital and all other conditions were lacking for large-scale cultivation. Incidentally, how much "politicians" nowadays "would like" to carry out parcellation, Saint Sancho could see from the fact that all the French bourgeois are dissatisfied with parcellation, both because it weakens competition among the workers and also for political reasons; further, from the fact that all reactionaries (as Sancho could see if only from the *Erinnerungen* of the old Arndt) regarded parcellation simply as the conversion of landed property into modern, industrial, marketable, desanctified property. We shall not here set forth for our saint the *economic* reasons why the bourgeoisie, as soon as it has attained power, must carry out this conversion, which can come about both by the abolition of land rents that exceed profit and by parcellation. Nor shall we explain to him that the form in which this conversion takes place depends on the level of development of industry, trade, shipping, etc., in the country concerned. The propositions cited above about parcellation are nothing more than a bombastic circumlocution of the simple fact that in various places "here and there" considerable parcellation exists — expressed in our Sancho's canonising manner of speech, which suits everything and nothing. For the rest, Sancho's propositions given above contain merely the fantasies of the German petty bourgeois about parcellation which, of course, is for him the alien, "the holy". Cf. "Political Liberalism".

2. The redemption of feudal obligations, a misery which occurs only in Germany, where the governments were only compelled to carry it through by the more advanced conditions in neighbouring countries and by financial difficulties — this

redemption is held by our saint to be something that "the political liberals" desire in order to produce "free people and good burghers". Sancho's horizon again does not go beyond the Pomeranian Landtag and the Saxon Chamber of Deputies. This German redemption of feudal obligations never led to any political or economic results and, being a half-measure, remained without any effect at all. Sancho knows nothing, of course, about the *historically* important redemption of feudal obligations in the fourteenth and fifteenth centuries, which was due to the commencing development of trade and industry and the landowners' need for money.

The very same people who, like Stein and Vincke, wanted the redemption of feudal obligations in Germany in order, as Sancho believes, to make good burghers and free people, found later on that in order to produce "good burghers and free people" feudal obligations ought to be restored, as is just now being attempted in Westphalia. From which it follows that "respect", like the fear of God, is useful for all purposes.

3. The "buying-up" of small landed property by the "large landowners" takes place, according to Sancho, because in practice "respect for property" does not occur. Two of the most common consequences of competition — concentration and buying-up — and *competition* as a whole, which does not exist without concentration, seem here to our Sancho to be *violations* of bourgeois *property*, which moves within the sphere of competition. Bourgeois property is already violated by the very fact of its existence. In Sancho's opinion, it is not possible to buy anything without attacking property.* How deeply Saint Sancho has penetrated into the concentration of landed property can already be deduced from the fact that he sees in it only the most obvious act of concentration, the mere "buying-up". Incidentally, from what Sancho says it is not possible to perceive to what extent small landowners cease to be owners by becoming day-labourers. Indeed, on the following page (p. 329) Sancho himself with great solemnity advances as an argument against Proudhon that they continue to be "owners of the share remaining to them in the utilisation of the land", namely owners of wages. "It can sometimes be observed in history" that large landed property swallows up small landed property, and then in turn the small swallows up the large, two phenomena which, in

---

* [The following passage is crossed out in the manuscript:] Saint Sancho arrives at this nonsense because he mistakes the juridical, ideological expression of bourgeois property for actual bourgeois property, and he cannot understand why the reality will not correspond to this illusion of his.

Saint Sancho's opinion, become peacefully resolved into the adequate reason that "in practice people respect nothing". The same thing holds good for the other manifold forms of landed property. And then the wise "if the small owners had", etc.! In the Old Testament we saw how Saint Sancho, in accordance with the speculative method, made earlier generations reflect on the experiences of later ones; now we see how, in accordance with his ranting method, he complains that the earlier generations have failed to bear in mind not only the thoughts of later generations about them, but also his own nonsense. What school-masterly *wisdom*" [a]! If the terrorists had considered that they would bring Napoleon to the throne, if the English barons at the time of Runnymede and Magna Charta had considered that in 1849 the Corn Laws[96] would be repealed, if Croesus had considered that Rothschild would surpass him in riches, if Alexander the Great had considered that Rotteck[b] would judge him and that his Empire would fall into the hands of the Turks, if Themistocles had considered that he would defeat the Persians in the interests of Otto the Child,[97] if Hegel had considered that he would be exploited in such a "vulgar" way by Saint Sancho, ... if, if, if! About what kind of "small owners" does Saint Sancho fancy that he is talking? About the propertyless peasants who only *became* "small owners" as a result of the parcelling out of large landed property, or about those who are being ruined nowadays as a result of concentration? For Saint Sancho these two cases are as like as two drops of water. In the first case, the small owners did not by any means exclude themselves from "large property", but each took possession of it insofar as he was not excluded by others and had the power to do so. This power, however, was not Stirner's vaunted power, but was determined by quite empirical relations, e.g., their development and the whole preceding development of bourgeois society, the locality and its greater or lesser degree of connection with the neighbourhood, the size of the piece of land taken into possession, and the number of those who appropriated it, the relations of industry, of intercourse, means of communication, instruments of production, etc., etc. That they had no intention of excluding themselves from large landed property is evident even from the fact that many of them became large landed proprietors themselves. Sancho makes himself ridiculous even in Germany by his unreasonable

---

[a] In the manuscript the Berlin dialect form *Jescheitheit* is used.— *Ed.*

[b] Karl Rotteck, *Allgemeine Weltgeschichte für alle Stände.—Ed.*

demand that these peasants should have jumped the stage of parcellation, which did not yet exist and was at that time the only revolutionary form for them, and that they should have thrown themselves at a bound into his egoism in agreement with itself. Disregarding this nonsense of his, it was not possible for these peasants to organise themselves communistically, since they lacked all the means necessary for bringing about the first condition of communist association, namely collective husbandry, and since, on the contrary, parcellation was only one of the conditions which subsequently evoked the need for such an association. In general, a communist movement can never originate from the countryside, but only from the towns.

In the second case, when Saint Sancho talks of the ruined small owners, these still have a common interest with the big landowners as against the wholly propertyless class and the industrial bourgeoisie. If this common interest is absent, they lack the power to appropriate large landed property, since they live scattered and their whole activity and way of life make association, the first condition for such appropriation, impossible for them, and such a movement, in its turn, presupposes a much more general movement which by no means depends on them.

Finally, Sancho's whole tirade amounts to this: that they ought merely to get rid of their respect for the property of others. We shall hear a little more about this later on.

In conclusion, let us take one more proposition *ad acta.* "*The point is that in practice people respect nothing,*" so, after all, it appears that it is not "just" a matter of "respect".

Treatise No. 2. Private property, state and right.

"If, if, if!"

"If" Saint Sancho had for one moment set aside the current ideas of lawyers and politicians about private property, and also the polemic against it, if he had once looked at this private property in its empirical existence, in its connection with the productive forces of individuals, then all his Solomon's wisdom, with which he will now entertain us, would have been reduced to nothing. Then it would hardly have escaped him (although like Habakkuk he is *capable de tout*[98] that private property is a form of intercourse necessary for certain stages of development of the productive forces; a form of intercourse that cannot be abolished, and cannot be dispensed with in the production of actual material life, until productive forces have been created for which private property becomes a restricting fetter. In that case it could not have escaped the reader also that Sancho ought to have occupied himself with material relations, instead of dissolving the whole world in a system of theological morality in order to set against it a new system of would-be egoistical morality. It could not have escaped him that it was a question of things altogether different from "respect" or disrespect. "If, if, if!"

Incidentally, this "if" is only an echo of Sancho's proposition given above; for "if" Sancho had done all that, he obviously could not have written his book.

Since Saint Sancho accepts in good faith the illusion of politicians, lawyers and other ideologists which puts all empirical relations upside-down, and, in addition, in the German manner adds something of his own, *private property* for him *becomes transformed* into *state property*, or *property by right*, on which he can now make an experiment to justify his equations given above. Let us first of all look at the transformation of private property into state property.

> "The question of property is decided only by force" (on the contrary, the question of force has so far been decided by property), "and since the state alone is the mighty one — irrespective of whether it is a state of burghers, a state of ragamuffins" (Stirner's "union") "or simply a state of human beings — it alone is the owner." (P. 333.)

Side by side with the fact of the German "state of burghers" here again fantasies invented by Sancho and Bauer appear on an equal footing, whereas no mention is made anywhere of the historically important state formations. First of all he transforms the state into a person, into "the Mighty one". The fact that the ruling class establishes its joint domination as public power, as the state, Sancho interprets and distorts in the German petty-bourgeois manner as meaning that the "state" is established as a third force against this ruling class and absorbs all power in the face of it. He proceeds now to confirm this belief of his by means of a series of examples.

Because property under the rule of the bourgeoisie, as in all epochs, is bound up with definite conditions, first of all economic, which depend on the degree of development of the productive forces and intercourse — conditions which inevitably acquire a legal and political expression — Saint Sancho in his simplicity believes that

> "the *state* links possession of property" (*car tel est son bon plaisir*[a]) "just as it links everything else, e.g., marriage, with certain conditions". (P. 335.)

---

[a] Because it chooses to do so — a paraphrase of the concluding words of French royal edicts.— *Ed.*

Because the bourgeois do not allow the state to interfere in their private interests and give it only as much power as is necessary for their own safety and the maintenance of competition and because the bourgeois in general act as citizens only to the extent that their private interests demand it, Jacques le bonhomme believes that they are "nothing" in face of the state.

"The state is only interested in being wealthy itself; whether Michael is rich and Peter poor is a matter of indifference to it ... in face of it both of them are nothing." (P. 334.)

On page 345 he derives the same wisdom from the fact that competition is tolerated in the state.

Because the board of a railway is concerned about its shareholders only insofar as they make their payments and receive their dividends, the Berlin school-master in his innocence concludes that the shareholders are "nothing in face of the board just as we are all sinners in the face of God". On the basis of the impotence of the state in face of the activities of private property-owners Sancho proves the impotence of private property-owners in face of the state and his own impotence in face of both.

Further, since the bourgeois have organised the defence of their own property in the state, and the "ego" cannot, therefore, take away his factory "from such and such a manufacturer", except under the conditions of the bourgeoisie, i.e., under the conditions of competition, Jacques le bonhomme believes that

"the state has the factory as property, the manufacturer holds it only in fee, as possession". (P. 347.)

In exactly the same way when a dog guards my house it "has" the house "as property", and I hold it only "in fee, as possession" from the dog.

Since the concealed material conditions of private property are often bound to come into contradiction with the *juridical illusion* about private property—as seen, for example, in expropriations—Jacques le bonhomme concludes that

"here the otherwise concealed principle that only the state is the property-owner whereas the individual is a feudal tenant, strikes the eye" (p. 335).

All that "strikes the eye here" is the fact that worldly property relations are hidden from the eyes of our worthy burgher behind the mantle of "the holy", and that he has still to borrow a "heavenly ladder" from China in order to "climb" to the "rung of civilisation" attained even by school-masters in civilised countries. In the same way as Sancho here transforms the contradictions belonging to the *existence* of private property into the *negation* of private property, he dealt, as we saw above, with the contradictions within the bourgeois family.[a]

Since the bourgeois, and in general all the members of civil society, are forced to constitute themselves as "we", as a juridical person, as the state, in order to safeguard their common interests and—if only because of the division of labour—to delegate the collective power thus created to a few persons, Jacques le bonhomme imagines that

"each has the use of property only so long as he bears within himself the *ego* of the state or is a loyal member of society.... He who is a state-ego, i.e., a good burgher or subject, he, as *such* an ego, not as his own, holds the fee undisturbed." (Pp. 334, 335.)

From this point of view, a person possesses a railway share only so long as he "bears within himself" the "ego" of the board; consequently it is only as a saint that one can possess a railway share.

Having in this way convinced himself of the identity of private and state property, Saint Sancho can continue:

"That the state does not arbitrarily take away from the individual that which he has from the state, only means that the state does not rob itself." (Pp. 334, 335.)

That Saint Sancho does not arbitrarily rob others of their property only means that Saint Sancho does not rob himself, for indeed he *"regards"* all property as his own.

One cannot demand of us that we should deal further with the rest of Saint Sancho's fantasies about the state and property, e.g., that the state "tames" and "rewards" individuals by means of property, that out of special malice it has invented high stamp duties in order to ruin the citizens if they are not loyal, etc., etc., and in general with the *petty-bourgeois German* idea of the *omnipotence* of the state, an idea which was already current among the old German lawyers and is here presented in the form of grandiloquent assertions.

Finally Saint Sancho also tries to confirm his adequately proved identity of state and private property by means of etymological synonymy; in doing which, however, he belabours his erudition *en ambas posaderas.*

---

[a] See this volume, pp. 194-96.— *Ed.*

"My private property is only that which the state allows me out of *its property, by depriving (privieren)* other state members of it: it is state property." (P. 339.)

By chance this is just the reverse of what happened. Private property in *Rome*, to which alone this etymological witticism can relate, was in the most direct contradiction to state property. True, the state gave the plebeians private property; in doing so it did not, however, deprive "others" of their private property but deprived these plebeians themselves of their state property (*ager publicus*[a]) and their political rights, and it was precisely on that account that they *themselves* were called *privati*, robbed ones, and not the fantastical "other state members" of whom Saint Sancho dreams. Jacques le bonhomme covers himself with shame in all countries, all languages and all epochs as soon as he begins to talk about positive facts concerning which "the holy" cannot have any knowledge *a priori*.

Desperation because the state swallows up all property drives Sancho back to his innermost "indignant" self-consciousness, where he is surprised to discover that he is a *man of letters*. He expresses his astonishment in the following remarkable words:

"In opposition to the state I feel ever more clearly that I still retain one great power, power over myself."

Further on this is developed thus:

"My thoughts constitute real property for me with which I can carry on trade." (P. 339.)

Thus, Stirner the "ragamuffin", the "man of only ideal wealth", arrives at the desperate decision to carry on trade with the curdled, sour milk of his thoughts.[99] But what cunning does he use if the state declares his thoughts to be contraband? Just listen to this:

"I renounce them" (which is undoubtedly very wise) "and exchange them for others" (that is, if anyone should be such a bad businessman as to accept his exchange[b] of thoughts), "which then become my new, purchased property." (P. 339.)

Our honourable burgher will not rest until he has it in black and white that he has bought his property honestly. Here one sees the consolation of the Berlin burgher in the face of all his

---

[a] Common land.— *Ed.*

[b] In the original a pun, for the German word *Wechsel*, used here, can mean either "change", "alteration", "exchange" or "bill of exchange".— *Ed.*

political calamities and police tribulations: "Thoughts are free of customs duty!"[a]

The transformation of private property into state property reduces itself, in the final analysis, to the idea that the bourgeois has possessions only as a member of the bourgeois species, a species which as a whole is called the state and which invests individuals with the fief of property. Here again the matter is put upside-down. In the bourgeois class, as in every other, it is only personal conditions that are developed into common and universal conditions under which the separate members of the class possess and live. Although previously philosophical illusions of this kind could be current in Germany, they have now become completely ludicrous, since world trade has adequately proved that bourgeois gain is quite independent of politics, but that politics, on the other hand, is entirely dependent on bourgeois gain. Already in the eighteenth century, politics was so dependent on trade that when, for example, the French Government wanted to raise a loan, the Dutch demanded that a private individual should stand security for the state.

That "my worthlessness" or "pauperism" is the "realisation of the value" or the "existence" of the "state" (p. 336) is one of the thousand and one Stirnerian equations which we mention here only because in this connection we shall hear something new about pauperism.

"Pauperism is *my worthlessness*, the phenomenon that I cannot realise my value. Hence state and pauperism are one and the same.... The state is always trying to *derive benefit* from me, i.e., to exploit me, make use of me, to utilise me, even though this utilisation consists merely in my providing *proles*[b] (proletariat). It wants me to be its creature." (P. 336.)

Apart from the fact that one sees here how little it depends on him to realise his value, although everywhere and at all times he can assert his peculiarity, and that here once again, in contradiction to former statements, essence and appearance are totally divorced from each other, we have again the above-mentioned petty-bourgeois view of our bonhomme that the "state" wants to exploit him. The only further point of interest to us is the ancient Roman etymological derivation of the word "proletariat", which is here naïvely smuggled into the modern state. Does Saint Sancho really not know that wherever the modern state has developed, "providing *proles*" is for the state,

---

[a] Martin Luther, *Von weltlicher Obrigkeit.— Ed.*

[b] Offspring.— *Ed.*

i.e., the official bourgeois, precisely the most unpleasant activity of the proletariat? Perhaps he ought to translate Malthus and Minister Duchâtel into German,[a] for his own benefit? Just now, Saint Sancho, as a German petty bourgeois, "felt" "ever more clearly" that "in opposition to the state he still retained one great power", namely—the power to think in defiance of the state. If he were an English proletarian he would have felt that he "retained the power" to produce children in defiance of the state.

Another jeremiad against the state! Another theory of pauperism! To start with he, as "ego", "creates" "flour, linen or iron and coal", thereby from the outset abolishing division of labour. Then he begins "to complain" "at length" that his work is not paid for at its value, and in the first instance he comes into conflict with those who pay for it. Then the state comes between them in the role of "conciliator".

"If I am not satisfied with the price it" (i.e., the state) "pays for my commodity and labour, if instead I myself endeavour to fix the price of my commodity, i.e., try to see that it is lucrative for me, I come into conflict in the first instance" (a great "in the first instance"!—not with the state, but) "with the buyers of the commodity." (P. 337.)

If then he wants to enter into "direct relation" with these buyers, i.e., "seize them by the throat", the state "intervenes", "tears man from man" (although it was not a matter of "man in general" but of worker and employer or, what he lumps together in confusion, of the seller and buyer of commodities); moreover, the state does this with the malicious intention "to put itself in the middle as *spirit*" (obviously the holy spirit).

"Workers who demand higher wages are treated as criminals as soon as they try to achieve this by *force.*" (P. 337.)

Once more we are presented with a bouquet of nonsense. Mr. Senior need never have written his letters on wages[b] if he had first entered into "direct relation" with Stirner, especially as in that case the state would hardly have "torn man from man". Sancho here gives the state a triple function. It first acts as a "conciliator", then as price fixer, and finally as "spirit", as the holy. The fact that, after having gloriously identified private and state property, Saint Sancho also makes the state fix the level of wages, is testimony equally to his great consistency and his

---

[a] Thomas Robert Malthus, *An Essay on the Principle of Population*; Charles Marie Duchâtel, *De la Charité.—Ed.*

[b] Nassau William Senior, *Three Lectures on the Rate of Wages.—Ed.*

ignorance of the affairs of this world. The fact that in England, America and Belgium "workers who try to gain higher wages by force" are by no means immediately treated as "criminals", but on the contrary quite often actually succeed in obtaining higher wages, is also something of which our saint is ignorant, and which disposes of his whole legend about wages. The fact that, even if the state did not "put itself in the middle", the workers would gain nothing by "seizing" their employers "by the throat", or at any rate much less than through association and strikes, that is, so long as they remain workers and their opponents capitalists—this is also something that could be comprehended even in Berlin. There is likewise no need to demonstrate that bourgeois society, which is based on competition, and its bourgeois state, owing to their whole material basis, cannot permit any struggle among the citizens except the struggle of competition, and are bound to intervene not as "spirit", but with bayonets if people "seize each other by the throat".

Incidentally, Stirner's idea that only the state becomes richer when individuals become richer on the basis of bourgeois property, or that up to now all private property has been state property, is an idea that again puts historical relations upside-down. With the development and accumulation of bourgeois property, i.e., with the development of commerce and industry, individuals grew richer and richer while the state fell ever more deeply into debt. This phenomenon was evident already in the first Italian commercial republics; later, since the last century, it showed itself to a marked degree in Holland, where the stock exchange speculator Pinto drew attention to it as early as 1750,[a] and now it is again occurring in England. It is therefore obvious that as soon as the bourgeoisie has accumulated money, the state has to beg from the bourgeoisie and in the end it is actually bought up by the latter. This takes place in a period in which the bourgeoisie is still confronted by another class, and consequently the state can retain some appearance of independence in relation to both of them. Even after the state has been bought up, it still needs money and, therefore, continues to be dependent on the bourgeoisie; nevertheless, when the interests of the bourgeoisie demand it, the state can have at its disposal more funds than states which are less developed and, therefore, less burdened with debts. However,

---

[a] Icaac Pinto, *Lettre sur la jalousie du commerce* in *Traité de la Circulation et du Crédit.*— Ed.

even the least developed states of Europe, those of the Holy Alliance, are inexorably approaching this fate, for they will be bought up by the bourgeoisie; then Stirner will be able to console them with the identity of private and state property, especially his own sovereign, who is trying in vain to postpone the hour when political power will be sold to the "burghers" who have become "angry".

We come now to the relation between private property and right, where we have to listen to the same stuff in another form. The identity of state and private property is apparently given a new turn. Political *recognition* of private property in law is declared to be the *basis* of private property.

"Private property lives by grace of right. It is guaranteed only in right—for possession is not yet property—it becomes mine only with the consent of right; it is not a fact, but a fiction, a thought. That is property by right, rightful property, *guaranteed* property; it is mine not thanks to me, but thanks to right." (P. 332.)

In this passage the previous nonsense about state property merely reaches still more comical heights. We shall, therefore, pass on at once to Sancho's exploitation of the fictitious *jus utendi et abutendi*.[a]

On page 332 we learn, besides the beautiful passage above, that property

"is unlimited power over something which I can dispose of as I please". But "power" is "not something existing of itself, but exists only in the powerful ego, in me, the possessor of power". (P. 366.) Hence property is not a "thing", "what is mine is not this tree, but my power over it, my ability to dispose of it". (P. 366.) He only knows "things" or "egos". "The power" which is "separated from the ego", given independent existence, transformed into a "spectre", is "right". "This perpetuated power" (treatise on right of inheritance) "is not extinguished even when I die, but is passed on or inherited. Things now really belong not to me, but to right. On the other hand, this is nothing but a delusion, for the power of the individual becomes permanent, and becomes a right, only because other individuals combine their power with his. The delusion consists in their belief that they cannot take their power." (Pp. 366, 367.) "A dog who sees a bone in the power of another dog stands aside only if it feels it is too weak. Man, however, respects the *right* of the other man to his bone.... And as here, so in general, it is called '*human*' when something *spiritual*, in this case right, is seen in everything, i.e., when everything is made into a spectre and treated as a spectre.... It is human to regard the individual phenomenon not as an individual, but as a universal phenomenon." (Pp. 368, 369.)

Thus once again the whole mischief arises from the faith of individuals in the conception of right, which they *ought* to get

---

[a] The right of using and consuming (also: abusing), i. e., of disposing of a thing at will.—*Ed.*

out of their heads. Saint Sancho only knows "things" and "egos", and as regards anything that does not come under these headings, as regards all relations, he knows only the abstract concepts of them, which for him, therefore, also become "spectres". "On the other hand", it does dawn on him at times that all this is "nothing but a delusion" and that the "power of the individual" very much depends on whether others combine their power with his. But in the final analysis everything is nevertheless reduced to the "illusion" that individuals "*believe* that they cannot take back their power". Once again the railways do not "actually" belong to the shareholders, but to the statutes. Sancho immediately puts forward the right of inheritance as a striking example. He explains it not from the necessity for accumulation and from the family which existed before right, but from the *juridical fiction* of the *prolongation of power* beyond death.* However, the more feudal society passes into bourgeois society, the more is this juridical fiction itself abandoned by the legislation of all countries. (Cf., for example, the Code Napoléon.) There is no need to show here that absolute paternal power and primogeniture — both natural feudal primogeniture and the later form — were based on very definite material relations. The same thing is to be found among ancient peoples in the epoch of the disintegration of the *community* in consequence of the development of *private* life (the best proof of this is the history of the Roman right of inheritance). In general, Sancho could not have chosen a more unfortunate example than the right of inheritance, which in the clearest possible way shows the dependence of right on the relations of production. Compare, for example, Roman and German right of inheritance. Certainly, no dog has ever made phosphorus, bonemeal or lime out of a bone, any more than it has ever "got into its head" anything about its "right" to a bone; equally, it has never "entered the head" of Saint Sancho to reflect whether the right to a bone which people, but not dogs, claim for themselves, is not connected with the way in which people, but not dogs, utilise this bone in production. In general, in this one example we have before us Sancho's whole method of criticism and his unshakeable faith in current illusions. The

---

* [The following passage is crossed out in the manuscript:] He could have learned from more advanced legal systems which adequately express modern property relations, e. g., from the *Code civil*, that... "the perpetuated power" which "is not extinguished even when I die" is, in the *Code civil*, reduced to a minimum, and the legal portion of children is a recognition of the material basis of the law and particularly of the law under bourgeois rule.

hitherto existing production relations of individuals are bound also to be expressed as political and legal relations. (See above.[a]) Within the division of labour these relations are bound to acquire an independent existence over against the individuals. All relations can be expressed in language only in the form of concepts. That these general ideas and concepts are looked upon as mysterious forces is the necessary result of the fact that the real relations, of which they are the expression, have acquired independent existence. Besides this meaning in everyday consciousness, these general ideas are further elaborated and given a special significance by politicians and lawyers, who, as a result of the division of labour, are dependent on the cult of these concepts, and who see in them, and not in the relations of production, the true basis of all real property relations. Saint Sancho, who takes over this illusion without examination, is thus enabled to declare that property by right is the basis of private property, and that the concept of right is the basis of property by right, after which he can restrict his whole criticism to declaring that the concept of right is a concept, a spectre. That is the end of the matter for Saint Sancho. To set his mind at rest, we can add that in all the early law books the behaviour of two dogs who have found a bone is regarded as right: *vim vi repellere licere*,[b] say the Pandects [100]; *idque jus natura comparatur*,[c] by which is meant *jus quod natura omnia animalia* (people and dogs) *docuit*[d]; but that later it is "just" the organised repulsion of force by force that becomes right.

Saint Sancho, who is now well under way, proves his erudition in the field of the history of right by disputing a "bone" with Proudhon.

Proudhon, he says, "tries to humbug us into believing that society is the original possessor and sole owner of imprescriptible right; that the so-called owner has committed theft with regard to society; that if society takes from any present-day owner his property, it does not steal anything from him, for it is only asserting its imprescriptible right. That is where one can get with the spectre of society as a *juridical person*". (Pp. 330, 331.)

In contrast to this Stirner "tries to humbug us into believing" (pp. 340, 367, 420 and elsewhere) that we, viz., the propertyless, presented the owners with their property, out of ignorance,

---

[a] See this volume, pp. 41-42.— *Ed.*
[b] It is permissible to repel force by force.— *Ed.*
[c] And this right is fixed by nature.— *Ed.*
[d] A right which nature has taught all living beings.— *Ed.*

cowardice or good nature, etc., and he calls on us to take back our gift. The difference between these two attempts at "humbugging" is that Proudhon bases himself on a historical fact, while Saint Sancho has only "got something into his head" in order to give the matter a "new turn". For recent investigations into the history of right have established that both in Rome and among the German, Celtic and Slav peoples the development of property had as its starting-point communal or tribal property and that private property strictly speaking arose everywhere by usurpation; Saint Sancho could of course not extract this from the profound idea that the concept of right is a concept. In relation to the legal dogmatists, Proudhon was perfectly right when he stressed this fact and in general combated them by means of their own premises. "That is where one can get with the spectre" of the concept of right as a concept. Proudhon could only have been attacked on account of his proposition quoted above if he had defended the earlier and cruder form of property against the private property that had developed out of this primitive communal system. Sancho sums up his criticism of Proudhon in the arrogant question:

"Why such a sentimental appeal for sympathy as if he were a poor victim of robbery?" (P. 420.)

Sentimentality, of which, incidentally, not a trace is to be found in Proudhon, is only permitted towards Maritornes. Sancho really imagines that he is a "whole fellow" compared with such a believer in apparitions as Proudhon. He considers his inflated bureaucratic style, of which even Frederick William IV would be ashamed, to be revolutionary. "Blessed are those that believe."[a]

On page 340 we learn:

"All the attempts to enact rational laws about property proceeded from the *bay of love* into a barren ocean of definitions."

A fitting companion to this is the equally bizarre statement:

"Intercourse hitherto has been based on love, on considerate behaviour, on care for one another." (P. 385.)

Saint Sancho here surprises himself with a striking paradox about right and intercourse. If, however, we recall that by "love" he understands love of "Man", love of something existing in and for itself, of the universal, that by love he understands the relation to an individual or thing regarded as

_____
[a] Luke 1:45 (paraphrased).— *Ed.*

essence, the *holy*, then this appearance of brilliance is dissipated. The oracular utterances quoted above are then reduced to the old trivialities which have bored us throughout "the book", i.e., that two things, about which Sancho knows nothing, viz., in this case hitherto existing right and hitherto existing intercourse, are the "holy", and that in general only "concepts have ruled the world" up to now. The relation to the holy, as a rule called "respect", can on occasion also be entitled "love". (See "Logic".)

Just one example of how Saint Sancho transforms legislation into a love relation, and trade into a love-affair:

> "In a Registration Bill for Ireland, the government put forward the proposal to give the suffrage to those who pay a tax of £5 for the poor. Consequently one who gives alms acquires political rights or, elsewhere, becomes a Knight of the Swan." (P. 344.)

It is to be noted here first of all that this "Registration Bill" granting "political rights" was a municipal or corporation Bill or, in more comprehensible language to Sancho, an "urban regulation", which was not designed to grant "political rights" but only urban rights, the right to elect local officials. Secondly, Sancho, who translates McCulloch, surely ought to know quite well the meaning of "to be assessed to the poor-rates at five pounds".[a] This does not mean "to pay a tax of £5 for the poor", but means to be entered on the list of those who pay this tax as the tenants of a house the annual rent of which amounts to £5. Our Berlin bonhomme does not know that the poor-rate in England and Ireland is a *local* tax which *varies* in amount in different towns and different years, so that it would be a sheer impossibility to connect any sort of right with the payment of a particular amount of tax. Finally, Sancho believes that the English and Irish poor-rate is an "*alms*"; whereas it only provides funds for a direct and open offensive war of the ruling bourgeoisie against the proletariat. It pays the cost of workhouses which, as is well known, are a Malthusian deterrent against pauperism. We see how Sancho "proceeds from the bay of love into a barren ocean of definitions".

It may be remarked in passing that German philosophy, because it took consciousness alone as its point of departure, was bound to end in moral philosophy, where the various heroes squabble about true morals. Feuerbach loves man for the sake

---

[a] McCulloch, *Statistical Account of the British Empire*. The quotation is in English in the manuscript.— *Ed.*

of man, Saint Bruno loves him because he "deserves" it (*Wigand*, p. 137[a]), while Saint Sancho loves "everyone", because he likes to do so, with the consciousness of egoism. ("The book", p. 387.)

We have already seen above — in the first treatise — how the small landed proprietors respectfully excluded themselves from large landed property. This self-exclusion from other people's property, out of respect, is depicted in general as the characteristic of bourgeois property. From this characteristic Stirner is able to explain to himself why it is that

"within the bourgeois system, in spite of its implication that everyone should be an owner, the majority have practically nothing". (P. 348.) This "occurs because the majority are pleased if they are owners at all, even if they are merely owners of a few rags". (P. 349.)

That the "majority" possess only "a few rags", Szeliga regards as a perfectly natural consequence of their love of rags.

Page 343: "Am I thus nothing but an owner? No, hitherto a person was merely an owner, secure in possession of a plot of land by allowing others also to possess their plot; now, however, *everything* belongs to me. I am the owner of everything that I need and can take possession of."

Just as Sancho previously made small landed proprietors respectfully exclude themselves from large landed property, and now makes the small landed proprietors exclude one another, so he could go into more detail and make respect responsible for the exclusion of commercial property from landed property, of industrial property from commercial property proper, etc., and thus arrive at a totally new political economy on the basis of the holy. He has only then to get respect out of his head in order to abolish at one stroke division of labour and the form of property that arises from it. Sancho gives an example of this new political economy on page 128 of "the book", where he buys a needle not from a shopkeeper,[b] but from respect, and not with money paid to the shopkeeper, but with respect paid to the needle. Incidentally, the *dogmatic* self-exclusion of each individual from other people's property which Sancho attacks is a purely juridical illusion. Under the modern mode of production and intercourse each person delivers a blow at this illusion and directs his efforts precisely to excluding all others from the property that at present belongs to them. How the matter stands with regard to Sancho's "property in everything" is clear enough from the supplementary clause:

[a] Bruno Bauer, "Charakteristik Ludwig Feuerbachs".— *Ed.*
[b] Here and below the word is in English in the original.— *Ed.*

"that I need and *can take possession of*". He explains this in more detail on page 353:

"If I say: the world belongs to me, *then, properly speaking, this too is empty talk*, which has meaning only insofar as I do not respect any property of others";

that is insofar as *no n-respect* of the property of others constitutes *his property*.

What irks Sancho about the private property that is so dear to him is precisely its exclusiveness, without which it would be nonsense — the fact that besides him there are also other private owners. For the private property of others is something holy. We shall see how in his "union" he gets over this inconvenience. We shall find that his egoistical property, property in the extraordinary sense, is nothing but ordinary or bourgeois property transfigured by his sanctifying fantasy.

Let us conclude with the following wisdom of Solomon:

"If people reach a stage where they lose respect for property, then each will possess property ... then [in this matter, too, *unions* will augment the means of the individual and safeguard his contested property." (P. 342.)][a]

[Treatise No. 3: On competition in the ordinary and extraordinary sense.]

One morning the writer of these lines, in suitable attire, went to see Herr Minister Eichhorn:

"Since things have come to nothing with the factory-owner" (for the Finance Minister had given him neither a site nor funds to build a factory of his own, and the Minister of Justice had not given him permission to take the factory away from the factory-owner — see above on bourgeois property[b]) "I will compete with this professor of law; the man is a blockhead, and I, who know a hundred times more than he does, will take his audience away from him."—"But, my friend, did you study at a university and get a degree?"—"No, but what of that? I fully understand all that is necessary for teaching."—"I'm sorry, but in this matter there is no free competition. I have nothing against you personally, but the essential thing is lacking—a doctor's diploma—and I, the state, demand it."—"So that is the freedom of competition," sighed the author. "Only the state, *my master*, gives me the possibility of competing." Whereupon he returned home downcast. (P. 347.)

In a more advanced country it would not have occurred to him to ask the state for permission to compete with a professor of law. But once he turns to the state as an *employer* and asks for remuneration, i.e., *wages*, thus entering the sphere of competition, then of course after his previous treatises about private property and *privati*, communal property, the proletariat, *lettres patentes*, the state and *status*, etc., one cannot

---

[a] Four pages of the manuscript are missing here.— *Ed.*

[b] See this volume, p. 377.— *Ed.*

suppose that his "solicitation will be successful". Judging by his past feats, the state can at best appoint him as custodian (*custos*) of "the holy" on some domanial estate in the backwoods of Pomerania.

By way of amusement we can "insert" here "episodically" Sancho's great discovery that there is no "other difference" between the "*poor*" and the "*rich*" "than that between the *resourceful*[a] and the *resourceless*"[b]. (P. 354.)

Let us plunge once more into the "barren ocean" of Stirner's "definitions" of competition:

> "Competition is connected *less*" (Oh, "less"!) "with the intention of doing a thing as well as possible, than with the intention of making it as *profitable*, lucrative, as possible. For that reason people study for the sake of a post (bread-and-butter study), cultivate obsequiousness and flattery, routine and knowledge of business; they work for appearance. Hence while apparently it is a matter of a *good performance*, in reality people aim only at a good stroke of business and monetary gain. Of course, no one wants to be a censor, but people want to get advancement ... people are afraid of being transferred or even more of being dismissed." (Pp. 354, 355.)

Let our bonhomme discover a textbook on political economy where even theoreticians assert that in competition it is a matter of a "good performance" or "of doing a thing as well as possible" and not of making "it as profitable as possible". Incidentally, in any such book he will find it stated that under the system of private property highly developed competition, for example in England, certainly causes a "thing" to be "done as well as possible". Small-scale commercial and industrial swindling flourishes only in conditions of restricted competition, among the Chinese, Germans and Jews, and in general among hawkers and small shopkeepers. But even hawking is not mentioned by our saint; he only knows the competition of super-numerary officials and school-masters on probation, he reveals himself here as a downright royal-Prussian junior official. He might just as well have given as an example of competition the endeavour of courtiers in every age to win the favour of their sovereign, but that lay much too far beyond his petty-bourgeois field of vision.

After these tremendous adventures with super-numerary officials, salaried accountants and registrars, Saint Sancho experiences his great adventure with the famous horse

---

[a] In the original *der Vermögende*, a capable, resourceful, powerful or wealthy person.— *Ed.*

[b] In the original *der Unvermögende*, an incapable, resourceless, powerless or destitute person.— *Ed.*

Clavileño, of which the prophet Cervantes has already spoken in the New Testament, Chapter 41. For Sancho mounts the high horse of political economy and determines the minimum wage by means of "the holy". True, here once again he reveals his innate timidity and at first refuses to mount the flying steed that carries him far above the clouds into the region "where hail and snow, thunder, lightning and thunderbolts are engendered". But the "Duke", i.e., the "state", encourages him and as soon as the bolder and more experienced Szeliga-Don Quixote has swung himself into the saddle, our worthy Sancho climbs behind him on to the horse's crupper. And when Szeliga's hand had turned the peg on the horse's head, the horse soared high into the air and all the ladies — especially Maritornes — cried after them: "May egoism in agreement with itself guide you, valiant knight, and you, still more valiant armour-bearer, and may you succeed in liberating us from the spectre of Malambruno, of 'the holy'. Only keep your balance, valiant Sancho, so that you do not fall and suffer the same fate as Phaeton, when he wanted to drive the chariot of the sun."

"If we assume" (he is already wavering hypothetically) "that just as *order* belongs to the *essence of the state, subordination* too is based on its *nature*" (a pleasant modulation between "essence" and "nature"—the "goats" which Sancho observed during his flight), "*then* we observe that the underprivileged are *excessively overcharged* and *defrauded* by the inferior" (it should probably read superior) "or privileged." (P. 357.)

"If we assume ... then we observe." It should read: then we assume. If we assume that "superior" and "inferior" exist in the state, then "we assume" likewise that the former are "privileged" compared with the latter. We can, however, ascribe the stylistic beauty of this sentence, as also the sudden recognition of the "essence" and "nature" of a thing, to the timidity and confusion of our Sancho while anxiously trying to retain his balance during his aerial flight, and to the rockets set alight under his nose. We are not even surprised that Saint Sancho derives the consequences of competition not from competition but from bureaucracy, and once again makes the state determine wages.*

---

* [The following passage is crossed out in the manuscript:] Here again he does not take into consideration that the "overcharging" and "defrauding" of the workers in the modern world is due to their lack of property and that the lack of property directly contradicts the assertions which Sancho attributes to the liberal bourgeoisie [...] the liberal bourgeoisie who claim to give property to everyone by parcelling out landed property.

He does not take into consideration that the continual fluctuations in wages explode the whole of his beautiful theory; a closer examination of industrial conditions would certainly have provided him with examples of a factory-owner being "overcharged" and "defrauded" by his workers according to the universal laws of competition, if these juridical and moral expressions had not lost all meaning within the framework of competition.

The dwarfish form to which competition has shrunk for Sancho once again demonstrates the naïve and petty-bourgeois manner in which world-embracing relations are reflected inside his unique skull, and the extent to which he as a school-master is bound to extract moral applications from all these relations and to refute them with moral postulates. We must give this precious passage *in extenso* "so that nothing should be lost".

> "As regards competition again, it exists precisely because not all persons *attend to their business* and *come to an understanding* with one another about it. Thus, for example, bread is needed by all the inhabitants of a town; hence they could easily come to an agreement to establish a public bakery. Instead, they leave the supply of bread to competing bakers. Similarly, they leave the supply of meat to the butchers, of wine to the wine merchants, etc.... If *I* do not concern myself with *my* business, then I have to *be content* with what *it suits* others to offer me. To have bread is my business, my wish and desire, and yet people leave it to the bakers, and hope at most, thanks to their contention, rivalry and their attempts to outstrip one another, in a word, thanks to their competition, to get an advantage which people could not count on under the guild-system, when the right to bake bread belonged *wholly and solely* to the guilds-men." (P. 365.)

It is characteristic of our petty bourgeois that he here recommends to his fellow-philistines, in place of competition, an institution like public bakeries, which existed in many places under the guild-system and which were put an end to by the cheaper competitive mode of production. That is to say, he recommends an institution of a local nature, which could only persist under narrowly restricted conditions and was inevitably bound to perish with the rise of competition, which abolished local narrowness. He has not even learned from competition that the "need" of bread, for example, differs from day to day, that it does not at all depend on him whether tomorrow bread will still be "his business" or whether others will still regard his need as their business, and that within the framework of competition the price of bread is determined by the costs of production and not by the whim of the bakers. He ignores all those relations which were brought about by competition: the abolition of local narrowness, the establishment of means of communication, highly developed division of labour, world intercourse, the proletariat, machinery, etc., and regretfully looks back to medieval philistinism. All he knows about competition is that it is "contention, rivalry and attempts to outstrip one another"; he is not concerned about its connection with division of labour, the relation between supply and demand, etc.* That the bourgeois, whenever their interests demanded it (and they are better judges of this than Saint Sancho), always "came to an understanding" insofar as this was possible in the framework of competition and private property, is proved by the joint-stock companies, which came into being with the rise of sea-borne trade and manufacture and took possession of all the branches of industry and commerce accessible to them. Such "agreements", which led among other things to the conquest of an empire in the East Indies,[101] are of course a small matter compared with the well-meaning fantasy about public bakeries, which is worthy of being discussed in the *Vossische Zeitung.*

As for the proletarians, they — at any rate in the modern form — first arose out of competition; they have already repeatedly set up collective enterprises which, however, always perished because they were unable to compete with the "contending" private bakers, butchers, etc., and because for proletarians — owing to the frequent opposition of interests among them arising out of the division of labour — no other "agreement" is possible than a political one directed against the whole present system. Where the development of competition enables the proletarians to "come to an understanding", they reach an understanding not about public bakeries but about quite different matters.** The lack of "agreement" between

---

* [The following passage is crossed out in the manuscript:] At the outset they could have "come to an understanding". That an "understanding" (to use this word with its moral connotations) is only made possible by competition and that because of the antagonistic class interests there can be no question of all people "coming to an understanding", as Sancho suggests, hardly troubles our sage. These German philosophers generally believe that their own petty parochial misery is of world-historical importance, while as regards the most far-reaching historical relations they imagine it was only for want of their wisdom that matters were not settled by "agreement" and everything cleared up. Sancho's example shows how far one can get with such fantasies.

** [The following passage is crossed out in the manuscript:] "They" should "come to an understanding" about a public bakery. It does not, of course, concern our Sancho that in each epoch those whom he calls "they" and "all" are themselves diverse individuals with diverse interests, living under diverse conditions. During the whole course of history until now individuals have always made the mistake that, from the very outset, they did not adopt the

competing individuals that Sancho notes here entirely corresponds to and contradicts his further exposition of competition, which we can enjoy in the "Commentary". (*Wigand*, p. 173.)

"Competition was introduced because it was looked upon as a blessing for all. People *came to an agreement* about it, attempts were made to approach it *jointly*... people *agreed* about it in much the same way as on a hunting expedition all the hunters taking part ... may find it expedient for their purpose to scatter in the forest and to hunt 'singly'.... True, it now turns out ... that in the case of competition not everyone gets ... his advantage."

"It turns out" that Sancho knows as much about hunting as he knows about competition. He is not speaking about a battue nor about hunting with hounds, but about hunting in the extraordinary sense. It only remains for him to write a new history of industry and commerce according to the above principles, and to set up a "union" for this kind of extraordinary hunting.

In the same calm, comfortable style appropriate to a parish magazine he speaks of the relation of competition to morality.

"Those corporeal goods which man as such" (!) "cannot maintain, we have the right to take away from him: this is the meaning of competition, of freedom of industry. Any of the spiritual goods that he cannot maintain devolve likewise upon us. But *sanctified* goods are inviolable. Sanctified and guaranteed — by whom?... By man or the concept, the concept of the matter under consideration." As such sanctified goods he cites "life", "freedom of the person", "religion", "honour", "sense of decency", "sense of shame", etc. ([Stirner, *Der Einzige und sein Eigentum*,] p. 325.)

In the advanced countries, Stirner "has the right" to take all these "sanctified goods", although not from "man as such", but from actual men, of course, by means of and under the conditions of competition. The great revolution of society brought about by competition, which resolved the relations of the bourgeois to one another and to the proletarians into purely monetary relations, and converted all the above-named "sanctified goods" into articles of trade, and which destroyed for the proletarians all naturally derived and traditional relations, e.g., family and political relations, together with their entire ideological superstructure — this mighty revolution did not, of course, originate in Germany. Germany played only a passive role in it; she allowed her sanctified goods to be taken from her without even getting the current price for them. Hence our German petty bourgeois knows only the hypocritical assertions

overwise "cleverness" with which, after the events, our German philosophers are expatiating about them.

of the bourgeoisie about the moral limits of competition observed by the bourgeoisie, which every day tramples underfoot the "sanctified goods" of the proletarians, their "honour", "sense of shame" and "freedom of the person", and which even deprives them of religious instruction. These would-be "moral limits" are regarded by Sancho as the true "meaning" of competition, and its reality is excluded from its meaning.

Sancho sums up the results of his investigation of competition as follows:

"Is the competition free which the state, this ruler, according to bourgeois principles, cramps by a thousand barriers?" (P. 347.)

Sancho's "bourgeois principle" of everywhere making the "state" the "ruler" and regarding the barriers of competition that arise from the mode of production and intercourse as barriers by which the "state" "cramps" competition, are here once more proclaimed with suitable "indignation".

"Recently" Saint Sancho has vaguely heard miscellaneous news "from France" (cf. *Wigand*, p. 190), *inter alia*, about the objectification of persons in competition and the difference between competition and emulation. But the "poor Berliner" has, "*out of stupidity*, spoilt these fine things" (*Wigand*, ibid., where it is his guilty conscience that speaks). "Thus, for example, he says" on page 346 of "the book":

"Is free competition actually free? Indeed, is it real competition, i.e., competition of *persons*, as it gives itself out to be, because it bases its right on this title?"

Madame Competition gives herself out to be something, because she (i.e., some lawyers, politicians and petty-bourgeois dreamers, trailing in the tail of her suite) bases her right on this title. With this allegory Sancho begins to adapt the "fine things" "from France" to suit the Berlin meridian. We shall skip the absurd assertion already dealt with above that "the state has no objection to make against me personally" and thus allows me to compete, but does not give me the "thing" (p. 347), and we shall pass straight on to his proof that competition is not at all a competition of persons.

"But is it *persons* who actually compete? No, it is again *only things*! In the first place — money, etc. There is always one who lags behind the other in the contest. But it makes a difference whether the means that are lacking can be gained through *personal power* or can only be obtained by grace, as a gift, and moreover by the poorer, for instance, being forced to leave, i.e., to present his wealth to the richer." (P. 348.)

As for the gift theory, we shall "spare him".[a] (*Wigand*, p. 190.) Let him look up the chapter on "contract" in any textbook of law and find out whether a "gift" he is "forced to present" is still a gift. In this way, Stirner "presents" us with our criticism of his book, for he "is forced to leave, i.e., to present", it to us.

The fact that of two competitors whose "things" are equal one ruins the other, does not exist for Sancho. That workers compete among themselves, although they possess no "things" (in Stirner's sense) is also a fact that does not exist for him. By doing away with the competition of workers among themselves, he is fulfilling one of the most pious wishes of our "true socialists", whose deepest thanks he is sure to receive. So it is "only things" and not "persons" that compete. Only weapons fight, not the people who use them, and who have learned to wield them. The people are only there to be shot dead. This is how the competitive struggle is reflected in the minds of petty-bourgeois school-masters who, faced with modern stock exchange barons and cotton-lords,[b] console themselves with the thought that they only lack the "things" in order to bring their "personal power" to bear against them. This narrow-minded idea appears still more comic if one looks a little more closely at the "things", instead of restricting oneself to the commonest and most popular, e.g., "money" (which, however, is not so popular as it seems). These "things" include, among others: that the competitor lives in a country and town, where he enjoys the same advantages as the competitors whom he encounters; that relations between town and countryside have reached an advanced stage of development; that he is competing under favourable geographical, geological and hydrographical conditions; that as a silk manufacturer he carries on his business in Lyons, as a cotton manufacturer in Manchester, or, in an earlier period, as a shipper in Holland; that division of labour in his branch of industry — as in other branches totally independent of him — has become highly developed; that the means of communication ensure him the same cheap transport as his competitors; and that he finds in existence skilful workers and experienced overseers. All these "things", which are essential for competition, and in general the ability to compete on the *world market* (which he does not know and cannot know

---

[a] In German, a pun on the word *schenken*, which means to give, to present, to make a gift of, but which in a certain context can also mean to spare, to let off.— *Ed.*

[b] This word is in English in the manuscript.— *Ed.*

because of his theory of the state and public bakeries, but which, unfortunately, determines competition and the ability to compete), are "things" that he can neither gain by "personal power" nor "get presented" to him by "grace" of the "state". (Cf. p. 348.) The Prussian state, which attempted to "present" all this to the *Seehandlung*,[102] could give him the best instruction on that subject. Sancho appears here as the royal Prussian philosopher of the *Seehandlung*, by giving a detailed commentary on the illusion of the Prussian state about its omnipotence and the illusion of the *Seehandlung* about its competitive capacity. Incidentally, competition certainly began as a "competition of persons" possessing "personal means". The liberation of the feudal serfs, the first condition of competition, and the first accumulation of "things" were purely "personal" acts. If, therefore, Sancho wishes to put the competition of persons in the place of competition of things, it means that he wishes to return to the beginning of competition, imagining in doing so that by his good will and his extraordinary egoistical consciousness he can give a different direction to the development of competition.

This great man, for whom nothing is holy and who is not interested in the "nature of things" and the "concept of the relation", has nevertheless in the end to declare the "nature" of the difference between personal and material to be holy, as also the "concept of the relation" between these two qualities, and so renounce the role of "creator" in respect of them. The difference — regarded by him as holy — which he notes in the passage quoted, can nevertheless be abolished without thereby committing "the most unmitigated profanation". Firstly he abolishes it himself by causing material means to be acquired through personal power and thus converts personal power into material power. He can then calmly address others with the moral postulate that they should adopt a personal attitude to him. In just the same way the Mexicans could have demanded that the Spaniards should not shoot them with rifles but attack them with their fists or, according to Saint Sancho's proposal, "seize them by the throat" in order to adopt a "personal" attitude to them.

If one person, thanks to good food, careful education and physical exercise, has acquired well-developed bodily powers and skill, while another, owing to inadequate and unhealthy food and consequent poor digestion, and as the result of neglect in childhood and over-exertion, has never been able to acquire the "things" necessary for developing his muscles — not to mention acquiring mastery over them — then the "personal power" of the first in relation to the second is a purely material one. It was not "through personal power" that he gained the "means that were lacking"; on the contrary, he owes his "personal power" to the material means already existing. Incidentally, the transformation of personal means into material means and of material means into personal means is only an aspect of competition and quite inseparable from it. The demand that competition should be conducted not with material means but with personal means amounts to the moral postulate that competition and the relations on which it depends *should* have consequences other than those inevitably arising from them.

Here is yet another, and this time the final summing-up of the philosophy of competition:

"Competition suffers from the drawback that not everyone has the means for competition, because these means are taken not from *personality*, but from *chance*. The majority are without means and therefore" (Oh, Therefore!) "impecunious". (P. 349.)

It has already been pointed out to him that in competition personality itself is a matter of chance, while chance is personality.[a] The "means" for competition which are independent of personality are the conditions of production and intercourse of the persons themselves, which within the framework of competition appear as an independent force in relation to these persons, as means which are accidental for them. The liberation of people from these forces comes about, according to Sancho, by people getting out of their heads the *ideas* about these forces, or rather the philosophical and religious distortions of these ideas — whether by etymological synonymy ("*Vermögen*" and "*vermögen*"), moral postulates (e.g., let each one be an all-powerful ego), or by making monkey faces and by sentimentally comic bragging against "the holy".

We have heard the complaint made before that in present-day bourgeois society the "ego", especially because of the state, cannot realise its value, i.e., cannot bring its "abilities" [*Vermögen*] into play. Now we learn in addition that "peculiarity" does not give the "ego" the means for competition, that "its might" is no might at all and that it remains "impecunious", although every object, "being *its* object, is also its *property*"*. It

* [The following passage is crossed out in the manuscript:] The difference between essence and appearance asserts itself here in spite of Sancho.

[a] See this volume, pp. 86-88.— *Ed.*

is a complete denial of egoism in agreement with itself. But all these "drawbacks" of competition will disappear, once "the book" has become part of the general consciousness of people. Until then Sancho persists in his trade in thoughts, without however achieving a "good performance" or "doing things as well as possible".

II. Rebellion

The criticism of society brings to an end the criticism of the old, holy world. By means of *rebellion* we make a leap into the new, egoistical world.

We have already seen in "Logic" [a] what rebellion is in general; it is refusal to respect the holy. Here, however, rebellion acquires in addition a distinct practical character.

Revolution   =Holy rebellion.
Rebellion   =Egoistical or worldly revolution.
Revolution   =Transformation of existing conditions.
Rebellion   =Transformation of me.
Revolution   =A political or social act.
Rebellion   =My egoistical act.
Revolution   =Overthrow of the existing [state of affairs].
Rebellion   =Existence of overthrow.

Etc., etc. Page 422 et seq. The method hitherto used by people to overthrow the world in which they found themselves had. of course, also to be declared holy, and a "peculiar" method of smashing the existing world had to be asserted against it.

Revolution "consists in a transformation of the existing conditions [*Zustand* [b]] or *status*, of the state or society; hence it is a *political* or *social* act". "Although the inevitable consequence" of rebellion "is a transformation of existing conditions, it is not this transformation that is its starting-point, but *people's dissatisfaction with themselves*". "It is an uprising of individuals, a *rising* without regard for the arrangements that develop out of it. Revolution aimed at new *arrangements*; rebellion leads to a position where we no longer *allow* others to arrange things for us, but arrange things for ourselves. It is not a struggle against what exists, for if it prospers what exists will collapse of itself; it is only the setting free of me from what exists. If I abandon what exists, then it is dead and putrefies. But since my aim is not to overthrow something that exists, but for me to rise above it, my aim and action are not political or social,

---

[a] See this volume, pp. 317-18.— *Ed.*
[b] *Zustand*—state of affairs, conditions.— *Ed.*

but *egoistical* for they are directed solely towards me and my peculiarity." (Pp. 421, 422.)

Les beaux esprits se rencontrent.[a] That which was proclaimed by the voice crying in the wilderness[b] is now come about. The impious John the Baptist "Stirner" has found his holy Messiah in the shape of "*Dr. Kuhlmann from Holstein*". Listen:

"You should not tear down or destroy what stands in your way, but avoid it and abandon it. And when you have avoided and abandoned it, it will disappear of itself, for it will no longer find sustenance." (*Das Reich des Geistes*[c], etc., Genf, 1845, p. 116.)

The difference between revolution and Stirner's rebellion is not, as Stirner thinks, that the one is a political and social act whereas the other is an egoistical act, but that the former is an act whereas the latter is no act at all. The whole senselessness of the antithesis that Stirner puts forward is evident at once from the fact that he speaks of "*the* Revolution" as a juridical person, which has to fight against "*what exists*", another juridical person. If Saint Sancho had studied the various *actual* revolutions and revolutionary attempts perhaps he might even have found in them the forms of which he had a vague inkling when he created his ideological "rebellion"; he might have found them, for example, among the Corsicans, Irish, Russian serfs, and in general among uncivilised peoples. If, moreover, he had concerned himself with the actual individuals "existing" in every revolution, and with their relations, instead of being satisfied with the pure ego and "*what exists*", i.e., substance (a phrase the overthrow of which requires no revolution, but merely a knight-errant like Saint Bruno), then perhaps he would have come to understand that every revolution, and its results, was determined by these relations, by needs, and that the "political or social act" was in no way in contradiction to the "egoistical act".

The depth of Saint Sancho's insight into "revolution" is shown in his statement:

"Although the consequence of rebellion is a transformation of existing conditions, [...] this transformation is not its starting point."

This implies, by way of antithesis, that the starting point of the revolution is "a transformation of existing conditions", i.e.,

---

[a] Noble minds think alike.— *Ed.*

[b] Mark 1:3.— *Ed.*

[c] Georg Kuhlmann. *Die Neue Welt oder das Reich des Geistes auf Erden.*— *Ed.*

that revolution originates in revolution. "The starting point" of rebellion, on the other hand, is "people's dissatisfaction with themselves". This "dissatisfaction with oneself" fits admirably with the earlier phrases about peculiarity and the "egoist in agreement with himself", who is always able to go "his own way", who is always delighted with himself and who at every instant is what he can be. Dissatisfaction with oneself is either dissatisfaction with oneself within the framework of a definite condition which determines the whole personality, e.g., dissatisfaction with oneself as a worker, or it is moral dissatisfaction. In the first case, therefore, it is simultaneously and mainly dissatisfaction with the existing relations; in the second case — an ideological expression of these relations themselves, which does not at all go beyond them, but belongs wholly to them. The first case, as Sancho believes, leads to revolution; for rebellion there remains, therefore, only the second case — *moral* dissatisfaction with oneself. "What exists" is, as we know, "the holy"; hence, "dissatisfaction with oneself" reduces itself to moral dissatisfaction with oneself as a holy one, i.e., one who believes in the holy, in what exists. It could only occur to a discontented school-master to base his arguments about revolution and rebellion on satisfaction and dissatisfaction, moods that belong wholly to the petty-bourgeois circle from which, as we continually find, Saint Sancho derives his inspiration.

We already know what meaning "going beyond the framework of what exists" has. It is the old fancy that the state collapses of itself as soon as all its members leave it and that money loses its validity if all the workers refuse to accept it. Even in a hypothetical form, this proposition reveals all the fantasy and impotence of pious desire. It is the old illusion that changing existing relations depends only on the good will of people, and that existing relations are ideas. The alteration of consciousness divorced from actual relations — a pursuit followed by philosophers as a profession, i.e., as a *business* — is itself a product of existing relations and inseparable from them. This imaginary rising above the world is the ideological expression of the impotence of philosophers in face of the world. Practical life every day gives the lie to their ideological bragging.

In any event, Sancho did not "rebel" against his own state of confusion when he wrote those lines. For him there is the "transformation of existing conditions" on one side, and "people" on the other side, and the two sides are entirely separate from each other. Sancho does not give the slightest thought to the fact that the "conditions" have always been the conditions of these people and it would never have been possible to transform them unless the people transformed themselves and, if it has to be expressed in this way, unless they became "dissatisfied with themselves" in the old conditions. He thinks he is dealing a mortal blow at revolution when he asserts that it aims at new arrangements, whereas rebellion leads to a position where we no longer allow others to arrange things for us, but arrange things for ourselves. But the very fact that "we" arrange things for "ourselves", that it is "we" who rebel, denotes that the individual, despite all Sancho's "repugnance", has to "allow" that "we" "arrange things" for him, and that therefore the only difference between revolution and rebellion is that in the former this is known, whereas in the latter people harbour illusions about it. Next Sancho leaves it open whether the rebellion "*prospers*" or not. One cannot understand why it should *not* "prosper", and even less why it should prosper, since each rebel goes his own way. Worldly conditions would have to intervene to show the rebels the necessity of a *joint* act, one which would be "political or social", irrespective of whether it arises from egoistical motives or not. A further "trashy distinction", based again on confusion, is that drawn by Sancho between the "overthrow" of what exists and "rising" above it, as though in overthrowing what exists he does not rise above it, and in rising above it, he does not overthrow it, if only insofar as it exists in him himself. Incidentally, neither "overthrow" by itself nor "rising" by itself tells us anything; that "rising" also takes place in revolution Sancho could have seen from the fact that "*Levons-nous!*"[103] was a well-known slogan in the French Revolution.

"Revolution bids" (!) "us to create *institutions*, rebellion urges us to *rise or rise up*.[a] Revolutionary minds were occupied with the choice of a *constitution*, and the entire political period teems with constitutional struggles and constitutional questions, just as socially-gifted persons revealed extraordinary inventiveness as regards social institutions (phalansteries and such-like). To *be without a constitution* is the endeavour of the rebel." (P. 422.)

That the French Revolution brought institutions in its train is a fact; that *Empörung* is derived from the word *empor*[b] is also a

---

[a] Stirner uses three words which have a common root: *Einrichtung*—arrangement, institution—and the synonyms *sich aufrichten* and *emporrichten*—to stand up, to raise oneself, to rise.— *Ed.*

[b] *Empörung*—rising, rebellion; *empor*—up, upwards.— *Ed.*

fact; that during the revolution and after it people fought for
constitutions is another fact, and equally so that various social
systems were outlined; and it is no less a fact that Proudhon
spoke about anarchy. From these five facts Sancho has
concocted the above-quoted passage.

From the fact that the French Revolution led to "institutions", Sancho concludes that this is a "bidding" of revolution in
general. From the fact that the political revolution was a political one in which the social transformation had also an official expression in the form of constitutional struggles, Sancho—faithfully following his history-broker[a]—deduces that
in it people fought over the best constitution. To this discovery
he links, by means of the words "just as", a mention of social
systems. In the epoch of the bourgeoisie, people occupied
themselves with constitutional questions, "just as" in recent
times various social systems have been devised. This is the train
of thought in the above-quoted passage.

It follows from what was said above against Feuerbach that
previous revolutions within the framework of division of labour
were bound to lead to new political institutions; it likewise
follows that the communist revolution, which removes the
division of labour, ultimately abolishes political institutions[b];
and, finally, it follows also that the communist revolution will
be guided not by the "social institutions of inventive socially-
gifted persons", but by the productive forces.

But "to be without a constitution is the endeavour of the
rebel"! He who is "born free", who is from the outset rid of
everything, endeavours at the end of time to get rid of the
constitution.

It should be mentioned also that all sorts of earlier illusions of
our bonhomme contributed to Sancho's concept of "rebellion".
They include, among others, his belief that the individuals who
make a revolution are linked by some ideal bond and that their
"raising the standard of revolt" is limited to inscribing on it a
new concept, fixed idea, spectre, or apparition—the holy.
Sancho makes them get this ideal bond out of their heads,
whereby in his imagination they become a disorderly mob which
can now only "rebel". In addition, he has heard that competition
is a war of all against all,[c] and this proposition, mixed with

---

[a] An allusion to Bruno Bauer.— *Ed.*
[b] See this volume, pp. 60-61.— *Ed.*
[c] Thomas Hobbes, *Elementa philosophica. De cive* [Praefatio ad lec-
tores].— *Ed.*

his desanctified revolution, constitutes the main factor of his "rebellion".

"When, for the sake of clarity, I try to think of a comparison, there comes to my mind, against my expectation, the foundation of Christianity." (P. 423.) "Christ", we learn here, "was not a revolutionary but a *rebel* who rose. Therefore, he was concerned about one thing *alone*: 'be ye wise as serpents'." (Ibid.)

In order to suit the "expectation" and the "alone" of Sancho the second half of the biblical text quoted (Matthew 10:16) "and harmless as doves" ought not to exist. Christ has to figure here for the second time as a historical person in order to play the same role as the Mongols and Negroes played above. Whether Christ is meant to clarify the rebellion or the rebellion to clarify Christ is not known. The Christian-German gullibility of our saint is concentrated in the statement that Christ "drained the sources of life of the entire heathen world, and without *them*" (this ought to read: without *him*) "the existing state was anyway bound to wither". (P. 424.) A withered flower of pulpit eloquence! See above on the "ancients". For the rest, *credo ut intelligam*[a], or, in order to find a "comparison for the sake of clarity".

Countless examples have already shown us that everywhere nothing but *sacred* history comes into our saint's mind and, indeed, in precisely those passages where the reader "has not expected" it. "Against expectation" it occurs to him again even in the "Commentary", where Sancho on page 154 makes the "Judaic reviewers" in ancient Jerusalem exclaim in opposition to the Christian definition "God is love": "Thus you see that it is heathen God that is proclaimed by the Christians; for if God is love, then he is the God Amor, the God of love!" — "Against expectation", however, the New Testament was written in Greek, and the "Christian definition" reads: ὁ θεὸς ἀγάπη ἐστίν[b] (1 John 4:16), whereas "the God Amor, the God of love" is called Ἔρως. Sancho has, therefore, still to explain how it is that the "Judaic reviewers" were able to achieve the transformation of ἀγάπη into ἔρως. In this passage of the "Commentary", Christ — again "for the sake of clarity" — is compared with Sancho, and at any rate it must be admitted that they have a striking resemblance to each other, both are "corpulent beings" and the joyful heir at least believes in the existence, or

---

[a] I believe in order to understand. The expression belongs to the medieval scholastic Anselm of Canterbury.— *Ed.*

[b] God is love.— *Ed.*

the uniqueness, of both of them. Sancho is the modern Christ, at this "fixed idea" of his the whole historical construction is "aimed".

The philosophy of rebellion, which has just been presented to us in the form of bad antitheses and withered flowers of eloquence, is in the final analysis only a boastful apology for the parvenu system (parvenu, *Emporkömmling, Emporgekommener, Empörer*[a]). Every rebel in his "egoistical act" is faced by a particular existing reality, over which he endeavours to rise, without regard to the general conditions. He strives to get rid of the existing world only insofar as it is a fetter, for the rest, he endeavours, on the contrary, to appropriate it. The weaver who "rises" to become a factory-owner thereby gets rid of his loom and abandons it; for the rest, the world goes on as before and our "prosperous" rebel offers to others only the hypocritical moral demand that they should become parvenus like himself.* Thus, all Stirner's belligerent rodomontades end in moral deductions from Gellert's fables and speculative interpretations of middle-class wretchedness.

So far we have seen that rebellion is anything you like, except action. On page 342 we learn that

"the procedure of seizure is not contemptible, but expresses the *pure action of the egoist in agreement with himself*".

This should surely read: of egoists in agreement *with one another*, since otherwise seizure amounts to the uncivilised "procedure" of thieves or to the civilised "procedure" of the bourgeois, and in the first case does not prosper, while in the second case it is not "rebellion". It is to be noted that corresponding to the egoist in agreement with himself, who does nothing, we have here the "*pure*" act, certainly the only act which could be expected from such an inactive individual.

We learn by the way what created the plebs, and we can be sure in advance that it was created by a "dogma", and faith in that dogma, in the holy, a faith which here for a change appears as consciousness of sin:

* [The following passage is crossed out in the manuscript:] These are the traditional moral principles of the petty bourgeois, who believes that the world will be set to rights, if everyone by himself tries to get as far as possible and for the rest does not trouble his head about the course of the world.

---

[a] A pun on Stirner's synonymy: *Emporkömmling* (upstart), *Emporgekommener* (one who has raised himself up), and *Empörer* (rebel).— *Ed.*

"Seizure is a *sin*, a crime — this is the dogma that alone creates a plebs ... the old consciousness of sin *alone* is to blame." (P. 342.)

The belief that consciousness is to blame for everything is his dogma, which makes him a rebel and the plebs a sinner.

In contrast to this consciousness of sin, the egoist incites himself, respectively the plebs, to seizure as follows:

"I tell myself: where my power extends, that is my property, and I claim as my property everything that I feel strong enough to reach", etc. (P. 340.)

Thus, Saint Sancho tells himself that he wants to tell himself something, calls on himself to have what he has, and formulates his real relation as a relation of power — a paraphrase which in general is the secret of all his rodomontades. (See "Logic"[a]) Then he — who at each instant is what he can be, and therefore has what he can have — distinguishes his realised, actual property, which he has in his capital account, from his possible property, his unrealised "feeling of strength", which he enters in his profit and loss account. This is a contribution to the science of book-keeping of property in the extraordinary sense.

The meaning of his solemn "telling" was revealed by Sancho in a passage already quoted:

"*I tell myself* ... then that is, properly speaking, idle talk."

Sancho continues:

"Egoism" says "to the propertyless plebs" in order to "exterminate" it: "Seize and take what you need!" (P. 341.)

How "empty" this "talk" is can be seen at once from the following example:

"I as little regard the wealth of the banker as something alien, as Napoleon did the lands of the kings. We" ("I" is suddenly transformed into "we") "are not at all *afraid to conquer* this wealth, and we also seek the means to do so. Thus, we divest it of its *alien character* which we were afraid of." (P. 369.)

How little Sancho has "divested" the wealth of the banker of its "alien character" he proves at once by his well-meaning advice to the plebs to "conquer" it by seizure. "Let him seize and see what is left in his hands!" Not the wealth of the banker but useless paper, the "corpse" of that wealth which is no more wealth than "a dead dog is a dog". The wealth of the banker is wealth only in the framework of the existing relations of production and intercourse and can be "conquered" only in the conditions of these relations and with the means which are valid for them. And if Sancho were to turn to some other wealth, he

---

[a] See this volume, pp. 318-319.— *Ed.*

would find that the prospect was no better. Thus, the "pure act of the egoist in agreement with himself" amounts in the final analysis to an extremely impure misunderstanding. "That is where one can get with the spectre" of the holy.

Having told himself what he wanted to tell himself, Sancho makes the rebellious plebs say what he has prompted it to say. The fact is that in case of a rebellion he has drawn up a proclamation together with instructions as to its use, which should be posted up in all village ale-houses and distributed throughout the countryside. The proclamation claims a place in *Der hinkende Botte*[104] and in the Duchy of Nassau's country almanac. For the time being Sancho's *tendances incendiaires* are limited to the countryside, to propaganda among agricultural labourers and dairy maids, not touching the towns, which is a further proof of the extent to which he has "divested" large-scale industry of its "alien character". Nevertheless we should like here to give as detailed an account as possible of this valuable document, which ought not to be lost, in order "to contribute to the spread of a well-deserved fame insofar as it lies in our power." (*Wigand*, p. 191.)

The proclamation is printed on page 358 et seq. [of ."the book"] and begins as follows:

"But what is it due to that your property is safe, you privileged ones?... It is due to the fact that we refrain from attacking, consequently, it is due to *our* protection.... It is due to the fact that you use *force* against us."

First it is due to the fact that we refrain from attacking, i.e., to the fact that we use force *against ourselves*, and then to the fact that *you* use force against us. *Cela va à merveille!* Let us continue.

"If you desire our respect, then *buy* it at a price acceptable to us.... We only want *good value.*"

First the "rebels" want to sell their respect at an "acceptable price" and then they make "good value" the criterion of the price. First an arbitrary price, then a price determined independently of arbitrariness by commercial laws, by the costs of production and the relation between supply and demand.

"We agree to leave you your property provided you properly compensate this leaving.... You will shout about force if we help ourselves ... without force we shall not get them" (i.e., the oysters that the privileged enjoy).... "We intend taking nothing from you, nothing at all."

First we "leave" it to you, then we take it away from you and have to use "force", and finally we prefer taking nothing from you after all. We leave it to you in the event of your giving it up yourself; in a moment of enlightenment, the only one we have, we see that this "leaving" amounts to "helping oneself" and use of "force", but in the end we cannot be reproached with "taking" anything from you. And there the matter must rest.

"We toil for twelve hours in the sweat of our brows and you offer us a few pence for it. In that case you should take an *equal amount* for your work too.... No *equality* at all!"

The "rebellious" agricultural labourers reveal themselves as true Stirnerian "creations".

"You do not like that? You imagine that our work is more than adequately paid with those wages, but that yours, on the other hand, deserves a wage of several thousand. But if you did not put such a high value on your work and allowed us to realise a better value for ours, we would, if need be, achieve something more important than you do for many thousand taler, and if you received only such wages as ours, you would soon become more diligent in order to earn more. If you were to do something that appears to us to be ten and a hundred times more valuable than our own work, ah" (ah, you good and faithful servant![a]) "then you should get a hundred times more for it; we, for our part, are also thinking of making you things for which you will pay us more than the usual daily wage."

First the rebels complain that they are paid too little for their work. At the end, however, they promise that only if they receive a higher daily wage, they will perform work for which it will be worth paying "more than the usual daily wage". Further, they believe they would achieve extraordinary things if only they were to receive better wages, although at the same time they expect extraordinary achievements from the capitalist only if his "wage" is reduced to the level of theirs. Finally, after having performed the economic feat of transforming profit — this necessary form of capital, without which they would perish together with the capitalist — into wages, they perform the miracle of paying "a hundred times more" than they receive for "their own work", i.e., a hundred times more than they earn. "This is the meaning" of the above phrase, if Stirner "means what he says". But if this is only a stylistic error on his part, if the rebels intend jointly to offer the capitalist a hundred times more than *each of them* earns, then Stirner is only making them offer the capitalist what each capitalist already has nowadays. For it is clear that the work of the capitalist, in combination with his capital, is worth ten or a hundred times more than that of a single person who is merely a worker. Hence in this case, as always, Sancho leaves everything as it was before.

---

[a] Matthew 25:21.— *Ed.*

"We shall get on with one another if only we agree that no one any longer needs to *present* anything to someone else. Then we shall presumably go as far as to pay a decent price even to cripples, the sick and the aged, to prevent them from dying of hunger and want, for if we wish them to live it is fitting that we should *pay for* the fulfilment of our desire. I say *pay for*, hence I do not mean any miserable *alms*."

This sentimental episode about cripples, etc., is intended to prove that Sancho's rebellious agricultural labourers have already "risen" to those heights of middle-class consciousness where they do not wish to present anything or be presented with anything, and where they consider that the dignity and interests of the two parties in a relation are assured as soon as this relation is turned into a purchase.

This thunderous proclamation of the people who, in Sancho's imagination, are in rebellion, is followed by directions for its use in the form of a dialogue between a landowner and his labourers, the master this time behaving like Szeliga and the labourers like Stirner. In these directions the English strikes and the French workers' coalitions are interpreted *a priori* in the Berlin manner.

Spokesman of the labourers: "What have you got?"

Landowner: "I have an estate of 1,000 morgen." [a]

Spokesman: "And I am your labourer, and henceforth I will only cultivate your land for a wage of a taler a day."

Landowner: "In that case I shall hire someone else."

Spokesman: "You won't find anyone, for we labourers will not work in future on any other conditions, and if you find anyone who agrees to take less, let him beware of us. Even a servant-girl now demands as much, and you will no longer find anyone for a lower wage."

Landowner: "Oh! Then I shall be ruined!"

Labourers (in chorus): "Don't be in such a hurry! You are sure to get as much as we get. And if not, we'll deduct sufficient for you to live like us.— We are not talking of equality!"

Landowner: "But I am accustomed to better living!"

Labourers: "We have nothing against that, but that's not our concern; if you can save more, all right. Do we have to hire ourselves out at a reduced price so that you can live well?"

Landowner: "But you uneducated people do not need so much!"

Labourers: "Well, we shall take a little more so as to be able to get the education that we may, perhaps, need."

Landowner: "But if you ruin the rich, who will support the arts and sciences?"

Labourers: "Well, our numbers must see to that. We'll all contribute, it will make a good round sum. Anyway, you wealthy people now buy only the trashiest books and pictures of tearful madonnas or a pair of nimble dancer's legs."

---

[a] An old Germanic land measure of varying size in different parts of the country. The Prussian morgen for example was 0.63 acre.— *Ed.*

Landowner: "Oh, miserable equality!"

Labourers: "No, dear worthy master, we are not talking of equality! We only want to be appraised according to our worth, and if you are worth more, then after all you will also be appraised more highly. We only want *good value* and intend to show ourselves worth the price you will pay."

At the end of this dramatic masterpiece Sancho admits that, of course, "unanimity of the labourers" will be "required". How this will come about we are not told. What we do learn is that the agricultural labourers have no intention of changing in any way the existing relations of production and intercourse, but merely want to force the landowner to yield them the amount by which his expenditure exceeds theirs. It is a matter of indifference to our well-meaning bonhomme that this excess of expenditure, if distributed over the mass of the proletarians, would give each of them a mere trifle and not improve his position in the slightest. The stage of development of agriculture to which these heroic labourers belong becomes evident immediately after the conclusion of the drama, when they are transformed into "domestic servants". They are living, therefore, under patriarchal conditions in which division of labour is still very little developed, and in which, incidentally, the whole conspiracy "will reach its final goal" by the landowner taking the spokesman into a barn and giving him a thrashing, whereas in more civilised countries the capitalist ends the matter by closing his enterprise for a time and letting his workers go and "play". Sancho's highly practical way of constructing his work of art, his strict adherence to the limits of probability, is evident not only from his peculiar idea of arranging a turn-out[a] of agricultural labourers, but especially from his coalition of "servant girls". And how complacent to imagine that the price of corn on the world market will depend on the wage demands of these agricultural labourers from Further Pomerania and not on the relation between supply and demand! A real sensation is caused by the surprising discourse of the labourers about literature, the latest art exhibition and the fashionable dancer of the day, surprising even after the unexpected question of the landowner about art and science. They become quite friendly as soon as they touch on this literary subject and for a moment the harassed landowner even forgets his threatened ruin in order to demonstrate his *dévoûment* to art and science. Finally the rebels give him an assurance of their upright character and make the reassuring statement that they are guided neither by vexatious

---

[a] Here and below the word is in English in the manuscript.— *Ed.*

interests nor subversive tendencies, but by the highest moral motives. All they ask is price according to worth and they promise on their honour and conscience to be worthy of the higher price. All this has the sole aim of ensuring for each his own, his honest and fair earnings, "honestly earned pleasure". That this price depends on the state of the labour-market, and not on the moral rebellion of a few literary-minded agricultural labourers, is, of course, a fact which our worthy folk could not be expected to know.

These rebels from Further Pomerania are so modest that despite their "unanimity", which gives them the power to do something very different, they prefer to remain servants with the "wage of a taler a day" as their highest desire. It is quite consistent, therefore, that they do not cross-examine the landowner, who is in their power, but he cross-examines them.

The "firm spirit" and "strong self-consciousness of the domestic servant" find expression also in the "firm", "strong" language in which he and his comrades speak. "Perhaps — well — our numbers *must* see to that — a good round sum — dear worthy master — after all." Previously we read in the proclamation: "If need be — ah — we *are thinking* of making — perhaps, maybe, etc." One would think that the agricultural labourers had also mounted the wonderful steed Clavileño.*

Our Sancho's whole noisy "rebellion", therefore, reduces itself in the final analysis to a turn-out, but a turn-out in the extraordinary sense, viz., a turn-out on Berlin lines. Whereas in civilised countries the real turn-out plays a smaller and smaller role in the labour movement, because the more widespread association of workers leads to other forms of action, Sancho tries to depict the petty-bourgeois caricature of a turn-out as the ultimate and highest form of the world-historic struggle.

The waves of rebellion now cast us on the shore of the promised land, flowing with milk and honey[a] where every true Israelite sits beneath his fig-tree and where the millennium of "agreement" has dawned.

---

* [The following passage is crossed out in the manuscript:] France produces relatively more than Further Pomerania. According to Michel Chevalier [*Cours d'Economie politique fait au Collège de France*], the entire annual product of France uniformly distributed among its population amounts to 97 francs a head, this means per family....

---

[a] Exodus 3:8.— *Ed.*

III. Union

In the section on rebellion we first of all collected examples of Sancho's bragging, and then traced the practical course of the "pure act of the egoist in agreement with himself". With regard to "union", we shall do the opposite: we shall first of all examine the actual institutions and then compare them with the illusions of our saint about them.

1. Landed Property

"If we no longer wish to leave the land to the landed proprietors, but want to appropriate it for *ourselves,* then we unite to this end and form a *union, société*" (society), "*which makes itself the owner*; if we are successful, the landed proprietors cease to be such." The "land" will then be the "property of the conquerors.... And the attitude to the land of these individuals collectively will be no less arbitrary than that of an isolated individual or so-called *propriétaire.* Hence, in this case too, *property* continues to exist, and indeed even as '*exclusive*' property, since *mankind,* that great society, excludes the *individual* from its property, leasing to him, perhaps, only a part of it, as a reward.... So it remains and so it will come to be. That in which *all* want to have a *share* will be taken away from the individual who wants to have it for himself alone and turned into *common property.* Since it is *common property* each has his *share* in it and this share is his property. Thus in our old conditions, a house belonging to five heirs is likewise their common property; one-fifth part of the income, however, is the property of each of them." (Pp. 329, 330.)

After our brave rebels have formed a union, a society, and in this form have won a portion of land for themselves, this "*société*", this juridical person, "makes *itself*" the "*proprietor*". To avoid any misunderstanding, he adds at once that "this society *excludes* the individual from the property, leasing to him, perhaps, only a part of it, as a reward". In this way Saint Sancho appropriates for himself and his "union" his notion of communism. The reader will recall that Sancho in his ignorance reproached the communists for wanting to make society the supreme owner that gives each individual his "property" in feudal tenure.

Further, Sancho offers his recruits the prospect of a "share in the common property". On a later occasion, this same Sancho says, again against the communists:

"Whether wealth belongs to the whole community, which allows me a portion of it, or to separate owners, for me the compulsion is the same, since in both cases I am powerless to decide about it."

(For this reason, too, his "collective" "takes away" from him what it does not want him to have in his exclusive possession, and so makes him feel the power of the collective will.)

Thirdly, we here again encounter the "exclusiveness" with which he has often reproached bourgeois property, so that "even the miserable spot on which he stands does not belong to him". On the contrary, he has only the right and power to squat on it as a miserable and oppressed corvée peasant.

Fourthly, Sancho here appropriates the feudal system which, to his great annoyance, he has discovered in all hitherto existing or proposed forms of society. The "society" of conquerors behaves much as did the "unions" of semi-barbarian Germans who conquered the Roman provinces and introduced there a crude feudal system which was still strongly alloyed with the old tribal mode of life. It gives every individual a piece of land "as a reward". At the stage where Sancho and the sixth-century Germans are, the feudal system still coincides in many respects with the system of "reward".

It goes without saying, incidentally, that the tribal property which Sancho here restores afresh to honour would be bound before long to be dissolved again in the conditions now existing. Sancho feels this himself, for he exclaims: "So it *remains* and" (a beautiful "and"!) "so it *will come to be*", and finally, he proves — by his great example of the house belonging to five heirs — that he has not the slightest intention of going outside the framework of our old relations. His whole plan for the organisation of landed property has only the aim of leading us by a historical detour back to petty-bourgeois hereditary tenure and the family property of German imperial towns.

Of our old relations, i.e., those now existing, Sancho has appropriated only the legal nonsense that individuals, or *propriétaires*, behave "arbitrarily" in relation to landed property. In the "union", this imagined "arbitrariness" is to be continued by "society". To the "union" it is so much a matter of indifference what happens to the land that "perhaps" "society" leases plots of land to individuals, or perhaps not. All that is quite immaterial.

Sancho, of course, cannot know that a definite structure of agriculture is linked to a definite form of activity and determined by a definite stage of the division of labour. But anyone else can see how little the small corvée peasants, as proposed here by Sancho, are in a position where "each of them can become an omnipotent ego", and how little their ownership of a miserable plot of land resembles the greatly praised "ownership of everything". In the real world, the intercourse of individuals depends on their mode of production, and therefore Sancho's "perhaps" completely overthrows —

perhaps — his whole union. But "perhaps", or rather undoubtedly, there emerges here Sancho's real view concerning intercourse in the union, namely, the view that the basis of egoistical intercourse is the holy.

Sancho brings to light here the first "institution" of his future union. The rebels who strove to be "without a constitution", "arrange things for themselves", by "choosing" for themselves a "constitution" of landed property. We see that Sancho was right in not placing any brilliant hopes in new "institutions". At the same time, however, we see that he ranks highly among the "socially-gifted persons" and is "extraordinarily inventive in regard to social institutions".

2. Organisation of Labour

"The organisation of labour concerns only such work as can be done for us by others, such as cattle-slaughtering, ploughing, etc.; other work remains egoistical because, for example, no one can compose your music for you, complete the sketches for your paintings, etc. No one can do Raphael's works for him. These are works of a unique individual which only this unique person is capable of producing, whereas the former work deserves to be called *human*" (on page 356 this is made identical with "*generally useful*") "since *peculiarity* is of little consequence here and almost *every person* can be trained to do it." (P. 355.)

"It is always expedient for us to come to an agreement about human labour, in order that it should not claim all our time and effort, as is the case under competition.... For whom, however, should time be gained? For what purpose does a human being need more time than is required to restore his exhausted labour-power? To this communism gives no reply. For what purpose? In order to enjoy himself as the unique, having done his share as human being." (Pp. 356, 357.)

"Through work I can fulfil the official duties of a president, minister, etc.; these posts require only a general education, namely, the education that is generally accessible.... Although, however, anyone could occupy these posts, it is only the unique power of the individual, peculiar to him alone, that gives them. as it were, life and significance. For performing his duties not as an ordinary man would do, but by exerting the power of his uniqueness, he does not get paid, if he is paid only as an official or minister. If he has acted to your satisfaction and you wish for your benefit to retain this power of the unique person, which is worthy of gratitude, then you ought to pay him not simply as a man who performs a merely human task, but as one who accomplishes something unique." (Pp. 362, 363.)

"If you are in a position to afford joy to thousands of people, then thousands will remunerate you for it; for it is in your power not to do it and therefore they have to pay you for the fact that you do it." (P. 351.)

"One cannot establish any general rate of payment for my uniqueness, as can be done for work I perform as a man. Only for the latter can a tariff be fixed. Therefore you may fix a general tariff for human work, but do not deprive your uniqueness of what is due to it." (P. 363.)

As an example of the organisation of labour in the union, the public bakeries already mentioned are cited on page 365. Under the conditions of vandal parcellation presupposed above, these public institutions must be a real miracle.

First of all human labour must be organised and thereby shortened so that Brother Straubinger,[105] having finished his work early, can "enjoy himself as the unique" (p. 357), but on page 363 the "enjoyment" of the unique one is reduced to his extra earnings. On page 363 it is stated that the vital activity of the unique person does not have to take place subsequently to human labour; the latter can be performed as unique labour, and in that case it requires an additional wage. Otherwise the unique one, who is interested not in his uniqueness but in a higher wage, could shelve his uniqueness and to spite society be satisfied with acting as an ordinary person, at the same time playing a trick on himself.

According to page 356, human labour coincides with generally useful labour, but according to pages 351 and 363 unique labour shows its worth by being paid for additionally as generally useful or, at least, useful to many people.

Thus, the organisation of labour in the union consists in the separation of human labour from unique labour, in the establishment of a tariff for the former and in haggling for an additional wage for the latter. This addition is again twofold, one part being for the unique performance of *human* labour and the other for the unique performance of *unique* labour. The resulting book-keeping is the more complicated because what was unique labour yesterday (e.g., spinning cotton thread No. 200) becomes human labour today, and because the unique performance of human labour requires a continual *moucharderie*[a] upon oneself in one's own interest and universal *moucharderie* in the public interest. Hence this whole great organisational plan amounts to a wholly petty-bourgeois appropriation of the law of supply and demand, which exists at present and has been expounded by all economists. The law which determines the price of those types of labour that Sancho declares unique (e.g., that of a dancer, a prominent physician or lawyer), he could have found already explained by Adam Smith,[b] and a tariff fixed for it by the American Cooper.[c] Modern economists explain on the basis of this law the high payment for what they call *travail improductif* and the low wages of the agricultural day-labourer, and in general all

---

[a] Spying.— *Ed.*

[b] Adam Smith, *An Inquiry into the Nature and Causes of the Wealth of Nations.— Ed.*

[c] Thomas Cooper, *Lectures on the Elements of Political Economy.— Ed.*

inequalities in wages. Thus, with God's help, we have again arrived at competition, but a competition which has so much come down in the world that Sancho can propose a fixed rate, the establishment of wages by law, as was the case of old in the fourteenth and fifteenth centuries.

It deserves mention also that the idea which Sancho puts forward here is also to be found as something completely new in the Herr Messiah — Dr. Georg Kuhlmann of Holstein.[a]

What Sancho here calls human labour is, apart from his bureaucratic fantasies, the same thing as is usually meant by machine labour, labour which, as industry develops, devolves more and more on machines. True, because of the above-described organisation of landownership, machines are an impossibility in the "union" and therefore the corvée peasants in agreement with themselves prefer to reach an agreement with one another about this work. As regards "presidents" and "ministers", Sancho — this poor localised being[b], as Owen puts it — forms his opinion only by his immediate environment.

Here, as always, Sancho is again unlucky with his practical examples. He thinks that "no one can compose your music for you, complete the sketches for your paintings. No one can do Raphael's works for him". Sancho could surely have known, however, that it was not Mozart himself, but someone else who composed the greater part of Mozart's *Requiem* and finished it,[106] and that Raphael himself "completed" only an insignificant part of his own frescoes.

He imagines that the so-called organisers of labour[107] wanted to organise the entire activity of each individual, and yet it is precisely they who distinguish between directly productive labour, which has to be organised, and labour which is not directly productive. In regard to the latter, however, it was not their view, as Sancho imagines, that each should do the work of Raphael, but that anyone in whom there is a potential Raphael should be able to develop without hindrance. Sancho imagines that Raphael produced his pictures independently of the division of labour that existed in Rome at the time. If he were to compare Raphael with Leonardo da Vinci and Titian, he would see how greatly Raphael's works of art depended on the flourishing of Rome at that time, which occurred under Florentine influence, while the works of Leonardo depended on

---

[a] Georg Kuhlmann, *Die Neue Welt oder das Reich des Geistes auf Erden.— Ed.*

[b] This phrase is in English in the manuscript.— *Ed.*

the state of things in Florence, and the works of Titian, at a later period, depended on the totally different development of Venice. Raphael as much as any other artist was determined by the technical advances in art made before him, by the organisation of society and the division of labour in his locality, and, finally, by the division of labour in all the countries with which his locality had intercourse. Whether an individual like Raphael succeeds in developing his talent depends wholly on demand, which in turn depends on the division of labour and the conditions of human culture resulting from it.

In proclaiming the uniqueness of work in science and art, Stirner adopts a position far inferior to that of the bourgeoisie. At the present time it has already been found necessary to organise this "unique" activity. Horace Vernet would not have had time to paint even a tenth of his pictures if he regarded them as works which "only this unique person is capable of producing". In Paris, the great demand for vaudevilles and novels brought about the organisation of work for their production; this organisation at any rate yields something better than its "unique" competitors in Germany. In astronomy, people like Arago, Herschel, Encke and Bessel considered it necessary to organise joint observations and only after that obtained some moderately good results. In historical science, it is absolutely impossible for the "unique" to achieve anything at all, and in this field, too, the French long ago surpassed all other nations thanks to organisation of labour. Incidentally, it is self-evident that all these organisations based on modern division of labour still lead to extremely limited results, and they represent a step forward only compared with the previous narrow isolation.

Moreover, it must be specially emphasised that Sancho confuses the organisation of labour with communism and is even surprised that "communism" gives him no reply to his doubts about this organisation. Just like a Gascon village lad is surprised that Arago cannot tell him on which star God Almighty has built his throne.

The exclusive concentration of artistic talent in particular individuals, and its suppression in the broad mass which is bound up with this, is a consequence of division of labour. Even if in certain social conditions, everyone were an excellent painter, that would by no means exclude the possibility of each of them being also an original painter, so that here too the difference between "human" and "unique" labour amounts to sheer nonsense. In any case, with a communist organisation of society, there disappears the subordination of the artist to local and national narrowness, which arises entirely from division of labour, and also the subordination of the individual to some definite art, making him exclusively a painter, sculptor, etc.; the very name amply expresses the narrowness of his professional development and his dependence on division of labour. In a communist society there are no painters but only people who engage in painting among other activities.

Sancho's organisation of labour shows clearly how much all these philosophical knights of "substance" content themselves with mere phrases. The subordination of "substance" to the "subject" about which they all talk so grandiloquently, the reduction of "substance" which governs the "subject" to a mere "accident" of this subject, is revealed to be mere "empty talk".* Hence they wisely refrain from examining division of labour, material production and material intercourse, which in fact make individuals subordinate to definite relations and modes of activity. For them it is in general only a matter of finding new phrases for interpreting the existing world — phrases which are the more certain to consist only of comical boasting, the more these people imagine they have risen above the world and the more they put themselves in opposition to it. Sancho is a lamentable example of this.

3. Money

"Money is a commodity and indeed an essential *means* or faculty, for it protects wealth against ossification, keeps it fluid and effects its circulation. If you know of a better means of exchange, all right; but it too will be a variety of money." (P. 364.)

On page 353 money is defined as "marketable property or property in circulation".

Thus the "union" retains money, this purely social property which has been stripped of all individuality. The extent to

* [The following passage is crossed out in the manuscript:] If Sancho had taken his phrases seriously he would have had to analyse the division of labour. But he wisely refrained from doing this and unhesitatingly accepted the existing division of labour in order to exploit it for his "union". A closer examination on the subject would, of course, have shown him that the division of labour is not abolished by "getting it out of one's head". The fight of the philosophers against "substance" and their utter disregard of the division of labour, the material basis which has given rise to the phantom of substance, merely prove that for these heroes it is a matter only of abolishing phrases and by no means of changing the conditions from which these phrases were bound to arise.

which Sancho is in the grip of the bourgeois outlook is shown by his question about a better means of exchange. Consequently, he first of all assumes that a means of exchange is necessary, and moreover he knows of no other means of exchange except money. The fact that ships and railways, which serve to transport commodities, are also means of exchange does not concern him. Hence in order to speak not merely of means of exchange, but particularly of money, he has to include the other attributes of money; that it is a means of exchange that is universally marketable and in circulation, that it keeps all property fluid, etc. These bring in also economic aspects which Sancho does not know but which actually constitute money; and with them the whole present situation, class economy, domination of the bourgeoisie, etc.

First of all, however, we learn something about the — extremely odd — course of monetary crises in the union.

The question arises:

"Where is money to be obtained?... People pay not with money, of which there may be a shortage, but with their ability [*Vermögen*[a]], thanks to which alone we are wealthy [*vermögend*].... It is not money that harms you, but your inability [*Unvermögen*] to obtain it."

Now comes the moral exhortation:

"Let your ability [*Vermögen*] have its effect, brace yourself, and you will not lack money [*Geld*], your money, money of your coining.... Know then that you have as much money as you have power; for the extent to which you can assert yourself [*Dir Geltung verschaffst*] determines how much you are worth [*giltst*].[b]" (Pp. 353, 364.)

The power of money, the fact that the universal means of exchange becomes independent in relation both to society and to individuals, reveals most clearly that the relations of production and intercourse as a whole assume an independent existence. Consequently, Sancho as usual knows nothing about the connection of money relations with production in general and intercourse. As a good citizen, he unhesitatingly keeps money in force; indeed it could not be otherwise with his view of division of labour and the organisation of landed ownership. The material power of money, which is strikingly revealed in monetary crises and which, in the form of a permanent scarcity of money, oppresses the petty bourgeois who is "inclined to

---

[a] A play on the word *Vermögen*—ability, faculty, power, wealth, means, property—and its derivatives.—*Ed.*

[b] A play on the words *Geld*—money; *sich Geltung verschaffen*—to assert oneself; and *gelten*—to be worth.—*Ed.*

make purchases", is likewise a highly unpleasant fact for the egoist in agreement with himself. He gets rid of the difficulty by reversing the ordinary idea of the petty bourgeois, thus making it appear that the attitude of individuals to the power of money is something that depends solely on their personal willing or running.[108] This fortunate turn of thought then gives him the chance of reading a moral lecture, buttressed by synonymy, etymology and vowel mutation, to the astounded petty bourgeois already disheartened by lack of money, thus debarring in advance all inconvenient questions about the causes of the pecuniary embarrassment.

The monetary crisis consists primarily in the fact that all "wealth" [*Vermögen*] suddenly becomes depreciated in relation to the means of exchange and loses its "power" [*Vermögen*] over money. A crisis is in existence precisely when one *can* no longer pay with one's "wealth" [*Vermögen*], but *must* pay with money. And this again does not happen because of a shortage of money, as is imagined by the petty bourgeois who judges the crisis by his personal difficulties, but because the specific difference becomes fixed between money as the *universal* commodity, the "marketable property and property in circulation", and all the other, *particular* commodities, which suddenly cease to be marketable property. It cannot be expected that, to please Sancho, we shall analyse here the causes of this phenomenon. Sancho first of all consoles the moneyless and hopeless small shopkeepers by saying that it is not money that causes the scarcity of money and the whole crisis, but their inability to obtain it. It is not arsenic that is to blame for someone dying who takes it, it is the inability of his organism to digest it.

After first defining money as an essential and indeed *specific* form of wealth [*Vermögen*], as the universal means of exchange, money in the ordinary sense, Sancho suddenly turns the thing round when he sees the difficulties this would lead to and declares all ability [*Vermögen*] to be money, in order to create the appearance of personal power. The difficulty during a crisis is precisely that "all wealth" [*Vermögen*] has ceased to be "money". Incidentally, this amounts to the practice of the bourgeois who accepts "all wealth" as means of payment so long as it is money, and who only begins to raise difficulties when it becomes difficult to turn this "wealth" into money, in which case he also ceases to regard it as "wealth". Further, the difficulty in time of crisis is precisely that you, petty bourgeois, whom Sancho addresses here, can no longer put into circulation

the money of your coining, your bills of exchange; but you are
expected to pay with money not coined by you and which shows
no evidence that it has passed through your hands.

Finally, Stirner distorts the bourgeois motto "You are worth
as much as the money you possess" into "You have as much
money as you are worth", which alters nothing, but only
introduces an appearance of personal power and thus expresses
the trivial bourgeois illusion that everyone is himself to blame if
he has no money. Thus Sancho disposes of the classic bourgeois
saying: *L'argent n'a pas de maître*,[a] and can now mount the
pulpit and exclaim: "Let your ability have its effect, brace
yourself, and you will not lack money." *Je ne connais pas de lieu
à la bourse où se fasse le transfert des bonnes intentions*.[b] He
had but to add: Obtain credit; knowledge is power[c]; it is harder
to earn the first taler than the last million; be moderate and save
your money and, most important of all, do not multiply
overmuch, etc.— to reveal not one ass's ear, but both at once.
In general, the man for whom everyone is what he can be and
does what he can do, ends all chapters with moral exhortations.

The monetary system in Stirner's union is, therefore,
the existing monetary system expressed in the euphemistic and
gushingly-sentimental manner of the German petty bourgeois.

After Sancho has paraded in this way with the ears of his ass,
Don Quixote-Szeliga draws himself up to his full height and
delivers a solemn speech about the modern knight-errant, in the
course of which money is transformed into Dulcinea del Toboso
and the manufacturers and *commerçants en masse* into knights,
namely, into *chevaliers d'industrie*. The speech has also the
subsidiary aim of proving that because money is an "essential
means", it is also "essentially a daughter".* And he stretched
out his right hand and said:

"On money depends fortune and misfortune. In the bourgeois period it is a
force because like a maiden" (a dairymaid; *per appositionem* Dulcinea) "it is
only wooed but is not indissolubly joined in marriage to anyone. All the romance
and chivalry of wooing a dear object is revived in competition. Money, an
object of ardent desire, is abducted by the bold *chevaliers d'industrie*". (P. 364.)

Sancho has now arrived at a profound explanation why
money in the bourgeois epoch is a power, namely, because in

* Cf. *Die heilige Familie*, p. 266.[d]

---

[a] Money has no master.— *Ed.*
[b] I do not know a place at the stock exchange where people trade in good
intentions.— *Ed.*
[c] This phrase is in English in the manuscript.— *Ed.*
[d] See Karl Marx and Frederick Engels, *Collected Works*, Vol. 4, p.
167.— *Ed.*

the first place fortune and misfortune depends on it and, secondly, because it is a *maiden*. He has further learned why he can lose his money, namely, because a maiden is not indissolubly joined in marriage to anyone. Now the poor wretch knows where he stands.

Szeliga, who has thus made the burgher into a knight, now in the following way makes the communist into a burgher and indeed into a burgher husband:

"He on whom fortune smiles leads the bride home. The ragamuffin is fortunate, he takes her into his household, *society*, and destroys the maiden. In his home she is no longer a bride, but a wife, and her maiden name disappears with her maidenhood. As a housewife, the money-maiden is called *labour*, for *labour* is the name of the husband. She is the property of the husband.

"To complete the picture, the child of labour and money is again a girl" ("essentially a daughter"), "an unmarried girl" (has Szeliga ever known of a girl coming "married" out of the maternal womb?) "and therefore money" (according to the above proof that all money is an "unmarried girl", it is self-evident that "all unmarried girls" are "money")—"therefore money, but having its *definite* descent from labour, its father" (*toute recherche de la paternité est interdite*[a]). "The shape of the face, the image, bears a different stamp." (Pp. 364, 365.)

This story of marriage, burial and baptism is surely of itself sufficient proof that it is "essentially a daughter" of Szeliga, and indeed a daughter of "definite descent". Its ultimate basis, however, lies in the ignorance of his former stableman, Sancho. This is clearly seen at the end, when the orator is again anxiously concerned about the "coining" of money, thereby betraying that he still considers that coins are the most important medium of circulation. If he had taken the trouble to examine a little more closely the economic relations of money, instead of weaving a beautiful, leafy bridal wreath for it,[b] he would have known that—without mentioning state securities, shares, etc.—the major part of the medium of circulation consists of bills of exchange, whereas paper money forms a comparatively small part, and coin a still smaller part. In England, for example, fifteen times as much money circulates in the form of bills of exchange and bank-notes as in the form of coin. And even as regards coin, it is determined exclusively by the costs of production, i.e., labour. Hence Stirner's elaborate process of procreation was superfluous here.

Szeliga's solemn reflections about a means of exchange based on labour but, nevertheless, different from the money of today,

---

[a] Any investigation regarding paternity is forbidden—the formula used in article 340 of the *Code Napoléon* (the French civil code).— *Ed.*

[b] Carl Maria von Weber, *Der Freischütz* (Libretto by Friedrich Kind), Act III, Scene 4, "Wedding Song".— *Ed.*

which he claims to have discovered among certain communists, only prove once again the simplicity with which our noble couple believe everything they read without even examining it.

When the two heroes ride homewards after this "knightly and romantic" campaign of "wooing", they are bringing back no "fortune", still less the "bride", and least of all "money", but at best one "ragamuffin" is bringing home the other.

4. State

We have seen that Sancho retains in his "union" the existing form of landownership, division of labour and money, in the way in which a petty bourgeois conceives these relations in his imagination. It is clear at a glance that with such premises Sancho cannot do without the state.

First of all his newly acquired property will have to assume the form of guaranteed, legal property. We have already heard his words:

"That in which all want to have a share will be taken away from the individual who wants to have it for himself alone." (P. 330.)

Here, therefore, the will of the whole community is enforced against the will of the separate individual. Since each of the egoists in agreement with themselves may turn out to be not in agreement with the other egoists and thus become involved in this contradiction, the collective will must also find some means of expression in relation to the separate individuals —

"and this will is called the *will of the state*". (P. 257.)

Its decisions are then *legal* decisions. The enforcement of this collective will in its turn requires repressive measures and public power.

"In this matter also" (in the matter of property) "the unions will multiply the means of the individual and *safeguard* his *disputed* property" (they guarantee, therefore, guaranteed property, i.e., legal property, i.e., property that Sancho possesses not "unconditionally", but "holds on feudal tenure" from the "union"). (P. 342.)

Obviously, the whole of civil law is re-established along with the relations of property, and Sancho himself, for example, sets forth the theory of contract fully in the spirit of the lawyers, as follows:

"It is of no importance, too, that I deprive myself of one or other freedom, for example, through any *contract*." (P.409.)

And in order to "safeguard" "disputed" contracts, it will also "be of no importance" if he has again to submit himself to a court and to all the actual consequences of a civil court case.

Thus, "little by little out of the twilight and the night" we come closer again to the existing relations, but only as these relations exist in the dwarfish imagination of the German petty bourgeois.

Sancho admits:

"In relation to freedom there is no essential difference between state and union. The latter cannot arise and exist without restricting freedom in various ways just as the state is incompatible with boundless freedom. Restriction of freedom is always unavoidable, for it is impossible to *get rid of* everything; one cannot fly like a bird just because one would like to fly, etc.... In the union there will still be a fair amount of compulsion and lack of freedom, for its aim is not freedom which, on the contrary, it sacrifices for the sake of peculiarity, but only for the sake of *peculiarity*." (Pp. 410, 411.)

Leaving aside for the time being the strange distinction between freedom and peculiarity, it should be noted that Sancho, without intending to do so, has already sacrificed his "peculiarity" in his union owing to its *economic* institutions. As a true "believer in the state", he sees a restriction only where political institutions begin. He lets the old society continue in existence and with it also the subordination of individuals to division of labour; in which case he cannot escape the fate of having a special "peculiarity" prescribed for him by the division of labour and the occupation and position in life that falls to his lot as a result of it. If, for example, it fell to his lot to work as an apprentice fitter in Willenhall,[109] then the "peculiarity" imposed on him would consist of a twisted hip-bone resulting in a "game leg"; if the "title spectre[a] of his book"[110] has to exist as a female throstle spinner, then her "peculiarity" would consist in stiff knees. Even if our Sancho continues his old vocation of a corvée peasant, already assigned to him by Cervantes, and which he now declares to be his own vocation, which he calls upon himself to fulfil, then, owing to division of labour and the separation of town and countryside, he will have the "peculiarity" of being a purely local animal cut off from all world intercourse and, consequently, from all culture.

Thus, in the union owing to its social organisation, Sancho *malgré lui* loses his peculiarity if, by way of exception, we take peculiarity in the sense of individuality. That owing to its political organisation, he then surrenders his freedom as well is quite consistent and only shows still more clearly how much he strives to retain the present state of affairs in his union.

Thus, the essential distinction between freedom and peculiar-

---

[a] Marie Dähnhardt, Stirner's wife.— *Ed.*

ity constitutes the difference between the present state of affairs and the "union". We have already seen how essential this distinction is. The majority of the members of the union, too, will possibly not be particularly embarrassed by this distinction and will hasten to decree their "riddance" from it, and if Sancho is not satisfied with that, they will show him on the basis of his own "book" that, firstly, there are no essences, but that essences and essential differences are "the holy"; secondly, that the union does not have to trouble about the "nature of the matter" and the "concept of the relation"; and, thirdly, that they in no way encroach on his peculiarity but only on his freedom to express it. They will perhaps prove to him, if it is his "endeavour to be without a constitution", that they restrict only his freedom by putting him in prison, striking blows at him, or tearing off his leg, and that he remains *partout et toujours* "peculiar", so long as he is still able to show the signs of life of a polyp, an oyster or even a galvanised dead frog. They will "set a definite price" on his work, as we have already heard, and "will not allow a truly *free*" (!) "realisation of his property", for thereby they restrict only his freedom, not his peculiarity. These are things for which Sancho, on page 338, reproaches the state. "What then should" our corvée peasant Sancho "do? He should be firm and pay no attention" to the union. (Ibid.) Finally, whenever he begins to grumble about the restrictions imposed on him, the majority will suggest that so long as he has the peculiarity of declaring that freedoms are peculiarities, they can take the liberty of regarding his peculiarities as freedoms.

Just as the difference mentioned above between human and unique labour was only a miserable appropriation of the law of supply and demand, so now the difference between freedom and peculiarity is a miserable appropriation of the relation between the state and civil society or, as Monsieur Guizot says, between *liberté individuelle* and *pouvoir public*. This is so much the case that in what follows he can copy Rousseau[a] almost word for word.

"The agreement [...] according to which everyone must sacrifice a part of his freedom" occurs "not at all for the sake of something universal or even for the sake of another person", on the contrary, "I only concluded it out of *self-interest*. As far as sacrificing is concerned, after all I merely sacrifice what is not in my power, i.e., I sacrifice nothing at all." (P. 418.)

Our corvée peasant in agreement with himself shares this quality with all other corvée peasants and, in general, with

---

[a] *Du Contrat social; ou, Principes du droit politique.—Ed.*

every individual who has ever lived on the earth. Compare also Godwin, *Political Justice*.[a]

Incidentally, Sancho appears to possess the peculiarity of imagining that according to Rousseau individuals concluded the contract for the sake of the universal, which never entered Rousseau's head.

One consolation, however, remains for him.

> "The state is *holy* ... the union, however, is ... *not* holy." And herein lies the "great difference between the state and the union". (P. 411.)

The whole difference, therefore, amounts to this, that the "union" is the actual modern state, and the "state" is Stirner's illusion about the Prussian state, which he confuses with the state in general.

5. Rebellion

Sancho quite rightly has so little faith in his subtle distinctions between state and union, holy and not holy, human and unique, peculiarity and freedom, etc., that in the end he takes refuge in the *ultima ratio* of the egoist in agreement with himself — in rebellion. This time, however, he rebels not against himself, as he earlier asserted, but against the union. Just as earlier Sancho sought to achieve clarity on all points in the union, so he does here, too, as regards rebellion.

> "If the community treats me unjustly, I rebel against it and defend my property." (P. 343.)
>
> If the rebellion does not "prosper", the union will "expel (imprison, exile, etc.) him". (Pp. 256, 257.)

Sancho here tries to appropriate the *droits de l'homme* of 1793, which included the right of insurrection [111]— a human right that, of course, bears bitter fruits for him who tries to make use of it at his "own" discretion.

Thus Sancho's whole union amounts to the following. Whereas in his previous criticism he regarded existing relations only from the aspect of illusion, when speaking of the union he tries to get to know the actual content of these relations and to oppose this content to the former illusions. In this attempt, our ignorant school-master was of course bound to fail ignominiously. By way of exception, he did once endeavour to appropriate the "nature of the matter" and the "concept of the relation", but

---

[a] William Godwin, *Enquiry Concerning Political Justice, and Its Influence on Morals and Happiness.— Ed.*

he failed to "divest" any matter or any relation of its "alien character".

Now that we have become acquainted with the union in its real form, it only remains for us to examine Sancho's enthusiastic ideas about it, i.e., the religion and philosophy of the union.

6. Religion and Philosophy of the Union

Here we again start from the point at which, above, we began the description of the union. Sancho employs two categories: property and wealth; the illusions about property correspond mainly to the positive data given on landed property, the illusions about wealth to the data on the organisation of labour and the monetary system in the union.

A. Property

Page 331: "The world belongs to me."

Interpretation of his hereditary tenure of a plot of land.

Page 343: "I am the owner of everything that I need",

a euphemistic way of saying that his needs are his possession and that what he needs as a corvée peasant is determined by his circumstances. In the same way the economists maintain that the worker is the owner of everything that he needs as a worker. See the discourse on the minimum wage in Ricardo.[a]

Page 343: "Now, however, everything belongs to me."

A musical flourish in honour of his rate of wages, his plot of land, his permanent lack of money, and his expulsion from everything that the "society" does not want him to have in exclusive possession. The same idea occurs on page 327, expressed thus:

"His" (i.e., of another person) "possessions are mine and I dispose of them as the owner to the extent of my power."

This pompous *allegro marciale* passes in the following way into a gentle cadence, in which it gradually collapses on its backside — Sancho's usual fate:

Page 331: "The world belongs to me. Do you" (communists) "say anything different with your opposite thesis: the world belongs to *all*? All are I, and once more I, etc." (for example, "Robespierre, for example, Saint-Just, and so on").

---

[a] David Ricardo, *On the Principles of Political Economy and Taxation.— Ed.*

Page 415: "I am I and you are I, but ... this I, in which we are all equal, is only my thought [...] a generality" (the holy).

The practical variation on this theme occurs on page 330, where the "individuals collectively" (i.e., all) are courterposed as a regulating force to the "isolated individual" (i.e., the I as distinct from all).

These dissonances are at last resolved in the soothing final chord, to the effect that what I do not possess is at any rate the property of another "ego". Thus, "ownership of everything" is only an interpretation of the statement that each person possesses exclusive property.

Page 336: "But property is only my property if I have unconditional possession of it. As the unconditional ego, I have property, I carry on free trade."

We already know that only freedom, and not peculiarity, is affected if freedom of trade and unconditionality are not respected in the union. "Unconditional property" is a fitting supplement to the "secure", guaranteed property in the union.

Page 342: "In the opinion of the communists, the community should be the owner. On the contrary, I am the owner and only come to an agreement with others about my property."

On page 329 we saw how "the *société* makes itself the *owner*" and on page 330 how it "excludes *individuals* from *its* property". In general, we saw that the tribal system of feudal tenure, the crudest beginnings of the system of feudal tenure, was introduced. According to page 416, the "feudal system = absence of property"; hence, according to the same page, "property is recognised in the union, and only in the union", and moreover for a conclusive reason: "because no one any longer holds his possession in feudal tenure from any being [*Wesen*]" (ibid.). That is to say, under the hitherto existing feudal system, the feudal lord was this "being", in the union it is the *société*. From this one may at least conclude that Sancho possesses an "exclusive" but by no means "secure" property in the "essence" [*Wesen*[a]] of past history.

In connection with page 330, according to which each individual is excluded from that which society does not consider it right for him to hold in his sole possession, and in connection with the state and legal system of the union, it is stated:

Page 369: "The rightful and legitimate property of another will only be that which you consider it right to recognise as his property. If you no longer consider it right, it loses its rightfulness for you and you will deride any claim to absolute right in it."

---

[a] A pun on the word *Wesen*, which can mean "being" or "essence".— *Ed.*

He thus proves the astounding fact that what is right in the union does not have to be right for him — an indisputable right of man. If there exists in the union the institution of the old French parliaments, which Sancho loves so much, then he can even have his dislike recorded and deposit the document in the office of the law courts, consoling himself with the thought that "one cannot get rid of everything".

These various statements appear to contradict themselves, one another and the actual state of things in the union. But the key to this riddle is to be found in the juridical fiction, already mentioned, that when Sancho is excluded from the property of others, he is merely coming to an agreement with these others. This fiction is expounded in more detail in the following statements:

Page 369: "This" (i.e., respect for the property of others) "comes to an end when I can leave the tree in question to another, just as I leave my stick, etc., to another, but do not from the outset regard it as something alien, i.e., holy. Rather ... it remains my property, no matter for what period I cede it to another; it is mine and remains mine. I *see* nothing alien in the wealth belonging to the banker."

Page 328: "I do not retreat timidly before thy and your property, but always *regard* it as my property, which I do not need to respect at all. Just do the same with what you call my property. With this *point of view* we shall most easily reach agreement with one another."

If, according to the rules of the union, Sancho is "given a drubbing" as soon as he tries to seize another's property, he will, of course, maintain that pilfering is a "peculiarity" of his; nevertheless, the union will decide that Sancho has merely taken a "liberty". And if Sancho takes the "liberty" of attempting to seize another's possessions, the union has the "peculiarity" of sentencing him to a flogging for it.

The essence of the matter is this. Bourgeois and, particularly, petty-bourgeois and small-peasant property is, as we have seen, retained in the union. Merely the *interpretation*, the "*point of view*", is different, for which reason Sancho always lays stress on the way of "regarding". "Agreement" is reached when this new philosophy of regarding enjoys the regard of the whole union. This philosophy consists of the following. Firstly, every relation, whether caused by economic conditions or direct compulsion, is regarded as a relation of "agreement". Secondly, it is imagined that all property belonging to others is relinquished to them by us and remains with them only until we have the power to take it from them; and if we never get the power, *tant mieux*. Thirdly, Sancho and his union in theory guarantee each other absence of respect, whereas in practice the union "reaches agreement" with Sancho with the aid of a stick. Finally, this "agreement" is a mere phrase, since everyone knows that the others enter into it only with the secret reservation that they will reject it on the first convenient occasion. I see in your property something that is not yours but mine; since every ego does likewise, they see in it the *universal*, by which we arrive at the modern-German philosophical interpretation of ordinary, special and exclusive private property.

The union's philosophy of property includes, *inter alia*, the following fancies derived from Sancho's system:

On page 342, that property can be acquired in the union through absence of respect; on page 351, that "we are all in the midst of abundance", and I "have only to help myself to as much as I can", whereas in actual fact the whole union belongs to Pharaoh's seven lean kine[112]; and finally that Sancho "cherishes thoughts" which are "written in his book" and which are sung on page 374 in the incomparable ode addressed to himself imitating Heine's three odes to Schlegel[a]: "*You, who* cherishes such thoughts as are written in your book ... you cherish nonsense!" Such is the hymn which for the time being Sancho addresses to himself, and about which the union will later "reach agreement" with him.

Finally, it is obvious even without reaching "agreement" that property in the extraordinary sense, about which we already spoke in the "Phenomenology",[b] is accepted in the union in lieu of payment, as "marketable" property and "property in circulation". Concerning simple facts, e.g., that I feel sympathy, that I talk to others, that my leg is amputated (or torn off), the union will reach agreement that "the feeling experienced by sentient beings is also mine, my property" (p. 387); that other people's ears and tongues are likewise my property, and that mechanical relations too are my property. Thus, appropriation in the union will consist chiefly in all relations being transformed into property relations by means of a facile paraphrase. This new mode of expressing "evils" that are already now rife is an "essential means or faculty" in the union and will successfully make up for the deficit in the means of existence that is inevitable in view of Sancho's "social gifts".

---

[a] Heine's "Sonettenkranz an A. W. von Schlegel" in his *Buch der Lieder*.— *Ed.*

[b] See this volume, pp. 276-78.— *Ed.*

B. Wealth

Page 216: "Let each of you become an *omnipotent ego!*"
Page 353: "Think about increasing your wealth!"
Page 420: "Keep up the value of your gifts;
"Keep up their price,
"Do not allow yourself to be compelled to sell below the price,
"Do not allow yourself to be persuaded that your commodity is not worth the price,
"Do not make yourself ridiculous by a ridiculously low price,
"Follow the example of the courageous man", etc.!
Page 420: "Increase the value of your property!"
"Increase your value!"

These moral sayings, which Sancho learned from an Andalusian Jewish huckster who drew up rules of life and trade for his son, and which Sancho now pulls out of his knapsack, form the main wealth of the union. The basis of all these statements is the great proposition on page 351:

"Everything that you are able to do [*vermagst*— inflected form of *vermögen*] is your wealth [*Vermögen*]."

This proposition is either meaningless, i.e., mere tautology, or is nonsense. It is tautology if it means: what you are able to do, you are able to do. It is nonsense if *Vermögen* No.2 is meant to denote wealth "in the ordinary sense", commercial wealth, and if the proposition is based, therefore, on the etymological similarity. The collision consists precisely in the fact that what is expected of my ability [*Vermögen*] is different from what it is capable of doing, e.g., it is demanded of my ability to write verses that it should make money out of these verses. My ability is expected to produce something quite different from the specific product of this special ability, viz., a product depending on extraneous conditions which are not subject to my ability. This difficulty is supposed to be resolved in the union by means of etymological synonymy. We see that our egoistical school-master hopes to occupy an important post in the union. Incidentally, this difficulty is only an apparent one. The usual pithy moral saying of the bourgeois: "Anything is good to make money of"[a] is here expounded at length in Sancho's solemn manner.

C. Morality, Intercourse, Theory of Exploitation

Page 352: "You behave egoistically when you regard one another neither as owners nor as ragamuffins or workers, but as part of your wealth, as *useful creatures*. Then you will not give anything either to the owner, the proprietor,

---

[a] The words in quotes are in English in the manuscript.— *Ed.*

for his property, or to the one who works, but only to him whom you can make use of. Do we need a king? the North Americans ask themselves, and they reply: 'He and his work are not worth a farthing to us'."

On the other hand, on page 229, he reproaches the "bourgeois period" for the following:

"Instead of taking me as I am, attention is paid only to my property, my qualities, and a marriage alliance[a] is concluded with me only for the sake of what I possess. The marriage is concluded, so to speak, with what I have and not with what I am."

That is to say, attention is paid solely to what I am for others, to my usefulness, I am dealt with as a useful creature. Sancho spits into the "bourgeois period's" soup, so that in the union he alone can devour it.

If the individuals of modern society regard one another as owners, as workers and, if Sancho wishes, as ragamuffins, this only means that they treat one another as useful creatures, a fact which can only be doubted by such a useless individual as Sancho. The capitalist, who "regards" the worker "as a worker", shows consideration for him only because he needs workers; the worker treats the capitalist in the same way, and the Americans too, in Sancho's opinion (we would like him to point out the source from which he took this historic fact), have no *use* for a king, *because* he is useless to them *as a worker*. Sancho has chosen his example with his usual clumsiness, for it is supposed to prove exactly the opposite of what it actually proves.

Page 395: "For me, you are nothing but food, just as I am eaten up and consumed by you. We stand in only one relation to one another: that of usefulness, utility, use."

Page 416: "No one is to me a person to be held in respect, not even my fellow-man; but, like other *beings*" (!), "he is solely an *object*, for which I may or may not have sympathy, an interesting or uninteresting object, a useful or useless creature."

The relation of "usefulness", which is supposed to be the *sole* relation of the individuals to one another in the union, is at once paraphrased as "*eating*" one another. The "perfect Christians" of the union, of course, also celebrate holy communion, only not by eating together but by eating one another.

The extent to which this theory of mutual exploitation, which Bentham expounded *ad nauseam*, could already at the beginning of the present century be regarded as a phase of the previous one is shown by Hegel in his *Phänomenologie*. See

---

[a] In the manuscript: *ehelicher Bund*, that is, "marriage alliance"; in Stirner's book: *ehrlicher Bund*, i.e., "honest alliance".—*Ed.*

there the chapter "The Struggle of Enlightenment with Superstition", where the theory of usefulness is depicted as the final result of enlightenment. The apparent absurdity of merging all the manifold relationships of people in the *one* relation of usefulness, this apparently metaphysical abstraction arises from the fact that in modern bourgeois society all relations are subordinated in practice to the one abstract monetary-commercial relation. This theory came to the fore with Hobbes and Locke, at the same time as the first and second English revolutions, those first battles by which the bourgeoisie won political power. It is to be found even earlier, of course, among writers on political economy, as a tacit presupposition. Political economy is the real science of this theory of utility; it acquires its true content among the Physiocrats, since they were the first to treat political economy systematically. In Helvétius and Holbach one can already find an idealisation of this doctrine, which fully corresponds to the attitude of opposition adopted by the French bourgeoisie before the revolution. Holbach depicts the entire activity of individuals in their mutual intercourse, e.g., speech, love, etc., as a relation of utility and utilisation. Hence the actual relations that are presupposed here are speech, love, definite manifestations of definite qualities of individuals. Now these relations are supposed not to have the meaning *peculiar* to them but to be the expression and manifestation of some third relation attributed to them, the *relation of utility or utilisation*. This *paraphrasing* ceases to be meaningless and arbitrary only when these relations have validity for the individual not on their own account, not as spontaneous activity, but rather as disguises, though by no means disguises of the category of utilisation, but of an actual third aim and relation which is called the relation of utility.

The verbal masquerade only has meaning when it is the unconscious or deliberate expression of an actual masquerade. In this case, the utility relation has a quite definite meaning, namely, that I derive benefit for myself by doing harm to someone else (*exploitation de l'homme par l'homme*[a]); in this case moreover the use that I derive from some relation is entirely extraneous to this relation, as we saw above in connection with ability [*Vermögen*] that from each ability a product alien to it was demanded, a relation determined by social relations[b]— and this is precisely the relation of utility. All

---

[a] "Exploitation of man by man". See *Doctrine de Saint-Simon. Exposition. Première année.— Ed.*

[b] See this volume, pp. 430-32.— *Ed.*

this is actually the case with the bourgeois. For him only *one* relation is valid on its own account—the relation of exploitation; all other relations have validity for him only insofar as he can include them under this one relation; and even where he encounters relations which cannot be directly subordinated to the relation of exploitation, .ie subordinates them to it at least in his imagination. The material expression of this use is money which represents the value of all things, people and social relations. Incidentally, one sees at a glance that the category of "utilisation" is first abstracted from the actual relations of intercourse which I have with other people (but by no means from reflection and mere will) and then these relations are made out to be the reality of the category that has been abstracted from them themselves, a wholly metaphysical method of procedure. In exactly the same way and with the same justification, Hegel depicts all relations as relations of the objective spirit. Hence Holbach's theory is the historically justified philosophical illusion about the bourgeoisie just then developing in France, whose thirst for exploitation could still be regarded as a thirst for the full development of individuals in conditions of intercourse freed from the old feudal fetters. Liberation from the standpoint of the bourgeoisie, i.e., competition, was, of course, for the eighteenth century the only possible way of offering the individuals a new career for freer development. The theoretical proclamation of the consciousness corresponding to this bourgeois practice, of the consciousness of mutual exploitation as the universal mutual relation of all individuals, was also a bold and open step forward. It was a kind of *enlightenment* which interpreted the political, patriarchal, religious and sentimental embellishment of exploitation under feudalism in a secular way; the embellishment corresponded to the form of exploitation existing at that time and it had been systematised especially by the theoretical writers of the absolute monarchy.

Even if Sancho had done the same thing in his "book" as Helvétius and Holbach did in the last century, the anachronism would still have made it ridiculous. But we have seen that in the place of active bourgeois egoism he put a bragging egoism in agreement with itself. His sole service—rendered against his will and without realising it—was that he expressed the aspirations of the German petty bourgeois of today whose aim it is to become bourgeois. It was quite fitting that the petty, shy and timid behaviour of these petty bourgeois should have as its counterpart the noisy, blustering and impertinent public boasting of "the unique" among their philosophical representatives. It is quite in accordance with the situation of these petty bourgeois that they do not want to know about their theoretical loud-mouthed champion, and that he knows nothing about them; that they are at variance with one another, and he is forced to preach egoism in agreement with itself. Now, perhaps, Sancho will realise the sort of umbilical cord that connects *his* "union" with the Customs Union.[113]

The advances made by the theory of utility and exploitation, its various phases are closely connected with the various periods of development of the bourgeoisie. In the case of Helvétius and Holbach, the actual content of the theory never went much beyond paraphrasing the mode of expression of writers belonging to the period of the absolute monarchy. It was a different method of expression which reflected the desire to reduce all relations to the relation of exploitation and to explain the intercourse of people from their material needs and the ways of satisfying them, rather than the actual realisation of this desire. The problem was set. Hobbes and Locke had before their eyes not only the earlier development of the Dutch bourgeoisie (both of them had lived for some time in Holland) but also the first political actions by which the English bourgeoisie emerged from local and provincial limitations, as well as a comparatively highly developed stage of manufacture, overseas trade and colonisation. This particularly applies to Locke, who wrote during the first period of the English economy, at the time of the rise of joint-stock companies, the Bank of England and England's mastery of the seas. In their case, and particularly in that of Locke, the theory of exploitation was still directly connected with the economic content.

Helvétius and Holbach had before them, besides English theory and the preceding development of the Dutch and English bourgeoisie, also the French bourgeoisie which was still struggling for its free development. The commercial spirit, universal in the eighteenth century, had especially in France taken possession of all classes in the form of speculation. The financial difficulties of the government and the resulting disputes over taxation occupied the attention of all France even at that time. In addition, Paris in the eighteenth century was the only world city, the only city where there was personal intercourse among individuals of all nations. These premises, combined with the more universal character typical of the French in general, gave the theory of Helvétius and Holbach its peculiar universal colouring, but at the same time deprived it of the positive economic content that was still to be found among the English. The theory which for the English was still simply the registration of facts becomes for the French a philosophical system. This generality devoid of positive content, such as we find it in Helvétius and Holbach, is essentially different from the substantial comprehensive view which is first found in Bentham and Mill. The former corresponds to the struggling, still undeveloped bourgeoisie, the latter to the ruling, developed bourgeoisie.

The content of the theory of exploitation that was neglected by Helvétius and Holbach was developed and systematised by the Physiocrats—who worked at the same time as Holbach—but because their basis was the undeveloped economic relations of France where feudalism, under which landowner-ship plays the chief role, was still unshaken, they remained in thrall to the feudal outlook insofar as they declared landowner-ship and land cultivation to be that [productive force] which determines the whole structure of society.

The theory of exploitation owes its further development in England to Godwin, and especially to Bentham. As the bourgeoisie succeeded in asserting itself more and more both in England and in France, the economic content, which the French had neglected, was gradually re-introduced by Bentham. God-win's *Political Justice* was written during the terror, and Bentham's chief works during and after the French Revolution and the development of large-scale industry in England. The complete union of the theory of utility with political economy is to be found, finally, in Mill.

At an earlier period political economy had been the subject of inquiry either by financiers, bankers and merchants, i.e., in general by persons directly concerned with economic relations, or by persons with an all-round education like Hobbes, Locke and Hume, for whom it was of importance as a branch of encyclopaedic knowledge. Thanks to the Physiocrats, political economy for the first time was raised to the rank of a special science and has been treated as such ever since. As a special branch of science it absorbed the other relations—political, juridical, etc.—to such an extent that it reduced them to economic relations. But it regarded this subordination of all relations to itself as only one aspect of these relations, and thereby allowed them for the rest an independent significance outside political economy. The complete subordination of all existing relations to the relation of utility, and its unconditional elevation to the sole content of all other relations, occurs for the first time in Bentham's works, where, after the French Revolution and the development of large-scale industry, the bourgeoisie is no longer presented as a special class, but as the class whose conditions of existence are those of the whole society.

When the sentimental and moral paraphrases, which for the French were the entire content of the utility theory, had been exhausted, all that remained for its further development was the question how individuals and relations were to be used, to be exploited. Political economy had meanwhile already provided the answer to this question; the only possible advance consisted in the inclusion of the economic content. Bentham achieved this advance. Political economy, however, had already given expression to the fact that the chief relations of exploitation are determined by production in general, independently of the will of individuals, who find them already in existence. Hence, no other field of speculative thought remained for the utility theory than the attitude of individuals to these important relations, the private exploitation of an already existing world by individuals. On this subject Bentham and his school indulged in lengthy moral reflections. The whole criticism of the existing world by the utility theory was consequently restricted within a narrow range. Remaining within the confines of bourgeois conditions, it could criticise only those relations which had been handed down from a past epoch and were an obstacle to the development of the bourgeoisie. Hence, although the utility theory does expound the connection of all existing relations with economic relations, it does so only in a restricted way.

From the outset the utility theory had the aspect of a theory of general utility, yet this aspect only became fraught with meaning when economic relations, especially division of labour and exchange, were included. With division of labour, the private activity of the individual becomes generally useful; Bentham's general utility becomes reduced to the same general utility which is asserted in competition as a whole. By taking into account the economic relations of rent, profit and wages, the definite relations of exploitation of the various classes were introduced, since the manner of exploitation depends on the social position of the exploiter. Up to this point the theory of utility was able to base itself on definite social facts; its further account of the manner of exploitation amounts to a mere recital of catechism phrases.

The economic content gradually turned the utility theory into a mere apologia for the existing state of affairs, an attempt to prove that under existing conditions the mutual relations of people today are the most advantageous and generally useful. It has this character among all modern economists.

But whereas the utility theory had thus at least the advantage of indicating the connection of all existing relations with the economic foundations of society, in Sancho the theory has lost all positive content; it is divorced from all actual relations and is restricted to the mere illusion cherished by the isolated bourgeois about his "cleverness", by means of which he reckons to exploit the world. Incidentally, it is only in a few passages that Sancho deals with the theory of utility even in this diluted form; almost the entire "book" is taken up, as we have seen, with egoism in agreement with itself, i.e., with an illusion about this illusion of the petty bourgeois. Even these few passages are finally reduced by Sancho to mere vapour as we shall see.

D. Religion

"In this community" (namely with other people) "I *perceive* nothing at all but a multiplication of my power, and I retain it only for so long as it is my multiplied power." (P. 416.)

"I no longer *abase* myself before any power, and *recognise* that all powers are only my power, which I have immediately to subdue if they threaten to become a power against me or over me; each of them *is permitted* to be only one of *my means* for achieving my purpose."

I "*perceive*", I "*recognise*", I "*have to* subdue" power "*is permitted* to be only one of my means". We have already been shown in connection with the "union" what these moral demands mean and how far they correspond to reality. This illusion about his power is closely connected with the other illusion: that in the union "substance" is abolished (see "Humane Liberalism"[a]), and that the relations of the union members never assume a rigid form in respect to separate individuals.

"The union, the association, this eternally fluid association of everything that exists.... Of course, society can arise also from union, but only as a fixed idea arises out of a thought.... If a union has crystallised into a society, it has ceased to be an association, for association is the unceasing process of associating with one another; it has reached the state of being associated, it has become society, the corpse of the union or association.... Neither a natural nor a spiritual bond holds the union together." (Pp. 294, 408, 416.)

---

[a] See this volume, pp. 252-53.— *Ed.*

As regards the "natural bond", it exists, despite Sancho's "ill will", in the form of corvée peasant economy and organisation of labour, etc., in the union; likewise the "spiritual bond" [a] in Sancho's philosophy. For the rest we need only refer to what we have already said several times, and repeated in connection with the union, about division of labour causing the relations to confront individuals as something existing independently of them.

"In short, society is *holy*, the union is your *own*; society uses you, you use the union", etc. [P. 418.]

E. Supplement to the Union

Whereas hitherto we were shown no other possibility of reaching the "union" than through rebellion, now we learn from the "Commentary" that the "union of egoists" already exists in "hundreds of thousands" of cases as one of the aspects of existing bourgeois society and that it is accessible to us even without any rebellion and any "Stirner". Then Sancho shows us

"such unions in actual life. Faust is within such unions when he exclaims: Here I am a *human being*" (!), "here I dare to be one, [b] here Goethe states it even in black and white" ("but the holy person is called Humanus, see Goethe", [c] cf. "the book").... "If Hess were to look attentively at real life, he would see hundreds of thousands of such egoistical unions — some of short duration, some enduring."

Sancho then makes some "children" meet for a game in front of Hess' window, and makes "a few friends" take Hess to a tavern and lets him associate with his "beloved".

"Of course, Hess does not notice how full of significance these trivial examples are and how, infinitely different they are from the holy societies and indeed from the fraternal, human society of holy socialists." (Sancho contra Hess, *Wigand*, pp. 193, 194.)

In just the same way, on page 305 of "the book", "association for material aims and interests" is graciously accepted as a voluntary union of egoists.

Thus the union here is reduced, on the one hand, to bourgeois associations and joint-stock companies and, on the other hand, to bourgeois clubs, picnics, etc. That the former belong wholly to the *present epoch* is well known, and that this

---

[a] Goethe, *Faust*, I. Teil, 2 "Studierzimmerszene".— *Ed.*

[b] Goethe, *Faust*, I. Teil, *"Osterspaziergang"*.— *Ed.*

[c] From Goethe's unfinished poem "Die Getheimnisse" (*Humanus*—a character in this poem).— *Ed.*

equally applies to the latter is also well known. Let Sancho look at the "unions" of an earlier epoch, e.g., of feudal times, or those of other nations, e.g., of the Italians, English, etc., right down to the "union" of children, in order to realise what the difference is. By this new interpretation of the union he confirms only his obdurate conservatism. Sancho, who incorporated the whole of bourgeois society, insofar as he liked it, into his allegedly new institution, here by way of supplement only assures us that in his union people will also enjoy themselves and indeed in quite the traditional way. Our bonhomme, of course, does not consider the question: what relations existing independently of him enable — or do not enable — him to "accompany a few friends to a tavern".

The idea of resolving the whole of society into voluntary groups — which is here, on the basis of hearsay accounts current in Berlin, turned into a Stirnerian idea — belongs to Fourier.[a] But with Fourier this view presupposes a complete transformation of society and is based on a criticism of the existing "unions", so much admired by Sancho, and of their infinite tedium. Fourier describes these present-day attempts at amusement in their connection with the existing relations of production and intercourse, and wages a polemic against them; Sancho, far from criticising them, wants on the contrary to transplant them in their entirety into his new "mutual agreement" institution for promoting happiness; he thereby only proves once again how strongly he is held in thrall to existing bourgeois society.

Finally, Sancho delivers the following *oratio pro domo*, i.e., in defence of the "union".

> "Is a union in which the majority allow themselves to be cheated in regard to their most natural and obvious interests, a union of egoists? Have egoists united where one is the slave or serf of another?... Societies in which the needs of some are satisfied at the expense of others, in which, for example, some can satisfy the need for rest by others having to work to the point of exhaustion.... Hess ... identifies ... these 'egoistical unions' of his with *Stirner's* union of egoists." ([*Wigand*,] pp. 192, 193.)

Sancho, therefore, expresses the pious wish that in his union, based on mutual exploitation, all the members will be equally powerful, cunning, etc., etc., so that each can exploit the others to exactly the same extent as they exploit him, and so that no one will be "cheated" in regard to his "most natural and obvious

---

[a] Charles Fourier, *Théorie de l'unité universelle.— Ed.*

interests" or be able to "satisfy his needs at the expense of others". We note here that Sancho recognises "natural and obvious interests" and "needs" of all — consequently, *equal* interests and needs. Further, we recall at once page 456 of the book, according to which "overreaching" is a "moral idea inculcated by the guild spirit", and for a man who has had a "wise education", it remains a "fixed idea from which no freedom of thought can give protection". Sancho "gets his thoughts from above and adheres to them". (Ibid.) This equal power of all consists, according to his demand, in that everyone should become "*omnipotent*", i.e., all should become *impotent* in relation to one another, a perfectly consistent postulate that coincides with the sentimental desire of the petty bourgeois for a world of hucksters, in which everyone gets his advantage. Or, on the other hand, our saint quite suddenly presupposes a society in which each can satisfy his needs unhampered, without doing so "at the expense of others", and in that case the theory of exploitation again becomes a meaningless paraphrase for the actual relations of individuals to one another.

After Sancho in his "union" has "devoured" and consumed the others, thereby transforming intercourse with the world into intercourse with himself, he passes from this indirect self-enjoyment to direct self-enjoyment, by consuming himself.

C. My Self-Enjoyment

The *philosophy* which preaches enjoyment is as old in Europe as the Cyrenaic school.[114] Just as in antiquity it was the *Greeks* who were the protagonists of this philosophy, so in modern times it is the *French*, and indeed for the same reason, because their temperament and their society made them most capable of enjoyment. The philosophy of enjoyment was never anything but the clever language of certain social circles who had the privilege of enjoyment. Apart from the fact that the manner and content of their enjoyment was always determined by the whole structure of the rest of society and suffered from all its contradictions, this philosophy became a mere *phrase* as soon as it began to lay claim to a universal character and proclaimed itself the outlook on life of society as a whole. It sank then to the level of edifying moralising, to a sophistical palliation of existing society, or it was transformed into its opposite, by declaring compulsory asceticism to be enjoyment.

In modern times the philosophy of enjoyment arose with the decline of feudalism and with the transformation of the feudal landed nobility into the pleasure-loving and extravagant nobles of the court under the absolute monarchy. Among these nobles this philosophy still has largely the form of a direct, naïve outlook on life which finds expression in memoirs, poems, novels, etc. It only becomes a real philosophy in the hands of a few writers of the revolutionary bourgeoisie, who, on the one hand, participated in the culture and mode of life of the court nobility and, on the other hand, shared the more general outlook of the bourgeoisie, based on the more general conditions of existence of this class. This philosophy was, therefore, accepted by both classes, although from totally different points of view. Whereas among the nobility this language was restricted exclusively to its estate and to the conditions of life of this estate, it was given a generalised character by the bourgeoisie and addressed to every individual without distinction. The conditions of life of these individuals were thus disregarded and the theory of enjoyment thereby transformed into an insipid and hypocritical moral doctrine. When, in the course of further development, the nobility was overthrown and the bourgeoisie brought into conflict with its opposite, the proletariat, the nobility became devoutly religious, and the bourgeoisie solemnly moral and strict in its theories, or else succumbed to the above-mentioned hypocrisy, although the nobility in practice by no means renounced enjoyment, while among the bourgeoisie enjoyment even assumed an official, economic form — that of *luxury*.*

---

* [The following passage is crossed out in the manuscript:] In the Middle Ages the pleasures were strictly classified; each estate had its own distinct forms of pleasure and its distinct manner of enjoyment. The nobility was the estate privileged to devote itself exclusively to pleasure, while the separation of work and enjoyment already existed for the bourgeoisie and pleasure was subordinated to work. The serfs, the class destined exclusively to labour, had only extremely few and restricted pleasures, which came their way mostly by chance, depended on the whim of their masters and other contingencies, and are hardly worth considering.

Under the rule of the bourgeoisie the nature of the pleasures depended on the classes of society. The pleasures of the bourgeoisie are determined by the material brought forth by this class at various stages of its development and they have acquired the tedious character which they still retain from the individuals and from the continuous subordination of pleasure to money-making. The present crude form of proletarian pleasure is due, on the one hand, to the long working hours, which led to the utmost intensification of the need for enjoyment, and, on the other hand, to the restriction — both qualitative and quantitative — of the means of pleasure accessible to the proletarian.

In general, the pleasures of all hitherto existing estates and classes had to be

It was only possible to discover the connection between the kinds of enjoyment open to individuals at any particular time and the class relations in which they live, and the conditions of production and intercourse which give rise to these relations, the narrowness of the hitherto existing forms of enjoyment, which were outside the actual content of the life of people and in contradiction to it, the connection between every philosophy of enjoyment and the enjoyment actually present and the hypocrisy of such a philosophy which treated all individuals without distinction — it was, of course, only possible to discover all this when it became possible to criticise the conditions of production and intercourse in the hitherto existing world, i.e., when the contradiction between the bourgeoisie and the proletariat had given rise to communist and socialist views. That shattered the basis of all morality, whether the morality of asceticism or of enjoyment.

Our insipid, moralising Sancho believes, of course, as his whole "book" shows, that it is merely a matter of a different morality, of what appears to him a new outlook on life, of "getting out of one's head" a few "fixed ideas", to make everyone happy and able to enjoy life. Hence the chapter on self-enjoyment could at most reproduce under a new label the same phrases and maxims which he had already so frequently had the "self-enjoyment" of preaching to us. This chapter has only one original feature, namely that he *deifies* and turns into philosophical German all enjoyment, by giving it the name "*self-enjoyment*". While the French philosophy of enjoyment of the eighteenth century at least gave a witty description of the gay and audacious mode of life that then existed, Sancho's whole frivolity is limited to such expressions as "consuming" and "squandering", to images such as the "light" (it should read a candle) and to natural-scientific recollections which amount either to belletristic nonsense such as that the plant "imbibes the air of the ether" and that "song-birds swallow beetles", or else to wrong statements, for example, that a candle burns itself. On the other hand, here we again enjoy all the solemn seriousness of the statements against "the holy", which, we are told, in the

---

either childish, exhausting or crude, because they were always completely divorced from the vital activity, the real content of the life of the individuals, and more or less reduced to imparting an illusory content to a meaningless activity. The hitherto existing forms of enjoyment could, of course, only be criticised when the contradiction between the bourgeoisie and the proletariat had developed to such an extent that the existing mode of production and intercourse could be criticised as well.

guise of "vocation — designation — task" and "ideal" has hitherto spoiled people's self-enjoyment. For the rest, without
dwelling on the more or less dirty forms in which the "self" in
"self-enjoyment" can be more than a mere phrase, we must
once more as briefly as possible outline for the reader Sancho's
machinations against the holy, with the insignificant modula-
tions occurring in this chapter.

To recapitulate briefly, "vocation, designation, task, ideal"
are either

1. the idea of the revolutionary tasks laid down for an
oppressed class by the material conditions; or

2. mere idealistic paraphrases, or also the apt conscious
expression of the individuals' modes of activity which owing to
division of labour have assumed independent existence as
various professions; or

3. the conscious expression of the necessity which at every
moment confronts individuals, classes and nations to assert
their position through some quite definite activity; or

4. the conditions of existence of the ruling class (as
determined by the preceding development of production),
ideally expressed in law, morality, etc., to which [conditions]
the ideologists of that class more or less consciously give a sort
of theoretical independence; they can be conceived by separate
individuals of that class as vocation, etc., and are held up as a
standard of life to the individuals of the oppressed class, partly
as an embellishment or recognition of domination, partly as a
moral means for this domination. It is to be noted here, as in
general with ideologists, that they inevitably put the thing
upside-down and regard their ideology both as the creative force
and as the aim of all social relations, whereas it is only an
expression and symptom of these relations.

As for our Sancho, we know that he has the most ineradicable
faith in the illusions of these ideologists. Because people,
depending on their various conditions of life, construct various
notions about themselves, that is about man, Sancho imagines
that the various ideas created the various conditions of life and
thus the wholesale manufacturers of these ideas, i.e., the
ideologists, have dominated the world. Cf. page 433.

"Thinkers rule in the world", "thought rules the world"; "priests or
school-masters" "stuff their heads with all sorts of trash", "they imagine a
human ideal" which other people have to take as a guide. (P. 442.) .

Sancho even knows exactly the conclusion by virtue of which
people were subjected to the fancies of the school-masters

and owing to their stupidity subjected themselves to these fancies:

"Because it is *conceivable* for me" (the school-master), "it is *possible* for people; because it is possible for people, it means that they *ought to* be such, it was their *vocation*; and, finally, it is only according to this *vocation*, only as *persons having a vocation*, that one must judge human beings. And the further conclusion? It is not the individual who is man, but it is a *thought*, an *ideal*, that is man — species — mankind." (P. 441.)

All collisions in which, owing to their actual conditions of life, human beings become involved with themselves or with others appear to our school-master Sancho as collisions between people and their ideas about the life of "Man", ideas which they either have put themselves into their heads or have allowed school-masters to put into their heads. If they managed to get these ideas out of their heads "how happily" "these unfortunate beings could live", what "capers" they could cut, whereas now they have to "dance to the pipe of the school-masters and bear-leaders"! (P. 435.) (The lowest of these "bear-leaders" is Sancho, for it is only *himself* whom he leads by the nose.) If, for example, people almost always and almost everywhere — in China as well as in France — did not get it into their heads that they suffer from over-population, what an overflowing abundance of the means of existence would these "unfortunate beings" suddenly have at their disposal.

Under the pretext of writing a treatise on possibility and reality, Sancho here once more attempts to put forward his old story of the rule of the holy in the world. For him everything a school-master gets into his head about me is possible, and then Sancho can easily prove that this possibility has no reality except in his head. His solemn assertion that "behind the word *possible* lay concealed the most momentous misunderstanding of thousands of years" (p. 441) is sufficient proof that it is impossible for him to conceal behind words the consequences of his abundant misunderstanding of thousands of years.

This treatise on the "coincidence of possibility and reality" (p. 439), on what people have the ability to be and what they are, a treatise that harmonises so well with his earlier insistent exhortations that one should bring all one's abilities into play, etc., leads him, however, to a few more digressions on the materialist *theory of circumstances*, which we shall presently deal with in more detail. But first, one more example of his ideological distortion. On page 428 he makes the question "how can one acquire life" identical with the question how is one to "create in oneself the true ego" (or "life"). According to the same page, "worrying about life" ceases with his new moral philosophy and the "squandering" of life begins. Our Solomon expresses still more "eloquently" the miraculous power of his allegedly new moral philosophy in the following saying:

"Regard yourself as more powerful than others say you are, then you will have more power; value yourself more and you will have more." (P. 483.)

See above, in the section on the "union", Sancho's method of acquiring property.[a]

Now for his *theory of circumstances.*

"Man has no vocation, but he has powers *which* manifest *themselves* where they exist, because their being consists solely in their manifestation, and they cannot remain inactive any more than life itself.... Everyone at each instant uses as much power as he has" ("increase your value, follow the example of the courageous man, let each of you become an omnipotent ego", etc.— Sancho said above).... "One's powers can indeed be intensified and multiplied, particularly by hostile resistance or friendly support; but where their application is missing one can be sure that they are absent. It is possible to strike fire from a stone, but without striking it, nothing comes out; similarly man needs an *impulse.* Since powers always prove to be operative of themselves, the injunction to use them would be superfluous and senseless.... Power is merely a simpler word for manifestation of power." (Pp. 436, 437.)

"Egoism in agreement with itself", which just as it pleases brings or does not bring its powers or abilities into play and which applies the *jus utendi et abutendi*[b] to them, here suddenly and unexpectedly comes to grief. Once they are present, the forces here all of a sudden act autonomously, without caring about Sancho's "pleasure", they act like chemical or mechanical forces, independently of the individual who possesses them. We learn further that a force is not present if its manifestation is missing; the correction being made that power requires an *impulse* for its manifestation. We do not learn, however, how Sancho will decide whether it is the *impulse* or the *power* that is lacking when the manifestation of power is deficient. On the other hand, our unique investigator of nature teaches us that "it is possible to strike fire from a stone", and, as is always the case with Sancho, he could not have chosen a more unfortunate example. Sancho, like a simple village school-master, believes that the fire he strikes in this way comes from the stone, where it was previously latent. But any fourth-form schoolboy could tell him that in this method of obtaining fire, a method long

---

[a] See this volume, pp. 426-31.— *Ed.*
[b] The right of use and of disposal.— *Ed.*

forgotten in all civilised countries, by the friction of steel and stone, particles which become red-hot owing to this friction are separated from the steel, and not from the stone; that, consequently, the "fire", which for Sancho is not a definite relation, at a definite temperature, of certain bodies to certain other bodies, in particular oxygen, but is an independent thing, an "element", a fixed idea, "the holy"—that this fire does not come either from the stone or from the steel. Sancho might just as well have said: one can make bleached linen from chlorine, but if the "impulse", viz., the *unbleached* linen, is lacking, then "nothing comes out". We shall take this opportunity, for Sancho's "self-enjoyment", of noting an earlier fact of "unique" natural science. In the ode on crime it is stated:

> "Is there not a distant peal of *thunder*
> And do you not *see* how the sky
> Filled with foreboding *is silent* and overcast?" (P. 319 of "the book".)

It thunders and the sky is silent. Hence Sancho knows of some other place than the sky from which thunder comes. Further, Sancho notices the silence of the sky by means of his organ of *sight*—a feat which no one will be able to imitate. Or perhaps Sancho *hears* thunder and *sees* silence, so that the two phenomena can take place simultaneously. We saw how Sancho in dealing with "apparitions" made mountains represent the "spirit of loftiness".[a] Here the silent sky represents for him the spirit of foreboding.

Incidentally, it is not clear why Sancho here rails against the "injunction to use one's powers". This injunction, after all, could possibly be the missing "impulse", which, it is true, fails to have effect in the case of a stone, but the efficacy of which Sancho could observe during the exercises of any battalion. That the "injunction" is an "impulse" even for his feeble powers follows also from the fact that for him it turns out to be a "stumbling block".[b]

Consciousness is also a power which, according to the doctrine which has just been enunciated, "always proves to be operative of itself". In accordance with this, therefore, Sancho ought not to have set out to change consciousness, but at most the "impulse" which affects consciousness; consequently Sancho would have written his whole book in vain. But in this

---

[a] See this volume, p. 165.— *Ed.*
[b] A pun on the word *Anstoss*—impulse, shock, scandal, offence; *Stein des Anstosses*—stumbling block.— *Ed.*

case, of course, he regards his moral preaching and "injunctions" as a sufficient "impulse".

"What an individual can become he will become. A born poet may be prevented, owing to unfavourable *circumstances*, from being abreast of the times and creating great works of art, for which much study is indispensable; but he will compose poetry whether he is an agricultural labourer or has the good fortune to live at the Weimar Court. A born musician will occupy himself with music, no matter whether on all instruments" (he found this fantasy about *"all* instruments" in Proudhon. See "Communism") "or only on a shepherd's reed" (Virgil's *Eclogues*, of course, again come into the mind of our school-master). "A born philosophical intellect can prove its worth either as a university philosopher or a village philosopher. Finally, a *born dunce* always remains a blockhead. Indeed, innate limited intellects undoubtedly form the most numerous class of mankind. *And why should not* the same differences occur in the *human species* as are unmistakably seen in every species of animals?" (P. 434.)

Sancho has again chosen his example with his usual lack of skill. If all his nonsense about born poets, musicians and philosophers is accepted, then this example only proves, on the one hand, that a born poet, etc., *remains* what he *is* from birth—namely a poet, etc.; and, on the other hand, that the born poet, etc., in so far as he *becomes*, develops, may, "owing to unfavourable circumstances", not become what *he could become*. His example, therefore, on the one hand, proves nothing at all and, on the other hand, proves the opposite of what it was intended to prove; and taking both aspects together it proves that either from birth or owing to circumstances, Sancho belongs to *"the most numerous class of mankind"*. However, he shares the consolation of being a *unique* "blockhead" with this class and with his own blockheadedness.

Here Sancho experiences the adventure with the magic potion which Don Quixote brewed from rosemary, wine, olive oil and salt. As Cervantes relates in the seventeenth chapter, after Sancho had drunk this mixture he spent two hours in sweats and convulsions pouring it out from both channels of his body. The materialist potion which our valiant armour-bearer imbibed for his self-enjoyment purges him of all his egoism in the extraordinary sense. We saw above that Sancho suddenly lost all his solemnity when confronted with the "impulse", and renounced his "ability", like of yore the Egyptian magicians when confronted with the lice of Moses.[a] Now we observe two new attacks of faint-heartedness, in which he also gives way "to unfavourable *circumstances*" and finally even admits that his

---

[a] Exodus 8:16-18.— *Ed.*

original physical organisation is something that becomes crippled without co-operation from him. What is left now to our bankrupt egoist? He has no power over his original physical organisation; nor can he control the "circumstances" and the "impulse" under the influence of which this organisation develops; "what he is at every instant" is not "his own creation", but something created by the interaction between his innate potentialities and the circumstances acting on them — all this Sancho concedes. Unfortunate "creator"! Most unfortunate "creation"!

But the greatest calamity comes at the end. Sancho, not satisfied that already long ago he received the full count of the *tres mil azotes y trecientos en ambas sus valientes posaderas*,[a] finally delivers himself another and mighty blow by proclaiming himself a *believer in species*. And what a believer in species! Firstly, he attributes division of labour to species by making it responsible for the fact that some people are poets, others musicians, and still others school-masters. Secondly, he ascribes to species the existing physical and intellectual defects of "the most numerous class of mankind" and makes it responsible for the fact that under the rule of the bourgeoisie the majority of individuals are like himself. According to his views on innate limited intellects, one would have to explain the present spread of scrofula from the fact that "the species" finds a special satisfaction in making innate scrofulous constitutions form "the most numerous class of mankind". Even the most ordinary materialists and medical men had got beyond such naïve views long before the egoist in agreement with himself was "called" upon by "the species", "unfavourable circumstances" and the "impulse" to make his *début* before the German public. Just as previously Sancho explained all crippling of individuals, and hence of their relations, by means of the fixed ideas of school-masters, without worrying about the origin of these ideas, so now he explains this crippling as merely due to the natural process of generation. He has not the slightest idea that the ability of children to develop depends on the development of their parents and that all this crippling under existing social relations has arisen historically, and in the same way can be abolished again in the course of historical development. Even naturally evolved differences within the species, such as racial differences, etc., which Sancho does not mention at all, can and must be abolished in the course of

---

[a] Three thousand and three hundred lashes upon his ample buttocks.— *Ed.*

historical development. Sancho — who in this connection casts a stealthy glance at zoology and so makes the discovery that "innate limited intellects" form the most numerous class not only among sheep and oxen, but also among polyps and infusoria, which have no heads at all — has perhaps heard that it is possible to improve races of animals and by cross-breeding to create entirely new, more perfect varieties both for human enjoyment and for their own self-enjoyment. "Why should not" Sancho be able to draw a conclusion from this in relation to people as well?

We shall take this opportunity to "introduce episodically" Sancho's "transformations" in relation to species. We shall see that his attitude to species is exactly the same as to the holy: the more he blusters against it, the more he believes in it.

No. I. We have already seen that species engenders division of labour and the crippling that takes place under existing social circumstances and *indeed in such a way* that the species together with its products is regarded as something immutable under all circumstances, as outside the control of people.

No. II.

"Species is already realised owing to inherent constitution; on the other hand, what you make of this constitution" (according to what was said above, this ought to be: what "circumstances" make of it) "is the realisation of you. Your hand is fully realised in the sense of species, otherwise it would not be a hand but, let us say, a paw…. You make of it what and how you wish it to be and what you can make of it." (*Wigand*, pp. 184, 185.)

Here Sancho repeats in a different form what was already said in No. I.

We have seen, therefore, from what has been said so far that species, independently of control by individuals and the stage of their historical development, brings into the world all physical and spiritual potentialities, the immediate existence of individuals and, in embryo, division of labour.

No. III. Species remains as "impulse", which is only a general term for the "circumstances" that determine the development of the original individual, again engendered by species. For Sancho species is here precisely the same mysterious force which other bourgeois call the nature of things and which they make responsible for all relationships that are independent of them as bourgeois, and whose interconnection, therefore, they do not understand.

No. IV. Species taken as "what is possible for man" and "required by man" forms the basis of the organisation of labour in "Stirner's union", where likewise what is possible for all and required by all is regarded as a product of species.

No. V. We have already heard about the role that agreement plays in the union.

Page 462: "If it is a matter of coming to an agreement or communicating with one another, then, of course, I can only make use of the *human* means that are at my disposal because I am at the same time a man" (i.e., a specimen of the species).

Here, therefore, *language* is regarded as a product of the species. That Sancho speaks German and not French, however, is something he in no way owes to the species, but to circumstances. Incidentally, in every modern developed language, partly as a result of the historical development of the language from pre-existing material, as in the Romance and Germanic languages, partly owing to the crossing and mixing of nations, as in the English language, and partly as a result of the concentration of the dialects within a single nation brought about by economic and political concentration, the spontaneously evolved speech has been turned into a national language. As a matter of course, the individuals at some time will take completely under their control this product of the species as well. In the union, language as such will be spoken, holy language, the language of the holy — Hebrew, and indeed the Aramaic dialect spoken by that "corporeal essence", Christ. This "occurred" to us here "against the expectation" of Sancho, and "indeed exclusively because it seems to us that it could help to clarify the remainder".

No. VI. On pages 277, 278, we learn that "the species reveals itself in nations, towns, estates, diverse corporations" and, finally, "in the family"; hence it is perfectly logical that up to now it has "made history". Thus, here all preceding history, up to the unfortunate history of the unique, becomes a product of the "species" and, indeed, for the sufficient reason that this history has sometimes been summed up under the title of the history of *mankind*, i.e., of the species.

No. VII. In what has been said so far Sancho has attributed to the *species* more than any mortal had ever done before him, and he now sums it up in the following proposition:

"Species is *nothing* ... species is only a *conception*" (spirit, spectre, etc.). (P. 239.)

Ultimately, then, this "*nothing*" of Sancho's, which is identical with a "*conception*", means nothing, for Sancho himself is "the creative nothing", and the species, as we have seen, creates a great deal, and in doing so it can therefore very well be "nothing". Moreover Sancho tells us on page 456:

"*Being* justifies nothing at all; something imagined *exists* just as well as something not imagined."

Starting with page 448, Sancho spins out a yarn lasting thirty pages in order to strike "fire" out of thought and criticism of the egoist in agreement with himself. We have already experienced too many expressions of his thought and criticism to give the reader further "offence"[a] with Sancho's beggar's broth. One spoonful of it will suffice.

"Do you believe that thoughts fly about freely for the taking, so that anyone can capture some of them and then put them forward against me as his inviolable property? Everything that flies about, all of it is — mine." (P. 457.)

Here Sancho poaches snipe existing only in the mind. We have seen how many of the thoughts flying about he has captured for himself. He fancied that he could catch them as soon as he put the salt of the holy on their tails. This colossal contradiction between his actual property in regard to thoughts and his illusions on that score may serve as a classic and striking example of his entire property in the extraordinary sense. It is precisely this contrast that constitutes his *self-enjoyment.*

6. SOLOMON'S SONG OF SONGS
OR
THE UNIQUE

Cessem do sabio Grego, e do Troiano,
As navegaçoẽs grandes que fizeram;
Calle-se de Alexandro, e de Trajano
A fama das victorias que tiveram,
....
Cesse tudo o que a Musa antigua canta,
Que outro valor mais alto se alevanta.
E vós, Spreïdes minhas...
Dai-me huma furia grande, e sonorosa,
E naõ agreste avena, on frauta ruda;

---

[a] A pun in the original: *Anstoss geben*—an expression frequently used by Stirner—can mean either "to give an impetus" or "to give offence".— *Ed.*

> Mas de tuba canora, e bellicosa
> Que o peito accende, e o côr ao getso muda,[a]

give me, o nymphs of the Spree, a song worthy of the heroes who fight on your banks against Substance and Man, a song that will spread over the whole world and will be sung in all lands — for it is a matter here of the man whose deeds are

> Mais do que promettia a força humana,[c]

greater than mere "human" power can perform, the man who

> ... edificára
> Novo reino que tanto sublimára,[d]

who has founded a new kingdom among a far-off people, viz., the "union" — it is a matter here of being a

> — tenro, e novo ramo florescente
> De huma arvore de Christo, mais amada,[e]

of the tender and young blossoming shoot of a tree especially loved by Christ, a tree which is nothing less than

> certissima esperança
> Do augmento da pequena Christiandade,[f]

the surest hope of growth for faint-hearted Christianity — in a word, it is a matter of something "unprecedented", the "unique".*

---

* Cf. Camoẽs, *Lusiadas*, 1, 1-7.

---

[a] Cease man of Troy, and cease thou sage of Greece,
To boast of Navigations great ye made;
Let the high Fame of Alexander cease,
And Trajan's Banners in the East display'd:
Cease All, whose Actions ancient Bards exprest:
A brighter Valour arises in the West.
And you (my Spree [b] Nymphs)...
Give me a mighty Fury, Nor rude Reeds
Or rustic Bag-Pipes sound, But such as War's
Lowd Instrument (the noble Trumpet) breeds,
Which fires the Breast, and stirs the blood to jars.
(This and the following quotations are from Luis de Camoẽs' *Lusiada*.) — *Ed.*
    [b] Marx and Engels substituted "Spree" — the river on which Berlin stands — for Tagus. — *Ed.*
    [c] Beyond what strength of human nature here. — *Ed.*
    [d] ... acquir'd
A modern Scepter which to Heaven aspired. — *Ed.*
    [e] ... fair and tender Blossom of that Tree
Belov'd by Him, Who dy'd on one for Man. — *Ed.*
    [f] ... certain Hope t'extend the Pale,
One day, of narrow Christianitie. — *Ed.*

Everything that is to be found in this unprecedented song of songs about the unique was in existence earlier in the "book". We mention this chapter only for the sake of good order; so that we should be able to do it properly we have left the examination of some points until now and we shall briefly recapitulate others.

Sancho's "ego" has gone through the full gamut of soul migration. We already met it as the egoist in agreement with himself, as corvée peasant, as trader in thoughts, as unfortunate competitor, as owner, as a slave who has had one of his legs torn out, as Sancho tossed into the air by the interaction between birth and circumstances, and in a hundred other shapes. Here it bids us farewell as an "*inhuman being*", under the same banner as that under which it made its entry into the New Testament.

"Only the *inhuman being* is the *real* man." (P. 232.)

This is one of the thousand and one equations in which Sancho expounds his legend of the holy.

The concept "man" is not the real man.

The concept "man"=Man.

Man=not the real man.

The real man=the non-man,

= the inhuman being.

"Only the inhuman being is the real man."

Sancho tries to explain to himself the harmlessness of this proposition by means of the following transformations:

"It is not so difficult to express in a few plain words what an inhuman being is; it is a man [...] who does not correspond to the concept of what is human. Logic calls this a nonsensical judgment. Would one have the right to pronounce this judgment that someone can be a man without being a man, if one did not admit the validity of the hypothesis that the concept of man can be separated from his existence, that the essence can be separated from the appearance? People say: so and so seems to be a man, but he is not a man. People have pronounced this nonsensical judgment throughout many centuries: moreover, during this long period of time there have only been inhuman beings. What individual did ever correspond to his concept?" (P. 232.)

This passage is again based on our school-master's fantasy about the school-master who has created for himself an ideal of "Man" and "put it into the heads" of other people, a fantasy which forms the basic theme of "the book".

Sancho calls it a hypothesis that the concept and existence, the essence and appearance of "man" can be separated, as though the possibility of this separation is not already expressed in the very words he uses. When he says *concept*, he is speaking of something different from *existence*; when he says *essence*, he is speaking of something different from *appearance*. It is not these *statements* that he brings into contradiction, but they themselves are the expressions of a contradiction. Hence the only question that could have been raised is whether it is permissible for him to range something under these points of view; and in order to deal with this Sancho would have had to consider the actual relations of people who have been given other names in these metaphysical relations. For the rest, Sancho's own arguments about the egoist in agreement with himself and about rebellion show how these points of view can be made to diverge, while his arguments about peculiarity, possibility and reality—in connection with "self-enjoyment"—show how they can be made simultaneously to coincide and to diverge.

The nonsensical judgment of the philosophers that he real man is not man is in the sphere of abstraction merely the most universal, all-embracing expression of the actually existing universal contradiction between the conditions and needs of people. The nonsensical form of the abstract proposition fully corresponds to the nonsensical character, carried to extreme lengths, of the relations of bourgeois society, just as Sancho's nonsensical judgment about his environment—they are egoists and at the same time they are not egoists—corresponds to the actual contradiction between the existence of the German petty bourgeois and the tasks which existing relations have imposed on them and which they themselves entertain in the form of pious wishes and desires. Incidentally, philosophers have declared people to be inhuman, not because they did not correspond to the concept of man, but because their concept of man did not correspond to the true concept of man, or because they had no true understanding of man. *Tout comme chez nous*,[a] in "the book", where Sancho also declares that people are non-egoists for the sole reason that they have no true understanding of egoism.

In view of its extreme triviality and indisputable certainty, there should have been no need to mention the perfectly inoffensive proposition that the *idea* of man is not the *real* man, that the idea of a thing is not the thing itself—a proposition

---

[a] A modified phrase from Nolant de Fatouville's comedy *Arlequin, empereur dans la lune*—"*tout comme ici*" (just as here) is the stock response made by the people listening to Harlequin's inventions about life on the moon.— *Ed.*

which is also applicable to a stone and to the idea of a stone, in accordance with which Sancho should have said that the real stone is non-stone. But Sancho's well-known fantasy that only because of the domination of ideas and concepts mankind has up to now been subjected to all sorts of misfortunes, makes it possible for him to link his old conclusions again with this proposition. Sancho's old opinion that one has only to get a few ideas out of one's *head* in order to abolish from the *world* the conditions which have given rise to these ideas, is reproduced here in the form that one has only to get out of one's head the idea of *man* in order to put an end to the actually existing conditions which are today called *inhuman* — whether this predicate "inhuman" expresses the opinion of the individual in contradiction with his conditions or the opinion of the normal, ruling society about the abnormal, subjected class. In just the same way, a whale taken from the ocean and put in the Kupfergraben,[115] if it possessed consciousness, would declare this situation created by "unfavourable circumstances" to be unwhale-like, although Sancho could prove that it is whale-like, if only because it is its, the whale's, own situation — that is precisely how people argue in certain circumstances.

On page 185, Sancho raises the important question:

"But how to curb the inhuman being who dwells in each individual? How can one manage not to set free the inhuman being along with the human being? All liberalism has a mortal enemy, an invincible opponent, as God has the devil; at the side of the human being there is always the inhuman being, the egoist, the individual. State, society, mankind cannot master this devil."

"And when the thousand years are expired, Satan shall be loosed out of his prison,

"And shall go out to deceive the nations which are in the four quarters of the earth, Gog and Magog, to gather them together to battle....

"And they went up on the breadth of the earth, and compassed the camp of the saints about, and the beloved city." (Revelation of St. John, 20:7-9.)

In the form in which Sancho understands it, the question again becomes sheer nonsense. He imagines that people up to now have always formed a concept of man, and then won freedom for themselves to the extent that was necessary to realise this concept; that the measure of freedom that they achieved was determined each time by their idea of the ideal of man at the time; it was thus unavoidable that in each individual there remained a residue which did not correspond to this ideal and, hence, since it was "inhuman", was either not set free or only freed *malgré eux*.

In reality, of course, what happened was that people won freedom for themselves each time to the extent that was dictated and permitted not by their ideal of man, but by the existing productive forces. All emancipation carried through hitherto has been based, however, on restricted productive forces. The production which these productive forces could provide was insufficient for the whole of society and made development possible only if some persons satisfied their needs at the expense of others, and therefore some — the minority — obtained the monopoly of development, while others — the majority — owing to the constant struggle to satisfy their most essential needs, were for the time being (i.e., until the creation of new revolutionary productive forces) excluded from any development. Thus, society has hitherto always developed within the framework of a contradiction — in antiquity the contradiction between free men and slaves, in the Middle Ages that between nobility and serfs, in modern times that between the bourgeoisie and the proletariat. This explains, on the one hand, the abnormal, "inhuman" way in which the oppressed class satisfies its needs, and, on the other hand, the narrow limits within which intercourse, and with it the whole ruling class, develops. Hence this restricted character of development consists not only in the exclusion of one class from development, but also in the narrow-mindedness of the excluding class, and the "inhuman" is to be found also within the ruling class. This so-called "inhuman" is just as much a product of present-day relations as the "human" is; it is their negative aspect, the rebellion — which is not based on any new revolutionary productive force — against the prevailing relations brought about by the existing productive forces, and against the way of satisfying needs that corresponds to these relations. The positive expression "human" corresponds to the definite relations *predominant* at a certain stage of production and the way of satisfying needs determined by them, just as the negative expression "inhuman" corresponds to the attempt to negate these predominant relations and the way of satisfying needs prevailing under them without changing the existing mode of production, an attempt that this stage of production daily engenders afresh.

For our saint, such world-historical struggles are reduced to a mere collision between Saint Bruno and "the mass". Cf. the whole criticism of humane liberalism, especially page 192 et seq.

Thus, our simple-minded Sancho with his naïve little statement about the inhuman being and with his talk of getting-man-out-of-one's-head, thanks to which the inhuman being also disappears and there is no longer any measure for individuals, finally arrives at the following result. He regards the physical, intellectual and social crippling and enslavement which as a result of the existing relations afflict an individual, as the individuality and peculiarity of that individual; like an ordinary conservative he calmly recognises these relations once he has freed his mind of all worry by getting out of his head the philosophers' idea of these relations. Just as here he declares fortuitous features imposed on the individual to be the latter's individuality, so earlier (cf. "Logic"), in connection with the ego, he abstracted not only from any fortuity, but also in general from any individuality.[a]

About the "inhuman" great result obtained by him Sancho sings in the following *Kyrie eleison*[b], which he puts into the mouth of "*the inhuman being*":

"I was despicable because I sought my *better self* outside me;
"I was the inhuman, because I dreamed of the *human*;
"I was like the pious ones who hunger for their *true ego* and always remain *poor sinners*;
"I thought of myself only in comparison with someone else;
"I was not all in all, I was not — *unique*.
"Now, however, I cease to appear to myself as the inhuman;
"I cease to measure myself by man and to let others measure me;
"I cease to recognise anything above myself —
"I was inhuman, but I am no longer inhuman, I am the *unique*!"
Hallelujah!

We shall not dwell further here on how "the inhuman"— which, it may be said in passing, put itself in the right frame of mind by "*turning its back*" "*on itself* and the critic", Saint Bruno — how "the inhuman" here "*appears*", or does not "appear" to *itself*. We shall only point out that the "unique" (it or he) is characterised here by his getting the holy out of his head for the nine-hundredth time, whereby, as we in our turn are compelled to repeat for the nine-hundredth time, everything remains as before, not to mention the fact that it is no more than a pious wish.

We have here, for the first time, the unique person. Sancho, who with the litany mentioned above has received the accolade of knighthood, now appropriates his new, noble name. Sancho

---

[a] See this volume, pp. 294-98.— *Ed.*
[b] Lord, have mercy.— *Ed.*

arrives at his uniqueness by getting "Man" out of his head. He thereby ceases "to think of himself only in comparison with someone else" and "to recognise something above him". He becomes incomparable. This is again the same old fantasy of Sancho's that it is not the needs of individuals, but concepts, ideas, "the holy"—here in the shape of "Man"—that are the sole *tertium comparationis* and the sole *bond* between individuals.* He gets an *idea* out of his head and thereby becomes *unique*.

To become "unique" in his sense of the word he must above all prove to us his *freedom from premises*.

Page 470: "*Your* thought has as its premise not *thought*, but *you*. But thus you nevertheless have yourself as a premise? Yes, but not to me, but to my thought. I am before my thought. It follows hence that no thought precedes my thinking, or that my thinking is without any premise. For the premise which I am for my thinking is not one *created by thinking*, not one that is *thought*, but ... is the owner of thinking, and proves only that thinking is nothing but— property."

"We are prepared to allow" that Sancho does not think before he thinks, and that he and everyone else is in this respect a thinker without premises. Similarly we concede that he does not have any thought as the premises of his existence, i.e., that he was not created by thoughts. If for a moment Sancho abstracts from all his thoughts — which with his meagre assortment cannot be very difficult — there remains his real ego, but his real ego within the framework of the actual relations of the world that exist for it. In this way he has divested himself for a moment of all dogmatic premises, but now for the first time the *real* premises begin to come to light for him. And these real premises are also the premises of his *dogmatic* premises which, whether he likes it or not, will reappear to him together with the real ones so long as he does not obtain different real premises, and with them also different dogmatic premises, or so long as he does not recognise in a materialistic way that the real premises are the premises of his thinking, and as a result his dogmatic ones will disappear altogether. Just as his development up to now and his Berlin environment have at

---

* [The following passage is crossed out in the manuscript:] Sancho, who notices nothing but "the holy", need not bother about the fact that it is through their needs that individuals are linked together, and that the development of the productive forces up to now implies the domination of one section over the other.

present led to the dogmatic premise of egoism in agreement with itself, so, despite all imaginary freedom from premises, this premise will remain with him as long as he fails to overcome its real premises.

As a true school-master, Sancho still continues to strive for the famous Hegelian "premiseless thinking", i.e., thinking without dogmatic premises, which in Hegel too is only a pious wish. Sancho believed he could achieve this by a skilful leap and even surpass it by going in pursuit of the premiseless ego. But both the one and the other eluded his grasp.

Then Sancho tries his luck in another fashion:

> Pages 214, 215: "Make full use" of the demand for freedom! "Who shall become free? You, I, we. Free from what? From everything that is not you, not I, not we. I, therefore, am the *core*.... What remains if I become free from everything that is not I? Only I and *nothing* but I."

> "So that was the poodle's core!
> A travelling scholar? The incident makes me laugh." [a]

"Everything that is not you, not I, not we" is, of course, here again a dogmatic idea, like state, nationality, division of labour, etc. Once these ideas have been subjected to criticism — and, in Sancho's opinion, this has already been done by "criticism", namely critical criticism — he again imagines that he is also free from the actual state, actual nationality and division of labour. Consequently the ego, which is here the "core", which "has become free from everything that is not I" — is still the above-mentioned premiseless ego with everything that it has not got rid of.

If, however, Sancho were once to tackle the subject of "becoming free" with the desire of freeing himself not merely from categories, but from actual fetters, then such liberation would presuppose a change common to him and to a large mass of other people, and would produce a change in the state of the world which again would be common to him and others. Although his "ego" "remains" after liberation, it is hereafter a totally changed ego sharing with others a changed state of the world which is precisely the premise, common to him and others, of his and their freedom, and it follows that the uniqueness, incomparability and independence of his "ego" again come to nothing.

---

[a] Goethe, *Faust*, I. Teil, 1. "Studierzimmerszene".— *Ed.*

Sancho tries again in a third fashion:

Page 237: "Their disgrace is not that they" (Jew and Christian) "*exclude* each other but that this only *half* occurs. If they could be perfect egoists they would *totally* exclude each other."

Page 273: "If one desires *only to resolve* the contradiction one grasps its meaning in too formal and feeble a way. The contradiction deserves rather to be *sharpened*."

Page 274: "Only when you recognise your contradiction fully and when everyone asserts himself from head to foot as *unique* will you no longer simply conceal your contradiction.... The final and most decisive contradiction — that between one unique person and another — goes basically beyond the bounds of what is called contradiction.... As a unique person you have nothing more in common with the other and, for that reason, nothing that makes you separate from him or hostile to him.... Contradiction disappears in perfect ... separateness or uniqueness."

Page 183: "I do not *want* to have or to be something *special* in relation to others; nor do I measure myself by others.... I want to be everything I can be, and to have everything I can have. What do I care whether others are or have *something similar* to me? They can neither be nor have something equal, the same. I do nothing detrimental to them any more than it is to the detriment of the cliff that I have the advantage of movement. If they could have it, they would have it. Doing nothing to the detriment of other people, that is the meaning of the demand to have no privileges.... One should not regard oneself as 'something *special*', e.g., Jew or Christian. Well, I *regard* myself not as something *special* but as *unique*. True, I have a resemblance to others; but this holds only for comparison or reflection; in fact, however, I am incomparable, unique. My flesh is not their flesh, my spirit is not their spirit. If you bring them under the *general concept* 'flesh', 'spirit', then those are your *thoughts*, which have *nothing* to do with my flesh, my spirit."

Page 234: "Human society perishes because of the egoists, for they no longer treat one another as human beings, but act egoistically as an ego against a you that is totally distinct from and hostile to me."

Page 180: "As though one individual will not always seek out another, and as though one person does not have to adapt himself to another, when he needs him. But the difference is that in this case the individual actually *unites* with another individual, whereas previously he was linked to him by a bond."

Page 178: "Only when you are unique can you in your intercourse with one another be what you actually are."

As regards Sancho's illusion about the intercourse of the unique ones "as what they actually are", about "the uniting of the individual with the individual", in short, about the "union", that has been completely dealt with. We shall merely point out: whereas in the union each regarded and treated the other merely as *his* object, *his* property (cf. page 167 and the theory of property and exploitation), in the "Commentary" (*Wigand*, p. 157), on the contrary, the governor of the island of Barataria realises and recognises that the other also belongs to himself, is *his* own, is unique, and in that capacity also becomes Sancho's *object*, although no longer Sancho's property. In his despair, he saves himself only by the unexpected idea that "because of this" he "forgets himself in sweet self-oblivion", a delight which he "affords himself a thousand times every hour" and which is still further sweetened by the sweet consciousness that nevertheless he has not "completely disappeared". The result, therefore, is the old wisdom that each exists for himself and for others.

Let us now reduce Sancho's pompous statements to their actual modest content.

The bombastic phrases about "contradiction" which has to be sharpened and taken to extremes, and about the "something special", which Sancho does not want to have as his advantage, amount to one and the same thing. Sancho wants, or rather *believes* he wants, that intercourse between individuals should be purely personal, that their intercourse should not be mediated through some third thing (cf. competition). This third thing here is the "something special", or the special, not absolute, contradiction, i.e., the position of individuals in relation to one another determined by present-day social relations. Sancho does not want, for example, two individuals to be in "contradiction" to one another as bourgeois and proletarian; he protests against the "special" which forms the "advantage" of the bourgeois over the proletarian; he would like to have them enter into a purely personal relation, to associate with one another merely as individuals. He does not take into consideration that in the framework of division of labour personal relations necessarily and inevitably develop into class relations and become fixed as such and that, therefore, all his talk amounts simply to a pious wish, which he expects to realise by exhorting the individuals of these classes to get out of their heads the idea of their "contradiction" and their "special" "privilege". In the passages from Sancho quoted above, everything turns only on people's *opinion of themselves*, and *his* opinion of them, what they want and what *he* wants. "Contradiction" and the "special" are abolished by a change of "*opinion*" and "*wanting*".

Even that which constitutes the advantage of an individual as such over other individuals, is in our day at the same time a product of society and in its realisation is bound to assert itself as privilege, as we have already shown Sancho in connection with competition. Further, the individual as such, regarded by himself, is subordinated to division of labour, which makes him one-sided, cripples and determines him.

What, at best, does Sancho's sharpening of contradiction and abolition of the special amount to? To this, that the mutual relations of individuals should be their *behaviour* to one another, while their mutual differences should be their *self-distinctions* (as one empirical self distinguishes *itself* from another). Both of these are either, as with Sancho, an ideological paraphrase of *what exists*, for the relations of individuals under all circumstances *can* only be their mutual behaviour, while their differences can only be their self-distinctions. Or they are the pious wish that they *should* behave *in such a way* and differ from one another *in such a way*, that their behaviour does not acquire independent existence as a social relationship independent of them, and that their differences from one another should not assume the material character (independent of the person) which they have assumed and daily continue to assume.

Individuals have always and in all circumstances "proceeded *from themselves*", but since they were not *unique* in the sense of not needing any connections with one another, and since their *needs*, consequently their nature, and the method of satisfying their needs, connected them with one another (relations between the sexes, exchange, division of labour), they *had to* enter into relations with one another. Moreover, since they entered into intercourse with one another not as pure egos, but as individuals at a definite stage of development of their productive forces and requirements, and since this intercourse, in its turn, determined production and needs, it was, therefore, precisely the personal, individual behaviour of individuals, their behaviour to one another as individuals, that created the existing relations and daily reproduces them anew. They entered into intercourse with one another as what they were, they proceeded "from themselves", as they were, irrespective of their "outlook on life". This "outlook on life" — even the warped one of the philosophers — could, of course, only be determined by their actual life. Hence it certainly follows that the development of an individual is determined by the development of all the others with whom he is directly or indirectly associated, and that the different generations of individuals entering into relation with one another are connected with one another, that the physical existence of the later generations is determined by that of their predecessors, and that these later generations inherit the productive forces and forms of intercourse accumulated by their predecessors, their own mutual relations being determined thereby. In short, it is clear that development takes place and that the history of a single individual cannot possibly be separated from the history of preceding or contemporary individuals, but is determined by this history.

The transformation of the individual relationship into its opposite, a purely material relationship, the distinction of individuality and fortuity by the individuals themselves is a historical process, as we have already shown [a], and at different stages of development it assumes different, ever sharper and more universal forms. In the present epoch, the domination of material relations over individuals, and the suppression of individuality by fortuitous circumstances, has assumed its sharpest and most universal form, thereby setting existing individuals a very definite task. It has set them the task of replacing the domination of circumstances and of chance over individuals by the domination of individuals over chance and circumstances. It has not, as Sancho imagines, put forward the demand that "I should develop myself", which up to now every individual has done without Sancho's good advice; it has on the contrary called for liberation from a quite definite mode of development. This task, dictated by present-day relations, coincides with the task of organising society in a communist way.

We have already shown above that the abolition of a state of affairs in which relations become independent of individuals, in which individuality is subservient to chance and the personal relations of individuals are subordinated to general class relations, etc.— that the abolition of this state of affairs is determined in the final analysis by the abolition of division of labour. We have also shown that the abolition of division of labour is determined by the development of intercourse and productive forces to such a degree of universality that private property and division of labour become fetters on them. We have further shown that private property can be abolished only on condition of an all-round development of individuals, precisely because the existing form of intercourse and the existing productive forces are all-embracing and only individuals that are developing in an all-round fashion can appropriate them, i.e., can turn them into free manifestations of their lives. We have shown that at the present time individuals *must* abolish private property, because the productive forces and forms of intercourse have developed so far that, under the domination of private property, they have become destructive forces, and because the contradiction between the classes has reached its extreme limit. Finally, we have shown that the abolition of private property and of the division of labour is

---

[a] See this volume, pp. 83-90.— *Ed.*

itself the association of individuals on the basis created by modern productive forces and world intercourse.[a] Within communist society, the only society in which the genuine and free development of individuals ceases to be a mere phrase, this development is determined precisely by the connection of individuals, a connection which consists partly in the economic prerequisites and partly in the necessary solidarity of the free development of all, and, finally, in the universal character of the activity of individuals on the basis of the existing productive forces. We are, therefore, here concerned with individuals at a definite historical stage of development and by no means merely with individuals chosen at random, even disregarding the indispensable communist revolution, which itself is a general condition for their free development. The individuals' consciousness of their mutual relations will, of course, likewise be completely changed, and, therefore, will no more be the "principle of love" or *dévoûment* than it will be egoism.

Thus, "uniqueness"— taken in the sense of genuine development and individual behaviour, as outlined above— presupposes not only things quite different from good will and right consciousness, but even the direct opposite of Sancho's fantasies. With him "uniqueness" is nothing more than an embellishment of existing conditions, a little drop of comforting balm for the poor, impotent soul that has become wretched through wretchedness.

As regards Sancho's *"incomparability"*, the situation is the same as with his "uniqueness". He himself will recall, if he is not completely "lost" in "sweet self-oblivion", that the organisation of labour in *"Stirner's* union of egoists" was based not only on the comparability of needs, but also on their *equality*. And he assumed not only equal needs, but also equal activity, so that one individual could take the place of another in "human work". And the extra remuneration of the "unique" person, crowning his efforts— what other basis had it than the fact that his performance was compared with that of others and in view of its superiority was better paid? And how can Sancho talk at all about incomparability when he allows *money*— the means of comparison that acquires independent existence in practice— to continue in being, subordinates himself to it and allows himself to be measured by this universal scale in order to be compared with others? It is quite evident that he himself gives the lie to his doctrine of incomparability. Nothing is easier than to call

---

[a] See Chapter I of Volume I.— *Ed.*

equality and inequality, similarity and dissimilarity, determinations of reflection. Incomparability too is a determination of reflection which has the activity of comparison as its premise. To show that comparison is not at all a purely arbitrary determination of reflection, it is enough to give just one example, *money*, the permanent *tertium comparationis* of all people and things.

Incidentally, incomparability can have different meanings. The only meaning in question here, namely "uniqueness" in the sense of originality, presupposes that the activity of the incomparable individual in a definite sphere differs from the activity of his *equals*. Persiani is an incomparable singer precisely because she is a *singer* and is compared with other singers, and indeed by people who are able to recognise her incomparability through comparison based on normal hearing and musical training. Persiani's singing and the croaking of a frog are incomparable, although even here there could be a comparison, but it would be a comparison between a human being and a frog, and not between Persiani and a particular unique frog. Only in the first case is it possible to speak of a comparison between individuals, in the second it is a matter only of their properties as species or genus. A third type of incomparability — the incomparability of Persiani's singing with the tail of a comet — we leave to Sancho for his "self-enjoyment", since at any rate he finds pleasure in "nonsensical judgments", although even this absurd comparison has a real basis in the absurdity of present-day relations. Money is the common measure for all, even the most heterogeneous things.

Incidentally, Sancho's incomparability amounts to the same empty phrase as his uniqueness. Individuals are no longer to be measured by some *tertium comparationis* independent of them, but comparison *should* be transformed into their self-distinction, i.e., into the free development of their individuality, which, moreover, is brought about by their getting "fixed ideas" out of their heads.

Incidentally, Sancho is acquainted only with the type of comparison made by scribblers and ranters, which leads to the magnificent conclusion that Sancho is not Bruno and Bruno is not Sancho. On the other hand, he is, of course, unacquainted with the sciences which have made considerable advances just by comparing and establishing differences in the spheres of comparison and in which comparison acquires a character of universal importance — i.e., in comparative anatomy, botany, philology, etc.

Great nations — the French, North Americans, English — are constantly comparing themselves with one another both in practice and theory, in competition and in science. Petty shopkeepers and philistines, like the Germans, who are afraid of comparison and competition, hide behind the shield of incomparability supplied them by their manufacturer of philosophical labels. Not only in their interests, but also in his own, has Sancho refused to tolerate any comparison.

On page 415 Sancho says:

"There exists no one *equal to me*",

and on page 408 association with "my equals" is depicted as the dissolution of society in intercourse:

"The child prefers *intercourse with his equals* to *society*."

However, Sancho sometimes uses "equal to me" and "equal" in general in the sense of "*the same*", e.g., the passage on page 183 quoted above:

"They can neither be nor have *something equal, the same*."

Here he arrives at his final "new turn of expression", which he uses especially in the "Commentary".

The uniqueness, the originality, the "peculiar" development of individuals which, according to Sancho, does not for example occur in all "human works", although no one will deny that one stove-setter does not set a stove in the "*same*" way as another; the "unique" development of individuals which, in the opinion of this same Sancho, does not occur in religious, political, etc., spheres (see "Phenomenology"), although no one will deny that of all those who believe in Islam not one believes in it in the "same" way as another and to this extent each of them is "unique", just as among citizens not one has the "same" attitude to the state as another if only because it is a matter of *his* attitude, and not that of *some-other*— all this much praised "uniqueness" which [according to Sancho] was so distinct from "*sameness*", *identity of the person*, that in all individuals who have so far existed he could hardly see anything but "specimens" of a species, is thus reduced here to the identity of a person with himself, as established by the police, to the fact that one individual is not some other individual. Thus Sancho, who was going to take the world by storm, dwindles to a clerk in a passport office.

On page 184 of the "Commentary" he relates with much unction and great self-enjoyment that he does not become replete when the Japanese Emperor eats, because his stomach and that of the Japanese Emperor are "unique", "incomparable stomachs", i.e., not the *same* stomachs. If Sancho believes that in this way he has abolished the social relations hitherto existing or even only the laws of nature, then his naïveté is excessively great and it springs merely from the fact that philosophers have not depicted social relations as the mutual relations of particular individuals identical with themselves, and the laws of nature as the mutual connections of these particular bodies.

The classic expression which Leibniz gave to this old proposition (to be found on the first page of any physics textbook as the theory of the impenetrability of bodies) is well known:

"Opus tamen est ... ut quaelibet monas differat ab alia quacunque, neque enim unquam dantur in natura duo entia, quorum unum exasse conveniat cum altero."[a] (*Principia Philosophiae seu Theses*, etc.)

Sancho's uniqueness is here reduced to a quality which he shares with every louse and every grain of sand.

The greatest disclaimer with which his philosophy could end is that it regards the realisation that Sancho is not Bruno, which is obvious to every country bumpkin and police sergeant, to be one of the greatest discoveries, and that it considers the fact of this difference to be a real miracle.

Thus the "critical hurrah" of our "virtuoso of thought" has become an uncritical miserere.

After all these adventures our "unique" squire again sails into the harbour of his native serf's cottage. "The title spectre of his book"[b] rushes out to meet him "joyfully". Her first enquiry is: how is the ass?

Better than his master, replies Sancho.

Thanks be to God for so much goodness. But tell me now, my friend, what profit have you got out of your squiredom? What new dress have you brought me?

I have brought nothing like that, replies Sancho, but I have brought "the creative nothing, the nothing from which I myself as creator create everything". This means you will yet see me in

------

[a] "However, every monad necessarily differs from every other; for in nature there are never two things that exactly coincide with each other." — *Ed.*

[b] An allusion to Stirner's wife, Marie Dähnhardt (see this volume, p. 424). — *Ed.*

the capacity of church father and archbishop of an island and, indeed, one of the best it is possible to find.

God grant it, my treasure, and may it be soon, for we sorely need it. But as regards the island you mention, I don't know what you mean.

Honey is not for the ass's mouth, replies Sancho. You will see it for yourself in due course, wife. But even now I can tell you that nothing is more pleasant in the world than the honour of seeking adventures as an egoist in agreement with himself and as the squire of the rueful countenance. True, most of these adventures do not "reach the final goal" so that "*human* requirement is satisfied" (tan como el *hombre* querria[a]), for ninety-nine adventures out of a hundred go awry and follow a tangled course. I know this from experience, for in some of them I was cheated and from others I went home soundly pounded and thrashed. But in spite of all that, it is a fine thing, for at any rate the "unique" requirement is always satisfied when one wanders through the whole of history, quoting all the books in the Berlin reading-room, getting an etymological night's lodging in all languages, falsifying political facts in all countries, boastfully throwing down gages to all dragons and ostriches, elfs, field hobgoblings and "spectres", exchanging blows with all church fathers and philosophers and yet, finally, paying for it only with your own body (cf. Cervantes, I, Chapter 52).

---

[a] As the human being desires.— *Ed.*

2. APOLOGETICAL COMMENTARY[116]

Although formerly, when in a state of humiliation (Cervantes, Chapters 26 and 29), Sancho had all kinds of "doubts" about accepting an ecclesiastical benefice, nevertheless, after pondering over the changed circumstances and his earlier preparation as beadle to a religious brotherhood (Cervantes, Chapter 21), he finally decided to "get" this doubt "out of his head". He became archbishop of the island of Barataria and a cardinal and as such sits with solemn mien and arch-ecclesiastical dignity among the foremost of our Council. Now, after the long episode of "the book", we return to this Council.

True, we find that "brother Sancho" in his new station in life has changed considerably. He now represents the *ecclesia triumphans*[a]—in contrast to the *ecclesia militans*,[b] in which he was before. Instead of the belligerent fanfares of "the book" there is a solemn seriousness; "Stirner" has taken the place of the "ego". This shows how true the French saying is: *qu'il n'y a qu'un pas du sublime au ridicule.*[c] Since he became a father of the church and began to write pastoral epistles, Sancho calls himself nothing but "Stirner". He learned this "unique" way of self-enjoyment from Feuerbach, but unfortunately it befits him no better than playing the lute does his ass. When he speaks of himself in the third person, everyone sees that Sancho the "creator", after the manner of Prussian non-commissioned officers, addresses his "creation" Stirner in the third person, and should on no account be confused with Caesar.[d] The

---

[a] Church triumphant.— *Ed.*

[b] Church militant.— *Ed.*

[c] There is only one step from the sublime to the ridiculous (an expression used by Napoleon on many occasions).— *Ed.*

[d] The reference is to Julius Caesar's *Commentarii de bello Gallico* (the author wrote in the third person about himself).— *Ed.*

impression is all the more comical because Sancho commits this inconsistency only in order to compete with Feuerbach. Sancho's "self-enjoyment" of his performance as a great man becomes here *malgré lui* an enjoyment for others.

The "*special*" thing that Sancho does in his "Commentary", insofar as we have not "used it up" already in the episode, consists in his regaling us with a new series of variations on the familiar themes already played with such long-winded monotony in "the book". Here Sancho's music, which like that of the Indian priests of Vishnu knows only one note, is played a few registers higher. But its narcotic effect remains, of course, the same. Thus, for example, the antithesis of "egoistical" and "holy" is again thoroughly kneaded, this time under the signboards of "interesting" and "uninteresting", and then of "interesting" and "absolutely interesting", an innovation which, incidentally, could only be of interest to lovers of unleavened bread, in common parlance matzos. One should not, of course, blame an "educated"[a] Berlin petty bourgeois for the belletristic distortion of the interested into the interesting.

All the illusions which, according to Sancho's pet crotchet, were created by "school-masters" appear here "as difficulties — *doubts*", which "only spirit created" and which "the poor souls who allowed themselves to be talked into these doubts" "should ... overcome" by "*light-heartedness*" (the famous getting out of one's head) (p. 162). Then comes a "treatise" in which he considers whether "doubts" should be got out of one's head by "thinking" or by "thoughtlessness", and a critical-moral adagio in which he laments in minor chords:

"Thought *must on no account* be suppressed by rejoicing." (P. 166.)

For the tranquillity of Europe, and especially of the oppressed old merry and young sorry England[b], as soon as Sancho has become somewhat accustomed to his episcopal *chaise percée*[c], he issues from this eminence the following gracious pastoral epistle:

"Civil society is not at all dear to Stirner, and *he has no intention of extending it so that it swallows up the state and the family*." (P. 189.)

Let Mr. Cobden and Monsieur Dunoyer bear this in mind. In his capacity of archbishop, Sancho immediately takes

---

[a] In the manuscript the Berlin dialect form *jebildeten* is used.— *Ed.*
[b] The phrase "old merry and young sorry England" is in English in the manuscript.— *Ed.*
[c] Night commode.— *Ed.*

control of the spiritual police, and on page 193 he gives Hess a reprimand for confusing matters, which "are contrary to police regulations" and the more unpardonable the greater the efforts that our church father continually makes to establish identity. To prove to this same Hess that "Stirner" also possesses the "heroic courage of lying", that orthodox quality of the egoist in agreement with himself, he sings on page 188: "But Stirner does not say *at all*—contrary to what Hess makes him say—that the whole mistake of previous egoists was merely that they were not *conscious* of their egoism." Cf. "Phenomenology" and the entire "book". The other quality of the egoist in agreement with himself—credulity—he displays on page 182, where he "*does not dispute*" Feuerbach's opinion that "*the individual* is a communist". A further exercise of his police powers consists in censuring (on page 154) all his reviewers for not having dealt "in more detail with egoism as Stirner *conceives* it". Indeed, they all made the mistake of thinking that it was a question of actual egoism, whereas it was merely a question of "Stirner's" conception of it.

The "Apologetical Commentary" also proves Sancho's aptitude for acting as a church father by beginning with a piece of hypocrisy:

"A brief reply may be of benefit, if not perhaps to the reviewers named, then at least to some other reader of the book." (P. 147.)

Here Sancho plays the devotee and asserts that he is prepared to sacrifice his valuable time for the "benefit" of the public, although he constantly assures us that he always has in view only his own benefit, and although he is only trying here to save his own clerical skin.

Thereby we have finished with the "special" of the "Commentary". The "*unique*" feature, which, however, occurs already in "the book", on page 491, has been kept by us in reserve not so much for the "benefit" of "some other reader" as for "Stirner's" own benefit. One hand washes the other, from which it indisputably follows that "the individual is a communist".

One of the most difficult tasks confronting philosophers is to descend from the world of thought to the actual world. *Language* is the immediate actuality of thought. Just as philosophers have given thought an independent existence, so they were bound to make language into an independent realm. This is the secret of philosophical language, in which thoughts in the form of words have their own content. The problem of descending from the world of thoughts to the actual world is turned into the problem of descending from language to life.

We have shown[a] that thoughts and ideas acquire an independent existence in consequence of the personal circumstances and relations of individuals acquiring independent existence. We have shown that exclusive, systematic occupation with these thoughts on the part of ideologists and philosophers, and hence the systematisation of these thoughts, is a consequence of division of labour, and that, in particular, German philosophy is a consequence of German petty-bourgeois conditions. The philosophers have only to dissolve their language into the ordinary language, from which it is abstracted, in order to recognise it as the distorted language of the actual world and to realise that neither thoughts nor language in themselves form a realm of their own, that they are only *manifestations* of actual life.

Sancho, who follows the philosophers through thick and thin, must inevitably seek the *philosopher's stone*, the squaring of the circle and elixir of life, or a *"word"* which as such would possess the miraculous power of leading from the realm of language and thought to actual life. Sancho has been so infected by his long years of association with Don Quixote that he fails to notice that this "task" of his, this "vocation", is nothing but the result of his faith in weighty philosophical books of knight-errantry.

Sancho begins by showing us once again the domination of the holy and of ideas in the world, this time in the new form of the domination of language or phrase. Language, of course, becomes a phrase as soon as it is given an independent existence.

On page 151, Sancho calls the modern world "a world of phrases, a world where in the beginning was the word". He describes in more detail the motives for his chase after the magic word:

"Philosophical speculation strove to find a *predicate* which would be so *universal* as to include everyone in itself.... In order that the predicate should include everyone in it, each should appear in it as *subject*, i.e., not merely as *what* he is, but as *who* he is." (P. 152.)

Since speculation "sought" such predicates, which Sancho had previously called vocation, designation, task, species, etc., therefore actual people up to now "*sought*" themselves "in the word, the logos, the predicate" (p. 153). Up to now one has used the *name* when one wanted to distinguish in language one

---

[a] See Chapter I of Volume I.— *Ed.*

individual from another, merely as an identical person. But Sancho is not satisfied with ordinary names; because philosophical speculation has set him the task of finding a predicate so universal that it would include in itself everyone as subject, he seeks the philosophical, abstract name, the "Name" that is above all names, the name of names, name as a category which, for example, would distinguish Sancho from Bruno, and both of them from Feuerbach, as precisely as their own proper names, and which would nevertheless be applicable to all three and also to all other people and corporeal beings—an innovation which would introduce the greatest confusion into all bills of exchange, marriage contracts, etc., and at one blow put an end to all notaries and registry offices. This miraculous name, this magic word, which in language spells the death of language, this asses' bridge leading to life and the highest rung of the Chinese celestial ladder is—*the unique*. The miraculous properties of this word are sung in the following stanzas:

"The unique one should be only the last, dying statement of you and me, should be only that statement which is transformed into opinion:
"a statement that is no longer a statement,
"a muted, mute statement." (P. 153.)
"With him" (the unique one) "what is not expressed is the chief thing." (P. 149.)
He "is without determination". (Ibid.)
"He points to the content, lying outside or beyond the concept." (Ibid.)
This is "a concept without determination and cannot be made more definite by any other concept". (P. 150.)
This is the philosophical "*christening*" of worldly names. (P. 150.)
"The unique is a word devoid of thought.
"It has no thought content."
"It expresses a person" "that cannot exist a second time, and consequently cannot be *expressed* either;
"For if he could be expressed actually and completely, then he would exist a second time, he would exist in the expression." (P. 151.)

Having thus sung the properties of this word, he celebrates in the following antistrophic stanzas the results obtained by the discovery of its miraculous power:

"With the unique one the realm of absolute thoughts is completed." (P. 150.)
"He is the keystone of our world of phrases." (P. 151.)
"He is logic that comes to an end as a phrase." (P. 153.)
"In the unique one, science can merge in life,
"By transforming its *this* into *such-and-such a one*,
"Who no longer seeks himself in the word, the logos, the predicate." (P. 153.)

True, as regards his reviewers Sancho has had the unpleasant experience of learning that the unique, too, can be "fixed as a concept", and "that is what the opponents do" (p. 149), who are so opposed to Sancho that they do not feel at all the expected magical effect of the magical word, but instead sing, as in the opera: *Ce n'est pas ça, ce n'est pas ça!* With great exasperation and solemn seriousness Sancho turns particularly against his Don Quixote-Szeliga, for in him the misunderstanding presupposes an open "rebellion" and a complete misapprehension of his position as a "creature".

"If Szeliga had understood that the unique, being a completely empty phrase or category, thereby is no longer a category, he might, perhaps, have recognised it as the name of that for which he still has no name." (P. 179.)

Here, therefore, Sancho expressly recognises that he and his Don Quixote are striving towards one and the same goal, with the only difference that Sancho imagines that he has discovered the true morning star, whereas Don Quixote, still in darkness

> ûf dem wildin leber-mer
> der grunt-lôsen werlde swebt.*ᵃ

Feuerbach said in his *Philosophie der Zukunft*,ᵇ p. 49:

"Being, based on sheer inexpressibles, is therefore itself something inexpressible. Yes, the inexpressible. Where words end, only there does life begin, only there can the secret of being be deduced."

Sancho has found the transition from the expressible to the inexpressible, he has found the word which is simultaneously more and less than a word.

We have seen that the whole problem of the transition from thought to reality, hence from language to life, exists only in philosophical illusion, i.e., it is justified only for philosophical consciousness, which cannot possibly be clear about the nature and origin of its apparent separation from life. This great problem, insofar as it at all entered the minds of our ideologists, was bound, of course, to result finally in one of these knights-errant setting out in search of a word which, as a *word*, formed the transition in question, which, as a word, ceases to be simply a word, and which, as a word, in a mysterious superlinguistic manner, points from within language to the actual object it denotes; which, in short, plays among words the same role as the Redeeming God-Man plays among people in

---

* Meister Kuonrat von Wurzeburc, *Diu guldin Smitte*, Verse 143.

ᵃ Swims in the wild liver-sea
of the unfathomable world.
(Liver-sea—mythical congealed sea in which ships stuck fast.)—*Ed.*
ᵇ Ludwig Feuerbach, *Grundsätze der Philosophie der Zukunft.—Ed.*

Christian fantasy. The emptiest, shallowest brain among the philosophers had to "end" philosophy by proclaiming his lack of thought to be the end of philosophy and thus the triumphant entry into "corporeal" life. His philosophising mental vacuity was already in itself the end of philosophy just as his unspeakable language was the end of all language. Sancho's triumph was also due to the fact that of all philosophers he was least of all acquainted with actual relations, hence philosophical categories with him lost the last vestige of connection with reality, and with that the last vestige of *meaning*.

So now go forth, pious and faithful servant Sancho, go or, rather, ride forth on your ass, to your unique's self-enjoyment, "use up" your "*unique*" to the last letter, the unique whose miraculous title, power and courage have already been sung by Calderón in the following words:

> The unique—
> El valiente campeon,
> El generoso adalid,
> El gallardo caballero,
> El ilustre Paladin,
> El siempre fiel Cristiano,
> El Almirante feliz
> De África, el Rey soberano
> De Alejandría, el Cadí
> De Berbería, de Egipto el Cid,
> Moravito, y *Gran Señor*
> *De Jerusalen.*[a]

"In conclusion, it would not be unsuitable to remind" Sancho, the Grand Seignior of Jerusalem, of Cervantes' "criticism" of Sancho in *Don Quixote*, Chapter 20, page 171, Brussels edition, 1617. (Cf. the "Commentary", p. 194.)

---

[a] The valiant fighter,
the generous leader,
the gallant knight,
the illustrious Paladin,
the always faithful Christian,
the fortunate Admiral
of Africa, the sovereign King
of Alexandria, the Judge
of Barbary, the Cid of Egypt,
Marabout, and *Grand Seignior of Jerusalem.*
Calderón, *La puenta de Mantible*, Act 1. The words "El siempre fiel Cristiano" ("The always faithful Christian") have been inserted by Marx and Engels.— *Ed.*

CLOSE OF THE LEIPZIG COUNCIL

After driving all their opponents from the Council, Saint Bruno and Saint Sancho, also called Max, conclude an eternal alliance and sing the following touching duet, amicably nodding their heads to one another like two mandarins.

Saint Sancho.

"The critic is the true spokesman of the mass.... He is its sovereign and general in the war of liberation against egoism." (The book, p. 187.)

Saint Bruno.

"Max Stirner is the leader and commander-in-chief of the Crusaders" (against criticism). "At the same time he is the most vigorous and courageous of all fighters." (*Wigand,*[a] p. 124.)

Saint Sancho.

"We pass on now to placing political and social liberalism before the tribunal of humane or critical liberalism" (i.e., critical criticism). (The book, p. 163.)

Saint Bruno.

"Confronted by the unique and his property, the *political* liberal, who desires to break down self-will, and the *social* liberal, who desires to destroy property, both collapse. They collapse under the critical" (i.e., stolen from *criticism*) "knife of the unique." (*Wigand,* p. 124.)

---

[a] Bruno Bauer, "Charakteristik Ludwig Feuerbachs".—*Ed.*

Saint Sancho.

"No thought is safe from criticism, because *criticism is the thinking mind itself...* Criticism, or rather he" (i.e., Saint Bruno). (The book, pp. 195, 199.)

Saint Bruno (interrupts him, making a bow).

"The *critical* liberal alone ... does not fall [before] criticism because *he himself* is [the critic]." [*Wigand,* p, 124.]

Saint Sancho.

"Criticism, and criticism alone, is *abreast of the times....* Among social theories, criticism is indisputably the most perfect.... In it the Christian principle of love, the true social principle, reaches its purest expression, and the last possible experiment is made to release people from exclusiveness [and] repulsion; it is a struggle against egoism in its simplest and therefore its *most rigid* form." (The book, p. 177.).

Saint Bruno.

"This ego is ... the completion and *culminating point* of a past historical epoch. The unique is the last refuge in the old world, the last hiding-place from which the old world can deliver its attacks" on critical criticism.... "This ego is the most extreme, the most powerful and most mighty egoism of the old world" (i.e., of Christianity).... "This ego is substance in its *most rigid rigidity.*" (*Wigand,* p. 124.)

After this cordial dialogue, the two great church fathers dissolve the Council. Then they silently shake hands. The unique "forgets himself in sweet self-oblivion" without, however, getting "completely lost", and the critic "smiles" three times and then "irresistibly, confident of victory and victorious, pursues his path".

Volume II

CRITIQUE OF GERMAN SOCIALISM
ACCORDING TO ITS VARIOUS PROPHETS

TRUE SOCIALISM

The relation between German socialism and the proletarian movement in France and England is the same as that which we found in the first volume (cf. "Saint Max", "Political Liberalism") between German liberalism, as it has hitherto existed, and the movement of the French and English bourgeoisie.[a] Alongside the German communists, a number of writers have appeared who have absorbed a few French and English communist ideas and amalgamated them with their own German philosophical premises. These "socialists" or "true socialists", as they call themselves, regard foreign communist literature not as the expression and the product of a real movement but as purely theoretical writings which have been evolved — in the same way as they imagine the German philosophical systems to have been evolved — by a process of "pure thought". It never occurs to them that, even when these writings do preach a system, they spring from the practical needs, the conditions of life in their entirety of a particular class in a particular country. They innocently take on trust the illusion, cherished by some of these literary party representatives, that it is a question of the "most reasonable" social order and not the needs of a particular class and a particular time. The German ideology, in the grip of which these "true socialists" remain, prevents them from examining the real state of affairs. Their activity in face of the "unscientific" French and English consists primarily in holding up the superficiality and the "crude" empiricism of these foreigners to the scorn of the German public, in eulogising "German science" and declaring that its mission is to reveal for the first time the *truth* of communism and socialism, the absolute, *true* socialism. They immediately set to work

---

[a] See this volume, pp. 208-09.— *Ed.*

discharging this mission as representatives of "German science", although they are in most cases hardly more familiar with "German science" than they are with the original writings of the French and English, which they know only from the compilations of Stein, Oelckers,[a] etc. And what is the "*truth*" which they impart to socialism and communism? Since they find the ideas contained in socialist and communist literature quite unintelligible — partly by reason of their ignorance even of the literary background, partly on account of their above-mentioned misunderstanding of this literature — they attempt to clarify them by invoking the German ideology and notably that of Hegel and Feuerbach. They detach the communist systems, critical and polemical writings from the real movement, of which they are but the expression, and force them into an arbitrary connection with German philosophy. They detach the consciousness of certain historically conditioned spheres of life from these spheres and evaluate it in terms of true, absolute, i.e., German philosophical consciousness. With perfect consistency they transform the relations of these particular individuals into relations of "Man"; they interpret the thoughts of these particular individuals concerning their own relations as thoughts about "Man". In so doing, they have abandoned the real historical basis and returned to that of ideology, and since they are ignorant of the real connection, they can without difficulty construct some fantastic relationship with the help of the "absolute" or some other ideological method. This translation of French ideas into the language of the German ideologists and this arbitrarily constructed relationship between communism and German ideology, then, constitute so-called "true socialism", which is loudly proclaimed, in the terms used by the Tories for the English constitution, to be "the pride of the nation and the envy of all neighbouring nations".

Thus "true socialism" is nothing but the transfiguration of proletarian communism, and of the parties and sects that are more or less akin to it, in France and England within the heaven of the German mind and, as we shall also see, of the German sentiment. True socialism, which claims to be based on "science", is primarily another esoteric science; its theoretical literature is intended only for those who are initiated into the mysteries of the "thinking mind". But it has an exoteric

---

[a] Lorenz von Stein, *Der Socialismus und Communismus des heutigen Frankreichs*. Theodor Oelckers, *Die Bewegung des Socialismus und Communismus.* — *Ed.*

literature as well; the very fact that it is concerned with social, exoteric relations means that it must carry on some form of propaganda. In this exoteric literature it no longer appeals to the German "thinking mind" but to the German "sentiment". This is all the easier since true socialism, which is no longer concerned with real human beings but with "Man", has lost all revolutionary enthusiasm and proclaims instead the universal love of mankind. It turns as a result not to the proletarians but to the two most numerous classes of men in Germany, to the petty bourgeoisie with its philanthropic illusions and to the ideologists of this very same petty bourgeoisie: the philosophers and their disciples; it turns, in general, to that "common", or uncommon, consciousness which at present rules in Germany.

The conditions actually existing in Germany were bound to lead to the formation of this hybrid sect and the attempt to reconcile communism with the ideas prevailing at the time. It was just as inevitable that a number of German communists, proceeding from a philosophical standpoint, should have arrived, and still arrive, at communism by way of this transition while others, unable to extricate themselves from this ideology, should go on preaching true socialism to the bitter end. We have, therefore, no means of knowing whether the "true socialists" whose works were written some time ago and are criticised here still maintain their position or whether they have advanced beyond it. We are not at all concerned with the individuals; we are merely considering the printed documents as the expression of a tendency which was bound to occur in a country so stagnant as Germany.

But in addition true socialism has in fact enabled a host of Young-German literary men,[117] quacks and other literati to exploit the social movement. Even the social movement was at first a *merely* literary one because of the lack of *real*, passionate, practical party struggles in Germany. True socialism is a perfect example of a social literary movement that has come into being without any real party interests and now, after the formation of the communist party, it intends to persist in spite of it. It is obvious that since the appearance of a real communist party in Germany, the public of the true socialists will be more and more limited to the petty bourgeoisie and the sterile and broken-down literati who represent it.

I
DIE RHEINISCHEN JAHRBÜCHER
or
THE PHILOSOPHY OF TRUE SOCIALISM

A. "COMMUNISMUS, SOCIALISMUS, HUMANISMUS"[a]
RHEINISCHE JAHRBÜCHER, 1. BD., P. 167 ET SEQ.

We begin with this essay because it displays quite consciously and with great self-confidence the national German character of true socialism.

Page 168: "It seems that the *French* do not understand their own men of genius. At this point *German science* comes to their aid and *in the shape of socialism presents the most reasonable social order*, if one can speak of a superlative degree of reasonableness."

"German science" here, therefore, presents a social order, in fact "the most reasonable social order", "*in the shape of* socialism". Socialism is reduced to a branch of that omnipotent, omniscient, all-embracing German science which is even able to set up a society. It is true that socialism is French in origin, but the French socialists were "*essentially*" *Germans*, for which reason the *real* Frenchmen "did not understand" them. Thus the writer can say:

"*Communism* is *French*, *socialism* is *German*; the French are lucky to possess so apt a social *instinct*, which will serve them one day as a substitute for *scientific investigation*. This result has been determined by the course of development of the two nations; the French arrived at *communism* by way of *politics*" (now it is clear, of course, how the French people came to communism); "the Germans arrived at *socialism*" (namely "true socialism") "by way of *metaphysics*, which eventually changed into anthropology. Ultimately both are resolved in *humanism*."

After having transformed communism and socialism into two abstract theories, two principles, there is, of course, nothing easier than to excogitate at will any Hegelian unity of these two opposites and to give it any vague name one chooses. One has thereby not only submitted "the course of development of the two nations" to a piercing scrutiny but has also brilliantly

---

[a] The author of this article is Hermann Semmig.— *Ed.*

demonstrated the superiority of the speculative individual over both Frenchmen and Germans.

Incidentally, the sentence is copied more or less literally from Püttmann's *Bürgerbuch*, p. 43 and elsewhere[a]; the writer's "scientific investigation" of socialism is likewise limited to a reinterpretative reproduction of ideas contained in this book, in the *Einundzwanzig Bogen* and in other writings dating from the early days of German communism.

We will only give a few examples of the objections raised to *communism* in his essay:

Page 168: "Communism does not combine the atoms into an organic whole."

The demand that the "atoms" should be combined into an "organic whole" is no more realistic than the demand for the squaring of the circle.

"Communism, as it is actually advocated in France, its main centre, takes the form of *crude* opposition to the egoistical dissipation of the shopkeeper's state; it never transcends this political opposition; it never attains to *unconditional, unqualified freedom*." (Ibid.)

Voilà the German ideological postulate of "unconditional, unqualified freedom", which is only the practical formula for "unconditional, unqualified thought". French communism is admittedly "crude" because it is the theoretical expression of a *real* opposition; however, according to the writer, French communism ought to have transcended this opposition by imagining it to be already overcome. Compare also *Bürgerbuch*, p. 43, etc.

"Tyranny can perfectly well persist within communism, since the latter refuses to permit the continuance of the species." (P. 168.)

Hapless species! "Species" and "tyranny" have hitherto existed *simultaneously*; but it is precisely because communism *abolishes* the "species" that it can allow "tyranny" to *persist*. And how, according to our true socialist, does communism set about abolishing the "species"? It "has the masses in view" (ibid.).

"In communism man is not *conscious* of his *essence* ... his dependence is reduced by communism to the *lowest, most brutal relationship*, to dependence on *crude matter*—the separation of *labour* and *enjoyment*. Man does not attain to *free* moral *activity*."

---

[a] This refers to the article "Ueber die Noth in unserer Gesellschaft und deren Abhülfe" by Moses Hess published in *Deutsches Bürgerbuch für 1845.— Ed.*

To appreciate the "scientific investigation" which has led our true socialist to this proposition, it is necessary to consider the following passage:

"French socialists and communists ... have by no means theoretically understood the *essence* of socialism ... even the radical" (French) "communists have still by no means transcended the antithesis of *labour* and *enjoyment* ... have not yet risen to the idea of *free activity*.... The only difference between communism and the world of the shopkeeper is that in communism the *complete alienation of real human property* is to be made independent of all fortuity, i.e., is to be *idealised*." (*Bürgerbuch*, p. 43.)

That is to say, our true socialist is here reproaching the French for having a correct consciousness of their actual social conditions, whereas they ought to bring to light "Man's" consciousness of "*his* essence". All objections raised by these true socialists against the French amount to this, that they do not consider Feuerbach's philosophy to be the quintessence of their movement as a whole. The writer proceeds from the already existing proposition of the separation of labour and enjoyment. Instead of starting with this proposition, he ideologically turns the whole thing upside-down, begins with the missing consciousness of man, deduces from it "dependence on crude matter" and assumes this to be *realised* in the "separation of labour and enjoyment". Incidentally we shall see later on where our true socialist gets to with his independence "from crude matter".

In fact, all these gentlemen display a remarkable delicacy of feeling. Everything shocks them, especially matter; they complain everywhere of crudity. Earlier we have already had a "*crude* antithesis", now we have "the *most brutal* relationship" of "dependence on *crude* matter".

> With gaping jaws the German cries:
> Too *crude* love must not be
> Or you'll get an infirmity.[a]

German philosophy in its socialist disguise appears, of course, to investigate "crude reality", but it always keeps at a respectable distance and, in hysterical irritation, cries: *noli me tangere!*[b].

After these scientific objections to French communism, we come to several historical arguments, which brilliantly demon-

---

[a] Modified quotation from Heine's poem "Sie sassen und tranken am Teetisch..." in *Lyrisches Intermezzo*. The first line of Heine's poem reads: "With gaping jaws the canon cries." — *Ed.*
[b] Touch me not! (John 20:17). — *Ed.*

strate the "free moral activity" and the "scientific investigation" of our true socialist and his independence of crude matter.

On page 170 he arrives at the "result" that the only communism which "exists" is "*crude* French communism" (crude once again). The construction of this truth *a priori* is carried out with great "social instinct" and shows that "man has become conscious of his essence". Listen to this:

"There is no other communism, *for* what Weitling has produced is only an elaboration of Fourierist and communist ideas with which he became acquainted in Paris and Geneva."

"There is no" English communism, "for what Weitling", etc. Thomas More, the Levellers,[118] Owen, Thompson, Watts, Holyoake, Harney, Morgan, Southwell, Goodwyn Barmby, Greaves, Edmonds, Hobson, Spence will be amazed, or turn in their graves, when they hear that they are no communists "for" Weitling went to Paris and Geneva.

Moreover, Weitling's communism does seem to be different in kind from the "crude French" variety, in vulgar parlance, from Babouvism, since it contains some of "Fourier's ideas" as well.

"The communists were particularly good at drawing up systems or even complete social orders (Cabet's *Icarie, La Félicité*,[a] Weitling). All systems are, however, dogmatic and dictatorial." (P. 170.)

By this verdict on systems in general true socialism has, of course, saved itself the trouble of acquainting itself at first hand with the communist systems. With one blow it has overthrown not only *Icarie* but also every philosophical system from Aristotle to Hegel, the *Système de la nature*,[b] the botanical systems of Linné and Jussieu and even the solar system. Incidentally, as to the systems themselves they nearly all appeared in the early days of the communist movement and had at that time propaganda value as popular novels, which corresponded perfectly to the still undeveloped consciousness of the proletarians, who were then just beginning to play an active part. Cabet himself calls his *Icarie* a *roman philosophique* and he should on no account be judged by his system but rather by his polemical writings, in fact his whole activity as a party leader. In some of these novels, e.g., Fourier's system, there is a vein of true poetry; others, like the

---

[a] Étienne Cabet, *Voyage en Icarie*; François de Chastellux, *De la Félicité publique.—Ed.*
[b] The author of this work is Paul Henri Holbach.— *Ed.*

systems of Owen and Cabet, show not a shred of imagination and are written in a business-like calculating way or else with an eye to the views of the class to be influenced, in sly lawyer fashion. As the party develops, these systems lose all importance and are at best retained purely nominally as catchwords. Who in France believes in Icarie, who in England believes in the plans of Owen, which he preached in various modifications with an eye to propaganda among particular classes or with respect to the altered circumstances of the moment? Fourier's orthodox disciples of the *Démocratie pacifique* show most clearly how little the real content of these systems lies in their systematic form; they are, for all their orthodoxy, doctrinaire bourgeois, the very antipodes of Fourier. All epoch-making systems have as their real content the needs of the time in which they arose. Each one of them is based on the whole of the antecedent development of a nation, on the historical growth of its class relations with their political, moral, philosophical and other consequences. The assertion that all systems are dogmatic and dictatorial gets us nowhere with regard to this basis and this content of the communist systems. Unlike the English and the French, the Germans did not encounter fully developed class relations. The German communists could, therefore, only base their system on the relations of the class from which they sprang. It is, therefore, perfectly natural that the only existing German communist system should be a reproduction of French ideas in terms of a mental outlook which was limited by the petty circumstances of the artisan.

"The *madness* of Cabet, who insists that everybody should subscribe to *his Populaire*", p. 168, is proof of the tyranny that persists within communism. If our friend first distorts the claims which a party leader makes on his party, impelled by particular circumstances and the danger of failing to concentrate limited financial means, and then evaluates them in terms of the "essence of man", he is indeed bound to conclude that this party leader and all other party members are "mad" whereas purely disinterested figures, like himself and the "essence of man", are of sound intellect. But let him find out the true state of affairs from Cabet's *Ma ligne droite.*

The whole antithesis of our author, and of German true socialists and ideologists in general, to the real movements of other nations is finally epitomised in one classic sentence. The Germans judge everything *sub specie aeterni*[a] (in terms of the

---

[a] From the standpoint of eternity (cf. Benedict Spinoza, *Ethica.* Pars quinta).— *Ed.*

essence of man), foreigners view everything practically, in terms of actually existing men and circumstances. The thoughts and actions of the foreigner are concerned with *temporariness*, the thoughts and actions of the German with *eternity*. Our true socialist confesses this as follows:

"The very name of communism, the contrary of competition, reveals its one-sidedness; but is this bias, which may *very well* have value *now* as a party name, to *last for ever?*"

After having thus thoroughly disposed of communism, the writer proceeds to its contrary, *socialism*.

"Socialism establishes that anarchic system which is an *essential characteristic* of the human race and the universe" (p. 170) and for that very reason has hitherto never existed for "the human race".

Free competition is too "crude" to be regarded by our true socialist as an "anarchic system".

"Relying entirely on the *moral core* of mankind, *socialism*" decrees that "the union of the sexes *is and should be* merely the highest intensification of love; *for* only what is natural is true and what is true is moral". (P. 171.)

The reason why "the union, etc., etc., is and should be", can be applied to everything. For example, "socialism, relying entirely on the *moral core*" of the apes, might just as well decree that the masturbation which occurs naturally among them "is and should be merely the highest intensification of" self-"love; *for* only what is natural is true and what is true is moral".

It would be hard to say by what standard socialism judges what is "natural".

"Activity and enjoyment coincide in the *peculiar nature* of man; they are determined by this and not by the products *external to us.*"

"But since these products are indispensable for activity, that is to say, for true life, and since by reason of the common activity of mankind as a whole they have, so to speak, detached themselves from mankind, they *are or should be* the common substratum of further development for all (*community of goods*)."

"Our present-day society has indeed relapsed into savagery to such an extent that some individuals fall upon the products of another's labour with beastly voracity and at the same time they indolently allow their own essence to decay (*rentiers*); as a *necessary consequence*, others are driven to *mechanical* labour; their property (their own human essence) has been stunted, not by idleness, but by exhausting exertion (*proletarians*).... The two extremes of our society, rentiers and proletarians, are, *however*, at the same stage of development. *Both are dependent upon things external to them*" or are "Negroes", as Saint Max would say. (Pp. 169, 170.)

The "results" reached above by our "Mongol" concerning "our Negroism" are the most perfect achievements which true socialism has, "so to speak, detached from itself, as a product indispensable for true life"; our Mongol, by reason of "the peculiar nature of man", believes that "mankind as a whole" is bound to "fall upon" them with "beastly voracity".

The four concepts — "rentiers", "proletarians", "mechanical" and "community of goods" — are for our Mongol at any rate "products external to him"; as far as they are concerned, his "activity" and his "enjoyment" consist in representing them simply as anticipated terms for the results of his own "mechanical labour".

Society, we learn, has relapsed into savagery and consequently the individuals who form this very society suffer from all kinds of infirmities. Society is abstracted from these individuals, it is made independent, it relapses into savagery on its own, and the individuals suffer only as a *result* of this relapse. The expressions — beast of prey, idle and possessor of "one's own decaying essence" — are the first result of this relapse; whereupon we learn to our horror that these expressions define the "rentier". The only comment necessary is that this "allowing one's own essence to decay" is nothing but a philosophically mystified manner of speaking used in an endeavour to comprehend "idleness", the actual character of which seems to be very little known.

The two expressions, "stunted growth of their own human essence as a result of exhausting exertion" and "being driven to mechanical labour", are the second "necessary consequence" of the first result of the relapse into savagery. These two expressions are a "necessary consequence of the fact that the rentiers allow their own essence to decay", and are known in vulgar parlance, we learn, once more to our horror, as "proletarians".

The sentence, therefore, contains the following sequence of cause and effect: It is a fact that proletarians exist and that they work mechanically. Why are proletarians driven to "mechanical labour"? Because the rentiers "allow their own essence to decay". Why is it that the rentiers allow their own essence to decay? Because "our present-day society has relapsed into savagery to such an extent". Why has it relapsed into savagery? Ask thy Maker.

It is characteristic of our true socialist that he sees "the extremes of *our* society" in the opposition of rentiers and proletarians. This opposition has pretty well been present at all fairly advanced stages of society and has been belaboured by all moralists since time immemorial; it was resurrected right at the beginning of the proletarian movement, at a time when the proletariat still had interests in common with the industrial and petty bourgeoisie. Compare, for example, the writings of

Cobbett and P. L. Courier or Saint-Simon, who originally numbered the industrial capitalists among the *travailleurs*[a] as opposed to the *oisifs*,[b] the rentiers. Stating this trivial antithesis, which moreover it expresses, not in ordinary language, but in the sacred language of philosophy, presenting this childish discovery in abstract, sanctified and quite inappropriate terms — this is what here, as in all other cases, the thoroughness of that German science which has been perfected by true socialism amounts to. The conclusion puts the finishing touch to this kind of thoroughness. Our true socialist here merges the totally dissimilar stages of development of the proletarians and the rentiers into "one stage of development", because he ignores their real stages of development and subsumes them under the philosophic phrase: "dependence upon things external to them". True socialism has here discovered the stage of development at which the dissimilarity of all the stages of development in the three realms of nature, in geology and history, vanishes into thin air.

Although he detests "dependence upon things external to him", our true socialist nevertheless admits that he is dependent upon them, "since products", i.e., these very things, "are indispensable for activity" and for "true life". He makes this shamefaced admission so that he can clear the road for a philosophical construction of the community of goods — a construction that lapses into pure nonsense so that we need merely draw the reader's attention to it.

We now come to the first of the passages quoted above. Here again, "independence from things" is claimed in respect of activity and enjoyment. Activity and enjoyment "are determined" by "the peculiar nature of man". Instead of tracing this peculiar nature in the activity and enjoyment of the men who surround him — in which case he would very soon have found how far the products external to us have a voice in the matter, too — he makes activity and enjoyment "coincide in the peculiar nature of man". Instead of visualising the peculiar nature of men in their activity and their manner of enjoyment, which is conditioned by their activity, he explains both by invoking "the peculiar nature of man", which cuts short any further discussion. He abandons the real behaviour of the individual and again takes refuge in his indescribable, inaccessible, peculiar nature. We see here, moreover, what the *true socialists*

---

[a] Workers.— *Ed.*
[b] Idlers.— *Ed.*

understand by "free activity". Our author imprudently reveals to us that free activity is activity which "is not determined by things external to us", i.e., *actus purus*, pure, absolute activity, which is nothing but activity and is in the last instance tantamount to the illusion of "pure thought". It naturally sullies the purity of this activity if it has a material basis and a material result; the true socialist deals only reluctantly with impure activity of this kind; he despises its product, which he terms "a mere *refuse* of man", and not "a result". (P. 169.) The subject from whom this pure activity proceeds cannot, therefore, be a real sentient human being; it can only be the thinking mind. This "free activity", thus translated into German, is nothing but the foregoing "unconditional, unqualified freedom" expressed in a different way. Incidentally, that this talk of "free activity", which merely serves the true socialists to conceal their ignorance of real production, amounts in the final analysis to "pure thought" is also shown by the fact that the writer gives us as his last word the postulate of true cognition.

"This separation of the *two principal parties of this age*" (namely, French crude *communism* and German *socialism*) "is a result of the *developments of the last two years*, which *started* more particularly with Hess' *Philosophie der That*, in Herwegh's *Einundzwanzig Bogen. Consequently* it was high time to throw a little more light on the shibboleths of the *social parties*." (P. 173.)

Here we have, on the one hand, the actually existing communist party in France with its literature and, on the other, a few German pseudo-scholars who are trying to comprehend the ideas of this literature philosophically. The latter are treated just as much as the former as a *"principal party* of this *age"*, as a party, that is to say, of infinite importance not only to its immediate antithesis, the French communists, but also to the English Chartists and communists, the American national reformers [119] and indeed to every other party "of this age". It is unfortunate that none of these know of the existence of this "principal party". But it has for a considerable time been the fashion among German ideologists for each literary faction, particularly the one that thinks itself "most advanced", to proclaim itself not merely "one of the principal parties", but actually *"the* principal party of this age". We have, among others, "the principal party" of critical criticism, the "principal party" of egoism in agreement with itself and now the "principal party" of the true socialists. In this fashion Germany can boast a whole horde of "principal parties", whose existence is known only in Germany and even there only among the small set of scholars, pseudo-scholars and literati. They all imagine that they are weaving the web of world history when, as a matter of fact, they are merely spinning the long yarn of their own imaginings.

This "principal party" of the true socialists is "a result of the developments of the last two years, which started more particularly with Hess' *Philosophie*". It is "a result", that is to say, of the developments "of the last two years" when our author first got entangled in socialism and found it was "high time" to *enlighten* himself "a little more", by means of a few "shibboleths", on what he considers to be "social parties".

Having thus dismissed communism and socialism, our author introduces us to the higher unity of the two, to *humanism*. Now we are entering the domain of "Man" and the entire true history of our true socialist will be enacted in Germany alone.

"All quibbles about names are resolved in *humanism*; wherefore communists, wherefore socialists? We are *human beings*" (p. 172) — *tous frères, tous amis*.

> Swim not, brothers, against the stream,
> That's only a useless thing!
> Let us climb up on to Templow hill
> And cry: God save the King![a]

Wherefore human beings, wherefore beasts, wherefore plants, wherefore stones? We are bodies!

There follows an historical discourse which is based upon German science and which "will one day help to replace the social instinct" of the French. Antiquity — naïveté, the Middle Ages — Romanticism, the Modern Age — Humanism. By means of these three trivialities, the writer has, of course, constructed his humanism historically and showed it to be the truth of the old *Humaniora*.[120] Compare "Saint Max" in the first volume for constructions of this kind; he manufactures such wares in a much more artistic and less amateurish way.

On page 172 we are informed that

"the final result of scholasticism is that cleavage of life which was abolished by Hess".

Here then, the cause of the "cleavage of life" is shown to be theory. It is difficult to see why these true socialists mention society at all if they believe with the philosophers that all *real* cleavages are caused by *conceptual cleavages*. On the basis of this philosophical belief in the power of concepts to make or destroy the world, they can likewise imagine that some individual "abolished the cleavage of life" by "abolishing"

---

[a] From Heine's poem "Verkehrte Welt" in his verse cycle *Zeitgedichte*.— *Ed.*

concepts in some way or other. Like all German ideologists, the true socialists continually mix up literary history and real history as equipotential. This habit is, of course, very understandable among the Germans, who conceal the abject part they have played and continue to play in real history by equating the illusions, in which they are so rich, with reality.

And now to the "last two years", during which German science has so thoroughly disposed of all problems that nothing remains to the other nations but to carry out its decrees.

"Feuerbach only partially completed, or rather only began, the task of anthropology, the regaining by man of his estranged essence" (the essence of man or the essence of Feuerbach?); "he destroyed the *religious* illusion, the theoretical abstraction, the God-Man, whereas Hess *annihilates* the *political* illusion, the abstraction of his ability [*Vermögen*[a]], of his activity" (does this refer to Hess or to man?), "that is, he *annihilates wealth*. It was the work of Hess which freed *man* from the last of the forces external to him, ana made him capable of moral activity — for all the unselfishness of earlier times" (before Hess) "was only an illusory unselfishness — and raised him once more to his former dignity; for was man ever previously" (before Hess) "esteemed for what he actually was? Was he not judged by what he possessed? He was esteemed for his money." (P. 171.)

It is characteristic of all these high-sounding phrases about liberation, etc., that it is always "man" who is liberated. Although it would appear from the pronouncements made above that "wealth", "money", and so on, have ceased to exist, we nevertheless learn in the following sentence:

"Now that these illusions" (money, viewed *sub specie aeterni*, is, indeed, an illusion, *l'or n'est qu'une chimère*[b]) "have been destroyed we can *think* about a new, *human* order of society." (Ibid.)

But this is quite superfluous since

"the recognition of the *essence of man* has as a necessary and natural result a life which is truly human". (P. 172.)

To arrive at communism or socialism by way of metaphysics or politics, etc., etc. — these phrases beloved of true socialists merely indicate that such and such a writer has adopted communist ideas (which have reached him from without and have arisen in circumstances quite different from his) translating them into the mode of expression corresponding to his former standpoint, and formulating them in accordance with this standpoint. Which of these points of view is predominant in a nation, whether its communist outlook has a political or

---

[a] *Vermögen* can mean ability, faculty, power, or fortune, wealth, property.— *Ed.*

[b] Gold is but a chimera. From Giacomo Meyerbeer's opera *Robert-le-Diable* (libretto Eugène Scribe and Germain Delavigne), Act I, Scene 7.— *Ed.*

metaphysical or any other tinge depends, of course, upon the whole development of the nation. The fact that the attitude of most French communists has a political complexion — this is, on the other hand, countered by the fact that very many French socialists have abstracted completely from politics — causes our author to infer that the French "have arrived at communism by way of politics", by way of their political development. This proposition, which has a very wide circulation in Germany, does not imply that the writer has any knowledge either of politics, particularly of French political developments, or of communism; it only shows that he considers politics to be an independent sphere of activity, which develops in its own independent way, a belief he shares with all ideologists.

Another catchword of the true socialists is "true property", "true personal property", "real", "social", "living", "natural", etc., etc., property, whereas it is very typical that they refer to private property as "*so-called* property". The Saint-Simonists were the first to adopt this manner of speaking, as we have already pointed out in the first volume; but they never lent it this German metaphysical-mysterious form; it was with them at the beginning of the socialist movement to some extent justified as a counter to the stupid clamour of the bourgeoisie.[a] The end to which most of the Saint-Simonists came shows at any rate the ease with which this "true property" is again resolved into "ordinary private property".

If one takes the antithesis of communism to the world of private property in its crudest form, i.e., in the most abstract form in which the real conditions of that antithesis are ignored, then one is faced with the antithesis of property and lack of property. The abolition of this antithesis can be viewed as the abolition of either the one side or the other; either property is abolished, in which case universal lack of property or destitution results, or else the lack of property is abolished, which means the establishment of true property. In reality, the actual property-owners stand on one side and the propertyless communist proletarians on the other. This opposition becomes keener day by day and is rapidly driving to a crisis. If, then, the theoretical representatives of the proletariat wish their literary activity to have any practical effect, they must first and foremost insist that all phrases are dropped which tend to dim the realisation of the sharpness of this opposition, all phrases which tend to conceal this opposition and may even give the

---

[a] See this volume, p. 249.— *Ed.*

bourgeois a chance to approach the communists for safety's sake on the strength of their philanthropic enthusiasms. All these bad qualities are, however, to be found in the catchwords of the true socialists and particularly in "true property". Of course, we realise that the communist movement cannot be impaired by a few German phrase-mongers. But in a country like Germany — where philosophic phrases have for centuries exerted a certain power, and where, moreover, communist consciousness is anyhow less keen and determined because class contradictions do not exist in as acute a form as in other nations — it is, nevertheless, necessary to resist all phrases which obscure and dilute still further the realisation that communism is totally opposed to the existing world order.

This theory of true property conceives *real* private property, as it has hitherto existed, merely as a semblance, whereas it views the concept abstracted from this real property as the *truth* and *reality* of the semblance; it is therefore ideological all through. All it does is to give clearer and more precise expression to the ideas of the petty bourgeois; for their benevolent endeavours and pious wishes aim likewise at the abolition of the lack of property.

In this essay we have had yet further evidence of the narrowly national outlook which underlies the alleged universalism and cosmopolitanism of the Germans.

> The land belongs to the Russians and French,
> The English own the sea.
> But we in the airy realm of dreams
> Hold sovereign mastery.
>
> Our unity is perfect here,
> Our power beyond dispute;
> The other folk in solid earth
> Have   meanwhile   taken   root.[a]

With infinite self-confidence the Germans confront the other peoples with this airy realm of dreams, the realm of the "essence of man", claiming that it is the consummation and the goal of all world history; in every sphere they regard their dreamy fantasies as a final verdict on the actions of other nations; and because everywhere their lot is merely to look on and be left high and dry they believe themselves called upon to sit in judgment on the whole world while history attains its ultimate purpose in Germany. We have already observed several times that the complement of this inflated and

---

[a] Heinrich Heine, *Deutschland. Ein Wintermärchen*, Caput VII.— *Ed.*

extravagant national pride is practical activity of the pettiest kind, worthy of shopkeepers and artisans. National narrow-mindedness is everywhere repellent. In Germany it is positively odious, since, together with the illusion that the Germans are superior to nationality and to all real interests, it is held in the face of those nations which openly confess their national limitations and their dependence upon real interests. It is, incidentally, true of every nation that obstinate nationalism is now to be found only among the bourgeoisie and their writers.

B. "SOCIALISTISCHE BAUSTEINE" [a]
RHEINISCHE JAHRBÜCHER, P. 155 ET SEQ.

In this essay the reader is first of all prepared for the more difficult truths of true socialism by a belletristic and poetic prologue. The prologue opens by proclaiming "happiness" to be the "ultimate goal of all endeavour, all movements, of all the arduous and untiring exertions of past millenniums". In a few brief strokes, so to speak, a history of the struggle for happiness is sketched for us:

"When the foundations of the old world crumbled, the human heart with all its yearning took refuge in the other world, to which it transferred its happiness." (P. 156.)

Hence all the bad luck of the terrestrial world. In recent times man has bidden farewell to the other world and our true socialist now asks:

"Can man greet the earth once more as the *land* of his happiness? Does he once more *recognise* earth as his original home? Why then should he still keep life and happiness apart? Why does he not break down the last barrier which cleaves earthly life into two hostile halves?" (Ibid.)

"Land of my most blissful feelings!" etc.

He now invites "Man" to take a walk, an invitation which "Man" readily accepts. "Man" enters the realm of "free nature" and utters, among other things, the following tender effusions of a true socialist's heart. [b]

"... gay flowers ... tall and stately oaks ... their satisfaction, their happiness lie in their life, their growth and their blossoming ... an infinite multitude of tiny

---

[a] "Cornerstones of Socialism"—title of an article by Rudolph Matthäi.— Ed.

[b] Paraphrase of the title of Wilhelm Wackenroder's book *Herzensergiessungen eines kunstliebenden Klosterbruders.— Ed.*

creatures in the meadows ... forest birds ... a mettlesome troop of young horses ... I see" (says "man") "that these creatures neither know nor desire any other happiness than that which lies for them in the expression and the enjoyment of their lives. When night falls, my eyes behold a countless host of worlds which revolve about each other in infinite space according to eternal laws. I see in their revolutions a unity of life, movement and happiness." (P. 157.)

"Man" could also observe a great many other things in nature, e.g., the bitterest competition among plants and animals; he could see, for example, in the plant world, in his "forest of tall and stately oaks", how these tall and stately capitalists consume the nutriment of the tiny shrubs, which might well complain: *terra, aqua, aere et igni interdicti sumus*[a]; he could observe the parasitic plants, the ideologists of the vegetable world, he could further observe that there is open warfare between the "forest birds" and the "infinite multitude of tiny creatures", between the grass of his "meadows" and the "mettlesome troop of young horses". He could see in his "countless host of worlds" a whole heavenly feudal monarchy complete with tenants and satellites, a few of which, e.g., the moon, lead a very poor life *aere et aqua interdicti*; a feudal system in which even the homeless vagabonds, the comets, have been apportioned their station in life and in which, for example, the shattered asteroids bear witness to occasional unpleasant scenes, while the meteors, those fallen angels, creep shamefaced through the "infinite space", until they find somewhere or other a modest lodging. In the further distance, he would come upon the reactionary fixed stars.

"All these beings find their happiness, the satisfaction and the enjoyment of their life in the exercise and manifestation of the vital energies with which nature has endowed them."

That is, "man" considers that in the interaction of natural bodies and the manifestation of their forces these natural bodies find their happiness, etc.

"Man" is now reproached by our true socialist with his discord:

"Did not man too spring from the primeval world, is he not a child of nature, like all other creatures? Is he not formed of *the same* materials, is he not endowed with *the same* general energies and properties that animate *all things*? Why does he still seek his earthly happiness in an earthly beyond?" (P. 158.)

"*The same* general energies and properties" which man has in common with "*all* things", are cohesion, impenetrability,

---

[a] We are banned from earth, water, air and fire.— *Ed.*

volume, gravity, etc., which can be found set out in detail on the first page of any textbook of physics. It is difficult to see how one can construe this as a reason why man should not "seek his happiness in an earthly beyond". However, he admonishes man as follows:

"Consider the lilies of the field."

Yes, consider the lilies of the field, how they are eaten by goats, transplanted by "man" into his buttonhole, how they are crushed beneath the immodest embraces of the dairymaid and the donkey-driver!

"Consider the lilies of the field, they *toil* not, neither do they *spin*: and thy Heavenly Father feedeth them."[a]

Go thou and do likewise!

After learning in this fashion of the unity of "man" with "all things", we now learn how he *differs* from "all things".

"But man *knows himself*, he is *conscious of himself*. Whereas in other beings, the instincts and forces of *nature* manifest themselves in isolation and unconsciously, they are united in man and become conscious ... his nature is the mirror of all nature, which *recognises itself* in him. Well then! If nature recognises itself in me, then I recognise myself in nature. I see in its life my own life[...]. We are thus giving living expression to that with which nature has imbued us." (P. 158.)

This whole prologue is a model of ingenuous philosophic mystification. The true socialist proceeds from the thought that the dichotomy of life and happiness must cease. To prove this thesis he summons the aid of nature presupposing that this dichotomy does not exist in nature and from this he deduces that since man, too, is a natural body and has the properties which such bodies generally possess, this dichotomy ought not to exist for him either. Hobbes had much better reasons for invoking nature as a proof of his *bellum omnium contra omnes*,[b] and Hegel, on whose construction our true socialist depends, for perceiving in nature the cleavage, the slovenly period of the Absolute Idea, and even calling the animal the concrete anguish of God. After shrouding nature in mystery, our true socialist shrouds human consciousness in mystery too, by making it the "mirror" of this mystified nature. Of course, when the manifestation of consciousness ascribes to *nature* the mental expression of a pious wish about human affairs, it is self-evident

---

[a] Cf. Matthew 6:28, 26.— *Ed.*

[b] Thomas Hobbes, *Elementa philosophica. De cive. Praefatio ad lectores.*— *Ed.*

that consciousness will only be the mirror in which nature contemplates itself. That "man" has to abolish in his own sphere the cleavage, which is assumed to be non-existent in nature, is now proved by reference to man in his quality as a mere passive mirror in which nature becomes aware of itself; just as it was earlier proved by reference to man as a mere natural body. But let us inspect the last proposition more closely; all the nonsense of these arguments is concentrated in it.

The first fact asserted is that man possesses self-consciousness. The instincts and energies of individual natural beings are transformed into the instincts and forces of "nature", which then, as a matter of course, "are manifested" *in isolation in* these individual beings. This mystification was needed in order later to effect a unification of these instincts and forces of "nature" in the human self-consciousness. Thereby the self-consciousness of man is, of course, transformed into the self-consciousness of nature within him. This mystification is apparently resolved in the following way: in order to pay nature back for finding *its* self-consciousness in man, man seeks his, in turn, in nature — a procedure which enables him, of course, to find nothing in nature except what he has imputed to it by means of the mystification described above.

He has now arrived safely at the point from which he originally started, and this way of turning round on one's heel is now called in Germany — *development*.

After this prologue comes the real exposition of true socialism.

First Cornerstone

Page 160: "Saint-Simon said to his disciples on his death-bed: 'My whole life can be expressed in one thought: all men must be assured the freest development of their natural capacities.' Saint-Simon was a herald of socialism."

This statement is now treated according to the true socialist method described above and combined with that mystification of nature which we saw in the prologue.

"Nature as the basis of all life is a unity which proceeds from itself and returns to itself, which embraces the immense multifariousness of its phenomena and apart from which nothing exists." (P. 158.)

We have seen how one contrives to transform the different natural bodies and their mutual relationships into multifarious "phenomena" of the secret essence of this mysterious "unity". The only new element in this sentence is that nature is first called "the *basis* of all life", and immediately afterwards we are informed that "apart from it nothing exists"; according to this it embraces "life" as well and cannot merely be its *basis*.

After these portentous words, there follows the pivotal point of the whole essay:

"Every one of these phenomena, every *individual life*, exists and develops only through its *antithesis*, its *struggle* with the external world, and it is based upon its *interaction* with the *totality of life*, with which it is in turn by its nature linked in a whole, *the organic unity of the universe*." (Pp. 158, 159.)

This pivotal sentence is further elucidated as follows:

"The individual life finds, on the one hand, its foundation, its source and its subsistence in the totality of life; on the other hand, the totality of life in continual struggle with the individual life strives to consume and to absorb it." (P. 159.)

Since this statement applies to *every* individual life, "therefore", it can be, and is, applied to men as well:

"Man can *therefore* only develop in and through the totality of life." (No. I, ibid.)

Conscious individual life is now contrasted with unconscious individual life; human society with natural life in general; and then the sentence which we quoted last is repeated in the following form:

"By reason of my nature, it is only in and through community with other men that I can develop, achieve self-conscious enjoyment of my life, and attain happiness." (No. II, ibid.)

This development of the individual in society is now discussed in the same way as "individual life" in general was treated above:

"In society, too, the opposition of individual life and life in general becomes the condition of conscious human development. It is through perpetual struggle, through perpetual reaction against society, which confronts me as a restricting force, that I achieve self-determination and freedom, without which there is no happiness. My life is a continuous process of liberation, a continuous battle with and victory over the conscious and unconscious external world, in order to subdue it and use it to enjoy my life. The instinct of self-preservation, the striving for my own happiness, freedom and satisfaction, these are *consequently* natural, i.e., reasonable, expressions of life." (Ibid.)

Further:

"I demand, *therefore*, from society that it should afford me the *possibility* of winning from it my satisfaction, my happiness, that it should provide a battlefield for my bellicose spirit. Just as the individual plant demands soil, warmth and sun, air and rain for its growth, so that it may bear leaves, blossoms and fruit, man too *desires* to find in society the *conditions* for the all-round development and satisfaction of all his needs, inclinations and capacities. It *must* offer him the possibility of winning his happiness. How he will use that chance, what he will make of himself, of his life, depends upon him, upon his individuality. I alone can determine my happiness." (Pp. 159, 160.)

There follows, as the conclusion of the whole argument, the statement by Saint-Simon which is quoted at the beginning of this section. The Frenchman's idea has thus been vindicated by German science. What does this vindication consist in?

The true socialist has already earlier imputed various ideas to nature which he would like to see realised in human society. While formerly it was the individual human being, whom he made the mirror of nature, it is now society as a whole. A further conclusion can now be drawn about human society from the ideas imputed to nature. Since the author does not discuss the historical development of society, contenting himself with this meagre analogy, it remains incomprehensible why society should not always have been a true image of nature. The phrases about society, which confronts the individual in the shape of a restricting force, etc., are therefore relevant to every form of society. It is quite natural that a few inconsistencies should have crept into this interpretation of society. Thus he must now admit that a *struggle* is waged in nature, in contrast to the harmony described in the prologue. Society, the "totality of life", is conceived by our author not as the interaction of the constituent "individual lives", but as a distinct existence, and this moreover separately interacts with these "individual lives". If there is any reference to real affairs in all this it is the illusion of the independence of the state in relation to private life and the belief in this apparent independence as something absolute. But as a matter of fact, neither here nor anywhere in the whole essay is it a question of nature and society at all; it is merely a question of the two categories, individuality and universality, which are given various names and which are said to form a contradiction, the reconciliation of which would be highly desirable.

From the vindication of "individual life" as opposed to the "totality of life" it follows that the satisfaction of needs, the development of capacities, self-love, etc., are "natural, reasonable expressions of life". From the conception of society as an image of nature, it follows that in all forms of society existing up to now, the present included, these expressions of life have attained full maturity and are recognised as justified.

But we suddenly learn on page 159 that "in our present-day society" these reasonable, natural expressions of life are nevertheless "so often repressed" and "usually only for that reason do they degenerate into an unnaturalness, malformation, egoism, vice, etc."

And so, since society does not, after all, correspond to its prototype, nature, the true socialist "demands" that it should conform to nature and justifies his claim by adducing the plant as an example — a most unfortunate example. In the first place, the plant does not "demand" of nature all the conditions of existence enumerated above; unless it finds them already present it never becomes a plant at all; it remains a grain of seed. Moreover, the state of the "leaves, blossoms and fruit" depends to a great extent on the "soil", the "warmth" and so on, the climatic and geological conditions of its growth. Far from "demanding" anything, the plant is seen to depend utterly upon the actual conditions of existence; nevertheless, it is upon this alleged demand that our true socialist bases his own claim for a form of society which shall conform to his individual "peculiarity". The demand for a true socialist society is based on the imaginary demand of a coco-nut palm that the "totality of life" should furnish it with "soil, warmth, sun, air and rain" at the North Pole.

This claim of the individual on society is not deduced from the real development of society but from the alleged relationship of the metaphysical characters — individuality and universality. You have only to interpret single individuals as representatives, embodiments of individuality, and society as the embodiment of universality, and the whole trick is done. And at the same time Saint-Simon's statement about the free development of the capacities has been correctly expressed and placed upon its true foundation. This correct expression consists in the absurd statement that the individuals forming society want to preserve their "peculiarity", want to remain as they are, while they demand of society a transformation which can only proceed from a transformation *of themselves.*

Second Cornerstone

> "You've forgotten the rest of the charming refrain?
> Well, just give it up and start over again!"[a]

"Infinite in their variety, all individual
Beings as unity taken together are World Organism" (P. 160.)

And so we find ourselves thrown back again to the beginning of the essay and have to go through the whole comedy of

---

[a] The refrain of a German nursery song.— *Ed.*

individual life and totality of life for the second time. Once more we are initiated into the deep mystery of the interaction of these two lives, *restauré à neuf* by the introduction of the new term *"polar relationship"* and the transformation of the individual life into a mere *symbol*, an *"image"* of the totality of life. Like a kaleidoscopic picture this essay is composed of reflections of itself, a method of argument common to all true socialists. Their approach to their arguments is similar to that of the cherry-seller who was selling her wares below cost price, working on the correct economic principle that it is the *quantity* sold that matters. As regards true socialism, this is the more essential because its cherries were rotten before they were ripe.

A few examples of this self-reflection follow:

Cornerstone No. I, pp. 158, 159.

"Every individual life exists and develops only through its antithesis ... is based upon its *interaction* with the *totality of life,*

"With which it is in turn, by its nature, linked in a *whole.*

"Organic unity of the universe.

"The individual life finds, on the one hand, its *foundation,* its source and its *subsistence* in the totality of life,

"On the other hand, the totality of life in continual *struggle* with the individual life strives to consume it.

"*Therefore* (p. 159):

"Human society is to *conscious* ... life what unconscious universal life in general is to the unconscious individual life.

"*I* can only *develop in and through community* with other men.... In society, too, the opposition of *individual life* and *life in general* becomes", etc....

"Nature ... is a *unity* ... which *embraces* the immense *multifariousness* of its phenomena."

Cornerstone No. II, pp. 160, 161.

"Every individual life exists and develops in and through the totality of life; the totality of life only exists and develops in and through the individual life." (Interaction.)

"The individual life develops ... as a *part* of life in general.

"The world organism is combined unity.

"Which" (the totality of life) "becomes the *soil* and *subsistence* of its" (the individual life's) "development ... that each is *founded* upon the other....

"That they *struggle* against one another and oppose one another.

"*It follows* (p. 161):

"That *conscious individual life* is also conditioned by the conscious totality of life and" ... (vice versa).

"*The individual human being develops only in and through society,* society", vice versa, etc....

"Society is a *unity* which embraces and *comprises* the *multifariousness* of individual human development."

But our author is not satisfied with this kaleidoscopic display. He goes on to repeat his artless remarks about individuality and universality in yet another form. He first puts forward these few arid abstractions as absolute principles and then concludes that the same relationship must recur in the real world. Even this gives him the chance of saying everything twice under the guise of making deductions, in abstract form and, when he is drawing his conclusion, in seemingly concrete form. Then, however, he sets about varying the concrete *names* which he has given to his two categories. Universality appears variously as nature, unconscious totality of life, conscious ditto, life in general, world organism, all-embracing unity, human society, community, organic unity of the universe, universal happiness, common weal, etc., and individuality appears under the corresponding names of unconscious and conscious individual life, individual happiness, one's own welfare, etc. In connection with each of these names we are obliged to listen to the selfsame phrases which have already been applied often enough to individuality and universality.

The second cornerstone contains, therefore, nothing which was not already contained in the first. But since the words *égalité, solidarité, unité des intérêts* are used by the French socialists, our author attempts to fashion them into "cornerstones" of true socialism by turning them into German.

"As a conscious member of society I recognise every other member as a being different from myself, confronting me and at the same time supported by and derived from the primary common basis of existence and equal to me. I recognise every one of my fellow-men as opposed to me by reason of his particular nature, yet equal to me by reason of his general nature. The recognition of human equality, of the right of every man to existence, depends *therefore* upon the consciousness that human nature is common to all; in the same way, love, friendship, justice and all the social virtues are based upon the feeling of natural human affinity and unity. If up to now these have been termed obligations and have been imposed upon men, *then* in a society founded upon the *consciousness* of man's inward nature, i.e., upon reason and not upon external compulsion, they will become free, natural expressions of life. In a society which conforms to nature, i.e., to reason, the conditions of existence must *accordingly* be equal for all its members, i.e., must be general." (Pp. 161, 162.)

The author displays a marked ability for first putting forward a proposition in assertive fashion and then legitimising it as a consequence of itself by inserting an *accordingly*, a *consequently*, etc. He is equally skilful at incidentally smuggling into his peculiar deductions traditional socialistic statements by the use of "if they have", "if it is"—"then they must", "then it will become", etc.

In the first cornerstone, we saw, on the one hand, the individual and, on the other, universality which confronted him as society. This antithesis now reappears in another form, the individual now being divided within himself into a particular and a general nature. From the *general* nature of the individual, conclusions are drawn about "human equality" and community. Those conditions of life which are common to men thus appear here as a product of "the essence of man", of *nature,* whereas they, just as much as the consciousness of equality, are historical products. Not content with this, the author substantiates this equality by stating that it rests entirely "on the primary common basis of existence". We learned in the prologue, p. 158, that man "is formed of the same materials and is endowed with the same general energies and properties that animate all things". We learned in the first cornerstone that nature is "the basis of all life", and so, the "primary common basis of existence". Our author has, therefore, far outstripped the French since, being "a conscious member of society", he has not only demonstrated the equality of men with one another; he has also demonstrated their equality with every flea, every wisp of straw, every stone.

We should be only too pleased to believe that "all the social virtues" of our true socialist are based "upon the feeling of natural human affinity and unity", even though feudal bondage, slavery and all the social inequalities of every age have also been based upon this "natural affinity". Incidentally, "natural human affinity" is an historical product which is daily changed at the hands of men; it has always been perfectly natural, however inhuman and contrary to nature it may seem, not only in the judgment of "Man", but also of a later revolutionary generation.

We learn further, quite by chance, that present-day society is based upon "external compulsion". By "external compulsion" the true socialists do not understand the restrictive material conditions of life of given individuals. They see it only as the compulsion exercised by the *state,* in the form of bayonets, police and cannons, which far from being the foundation of society, are only a consequence of its structure. This question has already been discussed in *Die heilige Familie* and also in the first volume of this work.

The socialist opposes to present-day society, which is "based upon external compulsion", the ideal of true society, which is based upon the "consciousness of man's *inward* nature, i. e., upon reason". It is based, that is, upon the consciousness of consciousness, upon the thought of thought. The true socialist does not differ from the philosophers even in his choice of terms. He forgets that the "inward nature" of men, as well as their "consciousness" of it, "i. e.", their "reason", has at all times been an historical product and that even when, as he believes, the society of men was based "upon external compulsion", their "inward nature" corresponded to this "external compulsion".

There follow, on page 163, individuality and universality with their usual retinue, in the form of individual and public welfare. You may find similar explanations of their mutual relationship in any handbook of political economy under the heading of competition and also, though better expressed, in Hegel.

For example, *Rheinische Jahrbücher*, p. 163:

"By furthering the public welfare, I further my own welfare, and by furthering my own welfare, I further the public welfare."

Cf. Hegel's *Rechtsphilosophie*, p. 248 (1833):

"In furthering my ends, I further the universal, and this in turn furthers my ends."

Compare also *Rechtsphilosophie*, p. 323 et seq., about the relation of the citizen to the state.

"Therefore, as a final consequence, we have the conscious unity of the individual life with the totality of life, harmony." (*Rheinische Jahrbücher*, p. 163.)

"As a final consequence", that is to say, of

"this polar relationship between the individual and the general life, which consists in the fact that sometimes the two clash and oppose one another, while at other times, the one is the condition and the basis of the other".

The "final consequence" of this is at most the harmony of disharmony with harmony; and all that follows from the constant repetition of these familiar phrases is the author's belief that his fruitless wrestling with the categories of individuality and universality is the appropriate form in which social questions should be solved.

The author concludes with the following flourish:

"*Organic society has as its basis universal equality and develops, through the opposition of the individuals to the universal, towards unrestricted concord, towards the unity of individual with universal happiness, towards social*" (!) "*harmony of society*" (!!), "*which is the reflection of universal harmony.*" (P. 164.)

It is modesty indeed to call this sentence a "cornerstone". It is the primal rock upon which the whole of true socialism is founded.

Third Cornerstone

"Man's struggle with nature is based upon the polar opposition of my particular life to, and its interaction with, the world of nature in general. When this struggle appears as conscious activity, it is termed *labour*." (P. 164.)

Is not, on the contrary, the idea of "polar opposition" based upon the observation of a struggle between men and nature? First of all, an abstraction is made from a fact; then it is declared that the fact is based upon the abstraction. A very cheap method to produce the semblance of being profound and speculative in the German manner.

For example:

Fact: The cat eats the mouse.

Reflection: Cat—nature, mouse—nature, consumption of mouse by cat=consumption of nature by nature=self-consumption of nature.

Philosophic presentation of the fact: Devouring of the mouse by the cat is based upon the self-consumption of nature.

Having thus obscured man's struggle with nature, the writer goes on to obscure man's conscious activity in relation to nature, by describing it as the *manifestation* of this mere abstraction from the real struggle. The profane word *labour* is finally smuggled in as the result of this process of mystification. It is a word which our true socialist has had on the tip of his tongue from the start, but which he dared not utter until he had legitimised it in the appropriate way. Labour is constructed from the mere abstract idea of Man and nature; it is thereby defined in a way which is equally appropriate and inappropriate to all stages in the development of labour.

"*Therefore*, labour is any conscious activity on the part of man whereby he tries to acquire dominion over nature in an intellectual and material sense, so that he may utilise it for the conscious enjoyment of his life and for his intellectual or bodily satisfaction." (Ibid.)

We shall only draw attention to the brilliant deduction:

"When this struggle appears as conscious activity, it is termed labour— *therefore* labour is any conscious activity on the part of man", etc.

We owe this profound insight to the "polar opposition".

The reader will recall Saint-Simon's statement concerning *libre développement de toutes les facultés*[a] mentioned above, and also remember that Fourier wished to see the present *travail*

---

[a] Free development of all capacities.— *Ed.*

répugnant replaced by *travail attrayant.*[a] We owe to the "polar opposition" the following philosophic vindication and explanation of these propositions:

"*But* since" (the "but" is meant to indicate that there is no connection here) "for *life* every *manifestation*, exercise and expression of its forces and faculties *s h o u l d* be a source of enjoyment and satisfaction, *it follows* that labour *should* itself be a manifestation and development of human capacities and *should* be a source of enjoyment, satisfaction and happiness. *Consequently*, labour *m u s t* itself become a *free* expression of life and *so* a source of enjoyment." (Ibid.)

Here we are shown what we were promised in the preface to the *Rheinische Jahrbücher,* namely, "how far German social science differs in its development up to the present from French and English social science" and what it means "to present the doctrine of communism in a scientific form".

It would be a lengthy and boring procedure to expose every logical lapse which occurs in the course of these few lines. But let us first consider the offences against *formal logic.*

To prove that labour, an expression of life, should be a source of enjoyment, it is assumed that life should afford enjoyment in *all* its expressions. From this the conclusion is drawn that life should be a source of enjoyment also in its expression as labour. Not satisfied with this periphrastic transformation of a postulate into a conclusion, the author draws a false conclusion. From the fact that "for life every manifestation should be a source of enjoyment", he deduces that labour, which is one of these manifestations of life, "should itself be a manifestation and development of human capacities", that is to say, of life once again. Hence it ought to be what it already is. How could labour ever be *anything but* a "manifestation of human capacities"? But he does not stop there. *Because* labour *should* be so, it "*must consequently*" be so, or still better: because labour "should be a manifestation and development of human capacities", *it must consequently* become something completely different, namely, "a free expression of life", which did not enter into the question at all before this. And whereas earlier the postulate of labour as enjoyment was directly deduced from the postulate of the enjoyment of life, the former postulate is now put forward as a consequence of the new postulate of "free expression of life in labour".

As far as the *content* of the proposition is concerned, one cannot quite see why labour has not always been what it ought

---

[a] "Repellent labour" replaced by "attractive labour" (Charles Fourier, *Nouveau monde industriel*).— *Ed.*

to be, why it must now become what it ought to be, or why it should become something which up to now it was not bound to be. But, of course, up to now the essence of man and the polar opposition of man and nature were not properly explained.

A "scientific vindication" of the communist view about the common ownership of the products of labour follows:

> "*But*" (the recurrent "but" has the same meaning as the previous one) "the product of labour must serve at one and the same time the happiness of the individual, of the labouring individual, and the general happiness. This is effected by reason of the fact that all social activities are complementary and reciprocal." (Ibid.)

This statement is merely a copy of what any political economy has to say in praise of competition and the division of labour; except that the argument has been weakened by the introduction of the word "happiness".

Finally, we are given a philosophic vindication of the French organisation of labour:

> "Labour as a free activity, which is enjoyable, affords satisfaction and at the same time serves the common weal, is the basis of the *organisation of labour*." (P. 165.)

But since labour *should* and *must* become a free activity "which is enjoyable", etc., and therefore this state of affairs has not yet been *reached*, one would have expected *on the contrary* the organisation of labour to be the basis of "labour as an enjoyable activity". But the *concept* of labour as such an activity is quite sufficient [for the writer].

At the end of the essay the author believes to have reached "results".

These "cornerstones" and "results", together with those other granite boulders which are to be found in the *Einundzwanzig Bogen,* the *Bürgerbuch* and the *Neue Anekdota,*[121] form the rock upon which *true socialism*, alias *German social philosophy*, will build its church.[a]

We shall have occasion to listen to a few of the hymns, a few of the fragments of the *cantique allégorique hébraïque et mystique*[b] which are chanted in this church.

---

[a] Cf. Matthew 16:18.—*Ed.*
[b] Evariste Parny, *La guerre des dieux*. Chant premier.—*Ed.*

IV

KARL GRÜN:

DIE SOZIALE BEWEGUNG IN FRANKREICH UND BELGIEN[a] (DARMSTADT, 1845)
or
THE HISTORIOGRAPHY OF TRUE SOCIALISM[122]

"In sooth, if it were not a matter of discussing the whole horde of them ... we should probably throw down our pen.... And now, with that same arrogance, it" (Mundt's *Geschichte der Gesellschaft*) "appears before a wide circle of readers, before that public which seizes voraciously upon everything displaying the word *social* because a sure instinct tells it what secrets of future times are hidden in this little word. Hence a double responsibility rests on the writer and he deserves double reproof, if he sets to work inexpertly!"

"We shall not reproach Herr Mundt with not knowing anything of the actual achievements of French and English social literature apart from what Herr *L. Stein* has revealed to him. When it appeared, Stein's book[b] was worthy of note.... But to coin phrases nowadays... about Saint-Simon, to call Bazard and Enfantin the two branches of Saint-Simonism, to follow this up with Fourier and to repeat idle chit-chat about Proudhon, etc.!... And yet we would willingly overlook this if he had only portrayed the *genesis* of social ideas in a new and original way."

With this haughty and Rhadamanthine pronouncement Herr Grün begins a review (in the *Neue Anekdota*, pp. 122, 123) of Mundt's *Geschichte der Gesellschaft*.

The reader will be amazed at the artistic talent shown by Herr Grün, who actually gives, in this guise, a criticism of his own book, which at that time was not yet born.

We observe in Herr Grün a fusion of true socialism with Young-German literary pretensions[123]—a highly diverting spectacle. The book mentioned above is in the form of letters to a lady, from which the reader may surmise that here the profound divinities of true socialism are garlanded with the roses and myrtles of "young literature". Let us hasten to pluck a few roses:

"The *Carmagnole* was running through my head ... in any case it is terrible that the *Carmagnole* should be permitted to take breakfast in the head of a German writer, even if not to take up permanent quarters there." (P. 3.)

---

[a] *The Social Movement in France and Belgium.—Ed.*
[b] *Der Socialismus und Communismus des heutigen Frankreichs.—Ed.*

"If I had old Hegel here, I should collar him: What! So nature is the otherness of mind? What! You dullard!" (P. 11.)

"Brussels is to some extent a reproduction of the French Convention; it has its parties of the Mountain and the Valley." (P. 24.)

"The Lüneburg Heath of politics." (P. 80.)

"Gay, poetic, inconsistent, fantastic chrysalis." (P. 82.)

"Restoration liberalism, the groundless cactus, which as a parasite coiled round the seats in the Chamber of Deputies." (Pp. 87, 88.)

That the cactus is neither "groundless", nor a "parasite", and that "gay", "poetic" or "inconsistent" "chrysalises" or pupae do not exist, does not detract from these lovely images.

"Amid this sea" (of newspapers and journalists in the Cabinet Montpensier[124]) "I myself, however, feel like a second Noah, despatching his doves to see if he can possibly build a dwelling or plant a vineyard anywhere or come to a reasonable agreement with the infuriated Gods." (P. 259.)

No doubt this refers to Herr Grün's activity as a newspaper correspondent.

"Camille Desmoulins was a *human being*. The Constituent Assembly was composed of *philistines*. Robespierre was a *virtuous magnetiser*. Modern history, in a word, is a life-and-death struggle against the shopkeepers and the magnetisers!!!" (P. 111.)

"Happiness is a plus, but a plus to the nth power." (P. 203.)

Hence, happiness $= +^n$, a formula which can only be found in the aesthetic mathematics of Herr Grün.

"Organisation of labour, what is it? And the peoples replied to the Sphinx with the voices of a thousand newspapers.... France sings the strophe, Germany the antistrophe, old mystic Germany." (P. 259.)

"North America is even more distasteful to me than the Old World because its shopkeeping egoism has on its cheeks the bloom of impertinent health ... because everything there is so superficial, so rootless, I might almost say so *provincial*.... You call America the New World; it is the oldest of all Old Worlds; our worn-out clothes set the fashion there." (Pp. 101, 324.)

So far we were only aware that unworn stockings of German manufacture were worn there; although they are of too poor a quality to set the "fashion".

"The logically stable security-mongering of these institutions." (P. 461.)

> Unless these flowers your heart delight
> To be a "man" you have no right![a]

What wanton grace, what saucy innocence! What heroic wrestling with aesthetic problems! This nonchalance and originality are worthy of a Heine!

---

[a] An adaptation of a couplet from Mozart's opera *The Magic Flute* (libretto by Emanuel Schikaneder), Act II, aria of Sarastro.— *Ed.*

We have deceived the reader. Herr Grün's literary graces are not an embellishment of the science of true socialism, the science is merely the padding between these outbursts of literary gossip, and forms, so to speak, its "social background".

In an essay by Herr Grün, "Feuerbach und die Socialisten", the following remark occurs (*Deutsches Bürgerbuch*, p. 74):

"When one *speaks* of Feuerbach one speaks of the entire work of philosophy from Bacon of Verulam up to the present; one defines at the same time the ultimate purpose and meaning of philosophy, one sees *man* as the final result of world history. To do so is a *more reliable, because a more profound*, method of approach than to bring up wages, competition, the faultiness of constitutions and systems of government.... We have gained *man*, man who has divested himself of religion, of moribund thoughts, of all that is foreign to him, with all their counterparts in the practical world; we have gained *pure, genuine man.*"

This one proposition is enough to show what kind of "reliability" and "profundity" one can expect from Herr Grün. He does not discuss small questions. Equipped with an unquestioning faith in the conclusions of German philosophy, as formulated by Feuerbach, viz., that "*man*", "pure, genuine man", is the ultimate purpose of world history, that religion is externalised [*entäusserte*] human essence, that human essence is human essence and the measure of all things — equipped with all the other truths of German socialism (see above) — i. e., that money, wage-labour, etc., are also externalisations [*Entäusserungen*] of human essence, that German socialism is the realisation of German philosophy and the theoretical truth of foreign socialism and communism, etc.[a] — Herr Grün travels to Brussels and Paris with all the complacency of a true socialist.

The powerful trumpetings of Herr Grün in praise of true socialism and of German science exceed anything his fellow-believers have achieved in this respect. As far as these eulogies refer to true socialism, they are obviously quite sincere. Herr Grün's modesty does not permit him to utter a single sentence that has not already been pronounced by some other true socialist in the *Einundzwanzig Bogen*, the *Bürgerbuch* and the *Neue Anekdota*. Indeed, he devotes his whole book to filling in an outline of the French social movement sketched in the *Einundzwanzig Bogen* (pp. 74-88) by Hess, and thereby answering a need expressed in the same work on page 88.[b] As regards the eulogies to German philosophy, the latter must

[a] See this volume, pp. 493-95.— *Ed.*
[b] Moses Hess, "Socialismus und Communismus".— *Ed.*

value them all the more, seeing how little he knows about it. The national pride of the true socialists, their pride in Germany as the land of "man", of "human essence", as opposed to the other profane nationalities, reaches its climax in him. We give below a few samples of it:

"But I should like to know whether they won't all have to learn from us, these French and English, Belgians and North Americans." (P. 28.)

He now enlarges upon this.

"The *North Americans* appear to me thoroughly prosaic and, despite their legal freedom, it is from us that they will probably have to learn their *socialism.*" (P. 101.)

Particularly because they have had, since 1829, their own socialist and democratic school,[125] against which their economist Cooper was fighting as long ago as 1830.

"The *Belgian* democrats! Do you really think that they are *half so far advanced* as we Germans are? Why, I have just had a tussle with one of them who considered the *realisation of free humanity* to be a chimera!" (P. 28.)

The nationality of "man", of "human essence", of "humanity" shows off here as vastly superior to Belgian nationality.

"*Frenchmen!* Leave Hegel in peace until you understand him." (We believe that *Lerminier's* criticism of the philosophy of law,[a] however weak it may be, shows more insight into Hegel than anything which Herr Grün has written either under his own name, or that of "Ernst von der Haide".) "Try drinking no coffee, no wine for a year; don't give way to passionate excitement; let Guizot rule and let Algeria come under the sway of Morocco" (how is Algeria ever to come under the sway of Morocco, even if the French were to relinquish it?); "sit in a garret and study the *Logik* and the *Phänomenologie.* And when you come down after a year, lean in frame and red of eye, and go into the street and stumble over some dandy or town crier, don't be abashed. For in the meantime you will have become great and mighty men, your mind will be like an oak that is nourished by miraculous" (!) "sap; whatever you see will yield up to you its most secret weaknesses; though you are created spirits, you will nevertheless penetrate to the heart of nature; your glance will be fatal, your word will move mountains, your dialectic will be keener than the keenest guillotine. You will present yourself at the Hôtel de Ville — and the bourgeoisie is a thing of the past. You will step up to the Palais Bourbon — and it collapses. The whole Chamber of Deputies will disappear into the void. Guizot will vanish, Louis Philippe will fade into an historical ghost and out of all these forces which you have annihilated there will rise victorious the absolute idea of free society. Seriously, you can only subdue Hegel by first of all becoming Hegel yourselves. As I have already remarked — Moor's beloved can only die at the hands of Moor."[b] (Pp. 115, 116.)

[a] Eugène Lerminier, *Philosophie du droit.— Ed.*
[b] Friedrich Schiller, *Die Räuber*, Act V, Scene 2.— *Ed.*

The belletristic aroma of these true socialist statements will be noticed by everyone. Herr Grün, like all true socialists, does not forget to bring up again the old chatter about the superficiality of the French:

"For I am fated to find the French mind inadequate and superficial, every time that I come into close contact with it." (P. 371.)

Herr Grün does not conceal from us the fact that his book is intended to glorify German socialism as the criticism of French socialism:

"The riff-raff of current German literature call our socialist endeavours an imitation of French perversities. No one has so far considered it worth while to reply to this. The riff-raff must surely feel ashamed, if they have any sense of shame at all, when they read *this book*. It probably never entered their head that *German socialism is a criticism of French socialism*, that far from considering the French to be the inventors of a new *Contrat social*, it demands that French socialism should *make good its deficiencies by a study of German science*. At this moment, an edition of a translation of Feuerbach's *Wesen des Christenthums* is being prepared here in Paris. May their German schooling do the French much good! Whatever may arise from the economic position of the country or the constellation of politics in this country, only the humanistic outlook will ensure a *human* existence for the future. The Germans, unpolitical and despised as they are, this nation which is no nation, will have laid the cornerstone of the building of the future." (P. 353.)

Of course, there is no need for a true socialist, absorbed in his intimacy with "human essence", to know anything about what "may arise from the economic position and the political constellation" of a country.

Herr Grün, as an apostle of true socialism, does not merely, like his fellow-apostles, boast of the omniscience of the Germans as compared with the ignorance of the other nations. Utilising his previous experience as a man of letters, he forces himself, in the worst globe-trotter manner, upon the representatives of the various socialist, democratic and communist parties and when he has sniffed them from all angles, he presents himself to them as the apostle of true socialism. All that remains for him to do is to teach them, to communicate to them the profoundest discoveries concerning free humanity. The superiority of true socialism over the French parties now assumes the form of the personal superiority of Herr Grün over the representatives of these parties. Finally, this gives him a chance not only of utilising the French party leaders as a pedestal for Herr Grün, but also of talking all sorts of gossip, thereby compensating the German provincial for the exertion which the more pregnant statements of true socialism have caused him.

"*Kats* pulled a face expressive of plebeian cheerfulness when I assured him of my complete satisfaction with his speech." (P. 50.)

Herr Grün lost no time in instructing Kats about French terrorism and "had the good fortune to win the approval of my new friend". (P. 51.)

His effect on *Proudhon* was important too, but in a different way.

"I had the infinite pleasure of acting, so to speak, as the *tutor* of the man whose acumen has not perhaps been surpassed since Lessing and Kant." (P. 404.)

Louis Blanc is merely "his swarthy young friend". (P. 314.)

"He asked very eagerly but also very ignorantly about conditions with us. We Germans know" (?) "French conditions almost as well as the French themselves; at least we study" (?) "them." (P. 315.)

And we learn of "Papa *Cabet*" that he "has limitations". (P. 382.) Herr Grün raised a number of questions, and Cabet

"confessed that he had not exactly been able to fathom them. *I*" (Grün) "had noticed this long ago; and that, of course, meant an end of everything, especially as it occurred to me that Cabet's mission had long ago been fulfilled." (P. 381.)

We shall see later how Herr Grün contrives to give Cabet a new "mission".

Let us first deal with the outline and the few well-worn general ideas which form the skeleton of Grün's book. Both are copied from Hess, whom Herr Grün paraphrases indeed in the most lordly fashion. Matters which are quite vague and mystical even in Hess, but which were originally — in the *Einundzwanzig Bogen* — worthy of recognition, and have only become tiresome and reactionary as a result of their perpetual reappearance in the *Bürgerbuch,* the *Neue Anekdota* and the *Rheinische Jahrbücher,* at a time when they were already out of date, become complete nonsense in Herr Grün's hands.

Hess synthesises the development of French socialism and the development of German philosophy — Saint-Simon and Schelling, Fourier and Hegel, Proudhon and Feuerbach. Compare, for example, *Einundzwanzig Bogen,* pp. 78, 79,[a] 326, 327[b]; *Neue Anekdota,* pp. 194, 195, 196, 202 ff.[c] (Parallels between Feuerbach and Proudhon, e.g., Hess: "Feuerbach is the German Proudhon", etc., *Neue Anekdota,* p. 202. Grün: "Proudhon is the French Feuerbach", p. 404.)

---

[a] Moses Hess, "Socialismus und Communismus".— *Ed.*
[b] Moses Hess, "Philosophie der That".— *Ed.*
[c] Moses Hess, "Ueber die sozialistische Bewegung in Deutschland".' — *Ed.*

This schematism in the form given it by Hess is all that holds Grün's book together. But, of course, Herr Grün does not fail to add a few literary flourishes to Hess' propositions. Even obvious blunders on the part of Hess, e.g., that theoretical constructions form the "social background" and the "theoretical basis" of practical movements (e.g., *Neue Anekdota*, p. 192) are copied faithfully by Herr Grün. (E.g., Grün, p. 264: "The social background of the political question in the eighteenth century ... was the simultaneous product of the two philosophic tendencies"—that of the sensationists and that of the deists.) He copies, too, the opinion that it is only necessary to put Feuerbach into practice, to apply him to social life, in order to produce the complete critique of existing society. If one adds the other critical remarks which Hess directed against French communism and socialism, for example: "Fourier, Proudhon, etc., did not get beyond the category of wage-labour" (*Bürgerbuch*, p. 46 and elsewhere[a]); "Fourier would like to present new associations of egoism to the world" (*Neue Anekdota*, p. 196); "Even the radical French communists have not yet risen above the opposition of labour and enjoyment. They have not yet grasped the *unity of production and consumption*, etc." (*Bürgerbuch*, p. 43); "Anarchy is the negation of the concept of political rule" (*Einundzwanzig Bogen*, p. 77), etc., if one adds these, one has pocketed the whole of Herr Grün's critique of the French. As a matter of fact he had it in his pocket before he went to Paris. In settling accounts with the French socialists and communists Herr Grün also obtains great assistance from the various traditional phrases current in Germany about religion, politics, nationality, human and inhuman, etc., which have been taken over by the true socialists from the philosophers. All he has to do is to hunt everywhere for the words "*Man*" and "human" and condemn when he cannot find them. For example: "You are political. Then you are narrow-minded." (P. 283.) In the same way, Herr Grün is enabled to exclaim: You are national, religious, addicted to political economy, you have a God—then you are not human, you are narrow-minded. This is a process which he follows throughout his book, thereby, of course, providing a thorough criticism of politics, nationality, religion, etc., and at the same time an adequate elucidation of the characteristics of the authors criticised and their connection with social development.

---

[a] Moses Hess, "Ueber die Noth in unserer Gesellschaft und deren Abhülfe".— *Ed.*

One can see from this that Grün's fabrication is on a much lower level than the work by *Stein*, who at least tried to explain the connection between socialist literature and the real development of French society. It need hardly be mentioned that in the book under discussion, as in the *Neue Anekdota*, Herr Grün adopts a very grand and condescending manner towards his predecessor.

But has Herr Grün even succeeded in copying correctly what he has taken over from Hess and others? Has he even incorporated the necessary material in the outline which he has taken over lock, stock and barrel in the most uncritical fashion? Has he given a correct and complete exposition of the individual socialist authors according to the sources? Surely this is the least one could ask of the man from whom the North Americans, the French, the English and the Belgians have to learn, the man who was the tutor of Proudhon and who perpetually brandishes his German thoroughness before the eyes of the superficial Frenchmen.

SAINT-SIMONISM

Herr Grün has *no* first-hand knowledge *of a single* Saint-Simonian *book*. His main sources are: primarily, the much despised *Lorenz Stein*; furthermore, Stein's chief source, *L. Reybaud*[a] (in return for which he proposes to make an example of Herr Reybaud and calls him a philistine, p. 260; on the same page he pretends that he only came across Reybaud's book by chance long after he had settled with the Saint-Simonists); and occasionally *Louis Blanc*.[b] We shall give direct proofs.

First let us see what Herr Grün writes about Saint-Simon's life.

The main sources for Saint-Simon's life are the fragments of his autobiography in the *Œuvres de Saint-Simon*, published by Olinde Rodrigues,[c] and the *Organisateur* of May 19th, 1830.[d] We have, therefore, all the documents here before us: 1) The original sources; 2) Reybaud, who summarised them; 3) Stein, who utilised Reybaud; 4) Herr Grün's belletristic edition.

---

    [a] Louis Reybaud, *Études sur les réformateurs ou socialistes modernes*. What edition the authors used is unknown.— *Ed.*
    [b] Louis Blanc, *Histoire de dix ans*.— *Ed.*
    [c] "Vie de Saint-Simon écrite par lui-même."— *Ed.*
    [d] "À un Catholique. Sur la vie et le caractère de Saint-Simon."— *Ed.*

Herr Grün:

"Saint-Simon took part in the American struggle for independence without having any particular interest in the war itself; it *occurred to him* that there was a possibility of linking the *two* great *oceans.*" (P. 84.)

Stein, page 143:

"First he entered military service ... and went to America with Bouillé.... In this war, the significance of which he, of course, realised.... The war, *as such,* he said, did not interest me, only the purpose of this war, etc." ... "After he had vainly tried to interest the Viceroy of Mexico in a plan to build a great canal linking the *two oceans.*"

Reybaud, page 77:

"Soldat de l'indépendance américaine, il servait sous Washington ... la guerre, en elle-même, ne m'intéressait pas, dit-il; mais le seul but de la guerre m'intéressait vivement, et cet intérêt m'en faisait supporter les travaux sans répugnance."[a]

Herr Grün only copies the fact that Saint-Simon had "no particular interest in the war itself"; he omits the whole point—his interest in the object of the war.

Herr Grün further omits to state that Saint-Simon wanted to win the Viceroy's support for his plan and thus turns the plan into a mere "idea". He likewise omits to mention that Saint-Simon did this only "*à la paix*",[b] the reason being that Stein indicates this merely by giving the date.

Herr Grün proceeds without a break:

"*Later*" (when?) "he *drafted* a plan for a Franco-Dutch expedition to the British Indies." (Ibid.)

Stein:

"He travelled to Holland in 1785, to *draft* a plan for a joint Franco-Dutch expedition against the British colonies in India." (P. 143.)

Stein is incorrect here and Grün copies him faithfully. According to Saint-Simon, the Duc de la Vauguyon had induced the States-General[126] to undertake a joint expedition with France to the British colonies in India. Concerning himself, he merely says that he "*worked*" (*poursuivi*) for the execution of this plan for a year".

Herr Grün:

"When in Spain, he *wished to dig* a canal from Madrid to the sea." (Ibid.)

---

[a] "A fighter for American independence, he served under Washington.... The war in itself did not interest me, he said, but I was keenly interested in the object of the war and this interest induced me to endure its hardships without demur."—*Ed.*

[b] After peace had been made.—*Ed.*

Saint-Simon wished to *dig a canal*? What nonsense! Previously, it *occurred to him* to do something, now he *wishes* to do something. Grün gets his facts wrong this time not because he copies Stein too faithfully as he did before, but because he copies him too superficially.

Stein, page 144:

"Having returned to France in 1786, he visited Spain the very next year to present to the Government a plan for the completion of a canal from Madrid to the sea."

Herr Grün could derive the foregoing sentence skimming through Stein, for with Stein it seems at least as if the plan of construction and the idea of the whole project originated with Saint-Simon. As a matter of fact, Saint-Simon merely drew up a plan to overcome the financial difficulties besetting the building of the canal, the construction of which had been started long ago.

Reybaud:

"Six ans plus tard il proposa au gouvernement espagnol un plan de canal qui devait établir une ligne navigable de Madrid à la mer."[a] (P. 78.)

The same mistake as that made by Stein.

Saint-Simon, page xvii:

"Le gouvernement espagnol avait entrepris un canal qui devait faire communiquer Madrid à la mer; cette entreprise languissait parce que ce gouvernement manquait d'ouvriers et d'argent; je me concertai avec M. le comte de Cabarrus, aujourd'hui ministre des finances, et nous présentâmes au gouvernement le projet suivant"[b] etc.

Herr Grün:

"In France he speculates *on* national domains."

Stein first of all sketches Saint-Simon's attitude during the revolution and then passes to his speculation in national domains, p. 144 et seq. But where Herr Grün has got the nonsensical expression: "to speculate *on* national domains", instead of *in* national domains, we can likewise explain by offering the reader the original:

---

[a] "Six years later, he put before the Spanish Government a plan for the construction of a canal with the object of establishing a navigable route from Madrid to the sea."— *Ed.*

[b] "The Spanish Government had undertaken the construction of a canal which was to link Madrid with the sea; the scheme came to a standstill since the Government lacked labour and funds; I joined forces with M. le Comte de Cabarrus, now Finance Minister, and we presented the following plan to the Government."— *Ed.*

Reybaud, page 78:

"Revenu à Paris, il tourna son activité vers des spéculations, et trafiqua *sur* les domaines nationaux."[a]

Herr Grün makes the foregoing statement without giving any explanation. He does not indicate why Saint-Simon should have speculated in national domains and why this fact, trivial in itself, should be of importance in his life. For Herr Grün finds it unnecessary to copy from Stein and Reybaud the fact that Saint-Simon wished to found a scientific school and a great industrial undertaking by way of experiment, and that he intended to raise the necessary capital by these speculations. These are the reasons which Saint-Simon himself gives for his speculations. (*Œuvres*, p. xix.)

Herr Grün:

"He marries so that he may be able to act as the host of science, to investigate the lives of men and exploit them psychologically." (Ibid.)

Herr Grün here suddenly skips one of the most important periods of Saint-Simon's life — the period during which he studied natural science and travelled for that purpose. What is the meaning of marrying *to be the host of science*? What is the meaning of marrying in order to exploit *men* (whom one does not marry) psychologically? The whole point is this: Saint-Simon married so that he could hold a salon and study there among others the men of learning.

Stein puts it in this way, page 149:

"He marries in 1801.... I made use of my married life to study the men of learning." (Cf. Saint-Simon, p. 23.)

Since we have now collated it with the original, we are in a position to understand and explain Herr Grün's nonsense.

The "psychological exploitation of *men*" amounts in Stein and in Saint-Simon himself merely to the observation of *men of learning* in their social life. It was in conformity with his socialist outlook that Saint-Simon should wish to acquaint himself with the influence of science upon the personality of men of learning and upon their behaviour in ordinary life. For Herr Grün this wish turns into a senseless, vague romantic whim.

Herr Grün:

"He becomes poor" (how, in what way?), "he works as a clerk *in a* pawnshop at a salary of a thousand francs a year — he, a count, a scion of

---

[a] "Having returned to Paris, he turned his attention to speculation and dealt *in* national domains" (*sur les domaines nationaux* literally translated means "*on* national domains").— *Ed.*

Charlemagne; *then*" (when and why?) "he lives on the bounty of a former servant of his; later" (when and why?) "he tries to shoot himself, is rescued and begins a new life of study and propaganda. Only now does he write his *two chief works.*"

"He becomes"—"then"—"later"—"now"— such phrases in the work of Herr Grün are to serve as substitutes for the chronological order and the connecting links between the various phases of Saint-Simon's life.

Stein, pages 156, 157:

"Moreover, there appeared a new and a fearful enemy—actual poverty, which became more and more oppressive.... After a distressing wait of six months ... he obtained a position—" (Herr Grün gets even the dash from Stein, but he is cunning enough to insert it after the pawnshop) "as clerk *in the* pawnshop" (not, as Herr Grün artfully writes, "in *a* pawnshop", since it is well known that in Paris there is only *one* such establishment, and that a public one) "at a salary of a thousand francs a year. How his fortune fluctuated in those days! The grandson of Louis XIV's famous courtier, the heir to a ducal coronet and to an immense fortune, by birth a peer of France and a Grandee of Spain, a clerk *in a* pawnshop!"

Now we see the source of Herr Grün's mistake regarding the pawnshop; here, in Stein, the expression is appropriate. To accentuate his difference from Stein, Grün only calls Saint-Simon a "count" and a "scion of Charlemagne". He has the last fact from Stein (p. 142) and Reybaud (p. 77), but they are wise enough to say that it was Saint-Simon himself who used to trace his descent from Charlemagne. Whereas Stein offers positive facts which make Saint-Simon's poverty seem surprising *under the Restoration*, Herr Grün only expresses his astonishment that a count and an alleged scion of Charlemagne can possibly find himself in reduced circumstances.

Stein:

"He lived two more years" (after his attempted suicide) "and perhaps achieved more during them than during any two decades earlier in his life. The *Catéchisme des industriels* was *completed*" (Herr Grün transforms this completion of a work which had long been in preparation into: "Only now did he write", etc.) "and the *Nouveau christianisme*, etc." (Pp. 164, 165.)

On page 169 Stein calls these two books "*the two chief works of his life*".

Herr Grün has, therefore, not merely *copied the errors of Stein* but has also *produced new errors* on the basis of obscure passages of Stein. To conceal his plagiarism, he selects only the outstanding facts; but he robs them of their factual character by tearing them out of their chronological context and omitting not only the motives governing them, but even the most vital connecting links. What we have given above is, literally, *all* that

Herr Grün has to relate about the life of Saint-Simon. In his version, the dynamic, active life of Saint-Simon becomes a mere succession of ideas and events which are of less interest than the life of any peasant or speculator who lived through those stormy times in one of the French provinces. After dashing off this piece of biographical hack-work, he exclaims: "this whole, *truly civilised* life!" He does not even shrink from saying (p. 85): "Saint-Simon's life is the mirror of Saint-Simonism itself"—as if Grün's "life" of Saint-Simon were the mirror of anything except Herr Grün's method of patching together a book.

We have spent some time discussing this biography because it is a classical example of the way in which Herr Grün deals *thoroughly* with the French socialists. Just as in this case, to conceal his borrowings, Herr Grün dashes off passages with an air of nonchalance, omits facts, falsifies and transposes, we shall watch him later developing all the symptoms of a plagiarist consumed by inward uneasiness: artificial confusion, to make comparison difficult; omission of sentences and words which he does not quite understand, being ignorant of the original, when quoting from his predecessors; free invention and embellishment in the form of phrases of indefinite meaning; treacherous attacks upon the very persons whom he is copying. Herr Grün is indeed so hasty and so precipitous in his plagiarism that he frequently refers to matters which he has never mentioned to his readers but which he, as a reader of Stein, carts round in his own head.

We shall now pass to Grün's exposition of the doctrine of Saint-Simon.

1. Lettres d'un habitant de Genève à ses contemporains[a][127]

Herr Grün did not gather clearly from Stein the connection between the plan for supporting the men of learning, outlined in the work quoted above, and the fantastic appendix to the brochure. He speaks of this work as if it treated mainly of a new organisation of society and ends as follows:

"The spiritual power in the hands of the men of learning, the temporal power in the hands of the property-owners, the franchise for all." (P. 35, cf. Stein, p. 151, Reybaud, p. 83.)

The sentence: "le pouvoir de nommer les individus appelés à remplir les fonctions des chefs de l'humanité entre les mains de

---

[a] *Letters of an Inhabitant of Geneva to His Contemporaries.*— Ed.

tout le monde",[a] which Reybaud quotes from Saint-Simon (p. 47) and which Stein translates in the clumsiest fashion, is reduced by Herr Grün to "the franchise for all", which robs it of all meaning. Saint-Simon is referring to the election of the Newton Council,[128] Herr Grün is referring to elections in general.

Long after dismissing the *Lettres* in four or five sentences copied from Stein and Reybaud, and having already spoken of the *Nouveau christianisme*, Herr Grün suddenly returns to the *Lettres*.

"But it is certainly not to be achieved by abstract learning." (Still less by concrete ignorance, as we observe.) "*For* from the standpoint of abstract science, there was *still* a cleavage between the 'property-owners' and '*everyone*'." (P. 87.)

Herr Grün forgets that so far he has only mentioned the "franchise for all" and has not mentioned "everyone". But since he finds "*tout le monde*" in Stein and Reybaud, he puts "everyone" in inverted commas. He forgets, moreover, that he has not quoted the following passage from Stein's book, that is the passage which would justify the "*for*" in his own sentence:

"He" (Saint-Simon) "*makes a distinction,* apart from the sages or the men of learning, between the *propriétaires* and *tout le monde*. It is true that *as yet* there is no clearly marked boundary between these two groups ... but, nevertheless, there lies in that indefinite idea of '*tout le monde*' the germ of that class towards the understanding and uplifting of which his theory was later directed, i.e., the *classe la plus nombreuse et la plus pauvre,*[b] and in reality, too, this section of the people was at that time only potentially present." (P. 154.)

Stein stresses the fact that Saint-Simon *already* makes a distinction between *propriétaires* and *tout le monde*, but *as yet* a very vague one. Herr Grün twists this so that it gives the impression that Saint-Simon *still* makes this distinction. This is naturally a great mistake on the part of Saint-Simon and is only to be explained by the fact that his standpoint in the *Lettres* is that of abstract science. But unfortunately, in the passage in question, Saint-Simon speaks by no means about differences in a future order of society, as Herr Grün thinks. He appeals for subscriptions to mankind as a whole, which, as he finds it, appears to him to be divided into three classes; not, as Stein believes, into *savants, propriétaires* and *tout le monde*; but 1) *savants* and *artistes* and all people of liberal ideas; 2) the

---

[a] "The power of nominating the persons who are to act as leaders of humanity should be in the hands of everyone."— *Ed.*
[b] The most numerous and poorest class.— *Ed.*

opponents of innovation, i.e., the *propriétaires*, insofar as they do not join the first class; 3) the *surplus de l'humanité qui se rallie au mot: Égalité*.[a] These three classes form *tout le monde*. Cf. Saint-Simon, *Lettres*, pp. 21, 22. Since moreover Saint-Simon says later that he considers his distribution of power advantageous to all classes, we may take it that in the place where he speaks of this distribution, p. 47, *tout le monde* obviously corresponds to the *surplus* which rallies around the slogan "equality", without, however, excluding the other classes.[b] Stein is roughly correct, although he pays no attention to the passage on pages 21 and 22. Herr Grün, who knows nothing of the original, clutches at Stein's slight error and succeeds in making sheer nonsense of his argument.

We soon come across an even more striking example. We learn unexpectedly on page 94, where Herr Grün is no longer speaking of Saint-Simon but of his school:

"In *one* of his books, Saint-Simon utters the *mysterious* words: 'Women will be admitted, they may even be nominated.' From this almost barren seed, the whole gigantic uproar of the emancipation of women has sprung up."

Of course, if in some work or other Saint-Simon had spoken of admitting and nominating women to some unknown position, these would indeed be "mysterious words". But the mystery exists only in the mind of Herr Grün. "One of Saint-Simon's books" is none other than the *Lettres d'un habitant de Genève*. In this work, after stating that everyone is eligible to subscribe to the Newton Council or its departments, he continues: "Les femmes seront admises *à souscrire*, elles pourront être *nommées*"[c]—that is, to a position in this Council or its departments, of course. Stein, as was fitting, quotes this passage in the course of his discussion of the book itself and makes the following comment:

Here, etc., "are to be found the *germs* of his later opinions and even those of his school; and even the first idea of the *emancipation of women*". (P. 152.)

In a note Stein points out quite rightly that for polemical reasons Olinde Rodrigues printed this passage in large type in his 1832 edition, since it was the only reference to the

---

[a] Rest of humanity which rallies around the slogan: *Equality.—Ed.*

[b] This sentence is omitted in the *Westphälische Dampfboot.—Ed.*

[c] "Women will be allowed *to subscribe*, it will be possible *to nominate* them."—*Ed.*

emancipation of women in Saint-Simon's work. To hide his plagiarism, Grün shifts the passage from the book to which it belongs to his discussion of the school, makes the above nonsense of it, changes Stein's "germ" into a "seed" and childishly imagines that this passage is the origin of the doctrine of the emancipation of women.

Herr Grün ventures an opinion on the contradiction which, he believes, exists between the *Lettres* and the *Catéchisme des industriels*; it consists in the fact that in the *Catéchisme* the rights of the *travailleurs* are asserted. He was bound to discover this difference, of course, because he derived his knowledge of the *Lettres* from Stein and Reybaud, and his knowledge of the *Catéchisme* similarly. Had he read Saint-Simon himself, he would have found in the *Lettres* not this contradiction, but a "seed" of the point of view developed among others in the *Catéchisme*. For example:

"Tous les hommes travailleront."[a] (*Lettres*, p. 60.) "Si sa cervelle" (the rich man's) "ne sera pas propre au travail, il sera bien obligé de faire travailler ses bras; car Newton ne laissera sûrement pas sur cette planète ... des ouvriers volontairement inutiles dans l'atelier."[b] (P. 64.)

2. Catéchisme politique des industriels[c]

As Stein usually quotes this work as the *Catéchisme des industriels*, Herr Grün knows of no other title. But since he only devotes ten lines to this work when he comes to speak of it *ex officio*, one might have at least expected him to give its correct title.

Having copied from Stein the fact that in this work Saint-Simon wants labour to govern, he continues:

"He now divides the world into idlers and industrialists." (P. 85.)

Herr Grün is wrong here. He attributes to the *Catéchisme* a distinction which he finds set out in Stein much later, in connection with the school of Saint-Simon.

Stein, page 206:

"Society consists at present only of idlers and workers." (Enfantin.)

---

[a] "All men will work."— *Ed.*
[b] "If his brain" ... "is not fitted for labour, he will be compelled to work with his hands; for Newton will assuredly not permit on this planet ... workers who, intentionally, remain idle in the workshops."— *Ed.*
[c] *Political Catechism of the Industrialists.*— *Ed.*

Instead of this alleged division, there is in the *Catéchisme* a division into three classes, the *classes féodale, intermédiaire et industrielle*; naturally, Herr Grün could not enlarge upon this without recourse to Stein, since he was not familiar with the *Catéchisme* itself.

Herr Grün then repeats once more that the content of the *Catéchisme* is the rule of labour and concludes his account of the work as follows:

"Just as republicanism proclaims: Everything for the people, everything through the people, Saint-Simon proclaims: Everything for industry, everything through industry." (Ibid.)

Stein, page 165:

"Since industry is the source of everything, everything must serve industry."

Stein rightly states (p. 160, note) that Saint-Simon's work *L'industrie*, printed as early as 1817, bears the motto: *Tout par l'industrie, tout pour elle.*[a] In his account of the *Catéchisme*, Herr Grün, therefore, not only commits the error mentioned above but also misquotes the motto of a much earlier work of which he has no knowledge whatever.

German thoroughness has in this way given an adequate criticism of the *Catéchisme politique des industriels*. We find however scattered throughout Grün's *omnium gatherum* isolated glosses which belong properly to this section. Chuckling over his own slyness, Herr Grün distributes the material which he finds in Stein's account of the work and elaborates it with commendable courage.

Herr Grün, page 87:

"Free competition was an impure and confused concept, a concept which contained in itself a new world of conflict and misery, the struggle between capital and labour and the misery of the worker who has no capital. Saint-Simon *purified the concept of industry; he reduced it to the concept of the workers*, he formulated the rights and grievances of the *fourth estate*, of the proletariat. He was forced to abolish the right of inheritance, since it had become an injustice towards the worker, towards the industrialist. This is the significance of his *Catéchisme des industriels*."

Herr Grün found the following observation in Stein's book (p. 169) with regard to the *Catéchisme*:

"It is, therefore, the true significance of Saint-Simon that he foresaw the inevitability of this contradiction" (between bourgeoisie and *peuple*).

This is the source of Herr Grün's idea of the "*significance*" of the *Catéchisme*.

---

[a] Everything through industry, everything for industry.— *Ed.*

Stein:

"He" (Saint-Simon in the *Catéchisme*) "begins with the *concept* of the industrial worker."

Herr Grün turns this into complete nonsense by asserting that Saint-Simon, who found free competition as an *"impure concept"*, "purified the *concept of industry* and reduced it to the *concept of the workers"*. Herr Grün shows everywhere that his concept of free competition and industry is a very "impure" and a very "confused" one indeed.

Not satisfied with this nonsense, Herr Grün risks a direct falsehood and states that Saint-Simon demanded the abolition of the right of inheritance.

On page 88 he tells us, still relying on his interpretation of Stein's version of the *Catéchisme*:

"Saint-Simon established the rights of the proletariat. He already formulated the new watchword: the *industrialists*, the *workers*, shall be raised to a position of supreme power. This was one-sided, but every struggle involves one-sidedness; he who is not one-sided cannot wage a struggle."

Despite his rhetorical maxim about one-sidedness, Herr Grün himself commits the one-sided error of understanding Stein to say that Saint-Simon wished to "raise" the real workers, the *proletarians*, "to a position of supreme power". Cf. page 102, where he says of Michel Chevalier:

"M. Chevalier still refers with great sympathy to the *industrialists*.... But to the disciple, the industrialists are no longer, *as they were for his master, the proletarians*; he includes capitalists, entrepreneurs and workers in one concept, that is to say, he includes the idlers in a category which should only embrace the poorest and most numerous class."

Saint-Simon numbers among the industrialists not only the workers, but also the *fabricants,* the *négociants,* in short, *all industrial capitalists;* indeed, he addresses himself primarily to them. Herr Grün could have found this on the very first page of the *Catéchisme.* But this shows how, without ever having seen the work, he concocts from hearsay fine phrases about it.

Discussing the *Catéchisme,* Stein says:

"After ... Saint-Simon comes to a *history of industry* in its relation to state authority ... he is the first to be conscious that in the science of industry there lies hidden a *political* factor.... It is undeniable that he succeeded in giving an important stimulus. For France possesses an *histoire de l'économie politique* only since Saint-Simon", etc. (Pp. 165, 170.)

Stein himself is extremely vague when he speaks of a "political factor" in "the science of industry". But he shows that he is on the right track by adding that the history of the state is intimately connected with the history of national economy.

Let us see how Herr Grün later, in his discussion of the school of Saint-Simon, appropriates this fragment of Stein:

"Saint-Simon had attempted a *history of industry* in his *Catéchisme des industriels* stressing the *political* element in it. The master himself paved the way, *t h e r e f o r e*, for *political economy*." (P. 99.)

Herr Grün "therefore" transforms the "political *factor*" of Stein into a "political *element*" and turns it into a meaningless phrase by omitting the details given by Stein. This "stone which the builders have rejected"[a] has indeed become for Herr Grün the "cornerstone" of his *Briefe und Studien*.[b] But it has also become for him a stumbling-block.[c] But that is not all. Whereas Stein says that Saint-Simon paved the way for a *history* of political economy by stressing the political factor in the science of industry, Herr Grün makes him the pioneer of *political economy itself*. Herr Grün argues something after this fashion: Economics existed already *before* Saint-Simon; but, as Stein relates, *Saint-Simon* stressed the political factor in industry, therefore he made economics political — political economics = political economy — hence Saint-Simon paved the way for political economy. In his conjectures Herr Grün undoubtedly displays a very genial spirit.

Just as he makes Saint-Simon the pioneer of political economy, he makes him the pioneer of scientific socialism:

"It" (Saint-Simonism) "contains ... scientific socialism, *for* Saint-Simon spent his whole life searching for the new science"! (P. 82.)

3. Nouveau christianisme [d]

With his customary brilliance, Herr Grün continues to give us extracts of extracts by Stein and Reybaud, to which he adds literary embellishments and which he dismembers in the most pitiless fashion. *One* example will suffice to show that he has never looked at the original of this work either.

"For Saint-Simon it was a question of establishing a unified view of life, such as is suitable to organic periods of history, which he *expressly* opposes to the critical periods. According to him, we have been living since Luther in a *critical*

---

[a] Cf. 1 Peter 2:7.— *Ed.*

[b] *Letters and Studies* is the subtitle of Grün's book, *Die Soziale Bewegung in Frankreich und Belgien.— Ed.*

[c] A pun on the words *Stein*, which in German means stone, *Eckstein*— cornerstone, and *Stein des Anstosses*— stumbling-block.— *Ed.*

[d] *New Christianity.— Ed.*

period; he thought to initiate a new *organic* period. *Hence* the *New Christianity."* (P. 88.)

At *no time* and in *no place* did Saint-Simon oppose organic to critical periods of history. This is a downright falsehood on the part of Herr Grün. *Bazard* was the first to make this distinction.[a] Herr Grün discovered from Stein and Reybaud that in *Nouveau christianisme* Saint-Simon commends the *criticism* of Luther, but finds his positive, dogmatic *doctrine* faulty. Herr Grün lumps that with what he remembers was said in the same sources about the *school* of Saint-Simon, and out of this he fabricates the above assertion.

After some florid comments on Saint-Simon's life and works produced by Herr Grün in the manner described earlier and based exclusively on Stein and the latter's primer, Reybaud, Herr Grün concludes by exclaiming:

"And those moral philistines, Herr Reybaud and the whole band of German parrots, thought that they had to defend Saint-Simon, by pronouncing with their usual wisdom that such a man, such a life, must not be measured by *ordinary* standards!—Tell me, are your standards made of wood? Tell the truth! We shall be quite pleased if they are made of good solid oak. Hand them over! We shall gratefully accept them as a precious gift. We shall not burn them, God forbid! We shall use them to measure the backs of the philistines." (P. 89.)

It is by affected bluster of this kind that Herr Grün attempts to prove his superiority over the men whom he has copied.

4. The School of Saint-Simon

Since Herr Grün has read just as much of the school of Saint-Simon as he read of Saint-Simon himself, that is nothing whatsoever, he should at least have made a proper summary of Stein and Reybaud, he should have observed the chronological order, he should have given a connected account of the course of the events and he should have mentioned the essential points. He does the contrary. Led astray by his bad conscience, he mixes everything up as far as possible, omits the most essential matters and produces a confusion even greater than that which we saw in his exposition of Saint-Simon. We must be still more concise here, for it would take a volume as thick as Herr Grün's to record every plagiarism and every blunder.

We are given no information about the period from the death of Saint-Simon to the July revolution[b]—a period which covers part of the most important theoretical development of Saint-

---

[a] See *Doctrine de Saint-Simon. Exposition. Première année.—Ed.*
[b] 1830.— *Ed.*

Simonism. And accordingly the Saint-Simonian criticism of existing conditions, the most important aspect of Saint-Simonism, is entirely omitted by Herr Grün. It is indeed hardly possible to say anything about it without a knowledge of the sources, and in particular of the newspapers.

Herr Grün opens his discourse on the Saint-Simonists with these words:

"To each according to his capacity, to each capacity according to its works: that is the practical dogma of the Saint-Simonists."

Like Reybaud (p. 96), Herr Grün presents this sentence as a transition from Saint-Simon to the Saint-Simonists and continues:

"It derives directly from the last words of Saint-Simon: all men must be assured the freest development of their faculties."

In this case Herr Grün wished to be different from Reybaud, who links the "practical dogma" with the *Nouveau christianisme*. Herr Grün believes this to be an invention of Reybaud's and unceremoniously substitutes the last words of Saint-Simon for the *Nouveau christianisme*. He did not realise that Reybaud was only giving a literal extract from the *Doctrine de Saint-Simon. Exposition. Première année*, p. 70.

Herr Grün cannot understand why Reybaud, after giving several extracts concerning the religious hierarchy of Saint-Simonism, should suddenly introduce the "practical dogma". Herr Grün imagines that the hierarchy follows directly from this proposition. But in fact, the proposition can refer to a new hierarchy only when taken in conjunction with the religious ideas of the *Nouveau christianisme*, whereas apart from these ideas, it can demand at most a purely secular classification of society. He observes on page 91:

"To each according to his capacity means to make the Catholic hierarchy the law of the social order. To each capacity according to its works means moreover to turn the workshop into a sacristy and the whole of civil life into a priestly preserve."

For in the above-mentioned extract from the *Exposition* quoted by Reybaud Herr Grün finds the following:

"L'église vraiment universelle va paraître ... l'église universelle gouverne le temporel comme le spirituel ... la science est sainte, l'industrie est sainte ... et tout bien est bien d'église et toute profession est une fonction religieuse, un grade dans la hiérarchie sociale.— *À chacun selon sa capacité, à chaque capacité selon ses œuvres.*" [a]

---

[a] "The truly universal Church shall appear ... the universal Church shall govern temporal as well as spiritual matters ... science shall be sacred, industry

To produce his own quite incomprehensible statement, Herr Grün had only to invert this passage and change the preceding sentences into conclusions of the final sentence.

Grün's interpretation of Saint-Simonism assumes "so confused and tangled a form" that on page 90 he first derives a "spiritual proletariat" from the "practical dogma", then from the spiritual proletariat he produces a "hierarchy of minds". Finally, out of the hierarchy of minds he produces the apex of the hierarchy. Had he read even only the *Exposition*, he would have seen that the religious approach of the *Nouveau christianisme*, together with the problem of how to determine *capacité*, necessitates the hierarchy and its apex.

Herr Grün concludes his discussion and criticism of the *Exposition* of 1828-29 with the single sentence: "*À chacun selon sa capacité, à chaque capacité selon ses œuvres.*" Apart from this he hardly even mentions the *Producteur* and the *Organisateur*. He glances at Reybaud and finds in the section "Third Epoch of Saint-Simonism", p. 126 (Stein, p. 205):

"... et les jours suivants le *Globe* parut avec le sous-titre de *Journal de la doctrine de Saint-Simon*, laquelle était *résumée* ainsi sur la première page:

Religion

Science   *Industrie*

Association universelle."[a]

Herr Grün passes from the above to the year 1831, without a break, and improves upon Reybaud in the following terms (p. 91):

"The Saint-Simonists put forward the following *outline* of their system; the formulation was largely the work of Bazard:

Religion

Science   *Industry*

Universal Association."

Herr Grün leaves out three sentences which are also to be found on the title-page of the *Globe* and which all relate to practical social reforms.[129] They are given by both Stein and

---

shall be sacred ... and all property shall be the property of the Church, every profession a religious function, a step in the social hierarchy.— *To each according to his capacity, to each capacity according to its works.*"—*Ed.*

[a] "...and during the following days the *Globe* appeared with the subtitle: *Journal of the Saint-Simonian Doctrine*, which was *summarised* as follows on the first page:

Religion

Science   *Industry*

Universal Association."— *Ed.*

Reybaud. This enables him to change what is, so to speak, the mere window-dressing of a journal into an "outline" of the system. He conceals the fact that it appeared on the title-page of the *Globe* and so can criticise the whole of Saint-Simonism, as contained in the mutilated title of this newspaper, with the clever comment that religion has *pride of place*. He could moreover have discovered from Stein that this is by no means true of the *Globe*. The *Globe* contains the most detailed and valuable criticism of existing conditions and particularly of economic conditions—a fact however which Herr Grün could not know.

It is difficult to say from where Herr Grün has obtained the new but important piece of information that the "formulation of the outline", four words in length, "was *largely* the work of *Bazard*".

Herr Grün now jumps from January 1831 back to October 1830:

"Shortly after the July revolution, during the *Bazard period*" (where does this period come from?), "the Saint-Simonists addressed a short but comprehensive statement of their beliefs to the Chamber of Deputies, after Messrs. Dupin and Mauguin had accused them from the tribune of preaching community of goods and wives."

The Address follows, with the comment by Herr Grün:

"How reasonable and measured it all is still! The Address presented to the Chamber was edited by Bazard." (Pp. 92-94.)

To begin with the concluding remark, Stein says, p. 205:

"Judging from its form and its attitude, we should not hesitate to ascribe it" (the document), "as does Reybaud, to Bazard *more* than to Enfantin."

And Reybaud says, p. 123:

"Aux formes, aux prétentions assez modérées de cet écrit il est facile de voir qu'il provenait *plutôt* de l'impulsion de M. Bazard que de celle de son collègue." [a]

With characteristic ingenuity and audacity, Herr Grün turns Reybaud's conjecture that Bazard *rather* than Enfantin was behind the Address into the certainty that he edited it in its entirety. The passage introducing the Address is translated from Reybaud, page 122:

---

[a] "From the form and the very moderate demands of this document, one can clearly see that it owes *more* to the initiative of M. Bazard than to that of his colleague."— *Ed.*

"MM. Dupin et Mauguin signalèrent du haut de la tribune une secte qui prêchait la communauté des biens et la communauté des femmes." [a]

Herr Grün merely leaves out the date given by Reybaud and writes instead: "shortly after the July revolution". Altogether, chronology does not suit Herr Grün's method of emancipating himself from those who have trodden the ground before him. In contradistinction to Stein he inserts in the text what Stein relegates to a note, he omits the introduction to the Address, he translates *fonds de production* (productive capital) as "*basic capital*" and *classement social des individus* (social classification of individuals) as "social order of individuals".

Some slipshod notes follow on the history of the school of Saint-Simon; they have been patched together from fragments of Stein, Reybaud and Louis Blanc with that artistic skill which we noticed in Grün's life of Saint-Simon. We leave it to the reader to look them up in the book for himself.

The reader now has before him all that Herr Grün has to say of the Bazard period of Saint-Simonism, i.e., the period from the death of Saint-Simon to the first schism. [130] Grün is now in a position to play an elegantly critical trump, and call Bazard a "poor dialectician". Then he continues:

"But so are the republicans. They only know how to die, Cato as much as Bazard; if they do not stab themselves to death, they die of *a broken heart*." (P. 95.)

"A few months after this quarrel, *his*" (Bazard's) "*heart was broken*." (Stein, p. 210.)

Such republicans as Levasseur, Carnot, Barère, Billaud-Varennes, Buonarroti, Teste, d'Argenson, etc., etc., show how correct Herr Grün's assertion is.

We are now offered a few commonplaces about Enfantin. Attention need only be drawn to the following discovery made by Herr Grün:

"Does this historical phenomenon not make it finally clear that religion is nothing but sensualism, that materialism can boldly claim the same origin as the sacred dogma itself?" (P. 97.)

Herr Grün looks complacently about him: "Has anyone else ever *thought of that*?" He would never have "thought of that" if the *Hallische Jahrbücher* had not already "thought of it" in

---

[a] "Messrs. Dupin and Mauguin drew attention from the tribune to a sect which was preaching community of goods and community of wives."— *Ed.*

connection with the Romantics.[a] One would have expected Herr Grün to have made some little intellectual progress since then.

We have seen that Herr Grün knows nothing of the whole economic criticism of the Saint-Simonists. Nevertheless, he manages to say something, with the help of Enfantin, about the economic consequences of Saint-Simon's theory, to which he has already made some airy references earlier. He finds in Reybaud (p. 129 et seq.) and in Stein (p. 206) extracts from Enfantin's *Political Economy*[b] but in this case, too, he falsifies the original; for the abolition of taxes on the most essential necessaries of life, which is correctly shown by Reybaud and Stein (who base their statements on Enfantin) to be a consequence of the proposals concerning the right of inheritance, is turned by Grün into an irrelevant, independent measure *in addition to* these proposals. He gives further proof of his originality by falsifying the chronological order; he refers first to the *priest* Enfantin and Ménilmontant and then to the *economist* Enfantin, whereas his predecessors deal with Enfantin's political economy during the Bazard period when they are discussing the *Globe*, for which it was written.[131] Just as here he includes the Bazard period in the Ménilmontant period so later, when referring to economics and to M. Chevalier, he brings in the Ménilmontant period. The occasion for this is the *Livre nouveau*,[132] and as usual he turns Reybaud's conjecture that M. Chevalier was the author of this work into a categorical assertion.

Herr Grün has now described Saint-Simonism "in its totality". (P. 82.) He has kept the promise he made "not to subject its literature to a critical scrutiny" (ibid.) and has therefore got mixed up, most uncritically, in quite a different "literature", that of Stein and Reybaud. He gives us by way of compensation a few particulars about M. Chevalier's economic lectures of 1841-42,[c] a time when the latter had long ceased to be a Saint-Simonist. For while writing about Saint-Simonism, Herr Grün had in front of him a review of these lectures in the *Revue des deux Mondes*. He has made use of it in the same way as he utilised Stein and Reybaud. Here is a sample of his critical acumen:

---

[a] This refers to Karl Rosenkranz's article "Ludwig Tieck und die romantische Schule".— *Ed.*

[b] Barthélemy-Prosper Enfantin, *Économie politique et Politique.— Ed.*

[c] Michel Chevalier, *Cours d'économie politique fait au Collège de France.— Ed.*

"In it he asserts that not enough is being produced. That is a statement worthy of the old economic school with its rusty prejudices.... As long as political economy does not understand that production is dependent upon consumption, this so-called science will not make any headway." (P. 102.)

One can see that with these phrases about consumption and production which he has inherited from true socialism, Herr Grün is far superior to any economic work. Apart from the fact that any economist would tell him that supply also depends on demand, i.e., that production depends on consumption, there is actually in France a special economic school, that of Sismondi, which desires to make production dependent on consumption in a form different from that which obtains under free competition; it stands in sharp opposition to the economists attacked by Herr Grün. Not till later, however, do we see Herr Grün speculating successfully with the talent[a] entrusted to him—the unity of production and consumption.

To compensate the reader for the boredom he has suffered from these sketchy extracts from Stein and Reybaud, which are moreover falsified and adulterated with phrases, Herr Grün offers him the following Young-German firework display, glowing with humanism and socialism:

"Saint-Simonism in its entirety as a social system was nothing more than a cascade of thoughts, showered by a beneficent cloud upon the soil of France" (earlier, pp. 82, 83, it was described as "a mass of light, but still a chaos of light" (!), "not yet an *orderly illumination*"!!). "It was both an overwhelming and a most amusing display. The author died before the show was put on, one producer died during the performance, the remaining producers and all the actors discarded their costumes, slipped into their civilian clothes, went home and behaved as if nothing had happened. It was a spectacle, an interesting spectacle, if somewhat confused towards the finale; a few of the performers overacted—and that was all." (P. 104.)

How right was Heine when he said about his imitators: "I have sown dragon's teeth and harvested fleas."

FOURIERISM

Apart from the translation of a few passages from the *Quatre mouvements*[b] on the subject of love, there is nothing here that cannot be found in a more complete form in Stein. Herr Grün

---

[a] Cf. Matthew 25:15-30 and Luke 19:13-26.—*Ed.*

[b] Charles Fourier, *Théorie des quatre mouvements et des destinées générales.—Ed.*

dismisses morality in a sentence which a hundred other writers had uttered long before Fourier:

"Morality is, according to Fourier, nothing but the systematic endeavour to repress the human passions." (P. 147.)

That is how Christian morality has always defined itself. Herr Grün makes no attempt to examine Fourier's criticism of present-day agriculture and industry and, as far as trade is concerned, he merely translates a few general remarks from the Introduction to a section of the *Quatre mouvements* ("Origine de l'économie politique et de la controverse mercantile", pp. 332, 334 of the *Quatre mouvements*). Then come a few extracts from the *Quatre mouvements* and one from the *Traité de l'association*, on the French Revolution together with the tables on civilisation, which are already known from Stein. The critical side of Fourier, his most important contribution, is thus dismissed in the most hasty and superficial fashion in twenty-eight pages of literal translation; and in these, with very few exceptions, only the most general and abstract matters are discussed, the trivial and the important being thrown together in the most haphazard way.

Herr Grün now gives us an exposition of Fourier's system. *Churoa*,[a] whose work is quoted by Stein, long ago gave us a better and more complete version. Although Herr Grün considers it "vitally necessary" to offer a profound interpretation of Fourier's series,[133] he can think of nothing better than to quote literally from Fourier himself and then, as we shall see later, to coin a few fine phrases about numbers. He does not attempt to show how Fourier came to deal with series, and how he and his disciples constructed them; he reveals nothing whatever about the inner construction of the series. It is only possible to criticise such constructions (and this applies also to the Hegelian method) by demonstrating how they are made and thereby proving oneself master of them.

Lastly, Herr Grün neglects almost entirely a matter which Stein at any rate emphasises in some measure, the opposition of *travail répugnant* and *travail attrayant*.

The most important aspect of the whole exposition is Herr Grün's criticism of Fourier. The reader may recollect what was said above concerning the sources of Grün's criticism. He will now see from the few examples which follow that Herr Grün

---

[a] August Ludwig Churoa, *Kritische Darstellung der Socialtheorie Fourier's.— Ed.*

first of all accepts the postulates of true socialism and then sets about exaggerating and distorting them. It need hardly be mentioned that Fourier's distinction between capital, talent and labour offers a magnificent opportunity for a display of pretentious cleverness; one can talk at length about the impracticability and the injustice of the distinction, about the introduction of wage-labour, etc., without criticising this distinction by reference to the *real* relationship of labour and capital. Proudhon has already said all this infinitely better than Herr Grün, but he failed to touch upon the real issue.

Herr Grün bases his criticism of Fourier's *psychology*—as indeed all his criticism—on the "essence of man":

"For human essence is all in all." (P. 190.)
"Fourier, too, appeals to this human essence and in his own way reveals to us its inner core" (!) "in his tabulation of the twelve passions; like all honest and reasonable people, he, too, desires to make man's inner essence a reality, a *practical reality.* That which is within must also be without, and thus *the distinction between the internal and the external must be altogether abolished.* The history of mankind teems with socialists, if this is to be their distinguishing feature.... The important thing about everyone is what he understands by the *essence of man.*" (P. 190.)

Or rather the important thing for the true socialists is to foist upon everyone thoughts about human essence and to transform the different stages of socialism into different philosophies of human essence. This unhistorical abstraction induces Herr Grün to proclaim the abolition of all distinction between the internal and the external, which would even put a stop to the propagation of human essence. But in any case, why should the Germans brag so loudly of their knowledge of human essence, since their knowledge does not go beyond the three general attributes, intellect, emotion and will, which have been fairly universally recognised since the days of Aristotle and the Stoics.[a] It is from the same standpoint that Herr Grün reproaches Fourier with having "cleft" man into twelve passions.

"I shall not discuss the completeness of this table, *psychologically* speaking; I consider it inadequate"—(whereupon the public can rest easy, "psychologically speaking").—"Does this number give us any knowledge of *what* man really is? Not for a moment. Fourier might just as well have enumerated the five

---

[a] The *Westphälische Dampfboot* has: "Or rather the important thing for the true socialists is to transform the different stages of socialism into different philosophies of human essence and since, according to the true socialists, 'human essence' — an unhistorical abstraction — has been revealed by Feuerbach, they have, as a result of this transformation, supplied a criticism of the socialist systems as well."— *Ed.*

senses; *the whole man* is seen to be contained in these, if they be properly explained and their human content rightly interpreted" (as if this "human content" is not entirely dependent on the stage of development which production and human intercourse have reached). "Indeed, it is in *one* sense alone that man is contained, in feeling; his feeling is different from that of the animal," etc. (P. 205.)

For the first time in his whole book, Herr Grün is obviously making an effort to say something about Fourier's psychology from the standpoint of Feuerbach. It is obvious too that this "whole man", "contained" in a single attribute of a real individual and interpreted by the philosopher in terms of that attribute, is a complete chimera. Anyway, what sort of man is this, "man" who is not seen in his real historical activity and existence, but can be deduced from the lobe of his own ear,[a] or from some other feature which distinguishes him from the animals? Such a man "is contained" in himself, like his own pimple. Of course, the discovery that human feeling is human and not animal not only makes all psychological experiment superfluous but also constitutes a critique of all psychology.

Herr Grün finds it an easy matter to criticise Fourier's treatment of love; he measures Fourier's criticism of existing amorous relationships against the fantasies by which Fourier tried to get a mental image of free love. Herr Grün, the true German philistine, takes these fantasies seriously. Indeed, they are the only thing which he does take seriously. It is hard to see why, if he wanted to deal with this side of the system at all, Grün did not also enlarge upon Fourier's remarks concerning education; they are by far the best of their kind and contain some masterly observations. Herr Grün, typical Young-German man of letters that he is, betrays, when he treats of love, how little he has learned from Fourier's critique. In his opinion, it is of no consequence whether one proceeds from the abolition of marriage or from the abolition of private property; the one must necessarily follow upon the other. But to wish to *proceed* from any dissolution of marriage other than that which now exists in practice in bourgeois society, is to cherish a purely literary illusion. Fourier, as Grün might have discovered in his works, always proceeds from the transformation of production.

Herr Grün is surprised that Fourier, who always starts with inclination (it should read: attraction), should indulge in all kinds of "mathematical" experiments, for which reason he calls him the "mathematical socialist", page 203. Even if he did not take into account Fourier's circumstances, he might well have

---

[a] G. W. F. Hegel, *Vorlesungen über die Naturphilosophie,* Einleitung, § 246, Zusatz.— *Ed.*

examined a little more closely the nature of attraction. He would very soon have discovered that a natural relation of the kind cannot be accurately defined without the help of calculation. He regales us instead with a philippic against number, a philippic in which literary flourishes and Hegelian tradition are intermixed. It contains passages such as:

Fourier "calculates the molecular content of your most abnormal taste".

Indeed, a miracle; and further:

"That civilisation, which is being so bitterly attacked, is based upon an unfeeling multiplication table.... Number is nothing definite.... What is the number one?... The number one is restless, it becomes two, three, four"

like the German country parson who is "restless" until he has a wife and nine children....

"Number stifles all that is essential and all that is real; can we halve reason or speak of a third of the truth?"

He might also have asked, can we speak of a green-coloured logarithm?...

"Number loses all sense in organic development"...

a statement of fundamental importance for physiology and organic chemistry. (Pp. 203, 204.)

"He who makes number the measure of all things becomes, nay, *is* an egoist."

By a piece of wilful exaggeration, he links to this sentence another, which he has taken over from Hess (see above[a]):

"Fourier's whole plan of organisation is based exclusively upon egoism.... Fourier is the very worst expression of civilised egoism." (Pp. 206, 208.)

He supplies immediate proof of this by relating that, in Fourier's world order, the poorest member eats from forty dishes every day, that five meals are eaten daily, that people live to the age of 144 and so on. With a naïve sense of humour Fourier opposes a Gargantuan view of man to the unassuming mediocrity of the men[b] of the Restoration period; but Herr Grün only sees in this a chance of moralising in his philistine way upon the most innocent side of Fourier's fancy, which he abstracts from the rest.

While reproaching Fourier for his interpretation of the French Revolution, Herr Grün gives us a glimpse of his own insight into the revolutionary age:

---

[a] See this volume, pp. 516-17.— *Ed.*

[b] In the *Westphälische Dampfboot* the following words enclosed in brackets have been inserted after "men": "(les infiniment petits [the infinitely small]. Béranger)".— *Ed.*

"If association had only been known of forty years earlier" (so he makes Fourier say), "the Revolution could have been avoided. But how" (asks Herr Grün) "did it come about that Turgot, the Minister, recognised the right to work and that, in spite of this, Louis XVI lost his head? After all, it would have been easier to discharge the national debt by means of the right to work than by means of hen's eggs." (P. 211.)

Herr Grün overlooks the trifling fact that the right to work, which Turgot speaks of, is none other than free competition and that this very free competition needed the Revolution in order to establish itself.

The substance of Herr Grün's criticism of Fourier is that Fourier failed to subject "ci?ilisation" to a "fundamental criticism". And why did he fail? Here is the reason:

"The *manifestations* of civilisation have been criticised but not its *basis*; it has been abhorred and ridiculed as it *exists*, but its *roots* have not been examined. Neither *politics* nor *religion* have undergone a searching criticism and for that reason the *essence of man* has not been examined." (P. 209.)

So Herr Grün declares that the real living conditions of men are *manifestations*, whereas religion and politics are the *basis and the root* of these manifestations. This threadbare statement shows that the true socialists put forward the ideological phrases of German philosophy as truths superior to the real expositions of the French socialists; it shows at the same time that they try to link the true object of their own investigations, human essence, to the results of French social criticism. If one assumes religion and politics to be the basis of material living conditions, then it is only natural that everything should amount in the last instance to an investigation of human essence, i.e., of man's consciousness of himself.— One can see, incidentally, how little Herr Grün minds what he copies; in a later passage and in the *Rheinische Jahrbücher*[a] as well, he appropriates, in his own manner, what the *Deutsch-Französische Jahrbücher* had to say about the relation of *citoyen* and *bourgeois*,[b] which directly contradicts the statement he makes above.

We have reserved to the end the exposition of a statement concerning production and consumption which true socialism confided to Herr Grün. It is a striking example of how Herr Grün uses the postulates of true socialism as a standard by which to measure the achievements of the French and how, by

---

[a] Karl Grün, "Politik und Socialismus".— *Ed.*

[b] See Marx's article "On the Jewish Question" (Karl Marx and Frederick Engels, *Collected Works*, Vol 3, pp. 146-74) and this volume, pp. 155-56 and p. 186.— *Ed.*

tearing the former out of their complete vagueness, he reveals them to be utter nonsense.

"Production and consumption can be separated temporally and spatially, in theory and in *external reality*, but in essence they are one. Is not the commonest occupation, e.g., the baking of bread, a productive activity, which is in its turn consumption for a hundred others? Is it not, indeed, consumption on the part of the baker himself, who consumes corn, water, milk, eggs, etc.? Is not the consumption of shoes and clothes production on the part of cobblers and tailors?... Do I not produce when I eat bread? I produce on an enormous scale. I produce mills, kneading-troughs, ovens and consequently ploughs, harrows, flails, mill-wheels, the labour of wood-workers and masons" ("and consequently", carpenters, masons and peasants, "consequently", their parents, "consequently", their whole ancestry, "consequently", Adam). "Do I not consume when I produce? On a huge scale, too.... If I read a book, I consume first of all the product of whole years of work; if I keep it or destroy it, I consume the material and the activity of the paper-mill, the printing-press and the bookbinder. But do I produce nothing? I produce perhaps a new book and thereby new paper, new type, new printer's ink, new bookbinding tools; if I merely read it and a thousand others read it too, we produce by our consumption a new edition and all the materials necessary for its manufacture. The manufacturers of all these consume on their part a mass of raw material which must be produced and which can only be produced through the medium of consumption.... In a word, *activity* and *enjoyment* are one, only a perverse world has torn them asunder and has thrust between them the concept of *value* and *price*: by means of this concept it has torn man asunder and with man, society." (Pp. 191, 192.)

Production and consumption are, in reality, frequently opposed to one another. But in order to restore the unity of the two and resolve all contradictions, one need only *interpret* these contradictions correctly and *comprehend* the true *nature* of production and consumption. Thus this German ideological theory fits the existing world perfectly; the unity of production and consumption is proved by means of examples drawn from present-day society, it exists *in itself*. Herr Grün demonstrates first of all that there actually does exist a relationship between production and consumption. He argues that he cannot wear a coat or eat bread unless both are produced and that there exist in modern society people who produce coats, shoes and bread which other people consume. This idea is, in Herr Grün's opinion, a new one. He clothes it in his classical, literary-ideological language. For example:

"It is believed that the enjoyment of coffee, sugar, etc., is mere consumption; but is this enjoyment not, in fact, production in the colonies?"

He might just as well have asked: Does not this enjoyment imply that Negro slaves enjoy the lash and that floggings are produced in the colonies? One can see that the outcome of such exuberance as this is simply an apology for existing conditions.

Herr Grün's second idea is that when he produces, he consumes, namely raw material, the costs of production in fact; this is the discovery that nothing can be created out of nothing, that he must have *material*. He would have found set out in any political economy, under the heading "productive consumption", the complicated relations which this involves if one does not restrict oneself, like Herr Grün, to the trivial fact that shoes cannot be made without leather.

So far, Herr Grün has realised that it is necessary to produce in order to consume and that raw material is consumed in the productive process. His real difficulties begin when he wishes to prove that he produces when he consumes. Herr Grün now makes a completely ineffective attempt to enlighten himself in some small degree upon the most commonplace and general aspects of the connection between supply and demand. He does discover that his consumption, i.e., his demand, produces a fresh supply. But he forgets that his demand must be *effective*, that he must offer an equivalent for the product desired, if his demand is to cause fresh production. The economists too refer to the inseparability of consumption and production and to the absolute identity of supply and demand, especially when they wish to prove that over-production never takes place; but they never perpetrate anything so clumsy, so trivial as Herr Grün. This is moreover the same sort of argument that the aristocracy, the clergy, the rentiers, etc., have always used to prove their own productivity. Herr Grün forgets, further, that the bread which is produced today by steam-mills, was produced earlier by wind-mills and water-mills and earlier still by hand-mills; he forgets that these different methods of production are quite independent of the actual eating of the bread and that we are faced, therefore, with an historical development of the productive process. Of course, producing as he does on "an enormous scale", Herr Grün never thinks of this. He has no inkling of the fact that these different stages of production involve different relations of production to consumption, different contradictions of the two; it does not occur to him that to understand these contradictions one must examine the particular mode of production, together with the whole set of social conditions based upon it; and that only by actually changing the mode of production and the entire social system based upon it can these contradictions be solved. While the other examples given by Herr Grün prove that he surpasses even the most undistinguished economists in banality, his example of the book shows that these economists are far more "humane" than he is. They do not demand that as soon as he has consumed a book he should produce another! They are content that he should produce his own education by his consumption and so exert a favourable influence upon production in general. Herr Grün's productive consumption is transformed into a real miracle, since he omits the connecting link, the cash payment; he makes it superfluous by simply ignoring it, but in fact it alone makes his demand *effective*. He reads, and by the mere fact of his *reading*, he enables the type-founders, the paper manufacturers and the printers to produce new type, new paper and new books. The mere fact of his consumption compensates them all for their costs of production. Incidentally, in the foregoing examination we have amply demonstrated the virtuosity with which Herr Grün produces new books from old by merely reading the latter, and with which he incurs the gratitude of the commercial world by his activities as a producer of new paper, new type, new printer's ink and new bookbinding tools. Grün ends the first letter in his book with the words:

"I am on the point of plunging into industry."

Herr Grün never once belies this motto of his in the whole of his book.

What did all his activity amount to? In order to prove the true socialist proposition of the unity of production and consumption, Herr Grün has recourse to the most commonplace economic statements concerning supply and demand; moreover, he adapts these to his purpose simply by omitting the necessary connecting links, thereby transforming them into pure fantasies. The essence of all this is, therefore, an ill-informed and fantastic transfiguration of existing conditions.

In his socialistic conclusion, he lisps, characteristically, the phrases he has learned from his German predecessors. Production and consumption are separated because a perverse world has torn them asunder. How did this perverse world set about it? It thrust a *concept* between the two. By so doing, it tore man *asunder*. Not content with this, it thereby tears society, i.e., itself, asunder, too. This tragedy took place in 1845.

The true socialists originally understood the unity of consumption and production to mean that activity shall itself involve enjoyment (for them, of course, a purely fanciful notion). According to Herr Grün's further definition of that unity, "consumption and production, economically speaking, must *coincide*" (p. 196); there must be no surplus of products over and above the immediate needs of consumption, which means, of course, the end of any movement whatsoever. With an air of importance, he therefore reproaches Fourier with wishing to *disturb* this unity by *over-production*. Herr Grün forgets that over-production causes crises only through its influence on the exchange value of products and that not only with Fourier but also in Herr Grün's perfect world exchange value has disappeared. All that one can say of this philistine rubbish is that it is worthy of true socialism.

With the utmost complacency, Herr Grün repeats again and again his commentary on the true socialist theory of production and consumption. For example, he tells us in the course of a discussion of Proudhon:

"Preach the social freedom of the consumers and you will have true equality of production." (P. 433.)

Preaching this is an easy matter! All that has hitherto been wrong has been that

"consumers have been uneducated, uncultured, they do not all consume in a *human way*". (P. 432.) "The view that consumption is the measure of production, instead of the contrary, is the death of every hitherto existing economic theory." (Ibid.) "The real solidarity of mankind, indeed, bears out the truth of the proposition that the consumption of each presupposes the consumption of all." (Ibid.)

Within the competitive system, the consumption of each presupposes more or less continuously the consumption of all, just as the production of each presupposes the production of all. It is merely a question of *how*, in what way, this is so. Herr Grün's only answer to this is the moral postulate of *human* consumption, the recognition of the "essential nature of consumption". (P. 432.) Since he knows nothing of the real relations of production and consumption, he has to take refuge in human essence, the last hiding-place of the true socialists. For the same reason, he insists on proceeding from consumption instead of from production. If you proceed from production, you necessarily concern yourself with the real conditions of production and with the productive activity of men. But if you proceed from consumption, you can set your mind at rest by merely declaring that consumption is not at present "human", and by postulating "human consumption", education for true consumption and so on. You can be content with such phrases, without bothering at all about the real living conditions and the activity of men.

It should be mentioned in conclusion that precisely those economists who took consumption as their starting-point happened to be reactionary and ignored the revolutionary element in competition and large-scale industry.

THE "LIMITATIONS OF PAPA CABET"
AND HERR GRÜN

Herr Grün concludes his digression on the school of Fourier and on Herr Reybaud with the following words:

> "I wish to make the organisers of labour *conscious of their essence*, I wish *to show* them *historically* where they have sprung from ... these hybrids ... who *cannot claim as their own even the least of their thoughts*. And later, perhaps, I shall find space to make an example of Herr Reybaud, not only of Herr Reybaud, but also of Herr Jay. The former is, in reality, not so bad, he is merely stupid; but the latter is more than stupid, he is learned.
> "And so".... (P. 260.)

The gladiatorial posture into which Herr Grün throws himself, his threats against Reybaud, his contempt for learning, his resounding promises, these are all sure signs that something portentous is stirring within him. Fully "conscious of his essence" as we are, we infer from these symptoms that Herr Grün is on the point of carrying out a most tremendous plagiaristic coup. To anyone who has had experience of his tactics, his bragging loses all ingenuousness and turns out to be always a matter of sly calculation.

"And so":

A chapter follows headed:

> "The Organisation of Labour!"

> "Where did this thought originate? — In France.— But how?"

It is also labelled:

> "Review of the Eighteenth Century."

"Where did this" chapter of Herr Grün's "originate? — In France.— But how?" The reader will find out without delay.

It should not be forgotten that Herr Grün wants to make the

French organisers of labour[134] conscious of their essence by an historical exposition in the profound German style. And so.

When Herr Grün realised that Cabet "had his limitations" and that his "mission had been completed long ago" (which he had known for a long time), it did not, "of course, mean an end of everything". On the contrary, by arbitrarily selecting a few quotations from Cabet and stringing them together he laid upon Cabet the new mission: to provide the French "background" to Herr Grün's German history of socialist development in the eighteenth century.

How does he set about his task? He reads *"productively"*.

The twelfth and thirteenth chapters of Cabet's *Voyage en Icarie* contain a motley collection of the opinions of ancient and modern authorities in favour of communism. He does not claim that he is tracing an historical movement. The French bourgeois view communism as a suspicious character. Good, says Cabet, in that case, men of the utmost respectability from every age will testify to the good character of my client; and Cabet proceeds exactly like a lawyer. Even the most adverse evidence becomes in his hands favourable to his client. One cannot demand historical accuracy in a legal defence. If a famous man happens to let fall a word against money, or inequality, or wealth, or social evils, Cabet seizes upon it, begs him to repeat it, puts it forward as the man's declaration of faith, has it printed, applauds it and cries with ironic good-humour to his irritated bourgeois: *"Écoutez, écoutez, n'était-il pas communiste?"* [a] No one escapes him. Montesquieu, Sieyès, Lamartine, even Guizot—communists all *malgré eux. Voilà mon communiste tout trouvé!* [b]

Herr Grün, in a productive mood, reads the quotations collected by Cabet, representing the eighteenth century; he never doubts for a moment the essential rightness of it all: he improvises for the benefit of the reader a mystical connection between the writers whose names happen to be mentioned by Cabet on one page, pours over the whole his Young-German literary slops and then gives it the title which we saw above.

And so.

---

[a] "Hear what he has to say! Was he not a communist?"—*Ed.*
[b] There's the communist all complete!—*Ed.*

Herr Grün:	*Cabet:*

Herr Grün introduces his review with the following words:	Cabet introduces his quotations with the following words:

| "The social idea did not fall from heaven, it is organic, i.e., it arose by a process of gradual development. I cannot write here its complete history, I cannot commence with the Indians and the Chinese and proceed to Persia, Egypt and Judaea. I cannot question the Greeks and Romans about their social consciousness, I cannot take the evidence of Christianity, Neo-Platonism and patristic philosophy,[135] I cannot listen to what the Middle Ages and the Arabs have to say, nor can I examine the Reformation and philosophy during the period of its awakening and so on up to the eighteenth century." (P. 261.) | "Vous prétendez, adversaires de la communauté, qu'elle n'a pour elle que quelques opinions sans crédit et sans poids; eh bien, je vais interroger devant vous l'histoire et tous les philosophes: écoutez! Je ne m'arrête pas à vous parler de plusieurs peuples anciens, qui pratiquaient ou avaient pratiqué la communauté des biens! Je ne m'arrête non plus aux Hébreux ... ni aux prêtres Égyptiens, ni à Minos ... Lycurgue et Pythagore ... je ne vous parle non plus de Confucius et de Zoroastre, qui l'un en Chine et l'autre en Perse ... proclamèrent ce principe."[a] (*Voyage en Icarie*, deuxième édition, p. 470.) |

After the passages given above, Cabet investigates Greek and Roman history, takes the evidence of Christianity, of Neo-Platonism, of the Fathers of the Church, of the Middle Ages, of the Reformation and of philosophy during the period of its awakening. Cf. Cabet, pp. 471-82. Herr Grün leaves others "more patient than himself" to copy these eleven pages, "provided the dust of erudition has left them the necessary humanism to do so" (that is, to copy them). (Grün, p. 261.) Only the social consciousness of the *Arabs* belongs to Herr Grün. We await longingly the disclosures about it which he has to offer the world. "I must restrict myself to the eighteenth century." Let us follow Herr Grün into the eighteenth century, remarking

---

[a] "You claim, foes of common ownership, that there is but a scanty weight of opinion in its favour. Well then, before your very eyes, I am going to take the evidence of history and of every philosopher. Listen! I shall not linger to tell you of those peoples of the past who practised community of goods! Nor shall I linger over the Hebrews ... nor the Egyptian priesthood, nor Minos ... Lycurgus and Pythagoras.... I shall make no mention of Confucius, nor of Zoroaster, who proclaimed, the one in China, the other in Persia ... this principle." — *Ed.*

only that Grün underlines almost the very *same words* as Cabet.[a]

Herr Grün:	Cabet:
"Locke, the founder of sensationism, observes: He whose possessions exceed his needs, oversteps the bounds of reason and of original justice and steals that which belongs to others. *Every surplus is usurpation,* and the sight of the needy must awaken remorse in the soul of the wealthy. Corrupt men, you who roll in luxury and pleasures, tremble lest one day the wretch who lacks the necessities of life *shall truly come to know the rights of man.* Fraud, faithlessness and avarice have produced that inequality of possessions *which is the great misfortune of the human race* by piling up all sorts of sufferings, on the one hand, beside riches, on the other, beside destitution. *The philosopher must, therefore, regard the use of money as one of the most pernicious inventions of human industry.*" (P. 266.)	"Mais voici Locke, écoutez-le s'écrier dans son admirable *Gouvernement civil*[b]: 'Celui qui possède au delà de ses besoins, passe les bornes de la raison et de la justice primitive et *enlève* ce qui *appartient aux autres.* Toute *superfluité* est une *usurpation,* et la vue de l'indigent devrait éveiller le remords dans l'âme du riche. Hommes pervers, qui nagez dans l'opulence et les voluptés, tremblez qu'un jour l'infortuné qui manque du nécessaire n'aprenne à connaître vraiment les *droits de l'homme.*' Écoutez-le s'écrier encore: 'La fraude, la mauvaise foi, l'avarice ont produit cette *inégalité dans les fortunes,* qui fait le *malheur de l'espèce humaine,* en amoncelant d'un côté tous les vices avec la richesse et de l'autre tous les maux avec la misère'" (of which Herr Grün makes nonsense). "'Le philosophe doit donc considérer l'usage de la *monnaie* comme une des plus *funestes* inventions de l'industrie humaine.'"[c] (P. 485.)

Herr Grün concludes from these quotations of Cabet's that Locke is "an opponent of the monetary system" (p. 264), "a

---

[a] The last part of this sentence from "remarking only that" to "Cabet" is omitted in the *Westphälische Dampfboot.—Ed.*

[b] *Two Treatises on Civil Government.—Ed.*

[c] "But here we have Locke, who exclaims in his admirable *Civil Government*: 'He who possesses in excess of his needs, oversteps the bounds of reason and of original justice and *appropriates the property of others.* All *excess* is *usurpation,* and the sight of the needy ought to awaken remorse in the soul of the wealthy. Perverse men, you who roll in riches and pleasures, tremble lest one day the wretch who lacks the necessities of life truly apprehend the *rights of man.'* Hear him exclaim again: 'Fraud, bad faith, avarice have produced that *inequality of means,* which, by piling on the one hand wealth and vice and on the other poverty and suffering, constitutes *the great misfortune of the human race....* The philosopher must, therefore, regard the use of *money* as one of the most *fatal* inventions of human industry.'"—*Ed.*

most outspoken opponent of money and of all property which exceeds the limits of need". (P. 266.) Locke was, unfortunately, one of the first scientific champions of the monetary system, a most uncompromising advocate of the flogging of vagabonds and paupers, one of the doyens of modern political economy.[a]

Herr Grün:

"Already *Bossuet,* the Bishop of Meaux, says in his *Politics Derived from Holy Scripture:* 'Without governments' ('without politics'—an absurd interpolation on the part of Herr Grün) 'the earth with all its goods would be the common property of men, just as much as air and light; no man, according to the original law of nature, has a particular right to anything. *All things belong to all men; it is from civil government that property results.*' A priest in the seventeenth century has the honesty to say such things as these; to express such views as these! And the German *Puffendorf,* whom one" (i.e., Herr Grün) "knows only through one of Schiller's epigrams,[b] was of the following opinion: '*The present inequality of means is an injustice* which involves all other inequalities by reason of the *insolence* of the rich and the *cowardice* of the poor.'" (P. 270.) Herr Grün adds: "We shall not digress; let us remain in France."

Cabet:

"Écoutez le baron de *Puffendorf,* professeur de droit naturel en Allemagne et conseiller d'état à Stockholm et à Berlin, qui dans son droit de la nature et des gens réfute la doctrine d'Hobbes et de Grotius sur la monarchie absolue, qui proclame l'égalité naturelle, la fraternité, la communauté des biens primitive, et qui reconnaît que la propriété est une institution humaine, qu'elle résulte d'un partage consenti pour assurer à chacun et surtout au travailleur une possession perpétuelle, indivise ou divise, et que par conséquent l'inégalité actuelle de fortune est une *injustice* qui n'entraîne les autres inégalités" (absurdly translated by Herr Grün) "que par *l'insolence des riches et la lâcheté des pauvres.*

"Et *Bossuet,* l'évêque de Meaux, le précepteur du Dauphin de France, le célèbre Bossuet, dans sa *Politique tirée de l'Ecriture sainte,* redigée pour l'instruction du Dauphin, ne reconnaît-il pas aussi que sans les gouvernements la terre et tous les biens seraient aussi *communs* entre les hommes que l'air et la lumière: Selon le droit primitif de la nature nul n'a le droit particulier sur quoi que *ce soit: tout est à tous,* et c'est du gouvernement civil que nait la propriété."[c] (P. 486.)

---

[a] The following note is added in brackets in the *Westphälische Dampfboot:* "Cf. Locke's book, *Some Considerations of the Consequences of the Lowering of Interest, etc.,* published in 1691, and also his *Further Considerations [Concerning Raising the Value of Money],* published in 1698." — *Ed.*

[b] Friedrich Schiller, "Die Philosophen".— *Ed.*

[c] "Listen to Baron von *Puffendorf,* a professor of natural law in Germany

The substance of Herr Grün's "digression" from France is that Cabet quotes a German. Grün even spells the German name in the incorrect French fashion. Apart from his occasional mistranslations and omissions, he surprises us by his improvements. Cabet speaks first of Pufendorf and then of Bossuet; Herr Grün speaks first of Bossuet and then of Pufendorf. Cabet speaks of Bossuet as a famous man; Herr Grün calls him a "priest". Cabet quotes Pufendorf with all his titles; Herr Grün makes the frank admission that one knows him only from one of Schiller's epigrams. Now he knows him also from one of Cabet's quotations, and it is apparent that the Frenchman, with all his limitations, has made a closer study than Herr Grün not only of his own countrymen, but of the Germans as well.

Cabet says: "I must make haste to deal with the great philosophers of the eighteenth century; I shall begin with Montesquieu." (P. 487.) In order to reach Montesquieu, Herr Grün begins with a sketch of the "legislative genius of the eighteenth century". (P. 282.) Compare their various quotations from Montesquieu, Mably, Rousseau, Turgot. It suffices here to compare Cabet and Herr Grün on Rousseau and Turgot. Cabet proceeds from Montesquieu to Rousseau. Herr Grün constructs this transition:

"Rousseau was the radical and Montesquieu the constitutional politician."

Herr Grün quotes from *Rousseau*:   *Cabet:*

"The greatest evil has already   "Écoutez maintenant *Rousseau*,
been done when one has to defend   l'auteur de cet immortel *Contrat*
the poor and restrain the rich,   *social* ... écoutez: 'Les hommes

---

and a Councillor of State in Stockholm and Berlin, a man who in his law of nature and nations refutes the doctrine of Hobbes and Grotius concerning absolute monarchy, who proclaims natural equality, fraternity, and primitive community of goods, and who recognises property to be a human institution, the result of a distribution of goods, by common consent, to the end that all, and particularly the workers, may be assured of permanent possession, undivided or divided, and that, in consequence, the existing inequality of possessions is an *injustice* which only involves the other inequalities in consequence of *the insolence of the rich and the cowardice of the poor.*

"And does not *Bossuet*, the Bishop of Meaux, the preceptor of the French Dauphin, the famous Bossuet, recognise also in his *Politique tirée de l'Ecriture sainte* — written for the Dauphin — that, were it not for governments, the earth and all goods would be as *common* to men as air and light; according to the primary law of nature, no one has a particular right to *anything*; *all things belong to all men* and it is from civil government that property springs." — *Ed.*

etc." ....
....
(ends with the words) "hence it
follows that the social state is only
advantageous to men if they all of
them [a] have something and none has
too much." According to Herr
Grün, Rousseau becomes "confused and quite vague when he has
to answer the question: what transformation does the previous form of
property undergo when primitive
man enters into society? What does
he answer? He answers: Nature has
made all goods common" ... (ends
with the words) "if a distribution
takes place the share of each becomes his property." (Pp. 284, 285.)

sont égaux en droit. La nature a
rendu tous les biens communs ...
dans le cas de partage la part de
chacun devient sa propriété. Dans
tous les cas la société est toujours
seule propriétaire de tous les
biens'" (a point omitted by Herr
Grün). "Écoutez encore: ..." (Cabet
ends) "'d'où il suit que l'état social
n'est avantageux aux hommes
qu'autant qu'ils ont tous quelque
chose et qu'aucun d'eux n'a rien de
trop.'
"Écoutez, écoutez encore Rousseau dans son *Économie politique*:
'Le plus grand mal est déjà fait
quand on a des pauvres à défendre,
et des riches à contenir'" [b] etc., etc.
(Pp. 489, 490.)

Herr Grün makes two brilliant innovations: firstly, he merges
the quotations from the *Contrat social* and the *Économie
politique* and, secondly, he begins where Cabet ends. Cabet
names the titles of the writings of Rousseau from which he
quotes, Herr Grün suppresses them. The explanation of these
tactics is, perhaps, that Cabet is speaking of Rousseau's
Économie politique, which Herr Grün does not know, even
from an epigram of Schiller. Although Herr Grün is conver-
sant with all the secrets of the *Encyclopédie* (cf. p. 263), it
was a secret for him that Rousseau's *Économie politique* is
none other than the article in the *Encyclopédie* on political
economy.

Let us pass on to *Turgot*. Herr Grün is not content here with
merely copying the quotations; he actually transcribes the
sketch that Cabet gives of Turgot.

---

[a] The parenthesis "(What grammar!)" is added in the *Westphälische
Dampfboot*.— Ed.

[b] "Listen now to *Rousseau*, the author of the immortal *Social Contract* — listen: 'Men are equal by right. Nature has made all goods common ... if
distribution takes place the share of each becomes his property. In all cases the
sole proprietor of all goods is society.' Listen again: ... 'hence it follows that the
social state is only advantageous to men inasmuch as they all have something
and none has too much'.
"Listen, listen again to Rousseau in his *Political Economy* [*Économie ou
Œconomie* (*Morale et Politique*)]: 'The greatest evil has already been done when
one has to defend the poor and restrain the rich.'" — Ed.

Herr Grün:	*Cabet:*
"One of the noblest and most futile attempts to establish a new order on the foundations of the old, everywhere on the point of collapse, was made by Turgot. It was in vain. The aristocracy brought about an artificial famine, instigated revolts, intrigued and spread calumnies against him until the debonair Louis dismissed his Minister.—The aristocracy would not listen, therefore, it had to suffer. Human development always avenges fearfully those good angels who utter the last urgent warning before a catastrophe. The French people blessed Turgot, Voltaire wished to kiss his hand before he died, the King had called him his friend.... Turgot, the Baron, the Minister, one of the last feudal lords, pondered the idea that a domestic press ought to be invented so as to make freedom of the press completely secure." (Pp. 289, 290.)	"Et cependant, tandis que le roi déclare que lui seul et son ministre (Turgot) sont dans la cour les amis du peuple, tandis que le peuple le comble de ses bénédictions, tandis que les philosophes le couvrent de leur admiration, tandis que Voltaire veut, avant de mourir, baiser la main qui a signé tant d'améliorations populaires, l'aristocratie conspire, organise même une vaste famine et des émeutes pour le perdre et fait tant par ses intrigues et calomnies qu'elle parvient à déchaîner les salons de Paris contre le réformateur et à perdre Louis XVI lui-même en le forçant à renvoyer le vertueux ministre qui le sauverait." (P. 497.) "Revenons à Turgot, baron, ministre de Louis XVI pendant la première année de son règne, qui veut réformer les abus, qui fait une foule de réformes, qui veut faire établir une nouvelle langue et qui, pour assurer la liberté de la presse, travaille lui-même à l'invention d'une presse à domicile."[a] (P. 495.)

Cabet calls Turgot a Baron and a Minister, Herr Grün copies this much from him, but by way of improving on Cabet, he changes the youngest son of the *prévôt* of the Paris merchants into "one of the *oldest* of the feudal lords". Cabet is wrong in attributing the famine and the uprising of 1775[136] to the machinations of the aristocracy. Up to the present, no one has discovered who was behind the outcry about the famine and the movement connected with it. But in any case the parliaments

---

[a] "Yet while the King declared that he and his Minister (Turgot) were the only friends the people had at court, while the people heaped blessings upon him, while the philosophers overwhelmed him with admiration, while Voltaire wished to kiss before he died the hand which had signed so many improvements for the people, the aristocracy conspired against him, even organised a vast famine, and stirred up insurrections in order to destroy him: by its intrigues and calumnies it succeeded in turning the Paris salons against the reformer and in destroying Louis XVI himself by forcing him to dismiss the virtuous Minister who would have saved him." "Let us return to Turgot, a Baron, a Minister of Louis XVI during the first year of his reign, one who desired to reform abuses, who carried through a mass of reforms, who wished to establish a new language; a man who actually tried to invent a domestic press in order to ensure the freedom of the press." — *Ed.*

and popular prejudice had far more to do with it than the aristocracy. It is quite in order for Herr Grün to copy this error of "poor limited Papa" Cabet. He believes in him as in a gospel. On Cabet's authority Herr Grün numbers Turgot among the communists, Turgot, one of the leaders of the physiocratic school. the most resolute champion of free competition, the defender of usury, the mentor of Adam Smith. Turgot was a great man, since his actions were in accordance with the time in which he lived and not with the illusions of Herr Grün, the origin of which we have shown already.

Let us now pass to the men of the French Revolution. Cabet greatly embarrasses his bourgeois opponent by numbering Sieyès among the forerunners of communism, by reason of the fact that he recognised equality of rights, and considered that only the state sanctions property. (Cabet, pp. 499-502.) Herr Grün, who "is fated to find the French mind inadequate and superficial every time that he comes into close contact with it", cheerfully copies this, and imagines that an old party leader like Cabet is destined to preserve the "humanism" of Herr Grün from "the dust of erudition". Cabet continues: "*Écoutez le fameux Mirabeau!*"[a] (P. 504.) Herr Grün says: "Listen to Mirabeau!" (p. 292) and quotes some of the passages stressed by Cabet, in which Mirabeau advocates the equal division of bequeathed property among brothers and sisters. Herr Grün exclaims: "Communism for the family!" (P. 292.) On this principle, Herr Grün could go through the whole range of bourgeois institutions, finding in all of them traces of communism, so that taken as a whole they could be said to represent perfect communism. He could christen the *Code Napoléon* a *Code de la communauté*.[b] And he could discover communist colonies in the brothels, barracks and prisons.

Let us conclude these tiresome quotations with *Condorcet*. A comparison of the two books will show the reader very clearly that Herr Grün now omits passages, now merges them, now quotes titles, now suppresses them, leaves out the chronological dates but meticulously follows Cabet's order, even when Cabet does not proceed strictly in accordance with chronology, and he achieves in the end nothing more than an abridgement of Cabet, poorly and timidly disguised.

---

[a] "Listen to the famous Mirabeau!"— *Ed.*

[b] A reference to Dezamy's main work, *Code de la Communauté*.— *Ed.*

Herr Grün:

"*Condorcet* is a radical Girondist. He recognises the injustice of the distribution of property, he absolves the poor from blame ... if the people are somewhat dishonest on principle, the cause lies in the institutions themselves.

"In his journal, *Social Education* ... he even tolerates large-scale capitalists....

"Condorcet moved that the Legislative Assembly should divide the 100 millions owned by the three princes who emigrated into 100,000 parts ... he organises education and the *establishment* of public assistance." (Cf. the original text.)

"In *his* report on public education to the Legislative Assembly, Condorcet says: 'The object of education and the duty of the political authorities ... is to offer every member of the human race the means of satisfying his needs, etc.'" (Herr Grün changes the report of the Committee *on* Condorcet's plan into a report by Condorcet himself.) (Grün, pp. 293, 294.)

Cabet:

"Entendez *Condorcet* soutenir dans sa réponse à l'académie de Berlin" ... (a long passage follows in Cabet, concluding:) "'C'est donc uniquement parce que les institutions sont mauvaises que le peuple est si souvent un peu voleur par principe.'

"Écoutez-le dans son journal *L'instruction sociale* ... il tolère même de grands capitalistes," etc.

"Écoutez l'un des chefs Girondins, le philosophe Condorcet, le 6 juillet 1792 à la tribune de l'assemblée législative: 'Décrétez que les biens des trois princes français (Louis XVIII, Charles X, et le prince de Condé'"—this is omitted by Herr Grün)"'soient sur-le-champ mis en vente ... ils montent à près de 100 millions, et vous remplacerez trois princes par cent mille citoyens ... organisez l'instruction et les *établissements* de secours publics.'

"Mais écoutez le comité d'instruction publique présentant à l'assemblée législative *son* rapport sur le plan d'éducation rédigé par Condorcet, 20 avril 1792: 'L'éducation publique doit offrir à tous les individus les moyens de pourvoir à leurs besoins ... tel doit être le premier but d'une instruction nationale et sous ce point de vue elle est pour la puissance politique un devoir de justice'",[a] etc. (Pp. 502, 503, 505, 509.)

---

[a] "Listen to *Condorcet*, who maintained in his reply to the Berlin Academy" ... "'It is therefore entirely because the institutions are evil that the people are so frequently a little dishonest on principle.'

"Listen to what he has to say in his journal *L'instruction sociale* ... he even tolerates large-scale capitalists....

"Listen to one of the Girondist leaders, the philosopher Condorcet, from the tribune of the Legislative Assembly, on the 6th July, 1792: 'Decree that the possessions of the three French princes (Louis XVIII, Charles X and the Prince of Condé) be immediately put up for sale ... they amount to almost 100 millions, and you will replace three princes by 100 thousand citizens ... organise education and *institutions* for public assistance.'

"But listen to the Committee of Public Education, presenting to the Legislative Assembly on the 20th April, 1792, *its* report on the plan of education drawn up by Condorcet: 'Public education should offer to every

By this shameless copying from Cabet, Herr Grün, using the historical method, endeavours to make the French organisers of labour conscious of their essence; he proceeds moreover according to the principle: *Divide et impera.* He unhesitatingly interpolates among his quotations his definitive verdict on persons whose acquaintance he made a moment ago by reading a passage about them; then he inserts a few phrases about the French Revolution and divides the whole into two halves by the use of a few quotations from Morelly. Just at the right moment for Herr Grün Morelly was *en vogue* in Paris, through the efforts of Villegardelle[a]; and the most important passages from Morelly's work had been translated in the Paris *Vorwärts*[b] long before Herr Grün came upon the scene. We shall adduce only one or two glaring examples of Herr Grün's slipshod method of translation.

Morelly:

"L'intérêt rend les cœurs *dénaturés* et répand l'amertume sur les plus doux liens, qu'il change en de pesantes chaînes *que détestent chez nous les époux en se détestant eux-mêmes.*"[c]

Herr Grün:

"Self-interest renders the heart *unnatural* and embitters the dearest ties, transforming them into heavy chains, *which our married people detest and they detest themselves into the bargain.*" (P. 274.)

Utter nonsense.

Morelly:

"Notre âme ... contracte une soif si furieuse qu'elle *se suffoque* pour l'étancher."[d]

Herr Grün:

"Our soul ... contracts ... so furious a thirst that *it suffocates itself in order to quench it.*" (Ibid.)

Again utter nonsense.

---

individual the means of providing for his needs ... such ought to be the first aim of national education and from this point of view it is a duty which justice demands of the political authorities.'"—*Ed.*

[a] Morelly, *Code de la Nature. Avec l'Analyse raisonnée du Système social de Morelly par Villegardelle.*—*Ed.*

[b] In the article "Auszüge aus Morelly's Code de la Nature".—*Ed.*

[c] "Self-interest *perverts* the heart and embitters our dearest ties, transforming them into heavy chains, *which in our society married couples detest and at the same time detest themselves.*"—*Ed.*

[d] "Our soul contracts such a terrific thirst that it *chokes* in quenching it."—*Ed.*

Morelly:

"Ceux qui *prétendent* régler les mœurs et dicter des lois", etc.[a]

Herr Grün:

"Those who *pretend* to control our morals and dictate our laws", etc. (P. 275.)

All three mistakes occur in a single passage of Morelly which takes up fourteen lines in Herr Grün's book. In his exposition of Morelly there are also numerous plagiarisms from Villegardelle.[b]

Herr Grün is able to sum up all his knowledge of the eighteenth century and of the Revolution in the following lines:

"Sensualism, deism and theism together stormed the old world. The old world crumbled. When a new world came to be built, deism was victorious in the Constituent Assembly, theism in the Convention, while pure sensualism was beheaded or silenced." (P. 263.)

Here we have the philosophic habit of dismissing history with a few categories proper to ecclesiastical history; Herr Grün reduces it to its basest form, to a mere literary phrase, which serves only to adorn his plagiarisms. *Avis aux philosophes!*[c]

We skip Herr Grün's remarks about communism. His historical notes are copied from Cabet's brochures, and the *Voyage en Icarie* is viewed from the standpoint adopted by true socialism (cf. *Bürgerbuch* and *Rheinische Jahrbücher*).[d] Herr Grün shows his knowledge of French, and at the same time of English, conditions by calling Cabet the "communist O'Connell of France" (p. 382), and then says:

"He would be ready to have me hanged if he had the power and knew what I think and write about him. These agitators are dangerous for men such as us, because their *intelligence is limited.*" (P. 382.)

PROUDHON

"Herr Stein revealed his intellectual poverty in no uncertain way by treating Proudhon *en bagatelle.*" (Cf. *Einundzwanzig Bogen*, p. 84.[e]) "One needs something more than Hegel's old twaddle to follow this logic incarnate." (P. 411.)

A few examples may show that Herr Grün remains true to his nature in this section too.

---

[a] "Those who *claim* to control our morals and dictate our laws", etc.— *Ed.*
[b] This sentence is omitted in the *Westphälische Dampfboot.*— *Ed.*
[c] A warning to the philosophers!— *Ed.*
[d] Karl Grün, "Feuerbach und die Socialisten" and "Politik und Socialismus".— *Ed.*
[e] Moses Hess, "Socialismus und Communismus".— *Ed.*

He translates (on pages 437-44) several excerpts from the economic arguments adduced by Proudhon to prove that property is intolerable and finally exclaims:

"To this critique of property, which is the *complete liquidation* of property, we need add nothing. We have no desire to write a new critique, abolishing in its turn equality of production and the isolation of equal workers. I have already in an earlier passage indicated what is necessary. The rest" (that is, what Herr Grün has not indicated) "we shall see when society is rebuilt, when true property relations are established." (P. 444.)

In this way Herr Grün tries to avoid a close investigation of Proudhon's economic arguments and, at the same time, to rise superior to them. Proudhon's whole set of proofs is wrong; however, Herr Grün will realise that, as soon as someone else has proved it.

The comments on Proudhon made in *Die heilige Familie*—in particular those stressing that Proudhon criticises political economy from the standpoint of political economy, and law from the legal standpoint[a]—are copied by Herr Grün. But he has understood so little of the problem that he omits the essential point, [namely] that Proudhon vindicates the *illusions* cherished by jurists and economists [as against] their practice; with regard to the foregoing statement he produces a set of nonsensical [phrases].

The most important thing in Proudhon's book *De la création de l'ordre dans l'humanité* is his *dialectique sérielle*, the attempt to establish a method of thought in which the *process* of thinking is substituted for independent thoughts. Proudhon is looking, from the French standpoint, for a dialectic method such as Hegel has indeed given us. A relationship with Hegel therefore really exists here and does not need to be constructed by means of some imaginative analogy. It would have been an easy matter to offer a criticism of Proudhon's dialectics if the criticism of Hegel's had been mastered. But this was hardly to be expected of the true socialists, since the philosopher Feuerbach himself, to whom they lay claim, did not manage to produce one. Herr Grün makes a highly diverting attempt to shirk his task. At the very moment when he should have brought his heavy German artillery into play, he decamps with an indecent gesture. First of all he fills several pages with translations, and then explains to Proudhon, with boisterous literary *captatio be-*

[a] See Karl Marx and Frederick Engels, *Collected Works*, Vol. 4, pp. 31-34.— *Ed.*

nevolentiae,[a] that his *dialectique sérielle* is merely an excuse for *showing off his learning.* He does indeed try to console Proudhon by addressing him as follows:

"Ah, my dear friend, make no mistake about being a *man of learning*" (or *"tutor"*). "We have had *to forget everything* that our school-masters and our university hacks" (with the exception of Stein, Reybaud and Cabet) "have tried to impart to us with such infinite labour and to our mutual disgust." (P. [457.])

As a proof that now Herr Grün no longer absorbs knowledge "with such infinite labour", although perhaps with just as much "disgust", we may note that he begins his socialist studies and letters in Paris on November 6th [and] by the following January 20th has "inevitably" [not] only concluded his *studies* but has also finished the [*exposition* of] his

"really complete impression of the entire process".

---

[a] Attempt to win good will.—*Ed.*

V

"DOCTOR GEORG KUHLMANN OF HOLSTEIN"

or

THE PROPHECIES OF TRUE SOCIALISM

DIE NEUE WELT ODER DAS REICH DES GEISTES AUF ERDEN. VERKÜN-DIGUNG[a][137]

"A man was needed" (so runs the preface) "who would give utterance to all our sorrows, all our longings and all our hopes, to everything, in a word, which moves our age most deeply. And in the midst of this stress and turmoil of doubt and of longing he had to emerge from the solitude of the spirit bearing the solution of the riddle, the living symbols of which encompass us all. This man, whom our age was awaiting, has appeared. *He is Dr. Georg Kuhlmann of Holstein.*"

August Becker, the writer of these lines, thus allowed himself to be persuaded, by a person of a very simple mind and very ambiguous character, that not a single riddle has yet been solved, not a single vital energy aroused — that the communist movement, which has already gripped all civilised countries, is an empty nut whose kernel cannot be discovered; that it is a universal egg, laid by some great universal hen without the aid of a cock — whereas the true kernel and the true cock of the walk is Dr. Georg Kuhlmann of Holstein!...

This great universal cock turns out, however, to be a perfectly ordinary capon who has fed for a while on the German artisans in Switzerland and who cannot escape his due fate.

Far be it from us to consider Dr. Kuhlmann of Holstein to be a commonplace charlatan and a cunning fraud, who does not himself believe in the efficacy of his elixir of life and who merely applies his science of longevity to the preservation of life in his own body — no, we are well aware that the inspired doctor is a *spiritualistic* charlatan, a *pious* fraud, a *mystical* old fox, but one who, like all his kind, is none too scrupulous in his choice of means, since his own person is intimately connected with his sacred mission. Indeed, sacred missions are always

---

[a] *The New World, or The Kingdom of the Spirit upon Earth. Annunciation.* — *Ed.*

intimately bound up with the holy beings who pursue them; for such missions are of a *purely* idealistic nature and exist *only* in the *mind*. All idealists, philosophic and religious, ancient and modern, believe in inspirations, in revelations, saviours, miracle-workers; whether their belief takes a crude, religious, or a refined, philosophic, form depends only upon their cultural level, just as the degree of energy which they possess, their character, their social position, etc., determine whether their attitude to a belief in miracles is a passive or an active one, i.e., whether they are shepherds performing miracles or whether they are sheep; they further determine whether the aims they pursue are theoretical or practical.

Kuhlmann is a very energetic person and a man of some philosophic education; his attitude to miracles is by no means a passive one and the aims which he pursues are very practical.

All that August Becker has in common with him is the national infirmity of mind. The good fellow

"pities those who cannot bring themselves to see that the will and the ideas of an age can only be expressed by individuals".

For the idealist, every movement designed to transform the world exists only in the head of some chosen being, and the fate of the world depends on whether this head, which is endowed with all wisdom as its own private property, is or is not mortally wounded by some realistic stone before it has had time to make its revelation.

"Or is this not the case?" adds August Becker defiantly. "Assemble all the philosophers and the theologians of the age, let them take counsel and register their votes, and then see what comes of it all!"

The whole of historical development consists, according to the ideologist, in the theoretical abstractions of that development which have taken shape in the "heads" of all "the philosophers and theologians of the age", and since it is impossible to "assemble" all these "heads" and induce them to "take counsel and register their votes", there must of necessity be one sacred head, the apex of all these philosophical and theological heads, and this *top head* is the speculative *unity* of all these *block-heads* — the saviour.

This "cranium" system is as old as the Egyptian pyramids, with which it has many similarities, and as new as the Prussian monarchy, in the capital of which it has recently been resurrected in a rejuvenated form. The idealistic Dalai Lamas have this much in common with their real counterpart: they would like to persuade themselves that the world from which they derive their subsistence could not continue without their holy excrement. As soon as this idealistic folly is *put into practice*, its *malevolent* nature is apparent: its clerical lust for power, its religious fanaticism, its charlatanry, its pietistic hypocrisy, its unctuous deceit. Miracles are the *asses' bridge* leading from the kingdom of the idea to *practice*. Dr. Georg Kuhlmann of Holstein is just such an asses' bridge — he is inspired — his magic words cannot fail to move the most stable of mountains. How consoling for those patient creatures who cannot summon up enough energy to blast these *mountains* with *natural powder*! What a source of confidence to the blind and timorous who cannot see the material coherence which underlies the diverse scattered manifestations of the revolutionary movement!

"There has been lacking, up to now, a rallying point," says August Becker.

Saint George overcomes all concrete obstacles with the greatest of ease by transforming all concrete things into ideas; he then pronounces himself the speculative unity of the latter, and this enables him to "rule and regulate them":

"The *society of ideas* is the world. And their unity *regulates and rules* the world." (P. 138.)

Our prophet wields all the power he can possibly desire in this "*society of ideas*".

"Led by our own idea, we will wander, hither and thither, and contemplate everything in the minutest detail, as far as our time requires." (P. 138.)

What a speculative unity of nonsense!

But paper is long-suffering, and the German public, to whom the prophet issued his oracular pronouncements, knew so little of the philosophic development in its own country that it did not even notice how, in his speculative oracular pronouncements, the great prophet merely reiterated the most decrepit philosophic phrases and adapted them to his practical aims.

Just as medical miracle-workers and miraculous cures are made possible by ignorance of the laws of the *natural* world, so *social* miracle-workers and miraculous social cures depend upon ignorance of the laws of the *social* world — and the witch-doctor of Holstein is none other than the *socialistic miracle-working shepherd* of Niederempt.

The first revelation which this miracle-working shepherd makes to his flock is as follows:

"I see before me an assembly of the *elect*, who have gone *before me* to work by word and deed for the salvation of our time, and who are now come to hear what *I* have to say concerning the weal and woe of mankind."

"Many have already spoken and written in the name of mankind, but *none* has yet given utterance to the real nature of man's suffering, his hopes and his expectations, nor told him how he may obtain his desires. That is precisely what *I* shall do."

And his flock believes him.

There is not a single original thought in the whole work of this "Holy Spirit"; he reduces out-of-date socialistic theories to abstractions of the most sterile and general kind. There is nothing original even in the form, the style. Others have imitated more happily the sanctified style of the Bible. Kuhlmann has taken Lamennais' manner of writing as his model, but he merely achieves a caricature of Lamennais. We shall give our readers a sample of the beauties of his style:

"Tell me, firstly, how feel ye when ye think of your eternal lot?

"Many indeed mock and say: 'What have I to do with eternity?'

"Others rub their eyes and ask: 'Eternity—what may this be? ...'

"How feel ye, when ye think of the hour when the grave shall swallow you up?"

"And I hear many voices." One among them speaks in this wise:

"Of recent years it hath been taught that the spirit is eternal, that in death it is only dissolved once more in God, from whom it proceedeth. But they who preach such things cannot tell me what then remaineth of me. Oh, that I had never seen the light of day! And assuming that I do not die — oh, my parents, my sisters, my brothers, my children, and all whom I love, shall I ever see you again? Oh, had I but never seen you!" etc.

"How feel ye, further, if ye think of infinity?" ...

We feel very poorly, Herr Kuhlmann — not at the thought of *death*, but at your *fantastic idea* of death, at your *style*, at the *shabby means* you employ to work upon the *feelings* of others.

"How dost feel," dear reader, when you hear a *priest* who paints hell very hot to terrify his sheep and make their minds very flabby, a priest whose eloquence only aims at stimulating the *tear glands* of his hearers and who speculates only on the *cowardice* of his congregation?

As far as the meagre *content* of the "Annunciation" is concerned, the first section, or the introduction to the *Neue Welt*, can be reduced to the simple thought that Herr Kuhlmann has come from Holstein to found the "Kingdom of the Spirit", the "*Kingdom of Heaven*" upon earth; that he was the first to know the real hell and the real heaven — the former being society as it has hitherto existed and the latter being future society, the "Kingdom of the Spirit" — and that he himself is the longed-for holy "spirit"....

None of these great thoughts of Saint George are exactly original and there was really no need for him to have bothered to come all the way from Holstein to Switzerland, nor to have descended from the "solitude of the spirit" to the level of the artisans, nor to have "revealed" himself, merely in order to present this "vision" to the "world".

However, the idea that Dr. *Kuhlmann of Holstein* is the "longed-for holy spirit" is his own exclusive property—and is likely to remain so.

According to Saint George's own "revelation", his Holy Scripture will progress in the following way:

"It will reveal" (he says) "the Kingdom of the Spirit in its earthly guise, that ye may behold its glory and see that there is no other salvation but in the Kingdom of the Spirit. On the other hand, it will *expose* your vale of tears that ye may behold your wretchedness and know the cause of all your sufferings. Then I shall show the way which leads from this sorrowful present to a joyful future. To this end, follow me in the spirit to a *height*, whence we may have a free prospect over the broad landscape."

And so the prophet permits us first of all a glimpse of his "*beautiful* landscape",[a] his *Kingdom of Heaven*. We see nothing but a misunderstanding of Saint-Simonism, wretchedly staged, with costumes that are a travesty of Lamennais, embellished with fragments from Herr Stein.

We shall now quote the most important revelations from the *Kingdom of Heaven*, which demonstrate the prophetic method. For example, page 37:

"The choice is *free and depends* on each person's inclinations. Inclinations *depend* on one's natural faculties."

"If in society," Saint George prophesies, "everyone follows his inclination, all the faculties of society without exception will be developed and *if this is so*, that which all need will continually be produced, in the realm of the spirit as in the realm of matter. For society always possesses as many faculties and energies as it has needs".... "*Les attractions sont proportionelles aux Destinées.*"[b] (Cf. also Proudhon.)

Herr Kuhlmann differs here from the socialists and the communists only by reason of a *misunderstanding*, the cause of which must be sought in his pursuit of *practical aims* and undoubtedly also in his narrow-mindedness. He confuses the *diversity* of faculties and capacities with the *inequality* of *possessions* and of *enjoyment* conditioned by possession, and *inveighs* therefore against *communism*.

"No one shall have there" (that is, under communism) "*any advantage* over another," declaims the prophet, "no one shall have *more possessions* and *live better* than another.... And if you cherish doubts about it and fail to join in their

---

[a] The phrase "beautiful landscape" (*schöne Gegend*) originated from a story about a woman who, trying to console the mother of a soldier killed in the Battle of Leipzig (1813), said: But it was a beautiful landscape.— *Ed.*

[b] The attractions correspond to the destinies. See Charles Fourier, *Théorie des quatre mouvements et des destinées générales.*— *Ed.*

vociferation, they will abuse you, condemn you, and persecute you and hang you on a gallows." (P. 100.)

Kuhlmann sometimes prophesies quite correctly, one must admit.

"In their ranks then are to be found all those who cry: Away with the Bible! Away, above all, with the Christian religion, for it is the religion of humility and servility! Away with all belief whatsoever! We know nothing of God or immortality! They are but figments of the imagination, exploited and continually concocted by deceivers and liars for their advantage" (it should read: which are exploited by the priests for their advantage). "In sooth, he who still believes in such things is the greatest of fools!"

Kuhlmann attacks with particular vehemence those who are on principle opposed to the doctrine of *faith, humility* and *inequality*, i.e., the doctrine of *"difference of rank and birth"*.

His socialism is based on the abject doctrine of predestined slavery — which, as formulated by Kuhlmann, reminds one strongly of *Friedrich Rohmer* — on the theocratic hierarchy and, in the last instance, on his *own sacred person!*

"Every branch of labour," we find on page 42, "is directed by the most skilled worker, who himself takes part in it, and in the realm of enjoyment every branch is guided by the *merriest member*, who himself participates in the enjoyment. But, as society is undivided and possesses only *one* mind, the whole system will be regulated and governed by *one* man—and he shall be the *wisest*, the *most virtuous* and the *most blissful*."

On page 34 we learn:

"If man strives after *virtue* in the *spirit*, then he *stirs* and *moves* his *limbs* and develops and moulds and forms everything in and outside himself according to his pleasure. And if he *experiences well-being* in the spirit, then he must also *experience* it in everything that lives in him. *Therefore*, man *eats* and *drinks* and *takes delight* therein; *therefore*, he *sings, plays* and *dances*, he *kisses, weeps* and *laughs*."

The knowledge of the influence which the *vision of God* exerts on the *appetite*, and which *spiritual blissfulness* exerts upon the *sex impulse* is, indeed, not the private property of Kuhlmannism; but it does shed light on *many an obscure passage* in the *prophet*.

For example, page 36:

"Both" (possession and enjoyment) "correspond to his labour" (that is, to man's labour). "Labour is the measure of his needs." (In this way, Kuhlmann distorts the proposition that a communist *society* has, *on the whole*, always as many faculties and energies as needs.) "For labour is the expression of the ideas and the instincts. And needs are based on them. But, *since* the faculties and needs of men are always different, and so apportioned that the former can only be developed and the latter satisfied, if each continually labours for all and the product of the labour of all is exchanged and apportioned in accordance with the deserts" (?) "of each—*for this reason* each receives only the *value* of his labour."

The whole of this tautological rigmarole would be — like the following sentences and many others which we spare the reader — utterly *incomprehensible*, despite the "sublime *simplicity* and *clarity*" of the "revelation" so praised by A. Becker, if we had not a *key* in the shape of the *practical aims* which the prophet is pursuing. This makes everything at once comprehensible.

> "Value," continues Herr Kuhlmann like an oracle, "determines itself according to the need of all." (?) "In value the work of each is always contained and for it" (?) "he can procure for himself whatever his heart desires."
> "See, my friends," runs page 39, "the society of true men always regards *life* as a *school* ... in which man must *educate* himself. And *thereby* it *wants* to attain *bliss*. But such" (?) "must *become evident* and visible" (?), "otherwise it" (?) "is *impossible*."

What Herr Georg Kuhlmann of Holstein has in view when he says that "such" (life? or bliss?) must "become evident" and "visible", because "it" would otherwise be "impossible" — that "labour" is "contained in value" and that one can procure for it (for what?) one's heart's desire — and finally, that "value" determines itself according to "need" — all this cannot be understood unless one once again takes into account the *crux* of the whole revelation, the *practical point* of it all.

Let us therefore try to offer a practical explanation.

We learn from August Becker that Saint George Kuhlmann of Holstein had no success in his own country. He arrives in Switzerland and finds there an entirely "new world", the communist societies of the German artisans. That is more to his taste — and he attaches himself without delay to communism and the communists. He always, as August Becker tells us, "worked unremittingly to develop his doctrine *further* and to *make it adequate* to the greatness of the times", i.e., he became a communist among the communists *ad majorem Dei gloriam*.

So far everything had gone well.

But one of the most vital principles of communism, a principle which distinguishes it from all reactionary socialism, is its empirical view, based on a knowledge of man's nature, that differences of *brain* and of intellectual ability do not imply any differences whatsoever in the nature of the *stomach* and of physical *needs*; therefore the false tenet, based upon existing circumstances, "to each according to his abilities", must be changed, insofar as it relates to enjoyment in its narrower sense, into the tenet, "*to each according to his need*"; in other words, a *different form* of activity, of labour, does not justify *inequality*, confers no *privileges* in respect of possession and enjoyment.

The prophet could not admit this; for the privileges, the advantages of his station, the feeling of being a chosen one, these are the very *stimulus* of the prophet.

"But such must become evident and visible, otherwise it is impossible."

Without practical advantages, without some *tangible stimulus*, the prophet would not be a prophet at all, he would not be a *practical,* but only a *theoretical,* man of God, a *philosopher.* The prophet must, therefore, make the communists understand that different forms of *activity* or *labour* give the right to different degrees of *value* and of *bliss* (or of enjoyment, merit, pleasure, it is all the same thing), and since each determines his own *bliss* and his *labour,* therefore, *he,* the prophet—this is the practical point of the revelation—can claim a *better life* than the *common artisan.**

After this, all the prophet's obscure passages become clear: that the "possession" and "enjoyment" of each should correspond to his "labour"; that the "labour" of each man should be the measure of his "*needs*"; that, therefore, each should receive the "value" of his labour; that "value" will determine *itself* according to "need"; that the work of each is "contained" in value and that he can procure for it what his "heart" desires; that, finally, the "bliss" of the chosen one must "become evident and visible", because it is otherwise "impossible". All this nonsense has now become intelligible.

We do not know the exact extent of the practical demands which Dr. Kuhlmann really makes upon the artisans. But we do know that his doctrine is a dogma fundamental to all spiritual and temporal craving for power, a mystic veil which is used to conceal all hypocritical pleasure-seeking; it serves to extenuate any infamy and is the source of many incongruous actions.

We must not omit to show the reader the way, which, according to Herr Kuhlmann of Holstein, "leads from this sorrowful present to a joyful future". This way is lovely and delightful as spring in a flowery meadow or as a flowery meadow in spring.

"Softly and gently, with sun-warmed fingers, it puts forth buds, the buds become flowers, the lark and the nightingale warble, the grasshopper in the grass is roused. Let the new world come like the spring." (P. 114 et seq.)

The prophet paints the transition from present social isolation to communal life in truly idyllic colours. Just as he has transformed real society into a "society of ideas", so that "led by his own idea he should be able to wander hither and thither,

---

* The prophet has moreover *openly* stated this in a lecture which has not been printed.

and contemplate everything in the minutest detail, as far as his time requires", so he transforms the real social movement which, in all civilised countries, already proclaims the approach of a terrible social upheaval into a process of *comfortable* and *peaceful conversion*, into a *still life* which will permit the owners and rulers of the world to slumber *peacefully*. For the idealist, the *theoretical abstractions* of real events, their ideal signs, are *reality*; *real events* are merely *"signs* that the old world is going to its doom".

"Wherefore do ye strive so anxiously for the things of the moment," scolds the prophet on page 118, "they are nothing more than signs that the *old* world is going to its doom; and wherefore do ye dissipate your strength in strivings which cannot fulfil your hopes and expectations?"

"Ye shall not tear down nor destroy that which ye find in your path, ye shall rather shun it and abandon it. And when ye have shunned it and abandoned it, then it shall cease to exist of itself, for it shall find no other nourishment."

"If ye seek truth and spread light abroad, then lying and darkness will vanish from your midst." (P. 116.)

"But there will be many who will say: 'How shall we build a new life as long as the old order prevails and hinders us? Must it not first be destroyed?' 'By no means,' answers the wisest, the most virtuous and the most blissful man. 'By no means. If ye dwell with others in a house that has become rotten and is too small and uncomfortable for you, and the others wish to remain in it, then ye shall not pull it down and dwell in the open, but ye shall first build a new house, and when it is ready ye shall enter it and abandon the old to its fate.'" (P. 120.)

The prophet now gives two pages of rules as to how one can *insinuate* oneself into the new world. Then he becomes aggressive:

"But it is not enough that ye should stand together and forsake the old world—ye shall also take up arms against it to make war upon it and to extend your kingdom and strengthen it. *Not by the use of force, however, but rather by the use of free persuasion.*"

But if *nevertheless* it comes about that one has to take up a *real* sword and hazard one's *real* life "to conquer heaven by force", the prophet promises his sacred host a Russian immortality (the Russians believe that they will rise again in their respective localities if they are killed in battle by the enemy):

"And they who shall fall by the wayside shall be born anew and shall rise more beauteous than they were before. Therefore" (therefore) "take no thought for your life and fear not death." (P. 129.)

Even in a conflict with *real* weapons, says the prophet reassuringly to his sacred host, you do not *really* risk your life; you merely *pretend* to risk it.

The prophet's doctrine is in every sense *sedative*. After these samples of his Holy Scripture one cannot wonder at the applause it has met with among certain *easy-going slowcoaches*.

Karl Marx

[THESES ON FEUERBACH^a]

1) *ad* Feuerbach [151]

1

The chief defect of all previous materialism (that of Feuerbach included) is that things [*Gegenstand*], reality, sensuousness are conceived only in the form of the *object, or of contemplation*, but not as *sensuous human activity, practice*, not subjectively. Hence, in contradistinction to materialism, the *active* side was set forth abstractly by idealism — which, of course, does not know real, sensuous activity as such. Feuerbach wants sensuous objects, really distinct from conceptual objects, but he does not conceive human activity itself as *objective* activity. In *Das Wesen des Christenthums*, he therefore regards the theoretical attitude as the only genuinely human attitude, while practice is conceived and defined only in its dirty-Jewish form of appearance.[152] Hence he does not grasp the significance of "revolutionary", of "practical-critical", activity.

2

The question whether objective truth can be attributed to human thinking is not a question of theory but is a *practical* question. Man must prove the truth, i.e., the reality and power, the this-worldliness of his thinking in practice. The dispute over the reality or non-reality of thinking which is isolated from practice is a purely *scholastic* question.

3

The materialist doctrine concerning the changing of circumstances and upbringing forgets that circumstances are

---

^a Original version.— *Ed.*

changed by men and that the educator must himself be educated. This doctrine must, therefore, divide society into two parts, one of which is superior to society.

The coincidence of the changing of circumstances and of human activity or self-change can be conceived and rationally understood only as *revolutionary practice.*

4

Feuerbach starts out from the fact of religious self-estrangement, of the duplication of the world into a religious world and a secular one. His work consists in resolving the religious world into its secular basis. But that the secular basis lifts off from itself and establishes itself as an independent realm in the clouds can only be explained by the inner strife and intrinsic contradictoriness of this secular basis. The latter must, therefore, itself be both understood in its contradiction and revolutionised in practice. Thus, for instance, once the earthly family is discovered to be the secret of the holy family, the former must then itself be destroyed in theory and in practice.

5

Feuerbach, not satisfied with *abstract thinking*, wants [*sensuous*] *contemplation*; but he does not conceive sensuousness as *practical*, human-sensuous activity.

6

Feuerbach resolves the essence of religion into the essence of *man*. But the essence of man is no abstraction inherent in each single individual. In its reality it is the ensemble of the social relations.

Feuerbach, who does not enter upon a criticism of this real essence, is hence obliged:

1. To abstract from the historical process and to define the religious sentiment [*Gemüt*] by itself, and to presuppose an abstract — *isolated*— human individual.

2. Essence, therefore, can be regarded only as "species", as an inner, mute, general character which unites the many individuals *in a natural way*.

7

Feuerbach, consequently, does not see that the "religious sentiment" is itself a social product, and that the abstract individual which he analyses belongs to a particular form of society.

8

All social life is essentially *practical*. All mysteries which lead theory to mysticism find their rational solution in human practice and in the comprehension of this practice.

9

The highest point reached by contemplative materialism, that is, materialism which does not comprehend sensuousness as practical activity, is the contemplation of single individuals and of civil society.

10

The standpoint of the old materialism is civil society; the standpoint of the new is human society, or social humanity.

11

The philosophers have only *interpreted* the world in various ways; the point is to *change* it.

Written in the spring of 1845
This version was first published
in 1924—in German and in Russian—
by the Institute of Marxism-
Leninism of the Central
Committee of the C.P.S.U. in *Marx-
Engels Archives*, Book I, Moscow

Printed according
to the manuscript

Karl Marx

[THESES ON FEUERBACH[a]]

Marx on Feuerbach

(Written in Brussels in the spring of 1845)

1

The chief defect of all previous materialism — that of Feuerbach included — is that things [*Gegenstand*], reality, sensuousness are conceived only in the form of the *object*, or of *contemplation*, but not as *human sensuous activity, practice*, not subjectively. Hence it happened that the *active* side, in contradistinction to materialism, was set forth by idealism — but only abstractly, since, of course, idealism does not know real, sensuous activity as such. Feuerbach wants sensuous objects, really distinct from conceptual objects, but he does not conceive human activity itself as *objective* activity. In *Das Wesen des Christenthums,* he therefore regards the theoretical attitude as the only genuinely human attitude, while practice is conceived and defined only in its dirty-Jewish form of appearance. Hence he does not grasp the significance of "revolutionary", of practical-critical, activity.

2

The question whether objective truth can be attributed to human thinking is not a question of theory but is a practical question. Man must prove the truth, i.e., the reality and power, the this-worldliness of his thinking in practice. The dispute over the reality or non-reality of thinking which isolates itself from practice is a purely scholastic question.

3

The materialist doctrine that men are products of circumstances and upbringing, and that, therefore, changed men are products of other circumstances and changed upbringing,

---

[a] Edited by Engels.— *Ed.*

forgets that it is men who change circumstances and that the educator must himself be educated. Hence, this doctrine is bound to divide society into two parts, one of which is superior to society (in Robert Owen, for example).

The coincidence of the changing of circumstances and of human activity can be conceived and rationally understood only as revolutionising practice.

4

Feuerbach starts out from the fact of religious self-estrangement, of the duplication of the world into a religious, imaginary world and a real one. His work consists in resolving the religious world into its secular basis. He overlooks the fact that after completing this work, the chief thing still remains to be done. For the fact that the secular basis lifts off from itself and establishes itself in the clouds as an independent realm can only be explained by the inner strife and intrinsic contradictoriness of this secular basis. The latter must itself, therefore, first be understood in its contradiction and then, by the removal of the contradiction, revolutionised in practice. Thus, for instance, once the earthly family is discovered to be the secret of the holy family, the former must then itself be criticised in theory and transformed in practice.

5

Feuerbach, not satisfied with *abstract thinking*, appeals to *sensuous contemplation*; but he does not conceive sensuousness as practical, human-sensuous activity.

6

Feuerbach resolves the essence of religion into the essence of man. But the essence of man is no abstraction inherent in each single individual. In its reality it is the ensemble of the social relations.

Feuerbach, who does not enter upon a criticism of this real essence, is hence obliged:

1. To abstract from the historical process and to define the religious sentiment [*Gemüt*] regarded by itself, and to presuppose an abstract — *isolated* — human individual.

2. The essence of man, therefore, can with him be regarded only as "species", as an inner, mute, general character which unites the many individuals only *in a natural way*.

7

Feuerbach, consequently, does not see that the "religious sentiment" is itself a *social product*, and that the abstract individual which he analyses belongs in reality to a particular form of society.

8

Social life is essentially *practical*. All mysteries which mislead theory into mysticism find their rational solution in human practice and in the comprehension of this practice.

9

The highest point attained by *contemplative* materialism, that is, materialism which does not comprehend sensuousness as practical activity, is the contemplation of single individuals in "civil society".

10

The standpoint of the old materialism is "*civil*" society; the standpoint of the new is *human* society, or associated humanity.

11

The philosophers have only *interpreted* the world in various ways; the point, however, is to *change* it.

Written in the spring of 1845

First published by Engels in   Printed according
the Appendix to the separate edition   to the book
of his *Ludwig Feuerbach und der
Ausgang der klassischen deutschen
Philosophie,* Stuttgart, 1888

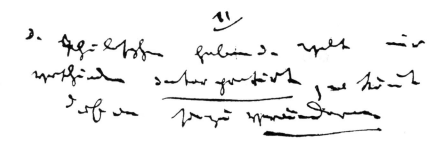

11

Die Philosophen haben die Welt nur verschieden *interpretirt*, es kommt darauf an sie zu *verädern*.

Facsimile of Thesis 11 on Feuerbach.
From Marx's notebook

GREAT BOOKS IN PHILOSOPHY PAPERBACK SERIES

ESTHETICS

❑ Aristotle—*The Poetics*
❑ Aristotle—*Treatise on Rhetoric*

ETHICS

❑ Aristotle—*The Nicomachean Ethics*
❑ Marcus Aurelius—*Meditations*
❑ Jeremy Bentham—*The Principles of Morals and Legislation*
❑ John Dewey—*Human Nature and Conduct*
❑ John Dewey—*The Moral Writings of John Dewey, Revised Edition*
❑ Epictetus—*Enchiridion*
❑ David Hume—*An Enquiry Concerning the Principles of Morals*
❑ Immanuel Kant—*Fundamental Principles of the Metaphysic of Morals*
❑ John Stuart Mill—*Utilitarianism*
❑ George Edward Moore—*Principia Ethica*
❑ Friedrich Nietzsche—*Beyond Good and Evil*
❑ Plato—*Protagoras, Philebus, and Gorgias*
❑ Bertrand Russell—*Bertrand Russell On Ethics, Sex, and Marriage*
❑ Arthur Schopenhauer—*The Wisdom of Life and Counsels and Maxims*
❑ Adam Smith—*The Theory of Moral Sentiments*
❑ Benedict de Spinoza—*Ethics and The Improvement of the Understanding*

LOGIC

❑ George Boole—*The Laws of Thought*

METAPHYSICS/EPISTEMOLOGY

❑ Aristotle—*De Anima*
❑ Aristotle—*The Metaphysics*
❑ Francis Bacon—*Essays*
❑ George Berkeley—*Three Dialogues Between Hylas and Philonous*
❑ W. K. Clifford—*The Ethics of Belief and Other Essays*
❑ René Descartes—*Discourse on Method and The Meditations*
❑ John Dewey—*How We Think*
❑ John Dewey—*The Influence of Darwin on Philosophy and Other Essays*
❑ Epicurus—*The Essential Epicurus: Letters, Principal Doctrines, Vatican Sayings, and Fragments*
❑ Sidney Hook—*The Quest for Being*
❑ David Hume—*An Enquiry Concerning Human Understanding*
❑ David Hume—*Treatise of Human Nature*
❑ William James—*The Meaning of Truth*
❑ William James—*Pragmatism*
❑ Immanuel Kant—*The Critique of Judgment*
❑ Immanuel Kant—*Critique of Practical Reason*
❑ Immanuel Kant—*Critique of Pure Reason*
❑ Gottfried Wilhelm Leibniz—*Discourse on Metaphysics and the Monadology*
❑ John Locke—*An Essay Concerning Human Understanding*
❑ George Herbert Mead—*The Philosophy of the Present*
❑ Michel de Montaigne—*Essays*
❑ Charles S. Peirce—*The Essential Writings*
❑ Plato—*The Euthyphro, Apology, Crito, and Phaedo*
❑ Plato—*Lysis, Phaedrus, and Symposium*
❑ Bertrand Russell—*The Problems of Philosophy*

- ❑ George Santayana—*The Life of Reason*
- ❑ Arthur Schopenhauer—*On the Principle of Sufficient Reason*
- ❑ Sextus Empiricus—*Outlines of Pyrrhonism*
- ❑ Ludwig Wittgenstein—*Wittgenstein's Lectures: Cambridge, 1932–1935*
- ❑ Alfred North Whitehead—*The Concept of Nature*

PHILOSOPHY OF RELIGION

- ❑ Jeremy Bentham—*The Influence of Natural Religion on the Temporal Happiness of Mankind*
- ❑ Marcus Tullius Cicero—*The Nature of the Gods* and *On Divination*
- ❑ Ludwig Feuerbach—*The Essence of Christianity* and *The Essence of Religion*
- ❑ Paul Henry Thiry, Baron d'Holbach—*Good Sense*
- ❑ David Hume—*Dialogues Concerning Natural Religion*
- ❑ William James—*The Varieties of Religious Experience*
- ❑ John Locke—*A Letter Concerning Toleration*
- ❑ Lucretius—*On the Nature of Things*
- ❑ John Stuart Mill—*Three Essays on Religion*
- ❑ Friedrich Nietzsche—*The Antichrist*
- ❑ Thomas Paine—*The Age of Reason*
- ❑ Bertrand Russell—*Bertrand Russell On God and Religion*

SOCIAL AND POLITICAL PHILOSOPHY

- ❑ Aristotle—*The Politics*
- ❑ Mikhail Bakunin—*The Basic Bakunin: Writings, 1869–1871*
- ❑ Jeremy Bentham—*The Rationale of Punishment*
- ❑ Edmund Burke—*Reflections on the Revolution in France*
- ❑ John Dewey—*Freedom and Culture*
- ❑ John Dewey—*Individualism Old and New*
- ❑ John Dewey—*Liberalism and Social Action*
- ❑ G. W. F. Hegel—*The Philosophy of History*
- ❑ G. W. F. Hegel—*Philosophy of Right*
- ❑ Thomas Hobbes—*The Leviathan*
- ❑ Sidney Hook—*Paradoxes of Freedom*
- ❑ Sidney Hook—*Reason, Social Myths, and Democracy*
- ❑ John Locke—*Second Treatise on Civil Government*
- ❑ Niccolo Machiavelli—*The Prince*
- ❑ Karl Marx (with Friedrich Engels)—*The German Ideology*, including *Theses on Feuerbach and Introduction to the Critique of Political Economy*
- ❑ Karl Marx—*The Poverty of Philosophy*
- ❑ Karl Marx/Friedrich Engels—*The Economic and Philosophic Manuscripts of 1844* and *The Communist Manifesto*
- ❑ John Stuart Mill—*Considerations on Representative Government*
- ❑ John Stuart Mill—*On Liberty*
- ❑ John Stuart Mill—*On Socialism*
- ❑ John Stuart Mill—*The Subjection of Women*
- ❑ Montesquieu, Charles de Secondat—*The Spirit of Laws*
- ❑ Friedrich Nietzsche—*Human, All-Too-Human*
- ❑ Friedrich Nietzsche—*Thus Spake Zarathustra*
- ❑ Thomas Paine—*Common Sense*
- ❑ Thomas Paine—*Rights of Man*
- ❑ Plato—*Laws*
- ❑ Plato—*The Republic*
- ❑ Jean-Jacques Rousseau—*Émile*
- ❑ Jean-Jacques Rousseau—*The Social Contract*
- ❑ Bertrand Russell—*Political Ideas*

- ❑ Mary Wollstonecraft—*A Vindication of the Rights of Men*
- ❑ Mary Wollstonecraft—*A Vindication of the Rights of Women*

GREAT MINDS PAPERBACK SERIES

ART

- ❑ Leonardo da Vinci—*A Treatise on Painting*

CRITICAL ESSAYS

- ❑ Desiderius Erasmus—*The Praise of Folly*
- ❑ Jonathan Swift—*A Modest Proposal and Other Satires*
- ❑ H. G. Wells—*The Conquest of Time*

ECONOMICS

- ❑ Charlotte Perkins Gilman—*Women and Economics: A Study of the Economic Relation between Women and Men*
- ❑ John Maynard Keynes—*The End of Laissez-Faire* and *The Economic Consequences of the Peace*
- ❑ John Maynard Keynes—*The General Theory of Employment, Interest, and Money*
- ❑ John Maynard Keynes—*A Tract on Monetary Reform*
- ❑ Thomas R. Malthus—*An Essay on the Principle of Population*
- ❑ Alfred Marshall—*Money, Credit, and Commerce*
- ❑ Alfred Marshall—*Principles of Economics*
- ❑ Karl Marx—*Theories of Surplus Value*
- ❑ John Stuart Mill—*Principles of Political Economy*
- ❑ David Ricardo—*Principles of Political Economy and Taxation*
- ❑ Adam Smith—*Wealth of Nations*
- ❑ Thorstein Veblen—*Theory of the Leisure Class*

HISTORY

- ❑ Edward Gibbon—*On Christianity*
- ❑ Alexander Hamilton, John Jay, and James Madison—*The Federalist*
- ❑ Herodotus—*The History*
- ❑ Thomas Paine—*The Crisis*
- ❑ Thucydides—*History of the Peloponnesian War*
- ❑ Andrew D. White—*A History of the Warfare of Science with Theology in Christendom*

LAW

- ❑ John Austin—*The Province of Jurisprudence Determined*

POLITICS

- ❑ Walter Lippmann—*A Preface to Politics*

PSYCHOLOGY

- ❑ Sigmund Freud—*Totem and Taboo*

RELIGION

- ❑ Thomas Henry Huxley—*Agnosticism and Christianity and Other Essays*
- ❑ Ernest Renan—*The Life of Jesus*
- ❑ Upton Sinclair—*The Profits of Religion*

- Elizabeth Cady Stanton—*The Woman's Bible*
- Voltaire—*A Treatise on Toleration and Other Essays*

SCIENCE

- Jacob Bronowski—*The Identity of Man*
- Nicolaus Copernicus—*On the Revolutions of Heavenly Spheres*
- Francis Crick—*Of Molecules and Men*
- Marie Curie—*Radioactive Substances*
- Charles Darwin—*The Autobiography of Charles Darwin*
- Charles Darwin—*The Descent of Man*
- Charles Darwin—*The Origin of Species*
- Charles Darwin—*The Voyage of the* Beagle
- René Descartes—*Treatise of Man*
- Albert Einstein—*Relativity*
- Michael Faraday—*The Forces of Matter*
- Galileo Galilei—*Dialogues Concerning Two New Sciences*
- Francis Galton—*Hereditary Genius*
- Ernst Haeckel—*The Riddle of the Universe*
- William Harvey—*On the Motion of the Heart and Blood in Animals*
- Werner Heisenberg—*Physics and Philosophy: The Revolution in Modern Science*
- Fred Hoyle—*Of Men and Galaxies*
- Julian Huxley—*Evolutionary Humanism*
- Thomas H. Huxley—*Evolution and Ethics* and *Science and Morals*
- Edward Jenner—*Vaccination against Smallpox*
- Johannes Kepler—*Epitome of Copernican Astronomy* and *Harmonies of the World*
- Charles Mackay—*Extraordinary Popular Delusions and the Madness of Crowds*
- James Clerk Maxwell—*Matter and Motion*
- Isaac Newton—*Opticks, Or Treatise of the Reflections, Inflections, and Colours of Light*
- Isaac Newton—*The Principia*
- Louis Pasteur and Joseph Lister—*Germ Theory and Its Application to Medicine* and *On the Antiseptic Principle of the Practice of Surgery*
- William Thomson (Lord Kelvin) and Peter Guthrie Tait—*The Elements of Natural Philosophy*
- Alfred Russel Wallace—*Island Life*

SOCIOLOGY

- Emile Durkheim—*Ethics and the Sociology of Morals*